Enterprise Architecture
A to Z

Enterprise Architecture
A to Z

Frameworks, Business Process Modeling,
SOA, and Infrastructure Technology

Daniel Minoli

CRC Press
Taylor & Francis Group
Boca Raton   London   New York

CRC Press is an imprint of the
Taylor & Francis Group, an **informa** business
AN AUERBACH BOOK

Auerbach Publications
Taylor & Francis Group
6000 Broken Sound Parkway NW, Suite 300
Boca Raton, FL 33487-2742

Library of Congress Cataloging-in-Publication Data

Minoli, Daniel, 1952-
  Enterprise architecture A to Z : frameworks, business process modeling, SOA, and infrastructure technology / Dan Minoli.
      p. cm.
  Includes bibliographical references and index.
  ISBN 978-0-8493-8517-9 (alk. paper)
  1. Information technology--Management. 2. Computer network architectures. 3. Information resources management. I. Title.

  T58.64.M56 2008
  004.068--dc22   2008013084

Visit the Taylor & Francis Web site at
http://www.taylorandfrancis.com

and the Auerbach Web site at
http://www.auerbach-publications.com

Contents

PART II: THE INFRASTRUCTURE LEVEL: MIGRATING TO STATE-OF-THE-ART ENVIRONMENTS IN ENTERPRISES WITH IT-INTENSIVE ASSETS: NETWORK VIRTUALIZATION

Preface

The goal of this text is to enlighten readers, CIOs, CTOs, and senior managers about a set of progressive approaches to designing state-of-the-art information technology (IT) infrastructures and data centers. We provide time-tested solid guidance to companies that perhaps prefer to get some fresh views on these weighty matters, rather than relying on consultants who have "answers" before the question is even asked, or other self-serving agents. This material is based on the author's hands-on practice in the architecture, grid computing, and networking arenas that spans three decades.

Driven by the need and desire to reduce costs, improve functionality, strengthen business continuity and disaster recovery, minimize risk, simplify architectures and operations, comply with regulatory requirements, build an open/standards-based environment, and pursue virtualization based on grid-oriented on-demand utility-based computing, organizations are faced with a set of decisions that require analytical scrutiny. This sets the backdrop for this book.

In this text we look at cost-saving trends in data center planning, administration, and management.

To set a baseline for the discussion, we open in Part I with an assessment of the role of enterprise architecture planning: Chapter 2 looks at enterprise architecture goals, roles, and mechanisms. Chapter 3 discusses The Open Group Architectural Framework (TOGAF). Chapter 4 looks at the Zachman Architectural Framework. Chapter 5 discusses official Enterprise Architecture standards. Chapter 6 provides a quick survey of enterprise architecture tools. Chapter 7 discusses business modeling and application development. Chapter 8 explores the issue of architecture fulfillment via Service-Oriented Architecture (SOA) Modeling.

Next, in Part II, we focus on infrastructure technologies. An assessment of high-speed communication mechanisms such as SANs, Gigabit Ethernet, and metro Ethernet, is provided (Chapter 9). This is followed by a discussion of WAN and Internet communication technologies (Chapter 10). Next, in Chapter 11, an assessment network virtualization via SOA modeling is discussed. Finally, in Chapter 12 we look at grid computing and server virtualization.

This text is intended for practitioners and decision makers in organizations who want to explore the overall opportunities afforded by newly emerged and emerging technologies to address pressing business needs while keeping costs in check. The book may be particularly useful for practitioners who are familiar with upper-layer architecture concepts (e.g., business process modeling, SOA, UML) and want to learn about lower-layer (technology infrastructure) architecture or vice versa.

About the Author

Daniel Minoli has many years of technical-hands-on and managerial experience (including budget or PL responsibility) in enterprise architecture, IT, telecom, and networking for financial companies and global carriers. He has worked at organizations such as AIG, Prudential Securities, and Capital One Financial, and carriers such as ARPA think tanks, Bell Telephone Laboratories, ITT, Bell Communications Research (now Telcordia), AT&T, Leading Edge Networks Inc., and SES Americom. Recently, he also played a founding role in the launching of two companies through the high-tech incubator Leading Edge Networks LLC, which he ran in the early 2000s: Global Wireless Services, a provider of secure broadband hotspot mobile Internet and hotspot VoIP services; and, InfoPort Communications Group, an optical and Gigabit Ethernet metropolitan carrier supporting data center/SAN/channel extension and Grid Computing network access services.

His work in enterprise architecture covers a number of layers of the TOGAF (The Open Group Architecture Framework) model, with special focus on the technology (infrastructure) architecture. This synthesis is based on his network infrastructure architecture mandate at Capital One Financial. Over the years he has done work in secure data centers, disaster recovery, business continuity, storage area networks, broadband communications, bandwidth-on-demand, and on-demand computing. His forward-looking disaster recovery work started in the early 1980s, and grid computing work started in the late 1980s. He has done work in platform architecture (blade technology, server consolidation, tiered storage, and processor and storage virtualization). He has also done work in Service-Oriented Architecture (SOA), business processing modeling (BPM), and Unified Modeling Language (UML), and has modeled the entire technology architecture of a financial firm (platforms, storage, networks, desktops, and databases) in ARIS and with an SOA focus. He is the author of the well-received 2005 Wiley book: *A Networking Approach to Grid Computing*. In 2004 he organized a session for the ENTNET (Enterprise Networking) Conference at SUPERCOMM on virtualization and Grid Computing applications for commercial users, and was the 2006 Tutorial Chair for the ENTNET 2006, again with a focus on virtualization and Grid Computing.

Mr. Minoli has also written columns for *ComputerWorld*, *NetworkWorld*, and *Network Computing* (1985–2006). He has taught at New York University (Information Technology Institute), Rutgers University, Stevens Institute of Technology, and Monmouth University (1984–2006). Also, he was a Technology Analyst-at-Large for Gartner/DataPro (1985–2001); based on extensive hands-on work at financial firms and carriers, he tracked technologies and wrote approximately 50 distinct CTO/CIO-level technical/architectural scans in the area of telephony and data systems, including topics on security, disaster recovery, IT outsourcing, network management, LANs, WANs (ATM and MPLS), wireless (LAN and public hotspot), VoIP, network design/economics, carrier networks (such as metro Ethernet and CWDM/DWDM), and e-commerce. Over the years he has advised venture capitalists for investments of $150M in a dozen high-tech companies, and has acted as expert witness in a (won) $11B lawsuit regarding a VoIP-based wireless Air-to-Ground communication system.

THE LOGICAL LEVEL

Chapter 1

Introduction: Enterprise Architecture and Technology Trends

Why is information technology (IT*) critical to organizations? What are the important trends in IT infrastructure technology? What are the technical and cost issues? How can a firm manage the infrastructure in an optimal manner that reduces costs and maximizes opportunity? Considering the answers to those questions, why are enterprise architecture (EA) methodologies important? Read on.

1.1 Introduction: The Criticality of Information Technology

Of late some have claimed that IT as applied to enterprise and institutional environments has become commoditized and it is no longer a strategic asset. Such statements originating from consultants, speakers, and magazine writers may well be off the mark. Although some commoditization has indeed occurred in the past ten years or so, in fact, it can be argued that not enough commoditization has yet taken place in IT, and more is needed. A lot of IT remains an art rather than a science: software solutions for a significant portion of a company's functions tend to be one-of-a-kind developments rather than being off-the-shelf standardized solutions. Furthermore, business demands required to support a service/consumer economy rely even more deeply than ever on having detailed real-time market and marketing information related, but not limited, to customer trends, needs, wishes, ability to pay, history, order taking, order tracking, supply-chain, physical

---

* When we use the term *information technology*, we mean the entire corporate activity and function related to computing, networking, and storage. This includes the people, the assets, the systems, the software, the applications, the practice, and the principles related to this function.

product delivery, and distributed (if not virtual) inventories. Additionally, consumers want to be able to check product offerings, status, availability, account and billing information, to name a few, in real-time and literally from anywhere. The support of this kind of business landscape and customer experience requires a sophisticated modern IT capability that is based on architecture-driven principles. A firm that can put together such a tightly woven, information-comprehensive infrastructure is well positioned to become an industry leader. Stated differently, given the competitive environment, it is far-fetched to believe that a firm can be a leader in its space or prosper if it does not have a well-planned, well-architected, best-in-class IT apparatus.

For example, consider the case of extending credit to consumers. If a firm can successfully perform data mining that goes deep beyond the openly available credit scores to establish a multidimensional risk decisioning process in regard to extending a specific individual a credit line, whereas every other competitor relies only on the one-dimensional openly available credit score, then that firm can, perhaps, quickly become an industry leader and build a multi-billion-dollar operation. This data-intensive operation requires a well-planned, well-architected, best-in-class IT corporate capability.

With a commodity, one can open up a product catalog or an online product portal, quickly determine which product meets one's needs, quickly undertake a feature customization, and speedily receive the product for actual use or deployment within days. The procurement of PC products is an example of a commoditized function at this time, as also the online purchase of a luxury car, boat, recreational vehicle, or modular home. In both cases one can look at a supplier's portal, see which off-the-shelf item out of a well-defined set of items available on the "shelf" satisfies the buyer's price/feature goal, apply some feature customization, and then immediately order the product; in the case of a PC, it typically arrives in a few days; in the case of a car, it could typically be delivered in a few weeks. That is not what happens when a large-size company needs, for example, to buy a billing system: such a project might require several hundred staff-years and cost several hundreds of millions of dollars, even when a core shell package might be available to build upon.

That IT does matter is established by the fact that there now exists a business environment that requires continual improvement and where the ultimate business goal is always a moving target that an organization must strive to achieve (but perhaps never truly attains.) First-generation (1G) IT evolved (in the 1970s) to meet 1G (batch-based) business processes. However, second-generation (2G) business processes emerged (in the 1980s and early 1990s). It is true that a firm would find it noncompetitive to try to address 2G business processes with 1G IT solutions, to the point that the firm could perhaps state that "those batch IT systems of the 1970s do not matter to the strategic needs of the 2G world"; but what a firm needed was not to declare that informatics did not matter, but to step up to develop 2G IT systems. Since the mid-1990s a third generation (3G) of business processes has emerged, based on online accessibility. Again, it is true that a firm would find it noncompetitive to try to address 3G business processes with 2G IT solutions, to the point that the firm could perhaps state that "those closed IT systems of the 1980s do not matter to the strategic needs of the 3G world"; but what a firm needs to do, then, is develop 3G IT systems. Now we are evolving to a 4G set of business processes, those based on a ubiquitous computing/location-based services/always-connected paradigm; 4G IT systems will be needed. And after that, past 2015, we will evolve to 5G business processes and 5G IT systems will be needed (what these are is anybody's guess, but it will happen). One does not want to fall in the trap of those physicists in the 19th century who stated that all that was there to be discovered in science was already discovered by then, or of those industrialists in the 1950s that stated that a handful of computers is all that the world would ever need. Fortunately, IT does move on and great new domains remain to be defined, appreciated, and conquered, to the financial benefit of the winners. At each stage IT is the strategic tool to conquer the new set of business opportunities; the world is not static and the "endgame" is not in sight.

To declare that "IT doesn't matter" is to assume that the "world comes to a stop" and nothing else happens hereafter in business, with the customer, with the environment, with the competition, and with regulations. So, although there were certain business expectations in the 1970s from customers, and IT systems were developed to support these (perhaps reasonably well), the underlying business processes have changed significantly since then. For example, in the 1970s one could generally only do banking Monday to Friday, 9:00 AM to 3:00 PM; the transaction had to be done face to face and in a bricks-and-mortar building. The customer's expectation was simply that if he or she walked into the bank, the bank would be able to reliably complete a transaction (e.g., a withdrawal) by having access to an up-to-date ledger. If the "world were to stop" then and nothing else ever changed, and a bank had developed an optimized IT system to support that paradigm, then in the early 1980s the bank could declare that there was no strategic value in spending more money in "tweaking" the 1G system. However, automated teller machines (ATMs) revolutionized the banking scene in the 1980s. Banks that could quickly and reliably bring this service to customers (by updating their IT systems) were the ones that thrived. Banks needed to make major investments in IT to serve the new customers' expectations. If the "world were to stop" in the late 1980s and nothing else ever changed, and a bank had developed an optimized IT system to support that ATM paradigm, then in the early 1990s the bank could declare that there was no strategic value in spending more money in "tweaking" the 2G system. However, the online approach to doing business (shopping, banking, paying, etc.) burst onto the scene in the 1990s. The same observations just made about necessary (new) IT investments apply. At this juncture, or soon hereafter, there may evolve an expectation for location-based services, such that when a consumer enters a space, say a mall, the consumer's PDA, iPod, cell phone, etc., starts telling the customer what services, sales, specials, etc., are available at that precise spot; if the customer walks 200 yards farther along, new information is then delivered to the customer. The customer may wish to make an on-the-spot purchase with a wireless financial transaction; then the customer may want the order shipped, again via a wireless interaction; then the customer may want to check how much money he or she has in the account; then the customer may want to see if money can be transferred on the spot for seven days to another bank that gives the customer a better interest rate—or transfer credit card balances to another credit card company with better rates. If that is the paradigm of the near future, then firms are well advised to start making major investments in IT now at all levels, to upgrade their 2.5G/3G systems to the 4G environment.

Perhaps what has worked against IT in large environments and has fed the recent chorus that "IT doesn't matter" is the fact that it continues to be difficult for decision makers to be able to get a good sense of what corporate IT resources (machine cycles, storage space, intranet use, etc.) really cost on an allocated run-time basis, and how chargebacks can be equitably passed back to the various business users across the company. The old saying that "a shoemaker's son always goes barefoot" seems, unfortunately, applicable here: IT runs all sorts of systems for the firm, but seems to be having a hard time designing a system to run "on itself" to collect appropriate measures of usage of resources and do a true cost-based allocation (which would have the benefit of providing true costs to business users and also be useful to drive new user behavior). Two symptomatic predicaments could be as follows: (1) having to collect and deal with several hundreds of IT usage measurements; or (2) being asked to develop a model for mainframe usage and work four months to "reinvent the wheel," when good measurements for mainframe usage were already developed four decades ago. There is no need to collect several hundreds of measurements: the IT industry could learn a lesson from the telecom industry in this regard. The telecom industry can charge back a user for the use of a broadband (say Asynchronous Transfer Mode) link between two distant cities by knowing just three things about the service that the user is employing: (1) access port speed, (2) average input rate, and (3) type of service, out of four possible service types. Why cannot the IT industry do something similar? The telecom carrier does not measure, for example, the instantaneous input rate, the specific kind of facility used to connect the user at site A, the specific kind of facility used to connect the user at site B, the amount of switch memory used at time t along the way, the amount of electrical power used by the switches along the way, the BTUs generated by the switches along the way (which needs to be then conditioned via HVAC systems), the length of the cabling within each central office along the way between the digital cross-connect system and the broadband switch, the number of retransmits that the user does at layer 2, the number of retransmits that the user does at layer 4, etc. The telecom industry does not collect or deal with several hundreds of parameters to compute a reasonably accurate bill for broadband transmission. Why do some firms need to collect several hundred parameters to provide a reasonably accurate chargeback to the business users? This only serves to obfuscate the value that IT can provide to an enterprise. Instead, a few well-chosen well-understood parameters should be used. A versatile enterprise architecture framework will go a long way to address this issue.

However, enough said about the dubious position that IT does not matter. Because it does matter, the fundamental question is then, "How do Fortune 5000 companies deal with it in the most versatile and profitable manner?" Earlier, we stated that a firm requires a well-woven information-comprehensive infrastructure to meet contemporary business demands. The problem is that many companies have hundreds, thousands, and even tens of thousands of applications to accomplish this, along with physical infrastructure assets valued at hundreds of millions of dollars. In turn, this creates an environment that is difficult to manage, optimize, and migrate to a (future) target state. What firms need is a well-planned, well-designed, best-in-class IT capability. To that end, it is the enterprise architecture plan that defines the organization's blueprint for optimal allocation of assets. This topic is the focus of this book.

1.2 IT Resources Requiring Proper Architectural Planning

Firms have made major investments in their IT resources in recent years. This text deals with optimizing the IT assets that a firm has deployed to run its business. This is accomplished, it is argued herewith, by properly architecting the IT environment, namely, by developing an enterprise architecture for all relevant assets, and then by implementing a roadmap for the proper realization of the architecture blueprint. At a broad level, enterprise architecture relates to understanding the universe of the distinct elements that comprise the enterprise and how those elements interrelate.

An enterprise, therefore, is any collection of departments or organizations that have a common set of goals/principles or a single bottom line. In that sense, an enterprise can be a whole corporation, a division of a corporation, a government agency, a single department, or a network of geographically distant organizations linked together by common objectives. Elements in this context encompass people, processes, business, and technology. Examples of elements include strategies, business drivers, principles, stakeholders, units, locations, budgets, domains, functions, processes, services, information, communications, applications, systems, infrastructure,* and so on [IEA200501]. Hence, enterprise architecture is the collection of business processes, applications, technologies, and data that supports the business strategies of an enterprise.

We begin this subsection by providing some heuristic ballpark estimates on the "size of the opportunity scope." This is information we have synthesized over the years in the context of first-pass quantification and modeling of IT assets. Although this information is approximate, it does show some of the macro-level trends.

Generally, we have found that for large companies the following applies at a broad level:

■ For manufacturing, education, legal, and transportation, companies tend, on average, to spend 2–3% of their gross yearly revenues on the (yearly) IT budget.
■ For marketing/service-based operations (publishing, reservation companies, hotels, average corporate establishment, etc.), companies tend, on average, to spend 3–6% of their gross yearly revenues on the (yearly) IT budget.
■ For information-intensive operations (banks, brokerage, insurance, credit cards, etc.), companies tend, on average, to spend 6–10% of their gross yearly revenues on the (yearly) IT budget.†

As a first pass, and for the typical firm, about 40% of this figure is for run-the-engine (RTE) costs and 60% for development of new applications (sometimes called *business process investments*) and for internal business user liaison (for many firms "internal selling/business user liaison" equates to 20% of this last figure or less; for some firms the "internal selling/business user liaison" equates—abnormally—to 40–50% of this last figure.)

Generally, for the RTE portion, 27–33% (30% as average) tends to be for staff payroll, 21–25% (23% as average) for equipment (yearly amortized figures), 15–19% (17% as average) for software licenses, 10–14% (12% as average) for communication, 10–16% (13% as average) for external support services (not including carriers), 4–6% (5% as average) for facilities (e.g., physical data center, backup site, offices, etc.) and miscellaneous.

As noted, communication services tend to be in the 12% range of the IT budget, split as follows: 83–87% (85% as average) voice services; 13–17% (15% as average) data/Internet services.

Finally, the embedded hardware investment of a firm can be taken to be 3–5 times the yearly amortized figures just quoted. The embedded applications investment can be taken to be 5–8 times the yearly application development figures just quoted.

All of this adds up to a lot of money. Table 1.1 provides an illustrative example. Again, this information is approximate, but it points to some general budgetary allocations. Because of the large budget figures involved, it makes sense to seek to optimize the environment and the architecture. Basically, all line items, including the staff line, can be addressed by the information contained in this book. Even a modest 5% improvement could save tens of millions of dollars in RTE expenses (e.g., $12, $16, and $20 million for lower-end, midrange, and higher-end, operation, respectively; see Table 1.1.)

---

* In this text, unless otherwise noted, the term *infrastructure* refers to the entire set of IT assets (software, hardware, data, etc.). The term *physical infrastructure* refers specifically to the physical infrastructure (the servers, the networks, the storage devices, etc.)
† Some researchers claim even higher spend rates.

Table 1.1   Example of an Information-Intensive Firm (e.g., a typical financial firm)

Firm's annual revenue	$10,000,000,000		
Lower-end operation			
IT budget (yearly)	$600,000,000		
RTE	$240,000,000		
Staff		$72,000,000	
Amortized IT hardware		$55,200,000	
Software licenses		$40,800,000	
Communications		$28,800,000	
Voice			$24,480,000
Data			$4,320,000
External services		$31,200,000	
Facilities, etc.		$12,000,000	
Development	$360,000,000		
Embedded hardware, range[a]	$165,600,000–$276,000,000		
Embedded applications, range[b]	$1,800,000,000–$2,880,000,000		
Midrange operation			
IT budget (yearly)	$800,000,000		
RTE	$320,000,000		
Staff		$96,000,000	
Amortized IT hardware		$73,600,000	
Software licenses		$54,400,000	
Communications		$38,400,000	
Voice			$32,640,000
Data			$5,760,000
External services		$41,600,000	
Facilities, etc.		$16,000,000	
Development	$480,000,000		
Embedded hardware, range[a]	$220,800,000–$368,000,000		
Embedded applications, range[b]	$2,400,000,000–$3,840,000,000		
Higher-end operation			
IT budget (yearly)	$1,000,000,000		
RTE	$400,000,000		
Staff		$120,000,000	
Amortized II hardware		$92,000,000	
Software licenses		$68,000,000	
Communications		$48,000,000	
Voice			$40,800,000
Data			$7,200,000
External Services		$52,000,000	
Facilities, etc.		$20,000,000	
Development	$600,000,000		
Embedded hardware, range[a]	$276,000,000–$460,000,000		
Embedded applications, range[b]	$3,000,000,000–$4,800,000,000		

Note: Top—lower-end operation; Center—midrange operation; Bottom—higher-end operation.
[a] 3–5 times yearly amortizes IT hardware
[b] 5–8 times yearly development budget

What organizations should seek to achieve is optimal management of the environment by developing an architecture that supports industry best practices; this allows the organization to reduce RTE costs, and often, enhances the firm's ability to meet evolving business needs and maximize functional enablements. IT assets, as noted earlier, encompass logical resources (applications, databases, etc.) and physical resources (processors, storage, networks, desktops, etc.).

1.3 What Is Enterprise Architecture?

We discuss more formally what an enterprise architecture is later in the book. For the time being, architecture can be seen as a blueprint for the optimal and target-conformant placement of resources in the IT environment for the ultimate support of the business function. As described in American National Standards Institute/Institute of Electrical and Electronics Engineers (ANSI/IEEE) Std 1471-2000, an **architecture** is "the fundamental organization of a system, embodied in its components, their relationships to each other and the environment, and the principles governing its design and evolution." A metaphor can be drawn by thinking of a corporate/IT blueprint for the planning of a city or a large development. Specifically, then, the blueprint provides the macro view of how elements (roads, lots, utilities—read: platforms, networks, applications, applications' logical components) fit, particularly in relation with one another. In this book we make use of terms such as "enterprise architecture, the current blueprint" (or "enterprise architecture," or "enterprise architecture description"), and "enterprise architecture blueprint for the target state" (or "target state enterprise architecture" or "target state enterprise architecture description".) See Appendix 1.1 for a more formal definition.

The goal of enterprise architecture is to create a unified IT environment (standardized hardware and software systems) across the firm or all of the firm's business units, with tight symbiotic links to the business side of the organization (which typically is 90% of the firm as seen earlier, at least by way of budget) and its strategy. More specifically, the goals are to promote alignment, standardization, reuse of existing IT assets, and the sharing of common methods for project management and software development across the organization. The end result, theoretically, is that the enterprise architecture will make IT cheaper, more strategic, and more responsive [KOC200502].

The purpose of enterprise architecture is to create a map of IT assets and business processes and a set of governance principles that drive an ongoing discussion about business strategy and how it can be expressed through IT. There are many different suggested frameworks to develop an enterprise architecture, as discussed later on. However, most frameworks contain four basic domains, as follows: (1) business architecture: documentation that outlines the company's most important business processes; (2) information architecture: identifies where important blocks of information, such as a customer record, are kept and how one typically accesses them; (3) application system architecture: a map of the relationships of software applications to one another; and (4) the infrastructure technology architecture: a blueprint for the gamut of hardware, storage systems, and networks. The business architecture is the most critical, but also the most difficult to implement, according to industry practitioners [KOC200502].

Figure 1.1 depicts the macro view of the environment. On the left-hand side of the figure one can see external entities that may drive a firm. These include the customers, the market, the industry the firm is in, the opportunities that may exist or may develop, competitors, regulators, and investors, among others. A firm has an existing or newly developed business strategy. The firm also has an existing set of business assets. The goal is to develop the IT infrastructure to support an

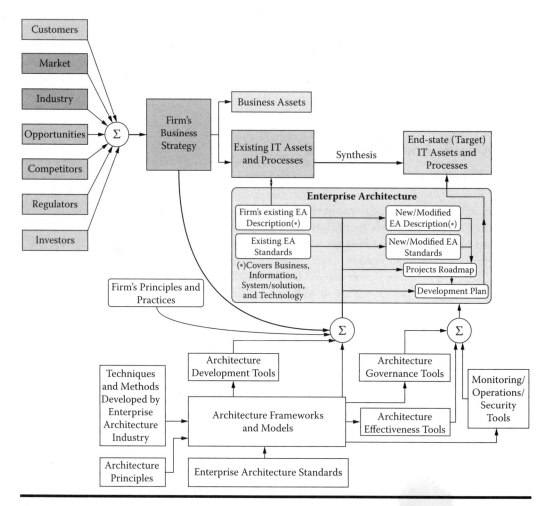

Figure 1.1   Macro view of the environment and of enterprise architecture.

end-state IT environment that enables, supports, and facilitates the business strategy. To this end, the enterprise may have developed an enterprise architecture, which is a blueprint of its information, systems, and technology environment. The blueprint also specifies the standards as related to these three categories (e.g., equipment standards, protocols standards, interface standards, etc.)

The firm may have developed the architecture using the industry mechanisms shown in the lower end of Figure 1.1. These include IT industry techniques and methods to develop an enterprise architecture; *architecture principles*; *enterprise architecture IT industry standards*; IT industry *enterprise architecture frameworks and models*; and *architecture development* tools.

As a new business strategy is developed by the firm, a new or modified enterprise architecture may be needed (this could be determined by a gap analysis). This enterprise architecture needs to take into account (as seen in the figure) the existing embedded base of IT assets, the existing enterprise architecture, the existing enterprise architecture standards, the firm's principles and practices, the desired business strategy, and the available frameworks/tools to develop a new enterprise architecture or modify the existing one.

The output of this synthesis will be a set of derived IT strategies, a new/modified enterprise architecture, a new/modified set of enterprise architecture standards, a roadmap describing the IT projects needed to effectuate (implement) the new architecture and achieve the target state, and a development/deployment plan. As the figure shows, there also are governance and effectiveness-assessment capabilities as well as an environment-monitoring function.

Part 1 of this book provides a survey of the architectural constructs that span the entire infrastructure, physical and logical; Part 2 focuses on actual technologies that can be used to develop an optimal physical infrastructure environment.

Layered frameworks and models for enterprise architecture have proved useful because layering has the advantage of defining contained, nonoverlapping partitions of the environment. There is a number of models/modeling techniques, for example, The Open Group Architecture Framework (TOGAF), the Federal Enterprise Architecture Framework (FEAF), and so on. However, there is at this time no complete industrywide consensus on what an architectural layered model should be, therefore various models exist or can be used. One case where standardization in the layered model has been accomplished is in the case of the Open Systems Interconnection Reference Model (OSIRM) published in 1984 by the International Organization for Standardization (ISO)*† (this model, however, only applies to communications). In the chapters that follow we discuss some formal models advanced or used in the industry to develop architecture planning tools. In the context of architecture, an important recent development in IT architecture practice has been the emergence of standards for architecture description, principally through the adoption by ANSI and the IEEE of ANSI/IEEE Std 1471-2000 *Recommended Practice for Architectural Description of Software-Intensive Systems*; one of the aims of this standard is to promote a more consistent, more systematic approach to the creation of views (a **view** is a representation of a whole system from the perspective of a related set of concerns) [TOG200502]. However, the adoption of this model is still far from being universal.

As noted, there are about a dozen-and-a-half enterprise architecture frameworks and new ones are being added over time (see Table 1.2). There is even a book with the title *How to Survive in the Jungle of Enterprise Architecture Frameworks: Creating or Choosing an Enterprise Architecture Framework* [SCH200501]. The most commonly used framework today, based on industry surveys, was the Zachman Framework, followed by organization's own locally developed frameworks, followed by TOGAF, and commercial-level Department of Defense Technical Reference Model (DoD TRM) (this covers about two-thirds of all enterprises.)

---

* The OSIRM is a set of internationally accepted standards that define a protocol model comprising seven hierarchically dependent layers. It is the foundation of protocol development work by the various standards agencies. A joint International Organization for Standardization (ISO)/International Telecommunications Union (ITU) standard for a seven-layer, architectural communication framework for interconnection of computers in networks. OSIRM-based standards include communication protocols that are mostly (but not totally) compatible with the Internet Protocol Suite, but also include security models, such as X.509, that are used in the Internet. The OSIRM layers, from highest to lowest, are (7) Application, (6) Presentation, (5) Session, (4) Transport, (3) Network, (2) Data Link, and (1) Physical. The model, originally developed in the 1980s, is defined in the following four documents: (1) ISO/IEC 7498-1:1994: Information technology—Open Systems Interconnection—Basic Reference Model: The Basic Model; (2) ISO 7498-2:1989: Information processing systems—Open Systems Interconnection—Basic Reference Model—Part 2: Security Architecture. (3) ISO/IEC 7498-3:1997: Information technology—Open Systems Interconnection—Basic Reference Model: Naming and addressing. (4) ISO/IEC 7498-4:1989: Information processing systems—Open Systems Interconnection—Basic Reference Model— Part 4: Management framework.

† Open Systems Interconnection (Networking) standards are defined by ISO to support the OSIRM architecture.

Table 1.2   Enterprise Architecture (EA) Frameworks (partial list)

1.   Zachman Enterprise Architecture Framework (ZIFA)
2.   The Open Group Architecture Framework (TOGAF)
3.   Extended Enterprise Architecture Framework (E2AF)
4.   Enterprise Architecture Planning (EAP)
5.   Federal Enterprise Architecture Framework (FEAF)
6.   Treasury Enterprise Architecture Framework (TEAF)
7.   Integrated Architecture Framework (IAF)
8.   Joint Technical Architecture (JTA)
9.   Command, Control, Communications, Computers, Intelligence, Surveillance, and Reconnaissance (C4ISR) and DoD Architecture Framework (DoDAF)
10. Department of Defense Technical Reference Model (DoD TRM)
11. Technical Architecture Framework for Information Management (TAFIM)
12. Computer Integrated Manufacturing Open System Architecture (CIMOSA)
13. Purdue Enterprise Reference Architecture (PERA)
14. Standards and Architecture for eGovernment Applications (SAGA)
15. European Union — IDABC & European Interoperability Framework
16. ISO/IEC 14252 (IEEE Std 1003.0)
17. IEEE Std 1471-2000 IEEE Recommended Practice for Architectural Description

Fundamentally, all models seek in some way to make use of the concept of a generic service/object-oriented architecture* (GSOA) in which sets of like functions are grouped into reusable service modules that can be described as objects; more complex capabilities are then built from appropriate assembly of these basic modules (just as, by analogy, matter is made up of various combinations of atoms of the elements). Although the idea of the service view is generally accepted at the "higher layers" of the model (e.g., the logical, computational, application, data, and business logic), we have advocated in recent years using the GSOA concepts also at the lower layers, where the actual IT technology resides (e.g., servers, networks, storage devices). This view can drive a move to a grid computing paradigm where physical IT assets are virtualized and distributed. Some of the enterprise architecture models have their genesis in the client-sever model developed in the late 1980s and early 1990s. However, some of the concepts have been modernized; for example, the client could be a browser-based access device, the server could be a Web server, and the exchange protocol could be Hypertext Transfer Protocol (HTTP); or both entities could be a server running some service-providing/service-requesting Web Service (WS) and the exchange protocol be Simple Object Access Protocol (SOAP).

Practitioners, however, need to have a pragmatic rather than academic view of all of these models; otherwise, one could end up spending an inordinate amount of time over several years developing a framework model (e.g., with principles, strategies, decisions, guidelines, standards, alternatives, justifications, etc.) and have little concrete to show (some firms have spent in the range of 100 staff-years to develop such a model with relatively little to show in the end). An analogy here with the well-established OSIRM mentioned earlier is useful. First, it should be noted that

---

* We employ the term GSOA to describe the general concept of service-oriented modeling of the enterprise architecture. We use the term SOA to refer specifically to the commercially available products to implement a GSOA paradigm, as discussed later in the book.

the model was quickly developed in the early 1980s. Second, the model was simple (a very thin standard). Third, the model has been standardized and universally accepted. Having said that, however, it needs to be noted that the raw OSIRM model by itself is of limited value; it would not have any major importance or consequence if it were not for the hundreds of supportive standards developed for Layer 1, Layer 2, Layer 3, etc., by all the standards-making organizations (not only ISO but also Telecommunication Standardization Sector of the International Telecommunication Union (ITU-T), IEEE, ANSI, Internet Engineering Task Force (IETF), etc.) What is useful is the full complement (the apparatus created by all) of the supportive standards, not the model itself.

A related observation in this context is as follows: the ultrarigorous attempt to model an entire enterprise (business/informatics) function with any one of the available models may be an extremely tedious effort and may become a moot point when the business climate changes every eighteen months, or even every six months. Because of the effort involved in the rigorous application of the modeling languages, an enterprise architecture organization may invest large amounts of time in undertaking a pedantic exercise that produces out-of-date results by the time it is completed. Results from the world of fuzzy set theory show that sometimes it is better to be in the "ballpark" rather than being "ultraprecise." We do agree that large-scale software development with fixed, well-established requirements (e.g., for things such as the next-generation jumbo jet, a nuclear power plant, a military system, or a space exploration platform) requires such rigor, but garden-variety business systems (e.g., order tracking, inventory system, customer records, etc.) may do fine with a somewhat more (but not totally) relaxed view. This is because requirements typically change even over a short period of time (new kinds of orders may be needed within six months, new kinds of items may be inventoried next year, new customer billing/information may be collected in nine months), and so an ultrarigorous effort at requirements documentation may not be worth it. Additionally, change control mechanisms may be difficult to implement over frequent variations over a short period of time. We are not suggesting not to go through the modeling effort; we are recommending not to spend hundreds of staff-years to develop a partial framework for the enterprise architecture.

A firm may have developed a full suite of architectures for the various framework layers or may only have a partially developed architecture, as illustrated in Figure 1.2. Figure 1.3 illustrates

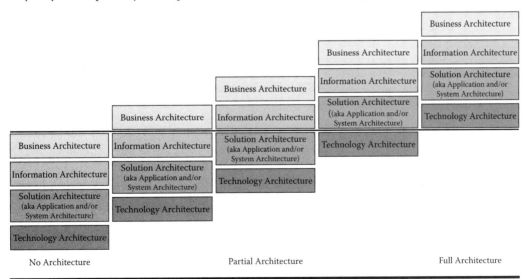

Figure 1.2 Maturity of enterprise architecture development at a firm.

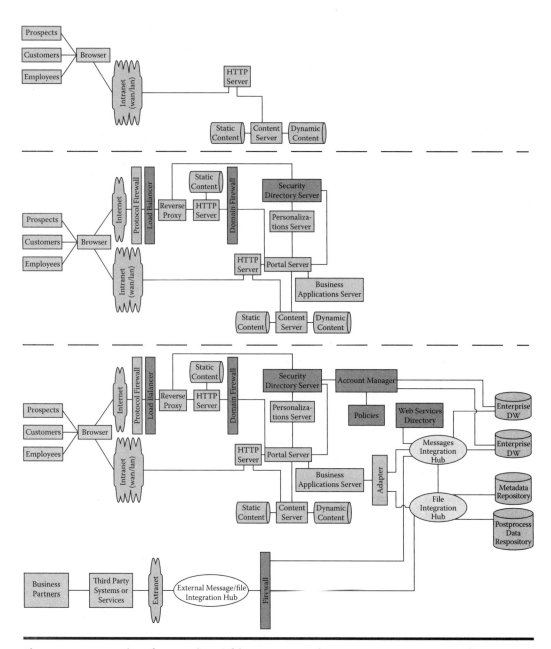

Figure 1.3 Necessity of enterprise architecture as environment grows more complex.

graphically the motivation for having an enterprise architecture: the top portion shows a rather simple application at a firm, where an architecture may be optional; the middle portion illustrates that over time the system and interrelations may grow more complex, and so an architecture blueprint is recommended; the bottom portion of the figure shows a full-grown application environment where an architecture blueprint is indispensable. Fortune 500 firms may have several dozens (if not hundreds) of applications with this type of complexity; trying to position oneself strategically in this environment without an enterprise architecture plan is completely futile. At this juncture it is not just the large organizations that have adopted enterprise architecture: smaller organizations are also adopting this approach (however, the architecture maturity is at a higher level in larger firms than in smaller firms) [IEA200501]. Every organization that seeks to manage its IT complexity in a cost-effective manner for rapid system deployment should consider making the appropriate investments in enterprise architecture.

Figure 1.4 shows some basic events that trigger a refresh of an enterprise architecture.

A final observation: any enterprise architecture must be seen (designed, delivered, and internally sold) as a deliverable product, something that can be "touched and used" not just an abstract conceptualization. In the IT context, an architecture needs to be perceived (seen) by users and stakeholders almost like another IT system application: it must have inputs, outputs, functionality, built-in data, etc. A simple conceptualization is difficult to be seen as adding value. If one is to consider the enterprise architecture as a set of "blueprint guidelines on how to build things, particularly showing the relationship of one IT entity with another," then the architecture should be perceived by the corporate user/developer to be like any other industry standard artifact (except that this applies internally to a firm rather than across the industry.) Such a standard is, in fact, a product: one can purchase a standard from ITU-T that is the definitive statement that a developer, say, of the Automatic Switched Optical Network (ASON), can use to develop globally conformant products. One can purchase a standard from the IEEE that is the definitive statement that a developer, say, of WiMax/802.16, can use to develop globally conformant products. So, we argue, the enterprise architecture description could well have the look-and-feel of an ISO, ITU-T, IEEE, ANSI, or IETF document with mandatory/optional capabilities, PICS Proforma, etc. If such ISO, IEEE, ANSI, IETF mechanisms are good enough to standardize products across an industry, or across several industries, or even across the world, why are these mechanism not good enough to standardize products inside a firm? Why does one need to reinvent, perhaps over several iterations, the set of architecture-supporting artifacts? This is what we meant earlier when we stated that there is, as of yet, not enough commoditization in IT: it is because often firms think that they are so different from one another that they have to reinvent how they undertake a common function, rather than use a standardized approach.

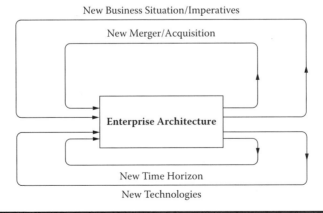

Figure 1.4 Some basic events that trigger a refresh of an enterprise architecture.

Next, we define a simple enterprise architecture model that we have used in recent years, which is depicted in Figure 1.5. This decomposition of the enterprise is modeled after TOGAF and is as follows:

- **Business Function:** This is a description of all business elements and structures that are covered by the enterprise.
- **Business Architecture:** An architectural formulation of the Business Function.
- **Information Function:** This is a comprehensive identification of the data, the data flows, and the data interrelations required to support the Business Function. The identification, systematization, categorization, and inventory/storage of information are always necessary to run a business, but these are essential if the data-handling functions are to be automated.
- **Information Architecture:** An architectural formulation of the Information Function via a data model.
- **(Systems/Application) Solution Function:** This is the function that aims at delivering/ supplying computerized IT systems required to support the plethora of specific functions needed by the Business Function.
- **(Systems/Application) Solution Architecture:** An architectural definition of the (Systems/ Application) Solution Function.
- **Technology Infrastructure Function:** The complete technology environment required to support the Information Function and the (Systems/Application) Solution Function.
- **Technology Infrastructure Architecture:** An architectural formulation (description) of the Technology Infrastructure Function.

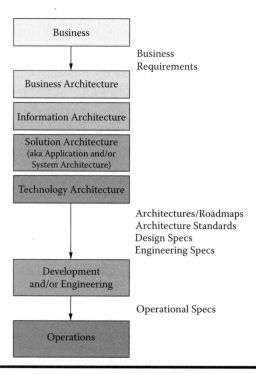

Figure 1.5 Enterprise architecture model, also showing architecture artifacts.

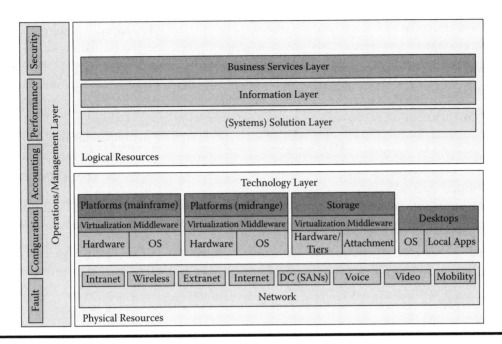

Figure 1.6 A layered model of the enterprise architecture.

These architecture sublayers are clearly related to one another via well-definable relations; integration of these sublayers is a necessity for a cohesive and effective enterprise architecture design. These layers are hierarchical only in the weak sense; hence, they can also be seen as domains (rather than layers per se.)

IT/networking security is also important, and firms need to have well-developed, comprehensive security architectures in place; this topic, however, is too extensive to be covered in this text.

Figure 1.6 partitions the IT space from an architectural perspective into logical resources, physical resources, and management resources. Physical resources in the Technology Layer provide the environment and services for executing applications; these resources encompass platforms (mainframe and midrange processors) along with hardware and operating system (OS) classifications; storage; desktops; and, networks (covering eight subcomponents). Notice the virtualization middleware, which we discuss later in the book. The Operations and Management Layer is a combination of processes and tools required to support the entire IT environment. It covers detection of faults and outages, configuration, administrative accounting, performance, and security.

As mentioned earlier, there are many models that can be used. The model of Figure 1.5 is loosely based on the Reference Model of Open Distributed Processing (ISO-RM-ODP) (ITU-T Rec. X.901-(aka) ISO/IEC 10746-1 through ITU-T Rec. X.904 (aka) ISO/IEC 10746-4), which provides a framework to support the development of standards to support distributed processing in heterogeneous environments. RM-ODP uses an object-modeling approach to describe distributed systems. Two structuring approaches are used to simplify the problems of design in large complex systems: (1) the "viewpoints" provide a way of describing the system; and (2) the "transparencies" identify specific problems unique to distributed systems. Each viewpoint is associated with a language that can be used to describe systems from that viewpoint. The five viewpoints in RM-ODP are the following:

1. The **enterprise** viewpoint, which examines the system and its environment in the context of the business requirements on the system, its purpose, scope, and policies. It deals with aspects of the enterprise, such as its organizational structure, that affect the system.
2. The **information** viewpoint, which focuses on the information in the system. How the information is structured, how it changes, information flows, and the logical divisions between independent functions within the system are all dealt with in the information viewpoint.
3. The **computational** viewpoint, which focuses on functional decomposition of the system into objects that interact at interfaces.
4. The **engineering** viewpoint, which focuses on how distributed interaction between system objects is supported.
5. The **technology** viewpoint, which concentrates on the individual hardware and software components that make up the system.

Having discussed this model, we alert the reader that the framework implied by Figures 1.5 and 1.6 is the one used in this text. Figure 1.7 shows how the key components of an architecture-enabled environment relate to one another.

Figure 1.8 illustrates some dos and don'ts in the process of developing or maintaining the enterprise architecture. Among other observations, the following are pertinent. Enterprise architecture must be more than just pretty pictures. Often, one sees lots of elaborate figures, charts, and presentations emerge from early enterprise architecture efforts at a firm, but unless the concepts are translated into actual decisions, migrations, and governance, such intriguing graphics will not lead to any concrete advancements and ameliorations. Enterprise architecture must help firms manage IT costs; it must help the organization decide where to make new IT investments, namely, where to "retain," "retire," or "rebuild" applications or infrastructure. Also, the architecture framework (just by) itself does not intrinsically save money for a firm: all of the follow-on artifacts must be developed, and, then, in turn applied to the environment, that is to say, implemented through funded efforts.

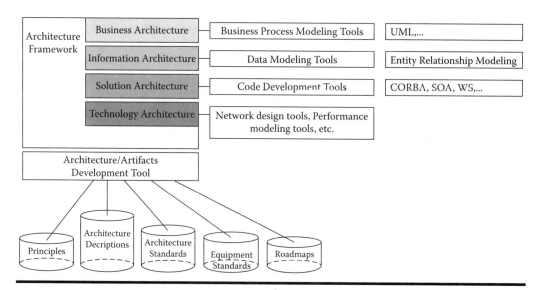

Figure 1.7   Key components of an architecture-enabled environment.

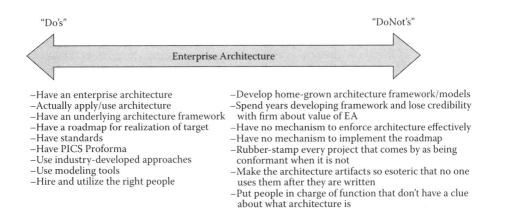

"Do's"   "DoNot's"

Enterprise Architecture

−Have an enterprise architecture
−Actually apply/use architecture
−Have an underlying architecture framework
−Have a roadmap for realization of target
−Have standards
−Have PICS Proforma
−Use industry-developed approaches
−Use modeling tools
−Hire and utilize the right people

−Develop home-grown architecture framework/models
−Spend years developing framework and lose credibility with firm about value of EA
−Have no mechanism to enforce architecture effectively
−Have no mechanism to implement the roadmap
−Rubber-stamp every project that comes by as being conformant when it is not
−Make the architecture artifacts so esoteric that no one uses them after they are written
−Put people in charge of function that don't have a clue about what architecture is

Figure 1.8 Some basic dos and don'ts in enterprise architecture.

1.4 Trends in Enterprise Architecture and Data Center Environments

In this section we highlight briefly some of the industry trends that are perceivable in the area of enterprise architecture and technology architecture (specifically, data center environments) at press time.

1.4.1 Enterprise Architecture

The following press time observations from *CIO* magazine do a good job of describing the environment and trends that impact enterprise architecture [KOC200501,KOC200502]:

Enterprise architecture has been around since the mid-1980s, but it has only recently begun to transform from an IT-centric exercise in mapping, controlling, standardizing and consolidating into something new—a function entrusted with creating a permanent process for alignment between IT and the business. This mandate is new, and forward-looking firms are just beginning to move beyond the IT architecture umbrella (which usually includes the data and infrastructure architectures).

However, practitioners believe that expanded role is not going to be successful if the Chief Information Officer (CIO) has not established institutionalized, repeatable governance processes that promote IT and business alignment at the highest level. The CIO has to report to the Chief Executive Officer (CEO) for enterprise architecture to be an alignment force. If CIOs cannot get access to strategic discussions, they cannot follow through on the next governance prerequisite to the new enterprise architecture: IT investment prioritization. If IT does not get access to the business at the highest level, IT is not going to get a clear idea of what the business really wants from IT. With a reasonable IT investment process in place at the highest level, enterprise architecture has a chance to move beyond IT architecture. But only if those who are part of the highest-level investment process are comfortable ceding some power and control to the architects. They need to make architecture review a condition for investment approval.

The executive committee holds the carrot (money) and they wave the stick, which is that before you come to us asking for money, you need to go through the architecture review process first. It is the only way to get midlevel business people to care about enterprise architecture. They do not care about IT architecture efforts that consolidate infrastructure or standardize applications because the savings do not impact them personally. They are focused on process. If the architects control investment and project review, they will start to care. Then it is up to the CIO to make sure that business people do not wind up hating the architects.

And enterprise architecture cannot become yet another effort to gain credibility for IT with the business. ... (one may) focus the enterprise architecture effort on IT architecture first before tackling the business and application architectures (i.e., before getting the business involved) because the business wanted proof that IT could deliver before giving up business people's time to the effort.

... Enterprise architecture has to offer more products and benefits to be accepted by the business. Architecture alone is not a viable sell. Service Oriented Architecture (SOA) is a great way to build enthusiasm for architecture among business people because it reduces IT to a vocabulary they can understand. ERP, CRM, legacy systems and integration are hidden beneath composite applications with names like "get credit rating" and "get customer record." Reuse becomes real and starts to impact midlevel business people directly because they can see how much faster they get new functionality from IT since "get customer" became a service in a repository that any developer can access when the need arises.

Advances in integration technology—primarily intelligent and flexible middleware and Web Services—are providing new ways for designing more agile, more responsive enterprise architectures that provide the kind of value the business has been seeking. With these new architectures, IT can build new business capabilities faster, cheaper and in a vocabulary the business can understand. These advances are giving new life to a couple of old concepts that could inspire new enterprise architecture efforts and revive failing ones. The first concept is services, better known today as SOA. SOA provides the value to the business that in the old enterprise architecture was rarely more than a vague promise. The idea behind services is simple: Technology should be expressed as a chunk of the business rather than as an arcane application...CIOs at large companies estimate that they may have on the order of 200 services sitting in a repository on their intranets, ranging from things like "credit check" to "customer record." Businesspeople can call for a service in a language they can understand, and IT can quickly link these with other services to form a workflow or, if need be, build a new application. These applications can be built quickly because complex, carefully designed interfaces allow developers to connect to the services without having to link directly to the code inside them. They do not even have to know how the service was built or in which type of language it was written. The second concept currently driving enterprise architecture is events. Pioneered by telecommunications carriers and financial services companies, this involves using IT systems to monitor a business process for events that matter—a stock-out in the warehouse, for example, or an especially large charge on a consumer's credit card—and automatically alert the people best equipped to do something about it. Together, services and events are revolutionizing the design of enterprise architecture, providing the kind of flexibility and value that CIOs, CFOs and CEOs have been looking for (but rarely have found) all these years. Services and events do not define enterprise architecture, but they can form its new core. CIOs who build enterprise architectures without a services-and-events approach will miss an opportunity to address the two most enduring—and accurate—complaints that the business has leveled at IT: slowness and inflexibility.

...In this evolving paradigm, enterprise architects have the opportunity to become the face of IT to the organization, consulting with business people to help them better articulate functional specifications. Technologies such as middleware, grid computing, Web Services (WS), enterprise architecture tools, and Business Process Management (BPM) tools are maturing to the point where architects can have a real strategic impact on the business and on IT. But not if governance has not been tackled first. CIOs need to do more to support their architects—the people who represent the future of the IT.

1.4.2 Technology Architecture

Although the entire IT environment greatly benefits from an architecture-based approach, as we will see in the next seven chapters, the second half of the book focuses principally on the technology infrastructure portion of the IT portfolio (the technology infrastructure architecture). This is relevant because as we saw earlier, a lot of the actual budget line-items are tied to this layer of the architecture. A press time survey of companies shows that having a technology architecture is as common as having the enterprise architecture as a whole*†[IEA200501].

In the early 1990s we published a fairly comprehensive book entitled *Enterprise Networking—From Fractional T1 to SONET, Frame Relay to BISDN* [MIN199301]. The text examined the plethora of evolving networking technologies that could be employed by large institutions to build out the (intranet) networking portion of the technology architecture. This present text extends the scope by examining late-decade networking, platform, and storage technologies. Also, this text extends a discussion of the enterprise architecture topic that was started by the author in a chapter entitled "Service Oriented Architecture Modeling: An Integrated Approach to Enterprise Architecture Definition That Spans the Business Architecture, the Information Architecture, the Solution Architecture, and the Technology Architecture," contained in the recently published *Handbook of IT and Finance* [MIN200701].

---

* The cited study obtained the following results: 15% of the surveyed companies had an enterprise architecture; 15% of the companies had a technology infrastructure architecture; 15% of the companies had a security architecture; 14% of the companies had an information-systems (solution, application) architecture; 13% of the companies had an information architecture/data model; 11% of the companies had a software architecture; and 10% of the companies had a business architecture.

† The cited study obtained the following results: 17% of the surveyed companies had an enterprise architecture; 14% of the companies had a technology infrastructure architecture; 10% of the companies had a security architecture; 14% of the companies had an information-systems (solution, application) architecture; 15% of the companies had an information architecture; 13% of the companies had a software architecture; and 12% of the companies had a business architecture.

New data center technologies such as blade servers, grid computing, IP storage, storage virtualization, tiered storage, Internet Fibre Channel Protocol (iFCP), Internet Small Computer System Interface (iSCSI), 10 Gigabit Ethernet (10GbE), storage attachment (only) via Storage Area Networks (SANs), MultiProtocol Label Switching backbone services, metro Ethernet services, and Voice-Over-IP (VoIP)/integrated networks are now become prominent for the technology layer of the enterprise architecture [MAC200501].

The following press time observations from a column for *NetworkWorld* by the author describes the technology environment and trends that likely will impact the technology architecture of an enterprise in the near future [MIN200601]:

Virtualization is a well known concept in networking, from Virtual Channels in Asynchronous Transfer Mode, to Virtual Private Networks, to Virtual LANs, and Virtual IP Addresses. However, an even more fundamental type of virtualization is achievable with today's ubiquitous networks: machine cycle and storage virtualization through the auspices of Grid Computing and IP storage. Grid Computing is also known as utility computing, what IBM calls on-demand computing.

Grid computing is a virtualization technology that was talked about in the 1980s and 1990s and entered the scientific computing field in the past ten years. The technology is now beginning to make its presence felt in the commercial computing environment. In the past couple of years there has been a lot of press and market activity, and a number of proponents see major penetration in the immediate future. IBM, Sun, Oracle, AT&T, and others are major players in this space.

Grid computing cannot really exist without networks (the "grid"), since the user is requesting computing or storage resources that are located miles or continents away. The user needs not be concerned about the specific technology used in delivering the computing or storage power: all the user wants and gets is the requisite "service." One can think of grid computing as a middleware that shields the user from the raw technology itself. The network delivers the job requests anywhere in the world and returns the results, based on an established service level agreement.

The advantages of grid computing are the fact that there can be a mix-and-match of different hardware in the network; the cost is lower because there is a better, statistically-averaged, utilization of the underlying resources; also, there is higher availability because if a processor were to fail, another processor is automatically switched in service. Think of an environment of a Redundant Array of Inexpensive Computers (RAICs), similar to the concept of Redundant Array of Inexpensive Drives (RAIDs).

Grid Computing is intrinsically network-based: resources are distributed all over an intranet, an extranet, or the Internet. Users can also get locally-based virtualization by using middleware such as VMware that allows a multitude of servers right in the corporate Data Center to be utilized more efficiently. Typically corporate servers are utilized for less than 30–40% of their available computing power. Using a virtualization mechanism the firm can improve utilization, increase availability, reduce costs, and make use of a plethora of mix-and-match processors; at a minimum this drives to server consolidation.

Security is a key consideration in grid computing. The user wants to get its services in a trustworthy and confidential manner. Then there is the desire for guaranteed levels of service and predictable, reduced costs. Finally, there is the need for standardization, so that a user with an appropriate middleware client software can transparently reach any registered resource in the network. Grid Computing supports the concept of the Service Oriented Architecture, where clients obtain services from loosely-coupled service-provider resources in the network. Web Services based on SOAP and Universal Description, Discovery and Integration (UDDI) protocols are now key building blocks of a grid environment.

These technologies will be discussed in Part 2 of this book.

1.5 Course of Investigation

Every organization that seeks to manage its IT complexity in a cost-effective manner and aims at rapid system deployment should consider making the appropriate investments in enterprise architecture. In this text we look at cost-saving trends in data center planning, administration, and management. We take a pragmatic approach to the discussion. We look at some of the framework models that have evolved, but we do not wish to become too abstract or formal. Nor do we want to take an overly high-level view of "nice chartware" that gets published by many of the vendors in the framework/architecture tools space. Appendix 1.2 provides for reference a partial list of books on enterprise architecture; approximately 60 books have appeared just in this decade. Effectively all of them, however, concentrate on the business, information (data), and system domains, not on the technology layer/domain; by contrast this treatise focuses on the Technology Infrastructure Architecture.

This book has two parts:

Part 1: The Logical Level: Enterprise Architecture A to Z: Frameworks, Business Process Modeling, and SOA

Part 2: The Infrastructure Level: Migrating to State-of-the-Art Environments in Enterprises with IT-Intensive Assets: Network Virtualization

To set a baseline for the discussion, we open in Part 1 of this text with an assessment of the role of enterprise architecture planning: Appendix 1.1 to this chapter provides a usable formal definition of an enterprise architecture; some of these concepts are used in other chapters. Chapter 2 looks at enterprise architecture goals, roles, and mechanisms. Chapter 3 discusses TOGAF. Chapter 4 looks at the Zachman Architectural Framework. Chapter 5 discusses some of the available official enterprise architecture standards. Chapter 6 provides a quick survey of enterprise architecture tools. Chapter 7 discusses business modeling and application development. Chapter 8 explores the issue of architecture fulfillment via SOA modeling.

Next, in Part 2, we focus on infrastructure technologies. An assessment of high-speed communication mechanisms such as SANs, Gigabit Ethernet, and metro Ethernet, is provided (Chapter 9). This is followed by a discussion of WAN and Internet communication technologies (Chapter 10).

Next, an assessment of networking virtualization via SOA constructs is provided (Chapter 11). Finally in Chapter 12 we look at grid computing and server virtualization. The appendix at the end of the book provides a short glossary of key terms and concepts used in the text.

As can be seen, we focus on the technology portion of the enterprise architecture; however, Part 1 provides a good view of the upper-layer modeling of a complete architecture. As we implied heuristically earlier, the technology portion of the architecture is where 40% of the budget is allocated and is where there is the most potential "churning" driven by incessant advancements in the constituent technologies.

Appendix 1.1: A Formal Definition of Architecture

Definition

What follows is a formal definition of an architecture; although we employ the term somewhat more loosely outside of this appendix, the mathematically precise definition we give here is worth considering.

Define a Function Block m at version n, FB(m,n), as comprising the following:

$$FB(m,n) = \{F(m,n), I(m,n,j), D(m,n,j), PI(m,n,j)\} \text{ for some } 1 \leq m \leq w$$

where

$F(m,n)$ is a set of (enterprise IT) functions that Function Block m can undertake at version n;

$I(m,n,j)$ is equal to "1" if Function Block FB(m,n) has an interface with Function Block FB(j,n) for j = 1, 2, …, x where x is the number of Function Blocks under consideration in this architecture, and "0" otherwise;

$D(m,n,j)$ is the set of data that is exchanged over interface $I(m,n,j)$ for all j where $I(m,n,j)$ = 1; and

$PI(m,n,j)\}$ is the protocol used to exchange data over interface $I(m,n,j)$ for all j where $I(m,n,j)$ = 1.

Finally, assume that a (nonoverlapping) partition exists such that {FB(m,n)} = P(1,n) U P(2,n) U P(3,n)… U P(y,n) for m = 1, 2, …, x.

Then, **enterprise architecture A(n)** is defined as

$$A(n) = \{P(k,n)\}, k = 1, 2, …, y$$

Note the following points:

1. We also call the set **{P(k,n)}, k = 1, 2, …, y** the *"architecture description."*
2. The set $\alpha(m,n)$ = {F(m,n), I(m,n,j), PI(m,n,j)} for some $1 \leq m \leq w$ (this is the same as FB(m,n) but with the omission of D(m,n,j) for all applicable values of j is also called the "set of *attributes of the architecture A(n)*"; basically, the attributes set is the set of function groupings, the constituent functions, the interfaces, and the protocols utilized over the interfaces.
3. The PI(m,n,j)} protocol set used to exchange data over interface I(m,n,j) for all j where I(m,n,j) = 1 is called the *set of EA standards*, or *standards set*.
4. If a canonical set of equipment E(n,m) is defined as follows:

$E(m,n) = \{E(m,n,i), i = 1,2, \ldots, z\}$, where $E(m,n,i)$ supports $FB(m,n)$ for some $i = 1, 2, \ldots, z$, and $E(m,n)$ is the only permitted equipment to support $FB(m,n)$, then this is known as the *approved equipment list* for Function Block m at time n. The set union of all $E(n) = \{E(n,m), m = 1, 2, \ldots, w\}$ is called the *enterprise approved equipment list.*

Example

A formal example follows:
   Define:

   $F(1,n)$ = corporate LAN at month n
   $F(2,n)$ = corporate WAN at month n
   $F(3,n)$ = corporate extranet at month n
   $F(4,n)$ = traditional corporate voice at month n

Then (assume):

   $I(1,2,n) = 1$
   $I(1,3,n) = 1$
   $I(1,4,n) = 0$
   $I(2,3,n) = 0$
   $I(2,4,n) = 0$
   $I(3,4,n) = 0$

Then:

   $D(1,2,n)$ = Encrypted files
   $D(1,3,n)$ = Encrypted files

Then:

   $PI(1,2,n)$ = TCP/IP with IPSec
   $PI(1,3,n)$ = TCP/IP with SSL

So,

   $FB(1,n) = \{F(1,n)$ = corporate LAN at month n, $I(1,2,n) = 1$, $I(1,3,n) = 1$, $I(1,4,n) = 0$, $D(1,2,n)$ = Encrypted files, $D(1,3,n)$ = Encrypted files, $PI(1,2,n)$ = TCP/IP with IPSec, $PI(1,3,n)$ = TCP/IP with SSL$\}$
   $FB(2,n) = \{F(2,n)$ = corporate WAN at month n, $I(2,3,n) = 0$, $I(2,4,n) = 0\}$
   $FB(3,n) = \{F(3,n)$ = corporate extranet at month n, $I(3,4,n) = 0\}$
   $FB(4,n) = \{F(4,n)$ = traditional corporate voice at month $n\}$

Finally, assume that $P(1,n) = \{FB(1,n), FB(2,n), FB(3,n)\}$ (these are the data networks) and $P(2,n) = \{FB(4,n)\}$ (the voice network).

$$A(n) = \{P(1,n), P(2,n)\}.$$

The standards set would be {PI(1,2,n) = TCP/IP with IPSec, PI(1,3,n) = TCP/IP with SSL}
An equipment list can be defined as follows (by way of an example):

$E(n,1) = \{E(1,n,1) = $ Cisco 4500, $E(1,n,2) = $ Cisco 6500, $E(1,n,3) = $ Cisco 3750$\}$
$E(n,2) = \{E(2,n,1) = $ Cisco IGX$\}$
$E(n,3) = \{E(3,n,1) = $ Cisco IGX$\}$
$E(n,4) = \{E(4,n,1) = $ Nortel PBX$\}$

This approach is pedantic, but rigorous.

Now, assume that at time $n + 1$ one added Voice-over-IP so that the LAN and WAN now "talk" to the voice network; also, it is desirable to view the voice network as a data network for the purpose of network management. This decision process (strategy) is external to the architecture itself; for example, a company (such as a system integrator) may want to deploy VoIP internally to gain experience with that technology to then sell that to prospective customers; again note that decision process (strategy) is external to the architecture itself.

Then we would have the following:

$I(1,2,n + 1) = 1$
$I(1,3, n + 1) = 1$
$I(1,4, n + 1) = 1$
$I(2,3, n + 1) = 0$
$I(2,4, n + 1) = 1$
$I(3,4, n + 1) = 0$

Then:

$D(1,2, n + 1) = $ encrypted files
$D(1,3, n + 1) = $ encrypted files
$D(1,4, n + 1) = $ compressed voice files
$D(2,4, n + 1) = $ compressed voice files

Then:

$PI(1,2, n + 1) = $ TCP/IP with IPSec
$PI(1,3, n + 1) = $ TCP/IP with SSL
$PI(1,4, n + 1) = $ RTP/UDP
$PI(2,4, n + 1) = $ RTP/UDP

So:

$FB(1,n) = \{F(1,n) = $ corporate LAN at month n, $I(1,2,n) = 1$, $I(1,3,n) = 1$, $I(1,4,n) = 1$, $D(1,2,n) = $ Encrypted files, $D(1,3,n) = $ Encrypted files, $D(1,4, n + 1) = $ compressed voice files, $PI(1,2,n) = $ TCP/IP with IPSec, $PI(1,3,n) = $ TCP/IP with SSL, $PI(1,4, n + 1) = $ RTP/UDP$\}$

$FB(2,n) = \{F(2,n) = $ corporate WAN at month n, $I(2,3,n) = 0$, $I(2,4,n) = 1$, $D(2,4, n + 1) = $ compressed voice files, $PI(2,4, n + 1) = $ RTP/UDP$\}$

FB(3,*n*) = {F(3,*n*) = corporate extranet at month *n*, I(3,4,*n*) = 0}
FB(4,*n*) = {F(4,*n*) = VoIP at month *n*}

Finally, assume that P*(1,*n*) = {FB(1,*n*), FB(2,*n*), FB(3,*n*), FB(4,*n*)} (these are the data networks). Hence:

$$A(n + 1) = \{P(1, n + 1)\}.$$

Now, a roadmap along with (migration) strategies would be needed to convert **A(*n*) = {P(1,*n*), P(2,*n*)}** to **A(*n* + 1) = {P*(1,*n* + 1)}.**

Figure A1.1.1 depicts pictorially an example of the changes to an architecture over time.

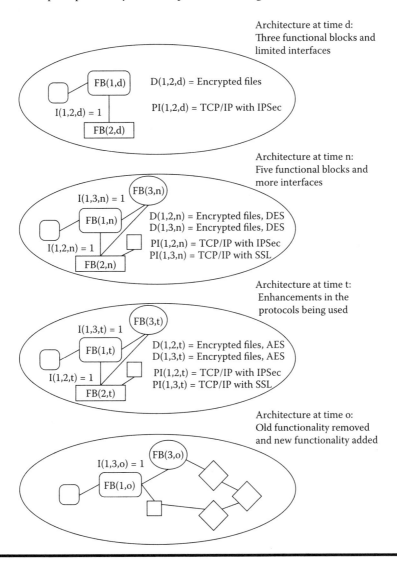

Figure A1.1.1   An example of the changes to an architecture over time.

Summary/Interpretation

An enterprise architecture at any instance *n* is an exact description of the functionality, the interfaces, the data, and the interface protocols supported by the (partitioned) set of functional elements in the environment, as of time instance *n*. Call that simply "enterprise architecture, the current blueprint," or just "enterprise architecture." One is then able to provide a description of a desired target state at time *n* + 1 or *n* + *j* in terms of possibly new functionalities, new interfaces, new data, new interface protocols, and possibly new partitioning of the set of functional elements. Call that the "enterprise architecture blueprint for the target state," or just "target state enterprise architecture."

Notice once again that (1) the strategy decision for wanting to define a certain "target state enterprise architecture" is actually external to the architecture itself (the architecture simply states how all the parts work together); and (b) the strategy steps needed to actually transition to the "target state enterprise architecture," the roadmap and the development plan, are also external to the architecture itself.

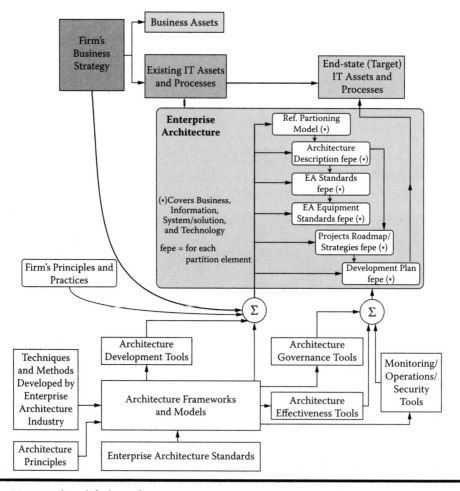

Figure A1.1.2 Pictorial view of concepts.

However, for practical considerations the following will be considered part of the enterprise architecture:

■ The enterprise architecture description (of the current or target state)
■ The enterprise standards set
■ The enterprise approved equipment list
■ The roadmap, along with (migration) strategies

See Figure A1.1.2.

The frameworks and models discussed in Chapter 2 provide ways of looking at the partition, the data representation, etc., and do not invalidate the formulation given earlier.

Appendix 1.2: Bibliography on Enterprise Architecture

The following is a partial list of books on enterprise architecture. Almost all of them concentrate on the business, information (data), and system domains, not on the technology layer/domain; by contrast this treatise focuses on the technology infrastructure architecture.

1. Alan Dennis and Roberta M. Roth, *Systems Analysis and Design,* Pub. Date: September 2005.
2. Alex Duong Nghiem and Alex Nghiem, *IT Web Services: A Roadmap for the Enterprise,* Pub. Date: September 2002.
3. Andrzej Targowski and Andrew Targowski, *Electronic Enterprise: Strategy and Architecture,* Pub. Date: September 2003.
4. Anneke G. Kleppe, Jos Warmer, and Wim Bast, *MDA Explained: The Model Driven Architecture: Practice and Promise,* Pub. Date: April 2003.
5. Brett McLaughlin and Mike Loukides (Eds.), *Building Java Enterprise Applications Volume I: Architecture,* Pub. Date: March 2002.
6. Chris Britton, *IT Architectures and Middleware: Strategies for Building Large, Integrated Systems,* Pub. Date: December 2000.
7. Chris Britton and Peter Bye, *IT Architectures and Middleware: Strategies for Building Large, Integrated Systems,* Pub. Date: May 2004.
8. Christophe Longepe, *Enterprise Architecture IT Project: The Urbanisation Paradigm,* Pub. Date: July 2003.
9. Clive Finkelstein, *Enterprise Architecture for Integration: Rapid Delivery Methods and Technologies,* Pub. Date: April 2006.
10. Dan Woods, *Enterprise Services Architecture,* Pub. Date: September 2003.
11. Dan Woods and Thomas Mattern, *Enterprise Services Architecture,* Pub. Date: April 2006.
12. Daniel Serain, I. Craig (Translator), *Middleware and Enterprise Application Integration: The Architecture of E-Business Solutions,* Pub. Date: September 2002.
13. David A. Chappell, *Enterprise Service Bus,* Pub. Date: June 2004.
14. David Frankel, Foreword by Michael Guttman, *Model Driven Architecture: Applying MDA to Enterprise Computing,* Pub. Date: November 2002.
15. David McCullough, *The Great Bridge: The Epic Story of the Building of the Brooklyn Bridge,* Pub. Date: June 2001.
16. David S. Frankel (Ed.), John Parodi (Ed.), *MDA Journal: Model Driven Architecture Straight from the Masters,* Pub. Date: November 2004.
17. Dennis M. Buede, *Engineering Design of Systems: Models and Methods,* Pub. Date: September 1999.
18. Dimitris N. Chorafas, *Enterprise Architecture: For New Generation Information Systems,* Pub. Date: December 2001.

19. Dirk Krafzig, Dirk Slama, and Karl Banke, *Enterprise SOA: Service Oriented Architecture Best Practices (The Coad Series)*, Pub. Date: November 2004.

20. Douglas K. Barry, Foreword by Patrick J. Gannon, *The Savvy Manager's Guide to Web Services and Service-Oriented Architectures*, Pub. Date: April 2003.

21. Eric A. Marks and Michael Bell, *Executive's Guide to Service-Oriented Architecture*, Pub. Date: April 2006.

22. Eric Newcomer, Greg Lomow, and David Chappell (Eds.), *Understanding SOA with Web Services (Independent Technology Guides Series)*, Pub. Date: December 2004.

23. Faisal Hoque, Foreword by Tom Trainer, Dale Kutnick (Introduction), *E-Enterprise: Business Models, Architecture, and Components*, Pub. Date: February 2000.

24. Fred A. Cummins, *Enterprise Integration: An Architecture for Enterprise Application and Systems Integration*, Pub. Date: January 2002.

25. George W. Anderson, *SAP Planning: Best Practices in Implementation*, Pub. Date: April 2003.

26. Gerhard Wiehler, *Mobility, Security and Web Services: Technologies and Service-Oriented Architectures for a New Era of IT Solutions*, Pub. Date: September 2004.

27. Gustavo Alonso, Fabio Casati, Harumi Kuno, and Vijay Machiraju, *Web Services Concepts, Architecture and Applications*, Pub. Date: October 2003.

28. Hugh Taylor, *Joy of SOX: Why Sarbanes-Oxley and Services Oriented Architecture May be the Best Thing That Ever Happened to You*, Pub. Date: April 2006.

29. Irv Englander and Arv Englander, *Architecture of Computer Hardware and Systems Software: An Information Technology Approach*, Pub. Date: April 1996.

30. Jaap Schekkerman, *How to Survive in the Jungle of Enterprise Architecture Frameworks: Creating or Choosing an Enterprise Architecture Framework*, Updated Edition Pub. Date: December 2003.

31. James McGovern, Scott W. Ambler, Michael E. Stevens, James Linn, and Vikas Sharan, *A Practical Guide to Enterprise Architecture (The Coad Series)*, Pub. Date: October 2003.

32. Jan Killmeyer Tudor, *Information Security Architecture: An Integrated Approach to Security in the Organization*, Pub. Date: September 2000.

33. Jane Carbone, *IT Architecture Toolkit*, Pub. Date: October 2004.

34. Jeff Garland and Richard Anthony, *Large-Scale Software Architecture: A Practical Guide using UML*, Pub. Date: December 2002.

35. Jeffrey A. Hoffer, Joseph S. Valacich, and Joey F. George, *Modern Systems Analysis and Design*, Pub Date: May 2004.

36. Jeffrey Hasan, Foreword by Keith Ballinger, *Expert Service-Oriented Architecture in C#: Using the Web Services Enhancements 2.0*, Pub. Date: August 2004.

37. Jeffrey L. Whitten and Lonnie D. Bentley, *Systems Analysis and Design Methods*, Pub Date: 2006.

38. John Blommers, Hewlett-Packard Professional Books, *Architecting Enterprise Solutions With Unix Networking*, Pub. Date: October 1998.

39. John Sherwood, Andrew Clark, and David Lynas, *Enterprise Security Architecture: A Business-Driven Approach*, Pub. Date: December 2005.

40. Kenneth E. E. Kendall and Julie E. Kendall, *Systems Analysis and Design*, Pub. Date: March 2004.

41. Kent Sandoe, Gail Corbitt, and Raymond Boykin, *Enterprise Integration*, Pub. Date: December 1999.

42. Khawar Zaman Zaman Ahmed and Cary E. Umrysh, *Developing Enterprise Java Applications with J2EE and UML*, Pub. Date: October 2001.

43. Laurie Kelly and Fenix Theuerkorn, *Lightweight Enterprise Architectures*, Pub. Date: June 2004.

44. Mark Goodyear, *Enterprise System Architectures*, Pub. Date: December 1999.

45. Martin Fowler, David Rice, Matthew Foemmel, Edward Hieatt, and Robert Mee, *Patterns of Enterprise Application Architecture*, Pub. Date: November 2002.

46. Melissa A. Cook, Hewlett Packard Staff, *Building Enterprise Information Architectures: Reengineering Information Systems*, Pub. Date: January 1996.

47. Norbert Bieberstein, Rawn Shah, Keith Jones, Sanjay Bose, and Marc Fiammante, *Service-Oriented Architecture (SOA) COMPASS: Business Value, Planning, and Enterprise Roadmap,* Pub. Date: October 2005.
48. Peter Bernus, Laszlo Nemes, Guenter Schmidt, and Gunter Schmidt (Eds.), *Handbook on Enterprise Architecture,* Pub. Date: September 2003.
49. Rahul Sharma, Beth Stearns, and Tony Ng, *J2EE Connector Architecture and Enterprise Application Integration,* Pub. Date: December 2001.
50. Ralph Whittle and Conrad B. Myrick, *Enterprise Business Architecture,* Pub. Date: August 2004.
51. Richard Hubert, Foreword by David A. Taylor, *Convergent Architecture: Building Model-Driven J2EE Systems with UML (OMG Press),* Pub. Date: November 2001.
52. Richard Monson-Haefel, Bill Burke, and Sacha Labourey, *Enterprise JavaBeans,* 4th Edition Pub. Date: June 2004.
53. Roel Wagter, Joost Luijpers, Klaas Brongers, Martin van den Berg, and Marlies Van Steenbergen, *Dynamic Architecture: How to Make Enterprise Architecture a Success,* Pub. Date: February 2005.
54. Scott A. Bernard, *An Introduction to Enterprise Architecture: Second Edition,* Pub. Date: September 2005.
55. Staff of Microsoft, *Microsoft .NET Core Requirements (MCAD/MCSD Self-Paced Training Kit Series),* Pub. Date: April 2003.
56. Steven H. Spewak, Steven C. Hill, and Hill Steve, *Enterprise Architecture Planning: Developing a Blueprint for Data, Applications, and Technology,* Pub. Date: May 1993.
57. Thomas Erl, *Service-Oriented Architecture: A Field Guide to Integrating XML and Web Services,* Pub. Date: April 2004.
58. Thomas Erl, *Service-Oriented Architecture: Concepts, Technology, and Design,* Pub. Date: August 2005.
59. Waqar Sadiq and Fred A. Cummins, *Developing Business Systems with CORBA with CD-ROM: The Key to Enterprise Integration,* Pub. Date: April 1998.

Chapter 2

Enterprise Architecture Goals, Roles, and Mechanisms

What does a corporate or institutional enterprise architecture corporate function address? What are the available architecture frameworks? What can tools do?

This chapter covers, at a macro level, the following: (1) techniques for developing an enterprise architecture by using an architecture framework; (2) tools for using the framework to instantiate the architecture; and (3) mechanisms for actually building out the architecture. We begin in Section 2.1 by reviewing some motivations as to why enterprise architectures are needed and some general approaches to the development effort, e.g., guiding principles and architecture techniques (see the lower portion of Figure 2.1). We then focus generically in Section 2.2 on architectural frameworks (e.g., Federal Enterprise Architecture Framework, Zachman Framework; see center-lower portion of Figure 2.1). In Section 2.3 we briefly discuss some governance approaches.

This discussion is completed over the next six chapters. Chapters 3 and 4 focus more directly on The Open Group Architecture Framework (TOGAF) and the Zachman Framework, respectively. Chapter 5 looks at what official architectural standards are available. Chapter 6 looks at tools (e.g., ARIS). Chapter 7 looks at business process modeling (BPM), relational/process modeling (UML), and requirements gathering and analysis. Chapter 8 looks at architecture fulfillment via service-oriented architecture (SOA) modeling; SOA is a method (but not the only one) to actually implement a portion or the entire enterprise architecture.

2.1 Enterprise Architecture

In this section we review some motivations as to why enterprise architectures are needed and some general approaches to the development effort, e.g., guiding principles and architecture techniques.

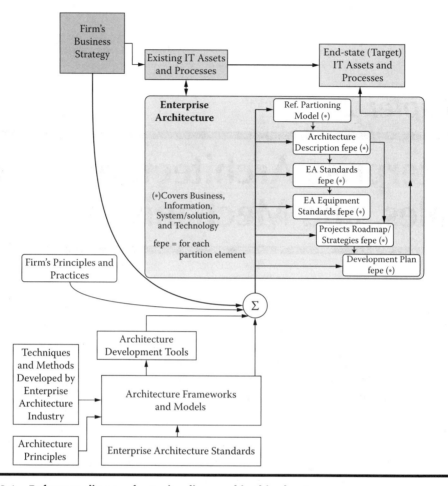

Figure 2.1 Reference diagram for topics discussed in this chapter.

2.1.1 Description of Enterprise

For the purpose of this book *enterprise* is any collection of corporate or institutional task-supporting functional entities that have a set of common goals or a single mandate. In this context, an enterprise is, but is not limited to, an entire corporation, a division or department of a corporation, a group of geographically dispersed organizations linked together by common administrative ownership, a government agency (or set of agencies) at any level of jurisdiction, a group of government agencies, and so on. This also encompasses the concept on an *extended enterprise*, which is a logical aggregation that includes internal business units of a firm along with partners and suppliers (sometimes customers are also considered part of an *extended enterprise*).

Large organizations and government entities may comprise multiple enterprises; however, there is often a lot in common about overall mission, and, hence, the ensuing need for (minimally) interoperable information systems, consistent data representations/extracts; in turn, this drives the desire for a common architecture framework. One of the many examples that could be given deals with having a set of common radio frequencies (and supportive infrastructure, whether that be physical, logical, or IT system level) that could be used by first responders. A common architecture supports cohesive multi-organizational operation. A common architectural framework, in turn, can provide a basis for the development of an architecture repository for the integration and reuse of models, designs, and baseline data.

In this book, in conformance with common parlance in the enterprise architecture context, the term *enterprise* is taken to denote the enterprise itself, as just defined, as well as all of its information systems and operational data; furthermore, the term is also employed to discuss a specific business domain within the enterprise at large, along with all the subtending information systems and data to support that specific function. In both cases, the architecture crosses multiple systems, and multiple functional groups within the enterprise.

2.1.2 Definition of Architecture

An enterprise architecture is a plan of record, a blueprint of the permitted structure, arrangement, configuration, functional groupings/partitioning, interfaces, data, protocols, logical functionality, integration, technology, of IT resources needed to support a corporate or organizational business function or mission. Typically, resources that need architectural formulations include applications, security subsystems, data structures, networks, hardware platforms, storage, desktop systems, to name just a few. The term *enterprise* is taken to be consistent with that given in Chapter 1. As described in ANSI/IEEE Std 1471-2000, an **architecture** is "the fundamental organization of a system, embodied in its components, their relationships to each other and the environment, and the principles governing its design and evolution."

As we discussed in Appendix 1.1 of Chapter 1, the following will be considered here as being part of the enterprise architecture:

- The enterprise architecture description (of the current or target state)
- The enterprise architecture standards set
- The enterprise approved equipment list
- The roadmap along with (migration) strategies

Areas where firms may look to develop an architecture include the following:

- **Business function:** This is a description of the all business elements and structures that are covered by the enterprise. These aspects capture the business logic functionality, specifically business processes. (In the language of Appendix 1.1 this would be called Business Functional Group.)
- **Information function:** This is a comprehensive identification of the data, the data flows, and the data interrelations required to support the business function. The identification, systematization, categorization, and inventory/storage of information are always necessary to run a business, but these are essential if the data-handling functions are to be automated. (In the language of Appendix 1.1 this would be called Information Functional Group.)
- **(Systems/application) Solution function:** This is the function that aims at delivering/supplying computerized IT systems required to support the plethora of specific functions needed by the business function. (In the language of Appendix 1.1 this would be called (Systems/Application) Solution Functional Group.)
- **Technology infrastructure function:** The complete technology environment required to support the information function and the (systems/application) solution function. (In the language of Appendix 1.1 this would be called Technology Functional Group.)

Subareas where firms may look to develop an architecture include, but are not limited to, the following:

- Presentation aspects of IT applications: These aspects define the logical interfaces between applications, and between applications and user systems.
- Application integration aspects: These aspects describe the interconnection mechanism of the business logic as implemented in IT applications (this supports the specification of interfaces, and messaging).
- Information management aspects: These aspects deal with the design and construction of data structures; data entities and relationships between data entities are defined via a data model.
- Technology infrastructure aspects: networks, platforms, storage, desktops, etc.

Architectures include the following (potentially along with other architectures to support the aspects just described):

- Business architecture: an architectural formulation of the business function.
- Information architecture: an architectural formulation of the Information Function via a data model.
- (Systems/application) solution architecture: an architectural definition of the (systems/application) solution function.
- Technology infrastructure architecture: an architectural formulation (description) of the technology infrastructure function.

The preceding paragraph points out that a firm will typically have several interlocking architectures that cover various aspects of the IT/enterprise function. For example, a presentation services architecture, an application integration architecture, an information/data architecture, a network architecture, a hardware platform architecture, etc. It is not possible or desirable to develop a massive architecture that covers everything. Figure 2.2 depicts the concept of multiple subarchitectures pictorially.

2.1.3 Motivations for Having an Enterprise Architecture

Enterprise architecture drives to standardization, which in turn drives to commoditization, as discussed in Chapter 1. Standardization results in (1) lower run-the-engine (RTE) costs and (2) faster rollout of a function, whether this is an atomic function such as "configure a server," "configure a storage partition," or a more complexly integrated function, such as a new software application. Figure 2.3 shows pictorially that although a completely rigid rollout of a standard may not always be optimal, a position where there is a large degree of standardization may be the overall optimal strategy. Architecture work is important for at least three reasons: It (1) enables communication among stakeholders, (2) facilitates early design decisions, and (3) creates a transferable abstraction of a system/environment description [FER200401]. The enterprise architecture will help firms manage their IT costs; it helps the organization decide where to make new IT investments, namely, where to retain, retire, or rebuild applications or infrastructure.

As information technology extends its reach into every facet of the enterprise and as the panoply of systems, applications, databases, servers, networks, and storage appliances become highly

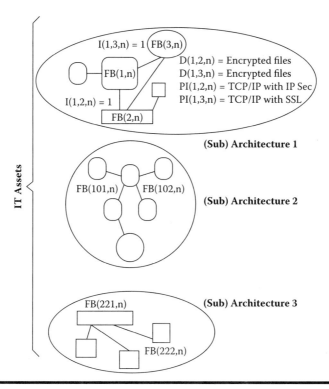

Figure 2.2   Collection of subarchitectures.

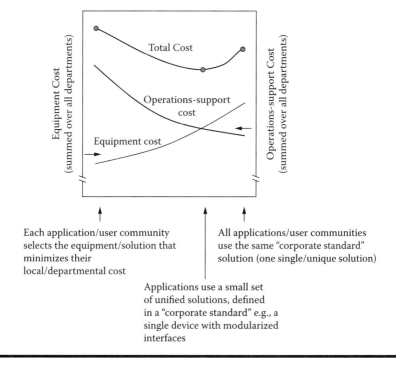

Figure 2.3   Optimality locus.

interconnected and highly interdependent at the logical and at the physical level, IT practitioners need to recognize the growing importance of enterprise architecture to the continued success and growth of the firm [ZIF200501]. Enterprise architecture work, when done correctly, provides a systematic assessment and description of how the business function operates at the current time; it provides a "blueprint" of how it should operate in the future, and, it provides a roadmap for getting to the target state. For example, for the U.S. Department of the Navy (DON) Enterprise Architecture development has been driven by a technology change, the implementation of the Navy Marine Corps Intranet (NMCI), and a mandate to reduce its application portfolio by 95%. The Application Rationalization Review conducted under the auspice of enterprise architecture initiatives indeed reduced the Navy and Marine Corps application portfolio from 100,000 applications to 60,000 applications; the final phase of these reviews will reduce the application portfolio to approximately 5000 supported applications [FEA200501].

Figure 2.4 shows how the IT budget maps (approximately) to the layers of the architecture and the supported functions. As can be seen, large fractions of the budget are allocated to activities related to the technology layer and to the development layer. Given the size of these allocations, it is useful to have a planned approach to the management of these IT resources.

Table 2.1 depicts the actual perceived value for the development of enterprise architecture, based on an extensive press time survey of large institutions around the globe and in several industry segments [IEA200501]. Table 2.2 identifies issues that are expected to be resolved by the development of enterprise architectures.

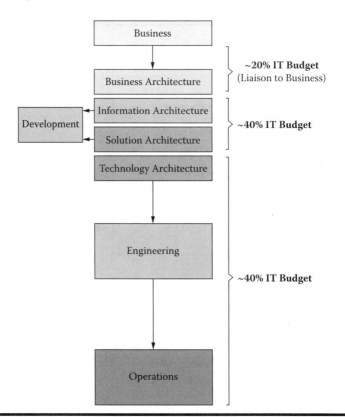

Figure 2.4 Mapping of IT budget to IT layers.

Table 2.1 Reasons Given for the Perceived Value of the Development of Enterprise Architecture in Large Corporations

Reason	Percentage of Companies
Supports decision making	16
Helps manage IT portfolio	14
Delivers blueprints for change	14
Helps manage complexity	12
Supports systems development	12
Delivers insight and overview of business and IT	11
Supports business and IT budget prioritization	11
Supports (out/in) sourcing	5
Helps affecting mergers and acquisitions	3
Other	2

Table 2.2 Issues That Firms Expect Enterprise Architecture to Help Tackle On

Specific Goals	Percentage of Companies
Business–IT alignment	20
Business change	15
Transformation roadmap	15
Infrastructure renewal	12
Legacy transformation	11
ERP implementation	11
Application renewal	10
Mergers/acquisition	4
Other	2

E-Government initiatives are driving the introduction of enterprise architecture. At press time about 1/4 of government agencies sampled were undertaking IT architectural efforts and about 1/6 of financial companies were also doing so; business segments such as insurance, telecom, utilities appear to be lagging, with only 1/50 of the establishments in each of these segments engaged in such efforts [IEA200501]. In the industry the function typically reports to the IT director/manager (in about a third of the companies that do have an architecture group); to the CIO (in about another third of the companies); and to a business manager, the CTO, the CEO, or the board of directors (in the rest of the companies). However, some see a recent shift of responsibilities from the CIO to a higher level, such as board members, or a shift to a federated environment that directly involves business managers.

What are the risks of not developing an enterprise architecture? Without enterprise architecture work, the following risks exist, among others:

- Locally optimal, rather than globally optimal solutions
- Expensive, nonshared, RTE-intensive solutions
- Closed vendor/proprietary environments—little leverage

- Solution band-aiding for the short term, but constraining in the long term
- Nonadherence to standards; complex solutions; plethora of one-off designs

Even if an organization outsources some (or all) of its IT functions and runs a set of these functions with an application service provider (ASP)-like arrangement, without architecture work the following risks exist:

- Vendor enslavement
- Suboptimal service from a cost, feature, and portability perspective
- Excessive, unhealthy reliance on vendor, which may not have a firm's best interests at heart
- Failure to follow industry standards or regulatory compliance
- Not achieving best-in-class/best-in-breed solutions
- Inappropriate visibility due to nonoptimal service level agreement (SLA) metrics

Even if an organization outsources some (or all) of its IT functions and runs a set of these functions with an asset-retention arrangement (in which the sources provide the personnel to run the function but the firm still owns the IT assets), without architecture work the following risks exist:

- Infrastructure becomes outdated and expensive
- Expensive, nonshared, RTE-intensive solutions
- Excessive, unhealthy reliance on vendor, which may not have firm's best interests at heart
- Failure to follow industry standards or regulatory compliance
- Not achieving best-in-class/best-in-breed solutions

In cases involving outsourcing, the planners need to take into account the end-to-end view and have the synthesis of an "extended enterprise" in mind. Here, certain portions of the environment will be directly controllable by the firm, whereas others will only be indirectly controllable. It is important to note, however, that in many (if not most) instances it is undesirable, in the long term, to not exercise any control even on the indirectly controllable portion of the operation.

The following are often-cited [ZIF200501] motivations/observations about enterprise architecture:

- Enterprise architecture is fundamental for successful participation in the global interaction of modern enterprises.
- Enterprise architecture is the principal structural mechanism for:
  - Establishing a basis for assimilating high rates of change
  - Advancing the state-of-the-art in enterprise design
  - Managing the knowledge base of the enterprise
  - Integrating the technology (automated or nonautomated) into the fabric of the enterprise
- Enterprise architecture is universal—that is, every enterprise of any substance and any expectation of longevity needs to employ architectural concepts.
- Enterprise architecture is cross-disciplinary, requiring integration of diverse skills, methods, and tools, within and beyond the technology community.

2.1.4 Role Enterprise Architecture Group

There are two polar-opposite approaches to the organizational role of the enterprise architecture function, along with something in between:

1. Mandate that absolutely no project can be approved for deployment if it does not conform to an architectural standard or go through an architectural assessment. Companies in this arena are either companies that have several decades of process-development history (but not limited to large manufacturing establishments), or companies that have a large installed base and so it make sense to test and validate a system for conformance before it is deployed in the field (e.g., traditional telecom carriers).
2. Strictly run the enterprise architecture function on a "pure advocacy basis": the group has no budgetary control and no (or very weak) enforcement control. Here, in effect, adherence to the architecture blueprint by the larger IT organization or by the business users, is pretty much voluntary; clearly, in this environment the function of the enterprise architecture group, unfortunately, often has relatively little overall impact. Companies in this arena tend to be younger companies that have grown to the ranks of Fortune 500 rather quickly and may only have a corporate history going back a decade or two.

The "in-between" formulation between these two extremes would say that firm placed IT subareas in two categories. For subareas in Category A the firm mandates that no project can be approved for deployment if it does not conform to an architectural standard or go through an architectural assessment. For subareas in Category B the firm runs the enterprise architecture function on an advocacy basis. It should be noted that the same kind of diagram as Figure 2.3 is applicable here: it would be optimal for the firm if a major portion (but not necessarily all) of the subareas were classified as Category A. We call this environment a Well Thought-Out Environment (WTE).

There is a fine balance between having an enterprise architecture group that "has no teeth" and one that is perceived to "have too much bite"; however, if the architecture group is to be successful, such a balance must be achieved. In some companies a developer or planner who wants to spend more than a quarter-of-a-million dollars on a project must get approval from the architecture group: to secure the funds, project leaders have to submit to a review process where the architects decide whether the project's goals and technology fit into the firm's overall business and technology strategy [KOC200502].

IT organizations need to take more leadership within the business context and achieve the "proper level of respect/confidence" within the organization. Respect and confidence are achieved by delivering products and services on a cost-effective, timely, and uncomplicated manner. IT cannot be "just taking orders" from the business side and constantly be in a "begging mode" where all they do is advocating this or advocating that; instead, IT must develop a corporate posture and positioning, based on sustained credibility and success, to be able to mandate various (architectural) solutions or approaches, and not just be in the advocacy role.

At first brush, standardizing, mapping, and controlling IT assets does not make the business more flexible, capable, or profitable for the immediate next quarter; as a result, IT architecture efforts at some firms fail or become completely IT-centric [KOC200502]. However, an analysis of (all sorts of) industry standardization efforts over the past 20 years shows unambiguously that not only do these efforts come to fruition in the sense of reducing costs over a period of perhaps three to five years, but entirely new functional enablements are fostered and triggered by the introduction of broadly available standardized techniques, platforms, data formats, protocols, and so on.

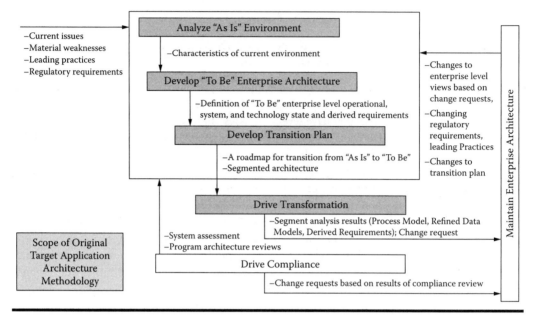

Figure 2.5 Synthesis of the enterprise architecture function as described in the FEAF.

In a well-thought-out environment, the enterprise architecture function develops and then "promulgates" high-level architectural requirements to in-house IT-services or to sourcing vendors to ensure best-in-class, industry-grade, reliable, open, measurable, portable, and replicable service environments. These guidelines aim at maximizing a firm's business/IT flexibility at any future point in time.

As a point of reference, Figure 2.5 depicts a synthesis of the enterprise architecture function as described in the FEAF [FEA200503].

In a well-thought-out organizational environment, when a new business imperative presents itself, a (high-level) enterprise architecture target is developed and architecture specifications (standards, or at least guidelines) are published; these specifications are then used by internal developers or by vendor management and sourcing vendors (when operating in an outsourcing mode) to deliver business service. The architecture is documented and published formally, with the goal of providing a "self-service" capability to consumers of these technical plans (e.g., developers).

The enterprise architecture function also develops SLA criteria. Enterprise architecture focuses on the form/syntax/scope of SLA (the business side of the firm would likely select actual values.) Enterprise Architecture will typically work closely with Vendor Management to implement solutions that support business operations in a symbiotic manner; it may assist in development of engineering specifications, RFPs, procurement plans, but in a consultative/support role.

In summary, enterprise architecture bears the fiduciary responsibility of helping the firm achieve the following:

1. Business and technology alignment:
   - Drive to provide a clear connection between the firm's business strategy and architecture work/deliverables
   - Maximize business opportunity/capabilities via open/non-vendor-proprietary solutions

- Recommend and publish medium-term and longer-term strategic directions based on business imperatives
- Undertake all pertinent technical due diligences at the enterprise architectural level
2. Develop a self-service architecture function (based on automated PICS Proforma mechanisms):
    - Recommend and publish medium-term and longer-term strategic directions that can be accessed and assessed by stakeholders in a simple and direct manner
    - Support adherence to enterprise standards
    - Manage internal governance of introduction of new services
3. Achieve optimality:
    - Secure optimal use of IT assets in the enterprise
    - Maximize business opportunity/capabilities via open/non-vendor-proprietary solutions
    - Achieve immediate/ongoing RTE savings via deployment of state-of-the-art/virtualized/shared assets and technologies

Some firms wonder if there is a need for enterprise architecture if the firm has outsourced (a certain portion of) the IT environment (either as an ASP model or as an asset-retention model). Indeed, enterprise architecture continues to have a role because from the perspective of the ultimate customer of the firm, it is the firm that provides them a service, even if a supplier handles some portion of the business process. In other words, the firm in question owns the entire business process end-to-end in the eyes of the customers even though some parts of the process are executed by a supplier. Therefore, a pragmatic architected end-to-end solution is required.

For example, if a customer of Bank X calls the bank's customer service number to review his or her account, and the telephone connection is noisy because the bank has outsourced the Contact Center to a large Contact Center provider Y, which in turn uses a hub-and-spoke Voice-over-IP (VoIP) service from carrier Z to connect remote or international sites where the provider's agents are located, the customer of Bank X will perceive Bank X as providing poor service, not the unknown suppliers Y or Z.

It follows that the firm's business processes and the underlying technology must be architected for end-to-end integrity. Some call this an "extended enterprise" environment. The roles of the enterprise architecture sourcing environment include the following:

- The enterprise architecture provides a holistic expression of the enterprise's key strategies and their impact on business functions and processes, taking the firm's sourcing goals into explicit consideration.
- The enterprise architecture assists the firm to establish technical guidelines of how the "service delivery function" (whether in-sourced, partially sourced, or fully sourced) needs to operate to deliver reliable, effective business services:
    - Establishes risk-monitoring mechanisms/flags (for example, over the past 15 years many sourcing deals have gone sour; how does the firm track/avoid predicament?)
    - Generates technical guidelines of how the "service delivery function" makes optimal use of IT assets, thereby maximizing cost-effectiveness, flexibility, and availability (for example, what happens if the supplier is only interested in profitability and fails to have a technically current/transferable technology?)
    - Generates technical guidelines on how to maximize business opportunities though open/non-vendor-proprietary solutions (for example, what happens if the supplier locks the firm in with a completely closed technology that nobody else has or is familiar with?)

- Develops high-level architectures that foster and engender best-in-class/best-in-breed service environments at sourcing partners (or in-sourced departments) to retain technically sound/nonobsolescent environments (for example, what happens if the supplier uses questionable/speculative technology such as a nonsecure connectivity service, an unreliable carrier, or outdated equipment?)
- Development of SLA schema/taxonomies/syntaxes to monitor that the service is achieved. Also, identify adequate reporting metrics (what happens if we fail to identify/enumerate the proper atomic components required for service unambiguous visibility?)
- Helps develop new technical business processes (for example, existing processes will become outdated/inefficient as a firm moves to a sourced environment. Who best to develop them but Enterprise Architecture?)
- Establishes a success-oriented technical environment (for example, how do we know that the vendor "is pulling wool over the firm's eyes" by promising something that in fact cannot be delivered?)
- Helps keep the vendor "technically honest" (for example, since time immemorial vendors have been self-serving; can we afford to give them carte blanche?)

■ Enterprise Architecture assists the firm to establish technical governance principles of how the "service delivery function" needs to design the service environment (at a high level) to meet technical and regulatory thresholds:
- Establish pertinent technical due-diligences mechanisms at the architectural level (consider an anecdotal example of wanting to source a truck-driving function. The firm would want to establish rules such as: drivers must have more than ten years' experience; drivers must not have been given more than two traffic tickets in ten years; drivers must not have had more than one accident in ten years; the firm shall carry business insurance; the trucks shall not pollute the environment and give bad publicity to the firm; etc.)

The business side of the firm clearly understands the kind of solutions required to meet business/financial imperatives. Hence, the role of Enterprise Architecture is to (1) determine which architectures are able to maximize their flexibility, positioning, and competitiveness; (2) articulate the value of these architectural visions; (3) develop appropriate technical approaches; and (4) socialize technical work through the IT and user organizations to secure sponsorship (and funds) to implement the roadmap.

In developing appropriate technical approaches, Enterprise Architecture should develop: (1) high-level architecture descriptions; along with (2) roadmaps and implementation plans. For environments where outsourcing is a factor, Enterprise Architecture should develop (1) service definition guidelines; (2) service acceptance principles; (3) service integrity criteria; (4) SLA criteria; (5) risk flags; and (6) metrics criteria/recommendations. Enterprise Architecture should also develop internal and external governance means/metrics/guidelines and socialize these with other teams.

With reference to the implementation of the architecture roadmap, typically, there will be an engineering/development organization that develops/builds systems and an operations organization that runs the IT systems and manages the data center and network. Enterprise Architecture should assist these other groups develop service-specific specifications, service acceptance specifications, service-reporting specifications, and request for proposal (RFP) generation. However, Enterprise Architecture should not be as involved with the development of budgets and implementation timetables. Enterprise Architecture may provide consultative assistance for RFP generation/vendor selection. The group also provides standards governance (products) and architecture governance (architecture).

Typically, there will be a Supply-Chain Management (purchasing) group at the firm: Enterprise Architecture may provide consultative assistance for RFP generation/vendor selection (done in conjunction with the Engineering/Development and Operations groups.)

Figure 2.6 depicts the four layer of the architecture partitions used in this book (Business Architecture, Information Architecture, Systems/Solution Architecture, and Technology Architecture) along with artifacts generated by the Enterprise Architecture group.

In cases where ASP suppliers or asset-retention suppliers have been engaged by the firm, Enterprise Architecture should help ensure that the high-level architecture plans, service definition guidelines, service acceptance principles, service integrity criteria, SLA criteria, risk flags, and metrics criteria/recommendations are properly addressed and implemented. This is done to mitigate the risks identified earlier, specifically, the goal of maintaining vendor independence/portability (see the left side of Figure 2.6).

Here, Enterprise Architecture should be able to cite demonstrated savings to the firm in using a recommended Architecture Approach A versus Architecture Approach B or no architecture at all. Also, it should be able to document improved flexibility/time-to-market/service availability in using recommended Architecture Approach A versus Approach B or no architecture at all.

Sometimes the following question is posed, "Why do I need enterprise architecture when I can get what I may need via an SLA with an outsourcer?" The answer to this question includes the following observations.

Typically, firms have outsourced the more routine, back-office, operations-oriented functions. They have not outsourced the more strategic-planning-oriented functions that support

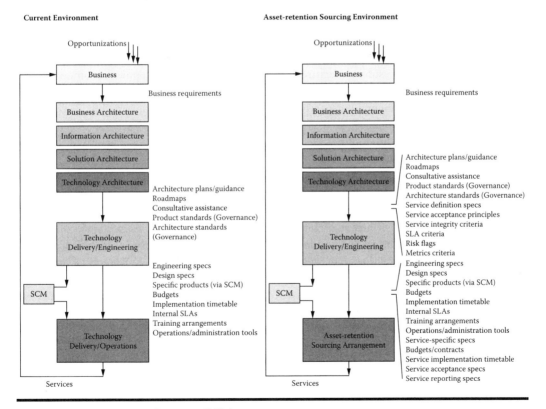

Figure 2.6   Functions and responsibilities.

the aforementioned activities. These more strategic functions are properly synthesized through an architectural capability that has the long-term technical integrity of the corporation in mind. SLAs do not address this issue; SLAs relate to a current capability; architecture work relates to future capabilities/positioning.

Architecture provides the "high-altitude/strategic view" of where the corporation should want to go. Outsourcers require proactive management to make sure that they do not deploy a set of technologies (on behalf of the enterprise) that may be constraining, suboptimal, short-sighted, self-serving, risky, premature, untested, etc. Many outsourcing deals have not delivered the intended value; hence, proactive management is important. This is done by specifying high-level technical/architecture directions and making sure they follow suit. Furthermore, the firm's target state is best developed by personnel who are intimately familiar with the firm's business and IT environment.

Besides the strategic function, Enterprise Architecture can assist the development of the "correct" set of SLAs. Specifically, the Enterprise Architecture group will work on the type, form, syntax, parameterization, and interdependence of SLA. For example, what would be the correct set of SLAs to guarantee that a host-based VoIP service has sufficient quality, reliability, security, etc.? Hence, the group will develop high-level architecture plans, service definition guidelines, service acceptance principles, service integrity criteria, SLA criteria, risk flags, and metrics criteria/recommendations. Enterprise Architecture also develops internal and external governance means/metrics/guidelines.

2.1.5 Organization-Specific Architecture Principles

2.1.5.1 Overview

It may be of some value to develop a set of organization-specific architectural principles that can be used to develop specific subarchitectures. These principles are philosophical positions of the firm with regard to particular issues of specific importance to a given organization. Architectural principles represent fundamental perspectives and practices believed to be valuable for the organization. Architectural principles can serve to provide a basis for decision making in regard to potential selections of attributes of the architecture (as we discussed in the appendix of Chapter 1, the attributes of the architecture A(n) represent the set of function groupings, the constituent functions, the interfaces, and the protocols utilized over the interfaces). In other words, they form the basis for making IT decisions related to the future (state). After defining and documenting the principles, an effort must be undertaken to define policies and procedures to support the proper application of the principles when an architecture or subarchitecture is developed.

Principles are general rules and guidelines that are stable and rarely amended. Principles describe and support the way that an organization undertakes its mission. Architectural principles must enjoy a level of consensus among the various elements of the enterprise. Each architectural principle needs to relate to the business objectives of the firm. However, principles are not expected to exhaustively define in an algorithmic manner the processes employed by the organization to carry out its work, but rather, they are part of a structured set of concepts, approaches, and philosophical ideas that collectively point the organization toward the goal.

Firm-specific principles are often defined in hierarchal tiers (or layers), although this is not mandatory. Suppose principles are organized as Tier 1 (e.g., Enterprise), Tier 2 (e.g., IT), and Tier 3 (Enterprise Architecture). Then, Tier 2 (e.g., IT) principles will be guided by, and elaborate on, the principles at the Tier 1 (e.g., Enterprise). Tier 3 (Enterprise Architecture) principles will be guided by the principles at the two higher levels. For example, a firm can have the following tier arrangement [TOG200501]:

- **Enterprise (business) principles** provide guidance for decision making throughout an enterprise, and impact how the organization sets about fulfilling its mission. **Enterprise principles** are used as a means of harmonizing decision making across a distributed organization. Included in this category are the business desiderata of the enterprise, e.g., business charter, business goals, strategic business directions, and some degree of service-delivery style/approach. Such enterprise-level principles are commonly found in governmental and not-for-profit organizations, but are also used in commercial organizations. In particular, they are a key element in a successful governance strategy related to architectural adherence by the firm. Generally, the definitional process for the generation and institutionalization of business principles is outside the scope of the architecture function.
- **IT principles** provide guidance on the use and deployment of all IT resources and assets across the enterprise. They are developed with the goal of making the information environment as productive and cost-effective as possible.
- **Architecture principles** provide guidance that relates to architecture efforts. These principles reflect a level of consensus across the enterprise, and embody the spirit and thinking of the enterprise architecture. The set of architecture principles focus on architecture-level issues but they can to also restate, or cross-refer, or embody a portion of the set of business principles. In any case, they must support the business principles; i.e., within an architecture project, the architect will normally need to ensure that the definitions of these business principles, goals, and strategic drivers are current, and clarify any areas of ambiguity. Architecture principles can be further partitioned as follows:
  - **Principles that govern the architecture process**, affecting the development, maintenance, and use of the enterprise architecture
  - **Principles that govern the implementation of the architecture**, establishing the first tenets and related guidance for designing and developing information systems.

Architectural principles are generally developed by the chief architect, in collaboration with the enterprise CIO, architecture board, and business stakeholders. Having too many principles can negatively impact the flexibility of the architecture development and maintenance process. Organizations should, therefore, define only high-level principles and limit the number to a dozen or at most two dozen. In addition to a definition statement, each principle could include information related to the rationale for choosing such a principle and also observations related to the possible downstream implications of the principle. This ancillary information serves to facilitate the acceptance of the principle and to support its application by explaining and justifying the rationale behind the guidelines embodied in the principle.

Two important observations here are that (1) principles are, basically, philosophical ideals/positions of the firm (specifically, of the firm's IT positions), and (2) the firm should not spend an inordinate amount of time to develop these. Certainly, it should not take three years and ten FTE (full time equivalents) to develop these. For example, it took this author one day to develop the following 16 enterprise architecture principles used in some applications (only the statement portion of the principle is shown):

1. The enterprise architecture shall be ***business-enabling***. It should help the company conduct its business in a reliable, expansive manner.
2. The enterprise architecture shall be ***value-enhancing***. It should help the company achieve increased value, either through improved cost, new functionality, or new flexibility, etc.
3. The enterprise architecture shall be ***brand-name advancing***. Clearly, it should help the company achieve added customer satisfaction and brand recognition.
4. The enterprise architecture shall be ***market-share expanding***. It should help the company open up new markets and reach a market faster in a more comprehensive manner.
5. The enterprise architecture shall be ***time-to-market facilitating***. It should help the company introduce new products faster, respond to changing consumer needs faster, etc.
6. The enterprise architecture shall be ***productivity-enhancing***. It should help the company conduct its business with fewer or less expensive resources.
7. The enterprise architecture shall be ***sourcing-enabling***. It should help the company rapidly and flexibly bring up a new outsourcing provider.
8. The enterprise architecture shall be ***process-simplifying***. It should help the company conduct its business in a simpler, more direct fashion.
9. The enterprise architecture shall be ***cost-effective***. It should help the company support transactions at a lower cost per transaction (for the same or better level of functionality).
10. The enterprise architecture shall be ***optimized***. It should help the company avail itself of ever-decreasing costs in technology to its benefit. It does so in a way that is the best compared to other approaches.
11. The enterprise architecture shall be ***global***. It should help the company reach/connect providers on multiple continents.
12. The enterprise architecture shall be ***multi-service***. It is often cheaper to have, say, one network that supports voice, video, and data, from a facilities, management, and planning/engineering point of view.
13. The enterprise architecture shall be ***scalable***. It should allow the company to rapidly add specific functionality in a forward-compatible, cost-effective, and rapid manner.
14. The enterprise architecture shall offer multiple levels of ***quality of service (QoS)***. It should help the company provide different grades of service to different transactions, products, or clientele.
15. The enterprise architecture shall be ***reconfigurable***. It should help the company quickly (and cost-effectively) redesign/reprovision the topology or relationship matrix to support rapidly evolving business needs.
16. The enterprise architecture shall be ***unified***. It should support a cohesive, consistent, well-architected, and well-planned networking infrastructure.

This is just an example. There are no fixed rules that limit the philosophical principles; they generally depend on the firm's mandate. For example, for a public agency the principles could relate to enhancing public safety. For a nonprofit the principles could relate to maximizing its value to the community. For a medical-oriented organization the principles could relate to optimizing health-care delivery. And so on. Again, these principles are nothing more than are philosophical positions of the firm and are to be used simply as a catalyst for architectural development, and the firm should not spend an inordinate amount of time to develop them. Also, the principle should neither be totally abstract or unrealistically ethereal nor ultraspecific or ultratechnical (see Figure 2.7).

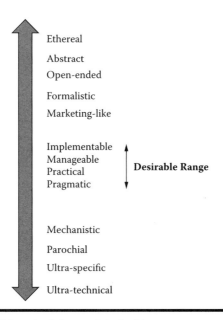

Ethereal

Abstract

Open-ended

Formalistic

Marketing-like

Implementable
Manageable
Practical
Pragmatic

Desirable Range

Mechanistic

Parochial

Ultra-specific

Ultra-technical

Figure 2.7   Gamut of possible principles and desirable range.

It is useful to have a systematic approach to defining principles. Using computer science terminology, one may define a principle, if the drafter of the principles so chooses, as an object with the following body parts:

PRx: = Name, Statement_body-part, Rationale_body-part, Implications_body-part

where [TOG200501]:

Name: Identity information (that distinguishes it from other principles/objects) that represents the essence of the rule. Additional observations: The name should be easy to remember. Specific technology platforms should not be mentioned in the name or statement of a principle. One should not use ambiguous words in the Name (and in the Statement_body-part) such as *support* and *open*. Avoid using unnecessary adjectives and adverbs.

Statement_body-part: Description that succinctly and unambiguously communicates the fundamental rule. For the most part, the statements for managing information are similar from one organization to the next. It is important that the statement be unambiguous.

Rationale_body-part: Description that highlights the business benefits of adhering to the principle, using business terminology. The drafter of the principle should point to the similarity of information and technology principles to the principles governing business operations. Also, the drafter of the principle should describe how it is related to other principles, and guidelines for a balanced interpretation. One should describe situations where one principle would be given precedence or carry more weight than another for making a decision.

Implications_body-part: Description that highlights the requirements, both for the business and IT, for implementing the principle—in terms of resources, costs, and activities/tasks. It will often be apparent that current systems, standards, or practices would be incongruent with the principle upon adoption. The impact to the business and consequences of adopting a principle should be clearly stated. The reader of the principle should readily discern the answer to "How does this affect me?" It is important not to oversimplify, trivialize, or judge the merit of the impact. Some of the implications will be identified as potential impacts only, and may be speculative rather than fully analyzed.

On the other hand, it is not obligatory that architectural principles exist at a firm; in this case the decisions related to attributes can be made based on the basis of some other mechanism (e.g., specific information about a particular subarea, specific financial business case as applicable to the subarea in question, specific information about a technology or solution, etc.) The fact that there is an absence of principle does not have to be taken as "an alarm bell"—it may simply be that given the relatively abstract formulation of the principles, the firm decides it is not worth the effort to define, maintain, and apply them to the daily decision-making process.

2.1.5.2 Additional Details

Architectural principles are intended to capture the fundamental truths about how the enterprise uses and deploys information technology resources and assets. Some useful guidance is provided in the TOGAF documentation about principles, which is applicable independently of the architectural framework model that is chosen by the enterprise (because principles are exogenous to the framework itself.) We include such guidance in this section [TOG200501].

Architectural principles need to be driven by overall IT principles and principles at the enterprise level, if they exist. Architectural principles are chosen to ensure alignment of IT strategies with business strategies and visions. Principles are often interrelated and must be developed and utilized as a cohesive set. Specifically, the development of architectural principles is typically influenced by the following:

- Enterprise mission and plans: The mission, plans, and organizational infrastructure of the enterprise
- Enterprise strategic initiatives: The characteristics of the enterprise—its strengths, weaknesses, opportunities, and threats—and its current enterprisewide initiatives (such as process improvement, quality management)
- External constraints: Market factors (time-to-market imperatives, customer expectations, etc.); existing and potential legislation
- Current systems and technology: The set of information resources deployed within the enterprise, including systems documentation, equipment inventories, network configuration diagrams, policies, and procedures
- Computer industry trends: Predictions about the usage, availability, and cost of computer and communication technologies, referenced from credible sources along with associated best practices presently in use

Simply having a set of written statements labeled as principles does not mean that the principles are good, even if people in the organization agree with it. A good set of principles is founded on the beliefs and values of the organization and expressed in language that the business side of the company understands and uses. This is driven by the fact that IT is a large line item in the budget, as high as 10% (as discussed in Chapter 1); therefore, it is important that the business side understand what they are getting for the money they allocate. Unfortunately, all too often conversation about IT effort is replete with an intolerably thick acronym alphabet soup.

Architectural principles (or even more generally, enterprise principles) need to drive behavior within the IT organization at the firm. Principles should be few in number, be forward-looking, and be endorsed and championed by senior IT and business management. They provide a foundation for making architecture and planning decisions, framing policies, procedures, and standards, and supporting resolution of contradictory situations. A poor set of principles will quickly fall into disuse, and the resultant architectures, policies, and standards will appear arbitrary or self-serving, and thus lack credibility. There are several criteria that characterize a good set of principles:

- **Understandability:** The underlying tenets can be quickly grasped and understood by individuals throughout the organization. The intention of the principle is clear and unambiguous, so that violations, whether intentional or not, are minimized.
- **Robustness:** Enables good-quality decisions about architectures and plans to be made, and enforceable policies and standards to be created. Each principle should be sufficiently definitive and precise to support consistent decision making in complex, potentially controversial situations.
- **Completeness:** Every potentially important principle governing the management of information and technology for the organization is defined. The principles cover every perceived situation.
- **Consistency:** Strict adherence to one principle may require a loose interpretation of another principle. The set of principles must be expressed in such a way that a balanced interpretation is possible. Principles should not be contradictory to the point where adhering to one principle would violate the spirit of another. Every word in a principle statement should be carefully chosen to allow consistent yet flexible interpretation.
- **Stability:** Principles should be enduring, yet able to accommodate changes. An amendment process should be established for adding, removing, or altering principles after they are ratified initially.

The architectural principles are used in a number of ways:

1. To provide a baseline within which the enterprise can start to make conscious decisions about IT.
2. As a guide to establishing relevant evaluation criteria, thus exerting strong influence on the selection of products or product architectures in the later stages of managing compliance with the IT architecture.
3. As drivers for defining the functional requirements of the architecture.
4. As an input to assessing both existing IT systems and the future strategic portfolio, for compliance with the defined architectures. These assessments will provide valuable insights into the transition activities needed to implement an architecture, in support of business goals and priorities.

5. The Rationale statements (discussed earlier) highlight the value of the architecture to the enterprise, and therefore provide a basis for justifying architectural activities.
6. The Implications statements (discussed earlier) provide an outline of the key tasks, resources and potential costs to the enterprise of following the principle. They also provide valuable inputs to future transition initiative and planning activities.
7. Support the architectural governance activities in terms of:
   - Providing a "back-stop" for the standard compliance assessments when some interpretation is allowed or required
   - Supporting the decision to initiate a dispensation request when the implications of a particular architecture amendment cannot be resolved within local operating procedures

From a pragmatic perspective, however, we strongly believe that just having a "nice set" of ideal target statements does not lead anywhere, unless the organization is willing to put "its money where the mouth is" and also runs the architecture function as a mandated compliance operation rather than just a "debate society to determine who has the best advocacy oratory and salesmanship skills." Architects in a firm need not have to be the best orators, advocacy mouthpieces, or salespeople; although these skills help, if 95% of the architects' time is "selling" and 5% is in the technical work, then such a function is really dysfunctional. We believe that the effort ratio allocation between "selling" and "doing the technical work" in an architecture organization needs to be more like "20% selling, 80% technical work." Therefore, the reader needs to be careful not to be oversold on the idea of generating an aesthetically beautiful set of principles because by itself this is only an academic exercise.

Appendix 2.1 shows a set of principles discussed under the TOGAF Model. Another example of architecture principles is contained in the U.S. government's Federal Enterprise Architecture Framework.

2.1.6 *Instituting Enterprise Architecture Mechanism in a Firm*

In consideration of the advantages to be gained by having an architected approach to IT, especially considering the relatively high budget figures involved in running an IT operation, as discussed in Chapter 1, the CIO may seek to establish an enterprise architecture capability within the firm. Generally, only a few senior individuals who have had previous experience in architecture are needed: a network architect, a platform architect, a security architect, a data architect, an integration architect, etc.

In recent years many firms have set out to install an enterprise architecture function. Some have attempted a centralized function with stringent governance powers. Others have tried a federated structure of architects from the different business units, working together to share best practices and coordinate architecture decisions across the firm. Yet others have tried a hybrid approach. Some argue that the hybrid approach is best [KOC200502]. In any event, because the IT department seems to be chronically tackling backlogs and is unable to meet requests from the business side in a timely manner (part of the reason being, perhaps, that IT often seeks to reinvent everything to perhaps get 95% of the users' needs over a long development cycle rather than using a commercial off-the-shelf (COTS) and getting 85% of the users' needs over a short development cycle), the Enterprise Architecture group should not be perceived as adding any (additional) delay or obstructing the IT initiatives.

Besides the dos and don'ts that we discussed in Chapter 1, what is needed is a relatively quick and effective exercise to achieve the following:

■ Develop and establish a set of organization-specific architectural principles (guidelines) (say, 0.5 staff-years of effort).
■ Select a framework from the set of available industry-defined frameworks (say, 1.0 staff-years of effort).
■ Identify the IT areas that are subject to architectural standardization (this is the partitioning/Functional Block discussion alluded to earlier, but it is also driven by the framework chosen—perhaps a dozen or so areas are identified) (say, 0.5 staff-years of effort).
■ Identify applicable industry standards (say, 0.5 staff-years of effort).
■ Select architectural description tools and install them (say, 1.0 staff-years of effort).
■ Establish governance mechanisms (and tools) and empower an Architecture Review Committee (say, 0.5 staff-years of effort).
■ Start the process of identifying in the current environment for the various areas identified earlier, but do not spend an inordinate amount of time documenting the "as is" environment (say, 2.4 staff-years for dozen or so areas identified).
■ Start the process of identifying the target environment for the various areas identified earlier, and publish target architectures (the "to be" environment) and architectural standards in such a manner that conformance by the developed is self-directed (namely, the architectures and standards contain unambiguous PICS Proforma) (say, 6 staff-years for dozen or so areas identified).

Notice that the effort discussed so far can be undertaken in about 13 staff-years of effort. Market research at the time of this writing found that nine out of ten companies surveyed had centralized enterprise architecture groups of fewer than ten people, regardless of company size [KOC200502]. This means that for the typical level of investment a firm can get the function established and running in one calendar year.

The refresh activities should be accomplishable for about 0.25–0.5 of a staff-year per architecture subarea. That implies that for a dozen or so areas identified, it will take about three to six staff-years. In turn this means that an organization of about ten people should be able to support this function. Large organizations have IT staffs that typically number in the several hundreds upward to a couple of thousand; ten people within such a pool should be financially acceptable in terms of the required investment.

Sometimes firms rely on consultative help from the outside to undertake the tasks of setting up an enterprise architecture initiative (from organizations such as Gartner, IBM, Forrester/Giga Research, Delloite & Touche, Accenture, Capgemini); what is important is that the function be established.

2.2 Enterprise Architecture Constructs

This section starts the discussion of the available industry machinery that can be used by firms to document their enterprise architecture work. We focus on architectural frameworks. A framework is intended to be a "language" to enable communication, research, and implementation of enterprise architecture constructs. Although some selection effort is needed, particularly by developing requirements for the framework that take into account the ultimate goal of the enterprise architecture function, the firm should not devote an inordinate amount of time to selecting the framework. Earlier we stated that a firm should try to select a framework from the set of available industry-defined frameworks with about 1.0 staff-years of effort. We noted in Chapter 1 that enterprise architecture must be more than just pretty pictures: firms need more than elaborate figures, charts, and presentations; unless the concepts are translated into actual decisions, migrations, and governance, such intriguing pictorials will not lead to any concrete results. Also, it needs to be reiterated that the architectural framework (just by) itself does not intrinsically save money for a firm: all of the follow-on artifacts must be developed, and then in turn applied to the environment, that is to say, implemented through funded efforts.

Leading organizations are seeking to organize architecture information using industry-proven frameworks and tools. This reduces replication of architecture documentation and improves the accessibility to architecture documents (these being captured under a system of record). Additionally, the use of tools reduces the cycle time for creating new artifacts, while at the same time establishing common nomenclature to foster consistency. At the same time, recent surveys have shown that a nontrivial fraction of organizations (about one-fifth) are defining their own enterprise architecture frameworks instead of adopting existing frameworks, and the trend seemed to be accelerating. The use of enterprise architecture repository tools is growing; however, again, at press time most organizations were still using Microsoft's Office and Visio products for capturing their enterprise architecture. On the other hand, the usage of standard business modeling techniques for modeling the results is broadly accepted, and Business Process Modeling Language (BPML) is today the standard in this area. OMG's Model-Driven Architecture and Unified Modeling Language (UML) are broadly accepted for modeling information systems [IEA200501].

2.2.1 Enterprise Architecture Principles

We discussed earlier that a firm may have firm-specific architectural principles that may depend on, among others, the industry the firm is in, the long-term mission of the firm, a short-term imperative of the firm, or a particular predicament the firm is in. In addition to the firm-specific architectural principles, the architecture framework may itself have (or may have been developed using) architectural principles in conjunction with subtending general business principles. Framework architectural principles provide a basis for decision making in regard to potential selections of attributes of the framework itself. These principles are not always explicitly stated in the frameworks, but they will have been used in the development and construction of the framework.

Framework architectural principles typically are similar to a core subset of firm-specific principles: e.g., "the framework shall be simple to use," "the framework shall be unambiguous," "the framework will facilitate (not hinder) the development of enterprise architectures for a wide range of enterprises," "the framework shall be stable," "the framework shall stand the test of time, and not be outdated within a couple of years as the underlying technology advances." Again, these principles are not necessarily explicitly stated, but they will have been used to derive the framework itself.

2.2.2 Enterprise Architecture Frameworks

There are many enterprise architecture frameworks, and new ones are being added every day. Some frameworks are given in the following list:

- The Open Group Architecture Framework (TOGAF)
- Zachman Enterprise Architecture Framework
- Extended Enterprise Architecture Framework (E2AF)
- Enterprise Architecture Planning (EAP)
- Federal Enterprise Architecture Framework (FEAF)
- Treasury Enterprise Architecture Framework (TEAF)
- Capgemini's Integrated Architecture Framework (IAF)
- Joint Technical Architecture (JTA)
- Command, Control, Communications, Computers, Intelligence, Surveillance, and Reconnaissance (C4ISR) and DoDAF
- Department of Defense Technical Reference Model (DoD TRM)
- Technical Architecture Framework for Information Management (TAFIM)
- Computer Integrated Manufacturing Open System Architecture (CIMOSA)
- Purdue Enterprise Reference Architecture (PERA)
- Standards and Architecture for eGovernment Applications (SAGA)
- European Union—IDABC & European Interoperability Framework
- ISO/IEC 14252 (IEEE Std 1003.0)
- IEEE Std 1471-2000 IEEE Recommended Practice for Architectural Description

Recent work shows that the most commonly used framework is the Zachman Framework, followed by the organization's own frameworks, followed by TOGAF, U.S. DoD (this covers about two-thirds of all enterprises.*) Generally, a framework is a detailed method and a set of supporting tools. Frameworks provide guidance on how to describe architectures; they typically do not provide guidance on how to construct or implement a specific architecture or how to develop and acquire systems or systems of systems [SYS200502].

Some see the architecture framework situation as a quagmire because of the overabundance of models and proposals [SYS200501]. Figure 2.8, loosely based on [SYS200501], depicts some of the relationships among the various models. In the material that follows we provide a brief overview of some of the more popular models.

2.2.2.1 *The Open Group Architecture Framework (TOGAF 8.1)*

The Open Group is a vendor-neutral and technology-neutral consortium seeking to enable access to integrated information, within and among enterprises, based on open standards and global interoperability. The Open Group had developed an architectural framework known as The Open Group Architecture Framework (TOGAF), Version 8.1 at time of book's publication. It is described in a set of documentation published by The Open Group on its public Web server, and may be used freely by any organization wishing to develop an enterprise architecture for use within that organization.

TOGAF Version 8.1 partitions the architecture into the Business Architecture, Data Architecture, Application Architecture, and Technical Architecture. These four domains track directly with the four domains that we are using in this text.

TOGAF was developed by The Open Group's own members. The original development of TOGAF Version 1 in 1995 was based on the Technical Architecture Framework for Information

---

* A press time survey showed the following statistics [IEA200501]: Zachman Framework: 25%; Organization's own: 22%; TOGAF: 11%; U.S., DoD Architecture Framework: 11%; E2AF: 9%; FEAF: 9%; IAF: 3%; TAFIM: 2%; TEAF: 0%; ISO/IEC 14252 (IEEE Std 1003.0): 0%; Other: 9%.

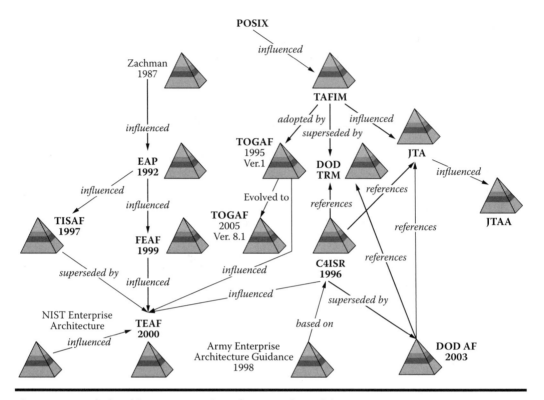

Figure 2.8   Relationships among various framework models.

Management (TAFIM), developed by the U.S. Department of Defense (DoD). The DoD gave The Open Group explicit permission and encouragement to create TOGAF by building on the TAFIM, which itself was the result of many years of development effort and many millions of dollars of U.S. government investment. Starting from this foundation, the members of The Open Group's Architecture Forum have developed successive versions of TOGAF each year and published each one on The Open Group's public Web site.

There are four main parts to the TOGAF document:

- **Part I: Introduction** provides a high-level introduction to some of the key concepts behind enterprise architecture and, in particular, the TOGAF approach.
- **Part II: Architecture Development Method** is the core of TOGAF. It describes the *TOGAF Architecture Development Method*—a step-by-step approach to developing an enterprise architecture.
- **Part III: Enterprise Continuum** describes the TOGAF Enterprise Continuum, a virtual repository of architecture assets, which includes the TOGAF Foundation Architecture, and the Integrated Information Infrastructure Reference Model.
- **Part IV: Resources** comprise the TOGAF Resource Base—a set of tools and techniques available for use in applying TOGAF and the TOGAF ADM.

TOGAF Version 8 is a superset of the well-established framework TOGAF Version 7. Version 8 uses the same underlying method for developing IT architectures that was evolved, with a particular focus on technical architectures, in the versions of TOGAF up to and including Version 7. However,

Version 8 applies that architecture development method to the other domains of an overall enterprise architecture—the business architecture, data architecture, and application architecture, as well as the technical architecture. The following significant additions have been made in Version 8.1:

1. Part II has a new section describing the requirements management process at the center of the ADM life cycle.
2. Part IV has a new structured section on architecture governance, comprising three subsections: (a) Introduction to Architecture Governance; (b) Architecture Governance Framework; and (c) Architecture Governance in Practice. Also, this part has a new section on architecture maturity models as well as a new section on TOGAF Architecture Skills Framework.

As noted earlier, TOGAF is the second most widely used framework. Chapter 3 covers this framework in detail.

2.2.2.2 Zachman Framework for Enterprise Architecture

The Zachman Framework for Enterprise Architecture (in short, the Zachman Framework) is a widely used approach for developing or documenting an enterprisewide architecture. John Zachman based his framework on practices in traditional architecture and engineering. The framework is a logical structure for classifying and organizing those elements of an enterprise that are significant to both the management of the enterprise and the development of its information systems. Figure 2.9 depicts the framework pictorially. The vertical axis provides multiple perspectives of the overall architecture, and on the horizontal axis a classification of the various artifacts of the architecture. Similar to other frameworks, its purpose is to provide a basic structure that supports the organization, access, integration, interpretation, development, management, and transformation of a set of architectural representations of the organization's information systems; such objects or descriptions of architectural representations are usually referred to as artifacts. The Zachman Framework is the most widely used framework today.

In 1987, John Zachman wrote, "To keep the business from disintegrating, the concept of information systems architecture is becoming less of an option and more of a necessity." From that assertion over 20 years ago, the Zachman Framework has evolved and become the model through which major organizations view and communicate their enterprise information infrastructure. The Zachman Framework draws upon the discipline of classical architecture to establish a common vocabulary and set of perspectives, a framework, for defining and describing today's complex enterprise systems. Enterprise architecture provides the blueprint, or architecture, for the organization's information infrastructure [ZIF200501].

The framework contains global plans as well as technical details, lists and charts as well as natural language statements. Any appropriate approach, standard, role, method, technique, or tool may be placed in it. In fact, the framework can be viewed as a tool to organize any form of metadata for the enterprise. The contents of some of the cells are well understood in the industry today. In fact, it is easy to purchase, off the shelf, application development tools and methodologies that support building the model [ZIF200501].

Chapter 3 covers this framework in detail.

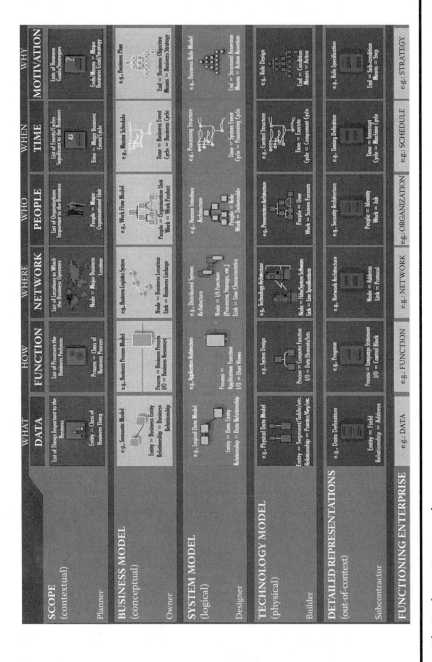

Figure 2.9 The Zachman Framework.

2.2.2.3 Extended Enterprise Architecture Framework (E2AF)

The Extended Enterprise Architecture[SM] (E2A) and Extended Enterprise Architecture Framework (E2AF) are developed by The Institute For Enterprise Architecture Developments (IFEAD). E2AF was in version 1.4 (at press time). E2AF addresses three major elements in a holistic way: the element of construction, the element of function, and the element of style. Style reflects the culture, values, norms, and principles of an organization.

Often, the term *enterprise architecture* deals with construction and function, without due consideration of the stylistic aspect. The stylistic aspect reflects the cultural behavior, values, norms, and principles of an organization in such a way that it reflects its corporate values. At the same time, the enterprise architecture addresses the aspects of business, information, information systems, and technology infrastructure in a holistic way covering the organization and its environment [IEA200501]. These domains are similar to the ones used in this text (see Figure 2.10). In this context enterprise architecture relates to understanding all of the different elements that go to make up the enterprise and how those elements interrelate; this is basically the definition we provide in Appendix 1.1.

Organizations can use this framework for their own purposes or in conjunction with their customers, by including a reference notice to IFEAD's copyrights. Organizations that want to use the framework for commercial purposes can get a license from IFEAD (http://www.enterprise-architecture.info/).

E2AF is based on the ideas described in IEEE 1471-2000 regarding views and viewpoints, and a transformation of these concepts into the enterprise architecture domain enables another perspective of viewpoints and views. Looking from the outside world at an enterprise, several groups of (extended) enterprise stakeholders influence the goals, objectives, and behavior of the enterprise. Even so, these groups of enterprise stakeholders have different concerns, and therefore different sets of viewpoints, when we analyze these extended enterprise stakeholders. The model clusters their concerns into four generic categories (Business, Information, Systems, and Infrastructure Technology), also as seen in Figure 2.10. The framework shows the drivers of the enterprise and makes possible an understanding of what motivates the (extended) enterprise stakeholders [IEA200501].

2.2.2.4 Department of Defense Architecture Framework (DoDAF)

In the mid-1990s, in response to requirements related to joint multi-service and multinational military operations, the DoD discerned the need for a standard architectural formulation to ensure that its military systems could interoperate. The Command, Control, Communications, Computers, Intelligence, Surveillance, and Reconnaissance (C4ISR) Architecture Framework, Version 1.0, was published in 1996 and it was reissued a year later in Version 2.0. On the basis of the experience with these frameworks, the DoD began work on a new version and published the DoD Architecture Framework (DoDAF), Version 1.0, in 2003.

The goal of DoDAF is to ascertain that the architectural descriptions developed by the various commands, services, and agencies are compatible and interrelatable and that the technical architecture views are usable and integrable across organizational domains. This framework addresses the military domain and is used primarily by the DoD.

Similar to any other architecture framework, it provides rules and guidance for developing and presenting architecture descriptions, including artifacts. It provides input on how to describe architectures, but it does not provide mechanisms in how to construct or implement a specific

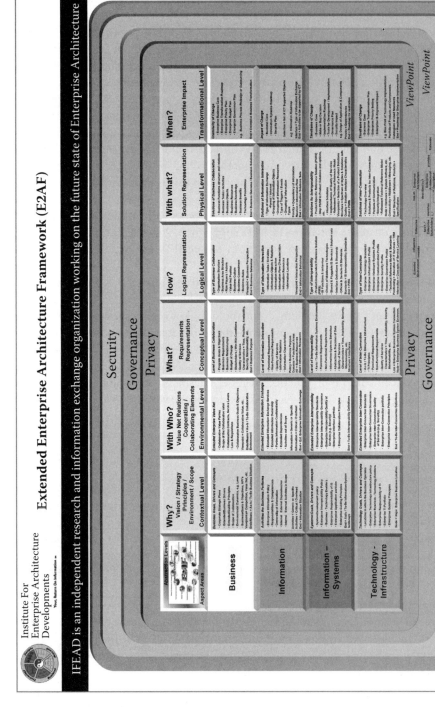

Figure 2.10   Extended Enterprise Architecture Framework (E2AF).

architecture or how to develop and acquire systems or systems of systems. DoDAF is organized into three parts. Volume I provides general guidance on the need for and use of architecture descriptions in DoD. Volume II provides definitions of the 26 products contained in the three views of the model (Operational View, Systems View, and Technical Standards View). Volume III is a deskbook that provides examples of architectures that are compliant, approaches to undertaking architecture development, and other support information. To comply with the framework, architecture descriptions must include the appropriate set of products and use the common terms and definitions specified in the framework.

As noted, DoDAF's architectural descriptions require the use of multiple views, each of which conveys different aspects of the architecture in several products (artifacts or models). DoDAF's integrated architecture comprises a number of views and the interrelationships between them. DoDAF defines the following views [SYS200502,DOD200301] (see Figure 2.11 [FEA200503]):

- **Operational View** depicts what is going on in the real world that is to be supported or enabled by systems represented in the architecture. Activities performed as parts of DoD missions and the associated information exchanges among personnel or organizations are the primary items modeled in operational views. The operational view reveals requirements for capabilities and interoperability.
- **Systems View** describes existing and future systems and physical interconnections that support the DoD needs documented in the operational view.
- **Technical Standards View** catalogs standard (commercial off-the-shelf [COTS], government off-the-shelf [GOTS]) system parts or components and their interconnections. This view augments the systems view with technical detail and forecasts of standard technology evolution.
- **All View** augments the other views by providing context, summary, or overview-level information, and an integrated dictionary to define terms.

The DoDAF comprises the types of guidance listed in Table 2.3.

The **Core Architecture Data Model** (CADM) (originally developed in the context of C4ISR) is a formal model of architecture products (artifacts), structures, and their respective interrelationships. It provides a common schema (database) for repositories of architectural information. A

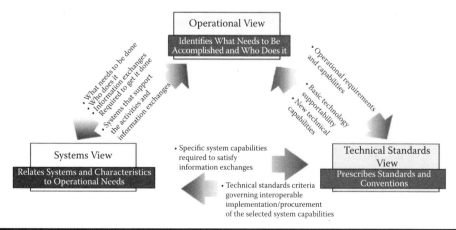

Figure 2.11   Views in DoDAF.

Table 2.3 DoDAF Architectural Guidance

Guidelines	A set of guiding principles and guidance for building architectures that are compliant with the framework (Volume I)
High-level process	Methodology for using the framework to develop architecture descriptions that fulfill a purpose
Architecture data and tools	Mechanisms that can serve as facilitators of the architecture description process
Architecture products	Description of the architectural artifacts (Volume II)

repository based on the CADM is able to store in a common manner architecture products (artifacts) from multiple framework-based architecture projects. This allows products from different projects, organizations, or services to be analyzed and compared. Furthermore, with a CADM-based repository, the extraction and presentation of an appropriate subset of the architectural information can be (partially) automated.

The DoDAF defines (Volume II) 26 different architecture products that are organized per the views (All, Operational, Systems, and Technical standards), as follows [SYS200502]:

- **All View**
  - **Overview and Summary Information:** Details scope, purpose, environment, and other summary-level formation for an architectural description.
  - **Integrated Dictionary:** Provides definitions of all terms used in all products.
- **Operational View**
  - **Operational Concept Graphic:** Provides a graphical and textual description of the operational concept.
  - **Operational Node Connectivity Description:** Lists the operational nodes, activities performed at each node, connectivity, and information needs between nodes.
  - **Operational Information Exchange Matrix:** Lists and describes information exchanged between nodes.
  - **Organizational Relationships Chart:** Lists organizations, roles, and relationships among organizations.
  - **Operational Activity Model:** Details the activities performed and their interrelationships, including input/output relationships.
  - **Operational Rules Model:** Identifies business rules that govern or constrain operations.
  - **Operational State Transition:** Identifies sequencing and timing of activities.
  - **Operational Event Trace:** Traces actions in a scenario or sequence of events.
  - **Logical Data Model:** Identifies data requirements of the operational view.
- **Systems View**
  - **Systems Interface Description:** Lists systems, system components, and their interconnections.
  - **Systems Communications Description:** Identifies system communications.
  - **Systems–Systems Matrix:** Lists connections between individual systems in a group.
  - **Systems Functionality Description:** Lists functions performed by individual systems and the related information flow.

- **Operational Activity-to-Systems Function Traceability Matrix:** Maps systems information back to the operational view.
- **Systems Data Exchange Matrix:** Provides detail of data moving between systems.
- **Systems Performance Parameters Matrix:** Lists performance characteristics of individual systems.
- **Systems Evolution Description:** Lists migration plans for systems.
- **Systems Technology Forecast:** Lists technologies and products that are expected to affect systems.
- **Systems Rules Model:** Describes constraints on system operation imposed by design or implementation.
- **Systems State Transition Description:** Describes system activity sequencing and timing.
- **Systems Event Trace Description:** Describes system-specific requirements on critical event sequences.
- **Physical Schema:** Describes the physical implementation of the logical data model from the operational view.
■ **Technical Standards View**
- **Technical Standards Profile:** Lists technical standards that apply to the architecture.
- **Technical Standards Forecast:** Describes emerging or evolving standards that might apply to the architecture.

2.2.2.5 Enterprise Architecture Planning (EAP)

EAP defines a process that emphasizes techniques for organizing and directing enterprise architecture projects, obtaining stakeholder commitment, presenting the plan to stakeholders, and leading the organization through the transition from planning to implementation. EAP was originally published in the early 1990s by S. Spewak [SPE199201]. EAP takes a business-data-driven approach aimed at ensuring quality information systems. EAP emphasizes (1) the definition of a stable business model, (2) data dependencies defined before system implementation, and (3) the order of implementation activities based on the data dependencies. EAP is a specific attempt to provide methodologies for specifying the top two rows of the Zachman Framework: Scope (Planner) and Business Model (Owner). Consequently, only the BPM is pursued, and no effort is devoted to technical design or implementation. EAP has been primarily used in business and industrial market segments.

The major principles that guide the application of the EAP framework include the following [SYS200502,SPE199201]:

- Enterprise data should be accessible whenever and wherever it is needed.
- Information systems should adapt to meet the needs of changing business needs.
- High data integrity and standards should exist across the enterprise.
- All enterprise data systems should be integrated.
- These critical success factors should be obtainable cost-effectively.

The synthesis of EAP is shown in Figure 2.12 [SYS200502]. Each block represents a phase of the process that focuses on how to define the associated architectures and development plans. The framework defines the roles and responsibilities for each phase along with descriptions of the artifacts that

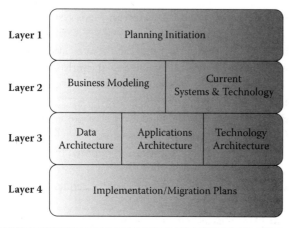

		Layer 1 represents project initiation. These activities determine an appropriate specific methodology, decide who should be involved, and which toolset to use. With this information collected, a workplan can be written and management buy-in can be sought.

Layer 1 — Planning Initiation

Layer 2 — Business Modeling | Current Systems & Technology

Layer 2 builds a knowledge base of the business processes and required information. The current systems baseline is also captured here. The baseline includes an inventory of application systems, data and technology platforms.

Layer 3 — Data Architecture | Applications Architecture | Technology Architecture

Layer 3 plans the future architecture. This includes defining the data architecture by understanding the major kinds of data needed by the business. The application architecture defines the major kinds of application needed to manage the data and support business processes. The technology architecture identifies the technology platforms needed to create an environment for the data and application architectures.

Layer 4 — Implementation/Migration Plans

Layer 4 addresses the implementation. This includes defining the sequence for implementing applications, creating a schedule for implementation, preparing a cost/benefit analysis, and defining a road map for migrating from the current state to the desired state.

Figure 2.12   EAP components.

need to be produced. Additional capabilities include mechanisms for carrying out the process steps and for undertaking cost estimates for each phase.

2.2.2.6 Federal Enterprise Architecture (FEA)

The goal of FEA is to improve interoperability within U.S. government agencies by creating one enterprise architecture for the entire federal government. The Clinger–Cohen Act (1996) legislated a chief information officer (CIO) for all federal agencies and makes him or her responsible for developing, maintaining, and facilitating the implementation of sound and integrated information technology and/or systems. Additional legislation that followed (Executive Order 13011 and the E-Government Act of 2002) established the Chief Information Officers Council as the principal interagency entity to improve agency practices for the management of IT. As part of its work the CIO Council authored the FEAF with the publication of "Federal Enterprise Architecture Framework, Version 1.1" in 1999 and "A Practical Guide to Federal Enterprise Architecture, Version 1.1" in 2001. The Office of Management and Budget (OMB) now reviews and approves the business cases for all major IT investments. The mandated applicability of FEA covers all organizations in the federal government.

Architectural principles include the following [FEA200101,SYS200502]:

- Architectures must be appropriately scoped, planned, and defined based on the intended use.
- Architectures must be compliant with the law as expressed in legislative mandates, executive orders, federal regulations, and other federal guidelines.
- Architectures should facilitate change.
- Architectures set the interoperability standard.
- Architectures provide access to information but must secure the organization against unauthorized access.
- Architectures must comply with the Privacy Act of 1974.
- Enterprise architectures must reflect the agency's strategic plan.
- Enterprise architectures coordinate technical investments and encourage the selection of proven technologies.

- Architectures continuously change and require transition.
- Architectures provide standardized business processes and common operating environments.
- Architecture products are only as good as the data collected from subject matter experts and domain owners.
- Architectures minimize the burden of data collection, streamline data storage, and enhance data access.
- Target architectures should be used to control the growth of technical diversity.

The Federal Enterprise Architecture is a collection of interrelated reference models designed to facilitate cross-agency analysis. It is intended for use in analyzing and optimizing IT operations (see Figure 2.13). The objectives of the FEAF are to enable the federal government and agencies to achieve the following [FEA200503]:

- Leverage technology and reduce redundant IT expenditures across the federal government
- Facilitate cross-agency IT integration and sharing of data
- Apply common architecture practices
- Assist agencies to meet their EA legislative mandates

The intent of the FEAF is to enable the federal government to define and align its business functions and supporting IT systems through a common set of reference models. These models are defined as follows [FEA200503]:

- Performance Reference Model (PRM): The PRM is a standardized framework to measure the performance of major IT investments and their contribution to program performance.
- Business Reference Model (BRM): The BRM is a function-driven framework for describing business operations of the federal government independent of the agencies that perform them.
- Service Component Reference Model (SRM): The SRM is a business- and performance-driven functional framework that classifies service components according to how they support business or performance objectives.

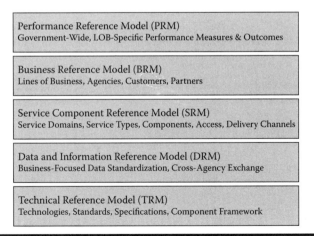

Figure 2.13   The Federal Enterprise Architecture.

■ Data Reference Model (DRM): The DRM is a model describing, at an aggregate level, the data and information that support program and business line operations.
■ Technical Reference Model (TRM): The TRM is a component-driven, technical framework used to identify the standards, specifications, and technologies that support and enable the delivery of service components and capabilities.

The Performance Reference Model (see Figure 2.14) is a framework to measure the performance of IT investments. The PRM aims at producing enhanced performance information to improve strategic and daily decision making. Its purpose is to improve the alignment (and better articulate the contribution) of inputs with outputs and outcomes, thereby creating a clear "line of sight" to desired results. It identifies performance improvement opportunities that span traditional organizational structures and boundaries. Agencies were required to use the PRM in their FY2005 IT initiatives.

The Business Reference Model is a function-driven agency-independent framework for describing the business operations of the federal government. The BRM Version 2.0 provides an organized, hierarchical construct for describing the day-to-day business operations of the government. The BRM is the first layer of the Federal Enterprise Architecture, and it is the main reference point for the analysis of data, service components, and technology. The BRM lists four Business Areas that provide a high-level view of the operations the federal government performs. The four business areas comprise a total of 39 external and internal Lines of Business and 153 SubFunctions. Starting with the FY2005 budget, agencies are required to map their major IT investments to BRM business lines.

The Service Component Reference Model is a business- and performance-driven, functional framework that classifies Service Components from the perspective of how they support business

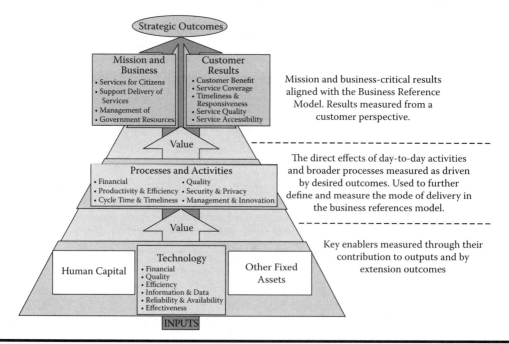

Figure 2.14   Performance Reference Model.

or performance objectives. It is intended to support the discovery of governmentwide business and application service components in IT investments and assets. The SRM is structured across horizontal and vertical service domains that, independent of the business functions, can provide a foundation to support the reuse of applications, application capabilities, components, and business services. The SRM defines "component" as a self-contained business process or service with predetermined functionality that may be exposed through a business technology or interface. There are fours levels in SRM [FEA200101,SYS200502]:

- Federated: A set of cooperating system-level components that resolve the business need of multiple end users, frequently from different organizations.
- Business Component System: A set of cooperating business components assembled to deliver a solution to a business problem.
- Business Component: The implementation of an autonomous business concept or business process.
- Distributed Component: A software element that can be called at run-time with a clear interface and a separation between interface and implementation. The most detailed level of granularity defined in the SRM.

The Technical Reference Model is a component-driven, technical framework employed to identify the standards, specifications, and technologies that support and enable the delivery of service components and capabilities. The TRM unifies existing capabilities by providing a foundation to advance the reuse of technology and component services from a governmentwide perspective. TRM has four tiers:

- Service Area: a technical tier that supports the secure construction, exchange, and delivery of business or service components. Each service area groups the requirements of component-based architectures within the federal government into functional areas.
- Service Category: a subtier of the service area to classify lower levels of technologies, standards, and specifications with respect to the business or technology function they serve.
- Standard: hardware, software, or specifications that are widely used and accepted (de facto) or are sanctioned by a standards organization (de jure).
- Specification: a formal layout/blueprint/design of an application development model for developing distributed component-based architectures.

2.2.2.7 Federal Enterprise Architecture Framework (FEAF)

As seen in a previous subsection, FEA seeks integrate the separate architectures of the various federal agencies. To support this goal, the government needs a collaboration tool for collecting and storing common architecture information; FEAF is such a tool. FEAF partitions a given architecture into business, data, applications, and technology architectures. FEAF includes the first three columns of the Zachman Framework and the EAP. FEAF allows the government to organize federal information for the entire federal government; promote information sharing among federal organizations; help federal organizations develop their architectures; help Federal organizations quickly develop their IT investment processes; and serve customer and taxpayer needs better, faster, and more cost-effectively.

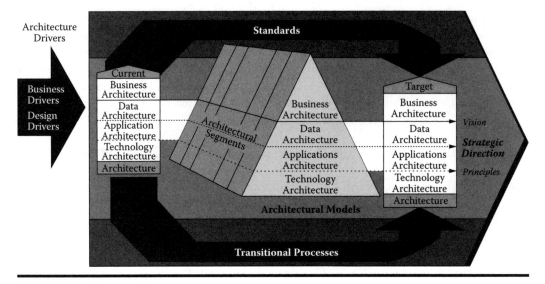

Figure 2.15   FEAF structure.

The major components of the FEAF are (also see Figure 2.15) [SYS200501,FEA200102]:

- **Architecture Drivers:** Represent external stimuli that cause the FEA to change.
- **Strategic Direction:** Ensures that changes are consistent with the overall federal direction.
- **Current Architecture:** Represents the current state of the enterprise. Full characterization may be significantly beyond its worth and maintenance.
- **Target Architecture:** Represents the target state for the enterprise within the context of the strategic direction.
- **Transitional Processes:** Apply the changes from the current architecture to the target architecture in compliance with the architecture standards, such as various decision-making or governance procedures, migration planning, budgeting, and configuration management and engineering change control.
- **Architectural Segments:** Focus on a subset or a smaller enterprise within the total federal enterprise.
- **Architectural Models:** Provide the documentation and the basis for managing and implementing changes in the federal enterprise.
- **Standards:** Include standards (some of which may be made mandatory), voluntary guidelines, and best practices, all of which focus on promoting interoperability.

2.2.2.8 Treasury Enterprise Architecture Framework (TEAF)

TEAF aims at guiding the planning and development of enterprise architectures in all bureaus and offices of the Treasury Department. TEAF (Version 1.0, July 2000) is an elaboration of an earlier (1997) Treasury model, TISAF; it also draws from FEAF. The purpose of the framework is to achieve the following:

- Provide guidance for Treasury Enterprise Architecture development and management
- Satisfy OMB and other federal requirements

- Support Treasury bureaus and offices with the implementation of their architectures based on strategic planning
- Show the benefits of incorporating enterprise architecture disciplines and tools into normal business operations
- Provide a structure for producing an EA and managing EA assets

The key principles in TEAF include [SYS200501,TEA200001]:

- Compliance with applicable laws, orders, and regulations is required.
- Business objectives must be defined before building IT solutions.
- Total business value is the primary goal that drives IT decisions.
- EA is an integral part of the Investment Management Process.
- Architectural decisions shall maximize interoperability and reusability.
- Standardization will be used to fulfill common requirements and provide common functions.
- Collaboration among Treasury IT organizations will facilitate sharing the information, data, and infrastructure required by the business units.
- COTS technology will be used, where appropriate, rather than customized or in-house solutions.
- Information and infrastructure are vital assets that must be managed, controlled, and secured.
- EA must be consistent with departmental guidance and strategic goals.

TEAF has three basic parts:

1. A definition of the framework
2. A set of activities that guide architecture planning and implementation
3. A set of guidelines that support strategic planning, EA management, EA implementation approach, and building a repository for EA products

The framework contains resources and work products that guide architecture development. The EA description must depict various perspectives of the Treasury from several different views. For instance, the Planner perspective must contain models that describe the enterprise functions, information, organization, and infrastructure from the perspective of the executives responsible for planning the work of the Treasury bureaus and offices. Similar models must be created for the perspectives of the Owner, Designer, and Builder. See Figure 2.16 for the reference model.

The activities within the EA development process include (1) defining an EA strategy; (2) defining an EA management process; (3) defining an EA approach; and (4) developing the EA repository. Although specific guidance is given for what should be in an EA, including strategy, work products, roles, and responsibilities, the TEAF leaves to each bureau the responsibility for choosing the how, when, and why. The TEAF provides guidance for the following: creating an enterprise architecture strategy, defining a road map for development, defining roles and responsibilities of participants, creating policies for configuration management, managing investments, creating an enterprise repository, and creating specific work products.

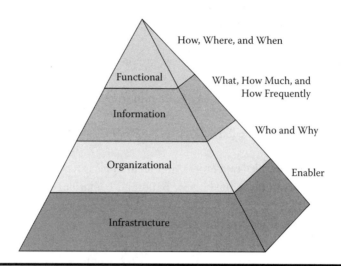

Figure 2.16   Reference model, TEAF.

2.2.2.9 ISO/IEC 14252 (IEEE Std 1003.0)

This 1996 ISO standard, "Guide to the POSIX Open System Environment," was the initial basis for a number of frameworks (as shown in Figure 2.8). For example, TOGAF was originally based on the U.S. DoD Technical Architecture Framework for Information Management (TAFIM), which was itself a development of ISO/IEC TR 14252. At a general level, ISO/IEC 14252, TAFIM and TOGAF have a similar reference model. ISO/IEC TR 14252, however, does not supply a diagram that provides a detailed partitioning of the application software, application platform, or external environment entities; the document does partition the application platform into a number of similar, though not identical, areas. ISO/IEC TR 14252 includes details related to service category definition and in the recommended family of standards and specifications. The ISO/IEC TR 14252 reference model implies no structure among the service categories, leaving that to individual system architectures and actual implementations.

2.3 Enterprise Architecture Governance

We have already hinted at the criticality of the governance process at the end of Chapter 1 and earlier in this chapter. This topic could well cover a chapter, and perhaps even a book. In the following text we simply scratch the surface.

Governance relates to the publication of the architecture (enterprise architecture description) of the current or target state, the enterprise standards set, the enterprise approved equipment list; and the roadmap along with (migration) strategies, and then having the mechanisms, the support, and the management commitment to effect enforcement or consistency with the enterprise architecture.

There are many ways of handling governance. One possible way is based on the federated approach described in FEA. The federal chief information officer (could be the firm's CIO) has issued an executive policy to ensure that all federal agencies (could be the firm's departments) apply minimal EA procedures. The policy states every federal agency (could be the firm's departments) should include the following [SYS200501,FEA200101]:

- Description of the purpose and value of an enterprise architecture
- Description of the relationship of the enterprise architecture to the agency's (department's) strategic vision and plans
- Description of the relationship of the enterprise architecture to capital planning, enterprise engineering, and program management
- Translation of business strategies into enterprise architecture goals, objectives, and strategies
- Commitment to develop, implement, and maintain an enterprise architecture
- Identification of enterprise architecture compliance as one criterion for new and ongoing investments
- Overview of an enforcement policy
- Security practices to include certification and accreditation

An Enforcement Policy defines the standards and process for determining the compliance of systems or projects to the FEAF (firm's enterprise architecture) and for resolving the issues of noncompliance. The Enforcement Policy should answer the following questions:

- How and when will projects submit project plans to be reviewed for enterprise architecture compliance?
- Who will be responsible for compliance assessment or justification of waivers?
- How will compliance and noncompliance be documented and reported?
- How will outstanding issues of noncompliance be resolved or waivers be processed and approved?
- Who will be responsible for processing, authorizing, and reassessing waivers?
- What will be the content and format of waiver submissions?
- If a waiver is granted, how will projects achieve compliance in the future?
- What are the ramifications if a noncompliant project is not granted a waiver (e.g., funding or deployment restrictions)?

The processes and procedures should allow for exceptions. In many cases, existing systems in the operations and maintenance phase should be granted exceptions or waivers from the technical standards and constraints of the enterprise architecture. Alignment of some legacy systems with new standards could be unreasonably costly and introduce additional risk to the business users [SYS200501].

However, a chronic granting of exceptions may defeat the purpose of having an enterprise architecture. We believe that the granted exceptions need to be less than 10% of the total set of activities, in most instances; otherwise, the lack of standardization will continue to proliferate. Sometimes a developer could find that using a nonstandard solution could be more locally optimal (read, cheaper) than using the company standard. In those cases the funding mechanism must be addressed by the chief architect: a (financially accommodating) mechanism must exist to "assist" the developer make the correct decision. For example, assume that the company was UNIX based but a desire may exist to move to Linux. Assume that the project would cost x under UNIX but $x + \Delta$ for Linux, considering that the developers/programmers are less familiar with the technology (as it might be new in that firm in question); or, it could take then $y + \Delta$ weeks to complete the project, compared with y weeks under the old technology. Then a way must be found to subsidize these developers (so that they have the money or they are not penalized for "overspending"), for the common good of the firm to move to the new, target-desired environment; the same would apply if the amount of time took longer.

The question may also arise if the Enforcement Policy should be managed at the firm's level or at the departmental level. In companies where there are good centralized controls or where the company operates a headquarter-driven operation, then a firm-level Enforcement Policy can be institutionalized. In companies where there are not good centralized controls or where the company operates a distributed, franchised, loosely coupled operation, then a department-level Enforcement Policy may have to be used.

Appendix 2.1: Firm-Specific Architectural Principles

This appendix expands the discussion on architectural principles, and is based on TOGAF documentation, with permission [TOG200501]. It provides an example that illustrates both the typical content of a set of architecture principles, and the recommended format.

Business Principles

1. Principle: **Primacy of principles**

   Statement: These principles of information management apply to all organizations within the enterprise.

   Rationale: The only way one can provide a consistent and measurable level of quality information to decision makers is if all organizations abide by the principles.

   Implications:

   Without this principle, exclusions, favoritism, and inconsistency would rapidly undermine the management of information.

   Information management initiatives will not begin until they are examined for compliance with the principles.

   A conflict with a principle will be resolved by changing the framework of the initiative.

2. Principle: **Maximize benefit to the enterprise**

   Statement: Information management decisions are made to provide maximum benefit to the enterprise as a whole.

   Rationale: This principle embodies "service above self." Decisions made from an enterprise-wide perspective have greater long-term value than decisions made from any particular organizational perspective. Maximum return on investment requires information management decisions to adhere to enterprisewide drivers and priorities. No minority group will detract from the benefit of the whole. However, this principle will not prevent any minority group from getting its job done.

   Implications:

   Achieving maximum enterprisewide benefit will require changes in the way one plans and manages information. Technology alone will not bring about this change.

   Some organizations may have to concede their own preferences for the greater benefit of the entire enterprise.

   Application development priorities must be established by the entire enterprise for the entire enterprise.

   Application components should be shared across organizational boundaries.

Information management initiatives should be conducted in accordance with the enterprise plan. Individual organizations should pursue information management initiatives that conform to the blueprints and priorities established by the enterprise. The plan will be changed as needed.

As needs arise, priorities must be adjusted. A forum with comprehensive enterprise representation should make these decisions.

3. Principle: **Information management is everybody's business**

   Statement: All organizations in the enterprise participate in information management decisions needed to accomplish business objectives.

   Rationale: Information users are the key stakeholders, or customers, in the application of technology to address a business need. To ensure that information management is aligned with the business, all organizations in the enterprise must be involved in all aspects of the information environment. The business experts from across the enterprise and the technical staff responsible for developing and sustaining the information environment need to come together as a team to jointly define the goals and objectives of information technology.

   Implications:

   To operate as a team, every stakeholder, or customer, will need to accept responsibility for developing the information environment.

   Commitment of resources will be required to implement this principle.

4. Principle: **Business continuity**

   Statement: Enterprise operations are maintained in spite of system interruptions.

   Rationale: As system operations become more pervasive, one becomes more dependent on them; therefore, one must consider the reliability of such systems throughout their design and use. Business premises throughout the enterprise must be provided the capability to continue their business functions regardless of external events. Hardware failure, natural disasters, and data corruption should not be allowed to disrupt or stop enterprise activities. The enterprise business functions must be capable of operating on alternative information delivery mechanisms.

   Implications:

   Dependency on shared system applications mandates that the risks of business interruption must be established in advance and managed. Management includes, but is not limited to, periodic reviews, testing for vulnerability and exposure, or designing mission-critical services to ensure business function continuity through redundant or alternative capabilities.

   Recoverability, redundancy, and maintainability should be addressed at the time of design.

   Applications must be assessed for criticality and impact on the enterprise mission, to determine what level of continuity is required and what corresponding recovery plan is necessary.

5. Principle: **Common-use applications**

   Statement: Development of applications used across the enterprise is preferred over the development of similar or duplicative applications that are only provided to a particular organization.

   Rationale: Duplicative capability is expensive and leads to proliferation of conflicting data.

Implications:

Organizations that depend on a capability which does not serve the entire enterprise must change over to the replacement enterprisewide capability. This will require establishment of and adherence to a policy requiring this.

Organizations will not be allowed to develop capabilities for their own use that are similar/duplicative of enterprisewide capabilities. In this way, expenditures of scarce resources to develop essentially the same capability in marginally different ways will be reduced.

Data and information used to support enterprise decision making will be standardized to a much greater extent than was previously done. This is because the smaller organizational capabilities that produced different data (which was not shared among other organizations) will be replaced by enterprisewide capabilities. The impetus for adding to the set of enterprisewide capabilities may well come from an organization making a convincing case for the value of the data/information previously produced by its organizational capability, but the resulting capability will become part of the enterprisewide system, and the data it produces will be shared across the enterprise.

6. Principle: **Compliance with law**

Statement: Enterprise information management processes comply with all relevant laws, policies, and regulations.

Rationale: Enterprise policy is to abide by laws, policies, and regulations. This will not preclude business process improvements that lead to changes in policies and regulations.

Implications:

The enterprise must be mindful to comply with laws, regulations, and external policies regarding the collection, retention, and management of data.

Education and access to the rules. Efficiency, need, and common sense are not the only drivers in architecture development. Changes in the law and changes in regulations may drive changes in the processes or applications.

7. Principle: **IT responsibility**

Statement: The IT organization is responsible for owning and implementing IT processes and infrastructure that enable solutions to meet user-defined requirements for functionality, service levels, cost, and delivery timing.

Rationale: Effectively align expectations with capabilities and costs so that all projects are cost-effective. Efficient and effective solutions have reasonable costs and clear benefits.

Implications:

A process must be created to prioritize projects

The IT function must define processes to manage business unit expectations

Data, application, and technology models must be created to enable integrated quality solutions and to maximize results.

8. Principle: **Protection of intellectual property**

Statement: The enterprise's intellectual property must be protected. This protection must be reflected in the IT architecture, implementation, and governance processes.

Rationale: A major part of an enterprise's intellectual property is hosted in the IT domain.

Implications:

Although protection of intellectual property assets is everybody's business, much of the actual protection is implemented in the IT domain. Even trust in non-IT processes can be managed by IT processes (e-mail, mandatory notes, etc.).

A Security Policy, governing human and IT actors, will be required that can substantially improve protection of intellectual property. This must be capable of both avoiding compromises and reducing liabilities.

Resources on such policies can be found at the SANS Institute (www.sans.org).

Data Principles

9. Principle: **Data is an asset**

   Statement: Data is an asset that has value to the enterprise and is managed accordingly.

   Rationale: Data is a valuable corporate resource; it has real, measurable value. In simple terms, the purpose of data is to aid decision making. Accurate, timely data is critical to accurate, timely decisions. Most corporate assets are carefully managed, and data is no exception. Data is the foundation of our decision making, so we must also carefully manage data to assure that one knows where it is, can rely upon its accuracy, and can obtain it when and where one needs it.

   Implications:

   This is one of three closely related principles regarding data: **data is an asset; data is shared;** and **data is easily accessible**. The implication is that there is an educational task to ensure that all organizations within the enterprise understand the relationship between value of data, sharing of data, and accessibility to data.

   Stewards must have the authority and means to manage the data for which they are accountable.

   One must make the cultural transition from "data-ownership" thinking to "data-stewardship" thinking.

   The role of data steward is critical because obsolete, incorrect, or inconsistent data could be passed to enterprise personnel and adversely affect decisions across the enterprise.

   Part of the role of the data steward, who manages the data, is to ensure data quality. Procedures must be developed and used to prevent and correct errors in the information and to improve those processes that produce flawed information. Data quality will need to be measured and steps taken to improve data quality—it is probable that policy and procedures will need to be developed for this as well.

   A forum with comprehensive enterprisewide representation should decide on process changes suggested by the steward.

   Because data is an asset of value to the entire enterprise, data stewards accountable for properly managing the data must be assigned at the enterprise level.

10. Principle: **Data is shared**

    Statement: Users have access to the data necessary to perform their duties; therefore, data is shared across enterprise functions and organizations.

    Rationale: Timely access to accurate data is essential to improving the quality and efficiency of enterprise decision making. It is less costly to maintain timely, accurate data in a single application, and then share it, than it is to maintain duplicative data in multiple applications. The enterprise holds a wealth of data, but it is stored in hundreds of incompatible stovepipe databases. The speed of data collection, creation, transfer, and assimilation is driven by the ability of the organization to efficiently share these islands of data across the organization.

Shared data will result in improved decisions because we will rely on fewer (ultimately one virtual) sources of more accurate and timely managed data for all of our decision making. Electronically shared data will result in increased efficiency when existing data entities can be used, without rekeying, to create new entities.

Implications:

This is one of three closely related principles regarding data: **data is an asset; data is shared;** and **data is easily accessible**. The implication is that there is an educational task to ensure that all organizations within the enterprise understand the relationship between value of data, sharing of data, and accessibility to data.

To enable data sharing one must develop and abide by a common set of policies, procedures, and standards governing data management and access for both the short and the long term.

For the short term, to preserve our significant investment in legacy systems, we must invest in software capable of migrating legacy system data into a shared-data environment.

One will also need to develop standard data models, data elements, and other metadata that define this shared environment, and develop a repository system for storing this metadata to make it accessible.

For the long term, as legacy systems are replaced, one must adopt and enforce common data access policies and guidelines for new application developers to ensure that data in new applications remains available to the shared environment and that data in the shared environment can continue to be used by the new applications.

For both the short term and the long term one must adopt common methods and tools for creating, maintaining, and accessing the data shared across the enterprise.

Data sharing will require a significant cultural change.

This principle of data sharing will continually "bump up against" the principle of data security. Under no circumstances will the data-sharing principle cause confidential data to be compromised.

Data made available for sharing will have to be relied upon by all users to execute their respective tasks. This will ensure that only the most accurate and timely data is relied upon for decision making. Shared data will become the enterprisewide "virtual single source" of data.

11. Principle: **Data is accessible**

Statement: Data is accessible for users to perform their functions.

Rationale: Wide access to data leads to efficiency and effectiveness in decision making, and enables timely response to information requests and service delivery. Information use must be considered from an enterprise perspective to allow access by a wide variety of users. Staff time is saved, and consistency of data is improved.

Implications:

This is one of three closely related principles regarding data: **data is an asset; data is shared;** and **data is easily accessible**. The implication is that there is an educational task to ensure that all organizations within the enterprise understand the relationship between value of data, sharing of data, and accessibility to data.

Accessibility involves the ease with which users obtain information.

The way information is accessed and displayed must be sufficiently adaptable to meet a wide range of enterprise users and their corresponding methods of access.

Access to data does not constitute understanding of the data. Personnel should be cautious not to misinterpret information.

Access to data does not necessarily grant the user access rights to modify or disclose the data. This will require an educational process and a change in the organizational culture that currently supports a belief in "ownership" of data by functional units.

12. Principle: **Data trustee**

Statement: Each data element has a trustee accountable for data quality.

Rationale: One of the benefits of an architected environment is the ability to share data (e.g., text, video, sound, etc.) across the enterprise. As the degree of data sharing grows and business units rely on common information, it becomes essential that only the data trustee make decisions about the content of data. Because data can lose its integrity when it is entered multiple times, the data trustee will have sole responsibility for data entry, which eliminates redundant human effort and data storage resources. (Note that a trustee is different from a steward—the trustee is responsible for accuracy and currency of the data, whereas responsibilities of a steward may be broader and include data standardization and definition tasks.)

Implications:

Real trusteeship dissolves the data "ownership" issues and allows the data to be available to meet all users' needs. This implies that a cultural change from data "ownership" to data "trusteeship" may be required.

The data trustee will be responsible for meeting quality requirements levied upon the data for which the trustee is accountable.

It is essential that the trustee have the ability to provide user confidence in the data based upon attributes such as "data source."

It is essential to identify the true source of the data so that the data authority can be assigned this trustee responsibility. This does not mean that classified sources will be revealed, nor does it mean the source will be the trustee.

Information should be captured electronically once and immediately validated as close to the source as possible. Quality control measures must be implemented to ensure the integrity of the data.

As a result of sharing data across the enterprise, the trustee is accountable and responsible for the accuracy and currency of their designated data elements, and subsequently, must then recognize the importance of this trusteeship responsibility.

13. Principle: **Common vocabulary and data definitions**

Statement: Data is defined consistently throughout the enterprise, and the definitions are understandable and available to all users.

Rationale: The data that will be used in the development of applications must have a common definition throughout the headquarters to enable sharing of data. A common vocabulary will facilitate communications and enable dialogue to be effective. In addition, it is required to interface systems and exchange data.

Implications:

We are lulled into thinking that this issue is adequately addressed because there are people with "data administration" job titles and forums with charters implying responsibility. Significant additional energy and resources must be committed to this task. It is a key to the success of efforts to improve the information environment. This is separate from but related to the issue of data element definition, which is addressed by a broad community—this is more like a common vocabulary and definition.

The enterprise must establish the initial common vocabulary for the business. The definitions will be used uniformly throughout the enterprise.

Whenever a new data definition is required, the definition effort will be coordinated and reconciled with the corporate "glossary" of data descriptions. The Enterprise Data Administrator will provide this coordination.

Ambiguities resulting from multiple parochial definitions of data must give way to accepted enterprisewide definitions and understanding.

Multiple data standardization initiatives need to be coordinated.

Functional data administration responsibilities must be assigned.

14. Principle: **Data security**

Statement: Data is protected from unauthorized use and disclosure. In addition to the traditional aspects of national security classification, this includes, but is not limited to, protection of predecisional, sensitive, source selection sensitive, and proprietary information.

Rationale: Open sharing of information and the release of information via relevant legislation must be balanced against the need to restrict the availability of classified, proprietary, and sensitive information.

Existing laws and regulations require the safeguarding of national security and the privacy of data, while permitting free and open access. Predecisional (work in progress, not yet authorized for release) information must be protected to avoid unwarranted speculation, misinterpretation, and inappropriate use.

Implications:

Aggregation of data, both classified and not, will create a large target requiring review and declassification procedures to maintain appropriate control. Data owners or functional users must determine if the aggregation results in an increased classification level. We will need appropriate policy and procedures to handle this review and declassification. Access to information based on a need-to-know policy will force regular reviews of the body of information.

The current practice of having separate systems to contain different classifications needs to be rethought. Is there a software solution to separating classified and unclassified data? The current hardware solution is unwieldy, inefficient, and costly. It is more expensive to manage unclassified data on a classified system. Currently, the only way to combine the two is to place the unclassified data on the classified system, where it must remain.

To adequately provide access to open information while maintaining secure information, security needs must be identified and developed at the data level, not the application level.

Data security safeguards can be put in place to restrict access to "view only," or "never see." Sensitivity labeling for access to predecisional, decisional, classified, sensitive, or proprietary information must be determined.

Security must be designed into data elements from the beginning; it cannot be added later. Systems, data, and technologies must be protected from unauthorized access and manipulation. Headquarters' information must be safeguarded against inadvertent or unauthorized alteration, sabotage, disaster, or disclosure.

Need new policies on managing duration of protection for predecisional information and other works in progress, in consideration of content freshness.

Application Principles

15. Principle: **Technology independence**

    Statement: Applications are independent of specific technology choices and therefore can operate on a variety of technology platforms.

    Rationale: Independence of applications from the underlying technology allows applications to be developed, upgraded, and operated in the most cost-effective and timely way. Otherwise, technology, which is subject to continual obsolescence and vendor dependence, becomes the driver rather than the user requirements themselves.

    Realizing that every decision made with respect to information technology makes one dependent on that technology, the intent of this principle is to ensure that application software is not dependent on specific hardware and operating system software.

    Implications:

    This principle will require standards that support portability.

    For COTS and GOTS applications, there may be limited current choices, as many of these applications are technology and platform dependent.

    Application programming interfaces (APIs) will need to be developed to enable legacy applications to interoperate with applications and operating environments developed under the enterprise architecture.

    Middleware should be used to decouple applications from specific software solutions.

    As an example, this principle could lead to use of JAVA, and future JAVA-like protocols, which give a high degree of priority to platform independence.

16. Principle: **Ease of use**

    Statement: Applications are easy to use. The underlying technology is transparent to users, so they can concentrate on tasks at hand.

    Rationale: The more a user has to understand the underlying technology, the less productive that user is. Ease of use is a positive incentive for use of applications. It encourages users to work within the integrated information environment instead of developing isolated systems to accomplish the task outside of the enterprise's integrated information environment. Most of the knowledge required to operate one system will be similar to others. Training is kept to a minimum, and the risk of using a system improperly is low.

    Using an application should be as intuitive as driving a different car.

    Implications:

    Applications will be required to have a common "look and feel" and support ergonomic requirements. Hence, the common look and feel standard must be designed and usability test criteria must be developed.

    Guidelines for user interfaces should not be constrained by narrow assumptions about user location, language, systems training, or physical capability. Factors such as linguistics, customer physical infirmities (visual acuity, ability to use keyboard/mouse), and proficiency in the use of technology have broad ramifications in determining the ease of use of an application.

Technical Principles

17. Principle: **Requirements-based change**

    Statement: Only in response to business needs are changes to applications and technology made.

Rationale: This principle will foster an atmosphere where the information environment changes in response to the needs of the business, rather than having the business change in response to information technology changes. This is to ensure that the purpose of the information support—the transaction of business—is the basis for any proposed change. Unintended effects on business due to information technology changes will be minimized. A change in technology may provide an opportunity to improve the business process, and hence, change business needs.

Implications:

Changes in implementation will follow full examination of the proposed changes using the enterprise architecture.

No funding for a technical improvement or system development is approved unless a documented business need exists.

Change-management processes conforming to this principle will be developed and implemented.

This principle may bump up against the responsive change principle. One must ensure the requirements documentation process does not hinder responsive change to meet legitimate business needs. The purpose of this principle is to keep the focus on business, not technology, needs—responsive change is also a business need.

18. Principle: **Responsive change management**

Statement: Changes to the enterprise information environment are implemented in a timely manner.

Rationale: If people are to be expected to work within the enterprise information environment, that information environment must be responsive to their needs.

Implications:

Process development for managing and implementing change must not create delays.

A user who feels a need for change will need to connect with a "business expert" to facilitate explanation and implementation of that need.

If one is going to make changes, one must keep the architectures updated.

Adopting this principle might require additional resources.

This will conflict with other principles (e.g., maximum enterprisewide benefit, enterprisewide applications, etc.).

19. Principle: **Control technical diversity**

Statement: Technological diversity is controlled to minimize the nontrivial cost of maintaining expertise in and connectivity between multiple processing environments.

Rationale: There is a real, nontrivial cost of infrastructure required to support alternative technologies for processing environments. There are further infrastructural costs incurred to keep multiple processor constructs interconnected and maintained.

Limiting the number of supported components will simplify maintainability and reduce costs.

The business advantages of minimum technical diversity include standard packaging of components, predictable implementation impact, predictable valuations and returns, redefined testing, utility status, and increased flexibility to accommodate technological advancements. Common technology across the enterprise brings the benefits of economies of scale to the enterprise. Technical administration and support costs are better controlled when limited resources can focus on this shared set of technology.

Implications:

Policies, standards, and procedures that govern acquisition of technology must be tied directly to this principle.

Technology choices will be constrained by the choices available within the technology blueprint. Procedures for augmenting the acceptable technology set to meet evolving requirements will have to be developed and emplaced.

There will be no freezing of the technology baseline. Technology advances will be welcomed and will change the technology blueprint when compatibility with the current infrastructure, improvement in operational efficiency, or a required capability has been demonstrated.

20. Principle: **Interoperability**

Statement: Software and hardware should conform to defined standards that promote interoperability for data, applications, and technology.

Rationale: Standards help ensure consistency, thus improving the ability to manage systems and improve user satisfaction, and protect existing IT investments, thus maximizing return on investment and reducing costs. Standards for interoperability additionally help ensure support from multiple vendors for their products, and facilitate supply-chain integration.

Implications:

Interoperability standards and industry standards will be followed unless there is a compelling business reason to implement a nonstandard solution.

A process for setting standards, reviewing and revising them periodically, and granting exceptions must be established.

The existing IT platforms must be identified and documented.

Chapter 3

The Open Group Architectural Framework

This chapter discusses in some depth The Open Group Architectural Framework (TOGAF). Currently, it is one of the most often used frameworks by organizations all over the world. TOGAF enables corporate architects and stakeholders to design, evaluate, and build a flexible enterprise architecture for the organization. Any organization undertaking, or planning to undertake, the design and implementation of an enterprise architecture for the support of mission-critical business applications using open systems building blocks can benefit from using TOGAF. Customers who design and implement enterprise architectures using TOGAF are assured of a design, and a procurement specification that facilitates open systems implementation and reduces risk. On the basis of its openness, we believe that in the future this model will become the most often used framework. The topic was briefly introduced in Chapter 2 and is expanded here.

This chapter is based on TOGAF documentation, with the permission of The Open Group. The Open Group* operates as a not-for-profit consortium committed to delivering greater business efficiency by bringing together buyers and suppliers of information systems to lower the barriers of integrating new technology across the enterprise.

3.1 Introduction and Overview

As we saw in previous chapters, there are four types of architectures that are commonly accepted as subsets of an overall enterprise architecture, all of which TOGAF is designed to support:

- A **business** (or **business process**) **architecture**—this defines the business strategy, governance, organization, and key business processes.
- An **applications architecture**—This kind of architecture provides a blueprint for the individual application systems to be deployed, their interactions, and their relationships to the core business processes of the organization.

---

* The Open Group has given us permission to reprint portions of their documentation. In the event of any discrepancy between these versions and the original document, The Open Group original is the referee document. The original document can be obtained online at http://www.opengroup.org/togaf.

■ A **data architecture**—This describes the structure of an organization's logical and physical data assets and data management resources.
■ A **technology architecture**—This describes the software infrastructure intended to support the deployment of core, mission-critical applications. This type of software is sometimes referred to as *middleware*.

The primary reason for developing an enterprise architecture is to support the business side of the organization by providing the fundamental technology and process structure for an IT strategy. This, in turn, makes IT a responsive asset for a successful up-to-date business strategy. Today's CEOs know that the effective management and exploitation of information through IT is the key to business success, and the indispensable means to achieving competitive advantage. An enterprise architecture addresses this need by providing a strategic context for the evolution of the IT system in response to the constantly changing needs of the business environment. Furthermore, a good enterprise architecture enables one to achieve the right balance between IT efficiency and business innovation. It allows individual business units to innovate safely in their pursuit of competitive advantage. At the same time, it assures the needs of the organization for an integrated IT strategy, permitting the closest possible synergy across the extended enterprise.

The technical advantages that result from a good enterprise architecture bring important business benefits:

■ A more efficient IT operation
  – Lower software development, support, and maintenance costs
  – Increased portability of applications
  – Improved interoperability and easier system and network management
  – A better ability to address critical enterprisewide issues such as security
  – Easier upgrade and exchange of system components
■ Better return on existing investment and reduced risk for future investment
  – Reduced complexity in IT infrastructure
  – Maximum return on investment in existing IT infrastructure
  – The flexibility to make, buy, or outsource IT solutions
  – Reduced risk overall in new investment, and the costs of IT ownership
■ Faster, simpler, and cheaper procurement
  – Simpler buying decisions, because the information governing procurement is readily available in a coherent plan
  – Faster procurement process—maximizing procurement speed and flexibility without sacrificing architectural coherence.

Architecture design is a technically complex process, and the design of heterogeneous, multi-vendor architectures is complex. Using an architecture framework will speed up and simplify architecture development, ensure more complete coverage of the designed solution, and make certain that the architecture selected allows for future growth in response to the needs of the business. TOGAF plays an important role in helping to systematize the architecture development process, enabling IT users to build open systems-based solutions to their business needs. Those IT customers who do not invest in enterprise architecture typically find themselves pushed to single-supplier solutions to ensure an integrated solution. At that point, no matter how ostensibly "open" any single supplier's products may be in terms of adherence to standards, the customer will be unable to realize the potential benefits of truly heterogeneous, multi-vendor open systems.

Typically, an architecture is developed because key people have concerns that need to be addressed by the IT systems within the organization. Such people are commonly referred to as the *stakeholders* in the system. The role of the architect is to address these concerns, by identifying and refining the requirements that the stakeholders have, developing views of the architecture that show how the concerns and the requirements are going to be addressed, and by showing the trade-offs that are going to be made in reconciling the potentially conflicting concerns of different stakeholders. Without the architecture, it is unlikely that all the concerns and requirements will be considered and met.

TOGAF consists of three main parts:

1. The **TOGAF Architecture Development Method (ADM)**, which explains how to derive an organization-specific enterprise architecture that addresses business requirements. The ADM provides the following:
   - A reliable, proven way of developing the architecture
   - Architectural views that enable the architect to ensure that a complex set of requirements are adequately addressed
   - Linkages to practical case studies
   - Guidelines on tools for architecture development

2. The **Enterprise Continuum**, a "virtual repository" of all the architecture assets—models, patterns, architecture descriptions, etc.—that exist both within the enterprise and in the IT industry at large, which the enterprise considers itself to have available for the development of architectures. At relevant places throughout the TOGAF ADM, there are reminders to consider which architecture assets from the Enterprise Continuum, if any, the architect should use. TOGAF itself provides two reference models for consideration for inclusion in an enterprise's own Enterprise Continuum:
   a. The **TOGAF Foundation Architecture**—an architecture of generic services and functions that provides a foundation on which specific architectures and architectural building blocks can be built. This foundation architecture in turn includes:
      i. The *TOGAF Technical Reference Model (TRM)*, which provides a model and taxonomy of generic platform services; and
      ii. The *TOGAF Standards Information Base (SIB)*, a database of open industry standards that can be used to define the particular services and other components of an enterprise-specific architecture
   b. The **Integrated Information Infrastructure Reference Model**, which is based on the TOGAF foundation architecture, and is specifically aimed at helping the design of architectures that enable and support the vision of "boundaryless information flow."

3. The **TOGAF Resource Base**, which is a set of resources—guidelines, templates, background information, etc.—to help the architect in the use of the ADM.

TOGAF is published by The Open Group on its public Web site, and may be reproduced freely by any enterprise wishing to use it to develop an enterprise architecture for use within that enterprise. Basically, information about the benefits and constraints of the existing implementation, together with requirements for change, are combined using the methods described in the TOGAF ADM, resulting in a "target architecture" or set of target architectures.

The TOGAF SIB provides a database of open industry standards that can be used to define the particular services and components required in the products purchased to implement the developed architecture. The SIB provides a simple and effective way to procure against an enterprise architecture.

3.2 The Role of Architecture Views

3.2.1 Introduction

Architecture views are representations of the overall architecture that are meaningful to one or more stakeholders in the system. The architect chooses and develops a set of views that will enable the architecture to be communicated to, and understood by, all the stakeholders, and enable them to verify that the system will address their concerns.

An architecture is usually represented by means of one or more architecture models that together provide a coherent description of the system's architecture. A single, comprehensive model is often too complex to be understood and communicated in its most detailed form, showing all the relationships between the various business and technical components. As with the architecture of a building, it is normally necessary to develop multiple *views* of the architecture of an information system, to enable the architecture to be communicated to, and understood by, the different stakeholders in the system.

For example, just as a building architect might create wiring diagrams, floor plans, and elevations to describe different facets of a building to its different stakeholders (electricians, owners, planning officials), so an IT architect might create physical and security views of an IT system for the stakeholders who have concerns related to these aspects.

3.2.2 TOGAF and Standards for IT Architecture Description

An important recent development in IT architecture practice has been the emergence of standards for architecture description, principally through the adoption by ANSI and the IEEE of ANSI/IEEE Std 1471-2000—Recommended Practice for Architectural Description of Software-Intensive Systems. One of the aims of this standard is to promote a more consistent, systematic approach to the creation of views. (At the present time, TOGAF encourages but does not mandate the use of ANSI/IEEE Std 1471-2000.)

Note: A short overview of ANSI/IEEE Std 1471-2000 can be found in Chapter 5; the reader may wish to skip forward temporarily to the end of Chapter 5 before proceeding with the following material.

Organizations that have incorporated, or plan to incorporate, ANSI/IEEE Std 1471-2000 into their IT architecture practice should find that none of the key concepts in TOGAF is incompatible with this standard, although some of the terminology used is not completely consistent with it.

TOGAF endeavors to strike a balance between promoting the concepts and terminology of ANSI/IEEE Std 1471-2000—ensuring that the usage of terms defined by ANSI/IEEE Std 1471-2000 is consistent with the standard—and retaining other commonly accepted terminology that is familiar to the majority of the TOGAF readership. An example of common terminology retained in TOGAF is the use of the terms *business architecture, technology architecture*, etc. These terms reflect common usage, but are at variance with ANSI/IEEE Std 1471-2000 (in which "architecture" is a property of something, not something in its own right). This situation will be reviewed in future versions of TOGAF. The process of gradual convergence between TOGAF and relevant standards for architecture description will continue as ANSI/IEEE Std 1471-2000 gains increased acceptance within the industry.

3.2.3 A Note on Terminology

It is arguable that the term *architecture* in TOGAF should be replaced by the term *view*, in accordance with ANSI/IEEE Std 1471-2000 recommended practice. There are practical problems with this.

First, there is the issue of common usage. Typically, an overall enterprise architecture comprising all four "architectures" (business, data, applications, and technology) will not be undertaken as a single project. Instead, each "architecture"—and in some cases, subsets of them—will be undertaken as individual projects. The ultimate deliverable of such a project is commonly referred to as an "architecture" (for example, a "business architecture"). Within such an "architecture" there will very likely be views, in the true ANSI/IEEE Std 1471-2000 sense. Second, such individual projects—leading to a "business architecture," or an "applications architecture," etc.—are often undertaken without any intent to develop all four "architectures" and integrate them into an overall enterprise architecture. (At least, there may be a long-term strategic goal to develop all four, but the initial development may be intended as a free-standing "architecture" and not a view of some larger entity.)

In summary, therefore, the choice of terminology will depend largely on the extent to which the enterprise concerned regards each of the architectures mentioned earlier as part of a larger "enterprise architecture."

As of press time, TOGAF retains the terminology of "business architecture," "technology architecture," etc., because the terminology associated with ANSI/IEEE Std 1471-2000 recommended practice is still relatively new to the industry and not yet in widespread use. This situation will be reviewed in future versions of TOGAF.

3.3 Basic TOGAF Concepts

The following concepts are central to the topic of views. These concepts have been adapted from more formal definitions contained in ANSI/IEEE Std 1471-2000—*Recommended Practice for Architectural Description of Software-Intensive Systems.*

A **system** is a collection of components organized to accomplish a specific function or set of functions.

The **architecture** of a system is the system's fundamental organization, embodied in its components, their relationships to each other and to the environment, and the principles guiding its design and evolution.

An **architecture description** is a collection of artifacts that document an architecture. In TOGAF, architecture views are the key artifacts in an architecture description.

Stakeholders are people who have key roles in, or concerns about, the system, for example, as users, developers, or managers. Different stakeholders with different roles in the system will have different concerns. Stakeholders can be individuals, teams, or organizations (or classes thereof).

Concerns are the key interests that are crucially important to the stakeholders in the system, and determine the acceptability of the system. Concerns may pertain to any aspect of the system's functioning, development, or operation, including considerations such as performance, reliability, security, distribution, and evolvability.

A **view** is a representation of a whole system from the perspective of a related set of concerns.

In capturing or representing the design of a system architecture, the architect will typically create one or more architecture **models**, possibly using different tools. A view will comprise selected parts of one or more models, chosen so as to demonstrate to a particular stakeholder or group of stakeholders that their concerns are being adequately addressed in the design of the system architecture.

A **viewpoint** defines the perspective from which a view is taken. More specifically, a viewpoint defines the following: how to construct and use a view (by means of an appropriate schema or template); the information that should appear in the view; the modeling techniques for expressing and analyzing the information; and a rationale for these choices (e.g., by describing the purpose and intended audience of the view).

- A *view* is what one sees. A *viewpoint* is where one is looking from—the vantage point or perspective that determines what one sees.
- Viewpoints are generic, and can be stored in libraries for reuse. A view is always specific to the architecture for which it is created.
- Every view has an associated viewpoint that describes it, at least implicitly. ANSI/IEEE Std 1471-2000 encourages architects to define viewpoints explicitly. Making this distinction between the content and schema of a view may seem at first to be an unnecessary overhead, but it provides a mechanism for reusing viewpoints across different architectures.

In summary, then, architecture views are representations of the overall architecture in terms meaningful to stakeholders. They enable the architecture to be communicated to and understood by the stakeholders, so they can verify that the system will address their concerns.

Note: The terms *concern* and *requirement* are not synonymous. A concern is an area of interest. So, system reliability might be a concern, or area of interest, for some stakeholders. The reason why architects should identify concerns and associate them with viewpoints is to ensure that those concerns will be addressed in some fashion by the models of the architecture. For example, if the only viewpoint selected by an architect is a structural viewpoint, then reliability concerns are almost certainly not being addressed, because they cannot be represented in a structural model. Within that concern, stakeholders may have many distinct requirements; different classes of users may have very different reliability requirements for different capabilities of the system.

Concerns are the root of the process of decomposition into requirements. Concerns are represented in the architecture by these requirements.

3.3.1 Viewpoint and View: A Simple Example

For many architectures, a useful viewpoint is that of business domains, which can be illustrated by an example from The Open Group itself.

The viewpoint is specified as follows:

Viewpoint element	Description
Stakeholders	Management board, chief information officer
Concerns	Show the top-level relationships between geographic sites and business functions
Modeling technique	Nested boxes diagram Blue = locations; brown = business functions Semantics of nesting = functions performed in the locations

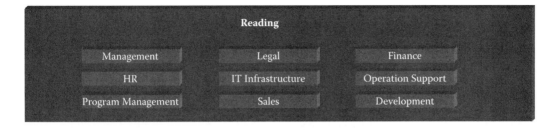

Figure 3.1 Example of a view—The Open Group business domains in 2001.

The corresponding view of The Open Group (in 2001) is shown in Figure 3.1.

3.4 Developing Views in the ADM

3.4.1 General Guidelines

The choice of which particular architecture views to develop is one of the key decisions that the architect has to make.

The architect has a responsibility for ensuring the *completeness* (fitness for purpose) of the architecture, in terms of adequately addressing all the pertinent concerns of its stakeholders, and the *integrity* of the architecture, in terms of connecting all the various views to each other, satisfactorily reconciling the conflicting concerns of different stakeholders, and showing the trade-offs made in so doing (as between security and performance, for example). The choice has to be constrained by considerations of practicality, and by the principle of fitness for purpose (i.e., the architecture should be developed only to the point at which it is fit for purpose, and not reiterated ad infinitum as an academic exercise).

As explained in the documentation on the Architecture Development Method, the development of architecture views is an iterative process. The typical progression is from business to technology, using a technique such as Business Scenarios to properly identify all pertinent concerns, and from high-level overview to lower-level detail, continually referring back to the concerns and requirements of the stakeholders, throughout the process.

Moreover, each of these progressions has to be made for two distinct environments: the existing environment (referred to as the *baseline* in the ADM) and the target environment. The architect must develop pertinent business and technical architecture views of both the existing system and the target system. This provides the context for the gap analysis that is part of the ADM, which establishes which elements of the current system must be carried forward and which must be removed or replaced.

3.4.2 The View Creation Process

As mentioned previously, at press time TOGAF encourages but does not mandate the use of ANSI/IEEE Std 1471-2000. The following description, therefore, covers both the situations, where ANSI/IEEE Std 1471-2000 has been adopted and where it has not.

IEEE 1471-2000 itself does not require any specific process for developing viewpoints or creating views from them. Where ANSI/IEEE Std 1471-2000 has been adopted and become a well-established practice within an organization, it will often be possible to create the required views for a particular architecture by following these steps:

1. Refer to an existing library of viewpoints.
2. Select the appropriate viewpoints (based on the stakeholders and concerns that need to be covered by views).
3. Generate views of the system by using the selected viewpoints as templates.

This approach can be expected to bring the following benefits:

■ Less work for the architects (because the viewpoints have already been defined and therefore the views can be created faster)
■ Better comprehensibility for stakeholders (because the viewpoints are already familiar)
■ Greater confidence in the validity of the views (because their viewpoints have a known track record)

However, situations can always arise in which a view is needed for which no appropriate viewpoint has been predefined. This is also the situation, of course, when an organization has not yet incorporated ANSI/IEEE Std 1471-2000 into its architecture practice and established a library of viewpoints. In each case, the architect may choose to develop a new viewpoint that will cover the outstanding need and then generate a view from it. (This is the ANSI/IEEE Std 1471-2000 recommended practice.) Alternatively, a more pragmatic approach can be equally successful: the architect can create an ad hoc view for a specific system and later consider whether a generalized form of the implicit viewpoint should be defined explicitly and saved in a library, so that it can be reused. (This is one way of establishing a library of viewpoints initially.)

Whatever the context, the architect should be aware that every view has a viewpoint, at least implicitly, and that defining the viewpoint in a systematic way (as recommended by ANSI/IEEE Std 1471-2000) will help in assessing its effectiveness (i.e., does the viewpoint cover the relevant stakeholder concerns?).

3.5 Core Taxonomy of Architecture Views

3.5.1 Overview

TOGAF's core taxonomy of architecture views defines the minimum set of views that should be considered in the development of an architecture. Because, in ANSI/IEEE Std 1471-2000, every view has an associated viewpoint that defines it, this may also be regarded as a taxonomy of viewpoints by those organizations that have adopted ANSI/IEEE Std 1471-2000.

3.5.2 Stakeholders

The minimum set of stakeholders for a system that should be considered in the development of architecture viewpoints and views comprises the following:

- Users
- System and software engineers
- Operators, administrators, and managers
- Acquirers

3.5.3 Views/Viewpoints

The architecture views, and corresponding viewpoints, that may be created to support each of these stakeholders fall into the following categories. (As mentioned previously, this may be regarded as a taxonomy of viewpoints by those organizations that have adopted ANSI/IEEE Std 1471-2000.)

- **Business Architecture Views**, which address the concerns of the users of the system, and describe the flows of business information between people and business processes
- **Data Architecture Views**, which address the concerns of database designers and database administrators, and system engineers responsible for developing and integrating the various database components of the system.
- **Applications Architecture Views**, which address the concerns of system and software engineers responsible for developing and integrating the various application software components of the system.
- **Technology Architecture Views**, which address the concerns of Acquirers (procurement personnel responsible for acquiring the commercial off-the-shelf (COTS) software and hardware to be included in the system), operations staff, systems administrators, and systems managers.

Examples of specific views that may be created in each category are given in Table 3.1, and explained in detail in the following subsection.

A mapping of these views to the schema of the well-known Zachman Framework is illustrated in Table 3.2.

The architect may or may not need to develop separate views for different stakeholders, for example, engineers and operations personnel. Engineering views provide information needed by engineering staff to design and implement the hardware and software system. Operations views provide information needed by operations staff to operate and administer the implemented system.

Table 3.1 Taxonomy of Architecture Views: An Example

To address the concerns of the following stakeholders…

Users, Planners, and Business Management	*Database Designers, Administrators, and System Engineers*	*System and Software Engineers*	*Acquirers, Operators, Administrators, and Managers*
…the following views may be developed:			
Business Architecture Views	*Data Architecture Views*	*Applications Architecture Views*	*Technology Architecture Views*
Business Function View	Data Entity View	Software Engineering View	Networked Computing/ Hardware View
Business Services View			
Business Process View			
Business Information View			
Business Locations View			Communications Engineering View
Business Logistics View	Data Flow View (organization data use)	Applications Interoperability View	
People View (organization chart)			Processing View
Workflow View			
Usability View			
Business Strategy and Goals View	Logical Data View	Software Distribution View	Cost View
Business Objectives View			
Business Rules View			Standards View
Business Events View			
Business Performance View	System Engineering View		
Enterprise Security View			
Enterprise Manageability View			
Enterprise Quality of Service View			
Enterprise Mobility View			

3.5.4 Description

The following description explains some of the views listed earlier. A more detailed description of each view, and guidelines for developing it, can be obtained by pursuing the relevant hyperlink in the following.

1. **Business Architecture Views** (see Appendix 3.1) address the concerns of **users, planners, and business managers,** and focuses on the functional aspects of the system from the perspective of the users of the system—that is, on what the new system is intended to do, including performance, functionality, and usability. These can be built up from an analysis of the existing environment and of the requirements and constraints affecting the new system.
   - The **People View** focuses on the human resource aspects of the system. It examines the human actors involved in the system.

Table 3.2 Taxonomy of Architecture Views to Zachman Framework: Mapping of Example

	Stakeholder	Data	Function	Network	People	Time	Motivation
Scope	*Planner*	Data Entity View (Class Model)	Business Function View	Business Locations View	People View (org chart)	Business Events View	Business Strategy and Goals View
			Business Services View	Enterprise Mobility View		Enterprise Quality of Service View	
Enterprise model	*Owner*	Data Flow View (organization data use)	Business Services View	Business Logistics View (business function to location mapping)	Workflow View	Business Performance View (master schedule)	Business Objectives View (SMART objectives from Business Scenario)
			Business Process View	Enterprise Mobility View		Enterprise Quality of Service View	
System model	*Designer*	Logical Data View	System Engineering View	System Engineering View	Usability View	System Engineering View	Business Rules View
			Software Engineering View				
						Processing View	
		Standards View	Application-to-application Communication View		Standards View	Standards View	Cost View

(continued)

Table 3.2 Taxonomy of Architecture Views to Zachman Framework: Mapping of Example (continued)

	Stakeholder	Data	Function	Network	People	Time	Motivation
		Standards View	Standards View	Enterprise Mobility View		Enterprise Quality of Service View	
Technology-constrained model	*Builder*	Physical Data View (out of TOGAF scope)	Software Distribution View	Networked Computing/ Hardware View Communications Engineering View	Usability View	Control structure (out of TOGAF scope)	Business Logic (rules) Design (out of TOGAF scope)
Detailed representations	*Subcontractor*	Data Definitions (out of TOGAF scope)	Application Program Code (out of TOGAF scope)	(out of TOGAF scope)	(out of TOGAF scope)	Timing Definitions (out of TOGAF scope)	Application Program (rules specification) (out of TOGAF scope)
Functioning enterprise		Enterprise Security View Enterprise Mobility View Enterprise Quality of Service View Enterprise Manageability View	Enterprise Security View Enterprise Mobility View Enterprise Quality of Service View Enterprise Manageability View	Enterprise Security View Enterprise Mobility View Enterprise Quality of Service View Enterprise Manageability View	Enterprise Security View Enterprise Mobility View Enterprise Quality of Service View	Enterprise Security View Enterprise Mobility View Enterprise Quality of Service View Enterprise Manageability View	Enterprise Security View Enterprise Mobility View Enterprise Quality of Service View

- The **Business Process View** deals with the user processes involved in the system.
- The **Business Function View** deals with the functions required to support the processes.
- The **Business Information View** deals with the information required to flow in support of the processes.
- The **Usability View** considers the usability aspects of the system and its environment.
- The **Business Performance View** considers the performance aspects of the system and its environment.

2. **Data Architecture Views and Applications Architecture Views** address the concerns of the **database designers and administrators**, and the **system and software engineers** of the system. They focus on how the system is implemented from the perspective of different types of engineers (security, software, data, computing components, communications), and how that affects its properties. Systems and software engineers are typically concerned with modifiability, reusability, and availability of other services:

   - The Data Flow View (see Appendix 3.2) deals with the architecture of storage, retrieval, processing, archiving and security of data. It looks at the flow of data as it is stored and processed, and at what components will be required to support and manage both storage and processing.
   - The Software Engineering View (see TOGAF Documentation for more information) deals with aspects of interest to software developers. It considers what software development constraints and opportunities exist in the new system, and looks at how development can be carried out, both in terms of technology and resources. The Software Engineering View is particularly important in that it provides a reference for selection of building blocks related to elements of the existing system that may be reused in the target architecture.
   - The System Engineering View (see TOGAF Documentation for more information) presents a number of different ways in which software and hardware components can be assembled into a working system. To a great extent the choice of model determines the properties of the final system. It looks at technology that already exists in the organization, and what is available currently or in the near future. This reveals areas where new technology can contribute to the function or efficiency of the new architecture, and how different types of processing platforms can support different parts of the overall system.

3. **Technology Architecture Views** address the concerns of the **acquirers, operators, communications engineers, administrators and managers** of the system.

   - The Communications Engineering View (see Appendix 3.3) addresses the concerns of the communications engineers. It examines various ways of structuring communications facilities to simplify the business of network planning and design. It examines the networking elements of the architecture in the light of geographic constraints, bandwidth requirements, and so on.
   - Acquirer's Views (see TOGAF Documentation for more information) address the needs of an acquirer or procurer, providing appropriate guidance for purchasing components that "fit" the architecture. Acquirer's views of the architecture are primarily concerned with costs, and standards that must be adhered to, for example:
     - The Cost View
     - The Standards View

These views typically depict building blocks of the architecture that can be purchased, and the standards that the building blocks must adhere to for the building block to be most useful.

4. **Composite Views**
   - The Enterprise Manageability View (see TOGAF Documentation for more information) addresses the concerns of the operations, administration, and management of the system, and concentrates more on the details of location, type, and power of the equipment and software to manage the health and availability of the system. It covers issues such as initial deployment, upgrading, availability, security, performance, asset management, and fault and event management of system components from the management perspective of the following subject matters: security, software, data, computing/hardware, and communications.
   - The Enterprise Security View (see TOGAF Documentation for more information) focuses on the security aspects of the system for the protection of information within the organization. It examines the system to establish what information is stored and processed, how valuable it is, what threats exist, and how they can be addressed.

Architects also have concerns of their own, which basically define the fitness for purpose of an effort. Architects must understand completeness, which means considering all relevant views, including the relationships between those views, and dealing with the conflicts that arise from those different views. Architects must also deal with the viability of the architecture; if the architecture is not capable of being implemented, then its value is in doubt.

3.6 Views, Tools, and Languages

The need for architecture views, and the process of developing them following the Architecture Development Method, are explained in the preceding text. This section describes the relationships between architecture views, the tools used to develop and analyze them, and a standard language enabling interoperability between the tools.

3.6.1 Overview

To achieve the goals of completeness and integrity in an architecture, architecture views are usually developed, visualized, communicated, and managed using a tool. In the current state of the market, different tools normally have to be used to develop and analyze different views of the architecture. It is highly desirable that an architecture description be encoded in a standard language, to enable a standard approach to the description of architecture semantics and their reuse among different tools. A viewpoint is also normally developed, visualized, communicated, and managed using a tool, and it is also highly desirable that standard viewpoints (i.e., templates or schemas) be developed, so that different tools that deal in the same views can interoperate, the fundamental elements of an architecture can be reused, and the architecture description can be shared among tools.

3.6.2 Views and Viewpoints

3.6.2.1 An Example

To illustrate the concepts of views and viewpoints, consider the example of a very simple airport system with two different stakeholders, the pilot and the air traffic controller.

The pilot has one view of the system, and the air traffic controller has another. Neither view represents the whole system, because the perspective of each stakeholder constrains (and reduces) how each sees the overall system. The view of the pilot comprises some elements not viewed by the controller, such as passengers and fuel, whereas the view of the controller comprises some elements not viewed by the pilot, such as other planes. There are also elements shared between the views, such as the communication model between the pilot and the controller and the vital information about the plane itself.

A viewpoint is a model (or description) of the information contained in a view. In the example above, one viewpoint is the description of how the pilot sees the system, and the other viewpoint is how the controller sees the system. Pilots describe the system from their perspective, using a model of their position and vector toward or away from the runway. All pilots use this model, and the model has a specific language that is used to capture information and populate the model. Controllers describe the system differently, using a model of the airspace and the locations and vectors of aircraft within the airspace. Again, all controllers use a common language derived from the common model to capture and communicate information pertinent to their viewpoint.

Fortunately, when controllers talk to pilots, they use a common communication language! (In other words, the models representing their individual viewpoints partially intersect.) Part of this common language is about location and vectors of aircraft, and is essential to safety.

So, in essence each viewpoint is an abstract model of how all the stakeholders of a particular type—all pilot, or all controllers—view the airport system. Tools exist to assist stakeholders, especially when they are interacting with complex models such as the model of an airspace or the model of air flight. The interface to the human user of a tool is typically close to the model and language associated with the viewpoint. The unique tools of the pilot are fuel, altitude, speed, and location indicators. The main tool of the controller is radar. The common tool is a radio.

To summarize from this example, one can see that a view can subset the system through the perspective of the stakeholder, such as the pilot versus the controller. This subset can be described by an abstract model called a viewpoint, such as an air flight versus an air space model. This description of the view is documented in a partially specialized language, such as "pilot-speak" versus "controller-speak." Tools are used to assist the stakeholders, and they interface with each other in terms of the language derived from the viewpoint ("pilot-speak" versus "controller-speak"). When stakeholders use common tools, such as the radio contact between pilot and controller, a common language is essential.

3.6.2.2 Views and Viewpoints in Information Systems

Now let us map the preceding example to information systems architecture. Consider two stakeholders in a new, small computing system: the users and the developers.

The users of the system have a view of the system, and the developers of the system have a different view. Neither view represents the whole system, because each perspective reduces how each sees the system. The view of the user consists of all the ways in which the person interacts with the system, not seeing any details such as applications or database management systems. The view of the developer is one of productivity and tools, and does not include things such as actual live data and connections with consumers. However, there are things that are shared, such as descriptions of the processes that are enabled by this system and communications protocols set up for users to communicate problems directly to development.

In the example presented, one viewpoint is the description of how the user sees the system, and the other viewpoint is how the developer sees the system. Users describe the system from their perspective, using a model of availability, response time, and access to information. All users of the system use this model, and the model has a specific language. Developers describe the system differently, using a model of software connected to hardware distributed over a network, etc. However, there are many types of developers (database, security, etc.) of the system, and they do not have a common language derived from the model.

3.6.2.3 The Need for a Common Language and Interoperable Tools for Architecture Description

Tools exist for both users and developers. Tools such as online help are there specifically for users, and attempt to employ the language of the user. Many different tools exist for different types of developers, but they suffer from the lack of a common language that is required to bring the system together. It is difficult, if not impossible, in the current state of the tools market to have one tool interoperate with another tool.

3.7 Conclusions

In general, TOGAF embraces the concepts and definitions presented in ANSI/IEEE Std 1471-2000, specifically the concepts that help guide the development of a view and make the view actionable. These concepts can be summarized as follows:

- Selecting a key stakeholder
- Understanding their concerns and generalizing/documenting those concerns
- Understanding how one models and deals with those concerns

In Appendices 3.1 through 3.4 we discuss a number of TOGAF-recommended views, some or all of which may be appropriate in a particular architecture development. This is not intended as an exhaustive set of views but simply as a starting point. Those described may be supplemented by additional views as required. These TOGAF subsections on views should be considered as guides for the development and treatment of a view, not as a full definition of a view. Each appendix describes the stakeholders related to the view, their concerns, the entities modeled, and the language used to depict the view (the viewpoint). The viewpoint provides architecture concepts from different perspectives, including components, interfaces, and allocation of services critical to the view. The viewpoint language, analytical methods, and modeling methods associated with views are typically applied with the use of appropriate tools.

Appendix 3.1: Developing a Business Architecture View

Stakeholder and Concerns

This view should be developed for the users. It focuses on the functional aspects of the system from the perspective of the users of the system. Addressing the concerns of the users includes consideration of the following:

- People—the human resource aspects of the system. It examines the human actors involved in the system.
- Process—deals with the user processes involved in the system.
- Function—deals with the functions required to support the processes.
- Business information—deals with the information required to flow in support of the processes.
- Usability—considers the usability aspects of the system and its environment.
- Performance—considers the performance aspects of the system and its environment.

Modeling the View

Business scenarios are an important technique that may be used before, and as a key input to, the development of the Business Architecture View, to help identify and understand business needs, and thereby to derive the business requirements and constraints that the architecture development has to address. Business scenarios are an extremely useful way to depict what should happen when planned and unplanned events occur. It is highly recommended that business scenarios be created for both planned and unplanned change. The following paragraphs describe some of the key issues that the architect might consider when constructing business scenarios.

Key Issues

The Business Architecture View considers the functional aspects of the system—that is, what the new system is intended to do. This can be built up from an analysis of the existing environment and of the requirements and constraints affecting the new system.

The new requirements and constraints will appear from a number of sources, possibly including:

- Existing internal specifications and lists of approved products
- Business goals and objectives
- Business process reengineering activities
- Changes in technology

What should emerge from the Business Architecture View is a clear understanding of the functional requirements for the new architecture, with statements such as "improvements in handling customer inquiries are required through wider use of computer/telephony integration."

The Business Architecture View considers the usability aspects of the system and its environment. It should also consider impacts on the user such as skill levels required, the need for specialized training, and migration from current practice. When considering usability, the architect should take into account:

- The ease of use of the user interface, and how intuitive it is
- Whether or not there is transparent access to data and applications, irrespective of location
- Ease of management of the user environment by the user
- Application interoperability through means such as drag and drop
- Online help facilities

- Clarity of documentation
- Security and password aspects, such as avoiding the requirement for multiple sign-on and password dialogues
- Access to productivity applications such as mail or a spreadsheet

Note that, although security and management are thought about here, it is from a usability and functionality point of view. The technical aspects of security and management are considered in the Security View and the Operations View.

Appendix 3.2: Developing a Data Flow View

Stakeholder and Concerns

This view should be developed for database engineers of the system. Major concerns for this view are understanding how to provide data to the right people and applications with the right interfaces at the right time. This view deals with the architecture of storage, retrieval, processing, archiving, and security of data. It looks at the flow of data as it is stored and processed, and at what components will be required to support and manage both storage and processing. In general, these stakeholders are concerned with assuring ubiquitous access to high-quality data.

Modeling the View

The subjects of the general architecture of a "database system" are database components or components that provide database services. The modeling of a "database" is typically done with entity-relationship diagrams and schema definitions, including document-type definitions.

Key Issues

Data management services may be provided by a wide range of implementations. Some examples are:

- Mega centers providing functionally oriented corporate databases supporting local and remote data requirements
- Distributed database management systems that support the interactive use of partitioned and partially replicated databases
- File systems provided by operating systems, which may be used by both interactive and batch-processing applications.

Data management services include the storage, retrieval, manipulation, backup, restart/recovery, security, and associated functions for text, numeric data, and complex data such as documents, graphics, images, audio, and video. The operating system provides file management services, but they are considered here because many legacy databases exist as one or more files without the services provided by a database management system (DBMS).

Major components that provide data management services that are discussed in this section are:

- Database management systems
- Data dictionary/directory systems
- Data administration
- Data security

These are critical aspects of data management for the following reasons. The DBMS is the most critical component of any data management capability, and a data dictionary/directory system is necessary in conjunction with the DBMS as a tool to aid the administration of the database. Data security is a necessary part of any overall policy for security in information processing.

Database Management Systems

A DBMS provides for the systematic management of data. This data management component provides services and capabilities for defining the data, structuring the data, accessing the data, as well as security and recovery of the data. A DBMS performs the following functions:

- Structures data in a consistent way
- Provides access to the data
- Minimizes duplication
- Allows reorganization, that is, changes in data content, structure, and size
- Supports programming interfaces
- Provides security and control

A DBMS must provide:

- Persistence—The data continues to exist after the application's execution has completed
- Secondary storage management
- Concurrency
- Recovery
- Data definition/data manipulation language (DDL/DML), which may be a graphical interface

Database Models

The logical data model that underlies the database characterizes a DBMS. The common logical data models are listed here and discussed in detail in the subsections that follow.

- Relational
- Hierarchical
- Network
- Object-Oriented
- Flat File

The Relational Model

A relational DBMS (RDBMS) structures data into tables that have certain properties:

- Each row in the table is distinct from every other row.
- Each row contains only atomic data; that is, there is no repeating data or such structures as arrays.
- Each column in the relational table defines named data fields or attributes.

A collection of related tables in the relational model makes up a database. The mathematical theory of relations underlies the relational model—both the organization of data and the languages that manipulate the data. Edgar Codd, then at IBM, developed the relational model in 1973. It has been popular, in terms of commercial use, since the early 1980s.

The Hierarchical Model

The hierarchical data model organizes data in a tree structure. There is a hierarchy of parent and child data segments. This structure implies that a record can have repeating information, generally in the child data segments. For example, an organization might store information about an employee, such as name, employee number, department, and salary. The organization might also store information about an employee's children, such as name and date of birth. The employee and children data forms a hierarchy, where the employee data represents the parent segment and the children data represents the child segment. If an employee has three children, then there would be three child segments associated with one employee segment. In a hierarchical database the parent–child relationship is one to many. This restricts a child segment to having only one parent segment. Hierarchical DBMSs were popular from the late 1960s, with the introduction of IBM's Information Management System (IMS) DBMS, through the 1970s.

The Network Model

The popularity of the network data model coincided with the popularity of the hierarchical data model. Some data were more naturally modeled with more than one parent per child. So, the network model permitted the modeling of many-to-many relationships in data. In 1971, the Conference on Data Systems Languages (CODASYL) formally defined the network model. The basic data modeling construct in the network model is the set construct. A set consists of an owner record type, a set name, and a member record type. A member record type can have that role in more than one set; hence, the multiparent concept is supported. An owner record type can also be a member or owner in another set. The CODASYL network model is based on mathematical set theory.

The Object-Oriented Model

An object-oriented DBMS (OODBMS) must be both a DBMS and an object-oriented system. As a DBMS it must provide the capabilities identified previously. OODBMSs typically can model tabular data, complex data, hierarchical data, and networks of data. The following are important features of an object-oriented system:

- Complex objects—e.g., objects may be composed of other objects.
- Object identity—Each object has a unique identifier external to the data.

- Encapsulation—An object consists of data and the programs (or methods) that manipulate it.
- Types or classes—A class is a collection of similar objects.
- Inheritance—Subclasses inherit data attributes and methods from classes.
- Overriding with late binding—The method particular to a subclass can override the method of a class at runtime.
- Extensibility—e.g., a user may define new objects.
- Computational completeness—A general-purpose language, such as Ada, C, or C++, is computationally complete. The special-purpose language SQL is not. Most OODBMSs incorporate a general-purpose programming language.

Flat Files

A flat file system is usually closely associated with a storage access method. An example is IBM's indexed sequential access method (ISAM). The models discussed earlier in this section are logical data models; flat files require the user to work with the physical layout of the data on a storage device. For example, the user must know the exact location of a data item in a record. In addition, flat files do not provide all of the services of a DBMS, such as naming of data, elimination of redundancy, and concurrency control. Further, there is no independence of the data and the application program. The application program must know the physical layout of the data.

Distributed DBMSs

A distributed DBMS manages a database that is spread over more than one platform. The database can be based on any of the data models discussed earlier (except the flat file). The database can be replicated, partitioned, or a combination of both. A replicated database is one in which full or partial copies of the database exist on the different platforms. A partitioned database is one in which part of the database is on one platform and parts are on other platforms. The partitioning of a database can be vertical or horizontal. A vertical partitioning puts some fields and the associated data on one platform and some fields and the associated data on another platform. For example, consider a database with the following fields: employee ID, employee name, department, number of dependents, project assigned, salary rate, and tax rate. One vertical partitioning might place employee ID, number of dependents, salary rate, and tax rate on one platform and employee name, department, and project assigned on another platform. A horizontal partitioning might keep all the fields on all the platforms but distribute the records. For example, a database with 100,000 records might put the first 50,000 records on one platform and the second 50,000 records on a second platform.

Whether the distributed database is replicated or partitioned, a single DBMS manages the database. There is a single schema (description of the data in a database in terms of a data model, e.g., relational) for a distributed database. The distribution of the database is generally transparent to the user. The term "distributed DBMS" implies homogeneity.

Distributed Heterogeneous DBMSs

A distributed, heterogeneous database system is a set of independent databases, each with its own DBMS, presented to users as a single database and system. "Federated" is used synonymously with "distributed heterogeneous." Heterogeneity refers to differences in data models (e.g., network and relational), DBMSs from different suppliers, different hardware platforms, or other differences. The simplest kinds of federated database systems are commonly called gateways. In a gateway, one vendor (e.g., Oracle) provides single-direction access through its DBMS to another database managed by a different vendor's DBMS (e.g., IBM's DB2). The two DBMSs need not share the same data model. For example, many RDBMS vendors provide gateways to hierarchical and network DBMSs.

There are federated database systems both on the market and in research that provide more general access to diverse DBMSs. These systems generally provide a schema integration component to integrate the schemas of the diverse databases and present them to the users as a single database, a query management component to distribute queries to the different DBMSs in the federation and a transaction management component to distribute and manage the changes to the various databases in the federation.

Data Dictionary/Directory Systems

The second component providing data management services, the data dictionary/directory system (DD/DS), consists of utilities and systems necessary to catalog, document, manage, and use metadata (data about data). An example of metadata is the following definition: a six-character long alphanumeric string, for which the first character is a letter of the alphabet and each of the remaining five characters is an integer between zero and nine; the name for the string is employee ID. The DD/DS utilities make use of special files that contain the database schema. (A schema, using metadata, defines the content and structure of a database.) This schema is represented by a set of tables resulting from the compilation of data definition language (DDL) statements. The DD/DS is normally provided as part of a DBMS but is sometimes available from alternate sources. In the management of distributed data, distribution information may also be maintained in the network directory system. In this case, the interface between the DD/DS and the network directory system would be through the API of the network services component on the platform.

In current environments, data dictionaries are usually integrated with the DBMS, and directory systems are typically limited to a single platform. Network directories are used to expand the DD/DS realms. The relationship between the DD/DS and the network directory is an intricate combination of physical and logical sources of data.

Data Administration

Data administration properly addresses the data architecture, which is outside the scope of TOGAF. We discuss it briefly here because of areas of overlap. It is concerned with all of the data resources of an enterprise, and as such there are overlaps with data management, which addresses data in databases. Two specific areas of overlap are the repository and database administration, which are discussed briefly in the following subsections.

Repository

A repository is a system that manages all of the data of an enterprise, which includes data and process models and other enterprise information. Hence, the data in a repository is much more extensive than that in a DD/DS, which generally defines only the data making up a database.

Database Administration

Data administration and database administration are complementary processes. Data administration is responsible for data, data structure, and integration of data and processes. Database administration, on the other hand, includes the physical design, development, implementation, security, and maintenance of the physical databases. Database administration is responsible for managing and enforcing the enterprise's policies related to individual databases.

Data Security

The third component providing data management services is data security. This includes procedures and technology measures implemented to prevent unauthorized access, modification, use, and dissemination of data stored or processed by a computer system. Data security includes data integrity (i.e., preserving the accuracy and validity of the data), and is also concerned with protecting the system from physical harm (including preventative measures and recovery procedures).

Authorization control allows only authorized users to have access to the database at the appropriate level. Guidelines and procedures can be established for accountability, levels of control, and type of control. Authorization control for database systems differs from that in traditional file systems because, in a database system, it is not uncommon for different users to have different rights to the same data. This requirement encompasses the ability to specify subsets of data and to distinguish between groups of users. In addition, decentralized control of authorizations is of particular importance for distributed systems.

Data protection is necessary to prevent unauthorized users from understanding the content of the database. Data encryption, as one of the primary methods for protecting data, is useful for both information stored on a disk and information exchanged on a network.

Appendix 3.3: Developing a Communications Engineering View

Stakeholder and Concerns

This view should be developed for the communications engineering personnel of the system, and should focus on how the system is implemented from the perspective of the communications engineer. Communications engineers are typically concerned with location, modifiability, reusability and availability of communications and networking services. Major concerns for this view are understanding the network and communications requirements. In general these stakeholders are concerned with assuring that the appropriate communications and networking services are developed and deployed within the system in an optimum manner.

Developing this view assists in the selection of the best model of communications for the system.

Key Issues

Communications networks consist of end devices (e.g., printers), processing nodes, communication nodes (switching elements), and the linking media that connect them. The communications network provides the means by which information is exchanged. Forms of information include data, imagery, voice, and video. Because automated information systems accept and process information using digital data formats rather than analog formats, the TOGAF communications concepts and guidance will focus on digital networks and digital services. Integrated multimedia services are included. The communications engineering view describes the communications architecture with respect to geography, discusses the Open Systems Interconnection (OSI) reference model, and describes a general framework intended to permit effective system analysis and planning.

Communications Infrastructure

The communications infrastructure may contain up to three levels of transport—local, regional/metropolitan, and global. The names of the transport components are based on their respective geographic extent, but there is also a hierarchical relationship among them. The transport components correspond to a network management structure in which management and control of network resources are distributed across the different levels.

The local components relate to assets that are located relatively close together, geographically. This component contains fixed communications equipment and small units of mobile communications equipment. Local area networks (LANs), to which the majority of end devices will be connected, are included in this component. Standard interfaces will facilitate portability, flexibility, and interoperability of LANs and end devices.

Regional and metropolitan area networks (MANs) are geographically dispersed over a large area. A regional or metropolitan network could connect local components at several fixed bases or connect separate remote outposts. In most cases, regional and metropolitan networks are used to connect local networks. However, shared databases, regional processing platforms, and network management centers may connect directly or through a LAN. Standard interfaces will be provided to connect local networks and end devices.

Global or wide area networks (WANs) are located throughout the world, providing connectivity for regional and metropolitan networks in the fixed and deployed environment. In addition, mobile units, shared databases, and central processing centers can connect directly to the global network as required. Standard interfaces will be provided to connect regional and metropolitan networks and end devices.

Communications Models

The geographically divided infrastructure described in the preceding subsection forms the foundation for an overall communications framework. These geographic divisions permit the separate application of different management responsibilities, planning efforts, operational functions, and enabling technologies to be applied within each area. Hardware and software components and services fitted to the framework form the complete model. The following subsections describe the OSI reference model and a grouping of the OSI layers that facilitates discussion of interoperability issues.

The OSI Reference Model

The Open Systems Interconnection (OSI) reference model is used for data communications in TOGAF. Each of the seven layers in the model represents one or more services or protocols (a set of rules governing communications between systems), which define the functional operation of the communications between user and network elements. Each layer (with the exception of the top layer) provides services for the layer above it. This model aims at establishing open systems operation and implies standards-based implementation. It strives to permit different systems to accomplish complete interoperability and quality of operation throughout the network.

The seven layers of the OSI model are structured to facilitate independent development within each layer and to provide for changes independent of other layers. Stable international standard protocols in conformance with the OSI reference model layer definitions have been published by various standards organizations. This is not to say that the only protocols which fit into TOGAF are OSI protocols. Other protocol standards such as TCP/IP can be described using the OSI seven-layer model as a reference. Most modern communication systems are in fact based on the TCP/IP suite of protocols.

Support and business-area applications, as defined in TOGAF, are above the OSI Reference Model protocol stack and use its services via the applications layer.

Communications Framework

A communications system based on the OSI reference model includes services in all the relevant layers, the support and business-area application software, which sits above the application layer of the OSI model, and the physical equipment carrying the data. These elements may be grouped into architectural levels that represent major functional capabilities, such as switching and routing, data transfer, and the performance of applications.

These architectural levels are:

The Transmission Level (below the physical layer of the OSI model) provides all of the physical and electronic capabilities, which establish a transmission path between functional system elements (wires, leased circuits, interconnects, etc.).

■ The Network Switching Level (OSI layers 1 through 3) establishes connectivity through the network elements to support the routing and control of traffic (switches, controllers, network software, etc.).

■ The Data Exchange Level (OSI layers 4 through 7) accomplishes the transfer of information after the network has been established (end-to-end, user-to-user transfer) involving more capable processing elements (hosts, workstations, servers, etc.).

■ In the TRM, OSI Application Layer Services are considered to be part of the application platform entity, because they offer standardized interfaces to the application programming entity.

■ The Applications Program Level (above the OSI) includes the support and business-area applications (non-management application programs).

The communications framework is defined to consist of the three geographic components of the communications infrastructure (local, regional, and global) and the four architectural levels (transmission, network switching, data exchange, and application program), and is depicted

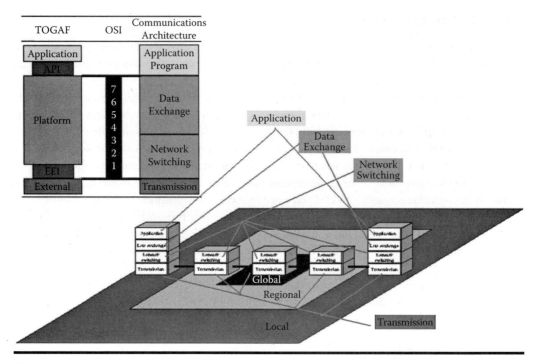

Figure A3.3.1 Communications framework.

in Figure A3.3.1. Communications services are performed at one or more of these architectural levels within the geographic components. Figure A3.3.1 shows computing elements (operating at the applications program level) with supporting data exchange elements, linked with each other through various switching elements (operating at the network switching level), each located within its respective geographic component. Figure A3.3.1 also identifies the relationship of The Open Group Architectural Framework to the communication architecture. The figure also depicts the External Environment Interface (EEI); as the term implies, this is the interface that supports information transfer between the Application Platform and the External Environment.

Allocation of Services to Components

The communications infrastructure consists of the local, regional, and global transport components. The services allocated to these components are identical to the services of the application program, data exchange, network switching, or transmission architectural levels that apply to a component. Data exchange and network switching level services are identical to the services of the corresponding OSI reference model layers. Typically, only network switching and transmission services are allocated to the regional and global components, which consist of communications nodes and transmission media. All services may be performed in the local component, which includes end devices, processing nodes, communications nodes, and linking media. Transmission, switching, transport, and applications are all performed in this component.

As noted earlier, the modeling makes use of the OSI reference model. However, nearly all contemporary commercial systems (and military systems, for that matter) use the TCP/IP protocol suite. Fortunately, there is a long-established mapping between the OSI layers and the protocols, such as TCP/IP, developed by the Internet Engineering Task Force (IETF).

Chapter 4

The Zachman Architectural Framework

This chapter discusses the Zachman Framework. Currently, it is the most often used framework by organizations all over the world. The framework can be used for developing or documenting an enterprisewide information systems architecture; it provides a view of the subjects and models that can be used to develop a complete architecture. The topic was briefly introduced in Chapter 2 and is expanded herewith. This chapter is based on materials from Zachman Institute for Architecture Advancement (ZIFA*).

4.1 Background

The Zachman Framework establishes a common vocabulary and set of perspectives for defining and describing complex enterprise systems. Since its first publication in 1987, the Zachman Framework has evolved and has become the model around which major organizations worldwide view and communicate their enterprise IT infrastructure. John Zachman based his framework on practices in traditional architecture and engineering. This resulted in an approach where a two-dimensional logical template is created to synthesize the framework. The vertical axis provides multiple perspectives of the overall architecture and the horizontal axis provides a classification of the various artifacts of the architecture.

As we discussed earlier in this text, the enterprise architecture provides the blueprint for the organization's information environment. The purpose of the framework is to provide a basic structure that supports the organization, access, integration, interpretation, development, management, and a (possibly changing) set of architectural representations of the organization's information systems. Such objects or descriptions of architectural representations are usually referred to as *artifacts*. The framework, then, can contain global plans as well as technical details, lists and charts, as well as natural language statements. Any appropriate approach, standard, role, method,

---

* The mission of ZIFA is to promote the exchange of knowledge and experience in the use, implementation, and advancement of the Zachman Framework for Enterprise Architecture.

technique, or tool may be placed in it. In fact, the framework can be viewed as a tool to organize any form of metadata for the enterprise. The framework has a set of rules that govern an ordered set of relationships that are balanced and orthogonal. By designing a system according to these rules, the architect can be assured of a design that is clean, easy to understand, balanced, and complete.

One of the drawbacks of the model is that there is not as much public, open documentation on it as there is on TOGAF.

4.2 Framework

The Zachman Framework describes a holistic model of an enterprise's information infrastructure from six perspectives: planner, owner, designer, builder, subcontractor, and the working system. There is no guidance on sequence, process, or implementation of the framework. The focus is on ensuring that all aspects of an enterprise are well organized and exhibit clear relationships that will ensure a complete system regardless of the order in which they are established [SYS200501,ZIF200501].

4.2.1 Principles

The major principles that guide the application of the Zachman Framework include the following [SYS200501,ZIF200501]:

1. A complete system can be modeled by depicting answers to the following questions: why, who, what, how, where, and when.
2. The six perspectives capture all the critical models required for system development.
3. The constraints for each perspective are additive; those of a lower row are added to those of the rows above to provide a growing number of restrictions.
4. The columns represent different abstractions in an effort to reduce the complexity of any single model that is built.
5. The columns have no order.
6. The model in each column must be unique.
7. Each row represents a unique perspective.
8. Each cell is unique.
9. The inherent logic is recursive.

4.2.2 Framework Structure

The Zachman Framework intends to provide an understanding of any particular aspect of a system at any point in its development. The tool can be useful in making decisions about changes or extensions. The framework contains six rows and six columns yielding 36 cells or aspects (see Figure 4.1).

The rows are as follows:

■ **Scope:** Corresponds to an executive summary for a planner who wants an estimate of the size, cost, and functionality of the system.
■ **Business model:** Shows all the business entities and processes, and how they interact.

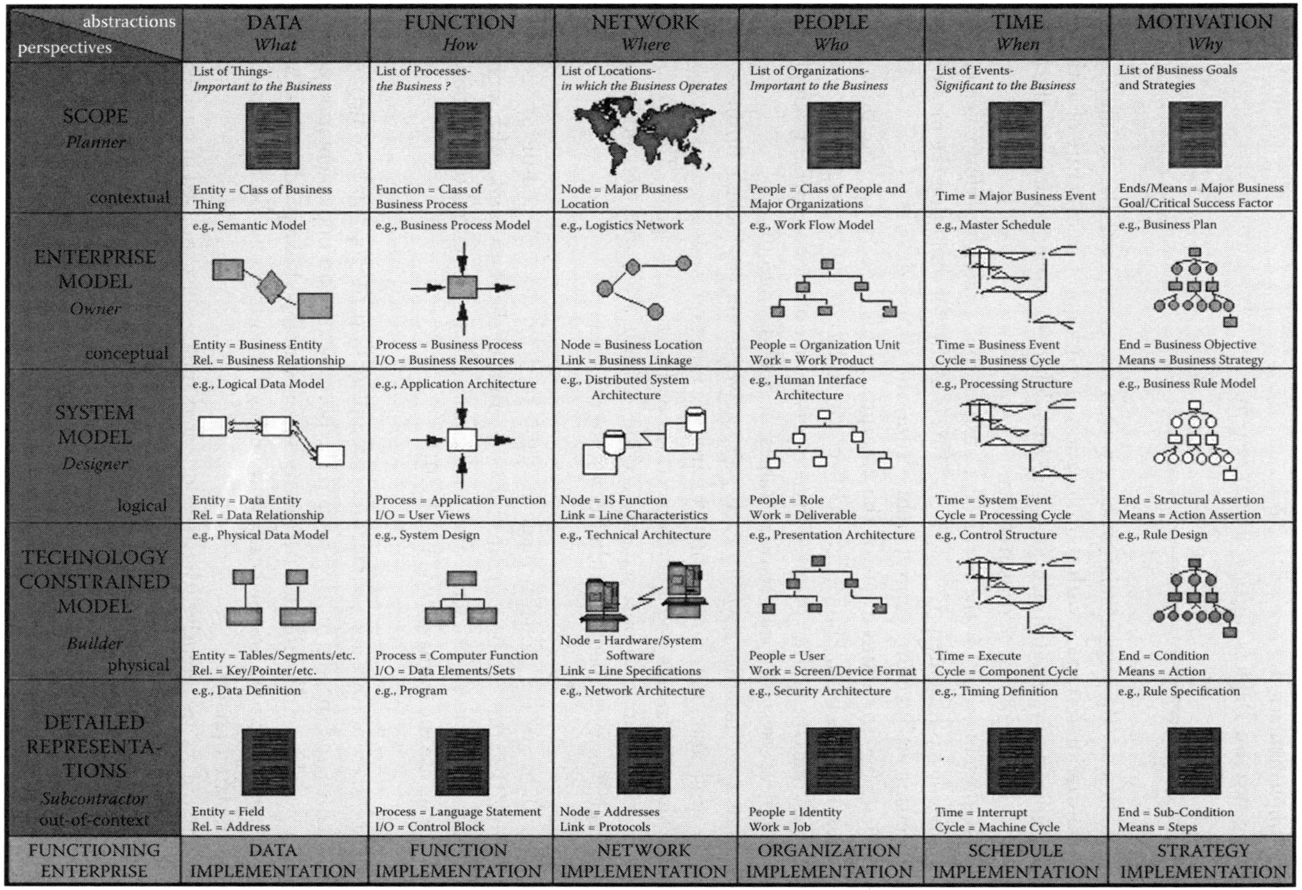

abstractions / perspectives	DATA *What*	FUNCTION *How*	NETWORK *Where*	PEOPLE *Who*	TIME *When*	MOTIVATION *Why*
SCOPE *Planner* — contextual	List of Things Important to the Business Entity = Class of Business Thing	List of Processes the Business ? Function = Class of Business Process	List of Locations- in which the Business Operates Node = Major Business Location	List of Organizations- Important to the Business People = Class of People and Major Organizations	List of Events- Significant to the Business Time = Major Business Event	List of Business Goals and Strategies Ends/Means = Major Business Goal/Critical Success Factor
ENTERPRISE MODEL *Owner* — conceptual	e.g., Semantic Model Entity = Business Entity Rel. = Business Relationship	e.g., Business Process Model Process = Business Process I/O = Business Resources	e.g., Logistics Network Node = Business Location Link = Business Linkage	e.g., Work Flow Model People = Organization Unit Work = Work Product	e.g., Master Schedule Time = Business Event Cycle = Business Cycle	e.g., Business Plan End = Business Objective Means = Business Strategy
SYSTEM MODEL *Designer* — logical	e.g., Logical Data Model Entity = Data Entity Rel. = Data Relationship	e.g., Application Architecture Process = Application Function I/O = User Views	e.g., Distributed System Architecture Node = IS Function Link = Line Characteristics	e.g., Human Interface Architecture People = Role Work = Deliverable	e.g., Processing Structure Time = System Event Cycle = Processing Cycle	e.g., Business Rule Model End = Structural Assertion Means = Action Assertion
TECHNOLOGY CONSTRAINED MODEL *Builder* — physical	e.g., Physical Data Model Entity = Tables/Segments/etc. Rel. = Key/Pointer/etc.	e.g., System Design Process = Computer Function I/O = Data Elements/Sets	e.g., Technical Architecture Node = Hardware/System Software Link = Line Specifications	e.g., Presentation Architecture People = User Work = Screen/Device Format	e.g., Control Structure Time = Execute Cycle = Component Cycle	e.g., Rule Design End = Condition Means = Action
DETAILED REPRESENTA-TIONS *Subcontractor* — out-of-context	e.g., Data Definition Entity = Field Rel. = Address	e.g., Program Process = Language Statement I/O = Control Block	e.g., Network Architecture Node = Addresses Link = Protocols	e.g., Security Architecture People = Identity Work = Job	e.g., Timing Definition Time = Interrupt Cycle = Machine Cycle	e.g., Rule Specification End = Sub-Condition Means = Steps
FUNCTIONING ENTERPRISE	DATA IMPLEMENTATION	FUNCTION IMPLEMENTATION	NETWORK IMPLEMENTATION	ORGANIZATION IMPLEMENTATION	SCHEDULE IMPLEMENTATION	STRATEGY IMPLEMENTATION

John A. Zachman, Zachman International

Figure 4.1 The Zachman Framework.

- **System model:** Used by a systems analyst who must determine the data elements and software functions that represent the business model.
- **Technology model:** Considers the constraints of tools, technology, and materials.
- **Components:** Represent individual, independent modules that can be allocated to contractors for implementation.
- **Working system:** Depicts the operational system.

The columns are as follows:

- **Who:** Represents the people relationships within the enterprise. The design of the enterprise organization has to do with the allocation of work and the structure of authority and responsibility. The vertical dimension represents delegation of authority, and the horizontal represents the assignment of responsibility.
- **When:** Represents time, or the event relationships that establish performance criteria and quantitative levels for enterprise resources. This is useful for designing the master schedule, the processing architecture, control architecture, and timing devices.
- **Why:** Describes the motivations of the enterprise. This reveals the enterprise goals and objectives, business plan, knowledge architecture, and knowledge design.
- **What:** Describes the entities involved in each perspective of the enterprise. Examples include business objects, system data, relational tables, or field definitions.
- **How:** Shows the functions within each perspective. Examples include business processes, software application function, computer hardware function, and language control loop.
- **Where:** Shows locations and interconnections within the enterprise. This includes major business geographic locations, separate sections within a logistics network, allocation of system nodes, or even memory addresses within the system.

Most of the guidance of the model is made available to firms through consulting services contracted through ZIFA; this can be somewhat of a downside of the framework. Although no architectural development process is described in publications, there are several observations that can help organizations use the framework [SYS200501].

- The perspectives or rows are abstract and incomplete near the top but become progressively more detailed and specific moving toward the bottom until an implementation emerges on the last row. This implies that the perspectives can be mapped to a product development life cycle where the top rows are used early on whereas the bottom rows become more important during the latter phases.
- The top two rows are intensively business oriented and can be expressed in business-oriented vocabularies, whereas the bottom four rows are in the technical domain.
- Although Zachman's models are explicitly procedural, there is no reason why the representation applied to each square in the framework could not be object oriented.
- Business concepts from the top row must be embedded into business objects and components in the bottom rows. The business concepts can be refined over time, but their relationships should not be changed. Generic software objects and components, along with those from a specific domain repository, can be selected to populate the foundation of the system, but specific application-oriented objects must be designed and integrated to implement the system under development.

■ Because the order of the columns has no prescribed meaning, they could be rearranged to more closely follow the order of object-oriented design. The requirements are captured in the *why* column, and the actors are associated with the *who* column. It is generally recommended that service identification precede objects, so the *how* and *what* columns can follow. Regardless of the chosen order, note that the columns are related as in the software: the data represent inputs and outputs of the services. The *when* column can precede the *where* column if that precedence is more meaningful to a particular software development process; the point being made is that the order of the columns can be used to facilitate discussion during object-oriented development.

Frameworks can be used recursively to manage the complexity of specifying an enterprise architecture. In this case, the top framework instance represents enterprise modeling of the entire business, the middle framework instance represents enterprise modeling of an independent division in another instance, and the bottom framework instance represents enterprise modeling of independent workstations. This is only an example of how a complex problem can be partitioned into simpler pieces, whereas each piece can be modeled in its own right with the Zachman Framework. One framework can be used to develop the technical architecture at a level that will apply to all divisions in the business. Another framework can be used to develop departmental networks, which must conform to all constraints specified at the enterprise level. Yet another framework can be used to develop and manage the configuration of an independent workstation, which conforms to all constraints developed at the division or departmental level. See Figure 4.2.

4.3 Architecture Implementation

There are two critical, distinctly different challenges facing the present-day enterprises. These challenges affect the enterprise's ability to operate effectively and dynamically respond to the ever-increasing rates of change in the competitive marketplace and regulatory environment. The enterprise must:

1. Begin making descriptive representations (models) of the enterprise explicit. This entails populating various cells of the Zachman Framework with instances of models, for example, defining specific models for the enterprise, with the intent of producing system implementations that more accurately reflect the intent of the enterprise, and of retaining the models to serve as a baseline for managing enterprise change.
2. Formalize and enhance the enterprise architecture process. Initially, this would entail defining for the enterprise, for example, the generic components (contents) of each of the cells of the framework, that is, defining what is important to capture in each cell when building instances of models for that enterprise. This would enable formalizing the management system (plans and controls) for building the enterprise models, for evaluating and deploying development methodologies and tools, for selecting or defining databases (repositories) for storing the enterprise models, for defining the roles, responsibilities and skills required within the architecture process, etc.

These two challenges go hand in hand. The enterprise must produce the models to deliver systems implementations in the short term and at the same time, for the long term, instantiate the architecture process to ensure ongoing coherence of system implementations and to build an enterprise environment conducive to accommodating high rates of change.

The contents of some of the cells are well understood in the industry today. In fact, it is easy to buy commercial off-the-shelf (COTS) application development tools and methodologies that support building the models shaded in Figure 4.1.

For example, Pinnacle Business Group (and its predecessor companies) invested a number of years in developing a robust methodology including tool support for doing the architecture planning (row 1), business process engineering (row 2) and application development (rows 3, 4, and 5) as shown in Figure 4.3.

Although many enterprises have been building information systems for a number of years, in general, few of them have actually understood enterprise models; that is, they have not understood the contents of the framework cells (and therefore have not understood their methodologies and tools), and neither have they had a disciplined architectural process in place. Therefore, there has been little cohesion in the resulting system implementations, regardless of how valid or robust the methodologies and tools are, and the systems have provided little lasting value as the enterprises have changed over time. Two programs can be undertaken to get the definition and establishment of the architecture work under way at a firm:

Architecture program 1—enterprise architecture process instantiation: This program would concentrate on defining appropriate contents of all the framework cells for the enterprise for the purpose of developing an enterprise architecture strategy which would include identifying the cells (models) in which to invest resources, skill/method/tool requirements, repository strategy, approach for maintaining continuity (integration) while building incrementally, sources of funding, roles and responsibilities, etc.

Architecture program 2—enterprise architecture quick start: This program focuses on developing the row 1 cells for the enterprise, evaluating the current systems environment and determining the enterprise priorities, to establish a context and to develop an implementation plan to deliver quick results. The plan could be expected to lead to validating any existing enterprise models; developing systems programs; doing appropriate, additional business process engineering; and subsequently building systems implementations consistent with the enterprise priorities.

A FRAMEWORK™ FOR ENTERPRISE ARCHITECTURE

	DATA — What	FUNCTION — How	NETWORK — Where	PEOPLE — Who	TIME — When	MOTIVATION — Why	
SCOPE (CONTEXTUAL) — Planner	List of Things Important to the Business; ENTITY = Class of Business Thing	List of Processes the Business Performs; Process = Class of Business Process	List of Locations in which the Business Operates; Node = Major Business Location	List of Organizations Important to the Business; People = Major Organization Unit	List of Events/Cycles Significant to the Business; Time = Major Business Event/Cycle	List of Business Goals/Strategies; Ends/Means = Major Business Goal/Strategy	**SCOPE (CONTEXTUAL)** / Planner
BUSINESS MODEL (CONCEPTUAL) — Owner	e.g., Semantic Model; Ent = Business Entity, Reln = Business Relationship	e.g., Business Process Model; Proc. = Business Process, I/O = Business Resources	e.g., Business Logistics System; Node = Business Location, Link = Business Linkage	e.g., Work Flow Model; People = Organization Unit, Work = Work Product	e.g., Master Schedule; Time = Business Event, Cycle = Business Cycle	e.g., Business Plan; End = Business Objective, Means = Business Strategy	**BUSINESS MODEL (CONCEPTUAL)** / Owner
SYSTEM MODEL (LOGICAL) — Designer	e.g., Logical Data Model; Ent = Data Entity, Reln = Data Relationship	e.g., Application Architecture; Proc. = Application Function, I/O = User Views	e.g., Distributed System Architecture; Node = I/S Function (Processor, Storage, etc), Link = Line Characteristics	e.g., Human Interface Architecture; People = Role, Work = Deliverable	e.g., Processing Structure; Time = System Event, Cycle = Processing Cycle	e.g., Business Rule Model; End = Structural Assertion, Means = Action Assertion	**SYSTEM MODEL (LOGICAL)** / Designer
TECHNOLOGY MODEL (PHYSICAL) — Builder	e.g., Physical Data Model; Ent = Segment/Table/etc., Reln = Pointer/Key/etc.	e.g., System Design; Proc. = Computer Function, I/O = Data Elements/Sets	e.g., Technology Architecture; Node = Hardware/Systems Software, Link = Line Specifications	e.g., Presentation Architecture; People = User, Work = Screen Format	e.g., Control Structure; Time = Execute, Cycle = Component Cycle	e.g., Rule Design; End = Condition, Means = Action	**TECHNOLOGY MODEL (PHYSICAL)** / Builder
DETAILED REPRESENTATIONS (OUT-OF-CONTEXT) — Sub-Contractor	e.g., Data Definition; Ent = Field, Reln = Address	e.g., Program; Proc. = Language Statement, I/O = Control Block	e.g., Network Architecture; Node = Address, Link = Protocol	e.g., Security Architecture; People = Identity, Work = Job	e.g., Timing Definition; Time = Interrupt, Cycle = Machine Cycle	e.g., Rule Specification; End = Sub-condition, Means = Step	**DETAILED REPRESENTATIONS (OUT-OF-CONTEXT)** / Sub-Contractor
FUNCTIONING ENTERPRISE	e.g. DATA	e.g. FUNCTION	e.g. NETWORK	e.g. ORGANIZATION	e.g. SCHEDULE	e.g. STRATEGY	**FUNCTIONING ENTERPRISE**

Figure 4.2   State of the art—methods and tools. © John A. Zachman, Zachman International

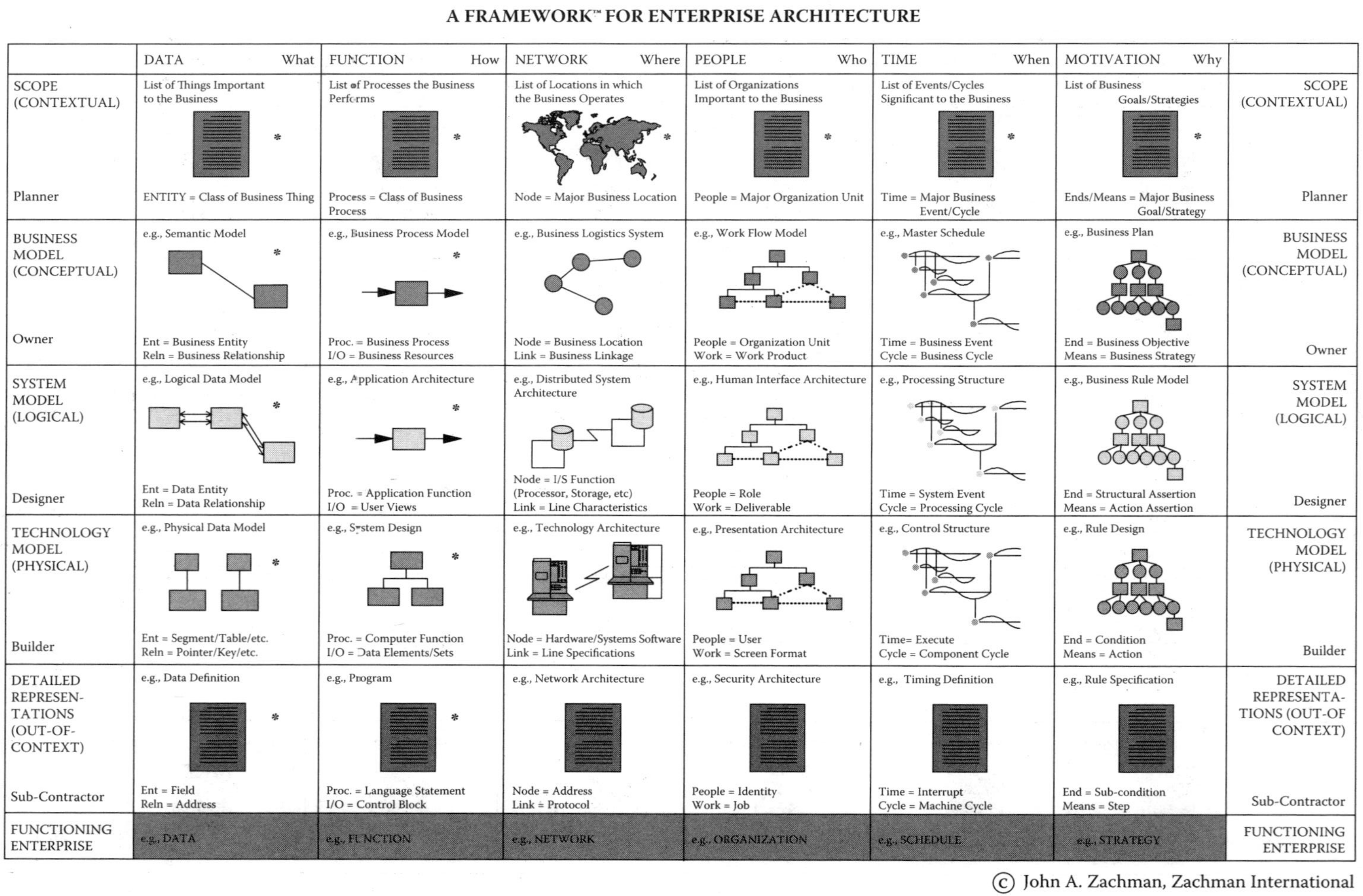

A FRAMEWORK™ FOR ENTERPRISE ARCHITECTURE

	DATA (What)	FUNCTION (How)	NETWORK (Where)	PEOPLE (Who)	TIME (When)	MOTIVATION (Why)	
SCOPE (CONTEXTUAL) / Planner	List of Things Important to the Business — ENTITY = Class of Business Thing	List of Processes the Business Performs — Process = Class of Business Process	List of Locations in which the Business Operates — Node = Major Business Location	List of Organizations Important to the Business — People = Major Organization Unit	List of Events/Cycles Significant to the Business — Time = Major Business Event/Cycle	List of Business Goals/Strategies — Ends/Means = Major Business Goal/Strategy	SCOPE (CONTEXTUAL) / Planner
BUSINESS MODEL (CONCEPTUAL) / Owner	e.g., Semantic Model — Ent = Business Entity, Reln = Business Relationship	e.g., Business Process Model — Proc. = Business Process, I/O = Business Resources	e.g., Business Logistics System — Node = Business Location, Link = Business Linkage	e.g., Work Flow Model — People = Organization Unit, Work = Work Product	e.g., Master Schedule — Time = Business Event, Cycle = Business Cycle	e.g., Business Plan — End = Business Objective, Means = Business Strategy	BUSINESS MODEL (CONCEPTUAL) / Owner
SYSTEM MODEL (LOGICAL) / Designer	e.g., Logical Data Model — Ent = Data Entity, Reln = Data Relationship	e.g., Application Architecture — Proc. = Application Function, I/O = User Views	e.g., Distributed System Architecture — Node = I/S Function (Processor, Storage, etc), Link = Line Characteristics	e.g., Human Interface Architecture — People = Role, Work = Deliverable	e.g., Processing Structure — Time = System Event, Cycle = Processing Cycle	e.g., Business Rule Model — End = Structural Assertion, Means = Action Assertion	SYSTEM MODEL (LOGICAL) / Designer
TECHNOLOGY MODEL (PHYSICAL) / Builder	e.g., Physical Data Model — Ent = Segment/Table/etc., Reln = Pointer/Key/etc.	e.g., System Design — Proc. = Computer Function, I/O = Data Elements/Sets	e.g., Technology Architecture — Node = Hardware/Systems Software, Link = Line Specifications	e.g., Presentation Architecture — People = User, Work = Screen Format	e.g., Control Structure — Time = Execute, Cycle = Component Cycle	e.g., Rule Design — End = Condition, Means = Action	TECHNOLOGY MODEL (PHYSICAL) / Builder
DETAILED REPRESENTATIONS (OUT-OF-CONTEXT) / Sub-Contractor	e.g., Data Definition — Ent = Field, Reln = Address	e.g., Program — Proc. = Language Statement, I/O = Control Block	e.g., Network Architecture — Node = Address, Link = Protocol	e.g., Security Architecture — People = Identity, Work = Job	e.g., Timing Definition — Time = Interrupt, Cycle = Machine Cycle	e.g., Rule Specification — End = Sub-condition, Means = Step	DETAILED REPRESENTATIONS (OUT-OF-CONTEXT) / Sub-Contractor
FUNCTIONING ENTERPRISE	e.g., DATA	e.g., FUNCTION	e.g., NETWORK	e.g., ORGANIZATION	e.g., SCHEDULE	e.g., STRATEGY	FUNCTIONING ENTERPRISE

© John A. Zachman, Zachman International

Figure 4.3 Robust top-down methodology and tool support. Cells with a bold asterisk (*) represent the top-down methodology.

Chapter 5

Official Enterprise Architecture Standards

In the previous three chapters we looked at some of the more common enterprise architecture frameworks. In this chapter we look at some of the underlying standards that have originated from the traditional standards-making bodies, specifically from standards development organizations (SDOs). Standards-based industry consensus on the approach to enterprise inter- and intradomain (or organization) integration is a prerequisite for real commercial acceptance and application of the enterprise architecture technology on a broad scale. Fortunately, there are several ongoing research activities in this arena seeking to establish common terminology and approach.

5.1 Introduction

Institutions for the development of de jure standards (e.g., see Table 5.1) have developed a number of "foundation standards" related to the definition of basic architectural concepts. Although frameworks are a step in the right direction, formal standardization is needed to provide for interoperability. This is critical for very large organizations and government agencies that may have dozens of dispersed divisions or agencies. The international standards organizations address the subject at different levels of abstraction, providing architectures, frameworks, and explicit standards for different application areas [KOS200301]. This work has been going on for about a decade.

Standards that have emerged span the following categories: modeling (specifically Business Process Modeling) and engineering (frameworks and languages), systems and subsystems (shop floor, control systems, and manufacturing data), IT services, and infrastructures (model execution and integration, open distributed processing, and others) [CHE200401]. Table 5.2 provides a short description of some of the key relevant standards [KOS200301]. Definitional problems remain to be resolved as they relate to inconsistency of contents between standards, inconsistency of terminology used in the different standards, and dearth of commercial applicability due to high level of abstraction of the standards.

Table 5.1   Key Standards-Making Organizations That Have Developed Enterprise Architecture Standards

American National Standards Institute (ANSI)	An association of manufacturers, users, and other stakeholders, which administers U.S. voluntary standards. ANSI is the U.S. representative of the International Organization for Standardization (ISO). ANSI has served in the capacity of administrator and coordinator of private sector voluntary standardization system in the United States for more than 80 years.
European Committee for Standardization (CEN)	CEN's mission is to promote voluntary technical harmonization in Europe in conjunction with worldwide bodies and its partners in Europe. Harmonization diminishes trade barriers, promotes safety, allows interoperability of products, systems and services, and promotes common technical understanding. CEN promotes voluntary technical harmonization in Europe in conjunction with worldwide bodies and its partners in Europe and the conformity assessment of products and their certification.
Institute of Electrical and Electronics Engineers (IEEE)	A U.S. organization for electrical engineering, the leading authority in technical areas ranging from telecommunications to aerospace and consumer electronics. The IEEE promotes standards related to electrical and information technologies. The 802 Committee is the developer of all local area network (LAN) standards to date, including the Ethernet family of specifications. They also handle standards in many other technical arenas.
International Organization for Standardization (ISO)	International organization for the development of de jure standards. An international, nonprofit standards organization whose membership includes standards organizations from participating nations. The American National Standards Institute (ANSI) is the U.S. representative. ISO is a voluntary, nontreaty, non-government organization, established in 1947, with voting members that are designated standards bodies of participating nations and nonvoting observer organizations. Legally, ISO is a Swiss, nonprofit, private organization. ISO and the IEC (the International Electrotechnical Commission) form the specialized system for worldwide standardization. National bodies that are members of ISO or IEC participate in developing international standards through ISO and IEC technical committees that deal with particular fields of activity. Other international governmental and non-governmental organizations, in liaison with ISO and IEC, also take part. The ISO standards development process has four levels of increasing maturity: Working Draft (WD), Committee Draft (CD), Draft International Standard (DIS), and International Standard (IS). In information technology, ISO and IEC have a joint technical committee, ISO/IEC JTC 1. DISs adopted by JTC 1 are circulated to national bodies for voting, and publication as an IS requires approval by at least three quarters of the national bodies casting a vote [SHI200001].
National Institute of Standards and Technology (NIST)	A U.S. agency (under Department of Commerce) that promotes U.S. economic growth by working with industry to develop and apply technology, measurements, and standards. Among many other roles, NIST has the responsibility for developing information security (INFOSEC) standards and guidelines for all federal computer systems, except national security systems.

Table 5.2   Standards-Related Efforts in Enterprise Engineering and Integration Item Description

Business Process Management Initiative (BPMI.org)	Defines the Business Process Modeling Language (BPML) and the Business Process Query Language (BPQL) that will enable the standards-based management of E-business processes with forthcoming Business Process Management Systems (BPMS).
CEN ENV 13550—Enterprise Model Execution and Integration Services	Identifies the requirements for a basic set of functionalities needed in enterprise engineering for creating and using enterprise models.
CEN-ISO DIS 19439—Framework for Enterprise Modeling	Describes the modeling framework that fulfils the requirements stated in ISO IS 15704 by identifying a three-dimensional structure with seven life cycle phases, three levels of genericity, and a minimum set of four model views.
CEN-ISO WD 19440—Constructs for Enterprise Modeling	Defines language constructs for enterprise modeling, supporting the enterprise model phases, view, and genericity dimensions defined in EN/ISO DIS 19439.
IEC/ISO 62264—Enterprise Control Systems Integration	A multipart set of standards that defines the interfaces between enterprise activities and control activities.
ISO 14258—Concepts and rules for enterprise models	Defines elements for enterprise modeling, concepts for life-cycle phases and guidelines and constraints for relating the real world to enterprise models through views.
ISO 15531—Manufacturing management data exchange: Resources usage management	A multipart set of standards that provides for the computer-interpretable representation and exchange of industrial manufacturing management data.
ISO 15704—Requirements for enterprise-reference architectures and methodologies	Places the concepts used in methodologies and reference architectures such as ARIS, CIMOSA, GRAI/GIM, IEM, PERA, and EN ISO DIS 19439 within an encompassing conceptual framework.
ISO 15745—Open systems application integration frameworks	A multipart set of standards that defines an application integration framework to enable a common environment for integrating applications and sharing life-cycle information in a given application domain. The standard consists of four parts: Part 1 (generic reference description), Part 2 (reference description for ISO 11898–based control systems), Part 3 (reference description for IEC 61158–based control systems), and Part 4 (reference description for Ethernet-based control systems.1
	The standard defines an Application Integration Framework (AIF)—a set of elements and rules for describing application interoperability profiles, which will enable a common environment for integrating applications and sharing life-cycle information in a given application domain [KOS200501].

(continued)

Table 5.2   Standards-Related Efforts in Enterprise Engineering and Integration Item Description (continued)

ISO 16100—Manufacturing software capability profiling	A multipart set of standards that specifies a manufacturing information model that characterizes software-interfacing requirements. • DIS Part 1—Framework—specifies a framework for interoperability of a set of software products used in the manufacturing domain and to facilitate its integration into manufacturing applications. • DIS Part 2—Methodology—specifies a methodology for constructing profiles of manufacturing software capabilities. • WD Part 3 (Interfaces—Protocols and Templates) specifies interoperability models of software unit object interfaces and related protocol options, as well as mappings from the interoperability models to models of capability classes, templates, and profiles. • Proposal Part 4—Conformance test methods, criteria, and reports. ISO 16100 specifies a framework for the interoperability of a set of software products used in the manufacturing domain and to facilitate integration into manufacturing applications. The framework addresses models for information exchange, software objects, interfaces, services, protocols, capability profiles, and conformance test methods. The standard specifies a methodology for constructing profiles of manufacturing software capabilities and requirements for interface services and protocols used to access and edit capability profiles and associated templates used in the capability profiling method. In addition, conformance test method and criteria for the capability profiling of a manufacturing software unit are specified [KOS200501].
ISO 18629—Process specification language	Part of a multipart set of standards that describes what elements interoperable systems should encompass.
ISO/IEC 15288—Life-cycle management	Identifies a framework for a system life cycle from the conception of ideas through to the retirement of a system.
ISO/IEC 15414—ODP Reference Model—Enterprise Language	A multipart set of standards that defines the reference model for Open Distributed Processing (ODP) comprising five viewpoints: enterprise, information, computation, engineering, and technology.
OMG—UML Profile for Business Process Definition	This Request For Proposals solicits submissions that specify a UML™ profile for business process definitions.

5.2 ISO 15704

One of the more inclusive standards to date is ISO 15704: "Requirements for enterprise-reference architectures and methodologies." Figure 5.1 identifies three categories of standards, which relate to the requirements for enterprise reference architectures specified in ISO 15704 using the structure

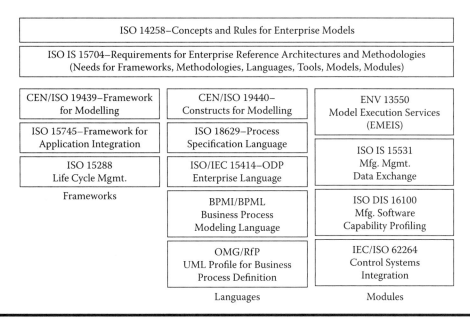

Figure 5.1 Standards related to enterprise engineering and integration.

defined in GERAM (Generalized Reference Architecture and Methodologies) developed by the IFAC/IFIP Task Force [KOS200301].

- **Framework:** The three standards structure elements for different tasks, although all are aimed at improving business process interoperability.
- **Languages:** The three standards and two consortia efforts provide language for modeling of various points of view. High-level enterprise description aimed on information and communication technology (ICT) aspects (ISO-IEC 15414), E-business (BPMI/BPML), user-oriented business process description (CEN/ISO 19440, OMG/RFP) and formal specifications (ISO 18629).
- **Modules:** The four standards are relevant for the subject of interoperability and integration, but there is even less coherence between these, than between those in the other two columns.

One of the key standards in the family encompassed by Figure 5.1 is preEN/ISO 19439: 2003: "Enterprise Integration—Framework for Enterprise Modeling." This framework defines the generic concepts that are required to enable the creation of enterprise models for industrial businesses (industrial enterprises). This modeling framework fulfils the requirements stated in ISO IS 15704, which have been derived from the framework of the Generalised Enterprise Reference Architecture (GERAM) proposed by the IFAC/IFIP Task Force. The standard defines a three-dimensional structure with seven life-cycle phases, three levels of genericity, and a minimum set of four model views [CIM200501]:

- **Model phase:** Enterprise models have a life cycle that is related to the life cycle of the entity being modeled. The enterprise model phases are Domain Identification, Concept Definition,

Requirements Definition, Design Specification, Implementation Description, Domain Operation, and Decommission Definition.

- **Model view:** The enterprise model view dimension enables the enterprise modeler and enterprise model user to filter their observations of the real world by particular views. The predefined views are Function View, Information View, Resource View, and Organization View/Decision View.
- **Genericity:** The genericity dimension provides for the progression from general concepts to particular models. The standard defines three levels of genericity: Generic Level, Partial Level, and Particular Level.

Another of the key standards in the family encompassed by Figure 5.1 is preEN/ISO 19440: "Enterprise Integration—Constructs for Enterprise Modelling," ISO TC 184/SC5/WG1-CEN TC 310/WG1, 2003. This standard defines constructs for enterprise modeling, supporting the three-dimensional structure enterprise model phases, views, and genericity defined in EN/IS19439. It contains definitions and descriptions of the core constructs necessary for computer-supported modeling of enterprises, possibly as a precursor to computer integration or mediated human system. The generic constructs of the modeling language are provided in textual description and with templates, containing header, attributes, and relationships. An overview of the modeling language constructs and their relationships is given in a UML meta model graphical representation. The list of core constructs comprises [CIM200501] Domain, Business Process, Enterprise Activity, Event, Enterprise Object, Object View, Product, Order, Resource, Capability, Functional Entity, Organizational Unit, and Organizational Cell. Furthermore, the core constructs have been identified for the different model phases.

5.3 Other ISO Standards

Next we briefly describe other ISO standards.

5.3.1 ISA-95.00.01-2000

ISA-95.00.01-2000, entitled "Enterprise-Control System Integration" (ISO/IEC JWG15) is a multipart set of proposed standards which has been developed with support of a large industry consortium. Part 1, Models and Terminology (ISA-95.00.01-2000), of this standard defines the interfaces between enterprise activities and control activities. Part 2, Object Model Attributes (ISA-95.00.02-2000), and Part 3, Infrastructures, are at a lower level of maturity; they are addressing numerous object models of the constructs, their attributes and the concepts identified in Part 1 [CIM200501]. Part 1 of the standard provides standard models and terminology for defining the interfaces between an enterprise's business systems and its manufacturing control systems, derived from the Purdue reference model. The models and terminology defined in this standard (1) emphasize good integration practices of control systems with enterprise systems during the entire life cycle of the systems, (2) can be used to improve existing integration capabilities of manufacturing control systems with enterprise systems, and (3) can be applied regardless of the degree of automation. The interfaces considered are the interfaces between levels 4 (business planning and logistics) and 3 (manufacturing operations and control) of the hierarchical model defined by this standard. The goal is to reduce the risk, cost, and errors associated with implementing these interfaces. The standard may be used to reduce the effort associated with implementing new product offerings. The goal is to have enterprise systems and control systems that interoperate and easily integrate. Besides terms and definitions, the standard addresses in its main chapters the concepts, enterprise-control system integration, hierarchy models, functional data flow model, and object models.

5.3.2 ENV 13350

ENV 13350, "Advanced Manufacturing Technology–Systems Architecture–Enterprise Model Execution and Integration Services" (CEN/TC310, 1999), describes the functionalities required for model development and execution, building on a set of model-related shared services, and in turn, base IT services that are to be provided by other standards. It identifies "those standards, services, protocols and interfaces which are necessary for the computer-based development and execution of enterprise models and model components" [CIM200501].

5.3.3 IS 15704

IS 15704, "Requirements for Enterprise Reference Architecture and Methodologies" (ISO TC 184/SC5/WG1, 1999), attempts to place the concepts used in methodologies and reference architectures such as ARIS, CIMOSA, GRAI/GIM, IEM, PERA, and ENV 40003 within an encompassing conceptual framework that allows the coverage and completeness of any such approach to be assessed. It draws heavily on the work of the IFAC/IFIP Task Force on Enterprise Integration and previous work from Purdue University. The conceptual framework is textual and relatively informal. It does not provide a basis for actual implementations and requires real understanding of the field to apply [CIM200501].

5.3.4 *ISO Reference Model for Open Distributed Processing*

The Reference Model of Open Distributed Processing (ISO-RM-ODP)(ITU-T Rec. X.901), aka ISO/IEC 10746-1 through ITU-T Rec. X.904 aka ISO/IEC 10746-4), provides a framework to support the development of standards to support distributed processing in heterogeneous environments. It uses formal description techniques for specification of the architecture. RM-ODP uses an object modeling approach to describe distributed systems. RM-ODP comprises four parts—an Overview of the reference model, the Descriptive Model, the Prescriptive Model, and the Architectural Semantics (see Table 5.3 [FAR199601]). These four parts provide the concepts and rules of *distributed processing* to ensure *openness* between interacting distributed application components. Two structuring approaches are used to simplify the problems of design in large complex systems: five "viewpoints" provide different ways of describing the system, and eight "transparencies" identify specific problems unique to distributed systems, which distributed system standards may wish to address. Each viewpoint is associated with a language, which can be used to describe systems from that viewpoint. The five viewpoints described by RM-ODP are [IES200501] as follows:

1. The *enterprise viewpoint*, which examines the system and its environment in the context of the business requirements on the system, its purpose, scope and policies. It deals with aspects of the enterprise such as its organizational structure, which affect the system.
2. The *information viewpoint*, which focuses on the information in the system. How the information is structured, how it changes, information flows, and the logical divisions between independent functions within the system are all dealt with in the information viewpoint.
3. The *computational viewpoint*, which focuses on functional decomposition of the system into objects which interact at interfaces.
4. The *engineering viewpoint*, which focuses on how the distributed interaction between system objects is supported.
5. The *technological viewpoint*, which concentrates on the individual hardware and software components that make up the system.

Table 5.3   RM-ODP Parts ([FAR199601])

Part 1 (ISO 10746-1/ ITU-T X.901)	Provides an overview and a guide to the use of other parts. It introduces the concept of information distribution. The application of standards for distributed information processing ranges from global communication networks to applications that run on them. It includes all types of application intercommunication and information media such as data, text, voice, video, hyper-media, etc. and all types of communication facilities. Thus, standardization of distribution aspects, i.e., processing, storage, user access, communication, interworking, identification, management and security aspects, supports the portability of applications and the interworking between ODP systems.
Part 2 (ISO 10746-2 / ITU-T X.902)	Provides the basic modeling concepts, whereas Part 3 prescribes the concepts, rules, and functions a system must adhere to so as to be qualified as an ODP System. The concepts, rules and functions are structured according to the RM-ODP concept of the "viewpoint."
Part 3 (ISO 10746-3 / ITU-T X.903)	For each of the viewpoints of Part 2, viewpoint-specific languages that use the terminology (descriptive concepts) of the ODP Part 2 are introduced in Part 3 to define viewpoint-specific concepts and rules. Apart from the viewpoint languages, the ODP functions such as distribution transparency functions, security functions, management functions, etc., are defined in Part 3. These functions constitute the building blocks of ODP systems (and are subject to separate standardization). The viewpoint approach is applied for the specification to the ODP functions. The object concept plays an important role in the modeling of ODP systems. An object-oriented approach has been adopted for modeling distributed systems in each viewpoint. An object stands for data abstraction, function encapsulation, and modularity. However, different interpretations of the concept of an object are possible, i.e., a real-world thing, the subject of concern, an idealized thing, a denotation of a model or program or the object itself as part of the real world.
Part 4 (ISO 10746-4 / ITU-T X.904)	It deals with how the modeling concepts of Part 2 and the viewpoint languages of Part 3 can be represented in standardized formal description techniques (FDTs) such as LOTOS, Estelle, and SDL.

5.4 IEEE 1471–2000 Standard

The IEEE Recommended Practice for Architectural Description of Software-Intensive Systems (IEEE Std 1471-2000 aka ANSI/IEEE Std 1471-2000) introduces a conceptual model that integrates mission, environment, system architecture, architecture description, rationale, stakeholders, concerns, viewpoints, library viewpoint, views, and architectural models facilitating the expression, communication, evaluation, and comparison of architectures in a consistent manner [FER200401]. IEEE 1471 contains a conceptual framework for architectural description and a statement of what information must be found in any IEEE 1471–compliant architectural description. The conceptual framework described in the standard ties together such concepts as system, architectural description, and view [CLE200501]. However, at face value, the emphasis is on architectures in support of software development. Also, the standard does not specify a delivery format for architectural description. In addition, it is difficult at the practical level to establish if an architecture is compliant with the principles of design imposed by a specific concern [FER200401].

In IEEE 1471, views have a central role in documenting the architecture. In this framework each view is "a representation of a whole system from the perspective of a related set of concerns." The architectural description of a system includes one or more views. In the framework, a view conforms to a *viewpoint*. A *viewpoint* is "a pattern or template from which to develop individual views by establishing the purposes and audience for a view and the techniques for its creation and analysis" [IEE200001,CLE200501]. In this framework the emphasis is on what drives the perspective of a view or a viewpoint. Viewpoints are defined with specific stakeholder concerns in mind, and the definition of a viewpoint includes a description of any associated analysis techniques, as illustrated in Figure 5.2 and 5.3 modeled from the standard. The framework is as follows:

- A system has an architecture.
- An architecture is described by one or more architecture descriptions.
- An architecture description is composed of one or more of stakeholders, concerns, viewpoints, views, and models.
- A stakeholder has one or more concerns.
- A concern has one or more stakeholders.
- A viewpoint covers one or more concerns and stakeholders.
- A view conforms to one viewpoint.

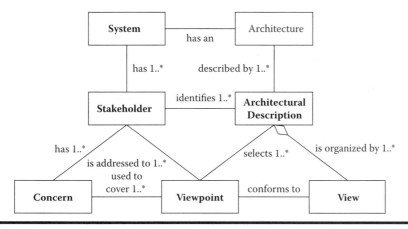

Figure 5.2   Conceptual framework of IEEE 1471 (partial view).

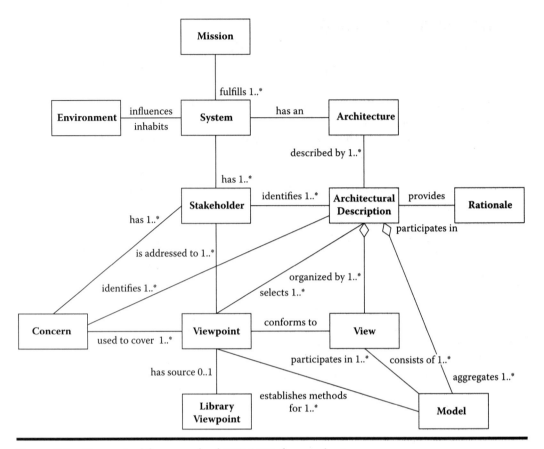

Figure 5.3 Conceptual framework of IEEE 1471 (larger view).

- A viewpoint defines the method of a model.
- A view has one or more models, and a model is part of one or more views.
- A viewpoint library is composed of viewpoints.

In addition to the conceptual framework, IEEE 1471 includes a statement of what information must be in any compliant architectural description, as follows [CLE200501]:

- **Identification and overview information.** This information includes the date of issue and status, identification of the issuing organization, a revision history, a summary and scope statement, the context of the system, a glossary, and a set of references.
- **Stakeholders and their concerns.** The architecture description is required to include the stakeholders for whom the description is produced and whom the architecture is intended to satisfy. It is also required to state "the concerns considered by the architect in formulating the architectural concept for the system." At a minimum, the description is required to address users, acquirers, developers, and maintainers.
- **Viewpoints.** An architecture description is required to identify and define the viewpoints that form the views contained therein. Each viewpoint is described by its name, the stakeholders and concerns it addresses, any language and modeling techniques to be used in

constructing a view based on it, any analytical methods to be used in reasoning about the quality attributes of the system described in a view, and a rationale for selecting it.

■ **Views.** Each view must contain an identifier or other introductory information, a representation of the system (conforming to the viewpoint), and configuration information.

■ **Consistency among views.** Although the standard is somewhat vague on this point, the architecture description needs to indicate that the views are consistent with each other. In addition, the description is required to include a record of any known inconsistencies among the system's views.

■ **Rationale.** The description must include the rationale for the architectural concepts selected, preferably accompanied by evidence of the alternatives considered and the rationale for the choices made.

Chapter 6

Enterprise Architecture Tools

This chapter provides a brief survey of (commercial) architecture description/development tools. The positioning of the tool in the overall context of the synthesis of the enterprise architecture is shown in Figure 6.1. Enterprise architectures aim at capturing detailed information about the business, the data, the systems, and the technology of an enterprise or some specific domain within the enterprise. Recent trends in enterprise architecture deal with the desire of

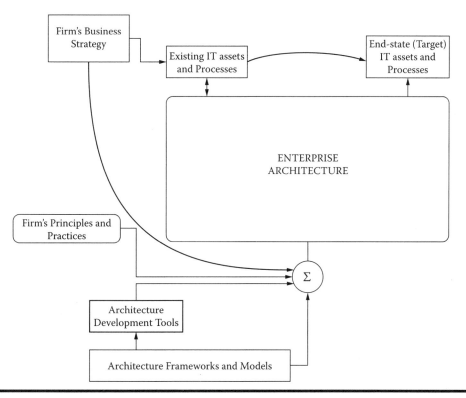

Figure 6.1   Positioning of the tool in the overall context of the synthesis of enterprise architecture.

creating holistic views that span all four of these layers. To accomplish this, after selecting an architecture framework (as discussed in the previous three chapters), architects need to utilize comprehensive modeling tools. Such tools support the development, storage, presentation and enhancement of enterprise architecture models, relationships, views, artifacts, roadmaps, and standards. That is, these tools support the systematization of the set of artifacts required to establish the "as is" environment, the "to be" target, the applicable standards, and the transition roadmap. Specifically, tools allow the firm to analyze and optimize the portfolio of business strategies, organizational structures, business processes/tasks and activities, information flows, applications, and technology infrastructure [IEA200502]. The practical adoption and use of enterprise architectural methodologies is dependent to a large degree on the availability of tools to support the development, storage, presentation and enhancement of enterprise architecture artifacts. However, having said that, planners need to be aware that the field of enterprise architecture tools is still in its infancy.

6.1 Overview

An enterprise architecture framework provides logical mechanisms for developing architectures in a uniform and consistent manner. One of the goals of the enterprise architecture function at the firm is to ascertain that the various architecture descriptions developed across the enterprise can be compared in a uniform manner and that the subarchitectures within each layer (business, data, applications, technology) can be integrated with one another as well as across domains, even when the architectures are developed by different architects. To facilitate the tasks of comparison and integration, the frameworks typically define a number of artifacts. The artifacts comprise a body of resources that need to be managed and controlled, particularly considering the obvious desire to reuse portions of the architecture or artifacts (and ultimately the assets themselves).

Automated tools can and should be used to generate architecture models and views, and to maintain the artifact in an easily accessible repository. Enterprise architecture tools are used to support the development, maintenance, and implementation of enterprise architectures. Tools can be classified into two main classes: (1) enterprise architecture repositories and (2) enterprise architecture modeling suites (in support of some enterprise architecture framework model). A firm may seek to identify a single multifunction tool for modeling architectures and generating the different architecture views; alternatively, the firm may employ a multi-tool toolset.

Press-time surveys show that a majority of the companies surveyed do not have formal tools to develop, store, maintain, and compare/analyze enterprise architecture artifacts and used instead simple word processing/graphics packages. Table 6.1 depicts relative penetration of tools based on press time surveys [IEA200501]. This predicament is an undesirable state of affairs because it limits the ability to develop a cohesive, interconnected set of descriptions. Firms should determine what tools are best suited for their environments and proceed to deploy these. To that end this chapter provides a quick snapshot of some of the available tools. This chapter is only an overview; planners should ultimately refer to the vendors' own product description information.

Considering the fact that the tools market is immature, many enterprises developing enterprise architectures are met with a challenge when it comes to selecting a tool and standardizing on it. The selection of a single tool has the advantage of reduced expenses associated with licenses,

Table 6.1   Use of Architecture Tools in Large Companies (survey at the time of this writing)

Architecture Tools		Penetration (percent)
Not a true tool	Microsoft Visio	33
	Microsoft Office Tools (Word, Excel, Powerpoint)	29
True tool	Telelogic System Architect	15
	ARIS Process Platform	5
	Casewise Modeler	2
	MEGA Architecture Tools	2
	Ptech Enterprise Framework	1
	Troux - METIS	1
Misc.	None	1
	Others	11

training, and maintenance; quantity discounts may become applicable. Also, a single tool has the obvious advantage of consistency and simplified data interchange. However, a single tool may not accommodate all of the requirements across the enterprise. Furthermore, recent history has shown that successful enterprise architecture teams are those that harmonize their architecture tools with their architecture maturity level, team/organizational capabilities, and objectives or focus. If different organizations within an enterprise are at different architecture maturity levels and have different objectives or focus (e.g., enterprise versus business versus technology architecture), it becomes difficult for one tool to satisfy all organizations' needs [TOG200501].

A number of frameworks (e.g., TOGAF) do not require or recommend any specific tool; other frameworks require a specific tool. Table 6.2 illustrates some of the decision points related to the selection of a tool by a firm.

6.2 Snapshot of Products

It is advantageous for a medium-to-large-size firm (or government branch) to consolidate the portfolio of business artifacts, especially as they are derived from the chosen framework, into a single standardized repository so that architects can model, manage, store, and share information. Tools can facilitate this artifact organization task.

Table 6.3 identifies some of the available tools and the supported frameworks, whereas Table 6.4 provides some additional information on some available tools. As noted, some tools are mostly graphical packages (supporting an object-oriented approach) that manage and organize document stores. Other more sophisticated tools support a "top-to-bottom approach," which can be employed for business, information, application, and infrastructure modeling, development, and deployment; these tools also embody data models and UML-based application development capabilities. Planners are encouraged to survey the field at the time that a purchase/deployment decision is being made because new products and features appear on a routine basis.

Table 6.2   Subset of Possible Selection Criteria for Tools (as suggested by TOGAF)

Functionality	Does the tool support the framework that the firm has chosen?
	Is the glossary extendable?
	Does the tool have the ability to represent architecture models and views in a way that can be understood by nontechnical stakeholders?
	Does the tool support meta-models, e.g., ability to configure and tailor models?
	Does the tool support enterprise use, e.g., multi-user collaboration support?
	Does the tool allow drill-down (e.g., conceptual, logical, physical, etc.)?
	Does the tool provide a mechanism for linking requirements (i.e., requirements of traceability security features) to the resulting enterprise architecture? For example, does it facilitate access control (such as different permissions for different roles)?
	Does the tool support a common language and notation?
	Support for visualization modeling?
	Can it be extended or customized, and does it provide utilities to do that?
	Does the tool track and audit changes?
	Does it provide a way for consistently naming and organizing those artifacts?
	Can those artifacts/components be easily viewed, used, and reused?
	Can it create an artifact inside the tool and export it to other commonly used tools, and have the users of those tools use the artifact intact?
	Does the tool use relevant industry standards (e.g., XML, HTML, UML, other industry standard)?
Tool architecture	Is the repository distributed or central? Dynamic or static?
	Does the tool function with multiple industry standard data stores, or is storage proprietary?
	Backwards compatibility with prior releases of the tool?
	Does the tool allow integration and consolidation of data into a central repository?
	Does the tool include version control?
	Is it accessible through a web client?
	What platforms (hardware, OS, DBMS, network) does it run on?
Cost	What is the acquisition cost?
	What is the total cost of ownership?

Table 6.3 Snapshot of Some Architecture Tools (information at the time of this writing; deemed reliable but not guaranteed)

Vendor	Products	Zachman	TOGAF	DoDAF	FEA	FEAF	FEAF/ TEAF	Vendor- Specific	Other	Not Specified
Adaptive	Adaptive EA Manager, Business Process Manager, IT Portfolio Manager	✓				✓				
Agilense	EA Webmodeler		✓	✓	✓		✓	✓	✓	
Casewise	Corporate Modeler Enterprise Edition	✓		✓	✓		✓	✓	✓	
Flashline	Flashline					✓				
Forsight	Modeling and Validation Tool			✓						
GoAgile	GoAgile MAP Product Suite									✓
IDS Scheer	ARIS Process Platform	✓	✓	✓	✓	✓	✓	✓		
LogicLibrary	Logidex									✓
Mega International	Mega (Process, Architect, Designer)	✓	✓	✓	✓	✓				
Popkin Software	System Architect Family	✓	✓	✓						
Proforma	Provision Modeling Suite	✓							✓	
Select Business Solutions	Select Component Architect	✓								
Simon Labs	Simon Tool	✓								
TeleLogic	Telelogic Enterprise Architect for DoDAF	✓	✓	✓				✓	✓	
Troux	Metis Product Family	✓		✓			✓			

Table 6.4 Sample Enterprise Architecture Tools (partial list compiled at the time of this writing)

Company/Product	Brief Description
Adaptive Inc.; Adaptations	Tool designed to solve specific business problems built on a vendor-specific reference model; customization and implementation services from Adaptive Solutions are used to deliver customer specific solutions.
Agilense; Enterprise Architecture WebModeler	Enterprise architecture management product. It provides a complete, easy to use, easy to deploy, end-user-focused enterprise architecture management tool. It supports multiple frameworks, including Zachman, TOGAF, DoDAF, FEAF/TEAF, and FEA.
Casewise; Corporate Modeler	Tool enables business and IT professionals to capture, analyze, simulate, and optimize business processes and supporting systems. The tool is designed to ensure a common understanding of the "as is" and "to be" situations and enables one to experiment with "what if" scenarios to formulate the best business and IT decisions. Corporate Modeler has an object repository, and its diagrams are well integrated with the repository.
Computer Associates (CA)	Offers several products, including AllFusion ERwin Data Modeler, AllFusion Modeling Suite, and AllFusion Process Modeler.
Federal Enterprise Architecture Management System (FEAMS)	A Web-based system designed to provide U.S. government agencies with access to initiatives aligned to the Federal Enterprise Architecture (FEA) and associated reference models. The tool includes multiple features to provide users with an intuitive approach to discover and potentially leverage components, business services, and capabilities across government agencies.
IDS Scheer; ARIS	ARIS Process Platform supports holistic management of business processes in a user-friendly manner. Enhancements have been made recently in the graphical editor to increase productivity. The software for business process management is now available in multiple natural languages. The IT City Planning capability supports integrated presentation, planning and optimization of heterogeneous IT environments.
LogicLibrary; Logidex	A software development asset (SDA) mapping and discovery engine that represents complex enterprise application environments in a graphical, intuitive fashion. Software development assets include executables (e.g., components, services, and frameworks) and their associated software development life-cycle artifacts (e.g., requirements documentation, UML models, and test plans), as well as knowledge assets (e.g., as best practices and design patterns).
MEGA International Ltd; MEGA 2005	MEGA 2005 provides an integrated modeling environment; it consists of three main products: MEGA Process, MEGA Architecture, and MEGA Designer, all sharing a common architecture. • MEGA Process—analyzes and documents strategy, value chains, and organizational processes. • MEGA Architecture—models and describes IT systems. • MEGA Designer—produces detailed architecture and specifications for applications, services, data, and databases. • Modules for personalization—making it possible to customize the tool for individual environments. • MEGA Simulation—for process optimization. • MEGA Business Data—defines business objects and data dictionaries.

Popkin Software; System Architect	Tool that integrates business and process modeling with an enterprise-development environment; allows the integrating business strategy, business analysis, systems analysis, and systems design techniques, leading to automatic code generation (UML and XML).
Proforma; ProVision	A modeling suite that provides an enterprisewide process modeling environment. Tool enables companies to quickly implement business processes and systems. ProVision's sharable repository of integrated strategy, process, and system models provides the framework to effectively model the enterprise and support application development.
Select Business Solutions; Select Enterprise	Select Enterprise provides a design environment for pragmatic business process design, UML, and database design. Select Component Architect offers an end-to-end design solution for business, data, object, component, and Web Services–based application development.
Sparx; Systems Enterprise Architect	Enterprise Architect is a complete UML modeling tool for the Windows platform; it supports system development, project management, and business analysis.
Telelogic; System Architect	Provides what the vendor calls a complete solution for enterprises to define, design, and deliver optimized business processes, software, products, and services.
Troux™ Technologies; Metis	Troux Technologies (by acquisition of Computas Technology's Metis® product suite) provides a tool that enables large enterprise and government agencies to have a mechanism for IT Governance and enterprise architecture management. Metis also includes a business process modeling (BPM) function that enables developers and business analysts to create models for business processes (e.g., event-driven business applications, collaborative workflows, and high-complexity systems). The Capital Asset Planning and Business Case (CAPBC) template provides the Federal Enterprise Architecture reference models and a way to import updated reference models from OMB. The UML template enables software developers using UML 2.0 for object-oriented.

Chapter 7

Business Process Modeling

This chapter deals with business process modeling (BPM) and requirements gathering/analysis in support of the business architecture. There are a number of modeling approaches; the chapter focuses on a handful of specific ones. Three topics are covered: (1) the Business Process Modeling Language (BPML) and the Business Process Modeling Notation (BPMN), both promulgated by the Business Process Management Initiative (BPMI.org)*; (2) the Unified Modeling Language™ (UML)†; and (3) the Model-Driven Architecture™ (MDA) (UML and MDA are both promulgated by the Object Management Group (OMG)). Figure 7.1 depicts the context of these tools, whereas Figure 7.2 provides a more inclusive snapshot of the environment.

Large enterprise applications must be more than just an aggregate of software modules: these applications must be structured (architected) in a way that the architecture enables scalability and reliable execution under normal or stressed conditions (of course, a well-designed architecture benefits any application, not just the large ones). The structure of these applications must be defined clearly and unambiguously so that (1) maintenance staff can quickly locate and fix any bugs that may show up long after the original programmers have moved on, and so that (2) developers can add new features that may be required over time by the business users. Another benefit of a architected structure is that it enables *code reuse:* design time is the best time to seek to structure an application as a collection of self-contained modules or components. Eventually, enterprises build up a library of models of components, each one representing an implementation stored in a

---

* In June of 2005, the Business Process Management Initiative (BPMI.org) and the Object Management Group™ (OMG™) announced the merger of their Business Process Management (BPM) activities to provide thought leadership and industry standards for this vital and growing industry. The combined group has named itself the Business Modeling & Integration (BMI) Domain Task Force (DTF). The BMI's combined activities continue BPMI's and OMG's work and focus on all aspects of business process management. BPMI's widely used standard for business modeling, Business Process Modeling Notation (BPMN), started the comment period required by OMG's fast-track "Request for Comment" (RFC) adoption process at the OMG's September 2005 Technical Meeting.

† The UML modeling format was originally introduced by Rational Software (now owned by IBM) and later adopted by the OMG as a standard.

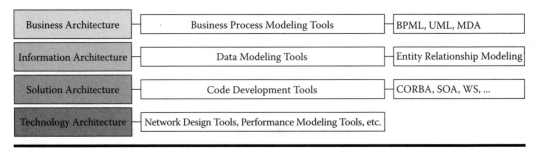

Figure 7.1   Context of tools with business process modeling.

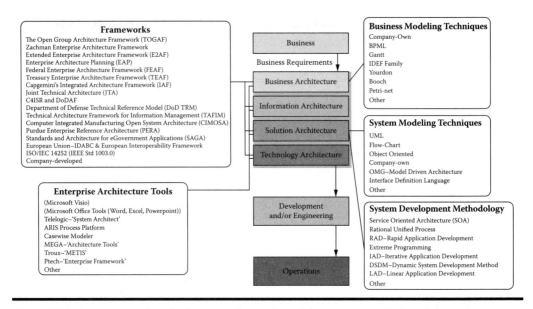

Figure 7.2   A snapshot of tools, frameworks, and models to support EA (partial view).

library of code modules. When another application needs the same functionality, the designer can quickly import this module from the library; at coding time, the developer can import the code module into the executable [OMG200501].

In this context, modeling is the process of architecting and structurally designing a software application before starting the coding phase. Modeling is a critical effort for large software projects, and it is also useful for medium projects. Using a model, developers can assure themselves that business functionality is complete and correct, that end-user needs are met, and that program design supports requirements for scalability, robustness, security, extendibility, and other characteristics, *before* implementation in code makes changes difficult and expensive to make. Models are useful because they allow one to work at a higher level of abstraction. A model may do this by hiding or masking details, bringing out the "big picture," or by focusing on different aspects of the prototype. Typically, one wants to be able to zoom out from a detailed view of an application to the environment where it executes, visualizing connections to other applications or, even further, to other sites. Alternatively, one may want to focus on different aspects of the application, such as the business process that it automates, or a business rules view.

Returning to the topics covered in this chapter, BPML is a metalanguage for the modeling of business processes; it provides an abstracted execution model for collaborative and transactional business processes based on the concept of a transactional finite-state machine. Its associated graphical notation, BPMN, is designed to be understandable by business users, by business analysts that create the initial drafts of the processes, by technical developers responsible for implementing the technology that will perform those processes, and by the business people who will manage and monitor those processes [BPM200501].

UML standardizes representation of object-oriented analysis and design. It lets architects and analysts visualize, specify, construct, and document applications in a standard way. The graphical language contains a dozen of diagram types including Use Case and Activity diagrams for requirements gathering, Class and Object diagrams for design, and Package and Subsystem diagrams for deployment. The key advantage of UML is that the models remain stable even as the technological landscape changes around them [OMG200501]. UML is a language with a broad scope that covers a diverse set of application domains; not all of its modeling capabilities are necessarily useful in all domains or applications; for this reason the language is structured modularly, with the ability to select only those parts of the language that are of direct interest.

MDA has the goal of unifying the modeling and middleware environments. MDA supports applications over their entire life cycle from analysis and design, through implementation and deployment, to maintenance and evolution. Based on UML models, MDA-based development seeks to integrate applications across the enterprise, and integrate the applications of one enterprise with applications of another [OMG200501]. Executable system code can be automatically generated by an MDA-based model (using an appropriate tool).

This chapter is only an introduction—it covers only some high-level aspects of these topics; interested readers should consult the cited documentation for detailed information. Note that to retain a manageable scope, this textbook does not discuss data modeling in support of the information architecture; the interested reader should look for this information in the appropriate literature. Also, the textbook does not cover the topic of application modeling to support the systems/solution architecture, except as achievable with UML/MDA, and except for service-oriented architecture (SOA) approaches, which are covered in Chapter 8.

7.1 Business Process Modeling

Business process modeling (BPM) seeks to standardize the management of business processes that span multiple applications, multiple data repositories, multiple corporate departments, or even multiple companies (or government agencies). BPM provides the foundation for interoperability, whether among departments or among affiliated organizations.

Business process modeling received a lot of attention in the early 1990s. Reengineering efforts arose in many quarters, including federal agencies that used the technique to rethink outdated ways of doing business. Staffers worked to document an organization's as-is environment and define the to-be environment, which aimed at supporting efficient processes and workflow arrangements. However, reengineering proved to be fairly time consuming and expensive; hence, the concept fell out of favor relatively quickly. At this juncture business process modeling is receiving a lot of renewed attention, driven by the Bush Administration's enterprise architecture mandate for government agencies. Business process modeling provides a way of visualizing the often-complex workflows within an organization. The idea is to create a graphical representation of business processes that describes activities and their interdependencies. The resulting diagram reveals inefficiencies and areas for improvement. Governmentwide enterprise architecture initiatives have rekindled interest in business process modeling because it helps create such architectures, which are models of agency information technology systems and business operations [MOO200401]. The Clinger–Cohen Act of 1996 requires agencies to create enterprise architectures. OMB is now mandating Clinger–Cohen compliance; that calls for as-is and to-be business process models to be supported by an economic analysis demonstrating the benefits of a given investment.

BPM typically has the following objectives:

1. Obtaining knowledge about the business processes of the enterprise
2. Utilizing business process knowledge in business process reengineering projects to optimize the operation
3. Facilitating the decision-making efforts of the enterprise
4. Supporting interoperability of the business processes

Ultimately, the idea of "reuse," with the goal of saving run-the-engine (RTE) costs, relies on (1) being able to apply a certain number of modeled processes from one department or application to another department or application, or (2) linking the various departmental models into an enterprise model. BPM is important within the context of an enterprise; however, the shift toward the "extended enterprise" paradigm makes objective #4, interoperability of business process models, even more critical. BPM standardization promotes inter- and intraenterprise business integration and collaboration, by developing shared models that support business modeling and the integration of systems, processes, and information across the enterprise, including business partners and customers [OMG200501]. International standards organizations and other advocacy groups deal with the subject at different levels of abstraction, providing architectures, frameworks, and explicit standards for different application arenas.

Modeling is a best-practices approach to ensure that enterprise IT systems deliver the functionality that a business requires, while at the same time enabling such systems to evolve in a controlled manner as business needs change over time. Systems that have been properly modeled are able to evolve more effectively over time, thus enabling firms to maximize the return on investment (ROI) for IT assets [SEI200201]. Clearly, one is interested in technology-independent representations of the business functionality and behavior. Models should enable the firm to represent exactly what a business application does in an industry-accepted manner.

For business process modeling, one therefore finds older (1990s vintage) and newer (2000s vintage) methods. Integrated Computer-Aided Manufacturing Definition (IDEF*) was the approach of choice in the 1990s and remains the only one compliant with Federal Information Processing Standards (FIPS). IDEF was developed 25 years ago and was prevalent in the 1990s; currently, IDEF plays a role in many enterprise architecture efforts. IDEF refers to a group of methods, each of which fulfills a specific purpose. IDEF0, for example, is used to model an organization's functions, whereas IDEF1x is used for data modeling. IDEF0 and IDEF1x are the most heavily used IDEF methods in government; both were published as FIPS in 1993. There are several tools that support IDEF [MOO200401]. However, joining IDEF now are two other techniques identified earlier: UML and BPMN. Many view IDEF as being "nonintuitive"; BPMN's creators recognized the need for a modeling notation that both business audiences and solution delivery specialists

---

* To be precise, IDEF is an abbreviation of another abbreviation. The workgroup Air Force Program for Integrated Computer-Aided Manufacturing (ICAM) developed ICAM definition language—ICAM Definition or IDEF. The IDEF is set of languages (IDEF 0,1,3,4,5). The mostly commonly used ones are IDEF 0 and IDEF 3. IDEF 0 is comparable to the UML Use Case diagram; IDEF 3 is comparable to the UML Activity diagram.

could interpret. The Business Process Management Initiative, which released BPMN 1.0 in 2003, describes the method as a common visual vocabulary for depicting business processes (companies such as Computer Sciences Corp., EDS, IBM Corp., Microsoft Corp. and Popkin Software reportedly support BPMN).

As noted, a number of approaches to BPM are available; these are modeling mechanisms that may be used to define a business architecture by a firm. Some of the newer BPM approaches are discussed in the sections that follow.

7.2 Business Process Modeling Standardization

7.2.1 Business Process Modeling Language

The Business Process Modeling Language (BPML) is one example of an effort at BPM standardization. BPML is a metalanguage for the modeling of business processes. It provides an abstracted execution model for collaborative and transactional business processes based on the concept of a transactional finite-state machine [BPM200501]. The language provides a model for expressing business processes and supporting entities. BPML defines a formal model for expressing abstract and executable processes that address all aspects of enterprise business processes, including activities of varying complexity, transactions and their compensation, data management, concurrency, exception handling, and operational semantics. BPML also provides a grammar in the form of an eXtensible Markup Language (XML) Schema for enabling the persistence and interchange of definitions across heterogeneous systems and modeling tools.

BPML itself does not define any application semantics such as particular processes or application of processes in a specific domain; rather, BPML defines an abstract model and grammar for expressing generic processes. This allows BPML to be used for a variety of purposes that include, but are not limited to, the definition of enterprise business processes, the definition of complex Web Services (WS), and, the definition of multiparty collaborations. A brief description of BPML follows, based on [BPM200201].

7.2.1.1 Activities

In BPML an activity is a component that performs a specific function. Complex activities are composed of other activities and direct their execution. A process is such a composition, and may itself be an activity within a larger process. The semantics of an activity definition apply to a process definition with a few exceptions.

7.2.1.2 Activity Types

An activity definition specifies the manner in which a given activity will execute. The behavior is defined by specifying the values of the activity's attributes. An activity type definition specifies the attributes that are used in the definition of an activity of that type, and how the values of these attributes affect the execution of that activity. The BPML specification defines 17 activity types, and three process types. All activity types are derived from a common base type. The base type defines the following attributes:

Attribute	Description
Name	The activity name (optional)
Documentation	Documentation (optional)
Other	Other attributes defined for the specific activity type

The *name* attribute provides a name that can be used to reference the activity definition or activity instance. Two activity definitions are distinct even if they have the same name. It is not an error if within a given context that name would reference both activity definitions. With the exception of process definitions, all activity definitions have an ordinal position within an activity list. If the *name* attribute is unspecified, the activity name is its ordinal position, for example, "1" for the first activity in the activity list, "2" for the second activity, and so forth. The *name* attribute is optional for all but process definitions. An activity type may define additional attributes that are specific to that type, for example, the *operation* attribute of the *action* activity, or the *condition* attribute of the *while* activity.

The syntax for the base type *bpml:activity* is as follows:

```
<{activity type}
name = NCName
{other attributes}>
Content: (documentation?, {other element}*)
</{activity type}>
```

Each activity type defines a syntax that specifies additional XML attributes and XML elements that represent values of the abstract model attributes. Other specifications may introduce additional activity types. The XML elements for these activity types are derived from the type *bpml:activity* and use the substitution group *bpml:otherActivity*. They must be defined in a namespace other than the BPML namespace.

The BPML specification defines simple activity types and complex activity types. A description follows.

7.2.1.2.1 Simple Activity Type

The verb list that follows identifies basic activity types.

action	Performs or invokes an operation involving the exchange of input and output messages.
assign	Assigns a new value to a property.
call	Instantiates a process and waits for it to complete.
compensate	Invokes compensation for the named processes.
delay	Expresses the passage of time.
empty	Does nothing.
fault	Throws a fault in the current context.
raise	Raises a signal.
spawn	Instantiates a process without waiting for it to complete.
synch	Synchronizes on a signal.

7.2.1.2.2 Complex Activity Type

The list that follows identifies complex activity types.

all	Executes activities in parallel.
choice	Executes activities from one of multiple sets, selected in response to an event.
foreach	Executes activities once for each item in an item list.
sequence	Executes activities in sequential order.
switch	Executes activities from one of multiple sets, selected based on the truth value of a condition
until	Executes activities once or more based on the truth value of a condition.
while	Executes activities zero or more times based on the truth value of a condition.

7.2.1.3 The Activity Context

Activities that execute in the same context use the context to exchange information through properties defined in that context. For example, an activity that receives an input message sets the value of a property from the contents of the input message. A subsequent activity uses the value of that property to construct and send an output message. The context defines common behavior for all activities executing in that context, such as handling of exceptional conditions and faults, providing atomic semantics, defining a time constraint, and so forth. The context in which an activity executes is referred to as its *current context*. Activities and contexts are composed hierarchically. The current context of an activity may be the child context of some other context, and the parent of multiple child contexts.

The term *downstream activity* refers to an activity that executes following another activity. The downstream activity may depend on the value of properties set by the current activity, a signal raised by the current activity, or the instantiation of another activity from the current activity. Activities that execute in the same context are grouped together into an *activity set*. The activity set is a composition of one or more activity definitions and the definition of the context in which these activities execute—their current context.

The activity set contains an *activity list*, an ordered list of activity definitions. Generally, activities from the activity list are executed in sequential order—an activity must complete before executing the next activity in the list. The BPML specification defines one activity that causes activities from the activity list to execute in parallel. The activity set may define activities that can be executed multiple times in parallel with other activities defined in the activity set. These activities are modeled as process definitions and are contained in the activity set's context definition. These are referred to as *nested processes*. The activity set may define activities that execute in response to exceptional condition and interrupt the execution of all other activities defined in the activity set. These activities are defined in a similar manner to nested processes and are referred to as *exception processes*.

The activity set construct is a composition of the following attributes:

Attribute	Description
context	A context definition (optional)
activities	One or more activity definitions (ordered)

The syntax for the activity set is given as follows:

```
Content: (context?, {any activity}+)
```

The *context* element is absent if the context definition contains no local definitions (an *empty context*). The activity list must contain at least one activity definition. Any activity type may be used in the activity list including activity types defined in other specifications, with the exception of process definitions. Nested process definitions appear inside the *context* element. The occurrence of the *bpml:activitySet* model group in the content of an XML element indicates that it contains an activity set.

7.2.1.4 Simple and Complex Activities

A simple activity is an activity that cannot be further decomposed. For example, the *action* activity that performs a single operation, or the *assign* activity that assigns a new value to a property (see Figure 7.3). A complex activity is a composition of one or more activities. They may be simple activities or complex activities that are recursively composed of simple and complex activities. A complex activity definition contains one or more activity sets and directs the execution of activities from one of these activity sets. A complex activity that contains multiple activity sets must select which one activity set to use. The *choice* activity waits for an event to be triggered and selects the activity set associated with that event handler. The *switch* activity evaluates conditions and selects the activity set associated with a condition that evaluates to true. All other complex activities defined in the BPML specification contain a single activity set (see Figure 7.3).

A complex activity determines the number of times to execute activities from the activity set. The *until* activity repeats executing activities until a condition evaluates to true. The *while* activity

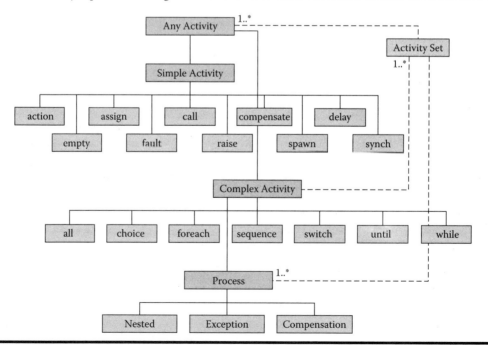

Figure 7.3   Activity types defined in the BPML specification.

repeats executing activities while the condition evaluates to true. The *foreach* activity repeats executing activities, once for each item in the item list. All other complex activities defined in the BPML specification execute activities from the activity set exactly once. A complex activity determines the order in which activities are executed. The *sequence* activity executes all activities from the activity set's list in sequential order. The *all* activity executes all activities from the activity set's list in parallel. All other complex activities defined in the BPML specification execute activities in sequential order. The complex activity completes after it has completed executing all activities from the activity set. This includes all activities that are defined in the activity list, and all processes instantiated from a definition made in the activity set's context. Nested processes and exception processes are considered activities of the activity set.

Simple activities generate faults if they cannot complete because of an unexpected error. Complex activities throw faults if one of their activities generate a fault and they cannot recover from that fault. The complex activity aborts when a fault is thrown by one of its activities. To abort, the complex activity terminates all of its executing activities.

7.2.1.5 Processes

A process is a type of complex activity that defines its own context for execution. Similar to other complex activity types, it is a composition of activities, and it directs their execution. A process can also serve as an activity within a larger composition, either by defining it as part of a parent process or by invoking it from another process. Processes are often defined as reusable units of work.

A process that is defined independently of other processes is called a *top-level process*, because its definition is found at the package level. A process that is defined to execute within a specific context is called a *nested process*, because its definition is part of that context's definition. An *exception process* is defined as part of a parent process to handle exceptional conditions that may interrupt activities executing in that process. A *compensation process* provides the compensation logic for its parent process. Exception processes and compensation processes are specific type of process definitions.

A process can be instantiated from the *call*, *compensate*, and *spawn* activities and from a schedule. Alternatively, it may define an instantiation event that responds to an input message, or instantiation event that responds to a raised signal. A BPML implementation that detects a process definition that violates one of the constraints defined in the BPML specification should flag the process definition as erroneous. It must not create instances from an erroneous process definition. A process definition is also erroneous if it references an erroneous process definition from the *call* and *spawn* activities.

Interested readers are referred to [BPM200201] for more information on BPML.

7.2.2 Business Process Modeling Notation

The Business Process Management Initiative (BPMI) has developed a standard modeling notation called the Business Process Modeling Notation (BPMN). This specification provides a graphical notation for expressing business processes in a Business Process Diagram (BPD). The BPMN specification also provides a binding between the notation's graphical elements and the constructs of block-structured process execution languages, including BPML and Business Process Execution Language for Web Services (BPEL4WS.) The first draft of BPMN became available in late

2002. This section is summarized from [BPM200301]; interested readers should consult the entire specification.

7.2.2.1 Introduction

The primary goal of BPMN is to provide a notation that is readily understandable by business users, from the business analysts who create the initial drafts of the processes, to the technical developers responsible for implementing the technology that will perform those processes, and finally, to the business people who will manage and monitor the processes. Thus, BPMN creates a standardized bridge for the gap between the business process design and process implementation. Another goal is to ensure that XML languages designed for the execution of business processes, such as BPEL4WS, can be visualized with a common notation.

This specification defines the notation and semantics of a BPD and represents the amalgamation of best practices within the business modeling community. The intent of BPMN is to standardize a business process modeling notation in the face of many different modeling notations and viewpoints. In doing so, BPMN provides a simple means of communicating process information to other business users, process implementers, customers, and suppliers. The membership of the BPMI Notation Working Group has expertise and experience with the many existing notations and has sought consolidate the best ideas from these divergent notations into a single standard notation. Examples of other notations or methodologies that were reviewed are UML Activity Diagram, UML Enterprise Distributed Object Computing (EDOC) Business Processes, Integrated Computer-Aided Manufacturing Definition (IDEF), Electronic Business using eXtensible Markup Language (ebXML) Business Process Specification Schema (BPSS) (ebXML BPSS*), Activity-Decision Flow (ADF) Diagram, RosettaNet, LOVeM, and Event-Process Chains (EPCs).

7.2.2.2 BPMN Overview

There has been much activity in the past few years in developing Web-service-based XML execution languages for BPM systems. Languages such as BPEL4WS provide a formal mechanism for the definition of business processes. The key element of such languages is that they are optimized for the operation and interoperation of BPM Systems. The optimization of these languages for software operations renders them less suited for direct use by humans to design, manage, and monitor business processes. BPEL4WS has both graph and block structures and utilizes the principles of

---

* The Electronic Business using eXtensible Markup Language (ebXML) project was started in 1999, jointly by OASIS and UN/CEFACT, the United Nations Centre for Trade Facilitation and Electronic Business, to provide a modular suite of specifications that enable enterprises of any size and in any location to conduct business over the Internet. The original project envisioned and delivered five layers of substantive data specification, including XML standards for: business processes, core data components, collaboration protocol agreements, messaging, registries, and repositories. The ebXML Business Process Specification Schema provides a generic framework for business process collaborations, both between two parties/partners (binary) and multiparty (expressed as two or more binary collaborations). This framework includes the means and descriptions by which one or more activities are performed in performing a business collaboration. This business collaboration could be part of an enterprise-to-enterprise collaboration (B2B) or within an enterprise for a collaboration that is required to be enforceable. The original BPSS version 1.01 was approved in 2001. ebXML has seen some adoption since its release, e.g., by General Motors, the U.S. Centers for Disease Control (CDC), and TransCanada Pipelines.

formal mathematical models. This technical underpinning provides the foundation for business process execution to handle the complex nature of both internal and business-to-business (B2B) interactions and take advantage of the benefits of Web Services. Given the nature of BPEL4WS, a complex business process could be organized in a potentially complex, disjointed, and unintuitive format that is handled well by a software system (or a computer programmer), but would be hard to understand by the business analysts and managers tasked to develop, manage, and monitor the process. Thus, there is a human level of "interoperability" or "portability" that is not addressed by these WS-based XML execution languages.

Business people are often comfortable with visualizing business processes in a flowchart format. There are thousands of business analysts studying the way companies work and defining business processes with simple flowcharts. This creates a technical gap between the format of the initial design of business processes and the format of the languages, such as BPEL4WS, that will execute these business processes. This gap needs to be bridged with a formal mechanism that maps the appropriate visualization of the business processes (a notation) to the appropriate execution format (a BPM execution language) for these business processes.

Interoperation of business processes at the human level, rather than the software engine level, can be solved with standardization of BPMN. BPMN provides a BPD, which is a diagram designed for use by the people who design and manage business processes. BPMN also provides a formal mapping to an execution language of BPM Systems (BPEL4WS). Thus, BPMN provides a standard visualization mechanism for business processes defined in an execution-optimized business process language.

BPMN provides businesses with the capability of understanding their internal business procedures in a graphical notation and will give organizations the ability to communicate these procedures in a standardized manner. Currently, there are many process modeling tools and methodologies. Given that individuals may move from one company to another and that companies may merge and diverge, it is likely that business analysts are required to understand multiple representations of business processes—potentially different representations of the same process as it moves through its life cycle of development, implementation, execution, monitoring, and analysis. Therefore, a standard graphical notation facilitates the understanding of the performance collaborations and business transactions within and between the organizations. This ensures that businesses understand their own environments and the environment of participants in their business, and will enable organizations to adjust to new internal and B2B business circumstances quickly. To do this, BPMN follows the tradition of flowcharting notations for readability but at the same time provides mapping to the executable constructs. BPMI has used the experience of the business process notations that preceded BPMN to create the next-generation notation that combines readability, flexibility, and expandability.

BPMN also advances the capabilities of traditional business process notations by inherently handling B2B business process concepts, such as public and private processes and choreographies, as well as advanced modeling concepts, such as exception handling and transaction compensation.

7.2.2.2.1 BPMN Scope

BPMN is constrained to support only the concepts of modeling that are applicable to business processes. This means that other types of modeling done by organizations for business purposes will be outside BPMN's scope; for example, the modeling of the following will not be a part of BPMN: organizational structures, functional breakdowns, and data models. In addition, although

BPMN will show the flow of data (messages) and the association of data artifacts to activities, it is not a data flow diagram.

7.2.2.2.2 Uses of BPMN

Business process modeling is used to communicate a wide variety of information to a wide variety of audiences. BPMN is designed to cover this wide range of usage and allows modeling of end-to-end business processes to allow the viewer of the diagram to be able to easily differentiate between sections of a BPMN diagram. There are three basic types of submodels within an end-to-end BPMN model:

- Private (internal) business processes
- Abstract (public) processes
- Collaboration (global) processes

7.2.2.2.2.1 Private (Internal) Business Processes

Private business processes are those that are internal to a specific organization and are the types of processes that have been generally called workflow or BPM processes. A single private business process will map to a single BPEL4WS document. If swimlanes are used, then a private business process will be contained within a single Pool. The Sequence Flow of the Process is therefore contained within the Pool and cannot cross its boundaries. Message Flow can cross the Pool boundary to show the interactions that exist among separate private business processes. Thus, a single BPMN diagram may show multiple private business processes, each mapping to a separate BPEL4WS process.

7.2.2.2.2.2 Abstract (Public) Processes

This represents the interactions between a private business process and another process or participant. Only those activities that are used to communicate outside the private business process are included in the abstract process. All other "internal" activities of the private business process are not shown in the abstract process. Thus, the abstract process shows to the outside world the sequence of messages that is required to interact with that business process. A single abstract process may be mapped to a single BPEL4WS abstract process (however, this mapping will not be done in this specification). Abstract processes are contained within a Pool and can be modeled separately or within a larger BPMN diagram to show the Message Flow between the abstract process activities and other entities. If the abstract process is in the same diagram as its corresponding private business process, then the activities that are common to both processes can be associated.

7.2.2.2.2.3 Collaboration (Global) Processes

A collaboration process depicts the interactions among two or more business entities. These interactions are defined as a sequence of activities that represents the message exchange patterns among the entities involved. A single collaboration process may be mapped to various collaboration languages, such as ebXML BPSS, RosettaNet, or the resultant specification from the W3C Choreography Working Group (however, these mappings are considered as future directions for BPMN). Collaboration processes may be contained within a Pool, and the different participant business interactions are shown as Lanes within the Pool. In this situation, each Lane would represent two participants and a direction of travel between them. They may also be shown as two or more Abstract Processes interacting through Message Flow. These processes can be modeled separately or within a larger BPMN diagram to show the Associations between the collaboration process activities and other entities. If the collaboration process is in the same diagram as one of its corresponding private business processes, then the activities common to both processes can be associated.

7.2.2.2.2.4 Types of BPD Diagrams

Within and between these three BPMN submodels, many types of diagrams can be created. The following are the types of business processes that can be modeled with BPMN (those with asterisks may not map to an executable language):

- High-level private process activities (not functional breakdown)*
- Detailed private business process
  - As-is, or old, business process*
  - To-be, or new, business process
- Detailed private business process with interactions among one or more external entities (or "black box" processes)
- Two or more detailed private business processes interacting
- Detailed private business process relationship with Abstract Process
- Detailed private business process relationship with Collaboration Process
- Two or more Abstract Processes*
- Abstract Process relationship with Collaboration Process*
- Collaboration Process only (e.g., ebXML BPSS, or RosettaNet)*
- Two or more detailed private business processes interacting through their Abstract Processes
- Two or more detailed private business processes interacting through a Collaboration Process
  - Two or more detailed private business processes interacting through their Abstract Processes and a Collaboration Process

BPMN is designed to allow all the foregoing types of diagrams. However, it should be cautioned that if too many types of submodels are combined, such as three or more private processes with message flow between each of them, then the diagram may become too hard for someone to understand. Thus, we recommend that the modeler pick a focused purpose for the BPD, such as a private process, or a collaboration process.

7.2.2.2.2.5 BPMN Mappings

Because BPMN covers such a wide range of usage, it will map to more than one lower-level specification language:

- BPEL4WS are the primary languages that BPMN will map to, but they only cover a single executable private business process. If a BPMN diagram depicts more than one internal business process, then there will a separate mapping for each of the internal business processes.
- The abstract sections of a BPMN diagram will be mapped to Web service interfaces specifications, such as the abstract processes of BPEL4WS.

■ The Collaboration model sections of a BPMN will be mapped to Collaboration models such as ebXML BPSS, RosettaNet, and the W3C Choreography Working Group Specification (when it is completed).

The BPMN specification will only cover the mappings to BPEL4WS. Mappings to other specifications will have to be a separate effort, or perhaps a future direction of BPMN (beyond Version 1.0 of the BPMN specification). One cannot predict which mappings will be applied to BPMN at this point, as process language specifications is a volatile area of work, with many new offerings and mergings.

A BPD is not designed to graphically convey all the information required to execute a business process. Thus, the graphic elements of BPMN will be supported by attributes that will supply the additional information required to enable a mapping to BPEL4WS.

7.2.2.2.3 Diagram Point of View

As a BPMN diagram may depict the processes of different Participants, each Participant may view the diagram differently; that is, the Participants have different points of view regarding how the processes will behave. Some of the activities will be internal to the Participant (meaning performed by or under control of the Participant), and other activities will be external to the Participant. Each Participant will have a different perspective as to which processes are internal and external. At runtime, the difference between internal and external activities is important in how a Participant can view the status of the activities or troubleshoot any problems. However, the diagram itself remains the same. Figure 7.4 displays as an example a simple Business Process that has two points of view. One point of view is of a Patient, the other is of the Doctor's office. The diagram shows the activities of both participants in the process, but when the process is actually being performed, each Participant will really have control over his or her own activities.

Although the diagram point of view is important for a viewer of the diagram to understand how the behavior of the process will relate to that viewer, BPMN does not currently specify any graphical mechanisms to highlight the point of view. It is open to the modeler or modeling tool vendor to provide any visual cues to emphasize this characteristic of a diagram.

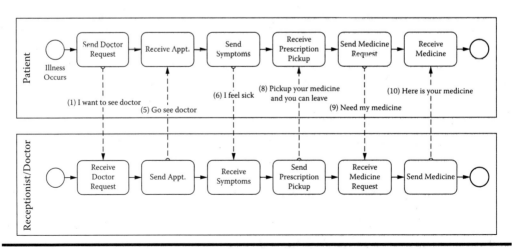

Figure 7.4   A business process diagram with two points of view.

7.2.2.2.4 Extensibility of BPMN and Vertical Domains

BPMN is intended to be extensible by modelers and modeling tools. This extensibility allows modelers to add nonstandard elements or artifacts to satisfy a specific need, such as the unique requirements of a vertical domain. While being extensible, BPMN diagrams should still have the basic look and feel, so that a diagram by any modeler should be easily understood by any viewer of the diagram. Thus, the footprint of the basic flow elements (Events, Activities, and Gateways) should not be altered, nor should any new flow elements be added to a BPD, because there is no specification as to how Sequence and Message Flow will connect to any new flow object. In addition, mappings to execution languages may be affected if new flow elements are added. To satisfy additional modeling concepts that are not part of the basic set of flow elements, BPMN provides the concept of Artifacts that can be linked to the existing flow objects through Associations. Thus, Artifacts do not affect the basic Sequence or Message Flow, nor do they affect mappings to execution languages. The graphical elements of BPMN are designed to be open to allow specialized markers to convey specialized information. For example, the three types of Events all have open centers for the markers that BPMN standardizes, as well as for user-defined markers.

7.2.2.3 Business Process Diagrams

This section provides a summary of the BPMN graphical objects and their interrelationships. One of the goals of BPMN is that the notation be simple and adoptable by business analysts. Also, there is a potentially conflicting requirement that BPMN provide the power to depict complex business processes and map to BPM execution languages. To help understand how BPMN can manage both requirements, the list of BPMN graphic elements is presented in two groups.

First, there are the core elements that support the requirement of a simple notation. These are the elements that define the basic look and feel of BPMN. Most business processes can be modeled adequately with these elements. Second, all the elements, including the core elements, help support the requirement of a powerful notation to handle more advanced modeling situations. Further, the graphical elements of the notation are supported by nongraphical attributes that provide the remaining information necessary to map to an execution language or for other business modeling purposes.

7.2.2.3.1 BPD Core Element Set

It should be emphasized that one of the drivers for the development of BPMN is to create a simple mechanism for creating business process models. Of the core element set, there are three primary modeling elements (flow objects):

- Events
- Activities
- Gateways

There are three ways of connecting the primary modeling elements:

- Sequence Flow
- Message Flow
- Association

There are two ways of grouping the primary modeling elements through Swimlanes:

■ Pools
■ Lanes

Table 7.1 displays a list of the core modeling elements that are depicted by the notation. Table 7.2 displays a more extensive list of the business process concepts that could be depicted through a business process modeling notation.

7.2.2.3.2 Flow Object Connection Rules

An incoming Sequence Flow can connect to any location on a flow object (left, right, top, or bottom). Likewise, an outgoing Sequence Flow can connect from any location on a flow object (left, right, top, or bottom). Message Flows also have this capability. BPMN allows this flexibility; however, we also recommend that modelers use judgment or best practices in how flow objects should be connected so that readers of the diagrams will find the behavior clear and easy to follow. This is even more important when a diagram contains Sequence Flows and Message Flows. In these situations it is best to pick a direction of Sequence Flow, either left to right or top to bottom, and then direct the Message Flow at a 90° angle to the Sequence Flow. The resulting diagrams will be much easier to understand.

7.2.2.3.2.1 Sequence Flow Rules

Table 7.3 displays the BPMN flow objects and shows how these objects can connect to one another through Sequence Flows. The symbol indicates that the object listed in the row can connect to the object listed in the column. The quantity of connections into and out of an object is subject to various configuration dependencies not specified here. Refer to the sections in the next chapter for each individual object for more detailed information on the appropriate connection rules. Note that if a subprocess has been expanded within a diagram, the objects within the subprocess cannot be connected to objects outside of the subprocess. Nor can Sequence Flows cross a Pool boundary.

7.2.2.3.2.2 Message Flow Rules

Table 7.4 displays the BPMN modeling objects and shows how they can connect to one another through Message Flows. The symbol indicates that the object listed in the row can connect to the object listed in the column. The quantity of connections into and out of an object is subject to various configuration dependencies that are not specified here. Refer to the sections in the next chapter for each individual object for more detailed information on the appropriate connection rules. Note that Message Flows cannot connect to objects that are within the same Participant Lane boundary.

7.2.2.4 Examples

The description given earlier is only a truncated synopsis of the modeling language. The interested reader should consult the full documentation. A handful of examples follow for illustrative purposes (Figures 7.5 through 7.10.) The figures that follow are just some examples.

Interested readers are referred to [BPM200301] for more information on BPMN.

Table 7.1 BPD Core Element Set

Element	Description	Notation
Event	An event is something that "happens" during the course of a business process. These events affect the flow of the process and usually have a cause (trigger) or an impact (result). Events are circles with open centers to allow internal markers to differentiate different triggers or results. There are three types of Events, based on when they affect the flow: Start, Intermediate, and End.	 ○
Activity	An activity is a generic term for work that the company performs. An activity can be atomic or nonatomic (compound). The types of activities that are a part of a Process Model are Process, Subprocess, and Task. Tasks and Subprocesses are rounded rectangles. Processes are either unbounded or a contained within a Pool.	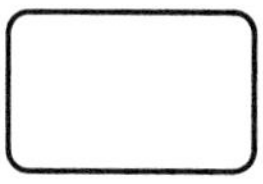 ▢
Gateway	A Gateway is used to control the divergence and convergence of Sequence Flow. Thus, it will determine branching, forking, merging, and joining of paths. Internal Markers will indicate the type of behavior control.	 ◇
Sequence Flow	A Sequence Flow is used to show the order that activities will be performed in a Process.	 ——→
Message Flow	A Message Flow is used to show the flow of messages between two entities that are prepared to send and receive them. In BPMN, two separate Pools in the diagram will represent the two entities (participants).	 ○----▷
Association	An Association is used to associate information with flow objects. Text and graphical nonflow objects can be associated with the flow objects.	⋯⋯→
Pool	A Pool is a "swimlane" and a graphical container for partitioning a set of activities from other Pools, usually in the context of B2B situations.	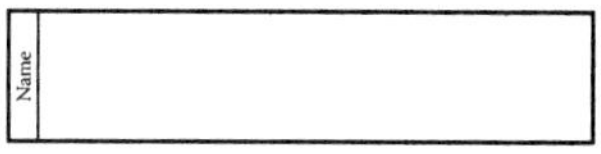 [Name]
Lane	A Lane is a subpartition within a Pool and will extend the entire length of the Pool, either vertically or horizontally. Lanes are used to organize and categorize activities.	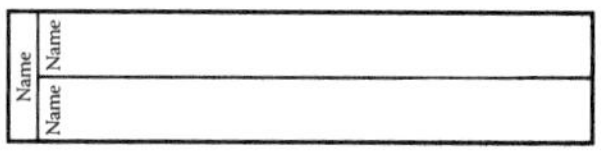 [Name/Name]

Table 7.2   BPD Complete Element Set

Element	Description	Notation
Event	An event is something that "happens" during the course of a business process. These events affect the flow of the process and usually have a cause (trigger) or an impact (result). There are three types of Events, based on when they affect the flow: Start, Intermediate, and End.	◯ Name or Source
Flow Dimension (e.g., Start, Intermediate, End)		
Start (None, Message, Timer, Rule, Link, Multiple)	As the name implies, the Start Event indicates where a particular process will start.	Start ◯
Intermediate (None, Message, Timer, Exception, Cancel, Compensation, Rule, Link, Multiple, Branching)	Intermediate Events occur between a Start Event and an End Event. It will affect the flow of the process, but will not start or (directly) terminate the process.	Intermediate ◎
End (None, Message, Exception, Cancel, Compensation, Link, Terminate, Multiple)	As the name implies, the End Event indicates where a process will end.	End ◯
Type Dimension (e.g., Message, Timer, Exception, Cancel, Compensation, Rule, Link, Multiple, Terminate)	Start and Intermediate Events have "Triggers" that define the cause of the event. There are multiple ways that these events can be triggered. End Events may define a "Result" that is a consequence of a Sequence Flow ending.	Message, Timer, Exception, Cancel, Compensation, Rule, Link, Multiple, Terminate

Element	Description	Notation
Task (Atomic)	A Task is an atomic activity that is included within a Process. A Task is used when the work in the Process is not broken down to a finer level of Process Model detail.	
Process/Subprocess (nonatomic)	A Subprocess is a compound activity that is included within a Process. It is compound in that it can be broken down into a finer level of detail (a Process) through a set of Subactivities.	See Next Two Figures
Collapsed Subprocess	The details of the Subprocess are not visible in the diagram. A "plus" sign in the lower-center of the shape indicates that the activity is a Subprocess and has a lower level of detail.	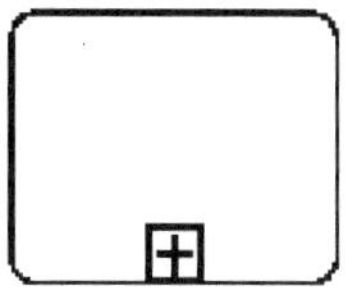
Expanded Subprocess	The boundary of the Subprocess is expanded and the details (a Process) are visible within its boundary. Note that Sequence Flow cannot cross the boundary of a Subprocess.	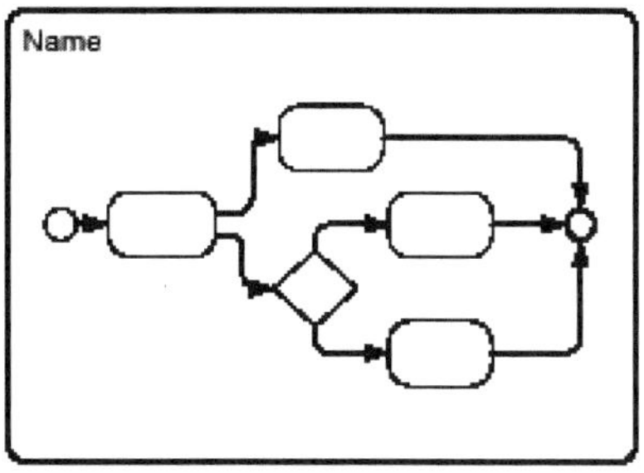 Name
Gateway	A Gateway is used to control the divergence and convergence of multiple Sequence Flows. Thus, it determines branching, forking, merging, and joining of paths.	

(continued)

Table 7.2   BPD Complete Element Set (continued)

Element	Description	Notation
Gateway Control Types	Icons within the diamond shape indicate the type of flow control behavior. The types of control include the following: • XOR – exclusive decision and merging. Both Data-Based and Event-Based. Data-Based can be shown with or without the "X" marker. • OR—inclusive decision • Complex—complex conditions and situations (e.g., 3 out of 5) • AND—forking and joining Each type of control affects both the incoming and outgoing Flow.	**Exclusive (XOR)** Data-Based ◇ or ⬨(X) **Event-Based** ◈ **Inclusive (OR)** ◉ **Complex** ✳ **Parallel (AND)** ⊕
Sequence flow	A Sequence Flow is used to show the order that activities will be performed in a Process.	See next seven figures
Normal flow	Normal Sequence Flow refers to the flow that originates from a Start Event and continues through activities via alternative and parallel paths until it ends at an End Event.	Name, Condition, Code, or Message ▸
Uncontrolled flow	Uncontrolled flow refers to flow that is not affected by any conditions or does not pass through a Gateway. The simplest example of this is a single Sequence Flow connecting two activities. This can also apply to multiple Sequence Flows that converge on or diverge from an activity. For each uncontrolled Sequence Flow a "Token" will flow from the source object to the target object.	Name, Condition, Code, or Message ▸

Element	Description	Notation
Conditional flow	Sequence Flow can have condition expressions that are evaluated at runtime to determine whether or not the flow will be used. If the conditional flow is outgoing from an activity, then the Sequence Flow will have a minidiamond at the beginning of the line (see figure to the right). If the conditional flow is outgoing from a Gateway, then the line will not have a minidiamond (see figure in the preceding row).	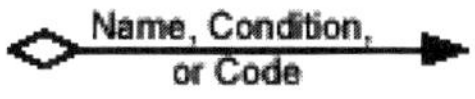 Name, Condition, or Code
Default flow	For Data-Based Exclusive Decisions, one type of flow is the Default condition flow. This flow will be used only if all the other outgoing conditional flows are not true at runtime. These Sequence Flows will have a diagonal slash added to the beginning of the line (see the figure to the right). Note that it is an open issue whether Default Conditions will be used for Inclusive Decision situations.	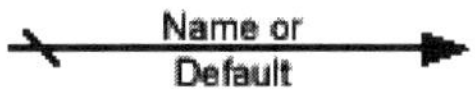 Name or Default
Exception flow	Exception flow occurs outside the normal flow of the Process and is based upon an Intermediate Event that occurs during the performance of the Process.	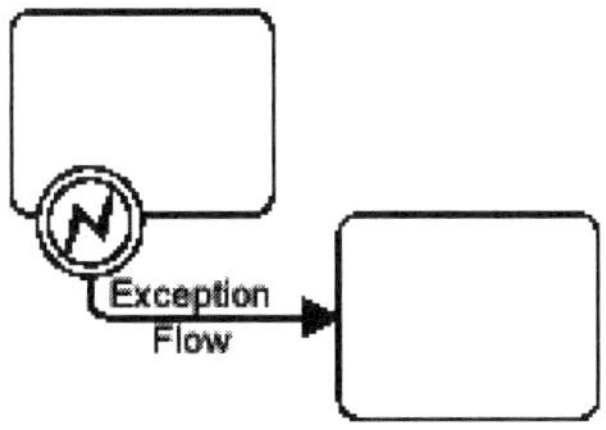 Exception Flow
Message flow	A Message Flow is used to show the flow of messages between two entities that are prepared to send and receive them. In BPMN, two separate Pools in the diagram represent the two entities.	 Name or Message

(continued)

Table 7.2 BPD Complete Element Set (continued)

Element	Description	Notation
Compensation Association	Compensation Association occurs outside the normal flow of the Process and is based upon an event (a Cancel Intermediate Event) that is triggered through the failure of a Transaction or a Compensate Event. The target of the Association must be marked as a Compensation Activity.	
Data Object	Data Objects are considered artifacts because they do not have any direct effect on the Sequence Flow or Message Flow of the Process, but they do provide information about what the Process does.	Name
For (AND-Split)	BPMN uses the term "fork" to refer to the dividing of a path into two or more parallel paths (also known as an AND-Split). It is a place in the Process where activities can be performed concurrently, rather than serially. There are two options: Multiple Outgoing Sequence Flow can be used (see figure at top right). This represents "uncontrolled" flow and is the preferred method for most situations. A Parallel (AND) Gateway can be used (see figure at bottom right). This will be used rarely, usually in combination with other Gateways.	
Join (AND-Join)	BPMN uses the term "join" to refer to the combining of two or more parallel paths into one path (also known as an AND-Join or synchronization). A Parallel (AND) Gateway is used to show the joining of multiple flows.	

Element	Description	Notation
Decision, Branching Point; (OR-Split)	Decisions are Gateways within a business process where the flow of control can take one or more alternative paths.	See next five rows.
Exclusive	An Exclusive Gateway (XOR) restricts the flow such that only one of a set of alternatives may be chosen during runtime. There are two types of Exclusive Gateways: Data-Based and Event-Based.	
Data-Based	This Decision represents a branching point where Alternatives are based on conditional expressions contained within the outgoing Sequence Flow. Only one of the Alternatives will be chosen.	
Event-Based	This Decision represents a branching point where Alternatives are based on an Event that occurs at that point in the Process. The specific Event, usually the receipt of a Message, determines which of the paths will be taken. Other types of Events can be used, such as Timer. Only one of the Alternatives will be chosen. There are two options for receiving Messages. Tasks of Type Receive can be used (see figure at top right). Intermediate Events of Type Message can be used (see figure bottom-right).	

(continued)

Table 7.2   BPD Complete Element Set (continued)

Element	Description	Notation
Inclusive	This Decision represents a branching point where Alternatives are based on conditional expressions contained within the outgoing Sequence Flow. In a sense it is a grouping of related independent Binary (Yes/No) Decisions. Because each path is independent, all combinations of the paths may be taken, from zero to all. However, it should be designed so that at least one path is taken. There are two versions of this type of Decision. The first uses a collection of conditional Sequence Flow, marked with minidiamonds (see top-right figure). The second uses an OR Gateway, usually in combination with other Gateways (see bottom-right picture).	
Merging (OR-Join)	BPMN uses the term merge to refer to the exclusive combining of two or more paths into one path (also known as an a OR-Join). A Merging (XOR) Gateway is used to show the merging of multiple flows. If all the incoming flow is alternative, then a Gateway is not needed; that is, uncontrolled flow provides the same behavior.	
Looping	BPMN provides two mechanisms for looping within a Process.	See Next Two Figures

Element	Description	Notation
Activity Looping	The properties of Tasks and Subprocesses will determine if they are repeated or performed once. There are two types of loops: Standard and Multi-Instance. A small looping indicator will be displayed at the bottom center of the activity.	
Sequence Flow Looping	Loops can be created by connecting a Sequence Flow to an "upstream" object. An object is considered to be upstream if it has an outgoing Sequence Flow that leads to a series of other Sequence Flows, the last of which is an incoming Sequence Flow for the original object.	
Multiple Instances	The attributes of Tasks and Subprocesses will determine if they are repeated or performed once. A small parallel indicator will be displayed at the bottom center of the activity.	
Process Break (something out of the control of the process makes it pause)	A Process Break is a location in the Process that shows where an expected delay will occur within it. An Intermediate Event is used to show the actual behavior (see top-right figure). In addition, a Process Break artifact, as designed by a modeler or modeling tool, can be associated with the Event to highlight the location of the delay within the flow.	

(continued)

Table 7.2   BPD Complete Element Set (continued)

Element	Description	Notation
Transaction	A transaction is an activity, either a Task or a Subprocess, that is supported by a special protocol that ensures that all parties involved have complete agreement that the activity should be completed or cancelled. The attributes of the activity will determine if the activity is a transaction. A double-lined boundary indicates that the activity is a Transaction.	
Nested Subprocess(Inline Block)	A nested Subprocess is an activity that shares the same set of data as its parent process. This is opposed to a Subprocess that is independent, reusable, and referenced from the parent process. Data needs to be passed to the referenced Subprocess, but not to the nested Subprocess.	There is no special indicator for nested Subprocesses
Group (a box around a group of objects for documentation purposes)	A grouping of activities that does not affect the Sequence Flow. The grouping can be used for documentation or analysis purposes. Groups can also be used to identify the activities of a distributed transaction that is shown across Pools.	
Off-Page Connector	Generally used for printing, this object will show where the Sequence Flow leaves one page and then restarts on the next. A Link Intermediate Event can be used as an Off-Page Connector.	

Element	Description	Notation
Association	An Association is used to associate information with flow objects. Text and graphical nonflow objects can be associated with the flow objects.	
Text Annotation (attached with an Association)	Text Annotations are a mechanism for a modeler to provide additional information for the reader of a BPMN Diagram.	Descriptive Text Here
Pool	A Pool is a "swimlane" and a graphical container for partitioning a set of activities from other Pools, usually in the context of B2B situations.	
Lanes	A Lane is a subpartition within a Pool and will extend the entire length of the Pool, either vertically or horizontally. Lanes are used to organize and categorize activities within a Pool.	

Table 7.3   Sequence Flow Connection Rules

From\To	○	▭	▭	◇	◯	◯
○		↗	↗	↗	↗	↗
▭		↗	↗	↗	↗	↗
▭		↗	↗	↗	↗	↗
◇		↗	↗	↗	↗	↗
◯		↗	↗	↗	↗	↗
◯						

Table 7.4   Message Flow Connection Rules

From\To	◯	▤ (Pool)	Name ▣	Name	◯	◯
◯						
▤ (Pool)	↗	↗	↗	↗	↗	
Name ▣	↗	↗	↗	↗	↗	
Name	↗	↗	↗	↗	↗	
◉						
◯	↗	↗	↗	↗	↗	

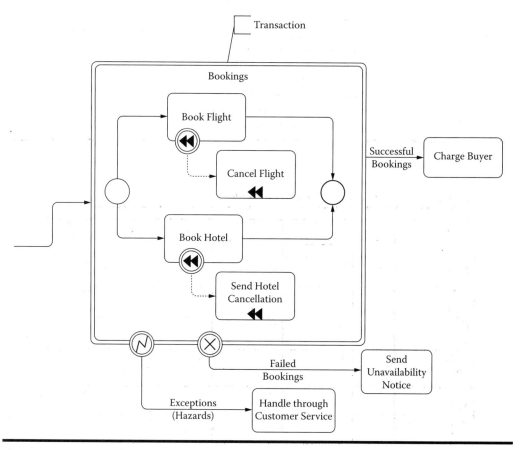

Figure 7.5   An example of a transaction expanded Subprocess.

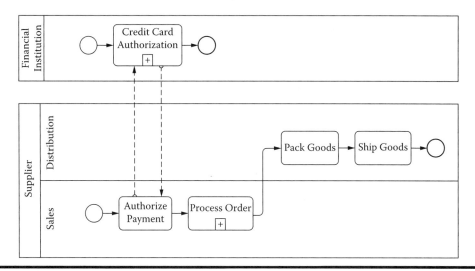

Figure 7.6   Message Flow connecting to flow objects within two Pools.

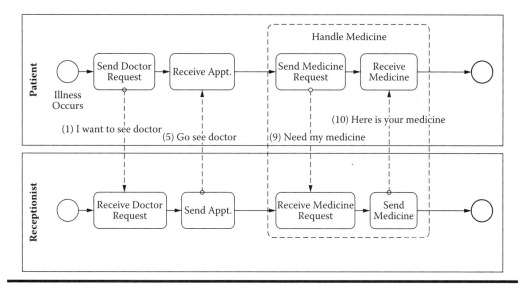

Figure 7.7   A Group around activities in different Pools.

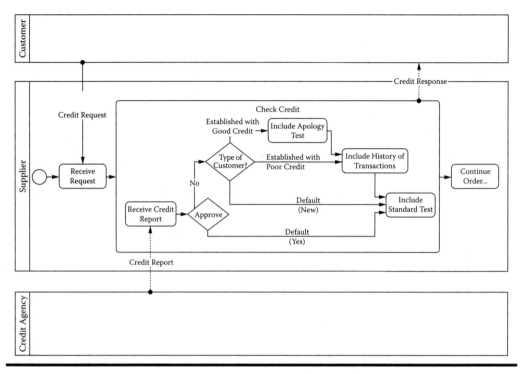

Figure 7.8   Message Flow connecting to boundary of Subprocess and Internal objects.

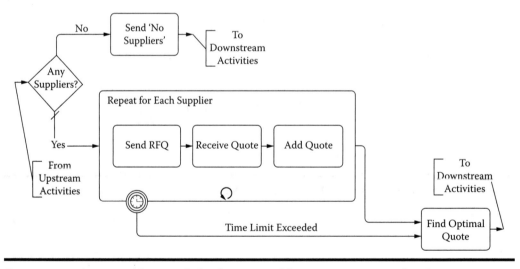

Figure 7.9   A Process with Expanded Subprocess without a Start Event and End Event.

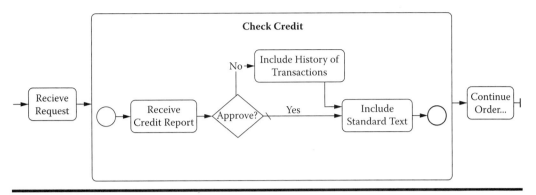

Figure 7.10   Example of Subprocess.

7.2.3 *Business Process Query Language*

The Business Process Query Language (BPQL) defines a standard interface to Business Process Management Systems (BPMSs). It allows system administrators to manage the BPMS and business analysts to query the instances of business processes it executes. BPQL is a management interface to a business process management infrastructure that includes a process execution facility (Process Server) and a process deployment facility (Process Repository). The BPQL interface to a Process Server enables business analysts to query the state and control the execution of process instances managed by the Process Server. This interface is based on the Simple Object Access Protocol (SOAP).

The BPQL interface to a Process Repository enables business analysts to manage the deployment of process models managed by the repository. This interface is based on the Distributed Authoring and Versioning Protocol (WebDAV). Process models managed by the Process Repository through the BPQL interface can be exposed as Universal Description, Discovery, and Integration (UDDI) services for process registration, advertising, and discovery purposes.

7.3 Unified Modeling Language™

The Unified Modeling Language™ (in Version 2.0 at press time) is OMG's most-used modeling specification. UML allows users to model the business process, application structure, application behavior, data structure, and architecture. Hence, UML can be utilized for the top three layers of the architecture, as seen in Figure 7.2. However, we discussed it here mostly in the context of the business process. UML, along with the Meta Object Facility (MOF™), also provides a foundation for OMG's Model-Driven Architecture, which unifies steps of development and integration from business modeling, through architectural and application modeling, to development, deployment, maintenance, and evolution. OMG is a not-for-profit computer industry specification consortium;

members define and maintain the various specifications discussed in this section (available for free). Software providers have built tools that conform to these specifications. Some of the key milestones of OMG accomplishments in the past few years include the following:

- 1989: OMG Established
- Standardization of Distributed Object Middleware
  - 1995: CORBA2
  - 2001: CORBA2.5
- Modeling Standardization
  - 1997: UML (Unified Modeling Language)
  - 1997: MOF
  - 1999: XMI
  - 2000: CWM
  - 2001: Application-specific UML Profiles (EDOC, EAI)
  - 2005: UML V2
- Architecture (Reference Model)
  - 1990: OMA (Object Management Architecture)
  - 2001: MDA (Model Driven Architecture)

UML is a visual language for specifying, constructing, and documenting the artifacts of systems. It is a general-purpose modeling language that can be used with all major object and component methods, and that can be applied to all application domains (e.g., health, finance, telecom, aerospace) and implementation platforms (e.g., J2EE, .NET). The OMG adopted the UML 1.1 specification in 1997; since then UML Revision Task Forces have produced several minor revisions. Under the stewardship of the OMG, UML has emerged as the software industry's dominant modeling language; it has been successfully applied to a wide range of domains, ranging from health and finance to aerospace to E-commerce. As should be expected, its extensive use has raised application and implementation issues by modelers and vendors. Consequently, in the early 2000s the OMG has sought to develop a new version, namely, UML 2.0. Version 2.0 started to be available in the 2004/5 timeframe and is now being rolled into other OMG constructs. With UML 2.0, both developers and tool vendors can use common semantics through integrated tools. UML 2.0 also defines compliance levels.

The observations that follow in this entire subsection are based on OMG information on UML and related capabilities [OMG200501].

7.3.1 Overview

UML helps firms specify, visualize, and document models of software systems, including their structure and design. (Firms can use UML for business modeling and modeling of other nonsoftware systems too.) Utilizing any one of the large number of UML-based tools on the market, firms can analyze their application's requirements and design a solution that meets these requirements while representing the results using UML's 12 standard diagram types.

Within UML one can model most types of applications, running on any type and combination of hardware, operating system, programming language, and network. UML's flexibility allows firms to model distributed applications that use any middleware on the market. Built upon the MOF metamodel, which defines *class* and *operation* as fundamental concepts, UML is a good fit for object-oriented (OO) languages and environments such as C++, Java, and C#; one can use it to model non-OO applications as well in, for example, Fortran, VB, or COBOL. *UML Profiles* (that is, subsets of UML tailored for specific purposes) help the developers model transactional, real-time, and fault-tolerant systems in a natural way. UML profiles are subsets of UML tailored to specific environments. For example, OMG has defined a profile for EDOC that is especially good at modeling collaborations, and a profile for Enterprise Application Integration (EAI), specialized for applications based on asynchronous communication [SEI200201].

The process of gathering and analyzing an application's requirements and incorporating them into a program design is a complex one. The industry currently supports many *methodologies* that define formal procedures specifying how to go about it. One characteristic of UML is that it is *methodology independent*. Regardless of the methodology that one uses to perform the analysis and design, architects can use UML to express the results; using XML Metadata Interchange (XMI), another OMG standard, one can transfer a UML model from one tool into a repository, or into another tool for refinement or the next step in the firm's chosen development process.

As noted, in the early 2000s OMG members started work on a major upgrade of UML (the most current version prior to the current UML v2.0 was UML v1.4). Four separate documents were defined as part of the upgrade: (1) UML Infrastructure, (2) UML Superstructure, (3) Object Constraint Language (OCL), and (4) UML Diagram Interchange. Adoption of the UML 2.0 Superstructure is complete (the Superstructure specification has been stable since it took its adopted form in 2004); adoption of the other three parts of UML 2.0 (also called UML2) was nearly complete at press time.

- The first specification, *UML 2.0: Infrastructure,* serves as the architectural foundation. It defines the foundational language constructs required for UML 2.0; specifically, it defines base classes that form the foundation not only for the UML 2.0 superstructure, but also for MOF 2.0.
- *UML 2.0: Superstructure* is the second of two complementary specifications. The superstructure defines the user-level constructs required for UML 2.0. It defines structure diagrams, behavior diagrams, interaction diagrams, and the elements that comprise them. The two complementary specifications constitute a complete specification for the UML 2.0 modeling language.
  (Note that as the two volumes cross-reference each other and the specifications are fully integrated, these two volumes could easily be combined into a single volume at a later time.)
- The *UML 2.0 OCL* allows setting of pre- and post-conditions, invariants, and other conditions.
- The *UML 2.0 Diagram Interchange* is a specification that extends the UML metamodel with a supplementary package for graph-oriented information, allowing models to be exchanged or stored/retrieved and then displayed as they were originally.

UML defines twelve types of diagrams, divided into three categories: four diagram types represent static application structure; five represent different aspects of dynamic behavior; and three represent ways one can organize and manage application modules. These are as follows:

- **Structural Diagrams** include the Class Diagram, Object Diagram, Component Diagram, and Deployment Diagram.

- **Behavior Diagrams** include the Use Case Diagram (used by some methodologies during requirements gathering); Sequence Diagram, Activity Diagram, Collaboration Diagram, and Statechart Diagram.
- **Model Management Diagrams** include Packages, Subsystems, and Models.

There are many UML tools on the market that allow architects to make practical use of the UML family of specifications. Some UML tools analyze existing source code and reverse-engineer it into a set of UML diagrams. UML has a focus on design rather than execution; however, some tools on the market execute UML models, typically in one of two ways:

1. Some tools execute a model interpretively in a way that lets the user confirm that it really does what the user wants, but without the scalability and speed that will be needed in the deployed application.
2. Other tools (typically designed to work only within a restricted application domain such as telecommunications or finance) generate program language code from UML, producing a bug-free, deployable application that runs quickly if the code generator incorporates best-practice scalable patterns for, e.g., transactional database operations or other common program tasks.

A number of tools on the market generate test and verification suites from UML models.

Middleware is important in software development, particularly in the context of enterprise application integration. According to observers, a few years ago the major problem a developer faced when starting a distributed programming project was finding a middleware with the needed functionality, that ran on the hardware and operating systems deployed at the firm. Today, faced with an array of middleware platforms, the developer has a number of different challenges: (1) selecting a specific middleware; (2) getting the middleware to work with the other platforms already deployed not only in his or her own shop, but also those of his customers and suppliers; and (3) interfacing or migrating to new environments or applications.

Keeping in mind the importance of middleware, it is worth noting that by design, UML is middleware-independent. A UML model can be either platform-independent or platform-specific, as one chooses. The Model-Driven Architecture development process, which UML supports, uses both of these forms. Every MDA standard or application is based, normatively, on a *Platform-Independent Model* (PIM); the PIM represents its business functionality and behavior very precisely but does not include technical aspects. From the PIM, MDA-enabled development tools follow OMG-standardized *mappings* to produce one or more *Platform-Specific Models* (PSMs), also in UML, one for each target platform that the developer chooses. (This conversion step is automated to a large degree: before the tool produces a PSM, the developer must annotate the base PIM to produce a more specific but still platform-independent PIM that includes details of desired semantics, and guides choices that the tool will have to make. Because of the similarities among middleware platforms of a given genre—component based or messaging based, for example—this guidance can be included in a PIM without rendering it platform specific. Still, developers have to fine-tune the produced PSMs to some extent, more in the early days of MDA but less and less as tools and algorithms advance.) The PSM contains the same information as an implementation, but in the form of a UML model instead of executable code. In the next step, the tool generates the running code from the PSM, along with other necessary files (including interface definition files if necessary, configuration files, makefiles, and other file types). After giving the developer an opportunity to hand-tune the generated code, the tool executes the makefiles to produce a deployable final application. MDA applications are *composable*: if one imports PIMs for modules, services, or other MDA applications into one's development tool, one can direct it to generate calls using whatever interfaces and protocols are required, even if these run cross-platform. MDA is revisited in Section 7.4.

At a macro level, developers my proceed as follows:

1. **Select a methodology:** A methodology formally defines the process that one uses to gather requirements, analyze them, and design an application that meets them in every way. There are many methodologies, each differing in some way or ways from the others. There are many reasons why one methodology may be better than another for one's particular project: for example, some are better suited for large enterprise applications, whereas others are built to design small embedded or safety-critical systems. Looking at other considerations, some methods better support large numbers of architects and designers working on the same project, whereas others work better when used by one person or a small group.

2. **Select a UML development tool:** Because most (although not all) UML-based tools implement a particular methodology, in some cases it might not be practical to select a tool and then try to use it with a methodology that it was not built for. (For other tool/methodology combinations, this might not be an issue, or might be easy to work around.) However, some methodologies have been implemented on multiple tools, so this is not strictly a one-choice environment.

7.3.2 Scratching the Surface of UML

This section provides a brief foray into UML. It is based on the *UML 2.0: Superstructure* [UML200501] and on the *UML 2.0: Infrastructure* [UMI200401]. The reader should consult these references for a complete coverage of the topic.

7.3.2.1 Conformance

As noted earlier, UML is a language with a broad scope that covers a diverse set of application domains. Not all of its modeling capabilities are necessarily useful in all domains or applications. This suggests that the language should be, and in fact is, structured modularly, with the ability to select only those parts of the language that are of direct interest. On the other hand, an excess of this type of flexibility increases the likelihood that two different UML tools will be supporting different subsets of the language, leading to interchange problems between them. Consequently, the definition of compliance for UML requires a balance to be drawn between modularity and ease of interchange. Experience has indicated that the ability to exchange models between tools is of paramount interest to a large community of users. For that reason, the UML specification defines a number of *compliance levels,* thereby increasing the likelihood that two or more compliant tools will support the same or compatible language subsets. However, in recognition of the need for flexibility in learning and using the language, UML also provides the concept of *language units*.

7.3.2.1.1 Language Units

The modeling concepts of UML are grouped into *language units*. A language unit consists of a collection of tightly coupled modeling concepts that provide users with the ability to represent aspects of the system under study according to a particular paradigm or formalism. For example, the State Machines' language unit enables modelers to specify discrete event-driven behavior using a variant of the well-known statecharts' formalism, whereas the Activities' language unit provides for modeling behavior based on a workflow-like paradigm. From the user's perspective, this partitioning of UML means that they need only be concerned with those parts of the language that they consider necessary for their models. If those needs change over time, further language units can be added to the user's repertoire as required. Hence, a UML user does not have to know the full language to use it effectively. In addition, most language units are partitioned into multiple increments, each adding more modeling capabilities to the previous ones. This fine-grained decomposition of UML serves to make the language easier to learn and use, but the individual segments within this structure do not represent separate compliance points. The latter strategy would lead to an excess of compliance points and result in the interoperability problems described earlier. Nevertheless, the groupings provided by language units and their increments do serve to simplify the definition of UML compliance.

7.3.2.1.2 Compliance Levels

The stratification of language units is used as the foundation for defining compliance in UML. The set of modeling concepts of UML is partitioned into horizontal layers of increasing capability called *compliance levels*. Compliance levels cut across the various language units, although some language units are only present in the upper levels. As their name suggests, each compliance level is a distinct compliance point. For ease of model interchange, there are just four compliance levels defined for the whole of UML:

- *Level 0 (L0)*: This compliance level is formally defined in the UML Infrastructure. It contains a single language unit that provides for modeling the kinds of class-based structures encountered in most popular object-oriented programming languages. As such, it provides an entry-level modeling capability. More importantly, it represents a low-cost common denominator that can serve as a basis for interoperability between different categories of modeling tools.
- *Level 1 (L1)*: This level adds new language units and extends the capabilities provided by Level 0. Specifically, it adds language units for use cases, interactions, structures, actions, and activities.
- *Level 2 (L2)*: This level extends the language units already provided in Level 1 and adds language units for deployment, state machine modeling, and profiles.
- *Level 3 (L3)*: This level represents the complete UML. It extends the language units provided by Level 2 and adds new language units for modeling information flows, templates, and model packaging.

The contents of language units are defined by corresponding top-tier packages of the UML metamodel, whereas the contents of their various increments are defined by second-tier packages within language unit packages. Therefore, the contents of a compliance level are defined by the set of metamodel packages that belong to that level.

As noted previously, compliance levels build on supporting compliance levels. The principal mechanism used in the UML specification for achieving this is *package merge*. Package merge allows modeling concepts defined at one level to be extended with new features. Most importantly, this is achieved in the context of the same namespace, which enables interchange of models at different levels of compliance. For this reason, all compliance levels are defined as extensions to a single core UML package that defines the common namespace shared by all the compliance levels (see Table 7.5 for an example).

Level 0 is defined by the top-level metamodel shown in Figure 7.11. In this model, UML is originally an empty package that simply merges in the contents of the Basic package from the UML Infrastructure. This package contains elementary concepts such as Class, Package, DataType, Operation, etc. (see the *UML 2.0 Infrastructure* specification for the complete list of contents).

At the next level (Level 1), the contents of the UML package, now including the packages merged into Level 0 and their contents, are extended with additional packages as shown in Figure 7.12. Note that each of the four packages shown in the figure merges in additional packages that are not shown in the diagram. They are defined in the corresponding package diagrams in this specification. Consequently, the set of language units that results from this model is more numerous than indicated by the top-level model in the diagram. The specific packages included at this level are listed in Table 7.6.

Table 7.5 Example Compliance Statement

	Compliance Summary		
Compliance level	*Abstract Syntax*	*Concrete Syntax*	*Diagram Interchange Option*
Level 0	YES	YES	YES
Level 1	YES	YES	NO
Level 2	YES	NO	NO

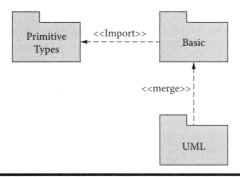

Figure 7.11 Level 0 package diagram.

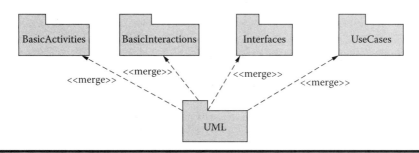

Figure 7.12 Level 1 top-level package merges.

Table 7.6 Metamodel Packages Added in Level 1

Language Unit	Metamodel Packages
Actions	Actions::BasicActions
Activities	Activities::FundamentalActivities
	Activities::BasicActivities
Classes	Classes::Kernel
	Classes:Dependencies
	Classes::Interfaces
General Behavior	CommonBehaviors::BasicBehaviors
Structures	CompositeStructure::InternalStructures
Interactions	Interactions::BasicInteractions
UseCases	UseCases

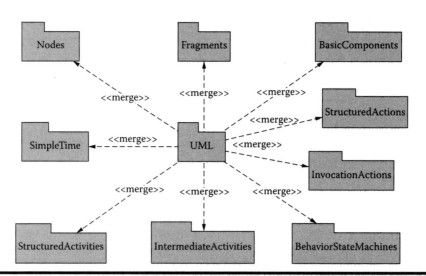

Figure 7.13 Level 2 top-level package merges.

Level 2 adds further language units and extensions to those provided by Level 1. Once again, the package UML now incorporates the complete Level 1 shown in Figure 7.13. The actual language units and packages included at this level of compliance are listed in Table 7.7.

Finally, Level 3, incorporating the full UML definition, is shown in Figure 7.14. Its contents are described in Table 7.8.

7.3.2.1.3 Meaning and Types of Compliance

Compliance to a given level entails full realization of all language units that are defined for that compliance level. This also implies full realization of all language units in all the levels below that level. "Full realization" for a language unit at a given level means supporting the complete set of

Table 7.7 Metamodel Packages Added in Level 2

Language Unit	Metamodel Packages
Actions	Actions::StructuredActions
	Actions::IntermediateActions
Activities	Activities::IntermediateActivities
	Activities::StructuredActivities
Components	Components::BasicComponents
Deployments	Deployments::Artifacts
	Deployments::Nodes
General Behavior	CommonBehaviors::Communications
	CommonBehaviors::SimpleTime
Interactions	Interactions::Fragments
Profiles	AuxilliaryConstructs::Profiles
Structures	CompositeStructures::InvocationActions
	CompositeStructures::Ports
	CompositeStructures::StructuredClasses
State Machines	StateMachines::BehaviorStateMachines

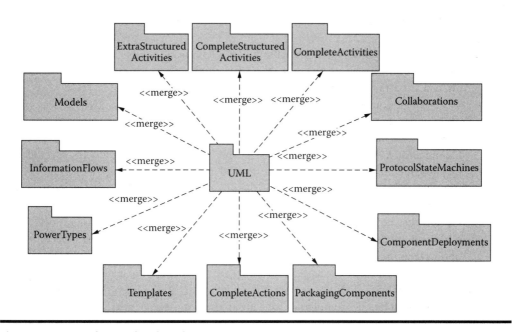

Figure 7.14 Level 3 top-level package merges.

modeling concepts defined for that language unit at that level. Thus, it is not meaningful to claim compliance with, say, Level 2, without also being compliant with the Level 0 and Level 1. A tool that is compliant at a given level must be able to import models from tools that are compliant with lower levels without loss of information.

Table 7.8   Metamodel Packages Added in Level 3

Language Unit	Metamodel Packages
Action	Actions::CompleteActions
Activities	Activities::CompleteActivities
	Activities::CompleteStructuredActivities
	Activities::ExtraStructuredActivities
Classes	Classes::AssociationClasses
	Classes::PowerTypes
Components	Components::PackagingComponents
Deployments	Deployments::ComponentDeployments
Information Flows	AuxilliaryConstructs::InformationFlows
Models	AuxilliaryConstructs::Models
State Machines	StateMachines::ProtocolStateMachines
Structures	CompositeStructures::Collaborations
	CompositeStructures::StructuredActivities
Templates	AuxilliaryConstructs::Templates

There are two types of compliance:

■ *Abstract syntax compliance*: For a given compliance level, this entails
  – Compliance with the metaclasses, their structural relationships, and any constraints defined as part of the merged UML metamodel for that compliance level
  – The ability to output models and to read in models based on the XMI schema corresponding to that compliance level
■ *Concrete syntax compliance*: For a given compliance level, this entails
  – Compliance with the notation defined in the "Notation" sections in this specification for those metamodel elements that are defined as part of the merged metamodel for that compliance level and, by implication, the diagram types in which those elements may appear.
  – Optionally, the ability to output diagrams and to read in diagrams based on the XMI schema defined by the Diagram Interchange specification for notation at that level. This option requires abstract syntax and concrete syntax compliance.

Concrete syntax compliance does not require compliance with any presentation options that are defined as part of the notation. Compliance for a given level can be expressed as follows:

■ Abstract syntax compliance
■ Concrete syntax compliance
■ Abstract syntax with concrete syntax compliance
■ Abstract syntax with concrete syntax and diagram interchange compliance

In the case of tools that generate program code from models or those that are capable of executing models, it is also useful to understand the level of support for the runtime semantics described in the various "Semantics" subsections of the specification. However, the presence of numerous variation points in these semantics (and the fact that they are defined informally using natural language) make it impractical to define this as a formal compliance type, because the number of possible combinations is very large. A similar situation exists with presentation options, because different implementers may make different choices on which ones to support. Finally, it is recognized that some implementers and profile designers may want to support only a subset of features from levels that are above their formal compliance level. (Note, however, that they can only claim compliance with the level that they fully support, even if they implement significant parts of the capabilities of higher levels.) Given this potential variability, it is useful to be able to specify clearly and efficiently which capabilities are supported by a given implementation. To this end, in addition to a formal statement of compliance, implementers and profile designers may also provide informal *feature support statements*. These statements identify support for additional features in terms of language units or individual metamodel packages, as well as for less precisely defined dimensions such as presentation options and semantic variation points.

7.3.2.2 Runtime Semantics of UML

It is useful to have a high-level view of the *runtime semantics* of UML. The term *runtime* is used to refer to the execution environment. Runtime semantics, therefore, are specified as a mapping of modeling concepts into corresponding program execution phenomena (there are other semantics relevant to UML specifications, such as the *repository semantics*, that is, how a UML model behaves in a model repository; however, those semantics are really part of the definition of the MOF).

7.3.2.2.1 The Basic Premises

There are two fundamental premises regarding the nature of UML semantics. The first is the assumption that all behavior in a modeled system is ultimately caused by actions executed by so-called active objects. This includes behaviors, which are objects in UML 2.0, that can be active and coordinate other behaviors. The second is that UML behavioral semantics only deal with *event-driven*, or discrete, behaviors. However, UML does not specify the amount of time between events, which can be as small as needed by the application, for example, when simulating continuous behaviors.

7.3.2.2.2 The Semantics Architecture

Figure 7.14 identifies the key semantic areas covered by the current standard and how they relate to one another. The items in the upper layers depend on the items in the lower layers, but not the other way around. (Note that the structure of metamodel package dependencies is somewhat similar to the dependency structure indicated here; however, they are not the same and should be distinguished—this is because package dependencies specify repository dependencies, not necessarily runtime dependencies.)

At the highest level of abstraction, it is possible to distinguish three distinct composite layers of semantic definitions. The foundational layer is structural. This reflects the premise that there is no disembodied behavior in UML—all behavior is the consequence of the actions of structural entities. The next layer is behavioral and provides the foundation for the semantic description of all the higher-level behavioral formalisms (the term *behavioral formalism* refers to a formalized framework for describing behavior, such as state machines, Petri nets, data flow graphs, etc.). This layer, represented by the shaded box in Figure 7.15, is the behavioral semantic base and consists of

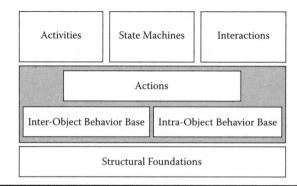

Figure 7.15   A schematic of the UML semantic areas and their dependencies.

three separate subareas arranged into two sublayers. The bottom sublayer consists of the *interobject behavior base*, which deals with how structural entities communicate with one another, and the *intraobject behavior base*, which addresses the behavior occurring within structural entities. The *actions* sublayer is placed on top of these two. It defines the semantics of individual actions. Actions are the fundamental units of behavior in UML and are used to define fine-grained behaviors. Their resolution and expressive power are comparable to the executable instructions in traditional programming languages. Actions in this sublayer are available to any of the higher-level formalisms to be used for describing detailed behaviors. The topmost layer in the semantics hierarchy defines the semantics of the higher-level behavioral formalisms of UML: *activities, state machines,* and *interactions.* Other behavioral formalisms may be added to this layer in the future.

7.3.2.2.3 The Basic Causality Model

The "causality model" is a specification of how things happen at runtime. It is briefly summarized here using the example depicted in the communication diagram in Figure 7.16. The example shows two independent, and possibly concurrent, threads of causally chained interactions. The first, identified by the thread prefix "A," consists of a sequence of events that commences with activeObject-1 sending signal s1 to activeObject-2. In turn, activeObject-2 responds by invoking operation op1( ) on passiveObject-1 after which it sends signal s2 to activeObject-3. The second thread, distinguished by the thread prefix "B," starts with activeObject-4 invoking operation op2( ) on passiveObject-1. The latter responds by executing the method that realizes this operation, in which it sends signal s3 to activeObject-2. The causality model is quite straightforward: Objects respond to messages that are generated by objects executing communication actions. When these messages arrive, the receiving objects eventually respond by executing the behavior that is matched to that message. The dispatching method by which a particular behavior is associated with a given message depends on the higher-level formalism used and is not defined in the UML specification (i.e., it is a semantic variation point).

The causality model also subsumes behaviors invoking one another and passing information to one another through arguments to parameters of the invoked behavior, as enabled by CallBehaviorAction. This purely "procedural," or "process," model can be used by itself or in conjunction with the object-oriented model of the previous example.

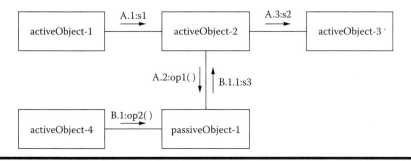

Figure 7.16 Example of threads of causally chained interactions.

7.3.2.3 The UML Metamodel

7.3.2.3.1 Models and What They Model

A model contains three major categories of elements: classifiers, events, and behaviors. Each major category models individuals in an incarnation of the system being modeled. A classifier describes a set of objects; an object is an individual thing with a state and relationships to other objects. An event describes a set of possible occurrences; an occurrence is something that happens that has some consequence within the system. A behavior describes a set of possible executions; an execution is the performance of an algorithm according to a set of rules. Models do not contain objects, occurrences, and executions, because they are the subject of models, not their content. Classes, events, and behaviors model sets of objects, occurrences, and executions with similar properties. Value specifications, occurrence specifications, and execution specifications model individual objects, occurrences, and executions within a particular context. The distinction between objects and models of objects, for example, may appear subtle, but it is important. Objects (and occurrences and executions) are the domain of a model and, as such, are always complete, precise, and concrete. Models of objects (such as value specifications) can be incomplete, imprecise, and abstract according to their purpose in the model.

7.3.2.3.2 Semantic Levels and Naming

A large number of UML metaclasses can be arranged into four levels with metasemantic relationships among the metaclasses in the different levels that transcend different semantic categories (e.g., classifiers, events, and behaviors). The specification attempts to provide a consistent naming pattern across the various categories to place elements into levels and emphasize metarelationships among related elements in different levels. The following four levels are important:

Type level—Represents generic types of entities in models, such as classes, states, activities, events, etc. These are the most common constituents of models because models are primarily about making generic specifications.

Instance level—These are the things that models represent at runtime. They do not appear in models directly (except very occasionally as detailed examples), but they are necessary to explain the semantics of what models mean. These classes do not appear at all in the UML2 metamodel or in UML models, but they underlie the meaning of models.

Value specifications—A realization of UML2, compared to UML, is that values can be specified at various levels of precision. The specification of a value is not necessarily an instance; it might be a large set of possible instances consistent with certain conditions. What appears in models is usually not instances (individual values) but specifications of values that may or may not be limited to a single value. In any case, models contain specifications of values, not values themselves, which are runtime entities.

Individual appearances of a type within a context—These are roles within a generic, reusable context. When their context is instantiated, they are also bound to contained instances, but as model elements they are reusable structural parts of their context; they are not instances themselves. A realization of UML2 was that the things called instances in UML1 were mostly roles: they map to instances in an instance of their container, but they are model elements, not instances, because they are generic and can be used many times to generate many different instances.

The specification establishes the following naming patterns:

Types: Instances: Values: Uses
Classifier, Class: Instance, Object : InstanceSpecification : Part, Role, Attribute, XXXUse (e.g., CollaborationUse)
Event: Occurrence: OccurrenceSpecification: various (e.g., Trigger)
Behavior: Execution: ExecutionSpecification: various (e.g., ActivityNode, State), XXXUse (e.g., InteractionUse)

The appearances category has too wide a variety of elements to reduce to a single pattern, although the form XXXUse is suggested for simple cases in which an appearance of an element is contained in a definition of the same kind of element. In particular, the word *event* has been used inconsistently in the past to mean both type and instance. The word *event* now means the type, and the word *occurrence* means the instance. When necessary, the phrases *event type* (for event) and *event occurrence* (for occurrence) may be used. Note that this is consistent with the frequent English usage *an event occurs* = the occurrence of an event of a given type; so, to describe a runtime situation, one could say "event X occurs" or "an occurrence of event X," depending on which form is more convenient in a sentence. It is redundant and incorrect to say "an event occurrence occurs."

7.3.2.4 UML Infrastructure Specification

The observations that follow in this entire subsection are based on OMG information [UMI200401]

7.3.2.4.1 Language Architecture

The UML specification is defined using a metamodeling approach (i.e., a metamodel is used to specify the model that comprises UML) that adapts formal specification techniques. Although this approach lacks some of the rigor of a formal specification method, it offers the advantages of being more intuitive and pragmatic for most implementers and practitioners.

7.3.2.4.1.1 Design Principles

The UML metamodel has been architected with the following design principles in mind:

■ Modularity—This principle of strong cohesion and loose coupling is applied to group constructs into packages and organize features into metaclasses.

■ Layering—Layering is applied in two ways to the UML metamodel. First, the package structure is layered to separate the metalanguage core constructs from the higher-level constructs that use them. Second, a four-layer metamodel architectural pattern is consistently applied to separate concerns (especially regarding instantiation) across layers of abstraction. These layers are referred to as M3, M2, M1, and M0.

■ Partitioning—Partitioning is used to organize conceptual areas within the same layer. In the case of the InfrastructureLibrary, fine-grained partitioning is used to provide the flexibility required by current and future metamodeling standards. In the case of the UML metamodel, the partitioning is coarser-grained to increase the cohesion within packages and relaxing the coupling across packages.

■ Extensibility—The UML can be extended in two ways:
  1. A new dialect of UML can be defined by using Profiles to customize the language for particular platforms (e.g., J2EE/EJB, .NET/COM+) and domains (e.g., finance, telecommunications, aerospace).
  2. A new language related to UML can be specified by reusing part of the InfrastructureLibrary package and augmenting with appropriate metaclasses and metarelationships. The former case defines a new dialect of UML, whereas the latter case defines a new member of the UML family of languages.

■ Reuse—A fine-grained, flexible metamodel library is provided that is reused to define the UML metamodel, as well as other architecturally related metamodels, such as the MOF and the Common Warehouse Model (CWM). (CWM is a metamodel that enables data mining across database boundaries; it is discussed in Section 7.4.2.4.)

7.3.2.4.1.2 Infrastructure Architecture

The Infrastructure of the UML is defined by the package *InfrastructureLibrary*, which satisfies the following design requirements:

■ Define a metalanguage core that can be reused to define a variety of metamodels, including UML, MOF, and CWM.

■ Architecturally align UML, MOF, and XMI so that model interchange is fully supported.

■ Allow customization of UML through Profiles and creation of new languages (family of languages) based on the same metalanguage core as UML.

As shown in Figure 7.17, Infrastructure is represented by the package *InfrastructureLibrary*, which consists of the packages *Core* and *Profiles*, the latter defining the mechanisms that are used to customize metamodels and the former containing core concepts used when metamodeling.

7.3.2.4.1.2.1 The *Core* Package

In its first capacity, the *Core* package is a complete metamodel specifically designed for high reusability, where other metamodels at the same metalevel either import or specialize its specified metaclasses. This is illustrated in Figure 7.18, where it is shown how UML, CWM, and MOF each depends on

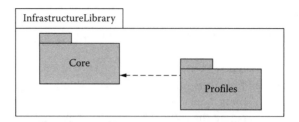

Figure 7.17 The *InfrastructureLibrary* packages.

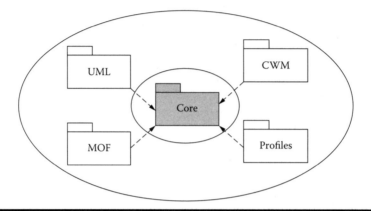

Figure 7.18 The role of the common *Core*.

a *common* core. Because these metamodels are at the core of MDA, the common core may also be considered the architectural kernel of MDA. The intent is for UML and other MDA metamodels to reuse all or parts of the *Core* package, which allows other metamodels to benefit from the abstract syntax and semantics that have already been defined.

To facilitate reuse, the *Core* package is subdivided into a number of packages: *PrimitiveTypes*, *Abstractions*, *Basic*, and *Constructs*, as shown in Figure 7.19. Some of these packages are then further divided into even more fine-grained packages to make it possible to pick and choose the relevant parts when defining a new metamodel. Note, however, that choosing a specific package also implies choosing the dependent packages. The package *PrimitiveTypes* simply contains a few predefined types that are commonly used when metamodeling, and is designed specifically with the needs of UML and MOF in mind. Other metamodels may need other or overlapping sets of primitive types. There are minor differences in the design rationale for the other two packages. The package *Abstractions* mostly contains abstract metaclasses that are intended to be further specialized or that are expected to be commonly reused by many metamodels. Very few assumptions are made about the metamodels that may want to reuse this package; for this reason, the package *Abstractions* is also subdivided into several smaller packages. The package *Constructs*, on the other hand, mostly contains concrete metaclasses that lend themselves primarily to object-oriented modeling; this package, in particular, is reused by both MOF and UML, and represents a significant part of the work that has gone into aligning the two metamodels. The package *Basic* represents a few constructs that are used as the basis for the produced XMI for UML, MOF, and other metamodels based on the *InfrastructureLibrary*.

In its second capacity, the *Core* package is used to define the modeling constructs used to create metamodels. This is done through instantiation of metaclasses in the *InfrastructureLi-*

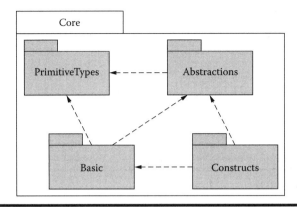

Figure 7.19   The *Core* packages.

brary. Whereas instantiation of metaclasses is carried out through MOF, the *InfrastructureLibrary* defines the actual metaclasses that are used to instantiate the elements of UML, MOF, CWM and, indeed, the elements of the *InfrastructureLibrary* itself. In this respect, the *InfrastructureLibrary* is said to be self-describing, or *reflective*.

7.3.2.4.1.2.2 The *Profiles* Package

As was depicted in Figure 7.17, the *Profiles* package depends on the *Core* package, and defines the mechanisms used to tailor existing metamodels toward specific platforms such as C++, Common Object Request Broker Architecture (CORBA), or Enterprise JavaBeans (EJBs), or domains, such as real-time, business objects, or software process modeling. The primary target for profiles is UML, but it is possible to use profiles together with any metamodel that is based on (i.e., instantiated from) the common core. A profile must be based on a metamodel such as the UML that it extends, and is not very useful stand-alone. Profiles have been aligned with the extension mechanism offered by MOF, but provide a more lightweight approach with restrictions that are enforced to ensure that the implementation and usage of profiles are straightforward and more easily supported by tool vendors.

7.3.2.4.1.2.3 Architectural Alignment between UML and MOF

One of the goals of the Infrastructure Specification has been to architecturally align UML and MOF. The first approach to accomplish this has been to define the common core, which is realized as the package *Core*, in such a way that the model elements are shared between UML and MOF. The second approach has been to make sure that UML is defined as a model that is based on MOF used as a metamodel, as illustrated in Figure 7.20. Note that MOF is used as the metamodel for not only UML, but also for other languages such as CWM.

Every model element of UML is an instance of exactly one model element in MOF. Note that the *InfrastructureLibrary* is used at both the M2 and M3 metalevels, because it is being reused by UML and MOF, respectively, as was shown in Figure 7.18. In the case of MOF, the metaclasses of the *InfrastructureLibrary* are used as is, whereas in the case of UML these model elements are given additional properties. The reason for these differences is that the requirements when metamodeling differ slightly from the requirements when modeling applications of a very diverse nature.

MOF defines, for example, how UML models are interchanged between tools using XMI. MOF also defines reflective interfaces (MOF::Reflection) for introspection that work for MOF itself, but also for CWM, UML, and any other metamodel that is an instance of MOF. It further defines an

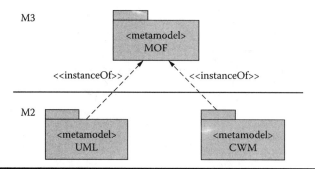

Figure 7.20 UML and MOF are at different metalevels.

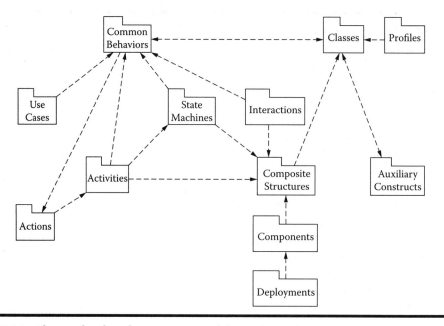

Figure 7.21 The top-level package structure of the UML 2.0 Superstructure.

extension mechanism that can be used to extend metamodels as an alternative to, or in conjunction with, profiles. In fact, profiles are defined to be a subset of the MOF extension mechanism.

7.3.2.4.1.2.4 Superstructure Architecture

The UML Superstructure metamodel is specified by the *UML* package, which is divided into a number of packages that deal with structural and behavioral modeling, as shown in Figure 7.21. Each of these areas is described in a separate chapter of the *UML 2.0: Superstructure* specification. Note that some packages are dependent on one another in circular dependencies. This is because the dependencies between the top-level packages show a summary of all relationships between their subpackages; there are no circular dependencies between subpackages of those packages.

7.3.2.4.1.2.5 Reusing Infrastructure

One of the primary uses of the UML 2.0 Infrastructure specification is that it should be reused when creating other metamodels. The UML metamodel reuses the *InfrastructureLibrary* in two different ways:

- All of the UML metamodel is instantiated from meta-metaclasses that are defined in the *InfrastructureLibrary*.
- The UML metamodel imports and specializes all metaclasses in the *InfrastructureLibrary*.

As was discussed earlier, it is possible for a model to be used as a metamodel, and here we make use of this fact. The *InfrastructureLibrary* is in one capacity used as a meta-metamodel and in the other capacity as a metamodel, and is thus reused in two dimensions.

7.3.2.4.1.2.6 The *Kernel* Package

The *InfrastructureLibrary* is primarily reused in the *Kernel* package of *Classes* in *UML 2.0: Superstructure*; this is done by bringing together the different packages of the Infrastructure using package merge. The *Kernel* package is at the very heart of UML, and the metaclasses of every other package are directly or indirectly dependent on it. The *Kernel* package is very similar to the *Constructs* package of the *InfrastructureLibrary*, but adds more capabilities to the modeling constructs that were not necessary to include for purposes of reuse or alignment with MOF.

Because the Infrastructure has been designed for reuse, there are metaclasses—particularly in *Abstractions*—that are partially defined in several different packages. These different aspects are for the most part brought together into a single metaclass already in *Constructs*, but in some cases this is done only in *Kernel*. In general, if metaclasses with the same name occurs in multiple packages, they are meant to represent the same metaclass, and each package where it is defined (specialized) represents a specific factorization. This same pattern of partial definitions also occurs in Superstructure, where some aspects of, for example, the metaclass *Class* are factored out into separate packages to form compliance points (see the following text).

7.3.2.4.1.2.7 Metamodel Layering

The architecture that is centered around the *Core* package is a complementary view of the four-layer metamodel hierarchy on which the UML metamodel has traditionally been based. When dealing with metalayers to define languages, there are generally three layers that always have to be taken into account:

- The language specification, or the metamodel
- The user specification, or the model
- Objects of the model

This structure can be applied recursively many times so that we get a possibly infinite number of metalayers; what is a metamodel in one case can be a model in another case, and this is what happens with UML and MOF. UML is a language specification (metamodel) from which users can define their own models. Similarly, MOF is also a language specification (metamodel) from which users can define their own models. From the perspective of MOF, however, UML is viewed as a user (i.e., the members of the OMG that have developed the language) specification that is based on MOF as a language specification. In the four-layer metamodel hierarchy, MOF is commonly referred to as a meta-metamodel, even though strictly speaking it is a metamodel.

7.3.2.4.1.2.8 The Four-Layer Metamodel Hierarchy

The meta-metamodeling layer forms the foundation of the metamodeling hierarchy. The primary responsibility of this layer is to define the language for specifying a metamodel. The layer is often referred to as M3, and MOF is an example of a meta-metamodel. A meta-metamodel is typically more compact than the metamodel that it describes, and often defines several metamodels. It is generally desirable that related metamodels and meta-metamodels share common design philosophies and constructs. However, each layer can be viewed independently of other layers, and needs to maintain its own design integrity.

A metamodel is an instance of a meta-metamodel, meaning that every element of the metamodel is an instance of an element in the meta-metamodel. The primary responsibility of the metamodel layer is to define a language for specifying models. The layer is often referred to as M2; UML and the OMG CWM are examples of metamodels. Metamodels are typically more elaborate than the meta-metamodels that describe them, especially when they define dynamic semantics. The UML metamodel is an instance of the MOF (in effect, each UML metaclass is an instance of an element in *InfrastructureLibrary*).

A model is an instance of a metamodel. The primary responsibility of the model layer is to define languages that describe semantic domains, i.e., to allow users to model a wide variety of different problem domains, such as software, business processes, and requirements. The things that are being modeled reside outside the metamodel hierarchy. This layer is often referred to as M1. A user model is an instance of the UML metamodel. Note that the user model contains both model elements and snapshots (illustrations) of instances of these model elements. The metamodel hierarchy bottoms out at M0, which contains the runtime instances of model elements defined in a model. The snapshots that are modeled at M1 are constrained versions of the M0 runtime instances.

When dealing with more than three metalayers, it is usually the case that the ones above M2 gradually get smaller and more compact the higher up they are in the hierarchy. In the case of MOF, which is at M3, it consequently only shares some of the metaclasses that are defined in UML. A specific characteristic about metamodeling is the ability to define languages as being reflective, i.e., languages that can be used to define themselves. The *InfrastructureLibrary* is an example of this, because it contains all the metaclasses required to define itself. When a language is reflective, there is no need to define another language to specify its semantics. MOF is reflective because it is based on the *InfrastructureLibrary*, and there is thus no need to have additional metalayers above MOF.

7.3.2.4.1.2.9 Metamodeling

When metamodeling, one primarily distinguishes between metamodels and models. As already stated, a model that is instantiated from a metamodel can in turn be used as a metamodel of another model in a recursive manner. A model typically contains model elements. These are created by instantiating model elements from a metamodel, i.e., metamodel elements.

The typical role of a metamodel is to define the semantics for how model elements in a model gets instantiated. As an example, consider Figure 7.22, where the metaclasses Association and Class are

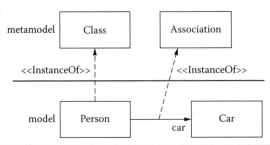

Figure 7.22   An example of metamodeling; note that not all InstanceOf relationships are shown.

both defined as part of the UML metamodel. These are instantiated in a user model in such a way that the classes Person and Car are both instances of the metaclass Class, and the association Person. car between the classes is an instance of the metaclass Association. The semantics of UML defines what happens when the user-defined model elements are instantiated at M0, and we get an instance of Person, an instance of Car, and a link (i.e., an instance of the association) between them.

The instances—sometimes referred to as *runtime instances*—that are created at M0 from, for example, Person should not be confused with instances of the metaclass InstanceSpecification that are also defined as part of the UML metamodel. An instance of an InstanceSpecification is defined in a model at the same level as the model elements that it illustrates, as is depicted in Figure 7.23, where the instance specification Mike is an illustration (or a snapshot) of an instance of class Person.

7.3.2.4.1.2.10 An Example of the Four-Level Metamodel Hierarchy

An illustration of how these metalayers relate to one another is shown in Figure 7.24. It should be noted that we are by no means restricted to only these four metalayers, and it would be possible to

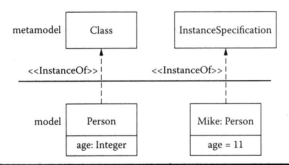

Figure 7.23   Giving an illustration of a class using an instance specification.

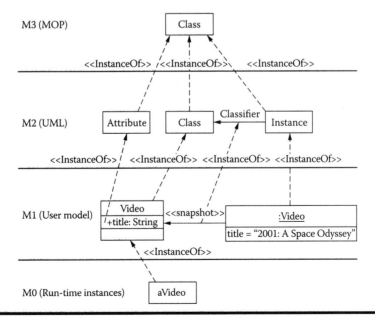

Figure 7.24   An example of the four-layer metamodel hierarchy.

define additional ones. As is shown, the metalayers are usually numbered from M0 and upward, depending on how many metalayers are used. In this particular case, the numbering goes up to M3, which corresponds to MOF.

7.3.2.4.2 Language Formalism

The UML specification is defined by using a metamodeling approach that adapts formal specification techniques. The formal specification techniques are used to increase the precision and correctness of the specification. This subsection explains the specification techniques used to define UML.

The following are the goals of the specification techniques used to define UML:

- Correctness—The specification techniques should improve the correctness of the metamodel by helping to validate it. For example, the well-formedness rules should help validate the abstract syntax and help identify errors.
- Precision—The specification techniques should increase the precision of both the syntax and semantics. The precision should be sufficient so that there is no syntactic nor semantic ambiguity for either implementers or users.
- Conciseness—The specification techniques should be parsimonious, so that the precise syntax and semantics are defined without superfluous detail.
- Consistency—The specification techniques should complement the metamodeling approach by adding essential detail in a consistent manner.
- Understandability—While increasing the precision and conciseness, the specification techniques should also improve the readability of the specification. For this reason a less than strict formalism is applied, because a strict formalism requires formal techniques.

The specification technique used describes the metamodel in three views using both text and graphic presentations. It is important to note that the current description is not a completely formal specification of the language, because to do so would have added significant complexity without clear benefit. The structure of the language is nevertheless given a precise specification, which is required for tool interoperability. The detailed semantics are described using natural language, although in a precise way so they can easily be understood. Currently, the semantics are not considered essential for the development of tools; however, this will probably change in the future.

7.3.2.4.2.1 Levels of Formalism

A common technique for specification of languages is to first define the syntax of the language and then to describe its static and dynamic semantics. The syntax defines what constructs exist in the language and how the constructs are built up in terms of other constructs. Sometimes, especially if the language has a graphic syntax, it is important to define the syntax in a notation-independent way (i.e., to define the abstract syntax of the language). The concrete syntax is then defined by mapping the notation onto the abstract syntax.

The static semantics of a language define how an instance of a construct should be connected to other instances to be meaningful, and the dynamic semantics define the meaning of a well-formed construct. The meaning of a description written in the language is defined only if the description is well formed (i.e., if it fulfills the rules defined in the static semantics).

The specification uses a combination of languages—a subset of UML, an object constraint language, and precise natural language to describe the abstract syntax and semantics of the full UML. The description is self-contained; no other sources of information are needed to read the document. Although this is a metacircular description, understanding this document is practical because only a small subset of UML constructs are needed to describe its semantics.

In constructing the UML metamodel, different techniques have been used to specify language constructs, using some of the capabilities of UML. The main language constructs are reified into metaclasses in the metamodel. Other constructs, in essence being variants of other ones, are defined as stereotypes of metaclasses in the metamodel. This mechanism allows the semantics of the variant construct to be significantly different from the base metaclass. Another more "lightweight" way of defining variants is to use meta-attributes. As an example, the aggregation construct is specified by an attribute of the metaclass *AssociationEnd*, which is used to indicate if an association is an ordinary aggregate, a composite aggregate, or a common association.

Interested readers are referred to [UML200501] and [UMI200401] for additional information on UML.

7.4 Model-Driven Architecture

7.4.1 MDA Background

The OMG Model-Driven Architecture™ (MDA) addresses the life cycle that spans design, deployment, integration, and management of applications. The OMG's MDA initiative is an evolving conceptual architecture for a set of industrywide technology specifications that support a model-driven approach to software development. Although MDA is not itself a technology specification, it represents an approach and a plan to achieve a cohesive set of model-driven technology specifications. MDA aims at unifying business modeling and supporting technology (from legacy systems to the newly introduced middleware platforms) into an industry-standard architecture [SEI200201]. Covering both the modeling and development arena, MDA is a comprehensive IT architecture that unifies business modeling and implementation into a synergistic environment (such environment is seen by proponents as being able to maximize IT ROI and give businesses that employ it a competitive advantage.) Figure 7.25 depicts the MDA environment graphically. The summary that follows is based in large part on OMG's information; additional details can be obtained by direct reference to these materials [MDA200301].

Before MDA became available, models and programming code were developed separately by different groups of people. Programmers regarded the models as guidelines or rough plans rather than firm requirements. Compared with development without modeling, this approach typically can be more expensive, and it can take longer to produce a final application. Here, a firm may find limited benefit from its modeling effort. MDA addresses this issue by codifying and standardizing the steps that take a model through development into implementation. MDA-based tools produce applications that meet the business requirements along with related nonfunctional requirements (e.g., scalability, reliability, security) that have been built into models by domain experts and IT architects. Models become the prime development artifact in this environment, not only defining and recording business requirements but also serving as the basis for development, maintenance, and evolution [SEI200201]. Typically, if a developer is building a Web Services application, for example, the developer is forced to assemble a number of legacy functions on legacy middleware to

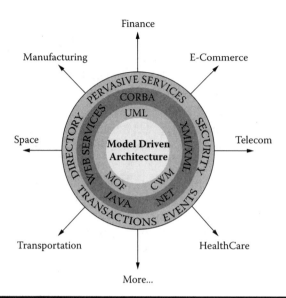

Finance

Manufacturing   E-Commerce

Space   Telecom

Transportation   HealthCare

More...

Figure 7.25   OMG Model-Driven Architecture.

a new front end; MDA is ideally suited to designing and building this kind of application. *UML 2.0: Infrastructure* supports MDA. MDA is now supported by many prominent software vendors.

OMG members voted to establish the MDA as the base architecture in late 2001. Software development in the MDA starts with a PIM of an application's business functionality and behavior, constructed using a modeling language based on OMG's MOF. The MDA approach is a way of developing applications and writing specifications, based on a PIM of the application or specification's business functionality and behavior. A complete MDA specification consists of a definitive platform-independent base model, plus one or more PSMs and sets of interface definitions, each describing how the base model is implemented on a different middleware platform. A complete MDA application consists of a definitive PIM, plus one or more PSMs and complete implementations, one on each platform that the application developer decides to support. MDA was defined and is nurtured by the OMG membership, which includes a diverse cross section of computer vendors, software suppliers, and many end users. MDA is defined by the *MDA Guide*, Version 1.0.1. OMG members were expecting to replace this interim version with an update, based on the Foundation Model also just mentioned, at the time of this writing.

MDA (as its name declares) is an architecture that works above the level of a middleware platform, including, for example, .NET and Web Services. A middleware platform is incorporated into the MDA as a platform-specific profile; OMG members may (in due course) define platform-specific profiles for .NET and Web Services.

MDA is both an OMG standard and a generic way to develop software. The OMG standard incorporates, among others, UML, MOF, the XMI, and the CWM. The two most important elements are UML and MOF, which helps to translate the models into specific code (XMI deals with sharing models and other development artifacts over the Web.) Some see MDA as helping UML to become more "real": prior to MDA one could use UML to develop graphs to help communicate concepts with stakeholders; however, the hard work of coding was a stand-alone effort. MDA makes modeling concrete, allowing UML to become, once again, a programming language. Among its other features, UML 2.0 improves the support for component-based software [AMB200301].

The MDA-based approach affords a number of benefits. Some benefits are business-oriented (for example, requirements built into the model always appear in the final implementation); others are technical (MDA-based applications are interoperable, portable, and middleware-platform-independent) [SEI200201]. MDA benefits include the following:

- In an MDA development project, attention focuses first on the application's business functionality and behavior, allowing stakeholders' investment to concentrate on the aspects that critically affect core business processes. Technical aspects, also critical but secondary to business functions, are well handled by automated or semiautomated development tools.
- An architecture based on the MDA is able to evolve over time; also, such an architecture makes it relatively easy to integrate applications and facilities across middleware boundaries.
- Domain facilities defined in the MDA provide interoperability: the application is available on a domain's preferred platform, and on multiple platforms whenever there is a need.

Additional benefits of MDAs include the following [SEI200201]:

- MDA-enabled tools follow OMG-standardized pathways to automate the transformation from the designers' business model into a firm-specific implementation, producing new applications faster, better, and cheaper.
- The MDA process ensures not only that the business requirements built into the design end up in the final implementation, but also that nonbusiness functional requirements carry through as well.
- Code generated by MDA-enabled development tools is derived from libraries based on patterns designed by the industry's best developers.
- MDA applications interoperate. The MDA was designed from the start for implementation in multiple middleware platforms, and codes cross-platform invocations when needed, not only within a given application, but also from one to another regardless of the target platform assigned to each.
- MDA applications are portable. As they are based on technology-independent business models, they can be generated on any middleware platform.
- MDA applications may well be future-proof. When new platforms are introduced (as they must over the next decades as networking continues to mature and computers become smaller, more specialized, and more ubiquitous), OMG is expected to add mappings for them, and tool vendors will implement them in their offerings. Using these new mappings, existing MDA-based applications can be made either to interoperate with others, or can be entirely reimplemented on the new platform.
- The MDA supports enterprise application integration. The entire enterprise's suite of applications can be thought as being a library of UML models. The developer selects the ones that need to work together, incorporates them into the MDA tool, and draws lines denoting the interoperability pathways. An MDA application does not have to make all of its invocations using the middleware of its PSM: the code database of an MDA tool includes invocation formats for every supported middleware platform. It follows that developers can pull models of existing applications and services from libraries into the project's environment as they construct new PIMs, and set up cross-platform invocations by simply drawing the connections in their new model. It is likely that some of these existing applications will not be on the same platform as the new PSM. Taking their cue from the actual middleware platform

of these existing applications, MDA tools will generate cross-platform invocations where needed. Legacy application based on a UML model and a supported middleware platform can be included in a company's circle of MDA interoperability by simply importing its model into MDA tools as PIMs for new applications are built.

To benefit an industry, a standard must be used by a critical mass of companies. Technology-specific standards will encounter challenges getting established where platform incompatibility prevents the achievement of this critical mass. Sometimes, the problem is more deep-rooted than this: in some industries, architecturally excellent standards were adopted in the formal sense but failed to win adherence because they were written for a platform that few companies were willing to support. MDA removes these roadblocks. Under MDA, the functional description of every standard is technology-independent, and the architecture is capable of producing interoperating implementations on multiple platforms. This allows an industry to define the business functionality and behavior of its standards as a PIM, and then produce PSMs and implementations on whatever platforms the participants require. In addition, technology-based standards become obsolete as their base platform ages. This is not a problem for MDA-based specifications: because they are based on platform-independent PIMs and can be made to interoperate with new platforms, or even reimplemented on them, through the MDA development process, MDA-based applications and specifications are truly "future-proof."

MDA development focuses first on the functionality and behavior of a distributed application or system, undistorted by idiosyncrasies of the technology platform or platforms on which it will be implemented. In this way, MDA separates implementation details from business functions. Thus, it is not necessary to repeat the process of defining an application or system's functionality and behavior each time a new technology (Web Services, for example) comes along. Other architectures are generally tied to a particular technology. With MDA, functionality and behavior are modeled just once. Mapping from a PIM through a PSM to the supported MDA platforms is being implemented by tools, easing the task of supporting new or different technologies. MDA models must be detailed because the application code will be generated from it and the code will include only functionality represented explicitly.

One can think of MDA as a stack with business at the top and technology at the bottom. Business domain experts work at the top, with the goal of modeling the needed business function. Here, UML-based tools provide support and the UML language's structure and narrower profiles (i.e., tailored subsets) provide guidance. The product of the first development step, termed the PIM, represents the business functionality and behavior that this MDA application will execute. As one moves down toward the bottom, the business domain recedes and technology takes over. In a perfectly efficient world, the MDA might jump directly from the business model at the top to the implementation at the bottom, but today the discontinuities are too great, so the MDA inserts an intermediate step. (The artifact produced in this step is termed the PSM.) Produced primarily by MDA-enabled tools following OMG-standardized mappings, the PSM provides a middle stage where skilled architects can mark up the model with their preferences or hints about how they want particular steps to be designed or executed. The completed PSM contains the same information set as a coded application, but in the form of a UML model instead of program language and makefiles. Taking advantage of the tight mapping, MDA-enabled development tools automate the conversion from PSM to code very well (this step is more mature than the PIM–PSM conversion in the previous step) [SEI200201].

Although it has always been true that UML models can be implemented on any platform, the continuing proliferation of middleware suggested that a platform-independent MOF-based model is the key to software stability; such a model remains fixed while the infrastructure landscape around it shifts over time. The MDA unites OMG's well-established modeling standards with middleware technology to integrate what one has built, with what the firm is building, with what the firm might build in the future. MDA designs portability and interoperability into the application at the model level.

Even though UML is usually thought of as the basis for MDA, it is actually MOF compliance that is formally required for a tool or tool chain to be labeled "MDA Compliant." The MOF is OMG's foundation specification for modeling languages; MOF compliance allows UML structural and behavioral models, and CWM data models, to be transmitted via XMI, stored in MOF-compliant repositories, and transformed and manipulated by MOF-compliant tools and code generators. Models in the context of the MDA Foundation Model are instances of MOF metamodels and therefore consist of model elements and links between them. This required MOF compliance enables the automated transformations on which MDA is built. UML compliance, although common, is not a requirement for MDA models. Additional OMG specifications populate the architecture. Development tools, provided by vendors, implement the supporting standards. Working synergistically, these tools constitute the working MDA modeling and development environment in which architects and developers create MDA applications.

Although not formally required, UML is still a key enabling technology for the MDA and the basis for nearly all MDA development projects. (Work in some specialized fields requires specially tailored modeling languages, although the additional capabilities added to UML by the 2.0 revision satisfies this need in many cases.) Hence, application development using the MDA is typically based on a normative, platform-independent UML model. By leveraging OMG's MOF and UML standards, MDA allows creation of applications that are portable across, and interoperate naturally across, a broad spectrum of systems from embedded, to desktop, to server, to mainframe, and across the Internet. Any modeling language used in MDA must be described in terms of the MOF language to enable the metadata to be understood in a standard manner, which is a precondition for the ability to perform automated transformations.

Patterns play a key role in most MDA-based development projects. Successful transformation from PIM to PSM, and from PSM to code, requires that the PIM contain enough detail to completely guide the software tools through the process. By incorporating this detail through the use of patterns instead of inserting it by hand, one can gain multiple benefits: architects do less work, the resulting PIM reflects the collective wisdom of many contributors, and the tools can work the pattern (parameterized as necessary in the UML models) through the transformations, ultimately pulling implementation code from a library written by experts and inserting it into the application.

In the MDA, middleware-specific models and implementations are secondary artifacts: a specification's PIM—the primary artifact—defines one or more PSMs, each specifying how the base model is implemented on a different middleware platform. Because the PIM, PSMs, and interface definitions are all part of an MDA specification, OMG now adopts specifications in multiple middleware platforms under the MDA. Suitable targets for MDA development projects and OMG specifications include WS, XML, .NET, EJB, and OMG's CORBA.

MDA enables cross-platform interoperability. In the MDA, the base specification of every service, facility, and application is a platform-independent model. Architects specify links from an application to needed services and facilities, and to other applications, as part of its model. As the PIM for the new MDA specification or application is transformed into a PSM and then a coded application by the MDA tool chain, interoperability with other applications and services is built into it according to these links, which are implemented properly regardless of the target's native middleware.

An extensive set of services is necessary to support distributed computing, both within an enterprise and among many over the Internet. In the MDA, these are known as *Pervasive Services*; a single implementation of each, regardless of the platform on which it runs, can service every application or client that needs its capabilities via MDA-generated cross-platform bridges. There are four Pervasive Services:

- Directory Services
- Transaction Services
- Security Services
- Distributed Event and Notification Services

Additional services are expected to be added as needed to keep the environment complete.

In terms of products, MDA is being implemented by tools—or tool chains, which may come from a single vendor or a number of vendors—that integrate modeling and development into a single environment that carries an application from the PIM, through the PSM, and then via code generation to a set of language and configuration files implementing interfaces, bridges to services and facilities, and possibly even business functionality. Several vendors already provide tools that support integration at about this level, including substantial code generation. Today's tools typically automate 50% to 70% of the PIM-to-PSM transformation; because the industry got started on the second step much earlier, automation of the PSM-to-code transformation is typically 100% or nearly so.

MDA development tools, available now from many vendors, convert the PIM first to a PSM and then to a working implementation on virtually any middleware platform: Web Services, XML/SOAP, EJB, C#/.Net, OMG's CORBA, or others. Portability and interoperability are built into the architecture. OMG Task Forces organized around industries including finance, manufacturing, biotechnology, space technology, and others use the MDA to standardize facilities in their domains.

7.4.2 MDA Support

This section identifies OMG elements that support/comprise MDA. These have been mentioned along the way, but are covered here as a group.

7.4.2.1 The Meta-Object Facility (MOF™)

In the MDA, models are first-class artifacts, integrated into the development process through the chain of transformations from PIM through PSM to coded application. To enable this, the MDA requires models to be expressed in a MOF-based language. This guarantees that the models can be stored in a MOF-compliant repository, parsed, and transformed by MOF-compliant tools, once rendered into XMI for transport over a network. This does not constrain the types of models you can use—MOF-based languages today model application structure, behavior (in many different ways), and data; OMG's UML and CWM are examples of MOF-based modeling languages but are not the only ones. The foundation for UML 2.0 is MOF 2.0.

As noted, each MDA-based specification has, as its normative base, two levels of models: a PIM, and one or more PSMs. For many specifications, these will be defined in UML, making OMG's standard modeling language a foundation of the MDA. (Use of UML, although common, is not a requirement; MOF is the mandatory modeling foundation for MDA.) Tailored to MDA requirements, UML 2.0 improves Business, Architectural, Structural, and Behavioral modeling and is being done in four parts. Several additional specifications help tailor the UML to support MDA:

- A Human-Usable Textual Notation (HUTN) enables a new class of model-editing programs and enhances the way models (if they are built using a MOF-based modeling language, of course) can be manipulated. Notation elements map one-to-one to the more verbose XMI, but the syntax of the HUTN is much more human-friendly.
- A standard Software Process Engineering Metamodel defines a framework for describing methodologies in a standard way. It does not standardize any particular methodology, but enhances interoperability from one methodology to another.

7.4.2.2 UML Profiles

UML Profiles tailor the language to particular areas of computing (such as Enterprise Distributed Object Computing) or particular platforms (such as EJB or CORBA). In the MDA, both PIMs and PSMs are defined using UML profiles; OMG is well along the way, defining a suite of profiles that span the entire scope of potential MDA applications. The current suite of profiles includes the following:

- The UML Profile for CORBA, which defines the mapping from a PIM to a CORBA-specific PSM.
- The UML Profile for CCM (the CORBA Component Model), OMG's contribution to component-based programming. EJBs are the Java mapping of CCM; an initial take on a profile for EJB appears as an appendix of the UML 2.0 Superstructure specification.
- The UML Profile for EDOC is used to build PIMs of enterprise applications. It defines representations for entities, events, process, relationships, patterns, and an Enterprise Collaboration Architecture. As a PIM profile, it needs mappings to platform-specific profiles. A mapping to Web Services is under way; additional mappings will follow.
- The UML Profile for EAI defines a profile for loosely coupled systems—that is, those that communicate using either asynchronous or messaging-based methods. These modes are typically used in Enterprise Application Integration, but are used elsewhere as well.
- The UML Profile for Quality of Service (QoS) and Fault Tolerance defines frameworks for real-time and high-assurance environments.
- The UML Profile for Schedulability, Performance, and Time supports precise modeling of predictable—that is, real-time—systems, precisely enough to enable quantitative analysis of their schedulability, performance, and timeliness characteristics.
- The UML Testing Profile provides important support for automated testing in MDA-based development environments.

7.4.2.3 XML Metadata Interchange (XMI™)

XMI defines an XML-based interchange format for UML and other MOF-based metamodels and models (because a metamodel is just a special case of a model), by standardizing XML document formats, DTDs, and schemas. In so doing, it also defines a mapping from UML to XML. Because one of OMG's XMI updates reflects the incorporation of XML Schemas, while MOF point updates were made periodically through OMG's established maintenance process, numbering of XMI and MOF versions diverged. The following table provides a mapping.

MOF 1.3	XMI 1.1
MOF 1.4 (current)	XMI 1.2
MOF 1.4 (current)	XMI 1.3 (adds Schema support)
MOF 1.4 (current)	XMI 2.0 (current; new format)
MOF 2.0 (in process)	XMI 2.1 (in process)

7.4.2.4 Common Warehouse MetaModel (CWM™)

The CWM standardizes a complete, comprehensive metamodel that enables data mining across database boundaries at an enterprise. Similar to a UML profile but in data space instead of application space, it forms the MDA mapping to database schemas. CWM does for data modeling what UML does for application modeling. The CWM is a formal OMG specification. A supplementary specification, CWM Metadata Interchange Patterns, defines patterns that smooth the way to data modeling tool interoperability.

7.4.2.5 CORBA®

Although MDA can target every middleware platform and will map to all that have significant market presence, CORBA plays a key role as a target platform because of its programming language, operating system, and vendor independence. CORBA is a vendor-independent middleware standard.

7.4.2.6 Writing Standards in the MDA

Applications and frameworks (that is, parts of applications that perform a particular function) can all be defined in the MDA as a base PIM that maps to one or more PSMs and implementations. Standards written this way enjoy two advantages:

- The base PIM is truly a business specification, defining *business functionality and behavior* in a technology-independent way. Technological considerations do not intrude at this stage, making it easy for business experts to model exactly the business rules they want into the PIM.
- Once business experts have completed the PIM, it can be implemented on virtually any platform, or on multiple platforms with interoperability among them, to meet the needs of the industry and companies that use it.

OMG Domain Task Forces, after years of writing specifications in only CORBA, are now writing their base specifications in the MDA to take advantage of these considerations. OMG recognizes (based on analogy with the CORBA-based Object Management Architecture) three levels of MDA-based specifications:

- The *Pervasive Services*, including enterprise necessities such as Directory Services, Transactions, Security, and Event handling (Notification).

- The *Domain Facilities*, in industries such as healthcare, manufacturing, telecommunications, biotechnology, and others.
- *Applications themselves*, perhaps created and maintained by a software vendor or end-user company or enterprise using MDA tools to run an MDA-based methodology, but not standardized by OMG.

7.4.2.7 The Pervasive Services

This category includes at least the following:

- Directory and Naming Services
- Event Handling/Notification Services

Additional pervasive services may be defined, either from the list of CORBA services already standardized by OMG or from other suggestions from OMG members. Transactions and Security, the other two most popular CORBA services, may or may not be part of this group—in the component world, transactionality and security are attributes of a running system rather than services that a program calls, because of the way the Component Container or Application Server is set up to run transactionally and securely as part of an application's environment. OMG members are already taking the group's well-established CORBA service specifications and mapping them back to PIMs, where they can serve all platforms through the MDA development pathway.

7.4.2.8 Domain-Specific Specifications

Various industry segments have typically defined computing standards based on a particular technology. This provides interoperability, but requires every company to use the same middleware. By defining standards in the MDA, industries avoid the underlying disadvantages that invariably arise: defined fundamentally as a PIM, their standard can be implemented equivalently and interoperably on multiple middleware platforms. Over time, if one or some of these platforms become obsolete, the industry can define new implementations on new platforms from the original PIM. Many industries are working on MDA standards at OMG, including telecommunications, biotechnology, manufacturing, healthcare, and finance [SEI200201].

Interested readers are referred to [MDA200301] for additional information on MDA.

Chapter 8

Architecture Fulfillment via Service-Oriented Architecture Modeling

Service-Oriented Architecture (SOA) techniques are applicable to the system layer (domain) of enterprise architecture as a system development methodology.* SOA is an approach to building IT systems out of common software modules (parts), called *services*. The goal of SOA-based development is to enable organizations to assemble business systems out of simpler cataloged modules. SOA methods are now being explored by enterprises with the goal of achieving flexibility, agility, and productivity enhancements in IT development. Indeed, in allowing reuse, SOA lowers long-term integration costs and provides faster delivery of business applications. This approach to development may typically require more upfront effort in design and planning when the paradigm is first adopted and applied, but, in theory, it enables organizations to increasingly build systems more rapidly and cheaply as the inventory of reusable modules grows over time.

Whereas this and related approaches (e.g., Common Object Request Broker Architecture [CORBA] mentioned in the previous chapter, and Web Services [WSs]) are generally applicable at the logical/software level, we have advocated over time and advocate herein that technology architecture can or should be viewed in terms of a similar service-modeling synthesis. Certainly, a service view of physical IT resources can help the introduction of virtualization/utility/grid methods in the area of computing, storage, and networking. In this situation, the service rendition modules are high-level hardware (rather than software) modules. However, the discussion that follows in the rest of the chapter is in the context of software development, because this is the most

---

* Press-time surveys showed that the top five system modeling techniques used by large institutions were as follows: Unified Modeling Language (UML) (about a third of the companies); flowchart (about one-fifth of the companies); object-oriented (about one-sixth of the companies); organization's own method (about one-tenth of the companies); and model-driven architecture (also about one-tenth of the companies) [KOS200301]. It should be noted that SOA as a system development methodology can actually be used in conjunction with any of these modeling approaches.

well-understood application of SOA principles. Nonetheless, the reader should keep in mind the additional applicability of the functional building-block concepts.

8.1 Background and Description

As already noted, SOA is an approach to software design ("architecture") in which applications are assembled from reusable components (called *services*). A service is a software building block that performs a distinct function—for example, retrieving customer information from a database, producing an invoice, performing a credit check, etc.—through a well-defined interface (basically, a description of how to call the service from other programs) [STA200504]. According to proponents, SOA is emerging as the premier integration and architecture framework in today's complex and heterogeneous computing environment. It can help organizations streamline processes so that they can do business more efficiently and adapt to changing needs, thus enabling the *software-as-a service* concept [MAH200501]. It should be clear that a SOA must be able to relate the business processes of an organization to the technical processes of that organization and map the workflow relationships between the two.

SOA describes an IT systems architecture based on the principle of delivering reusable business services that are assembled from software subcomponents in such a way that the providers and the consumers of the business services are loosely coupled. Specifically, with SOA the providers and consumers do not need to have in-depth knowledge of the technology, platform, location, or environment choices of each other. SOA promotes loose coupling between software components so that they can be reused [MAH200501].

More generally, a SOA is a way of connecting applications across a network via a common communications protocol. From this perspective, it is an architectural style for building integrated software applications that use services available in a network, such as the Internet or the corporate intranet. In theory, this lets developers treat applications as network services that can be concatenated to create a complex business process more quickly than by using other methods. CORBA-based object request brokers is one example of a service-oriented architecture. More recently, companies have been using WS to connect applications. A demonstrable advantage of SOA is code reuse—developers have only to figure out the interfaces for existing applications rather than writing new applications from the ground up each time new business rules are developed [STA200601]. The SOA model fosters a division of labor as it relates to system development: the developer focuses on creating functional units (services), and the architect focuses on how the units fit together.

SOA is a component model that interrelates an application's different functional units, called services, through well-defined interfaces and contracts. The interface is defined in a neutral manner that is independent of the hardware platform, operating system, and programming language in which the service is implemented. This allows services, built on a variety of such systems, to interact with each other in a uniform and universal manner. This feature of having a neutral interface definition that is not strongly tied to a particular implementation is known as *loose coupling* between the services. The benefit of a loosely coupled system is its agility and ability to survive evolutionary changes in the structure and implementation of the internals of each service that make up the whole application. Tight coupling, on the other hand, means that the interfaces between the different components of an application are tightly interrelated in function and form, thus making them brittle when any form of change is required to parts of or the whole application. The need for loosely coupled systems arose from the need for business applications to become more

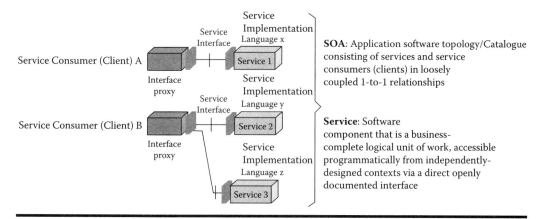

Figure 8.1   SOA elements.

agile [STA200602]. Previous attempts at integration did not enable open interoperable solutions because they relied on proprietary application programming (or programmer) interfaces (APIs) and required a high degree of coordination between functional groups.

A service is a software building block that performs a distinct function, such as retrieving customer information from a database, through a well-defined interface (a description of how to call the service from other services). Some define SOA as a software application topology (a catalogue) consisting of services and service consumers (users, clients) in a one-to-one (loosely coupled) relationship. The overall SOA-based application transparently incorporates the underlying services even when running on different hardware or software platforms (see Figure 8.1). Note that although SOA-based systems do not exclude the fact that individual services can themselves be built with object-oriented designs, the overall design in SOA is service-oriented. Because SOA allows for objects within the system, it is object-based, but, as a whole, it is not object-oriented in the strict sense of the term [STA200602].

Although the SOA concept of building systems out of common parts has been available for over a decade and a half, only recently has its practical implementation become feasible or cost-effective. Many companies have launched SOA initiatives in the recent past, and other companies are contemplating to embark on them. In a 2003 report, *Service-Oriented Architecture: Mainstream Straight Ahead*, Gartner, Inc., predicted, "by 2008, SOA will be the prevailing software engineering practice, ending the 40-year domination of monolithic software architecture" [STA200504]. Although these predictions may have been somewhat optimistic, recent market research suggests that a fair percentage of Fortune 500 companies are exploring the opportunities offered by SOA and WSs. This is driven by the fact that there is a need to create and enhance enterprise solutions on a short fuse to keep up with the changing business environment. Developers look at the potential of achieving such agility by reusing an enterprise's existing IT assets (e.g., legacy applications, middleware, mobile platforms, mismatched datasets, and so on) in the rapid assembly of composite applications at considerably reduced cost and with considerably less technical skill requirements [STA200505].

Over the years, software developers have sought to uncover ways of creating software that is easy to maintain, extend, and integrate with other systems. In this quest, various approaches to designing and writing software have been followed [STA200601]:

1. In the early stages of the business software industry (1960s and 1970s), programmers learned that organizing codes into modules made it easy to maintain and reuse discrete pieces of functionality. This led to the development of libraries of codes that could be (re)utilized by applying some (nontrivial amount of) customization.

2. The next major revolution in software design was object orientation (1980s). The software was modeled on the lines of real-world and virtual objects, where an "object" had properties that defined its state as well as the methods to change that state. Objects could be extended as required. The implementation details of an object were hidden from consumers and could be changed as long as the object's signature remained the same. This led to even greater ease of maintenance and extensibility. This paradigm was extended to distributed object systems where objects could reside on different machines across a network and communicate with each other using various remote access protocols.

3. The industry gradually realized that there was a market for pieces of functionality that could be plugged into software applications and customized for a specific application need. This led to the concept of software components.

4. Service orientation is yet another approach to development, where software functionality is defined as a set of services (1990s and 2000s). SOA is an alternative model to the more traditional tightly coupled object-oriented models that emerged in the earlier decades [STA200602].

SOA is an evolution of client/server architecture (e.g., [MIN199701]). In client/server systems, the user interface, business logic, and data management functions are separated in such a manner that each can be implemented using the platforms and technologies best suited to the task. With SOA, these functions (specifically, the business/application logic) are decomposed to finer levels of granularity. For example, rather than implementing business logic in a monolithic software module or application server, a SOA-based system incorporates services running on different software platforms, including (possibly) those provided remotely by an application service provider (ASP) (e.g., a WS) or a grid computing mechanism. Given a certain application, SOA not only needs to identify the service components, but it also needs to describe how the overall application performs its workflow between services.

As is the case in nearly all IT, telecom, networking, and Internet environments, standardization is critical for the successful market penetration of SOA. Specifically, one needs to have a standard way to represent a software component. CORBA (already mentioned in the previous chapter) is a late-1980s standard advanced by IBM, among others. Although it was a useful attempt at first, CORBA has been viewed as difficult to use; hence, it has not become a widespread standard. In the 1990s, Microsoft introduced an alternative: Distributed Component Object Model (DCOM). Unfortunately DCOM did not support CORBA. This predicament forestalled immediate advancements in the field. By the late 1990s, developers realized that relatively simple standards such as Hypertext Markup Language (HTML) and Hypertext Transfer Protocol (HTTP) can be used to link the end users and information sources. They started to investigate how to take the same technologies that were propelling the Internet and use them to link computer systems together. This eventually gave rise to WSs.

SOA itself is an abstract construct of how software should be put together. It relies on the more concrete ideas and technologies implemented in XML and WS to exist in software form. In addition, it also requires the support of security, policy management, reliable messaging, and accounting systems to work effectively. One can improve on it even further with the addition of distributed transactional processing and distributed software state management [STA200602].

WSs are achievable on the World Wide Web (WWW) or corporate intranet, and are based on technologies that originated from the Web. The key elements of WS are the Web Services Definition Language (WSDL), which is a standard way to represent software parts; the Simple Object Access Protocol (SOAP), which is a lightweight protocol for exchange of information in a decentralized, distributed environment; and the Universal Description, Discovery, and Integration (UDDI), which is a service registration mechanism. WSs are delivered over a network using technologies such as eXtensible Markup Language (XML), WSDL, SOAP, and UDDI. SOA enables companies to create standard components in the form of WSs that are accessible through a standard protocol, specifically SOAP. These components are accessed over an interface that uses a common protocol and are all registered in the same way in the centralized (services) directory. By describing interfaces in an XML-based language, specifically WSDL, SOA services make use of a more dynamic and flexible interface system than the older Interface Definition Language (IDL) found in CORBA* [STA200602].

WSs are software systems designed to support interoperable machine-to-machine interactions over a network. This interoperability is gained through the just-named set of XML-based open standards (WSDL, SOAP, and UDDI.) These standards provide a common approach for defining, publishing, and using WSs. Once a WS is discovered, the client makes a request to the WS. The WS (server) processes the request and sends the response back to the client. The Web Services Interoperability Organization (WS-I) (www.ws-i.org) is an open, industry organization committed to promoting interoperability among WSs based on common, industry-accepted definitions and related XML standards support. WS-I creates guidelines and tools to help developers build interoperable WSs. It addresses the interoperability need through profiles. The first profile, WS-I Basic Profile 1.0 (which includes XML Schema 1.0, SOAP 1.1, WSDL 1.1, and UDDI 2.0), attempts to improve interoperability within its scope, which is bounded by the specifications referenced by it [MAH200501].

WS provides a standards-based approach to defining and invoking aggregates of functional codes, whereas SOA offers a way to transform IT assets into a reusable collection of components assembled into various business-oriented services providing a mechanism for dealing with change in a responsive and cost-effective manner [STA200502]. Three factors have converged to make WS a broadly deployed technology [STA200503]:

- In the past few years, there has been a lot of activity related to standards that make it practical to implement a SOA. The result is a good level of interoperability between different products and platforms. In turn, this standards work is increasing the industry momentum behind SOA.
- Software vendors have brought products to market that make SOA real and useful. No longer just an idea, SOA is increasingly proving to be a cost-effective methodology for software development.
- Unlike earlier approaches, SOA is business focused. The services in SOA are business services—such as "Check credit" or "Create invoice"—not low-level bits of codes. This provides a common language for them to talk about requirements. In turn, this also makes it easier for business leaders to accept and adopt SOA; acceptance and adoption by management is vital for any technology to thrive.

---

* CORBA-based applications have many of the necessary mechanisms to interface into SOA-based environments. However, although the IDL is conceptually similar to WSDL, it is not exact and thus needs to be mapped to WSDL as an intermediary step. Additionally, the higher-level SOA protocols, such as for process and policy management, need to be used rather than the similar concepts within CORBA.

UML and MDA, discussed in the previous chapter, take a view that is consistent with this modeling approach. MDA has parallels to a number of concepts in SOA. It does not distinguish between services and objects, but allows models to be composed of other subset models themselves, similar to concepts in SOA. In MDA, a software process can be defined as a model that can be translated into actual software components of an application (MDA creates a model that is compiled into a software application, which in turn is compiled into an executable that can run on a physical platform).

Note that WSs are not strictly necessary to build an SOA; however, a standard set of protocols and technologies is desirable for effectively managing the services in such a SOA environment. WSs simplify and standardize the interface and invocation mechanism. The reader should keep in mind that SOA is an actual architecture, namely, it is a description of how the parts fit together, the functional groupings, the protocols and data used between functional groupings, etc.; so it is more than just a set of protocols. Also, note that WSs do not on their own address the operational and management issues; these capabilities must be added to the framework to make an SOA practical [STA200502].

So, as we have seen, SOA is a style that architects applications in such a way that the applications can be composed of discrete software agents that have simple, well-defined interfaces and are orchestrated through a loose coupling to perform a required function. There are two roles in SOA: a service provider, and a service consumer. A software module may play both roles [STA200601]. In SOA, software is organized into modular components. As noted, this is not a novel concept, but the difference is that the components, or services, are loosely coupled. Loose coupling means that the services can be linked together dynamically at runtime, with few dependencies on how the services are actually implemented [STA200504]. CORBA and DCOM have tightly coupled interfaces. With these approaches, one has to know where all of the objects reside on the network; further, all objects have to be CORBA or DCOM objects (later efforts from third-party developers bridged CORBA and DCOM). In comparison, SOA allows WSs to be accessed in an objective model neutral way. A Java application can call Microsoft .NET, CORBA-compliant, or even legacy COBOL applications by using XML-based messaging [PAT200501].

A service is an implementation of a well-defined business function that operates independent of the state of any other service. It has a clearly defined set of platform-independent interfaces and operates through a predefined contract with the consumer of the service. Because the services are loosely coupled, it need not know the technical details of another service to work with it—all interaction takes place through the interfaces [STA200601]. In SOA, IT components are formed into services that support what is relevant to the business operation—for example, get customer address, do credit check, check inventory, invoke shipping function, update online invoice, etc. In turn, these business services can themselves be used as part of other services, forming the so-called composite service. In this arrangement, the "get customer address" service can be invoked by any application on any platform without any knowledge by the invoking entity of the specific technical details. All the caller needs to know is what (standard) invocation procedure and what inputs and outputs are required for this particular service (see Figure 8.2).

Communication is carried out by the SOA communications layer, for example, a message-based backbone. Data between the consumer and the service is transacted in the XML format using one of several protocols; the commonly used ones for WS are SOAP and Representational State Transfer (REST). REST makes use of the existing Internet infrastructure (specifically HTTP), whereas SOAP is independent of the network layer and can use a variety of network protocols; it offers potentially more functionality (SOAP is not an absolute requirement, but it is a common messaging system used in SOA). See Figure 8.3.

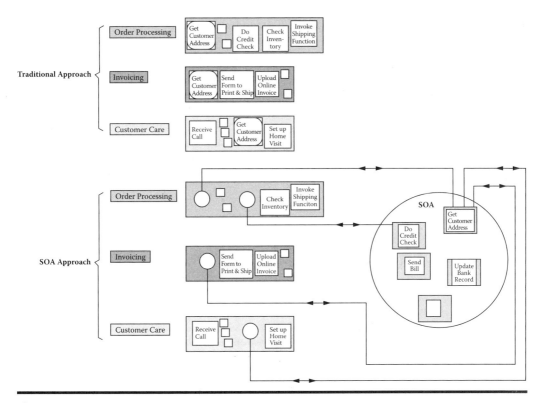

Figure 8.2   SOA reuse.

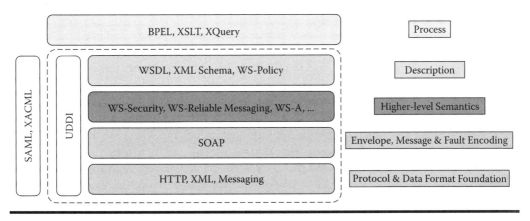

Figure 8.3   WS standards stack.

WSs provide the underpinning technology for SOA: the standard invocation mechanism defined by WSDL, and the standard communications protocol provided by SOAP (UDDI support WSs location management). WSs are not the only way to implement SOA; CORBA and Message-Oriented Middleware (MOM) systems such as the IBM MQ (Message Queue) Series and Java Messaging Service (JMS) can also be used. However, contemporary implementations tend to be almost exclusively WS based. SOA is not language specific, except that it makes use of XML and WSDL. Services can be implemented in any programming language as long as the language can generate and interact with WSDL. (Services in SOA can be implemented in almost any variety of programming languages and platforms that support WSDL.)

The distinction between SOA services and WSs has to do with that between a concept and its implementation. At the conceptual level, it is not the intent of SOA to exactly define how services are specifically expected to interact; it only defines how services can understand each other and how they interact. WSs have specific guidelines on how messaging between services needs to take place (most commonly seen in SOAP messages delivered over HTTP). WSs are one method for implementing SOA; they provide a tactical implementation of a SOA model. As noted, however, WS is just *one* method for implementing SOA. Other protocols that also directly implement service interfaces with WSDL and communicate with XML messages can also be involved in SOA (e.g., CORBA and the IBM MQ systems). Thus, WSs are a specific and practical approach to SOA implementation.

8.2 Benefits of Using SOA Machinery

There are five basic benefits in using SOA, in addition to several ancillary benefits: (1) business-centric perspective in software development, (2) lower incremental cost for development, (3) lower training and skill requirements, (4) lower maintenance costs, and (5) faster development cycle (Table 8.1 identifies some of the other benefits of using SOA [STA200601]).

The advantage of the SOA model is that it can take a business-centric perspective of business operations and processes rather than application- and programming-centric perspectives. This allows business managers in the firm to identify what needs to be added, modified, or removed based on the workings of the business. The software systems can then be structured to fit the business processes rather than the other way around, as commonly seen in many existing software platforms [STA200602].

By developing a catalogue of services, a developer designing a new system has a collection of existing software services from which to assemble certain portions of the system—possibly most of it. Over time, the fraction of the system that could be built from preexisting software services will increase. (As projects create new service modules, these will add to the catalogue and be available for reuse.) Figure 8.4 illustrates this concept; the figure actually illustrates a technology architecture layer example. Of course, the utilization of a service catalog is at the System Architecture layer, where most people typically see such application, and where the discussion of this chapter focuses on. Figure 8.5 illustrates that as time goes by, the incremental effort to develop a new system will decline in the SOA environment compared with the non-SOA environment. With reusability, the cost to bring each new additional application online decreases, and the total cost of development is less than delivering each additional application independently. Defining a service that can be invoked in standard fashion multiple applications enables the removal of a major portion of the redundant code that is inherent in many IT applications.

Because of the common WS protocol interface and environment, SOA generally reduces the number of programming skill sets that a firm needs to nurture, assuming that the service catalogue is already built. This reduces the training required for the system development team. With SOA, the company generally only needs developers who understand WSs; even if some staff are required to understand the languages used in developing the service modules, fewer people will be needed compared to a full-fledged development environment.

SOA allows for the reuse of existing assets, where new services can be created from an existing IT infrastructure of systems. It enables businesses to leverage existing investments by allowing

Table 8.1   Benefits of SOA (partial list)

Platform independence	Because WSs can be published and used across development and operating platforms, an enterprise can leverage its existing legacy applications that reside on different types of servers and build additional functionality without having to rebuild the entire system. It also helps an enterprise to integrate its applications with those of its partners.
Focused developer roles	Because a service is a discrete implementation independent of other services, developers in charge of a service can focus completely on implementing and maintaining that service without having to worry about other services as long as the predefined contract is honored.
Location transparency	WSs are often published in a directory where consumers can look them up. The advantage of this approach is that the WS can change its location at any time. Consumers of the service will be able to locate the service through the directory.
Code reuse	Because SOA breaks down an application into small, independent pieces of functionality, the services can be reused in multiple applications, thereby bringing down the cost of development.
Greater testability	Small, independent services are easier to test and debug than monolithic applications. This leads to more reliable software.
Parallel development	Because the services are independent of each other, and contracts between them are predefined, the services can be developed in parallel. This shortens the software development life cycle considerably.
Better scalability	Because the location of a service does not matter anymore, the service can be transparently moved to a more powerful server to serve more consumers if required. Also, there can be multiple instances of the service running on different servers; this increases scalability.
Higher availability	Because the location of a service does not matter, and one can have multiple instances of a service, it is possible to ensure high availability.

them to reuse existing applications and promises interoperability between heterogeneous applications and technologies [MAH200501]. SOA designs, when done right, can leverage existing software applications by service, enabling and integrating them through a SOA, such as using them in enterprise application integration (EAI), business process management, and business activity monitoring [PAT200501].

If there is only one copy of a business service when new functionality or fixes are needed, maintenance programmers are required to make changes only to one software module instead of making changes to multiple modules. Therefore, application maintenance costs are reduced, and new changes can be accommodated quickly and easily [STA200502].

SOA enables developers to build systems more rapidly than in a traditional environment. For example, when one is using the same module repeatedly, bugs only have to be identified and fixed once. When properly implemented, SOA allows business IT systems to be more agile to the changes in the business. By allowing well-defined functional relationships and yet flexible

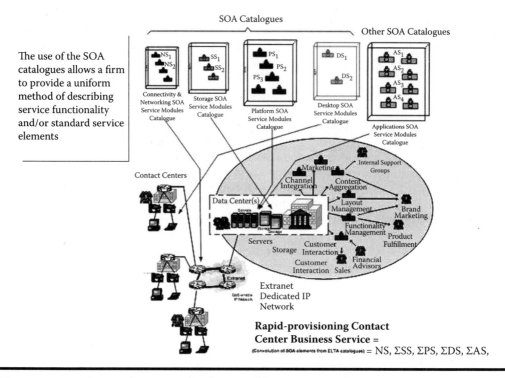

The use of the SOA catalogues allows a firm to provide a uniform method of describing service functionality and/or standard service elements

Figure 8.4 Service catalogue—Technology Architecture example.

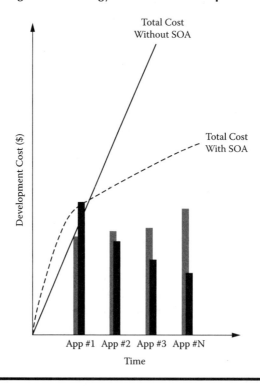

Figure 8.5 Cost of developing applications with and without SOA.

specific implementations, IT systems can take advantage of the capabilities of existing systems, while at the same time permitting changes to the interaction syntax [STA200602].

In an extended enterprise context, the workflow of a business includes operations not just between corporate departments, but also with other external partners. SOA can help in this situation, but one has to define the policies of how relationships between services should transpire, often in the form of service level agreements and operational policies [STA200602].

8.3 SOA Machinery

Next, we examine what machinery a firm needs to create a SOA-based enterprise architecture. This machinery includes services, a registry, messaging, management, orchestration, analytics, and an efficient user interface (see Figure 8.6), as covered in [STA200503], on which this discussion is based.

8.3.1 Services

As a first step, firms need to create the service catalogue that contains the building blocks of new systems. In some cases, companies might build services from the ground up in Java or .NET. In others, firms might use products to expose existing application functionalities into WSs. In still other cases, organizations might access external services provided by ASPs.

As we have discussed in the previous section, a service is an implementation of a well-defined business functionality, and such services can be used by clients in different applications or business processes [MAH200501]. A SOA service can be a simple object, a complex object, a collection of objects, a process containing many objects, processes containing other processes, and even a whole collection of applications outputting a single result. Outside the service, it is seen as a single entity, but within itself, it can have any level of complexity as necessary. Although SOA and WSs are independent of the programming languages, it needs to be noted that Java is a popular development language. The availability of well-defined Java interfaces along with off-the-shelf Java implementations of the various protocols gives Java an advantage in SOA development. In the context of SOA, Java is typically used in the functional development of

Figure 8.6   SOA machinery.

each service, manipulating data objects, and interaction with other objects that are logically encapsulated within the service [STA200602]. Java 2 Platform, Enterprise Edition (J2EE) can be used to develop state-of-the-art WSs to implement SOA. Additional facts about SOA services are as follows [MAH200501]:

- Services are software components with well-defined interfaces that are implementation-independent. An important aspect of SOA is the separation of the service interface (the what) from its implementation (the how). Such services are used by clients who are not concerned with how these services will execute their requests.
- Services are self-contained (perform predetermined tasks) and loosely coupled (for independence).
- Services can be dynamically discovered.
- Composite services can be built from aggregates of other services.

Although any functionality can be made into a service, the challenge is to define a service interface that is at the right level of abstraction. Services should provide coarse-grained functionality [MAH200501]. A SOA-based system will typically comprise the elements and services depicted in Table 8.2.

Table 8.2 Typical SOA Elements and Services

Enterprise Service Bus (ESB)	Delivers all of the interconnectivity capabilities required to leverage the services implemented across the entire architecture, including transport, event, and mediation services.
Interaction services	Provide the capabilities required to deliver IT functions and data to end users for meeting their specific usage preferences.
Process services	Provide the control services required to manage the flow and interactions of multiple services in ways that implement business processes.
Information services	Provide the capabilities required to federate, replicate, and transform various data sources that can be implemented in a variety of ways.
Access services	Provide bridging capabilities between legacy applications, prepackaged applications, enterprise data stores, and the ESB to incorporate services that are delivered through existing applications into SOA.
Partner services	Provide the document, protocol, and partner management capabilities required for business processes that involve interactions with outside partners and suppliers.
Business application services	Provide runtime services required for new application components to be included in the integrated system.
Infrastructure services	Provide the ability to optimize throughput, availability, and performance.

8.3.2 Registry

The second step is to "publish" services in a registry or a catalog. The registry concept is similar to the idea of a Yellow Pages directory. SOA uses the find–bind–execute paradigm as shown in Figure 8.7. In this paradigm, service providers register their services in a public registry. This registry is used by consumers to find services that match certain criteria. If the registry has such a service, it provides the consumer with a contract and an endpoint address for that service [MAH200501]. Figure 8.8 shows this machinery in a WS environment.

UDDI specifications define a registry service for WSs and for other electronic and nonelectronic services. A UDDI registry service is a WS itself and manages information about service providers, service implementations, and service metadata. Service providers can use UDDI to advertise the services they offer. Service consumers can use it to discover the services that suit their requirements and to obtain the service metadata needed for using those services. UDDI creates a standard interoperable platform that enables companies and applications to quickly, easily, and dynamically find and use WSs over the Internet. It also allows operational registries to be maintained for different purposes in different contexts. It is a cross-industry effort driven by major

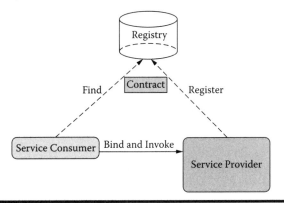

Figure 8.7   SOA's find–bind–execute paradigm.

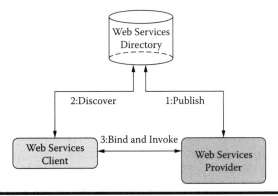

Figure 8.8   WS's publish–discover–invoke model.

platform and software providers, marketplace operators, and e-business leaders within the OASIS standards consortium [OAS200601]. The UDDI specifications define:

1. SOAP APIs that applications use to query and publish information to a UDDI registry
2. XML Schema schemata of the registry data model and SOAP message formats
3. WSDL definitions of the SOAP APIs
4. UDDI registry definitions of various identifier and category systems that may be used to identify and categorize UDDI registrations

SOA systems must be asynchronous, because applications and objects can be called at any time, and an application has no way of knowing when it will get back information it requested. This is done through a service registry. Basic UDDI registries focus on registration of service descriptions, i.e., WSDL descriptions. SOA registries need to contain much more service-related metadata, such as, but not limited to, XML schemas, Business Process Execution Language (BPEL) descriptions, and eXtensible Style Language transformation (XSLT) transforms. A WS registry helps track and manage WS access and SOA governance. The registry provides a central location to discover and access reusable WSs [PAT200501].

8.3.3 Messaging

Enterprises need a mechanism (which some call a *service bus* or *enterprise service bus*) that enables WS components to communicate with each other reliably through a middleware infrastructure. This infrastructure should support a variety of interaction patterns—request/reply, publish/subscribe, etc.—as well as handle transformations and transactions to support the applications that are based on the underlying services.

The Enterprise Service Bus (ESB), a middleware concept, is a hub for integrating different kinds of services through messaging, event handling, and business performance management. ESB plays a useful role in SOA and WS. It provides an abstraction layer above an enterprise messaging system that allows developers to exploit the value of messaging without writing specific codes [LUO200501]. It can be used for the proper control, flow and, possibly, translations of messages between services, using a number of possible messaging protocols. EBS enables one to establish proper control over service-to-service messaging and supports security, policy, reliability, and accounting. The ESB is not absolutely required but is a vital component for properly managing business processes in SOA. The ESB itself can be a single engine or even a distributed system consisting of many peers and subpeers, all working together to keep the SOA system operational. Conceptually, ESB has evolved from the store-and-forward mechanism found in earlier computer science concepts, such as the message queue and distributed transactional computing [STA200602].

ESB enables standards-based integration in SOA. One can think of it as a WS-capable middleware infrastructure that supports communication among application components and mediates application interactions. At a higher level, the core functionality of an ESB includes the ability to connect resources (via adapters or specific communication protocols), mediate communication among services (perhaps through routing, mapping, or transformations), coordinate or orchestrate processes (specifying what service is invoked when), and manage (such as security of) quality of services. The result is a more flexible approach to application integration. ESBs are not ideal for every type of integration solution; there are still many other traditional integration alternatives such as WebSphere MQ or old-style EAI solutions. For example, ESBs may not be required if an organization has stable business requirements and a low rate of change, smaller applications with limited services, or limited throughput and latency requirements, or has already standardized on a platform or integration vendor. However, ESBs can be particularly helpful in a variety of other deployment scenarios, such as the integration of larger applications with multiple services or event types and situations where an organization has frequent changes in business requirements or the need for higher levels of business agility, the need to integrate across applications or services from multiple providers, or a tops-down strategy to move to a SOA-based architecture [KEL200501].

8.3.4 Management

Enterprises need a service level management infrastructure (e.g., security, monitoring, manageability, and versioning) to provide views on functional activities so as to achieve robustness and reliability, especially for mission-critical systems based on WSs.

8.3.5 Orchestration

At some point along the development path, a firm will need to assemble appropriate services drawn from the catalogue into new "composite applications." To address new business process requirements, an enterprise will need to "orchestrate" a number of constituent services (basically, linking them together using business process modeling tools).

Grid computing and autonomic computing also support the concept of SOA [MIN200501]: SOA applications can be a consumer of the services of a grid, and autonomic computing can be utilized to maintain policies. Grid computing is a form of distributed computing, typically where the resources belong to distinct organizations and are located remotely with respect to one another (grid computing can also be implemented locally within a data center as a way to homogenize a set of processors to that of applications so as to increase utilization and availability; however, we are not focusing on these forms of grid computing at this juncture). Grids rely on well-defined services provided by different institutions or entities. Often grids are used for computation-intensive tasks such as scientific modeling or data mining. A grid can serve as a framework where some or all of the individual services are implemented in a distributed fashion so that the interactions between services can provide computational support to SOA applications. From a slightly different perspective, the grid itself can be built on SOA principles; here, the individual components of the grid can communicate using WS and interact according to SOA methodologies.

8.3.6 Analytics

An enterprise also needs to be able to extract events that provide real-time views to the system. Some call this *business activity monitoring* or *complex event processing*.

8.3.7 User Interface

The enterprise will need to expose the complex services that constitute the composite application possibly through a Web-based portal.

8.4 Challenges to Full-Fledged SOA Deployment

As might be expected, there are some practical challenges associated with the effective deployment of SOA and WSs in enterprise environments. SOA and WS deployments may be attractive in terms of productivity and flexibility, but the issues of scalability and mission criticality have to be taken into account; otherwise, as implementations expand, the result may be overall performance issues and application brittleness [STA200502].

According to some observers, an enablement gap exists between the practical reality and vision of SOA. Specifically, one needs to establish how services with no knowledge of one another will interoperate semantically. One needs to refine low-level services into the coarser business-oriented granularity of enterprise-class services. One also needs to provide centralized and managed access to WS and other software services in the firm's repository [STA200505]. A small set of considerations are discussed in the following text.

It is relatively easy to create a WS, particularly given the plethora of tools that support these development tasks. Often, various groups across the IT operations in a firm start building WSs and make them available for (re)use. Initially this fosters reuse, but if control measures are not instituted, the situation can quickly deteriorate. The ad hoc creation of WSs across the enterprise can result in complexity—for example, an incomplete understanding of what services are available, who is using what service, and which services are secure. Many SOA implementations are becoming more complex than the architectures they are replacing. The key to a successful SOA implementation is to minimize complexity and follow standards [STA200502,MEY200501]. If the environment is not managed properly, SOA-based implementations can give rise to unstable systems.

Another problem relates to controls vis-à-vis policy implementation. For example, a firm may introduce, at some point, a (new) business policy requirement, say, based on regulatory inputs, that affirms that customer information must never be transmitted in an unencrypted manner. A WS may support a function of interest, e.g., it may transfer data remotely, which works fine for general non-customer-specific data; but what assurances are there that the service in question is not used to handle a customer-specific data?

Yet another issue relates to the operational monitoring and management of WSs. For example, a number of applications supporting different enterprise functions or departments may be invoking a common WS; however, different quality of service requirements or expectations may exist. A reliable mechanism needs to be put in place to address these expectations.

Broadly speaking, to address these issues, firms need a WS framework that addresses (1) the registration of WSs across the enterprise, (2) monitoring of those WSs in the operations context, and (3) WS governance. Specifically, a SOA management framework is required that provides the following functionalities [STA200502]:

- Registration of all services across the enterprise
- Change of management and versioning support
- Security facilities
- Service monitoring
- Service management and event handling
- Service administration tools

8.5 Building SOA Environments

As we have seen, SOA is usually realized through WSs. But according to some practitioners, WS specifications may add to the confusion of how to best utilize SOA to solve business problems. For a smooth transition to SOA, developers at the firm should keep in mind the following [MAH200501]:

- WSs are the preferred way to realize SOA (other approaches may be more difficult).
- SOA is more than just deploying software. Organizations need to analyze their design techniques and development methodology, and partner/customer/supplier relationship.
- Moving to SOA should be done incrementally, and this requires a shift in how we compose service-based applications while maximizing existing IT investments.

Building SOA follows the phases of the following software life cycle [STA200602]: (1) model, (2) assemble, (3) deploy, (4) manage, and (5) process and governance. SOA development begins with the model phase by gathering business requirements and designing business processes. Once the process is optimized, it is implemented by assembling new and existing services to form the business process. The assets are then deployed into a secure and integrated services environment. Once deployed, they can be managed and monitored as business processes from both IT and business perspectives. Information gathered during the manage phase is fed back into the life cycle for a continuous process improvement. Underpinning all of these life-cycle stages are governance and processes, which provide the guidance and oversight for the SOA project [STA200602].

To develop an effective SOA environment, information analysts and software architects should be knowledgeable of MDA and UML V2.0 (discussed in the previous chapter). The software developer and programmer should be familiar with the programmatic interfaces for WS, MQ, and other protocols; they should also know what mechanisms are required to develop secure interactions; they should also be familiar with the concepts of workflow processing. The systems administrator should also know how application security and trust models work, and how application use policies affect the operating system platforms and network systems.

The essence of SOA is to be able to come up with a service portfolio that might be reused to realize multiple higher-level business processes. The implementation of the service also needs to be well thought out so that the artifacts (for example, components) are also inherently reusable across multiple service implementations [MIT200601].

Figure 8.9 provides a higher-level view of the various SOA layers [MIT200601]. The figure illustrates how steps within a business process can be realized through either a single service or through a composition of multiple services. It also shows how a service might be realized or implemented by components. These components might be assets harvested from existing assets (such as legacy systems), components from packaged or commercial off-the-shelf (COTS) applications, and those developed completely from the ground up. Starting with a candidate service portfolio is an essential step toward the ultimate goal of building an enterprise service portfolio [MIT200601].

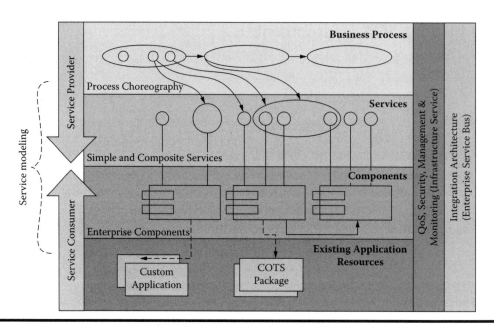

Figure 8.9 SOA layers. (From T. Mitra, Business-Driven Development, January 13, 2006, *IBM developerWorks*, On-line Magazine, http://www-128.ibm.com/developerworks/webservices/library/ws-bdd/)

The topic of SOA, specifically in the context of network services, is revisited in Chapter 11.

THE INFRASTRUCTURE LEVEL

Chapter 9

Evolving SAN, GbE/10GbE, and Metro Ethernet Technologies

This chapter is a survey of telecom and networking technologies that are applicable to enterprise environments. The author published one of the very first books on the topic in the early 1990s entitled *Enterprise Networking: Fractional T1 to SONET, Frame Relay to BISDN* (Artech House, 1993). This chapter updates that perspective for the contemporary reader, at least for a handful of telecommunications domains. After a brief overview we provide a bottom-line section in which readers interested in general trends for technology architecture planning in reference to enterprise networks, specifically *for local area networks (LANs) and storage area networks (SANs),* can find guidance. This is followed by sections that provide more in-depth technical details; readers just interested in the bottom line may chose to skip this material or skim through it. Chapter 10 looks at wide area network (WAN) trends.

Communication services and technologies can be classified in terms of administrative domain and geographic reach:

	Local Reach	Long-Haul Reach
Private networks	Local area network (LAN) Storage area network (SAN) for intra-data-center connectivity	Metro: metropolitan area networks (MANs) Regional/national: wide area networks (WANs)
Public/carrier networks	Local access infrastructure	Backbone infrastructure

More refined taxonomies are possible: for example, Figure 9.1 depicts a finer-grained taxonomy of communication services; however, this chapter focuses mostly on data-center services in support of system-to-system interconnection.

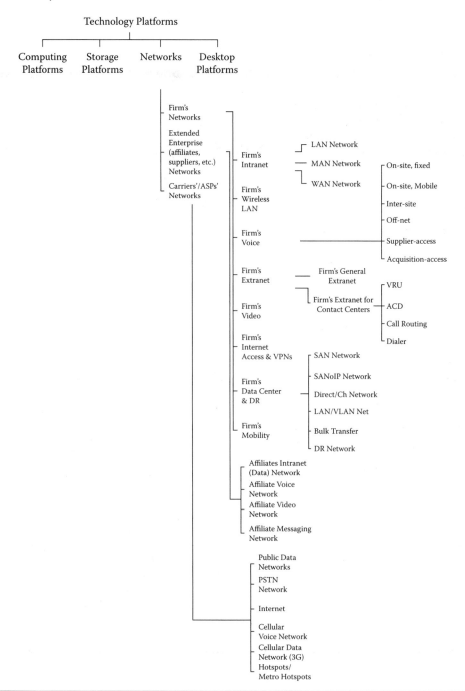

Figure 9.1   Network assets in a typical large firm.

At this juncture, connectivity is fundamental to nearly all business environments, not only for IT system support (for local or remote access; for thin, thick, or mobile clients; for back-office-based or Web Service [WS]-based system-to-system integration), but also for voice, video, and mobility services. Networking is part of the technology architecture.

As we hinted along the way, one can (should) see networking services as comprising SOA (technology) components that support required functionality for the developer, without requiring the developer to understand the technical minutiae of the networking technology (see Figure 9.2). On the other hand, to view networking simply as "pipes" or "plumbing" can be detrimental to an organization because of the host of implications related to (system) communication performance, functionality, cost, security, portability, extended-enterprise connectivity requirements, mobility, integration, data backup, global reach, consumer access, and other issues. Hence, a balanced view is optimal. Finally, Figure 9.3 depicts a multidomain view (networks, platforms) of the key infrastructure IT assets to provide end-to-end services.

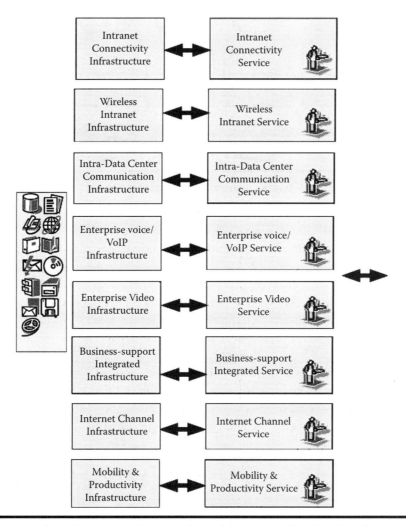

Figure 9.2   A service-oriented architecture view of the networking functionality.

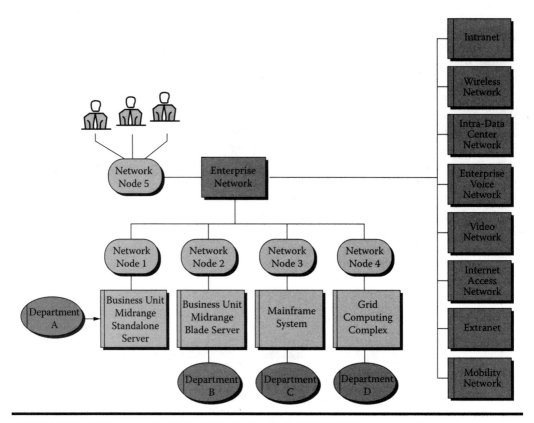

Figure 9.3   A Multidomain (networks, platforms) view of IT assets.

The intranet typically comprises (several) LANs, MANs, and WANs; these are owned by one administrative entity. Extranets can have the same geographic reach as intranets, but they are owned by a combination of administrative entities. Voice and video used to be separate infrastructures, but with a move to Voice-over-IP (VoIP), the intranet will be used to carry all three media (voice, video, and data). The data center network is typically made up of/supported by SANs.

The main theme of the telecom and networking industry for the rest of this decade is expected to be the introduction of *broadband* IP/Ethernet-based converged* transmission technologies in enterprise networks both at the local and at the long-haul level.† This chapter focuses on that broadband theme. It covers local technologies, including high-speed LANs and SANs. Gigabit Ethernet (GbE) and 10 Gigabit Ethernet (10GbE) LANs are covered. Optical transmission technology is fundamental to many types of networks, including all four elements of the taxonomy described earlier. Hence, we begin the chapter with a relatively brief discussion of basic optical concepts. A section on GbE/10GbE follows. Finally, a discussion of 10 Gbps Fibre Channel (FC) SAN technology is provided.

---

* Do not read the word *broadband* to mean "cable TV based." The word always had, and should always have, a broader meaning.

† Eventually there will also be generally available *higher speed data services for residential users*. This topic, however, is not covered here.

9.1 Overview of Networking

9.1.1 Background

Looking out over the next three to five years to 2012, one can assume that there are *not* going to be any major communications-related breakthroughs: the laser is not poised to be invented, the microprocessor is not poised to be introduced, the Internet is not poised to be commercialized, more fiber is not poised to be deployed in conjunction with a capacity-driven need for higher and higher transmission speeds, and, cellular telephony is not poised to be launched. Given these observations, what will likely be the industry focus for the next three to five years? We believe that in the public network arena the focus of carriers and service providers will be on *applications* and on *profit-based use of the deployed inventory of long-haul and transoceanic capacity*, which, according to some published reports, still remains largely idle. A secondary set of technical advancements expected to occur in the next five years include new consumer-level services, such as (1) IP-based TV (IPTV) distribution, (2) broad-coverage third-generation (3G) cellular data transmission for mobile e-mail and Web access, and, (3) a transition to VoIP as the protocol of choice for voice transmission. As noted, for private (enterprise) networks the main short-term emphasis both at the local and at the long-haul level is expected to be the introduction of broadband IP/Ethernet-based converged communication technologies.

A synthesis of networking services for both LAN and MAN/WAN applications can start with a technology assessment of optics. Upon these "Layer 0" mechanisms one can then place an all-optical (Layer 1) network that has the characteristic of being photonic (light-based) end to end. An optical network runs more efficiently if lambdas* can be switched and provisioned in real-time. While waiting for an all-optical network, users can employ Dense (or Coarse) Wavelength Division Multiplexing (DWDM/CWDM) capabilities in support of broadband applications. Because of the major embedded base of Synchronous Optical Network/Synchronous Digital Hierarchy (SONET/SDH) equipment, these time division multiplexing (TDM)-based services are here to stay in the MAN/WAN context in the short run; however, carriers and suppliers may soon contemplate the introduction of next-generation (next-gen) SONET technologies.†

A synthesis of networking services for WAN applications can then proceed by assessing key services at Layer 2 that are expected to play a role in the present decade: Frame Relay (FR), Asynchronous Transfer Mode (ATM), and Multi-Protocol Label Switching (MPLS) (FR and ATM were developed or deployed in the last decade and will continue to have some importance for the foreseeable future; however, they are on the decline, whereas MPLS/IP is on the ascendancy.) The fact remains, however, that many end users are still tied to T1-based (1.544 Mbps) dedicated-line technology‡ (other services still being expensively priced); carriers need to look at the practical/affordability level of how to move beyond T1 to open up new revenue possibilities.

One can also proceed with the Layer 2 assessment by looking at advances in LAN technologies, particularly GbE and 10GbE. Beyond LANs, and considering the advantages of an Ethernet-based approach to communications, there also has been considerable interest in the past few years

---

* The term *lambda* is jargon for a dedicated light beam within a fiber-optic cable.

† Wireless technologies such as Wireless Personal Networks (WPAN), Wireless LANs (WLAN), Wireless Wide Area Networks (WWAN), fixed wireless, and Free Space Optics are other Layer 1 bearers that will continue to acquire importance in coming years. These technologies, however, are not discussed in this chapter.

‡ E1 (2.048 Mbps) systems in Europe.

in a novel Layer 2 WAN/long-haul service: Transparent LAN services (TLSs) (also known as Ethernet Private Line Service). New technologies such as GbE, Rapid Spanning Tree Protocol (RSTP), and MPLS, in fact, facilitate the deployment of TLS. Recently there has been a flurry of industry activity in deploying new metro Ethernet technologies (including virtual local area networks [VLANs], GbE, and Resilient Packet Ring [RPR]*).

Layer 3/4 technologies such as IPv4, IPv6, Transmission Control Protocol (TCP), and Real Time Protocol (RTP) are important. Security technologies are important in their own merit, but also in support of virtual private networks (VPNs) over the Internet. Layer 3 (and also Layer 2) VPNs are expected to see increased usage over the decade. Quality of service (QoS) in packet networks is critical both for the support of VPNs and for the support of packetized voice and multimedia. QoS-enabled services typically provide a set of differentiated transmission capabilities (e.g., bronze, silver, gold) on parameters such as latency, jitter, and packet loss. Carriers also want to look at VoIP, particularly with an eye to new services such as advanced call centers using VoIP technology; furthermore, carriers also want to look at digital video, including IPTV.

Table 9.1 is a categorization by topic of over 40,000 articles published by a well-known networking industry Web site in 2006; this table is intended to give the reader a "real feel" for what was important at press time and likely will continue to be important in the near future.

Carriers and service providers will need to deploy new broadband technologies in a rational, analytical, and cost-effective manner to support these major trends. Also, what is important for carriers is the introduction of new revenue-generating services and the shift away from a transmission-capacity-size-based pricing model, just as these carriers have graduated to a large degree from a distance-based pricing long-haul model that was in place at least from the 1930s through the mid-1990s. There is an understanding in some circles that unless the telecom industry learns to exist in an environment where either the transmission bandwidth provided to the user doubles every 18 months, while maintaining the same price, or where the carrier is able to accept a halving of the price for the same transmission bandwidth every 18 months (a model that has existed and has been successfully dealt with in the chip/computer/consumer-electronics space), the ravages of events covered in Chapter 11, the industry contractions caused by mergers and the customer inconveniences or abandonment that ensue, will be an ever-present predicament.

Many investors and institutions lost money in the myriad of companies they funded in the 1996–2001 period to go build, and clearly overbuild, the physical-layer infrastructure (the fiber, the optical transmission equipment, Digital Subscriber Line, and the fixed-radio transmission systems), the data-link layer infrastructure (the switches), the network layer infrastructure (the routers, the ISP networks, and the modem dial-in pools), and the Internet applications (the dot.com companies). It turns out that these investors have given, in effect, a "gift" to consumers and users: a large supply of fiber-based broadband global connectivity that would not otherwise have been possible without "irrational (over)exuberance." The opportunity for all, for carriers, for planners, and practitioners, is to put the existing bandwidth glut to work for them and their organizations. It is a unique opportunity.

For the foreseeable future, there has to be an acceptance on the part of networking and telecom planners that although IP-based services consume 20 times more bandwidth globally than voice, voice services (averaged across all carriers) will continue to represent about 80% of the carriers' income; enterprise data services (also averaged across all carriers) will continue to represent about 15% of the carriers' income; and, Internet services represent, on the average, 5% of the carriers' income. Although single-digit shifts in percentages may occur in the next few

---

* RPR is not covered here.

Table 9.1 Technology Emphasis in Networking Space at Publication Time—Top 101 Issues

Percentage of Articles (%)	Networking Technology Area
4.29	Voice-over-IP (VOIP) equipment
4.14	Multi-Protocol Label Switching (MPLS)*
3.42	Optical components*
3.32	SONET/SDH Test & measurement equipment
3.15	Communication chip sets
2.98	VoIP services
2.78	Dense Wavelength Division Multiplexing (DWDM)*
2.58	Access technologies*
2.57	Security
2.45	Broadband wireless
2.41	Access equipment*
2.12	Edge routers*
2.01	Operation Support Systems (OSSs) Test & Measurement
1.97	10-Gbit/s Ethernet switches*
1.96	Core routers*
1.90	Operations Support Systems (OSSs)
1.88	IP technologies
1.79	SSL VPN
1.70	Metro optical switches, ROADMs*
1.67	IPSec VPN
1.66	Transceivers
1.61	Ethernet services*
1.61	SONET/SDH*
1.55	Cable/MSO equipment
1.53	Optical equipment and Test & measurement equipment
1.51	Core optical switches*
1.45	Lasers*
1.28	Network processors
1.25	Softswitches
1.25	Cable modem termination systems
1.19	Multi-service provisioning platforms
1.17	Video on Demand (VoD)
0.99	Video equipment
0.98	Digital Subscriber Line (DSL)
0.93	Video services
0.93	Ethernet equipment*
0.93	Metro WDM equipment*
0.87	Traffic managers
0.78	Optical switches and cross-connects*
0.76	Multi-service switches
0.73	Digital Subscriber Line Access Multiplexers (DSLAMs)
0.72	Provisioning systems
0.72	Transmission fiber*

(continued)

Table 9.1   Technology Emphasis in Networking Space at Publication Time—Top 101 Issues (continued)

Percentage of Articles (%)	Networking Technology Area
0.71	IPTV
0.71	ATM switches
0.71	Multi-service provisioning platforms & add/drop muxes
0.70	Service activation systems
0.65	Long-haul WDM equipment*
0.64	IP equipment
0.62	Test & measurement products
0.60	Optical amplifiers*
0.58	Optical equipment*
0.58	Optical Switches & OADMs*
0.57	Mux/demuxes
0.53	Billing systems
0.50	40-Gbps optical transmission*
0.48	VoIP software
0.47	FTTx
0.46	IMS
0.46	Fixed/mobile convergence
0.45	TV
0.45	Ethernet chips
0.40	CWDM*
0.39	QOS*
0.38	Residential services
0.38	SONET/SDH chips*
0.38	Revenue assurance & fraud management
0.36	Passive Optical Network (PON)
0.33	Mediation systems
0.32	B-RASs
0.29	Performance monitoring
0.29	IP software
0.28	Enterprise networking*
0.28	Set-top boxes
0.27	Ethernet technologies*
0.26	Wavelength services*
0.25	Variable optical attenuators*
0.24	Modulators
0.24	SIP
0.23	Dispersion compensators
0.22	Video software
0.21	Broadband loop carriers/multi-service access nodes
0.21	Session border controllers
0.19	Broadcast video equipment (including encoding)
0.18	Service delivery platforms (SDPs)

Percentage of Articles (%)	Networking Technology Area
0.18	Media gateways
0.17	WiMax
0.15	Wholesale VoIP services
0.15	Optical channel monitors
0.15	Ethernet Passive Optical Networks (PONs)*
0.15	Optical technologies
0.14	Access devices
0.14	Generalized MPLS (GMPLS)*
0.14	VoIP equipment and test & measurement equipment
0.13	Middleware & business support systems
0.13	Multi-service edge equipment
0.13	Centrex
0.12	Wireless LAN
0.12	Layer 3 VPNs
0.11	Digital Subscriber Line (DSL) chips
0.11	Service Oriented Architectures (SOA)*

Note: Asterisked items are covered in this book.

years, the price erosion is such that the net impacts may well cancel out, and the ratios remain relatively close to the ones cited.

In summary, networking technologies that are expected to be important for the rest of the decade include the following: optical networking (all-optical and switched lambdas also known as Optical Transport Network*); GbE and 10GbE in the LAN and in the WAN; and new customer-practical connectivity options (such as multilink Frame Relay, TLS, and MPLS.) VPNs will likely achieve increased penetration both as stand-alone services as well as a way to support secure communications. QoS is important both for VPN support as well as for packet voice and digital video/multimedia applications. Many of these themes are examined in this chapter. Figure 9.4 depicts a typical contemporary environment; it depicts a converged voice/data intranet and shows all four of the classification elements introduced earlier.

9.1.2 What This Chapter Covers

This chapter is intended to provide an input to practitioners in this field, to assist them to realize where the industry may be headed in the next few years. As noted, customers now look to deploy broadband services: broadband is needed in both the LAN as well as in the WAN environment. Section 9.2 provides an encapsulated bottom line for infrastructure architects seeking guidance. The rest of the chapter provides technical details. Transmission technologies represent a foundation upon which other services can be delivered; hence, Section 9.3 discusses advances in optics that support broadband services in the LAN and WAN space. These optical transmission technologies are used in support of enterprise-, metro-, wide-, and global-area (Internet) services that firms will typically utilize to construct their intranet. Section 9.4 examines LAN technology,

---

* Some call this the Intelligent Optical Network.

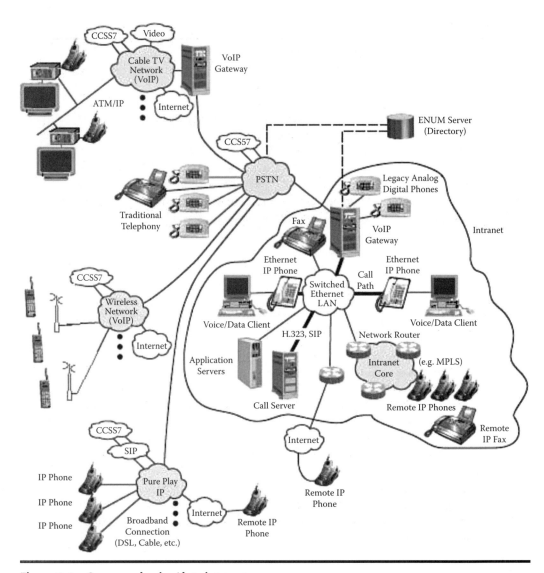

Figure 9.4   Converged voice/data intranet.

particularly GbE and 10 GbE. Section 9.5 examines SAN technology. The reader can use the acronym summary appendix as an aid. This chapter only gives a summary of these topics.

9.2 The Technology Architecture Bottom Line for LANs and SANs

A lot of information is presented in this chapter. An encapsulated bottom line for infrastructure architects seeking guidance is given in the following list. From an architecture-planning roadmap development perspective, the following is a list of possible strategies, based on the technology/ issues covered in the rest of the chapter:

- Deploy GbE or 10GbE in the campus (backbone).
- Deploy GbE or 10GbE in the data center to connect servers or blade server clusters.
- Use FC/SAN technology for connecting virtualized or nonvirtualized storage devices in the data center. Plan the use of 10 Gbps FC.
- Use IP-tunneled SANs for data-center-level connectivity beyond the local data center (e.g., for disaster recovery/data replication applications).
- Deploy power over Ethernet at the enterprise level.
- Deploy LAN QoS (IEEE 802.1p/1Q).
- Use VLANs for administrative purposes, but do so sparingly.
- Use the Rapid Spanning Tree Algorithm for faster convergence (both at the local and metro levels).
- Use state-of-the-art Layer 2 closet switches to support enterprisewide Ethernet connectivity; also seek to deploy closet-level routing (blades) and centralized wireless LAN management (blades) in the Layer 2 switch.
- Use metro Ethernet services when available for the majority of high-speed connections; when Ethernet is not available or usable, utilize SONET/SDH or OTN.

To aid readability, an acronym glossary is provided at the end of the chapter.

9.3 Introduction to Optical Transmission

This section looks at fundamental optical concepts that support the advances in broadband connectivity that, in turn, make possible new high-end LAN, MAN, and WAN services. Although these technologies are (also) used in high-end LANs, the major application of optical transmission is for the WAN environment. In optical transmission the signal is sent in digital form ("1" representing a light burst and "0" the absence of light) at high pulsing/clock rates over an optical cable (waveguide.)

Major advances in fiber-optic transmission technologies have occurred during the past decade, particularly in the context of "dense" multiplexing and the resulting ability to carry increased information over a single fiber pair. One can now routinely support 10 Gbps (work aimed at supporting 40 Gbps is under way) on a single beam of "light." Multiplexing systems allow the carriage of numerous (i.e., 8–160) beams onto a single fiber pair (or even a single fiber), providing near-terabit per-second speeds. The basic components of a fiber-optic system are a transmitter (laser diode [LD] or light-emitting diode [LED]), a fiber-optic waveguide (single-mode fiber [SMF] or multimode fiber [MMF]), and a receiver (photodetector diode). Typically, termination multiplexing equipment is located at the end of the link to support tributary lower-speed signals. This transmission/multiplex equipment generates electrical signals that the fiber-optic transmitter converts to optical signals for transmission over the optical fiber. The far-end receiver converts the optical signal back to electrical signals for distribution to the various ancillary devices. People are now looking at end-to-end optical systems without intervening electronics. Unrepeated distances have increased significantly over the years, and repeaters increase the distances to thousands of miles. Currently, many providers install a fiber infrastructure based on cables with a very high fiber count, on the order of 500 or even 1000; this deployment strategy provides tremendous bandwidth opportunities, particularly in the long-haul portion of the network. For LAN applications the issues just listed (very long distance, very high data rate, and tributary multiplexing) are less important; in LAN environments one is interested in a short-range, inexpensive, very-high-speed (but not ultrahigh) point-to-point link for data center, campus, or building connectivity.

9.3.1 Optical Fibers

Refraction is one of the most important properties of interest in optical communication. The index of refraction is defined relative to two media and represents the ratio of the speeds of light propagation in the two media. The difference in index of refraction gives the optical fiber its transmission (waveguide) properties. Refraction occurs because light moves faster through some materials than through others. The optical fiber is constructed with a cylindrical core of a higher index of refraction than the cladding material. Optical fibers used in carrier applications are based on silica; silica has a low optical signal loss in the infrared region of the electro-optical spectrum ranging from 0.80 to 1.60 μm (800 to 1600 nm) in terms of signal wavelength. The index of refraction of either the core or the cladding (or both) are changed from the values of pure silica by the incorporation of small amounts of dopant materials, such as germanium and phosphorus.

The fiber's core is made of transparent glass with a relatively high index of refraction; cladding is made of glass with a relatively lower index. The fiber (core plus cladding) acts as a waveguide for the signal. Because there is a difference of speed in the two media (core and cladding), the light is reflected and refracted at the boundary; the goal is to achieve total internal reflection, so that the light beam is projected forward. This occurs when the angle of refraction is 90°. Because, by design, the index of refraction changes "abruptly" at the core–cladding boundary, the resulting fiber is called *step-index* fiber. There is also a fiber type that exhibits a gradual change in the index across the cross section of the fiber; this is called *graded index* fiber.

Two types of (silica-based) optical (step index) fiber exist: MMF and SMF (see Figure 9.5). The transmission properties characteristic of the two types of optical fiber arise from the differing core diameters and refraction index profiles. Multimode fibers have various ratios of core to cladding diameter, the most common ratio being 62.5/125 μm (multimode fibers are more typical of LANs). The core carries multiple "modes" or rays of light. When the core is made smaller, there are fewer modes that carry energy. If the core is made small enough, then the fiber only carries one mode. When the core dimension is only a few times larger than the wavelength of the signal to be transmitted, only one of the originating rays ("modes") will be transmitted; this results in low loss (the others rays are attenuated in the proximity of the source). For wavelengths of 1.3 to 1.55 μm, the core needs to be less than 10 μm in diameter for single-mode transmission properties to hold. At this diameter a problem known as *modal dispersion* that affects multimode fiber disappears. With a single-mode fiber the information capacity is much higher; however, because the core is so small, more expensive light sources and connectors are required.

Depending on different service demands, optical cables contain different fiber types such as (see Table 9.2) standard single-mode fiber according to ITU-T G.652, nonzero dispersion-shifted single-mode according to ITU-T G.655, or fibers without hydrogen-oxide (OH)-peak. The main transmission fiber types are standard fiber (NDSF—Non Dispersion Shifted Fiber, e.g., Corning SMF-28), Dispersion Shifted Fiber (DSF), and the various types of Non Zero Dispersion Shifted Fiber (NZDSF, e.g., Corning LEAF or LS or Alcatel Lucent Truewave). New transmission fiber types with lower loss in the 1.4 micron region are beginning to emerge together with fibers specialized for the metro space. In this space, however, NDSF is still the most widely used fiber.

Corning SMF-28e fiber has become available in the past few years.* SMF-28e fiber supports low-water-peak performance across the entire operating wavelength range, including a specified attenuation at 1383 nm of less than or equal to 0.31 dB/km with a hydrogen-induced attenuation increase of less than or equal to 0.01 dB/km. This fiber belongs to the family of Extended

---

* Corning introduced SMF-28 fiber, the world's most extensively deployed fiber, in 1986.

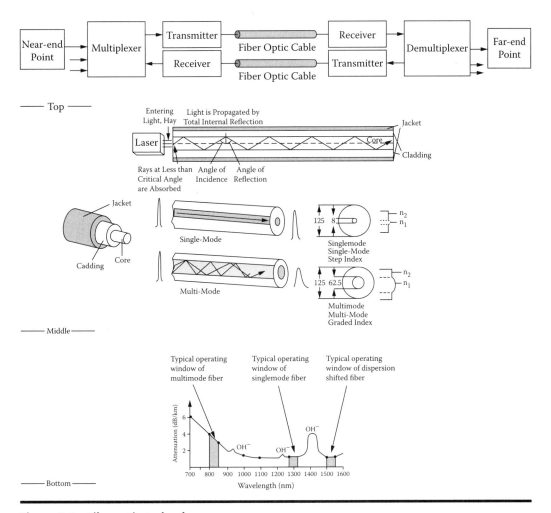

Figure 9.5   Fiberoptic technology.

Table 9.2   Standards for Basic Fiber Types

	Std SMF	*Extended Wavelength Band (EWB) SMF*
IEC (Category) 6073-2-50	B1.1	B1.3 (extended wavelength band)
ITU G652	G.652.B	G.652.C (extended wavelength band)
TIA 492CAAB (Class)	IVa	IVa (dispersion-unshifted with low water peak)

Wavelength Band (EWB) fibers. SMF-28e fiber is an ITU, G.652.C fiber. The additional operating wavelength potential opened by low attenuation in the water peak region combined with the emergence of systems designed to operate over those wavelengths translate into more options for network designers. Network designers may choose to transmit more channels on a single fiber, to increase channel spacing to facilitate CWDM or to reserve the additional wavelengths for future use.

9.3.1.1 Signal Degradation

The fiber medium degrades signal quality, as is the case in other media, although degradation is much less than that of other media. This greatly reduced attenuation is the reason why optical fiber can carry a signal over a longer distance or at much higher bandwidth than copper cables: (1) attenuation of a signal or waveform; and (2) distortion of its shape. Attenuation is a well-understood phenomenon: it is loss of light energy as it travels along the waveguide, that is, along the fiber strand. Two strands are used for each communication link: one for the transmit side and one for the receive side. Energy is lost because of impurities, imperfections, and physical phenomena. For single-mode systems running up to 0.5 Gbps, link length before regeneration is limited by loss rather than by dispersion. At higher bit rates, however, the length is limited by dispersion. Length issues are generally more of concern for long-haul systems; however, there are situations where they also impact metropolitan applications.*

9.3.1.2 Dispersion Phenomena

Next we discuss the distortion issues. Light not only becomes weaker when it goes through a long segment of fiber, but individual pulses of light in a digital signal may become broadened or blurred, so that they overlap. Either effect makes a signal more difficult to decipher at the remote end; in turn, this results in higher bit error rate (BER). The term that describes the principal cause of waveform distortion is *dispersion*.

Bandwidth is limited by the amount of pulse spreading and the response of source and detector. The total dispersion (pulse spreading or broadening) and the related fiber bandwidth are characterized by two key effects: *modal dispersion* (also called intermode or multimode dispersion) for multimode transmission systems, and *chromatic dispersion* (also called intramode or spectral dispersion) for single-mode transmission systems.

When a very short pulse of light is injected into an optical fiber, the optical energy does not all reach the far end at the same time. This causes the exit pulse to be broadened, that is, to be dispersed. Intramodal distortion is manifested in two ways: (1) as material dispersion resulting from slightly different indices of refraction that fiber presents to different wavelengths of light and (2) waveguide dispersion resulting from the longer path taken by longer wavelengths that reflect at more oblique angles with cladding.

Optical fibers are assigned dispersion ratings expressed either in (1) bandwidth in megahertz (MHz) per kilometer or (2) in time spread in picoseconds per kilometer. In the latter case, the dispersion of a fiber is measured in picoseconds of pulse spreading per kilometer of fiber per nanometer of source spectral width.

9.3.1.3 Intermodal Delay Distortion

In a simple step-index multimode fiber (which, as noted, has a large, uniform core), rays of light propagate through the core at different angles. Rays that go straight through the core have a shorter path than those at large angles which bounce off the inside wall of the core; hence, straight rays traverse the fiber faster. Step-index multimode fiber supports transmission of any light ray that enters optical fiber within an angle of acceptance. High-order modes travel over a longer

---

* For example, there are technical factors limiting transmission of 10 Gbps on a multimode fiber to around 82 m; new optimized multimode fibers are needed to reach (certain standards-driven goals of 300 m).

distance than low-order modes, and therefore, they arrive out of phase at any given point along the fiber. This causes intermodal delay distortion, and thus limits the bandwidth capacity of the fiber. Low-order modes, those launched into fiber at small angles with respect to the axis, travel a shorter ray distance to reach a given point along the fiber than do high-order modes launched at large angles. Intermodal distortion constricts the bandwidth of the cable because waves that start at the same instant arrive out of phase at the remote end, causing distortion.

The problem can be reduced by using a graded-index fiber; however, this type of fiber has relatively little if any commercial deployment at this time. With this kind of fiber, high-angle rays, with a longer physical distance to travel, spend more time in regions of the silica/glass with a lower index of refraction, where the speed of light is faster. This compensating effect gives all rays almost the same transit time; the result is that graded-index fiber has a much higher information capacity than step-index fiber. The compensation is never perfect, and a practical graded-index multimode optical fiber still cannot carry large data rates more than a few kilometers before distortion makes data unintelligible. Furthermore, it is more difficult to manufacture this type of fiber.

9.3.1.4 Chromatic Dispersion

Even in a single-mode fiber, all energy in a pulse does not reach the remote end at the same time. This phenomenon is called *chromatic dispersion*. Chromatic dispersion arises because although there is only one mode, the light pulse usually is composed of a small spectrum of wavelengths, and different wavelengths travel at different speeds in fiber. Chromatic dispersion is defined as the slope of the transit time versus wavelength curve for a given fiber substance.

Chromatic dispersion limits the bandwidth that can be secured over single-mode fibers. It results from the wavelength dependence of the velocity at which the optical signal travels: optical rays with different wavelengths travel along fiber at different velocities in different media. Because the optical sources (laser diodes) used produce signals over a range of wavelengths (e.g., from laser-diode "chirping"), and because each wavelength component of the pulse travels at a slightly different velocity, the pulse spreads in time as it travels down the fiber. In the visible spectrum of light, material dispersion causes longer wavelengths to travel faster than shorter ones. However, in the near-infrared region around wavelengths of 1.1 to 1.3 microns, the opposite happens: longer wavelengths tend to travel slower. There is also a temperature dependence to chromatic dispersion; although this dependence can generally be ignored for speeds up to 10 Gbps, it becomes an issue for higher speeds, e.g., OC-768/40 Gbps (its impact is 16 times more severe at 40 Gbps than at OC-192/10 Gbps*). There are three general ways to reduce the effect of chromatic dispersion:

1. Use a light source with only one wavelength. This approach, however, is not completely implementable, because every source has some spectral spread. The simplest lasers to manufacture are multi-longitudinal-mode lasers, which produce light at a number of different wavelengths spread over 5 to 10 nanometers or more. More sophisticated designs (distributed feedback, external cavity, etc.) reduce the spectrum to a single line, narrow enough so that chromatic dispersion can be ignored in most applications; these devices, however, are expensive.
2. This is the more common method. Choose a transmitter center wavelength and fiber design so that the effect is minimized. Silica-based optical fiber has low loss at 1300 nm, and even

---

* OC-x denotes, among other things, a clocking rate at 52,840,000x; e.g., OC-3 operates at 155.52 Mbps. See Section 9.3.3.5.

lower loss at 1550 nm, making these good-operating-wavelength regions. Close to 1300 nm, two signals 10 nm apart in wavelengths (a typical laser line width) will have little difference in velocity. In contrast, a laser pulse with a 1 nm spectral width centered at 1550 nm will be broadened by 16 ps after traveling 1 km. If spectral width is 10 nm and fiber length is 10 km, the pulse will be broadened by 1600 ps (1.6 ns). Negative values of chromatic dispersion have the same effect as positive values (sign indicates if longer or shorter wavelengths travel faster).

3. Utilize a certain amount of Dispersion Compensation Fiber (DCF) at the receiving end. When utilizing WDMs, multiple wavelengths travel down a fiber by design. By properly selecting a terminating fiber that "has the opposite effect" of the transmission fiber in terms of dispersion, one can reduce the impact of the dispersion phenomenon. The add-on fiber takes the rays that traveled faster and slows them down more than the rays that traveled slower. Unfortunately, a rather long spool of fiber (placed in a "pizza box") is needed, sometimes several kilometers long. These pizza boxes have to be selected on the basis of length of the transmission link. One of the issues is that these add-on fibers further impact attenuation (because the added fiber must be taken into account in the power budget). A relatively new approach is to use tunable dispersion compensators.

Returning to chromatic dispersion on non-WDM-used fiber, the optimal center wavelength for the transmitter is the point where chromatic dispersion is zero. This wavelength is called λ_0, or the zero-dispersion point (ZDP). This value varies from optical fiber to optical fiber and is an important parameter for fiber manufacturers to control. ZDP occurs naturally in pure silica glass at 1.27 microns. Because, in principle, single-mode fibers work with a single coherent wavelength, one way to exploit ZDP is to find a laser that emits light at 1.27 microns. However, when searching for greatest overall efficiency, other factors need to be considered. Usually, glass waveguides suffer from losses due to Rayleigh scattering, which occurs because of density and compositional variation within glass (Rayleigh scattering reduces as wavelengths grow longer.) To take advantage of this, dopant materials can be added to glass until its ZDP is shifted into the range between 1.3 and 1.6 microns. Many formulations of glass reach their lowest possible absorption in this range (below this, molecular thermal scattering becomes a problem). Some care in manufacture must be taken to avoid impurities in glass that increase absorption.

Ideally (in non-WDM situations), the laser would operate at the ZDP wavelength, so that the bandwidth would be very high; however, owing to manufacturing variations and aging, laser operating wavelengths cover a broad range of operating wavelengths. For a given transmission path length, a single-mode fiber-optic system exhibits less pulse broadening than multimode systems, provided the central wavelength is sufficiently close to the fiber's ZDP.

For long-distance applications it is desirable to operate at 1550 nm because of lower attenuation compared to 1300 nm. However, simple step-index single-mode fiber shows a large chromatic dispersion at 1550 nm. It is possible to design more sophisticated index profiles so that the point where chromatic dispersion is zero falls near 1550 nm instead of 1300 nm. This optical fiber is called a *dispersion-shifted fiber*. This fiber may give significantly longer unrepeatered distances at higher information transmission rates than the unshifted fiber when conventional LDs or LEDs are used. Segmented-core fiber is a fiber that is designed to operate as a low-loss single-mode fiber at 1300 and 1550 nm, while maintaining zero-dispersion wavelength in a 1550 nm window. In addition, this fiber performs as a high-bandwidth "few-mode" fiber near 800 nm, where inexpensive light sources are available. Segmented-core fiber allows mode equalization over a large range of wavelengths. This fiber can be used in high-performance long-haul or in subscriber-loop applications at longer wavelengths.

In conclusion, chromatic dispersion can be managed. At higher speeds the issue becomes more pressing (particularly at 40 Gbps on nondispersion shifted fiber; operation at OC-768 is 16 times more sensitive to the problem than operation at OC-192). Managing chromatic dispersion imposes a cost and a loss premium.

9.3.1.5 Polarization Mode Dispersion (PMD)

Polarization mode dispersion (PMD) is caused by slight fiber asymmetry: during fabrication or during the drawing process, a non-totally-circular core or cladding may result. PMD is the result of the accumulation of weak birefringence along the various fiber spans (a link of any length exceeding 2 or 4 km will comprise spliced fibers that originate from different manufacturing events). An input light pulse of an initial polarization will decompose into two pulses with two different polarizations separated in time. The time separation leads to decreased system margin or even outages. This issue becomes more pronounced and problematic at higher speeds (i.e., OC-192 and OC-768.)

In addition to noncircular cores and cladding from the manufacturing process, bends or twist-induced stresses also introduce PMD. Furthermore, PMD also depends on the temperature of the fiber, sometimes making transmission problematic on a seasonal basis. Systems components such as isolators and circulators also have a bearing on the issue. The problem is more pronounced on older fibers and systems. At this time fiber can be drawn in a manner that minimizes PMD; also, components can be manufactured that keep PMD low. Older fibers have PMD in the range of 0.5 ps/km$^{1/2}$; newer fibers range around 0.1 ps/km$^{1/2}$; the expectation is that this figure will decrease to 0.05 for future fibers. Forward error correction (FEC) methods may also be used as an effective tool against nonlinear effects. Tunable PMD compensators are also being developed at this time.

9.3.1.6 Single-Mode Fibers

As noted, single-mode fibers are designed in such a fashion that only one mode propagates. Here, the information transmission capacity is limited by the phenomenon of chromatic dispersion, which, as discussed earlier, is a result of the wavelength-dependant velocities of propagation in the fiber material. Conventional single-mode fiber (e.g., SMF-28) has its minimum chromatic dispersion (that is to say, its maximum transmission capacity) near 1.31 μm (see Figure 9.5).

Conventional single-mode fibers are classified as either matched-cladding or depressed-cladding designs. In the former type, the cladding has the same index of refraction from the core-cladding interface to the outer surface of the fiber. In the latter type, there are two layers of cladding material: the index of refraction of the inner cladding, which is adjacent to the fiber core, is lower than that of the outer cladding (typically undoped silica).

Single-mode fibers are characterized by the mode field diameter (MFD) and by the cutoff wavelength. The MFD is a measure of the width of the guided optical power's intensity distribution in the core and cladding. Typical values for the MFD are in the 10.0 μm range. The cutoff wavelength is the wavelength below which a single-mode fiber propagates more than one mode and above which only a single (fundamental) mode can operate.

As noted earlier, dispersion-shifted fiber is designated so that the wavelength of minimum dispersion is "shifted" to 1.55 μm. At this wavelength, the attenuation can be significantly lower than at 1.31 μm. Single-mode fibers can also be designated as dispersion-flattened fibers. Dispersion-flattened single-mode fibers are attractive: the dispersion is low in both the 1.31-μm window and in the 1.55-μm window.

9.3.1.7 Multimode Fibers

Multimode fibers support dozens of propagating modes, each of which travels at a slightly different velocity. These fibers tend to be used in GbE and 10GbE LAN applications, although these also can utilize single-mode fiber. The core diameter of the multimode fiber normally used is 62.5 μm, but other special designs of multimode fibers exist. Multimode fiber can be of the step-index or graded-index type, although most fiber deployed is of the former kind. As noted earlier, the graded-index multimode fiber is designed to reduce pulse distortion by nearly equalizing the velocities of the modes propagating in the fiber. With this graded-index fiber, the index of refraction decreases approximately parabolically from the center of the core to the boundary between the core and the cladding material. However, the equalization of mode velocities is not perfect, and the information transmission capacity of multimode fibers is substantially less than that of single-mode fibers.

Roughly speaking, 850 and 1310 nm multimode systems can operate at distances from a few hundred meters to a couple of kilometers; see Table 9.3 [BIR200601] for examples (also see Figure 9.5). 1310 nm FP laser single-mode systems can range from 10 to 40 km; Distributed Feedback Lasers (DFBs) can reach up to 100 km with good fiber. If the distance spanned exceeds these limits, the light must be amplified directly (with an Erbium Doped Fiber Amplifier) or converted to electricity, regenerated, amplified, and converted back to light.

9.3.2 Transmission Approaches

There are two basic approaches to optical transmission: noncoherent and coherent transmission. We focus here only on noncoherent because it is the norm for commercial systems. Noncoherent methods involve on-off keying and direct detection of signal; this is a variant of amplitude modulation, specifically, a unipolar digital scheme of amplitude shift keying (ASK). The amount of information transmitted is based on the source/reception clocking. Building on this basic method, several noncoherent optical channels can be operated over the low-loss/low-dispersion ranges of an optical fiber. This requires filters to separate the optical channels. Such devices (filters) are

Table 9.3 Distances Supported by Multimode Fiber

Application	Wavelength	Distance
10 Mbps Ethernet, 10Base-FL	850 nm MM	2000 m
100 Mbps Fast Ethernet, 100Base-FX	1310 nm MM	2000 m
100 Mbps Fast Ethernet, 100Base-SX	850 nm MM	300 m
Gigabit Ethernet, 1000Base-SX	850 nm MM	220 m/550 m[a]
Gigabit Ethernet, 1000Base-LX	1310 nm SM	550 m

[a] 62.5μm/50 μm fiber.

called WDMs. Initially, such multiplexers were designed to support two channels in the 1.30 μm wavelength region and three channels in the 1.50 μm region. Commercial products now support several dozen channels, and laboratory tests have demonstrated the possibility of using several hundred channels of 1 to 10 Gbps utilizing "narrow-spectrum" lasers and direct detection.

Even this multiplexing, however, does not use the available fiber bandwidth to its maximum potential (100 channels at 10 Gbps would equate to 1 terabit per second, or 0.001 petabit per second). First, there are several limitations such as source spectra, multiplexer filter technique, modulation-induced effects such as frequency chirp and mode-partition noise, and fiber dispersion characteristics. Second, the available fiber bandwidth can be estimated from looking at wavelength regions having low loss (less than 0.5 dB/km or so), such as from 1.27 to 1.35 μm and from 1.48 to 1.60 μm. These regions provide a total wavelength band of 200 nm and corresponds to a frequency bandwidth of about 29 terahertz; yet, it is used to support the few (dozen) noncoherent channels [BEL199001].

Optical line signals are usually in the form of Return to Zero (RZ) or Non-Return-to-Zero (NRZ) pulses. The RZ pulses typically have an average 50% duty cycle (duty cycle is the fraction of time that the light source is "on" compared with the assigned time slot.) For "off," the light from an LED is turned off; on the other hand, lasers are only dimmed (NRZ) to about 10 dB below the "on" level. Line signals are also used for clock recovery: the clock recovery circuit requires a minimum number of transitions between 0's and 1's and only short runs of contiguously successive 1's or 0's. To meet these conditions, line signals are typically scrambled to provide a balance between 0's and 1's.

9.3.3 Fiber-Optic Active Components

Optical transmitters convert digital electrical signals into pulsed optical signals; furthermore, they couple these signals into the fiber waveguide for transmission. The two major kinds of semiconductor transmitter in use are LEDs and LDs. These transmitters have the necessary design characteristics of small size, conversion efficiency, coupling efficiency, speed, electrical amenability, environmental resistance, and reliability. LDs are typically used with single-mode fibers, and LEDs are typically used with multimode fibers (however, other combinations are possible). Efforts have been under way for a number of years to integrate the optics and electronics monolithically in an electro-optical chip to provide for higher-bit-rate transmission.

9.3.3.1 Light-Emitting Diodes

Light-emitting diodes (LEDs) come in two types: *surface emitters* and *edge emitters*. The surface-type emission pattern is typically 120° × 120°. Light emission occurs at currents of 100 mA. The peak power coupled into multimode fiber is about –10 to –20 dBm; the power coupled into single-mode fiber is about –27 to –37 dBm. The spectral (noise) width of the emission is about 35 to 50 nm for short wavelengths, and about 80 to 120 nm for long wavelengths. The edge-emitting diode has a more "focused" emission pattern, typically 120° × 30° m; therefore, the power coupled into the fiber is up to 10 dB greater than for surface emitters. The spectral width is about 30 to 90 nm over the band of interest. The spectral width of the LED source and the dispersion characteristic of the fiber limit the bandwidth that can be used. The LED structure is similar to that for lasers, and care must be taken to prevent unwanted laser action. The LEDs are operated with a small forward bias (low light emission) to overcome a turn-on delay. Also, because the output optical power varies with dc voltage and with temperature, compensation of the LED is required. A thermoelectric cooler may also be used to stabilize the LED temperature over a range of temperature differences between the LED and the ambient.

9.3.3.2 Laser Diodes

Semiconductor laser diodes (LDs) have a typical emission pattern of 30° × 30°; this provides for higher coupling efficiency than for LEDs, particularly for single-mode fibers. LDs give a peak power of –10 to +10 dBm, typically near 0 dBm, coupled into either multimode or single-mode fibers. The spectra of LDs are much narrower than for LEDs, ranging from 3 to 5 nm for typical multi-longitudinal-mode lasers and 1 nm or less for single-longitudinal-mode laser. The LD relies on mirrors formed by cleaved crystal facets at each end of the optical cavity. In this design, the 3-to-5-nm-wide emitted spectrum is made up of a group of lines with the lines separated by the mode spacing of the cavity. Efforts to narrow the spectrum to permit greater bandwidth and repeater spacing have resulted in other structural designs. Multimode laser operation produces mode-partition noise. This means that the relative intensity of the various modes fluctuates, with the total optical power remaining constant. This fluctuation degrades system performance. Single-frequency lasers eliminate this noise: they reduce the dispersion bandwidth impairment to only that associated with the spectrum produced by the modulation. Further bandwidth impairments are caused by laser chirp, which is a frequency change in the laser output caused by "on" and completely "off" signaling. The change increases undesired spectral lines. This effect can be suppressed by keeping the laser in the light-emitting state and changing the light intensity for signaling.

9.3.3.3 Tunable Lasers

With the advent of DWDM, the need arises to have tunable lasers that can be used in lieu of a large inventory of fixed-wavelength line cards. Today's DFBs are unique to a given wavelength; a DWDM system with 100 channels (as an example) presents a daunting challenge to the service provider in terms of spares and maintenance. In case of an outage on a system, the carrier must find the exact replacement laser. Tunable lasers also reduce system maintenance and troubleshooting activities, thereby reducing system operating and maintenance costs. A tunable laser is a single replacement for all static sources; sparing is done with a single, common, configurable card. Tunable lasers are also at the basis for bandwidth (lambda) on demand and the Optical Transport Network (OTN).* In this fashion, the transport nodes can match available capacity to real-time demand. Routes can be set up across the network for an end-to-end "lambda" circuit; this also allows dynamic setup and teardown of lambdas based on downstream requirements. Proponents see these services entering the market on a wide scale shortly. Also, these devices support wavelength conversion, wavelength switching, and wavelength add/drop. The Intelligent Optical Network is an architecture that is based on all optical communication along with a control mechanism for both the User-Network Interface (UNI) as well as for the Network Node Interface (NNI).

Tunable laser families include DFB; Distributed Bragg Reflector (DBR); Vertical Cavity Surface Emitting Laser (VCSEL), and External Cavity Diode Laser (ECDL). The least expensive fiber-optic transmitters, the LEDs, are used for multimode transmission at 850 or 1310 nm, but are limited in

---

* OTN is a set of recommendations from the ITU-T on the "next-generation" optical network transport system (beyond SONET/SDH).

speed. Fabry–Perot (FP) laser diodes are relatively inexpensive and are typically used for single-mode transmission at 1310 nm. DFB laser diodes are most expensive and are used for single-mode transmission at 1550 nm. VCSEL is now popular for GbE operation at 850 nm. To give a rough view of the relative costs involved with these transmitters at press time, the original equipment manufacturer (OEM) cost in volume of an LED transmitter/receiver (transceiver) component is about $20; an FP laser transceiver, $100; a DFB laser, $600; and a gigabit VCSEL, $70 [BIR200601]. The receivers in these types of relatively inexpensive transceivers are similar; they consist of a special diode that converts photons into electrons. Quality receivers are able to detect light levels down to hundreds of nanowatts. Note that the receiver does not care if the transmitter is multimode or single-mode; it just knows that photons arrive, regardless of the path they take to get there.

9.3.3.4 Fiber-Optic Receivers

Optical receivers are coupled to the fiber strand as a unit. These receivers convert on-off light pulses by photodetection into electrical signals. The electrical signals are processed by electronics components to provide the output data stream. There are two kinds of photodetector diode, the PIN* (Positive Intrinsic Negative) and the APD† (Avalanche Photodetector Diode) type. Typically, the APD type can detect a lower optical signal power than the PIN type by about 10 dB (at 10^{-9} BER). An ideal receiver should offer good sensitivity (low received power for 10^{-9} BER), wide dynamic range, relatively low cost to manufacture and operate, reliability, low dependence on temperature, etc. None of the diodes currently in production have all of the ideal characteristics. For example, the APD has the highest sensitivity and good dynamic range but is difficult to produce, whereas InGaAs photoconductors have poorer sensitivity but are simpler and have the potential to be integrated with low-noise amplifiers. Over time, advances are expected to provide improved receivers with integrated optic and electronic circuits.

9.3.3.5 Technologies Supporting SONET and WDM Systems

9.3.3.5.1 The Basics of SONET

SONET/SDH is an interworking multiplexing and operations standard developed in the late 1980s and early 1990s that defines data rates, optical characteristics, and operations protocols (over a data communications channel) to support multi-vendor optical transmission. The common data rates are shown in Table 9.4. SONET technology is used in the United States and SDH in the rest of the world.

In SONET, the basic signal rate is 51.84 Mbps. This rate is known as the STS-1 rate. SONET resides at the Physical Layer in the Open Systems Interconnection Reference Model. Similar to other physical layer transport, it describes transmission speed, line encoding, and signal multiplexing. SONET defines this as the Optical Carrier (OC) signals, frame format, and the Operations Administration Maintenance and Provisioning (OAM&P) protocol. The fiber-optic transmission rates vary from OC-1 through OC-192.

SONET divides the fiber path into multiple logical channels called *tributaries*. A tributary's basic unit of transmission is the STS-1 (Synchronous Transport Signal Level 1) or OC-1 (optical carrier level 1) signal. Both operate at 51.84 Mbps; STS describes electrical signals, and OC refers

---

* Composition: InGaAs.

† Composition: Ge.

Table 9.4　Common Data Rates

Nomenclature	Data Rate (Mbps)
OC-1/STS-1	51.84
OC-3/STS-3/STM-1	155.52
OC-12/STS-12/STM-4	622.08
OC-48/STS-48/STM-16	2,488.32
OC-192/STS-192/STM-64	9,953.28
OC-768/STS-768/STM-256	39,813.12

to the same traffic once it has been converted into optical signals. SONET also allows channels to be multiplexed, so an OC-12 circuit, for instance, might carry traffic from four OC-3 links. A circuit also can carry a single channel, in which case the line is said to be concatenated; circuits are described as OC-3c, OC-12c, and so on.

Frame format structure is based on the STS-1 equivalent of 51.84 Mbps. Higher-level signals are integer multiples of the base rate, 51.84 Mbps. For example, an STS-3 is 3 × 51.84 =155 Mbps. The STS-1 signal is divided into two main parts, transport overhead and synchronous payload overhead (SPE). The SPE is further divided into two-parts: the STS Path Overhead (POH) and the payload. The payload is the data being transported and switched through the SONET network without being demultiplexed at the terminating locations.* As a result of this ability, SONET is said to be service independent or transparent.

The STS-1 has a sequence of 810 bytes (6480 bits) that includes overhead bytes and the envelope capacity for transporting payload. The frame consists of a 90 column by 9 row structure with a frame length of 125 ms, (8000) frames per second, thus (9) × (90 bytes/frame) × (8 bits/byte) × (8000 frames/s) = 51.84 Mbps. The order of transmission of bytes is row-by-row from top to bottom and from left to right. The STS payload pointer provider contained in the transport overhead designates the location of the byte where the STS-1 SPE begins. The STS POH is associated with each payload and is used to communicate various information, such as the pick-up and drop-off points. The higher STS-N signals are generated through byte-interleaving STS-1 modules. SONET provides overhead information that allows simpler multiplexing and greatly expanded operations, administration, maintenance, and provisioning capabilities. Overhead can be divided into several layers.

Path Level overhead is carried from end to end. It is added to DS-1 signals when they are mapped to Virtual Tributaries (VT) of the STS-1 payloads that travel end to end. Line overhead is for an STS-n signal between STS-n multiplexers (18 bytes). This data is accessed, generated, and processed by the line-terminating equipment. This data supports locating the SPE in the frame, multiplexing the signals, automatic protection switching (in case the ring fails), and line maintenance. Section overhead is used for the communication between network elements (9 bytes). This data is accessed, generated, and processed by section-terminating equipment. This information supports performance monitoring of signal, framing, and for alarms, controls, monitoring, and administration needs.

Pointers are contained in the line overhead. They compensate for the frequency and phase variations of asynchronous signals. This is accomplished through bit stuffing. The SPE payload pointer indicates where in the payload STS-1 or VT starts, and the bit stuffing allows for the alignment of the payload. If the timing of the signal is slow or fast, bit stuffing is implemented to

* Material for the rest of this subsection based in part on [KOU199901].

align the signal. They also indicate where the signal begins, allowing for easy extraction or insertion into the network. Pointers allow for the extraction of DS-1 without the need of multiplexing. STS POH is the first column of the SPE. It provides the communication between the creation of the STS SPE and its point of disassembly. This supports monitoring of payload, path status, path trace, and mapping status of the content within the payload. VT POH is created when a lower level signal less than the 51.84 Mbps must be transported, such as a DS-1. This pointer maps the DS-1; it provides information such as origin and destination.

The optical layers that define SONET are as follows:

- Path Layer—The Path Layer deals with the transport of services between the PTEs (path terminating equipment). It multiplexes or demultiplexes the STS payload. The terminating equipment assembles 28 1.544 Mbps DS-1 signals into a 51.84 Mbps STS-1 signal. The function of the Path Layer is to map the signals into a format required by the Line Layer. More specifically, its main functions are as follows: Read, interpret, and modify the path overhead for performance and automatic protection switching.
- Line Layer—The Line Layer deals with the transport of the Path Layer payload and its overhead across the physical medium. The main function of the Line Layer is to provide synchronization and to perform multiplexing for the Path Layer. Its main functions are protection switching, synchronization, multiplexing, line maintenance, and error monitoring.
- Section Layer—The Section Layer deals with the transport of an STS-N frame across the physical medium. Its functions are framing, scrambling, error monitoring, and section maintenance.
- Photonic Layer—The Photonic Layer mainly deals with the transport of bits across the physical medium. Its function is the conversion between STS signal and OC signals. Its main functions are: wavelength, pulse shape, and power levels.

The multiplexing principles of SONET are as follows:

- Mapping—process whereby tributaries are adapted into VTs by adding justification bits and POH information.
- Aligning—process whereby a pointer is included in the STS path or VT POH, to allow the first byte of the VT to be located.
- Multiplexing—process whereby multiple lower-order Path Layer signals are adapted into a higher-order path signal, or when the higher-order path signals are adapted into the line overhead.
- Stuffing—SONET has the ability to handle various input tributary rates from asynchronous signals; as the tributary signals are multiplexed and aligned, some spare capacity has been designed into the SONET frame to provide enough space for all these various tributary rates; therefore, at certain points in the multiplexing hierarchy, this space capacity is filled with fixed stuffing bits that carry no information but are required to fill up the particular frame.

9.3.3.5.2 The Basics of WDM

WDM is a multiplexing technology, as the name implies. Optical multiplexers aggregate multiple signals (lambdas) onto a single waveguide (here, the fiber). Demultiplexers separate the combined signal into individual signals (lambdas) and output ports/fibers. Three basic categories of multiplexers are *star couplers*, *thin-film filters*, and *phased array*. A star coupler is an all-fiber technology that is inexpensive and robust, but suffers from high signal loss. Typically, it is used for low-count systems. Thin-film

Table 9.5   System-Level Evolution over Time (1977–2010)

Phase 1 (1977–Present):	Asynchronous TDM (optical DS3s, etc.)
Phase 2 (1989–Present):	Synchronous TDM (SONET/SDH)
Phase 3 (1990–Present):	Wave Division Multiplexing
Phase 4 (1994–Present):	Dense Wave Division Multiplexing
Phase 5 (2001–Present):	Optical Transport Network (OTN)

Note: "Present" means this technology is still in use.

filters are manufactured according to well-known semiconductor processes. They are a robust and proven technology that allows the network designer to "pay as one scales." This technology can be used up to about 40 lambdas. Planar array waveguides are a silicon semiconductor technology that can be used for midrange systems (16–40 lambdas); it is cheaper on a per-channel basis than thin-film filters, but one must pay for the entire capability (wafer) up front. Other technologies used in WDM include bulk gratings, fiber Bragg gratings, Mach–Zehnder structures, and combination of Mach–Zehnder structures and fiber Bragg gratings.

WDM can be viewed as a sublayer to SONET: WDM can replace a number of distinct SONET transmission systems with a single WDM transmission system and a single fiber pair that support the (numerous) constituent SONET end systems. DWDM systems have seen major deployment in the United States starting in the late 1990s. Table 9.5 provides a view of the system-level evolutions over time.

By using frequency division multiplexing (FDM) techniques on a fiber transmission system, one can achieve "fiber-optic pair gain," where multiple signals ("lambdas") operating at different frequencies can each carry OC-48 or OC-192 channels between endpoints. Signal spacings have improved to the 100, 50, and even 25 GHz range. In a long-haul applications, optical amplification that is used in conjunction with WDM enables the network planner to either space out hub, regeneration, or amplification sites or skip amplification at some sites using techniques such as Raman amplification.

9.3.3.6 MAN, WAN, and Internet

The optical transmission technologies discussed earlier are used to support metro-, wide-, and global-area (Internet) services from carriers that firms will typically utilize to construct their intranet.

9.4 Advances in LAN Technology, Applications, and Opportunities

As companies contemplate the introduction of high-data-rate applications as well as multimedia applications, two key features are needed end to end: (1) high network throughput, and (2) transmission QoS. Both of these capabilities can be compromised if there is a shortcoming at any point along the way in the initial LAN, in the access network, in the backbone network, in the hand-off carrier's network, or in the far-end LAN. These capabilities have to be truly end to end; this is why it is important to understand how these capabilities are supported at the outset, on the originating LAN.

Major advancements in LAN systems have taken place in the past decade. Recent advances include the following: (1) increased aggregate bandwidth and the near elimination of contention-based designs; (2) faster convergence to restored topologies via the Rapid Spanning Tree Algorithm (RSTA); (3) better WAN interface, particularly at 10 Gbps speeds; (4) QoS support via the IEEE 802.1Q/p standards; and (5) wireless LANs (not covered here).

9.4.1 Increased Aggregate Bandwidth

This section looks at increased aggregate bandwidth LANs and the near elimination of contention-based designs in corporate enterprise applications. One area where contention-based designs continues to apply, however, is wireless; hence, some treatment of the traditional Carrier Sense Multiple Access with Collision Detect (CSMA/CD) is provided in this section.

9.4.1.1 Review of Traditional LAN Technology

9.4.1.1.1 History

A brief overview of classical LAN technology is presented in this section.* The original work that eventually led to the Ethernet specification began in the early 1970s at Xerox Palo Alto Research Center; this work built upon the Aloha System radio work done in the late 1960s and early 1970s. In 1976 Xerox built a LAN on a 1 km cable to interconnect about 100 workstations with about 3 Mbps throughput. This throughput was achieved using CSMA/CD sense channel (1-persistent with abort on collision). This work was improved upon by Digital Equipment Corporation, Intel, and Xerox, and in 1980 Ethernet Version 1 was released, supporting 10 Mbps. The specification was further updated, and in 1982 Ethernet Version 2 was released. However, by this time there were dozens of competing architectures on the market.

To stabilize the situation, the Institute of Electrical and Electronics Engineers (IEEE) became involved. By 1985, the IEEE 802.3 specification was completed and provided a specification for Ethernet LAN connectivity over thick and thin coax. In 1990, the specification was updated to include Ethernet over unshielded twisted pair (UTP) copper wiring, with the release of the 10BASE-T standard. The current IEEE 802.3 specification includes thick coax, thin coax, twisted pair cabling, and fiber, with speeds of 10 Mbps, 100 Mbps (Fast Ethernet), 1000 Mbps (Gigabit Ethernet—GbE), and 10,000 Mbps for the recently completed 10 Gbps standard (10GbE). The IEEE Committee is now looking at future enhancements in the 40 or perhaps 100 Gbps range.

Distinct LAN segments are interconnected using bridges. The first Ethernet bridges were developed by the Digital Equipment Corporation around the same time as Ethernet, namely, in the early 1980s. The 1990s saw the emergence of multi-port bridges that had as many ports as users; these have been called Layer 2 Switches (L2S), and are now broadly deployed.

The IEEE protocol suite comprises a media access control (MAC) layer that may directly include a PHY (physical layer) specification. More recent specifications make the PHY a separate sublayer (in fact, there may be a number of PHYs associated with a given Ethernet family). Figure 9.6 depicts the IEEE protocol model across several LAN technologies. Figure 9.7 shows the sublayering of the MAC/PHY layers.

---

* For example, see D. Minoli, *First, Second, and Next Generation LANs,* McGraw-Hill, New York, 1994, and D. Minoli and A. Alles, *LAN, LAN Emulation, and ATM,* Artech House, Norwood, Massachussets, 1997.

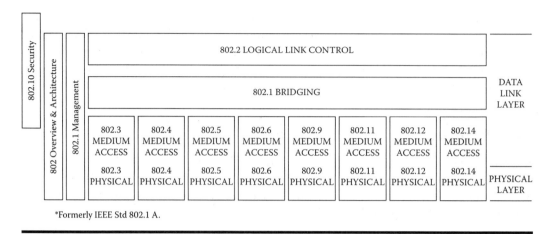

*Formerly IEEE Std 802.1 A.

Figure 9.6   IEEE protocol architecture.

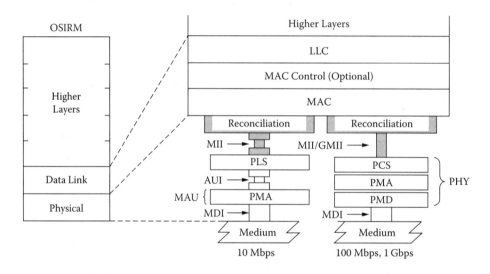

AUI = Attachment Unit Interface
GMI = Gigabit Media Independent Interface
MAU = Medium Attachment Unit
MDI = Medium Dependent Interface
MII = Media Independent Interface
LLC = Logical Link Control
MAC = Media Access Control
OSIRM = Open System Interconnection Reference Model

PCS = Physical Coding Sublayer
PHY = Physical Layer Device
PLS = Physical Layer Signaling
PMA = Physical Medium Attachment
PMD = Physical Medium Dependent

Figure 9.7   IEEE 802.3 protocol model.

9.4.1.1.2 Protocol Layers

The PHY covers the electrical, mechanical, and functional specifications of the cable used and the characteristics of the signal being transmitted. IEEE 802.3 includes specifications such as the maximum length of Ethernet cabling and maximum number of devices that can be connected to each cable. IEEE Standard 802.3 does not use straight binary (two states*) encoding (e.g., with 0 volts for a 0 bit and 5 volts for a 1 bit), because this leads to ambiguities caused by the fact that devices cannot tell the difference between the idle state (0 volts) and a 0 bit being sent, particularly with reference to tracking or deriving "clock" (that is, synchronization information). Instead, the IEEE 802.3 standard utilizes Manchester encoding. Manchester encoding works as follows: each bit period is divided into two equal intervals. A 1 bit is sent by having the voltage level of the first half of the bit interval set high and that of the second interval set low. With a 0 bit, the first interval is set low and the second interval set high. With this approach it is easy to synchronize the receiver (track clock) with the sender, because during every bit interval there is a transition. This way it is straightforward to distinguish between an idle period and a transmission of a 0 bit. However, Manchester encoding requires twice the bandwidth of unipolar binary encoding.

The functions of the MAC layer are as follows:

- Addressing of destination stations (both as individual stations and as groups of stations); each LAN device (e.g., PC, switch port, router port) has a network interface card (NIC), which contains a unique 48-bit address configured into the ROM when the NIC is manufactured.
- Control of access to the physical transmission medium, particularly in the contention-based environment of shared LANs.
- Conveyance of source-station addressing information.
- Filtering of frames according to their destination addresses to reduce the extent of propagation of frames in parts of a LAN that do not contain communication paths leading to the intended destination end stations. A frame unit of data transmission on an IEEE 802 LAN MAC that conveys a protocol data unit (PDU) between MAC Service users. There are three types of frame: *untagged, VLAN(Virtual LAN)-tagged,* and *priority-tagged.* These frames are defined in IEEE 802.1Q.
- Frame delimiting and recognition.
- Protection against errors.
- Transparent data transfer of Logical Link Control (LLC) PDUs, or of equivalent information in the Ethernet sublayer.

At Layer 2 (the "upper part" of the MAC layer), the "original" Ethernet Version 2 frame format is almost identical to the current IEEE 802.3 frame format (see Figure 9.8). Both Ethernet frames have a header containing the Destination Node Address (where it is going), followed by the Source Node Address (where it came from). The difference between them is that Ethernet Version 2 has an *EtherType* field containing a two-byte code describing the protocol inside the data section of the frame (e.g., the code for IPv4 is hexadecimal 0800, represented as 0x0800). The *EtherType* codes were originally administered by the Xerox Corporation, but they are now administered by the IEEE Type Field Registrar, which also administers the allocation of Ethernet NIC addresses to manufacturers. By contrast, the IEEE 802.3 *Length/Type Field* is a two-byte field that takes on one of two meanings, depending on its numeric value. The *Type Field* provides a context for interpretation of the data field of the frame (protocol identification). For numeric evaluation, the first byte is the most significant octet of this field. When the value of this field is greater than or equal to 1536 decimal (equal to 0600 hexadecimal, 0x0600), the *Type Field* indicates the nature of the MAC client protocol (Type interpretation). Well-known protocols already have a *Type Field*. The "length" and "type" interpretations of this field are mutually exclusive. Hence, when the value of

---

* This is also known as *unipolar.*

6 Bytes	6 Bytes	2 Bytes	46 to 1500 Bytes
Destination	Source	Ethertype	Data

(a) Ethernet Version 2

6 Bytes	6 Bytes	2 Bytes	1 Byte	1 Byte	1 Byte	43 to 1500 Bytes
Destination	Source	Length/Type	DSAP	SSAP	CTRL	Data

(b) IEEE 802.3 with 802.2 LLC

Figure 9.8   Ethernet versus IEEE 802.3 frames.

the two-byte field is equal to or greater than 0x0600, then it is a *Type Field* and the value of the *Type Field* is obtained from the IEEE Type Field Registrar.

9.4.1.1.3 Logical Link Control

IEEE 802.3 is intended for use with 802.2 LLC headers and therefore has a 2-byte *Length Field* specifying the length of the data carried by the frame. IEEE 802.3 also uses the first three bytes of the data field for Destination Source Service Access Point (DSAP) and Source Service Access Point (SSAP), and Control. This is followed by the data transported by the frame. The minimum frame length is 60 bytes. One of the functions of the LLC is to identify the protocol that is being carried in the payload. As alluded to earlier, protocol identification is accomplished as follows:

- Ethernet Type-encoding: The use of the Type interpretation of an IEEE 802.3 *Length/Type Field* value in a frame as a protocol identifier associated with the MAC Service user data carried in the frame. Ethernet Type-encoding can be used with MAC Service user data carried on non-IEEE 802.3 MACs by means of the SubNetwork Access Protocol (SNAP)-based encapsulation techniques specified in ISO/IEC 11802-5, IETF RFC 1042, and IETF RFC 1390.
- LLC encoding: The use of LLC addressing information in a frame as a protocol identifier associated with the MAC Service user data carried in the frame.

9.4.1.1.4 Carrier Sense Multiple Access with Collision Detect

The IEEE 802.3 standard uses the random access technique CSMA/CD at the upper part of the MAC layer to achieve multiplexing of the channel in the shared (but not in the switched) LAN environment. This is a distributed contention method, enabling, in normal circumstances, "fair" access to the shared medium. These days users tend to be in their own dedicated segments; hence, the contention mechanism is idle (unused) in those segments. However, if one employs any portion of a shared link, then contention still plays a role.

With CSMA/CD all LAN devices transmit on a common channel. Devices avoid collision by sensing the state of the channel before transmission. When a device wants to transmit, it listens to the cable. If the cable is in use, the device waits until it is idle, otherwise it transmits immediately:

- Send data frame if channel is sensed idle.
- Defer data frame transmission and repeat sensing if channel is sensed busy.

If multiple devices begin transmitting simultaneously, a *collision* will occur. Channel information is one propagation delay "away"; this propagation time interval is called "a." The LAN device listens to the cable after it transmits a frame to detect a collision. After a collision all LAN devices stop transmitting and wait a random amount of time before trying to transmit again (that is, if collision occurs, repeat sensing after random backoff for retransmission). This technique offers increased channel capacity compared to the basic Aloha scheme if the propagation delay is much less than the frame duration (a << 1).

Two key consequences of the classical CSMA/CD mechanism are as follows:

- Collision management channel overhead, decreasing the maximum actual throughput well below the channel rate.
- Unpredictable inter-PDU delay, making it somewhat ill-suited for multimedia and video applications.

As noted earlier, switched LANs (LANs where each station is on its own dedicated segment) do not make use of the CSMA/CD contention-resolution capability, because there is no risk or possibility of such contention. GbE supports both a shared contention-based (half-duplex) as well as a switched (full-duplex) configuration; 10GbE only supports a full-duplex configuration. Wireless LANs are usually shared (half-duplex). Over the years Ethernet has metamorphosed itself into something that only vaguely resembles the original: in the end, only the protocol model, the addressing, the MAC layer framing, the network management MIB (Management Information Base), the bridging principles, and some of the PHYs/physical media are retained.

As noted later, GbE maintains the minimum and maximum frame sizes of Ethernet. Because GbE is ten times faster than Fast Ethernet, keeping the same slot size requires the maximum cable length to be reduced to approximately 10 m, which is not very useful. Thus, GbE uses a bigger slot size of 512 bytes. To maintain compatibility with Ethernet, the minimum frame size is not increased, but instead, the "carrier event" is extended. If the frame is shorter than 512 bytes, it is padded with extension symbols.* These are special symbols that cannot occur in the payload. This process is called *carrier extension*. For carrier-extended frames, the nondata extension symbols are included in the collision window; that is, the entire extended frame is considered for collision and dropped. However, the Frame Check Sequence (FCS) is calculated only on the original frame (without extension symbols). The extension symbols are removed before the FCS is calculated and

---

* In half-duplex mode, at an operating speed of 1 Gbps, the minimum frame size is insufficient to ensure the proper operation of the CSMA/CD protocol for the desired network topologies. In other, the slotTime employed at slower speeds is inadequate to accommodate network topologies of the desired physical extent. To eliminate this problem, the MAC sublayer appends a sequence of extension bits to frames less than slotTime bits in length so that the duration of the resulting transmission is sufficient to ensure proper operation of the CSMA/CD protocol. Carrier Extension provides a means by which the slotTime can be increased to a sufficient value for the desired topologies, without increasing the minFrameSize parameter, as this would have deleterious effects. Nondata bits, referred to as extension bits, are appended to frames that are less than slotTime bits in length, so that the resulting transmission is at least one slotTime in duration. Carrier Extension can be performed only if the underlying physical layer is capable of sending and receiving symbols that are readily distinguished from data symbols, as is the case in most physical layers that use a block encoding/decoding scheme. The maximum length of the extension is equal to the quantity (slotTime − minFrameSize).

checked by the receiver. The LLC layer is not aware of the carrier extension. Another technique is also used, namely, packet bursting. Packet bursting is carrier extension in conjunction with a bursting (grouping) of packets. When a station has a number of packets to transmit, the first packet is added to the slot time using carrier extension, if necessary; subsequent packets are transmitted back to back with the minimum interpacket gap until a burst timer of 1500 bytes expires. Packet bursting substantially increases the throughput of a shared (half-duplex) GbE [SHA200101].

9.4.1.1.5 Bridging

Traditional shared LANs quickly become congested. Managing and troubleshooting a bridged enterprise becomes more difficult as the number of users increases because one misconfigured or malfunctioning workstation can disable an entire broadcast domain for an extended period of time. To relieve this congestion, the administrator is forced to segment the LAN cable into smaller runs and segregate users onto these newly created segments. In designing a bridged campus, each bridged segment typically corresponds to a workgroup. It follows that in a traditional (shared) LAN the workgroup server is placed in the same segment as the clients, allowing most of the traffic to be contained; this design approach is referred to as the 80/20 rule and refers to the goal of keeping at least 80% of the traffic contained within the local segment.

The amount of broadcast traffic sets a practical limit to the size of the broadcast domain. Hence, a traditional approach used in the late 1980s and early 1990s was to partition the LAN into a number of segments. Naturally, people still need to be able to communicate with one another. Therefore, forwarding devices known as bridges, or MAC bridges, were used to interconnect the disconnected islands of users or segments. More recently, either each user is on his or her own segment, or the subnets are separated into IP subnets that are then reconnected with a router. Today, users tend to be placed on microsegments; in fact, these microsegments support a single user. The multitude of users are then connected to each other via a Layer 2 switch—LAN switches typically perform cut-thru of 802.3 frames after reception of the destination *MAC address* (first six bytes of the *frame*). LAN switch cut-thru is not described in 802.1D but is left as a device-specific feature. The frame check is not performed for frames that are cut-thru.

Bridges provide a means to extend the LAN environment physically and to provide improved performance. IEEE 802 LANs of all types can be interconnected using MAC bridges. Each individual LAN has its own independent MAC. The bridged network of LANs (also referred to here as a *bridged system)* allows communication between stations (and servers) attached to separate LANs as if they were attached to a single LAN. Bridges operate at the MAC layer. They provide frame-forwarding (relaying) functions within the MAC; each network retains its independent MAC. Hence, a bridge (more precisely known as a *MAC bridge*) interconnects the distinct LANs by relaying frames between the separate MAC sublayers.

A bridged LAN allows the interconnection of stations attached to separate LANs as if they were attached to a single LAN, although they are in fact attached to separate LANs each with its own MAC. A MAC bridge operates below the MAC Service Boundary, and is transparent to protocols operating above this boundary, in the LLC sublayer or network layer (ISO/IEC 7498-1: 1994). The presence of one or more MAC bridges can lead to differences in the QoS provided by the MAC sublayer; it is only because of such differences that MAC bridge operation is not fully transparent. The specification is included in IEEE Std 802.1D, 1998 edition (the standard was originally published in the mid-1980s). The original IEEE 802.1D standard contains the specifications for the operation of MAC bridges; this has recently been extended to include support for traffic classes and dynamic multicast filtering [ISO199301,ISO199801].

As the network grows and a variety of bridged islands and bridges grow around the organization, a complex topology may arise. The network administrator will then need to establish some sort of "reliable" physical topology to interconnect the bridges (reliable means having more than a single uplink to other devices or to a backbone network). Figure 9.9 depicts some examples of such a reliable topology. However, the issue of forwarding loops arises in a general topology. Consequently, an algorithm is needed to place some of the physical links into a "blocked" state until such time as a link fails and the "backup blocked" link is placed in service (that is, frames can be forwarded over it). This algorithm is the Spanning Tree Algorithm (STA). The two key function of the STA are (1) to find an "active" topology without any loops, that is to say, a "spanning tree" (from the mathematical discipline of Graph Theory); and (2) have a mechanism to discover failures around the network. The protocol used to support the STA is called the Spanning Tree Protocol (STP). Figure 9.10 depicts one possible (of many) spanning tree that may be developed for the topologies shown in the previous figure.

The IEEE 801.2D standard defines an architecture for the interconnection of (IEEE 802-conformant) LANs. The interconnection is achieved below the MAC Service (i.e., MAC layer) and is therefore transparent to the LLC and all upper layers. The standard includes an STA that ensures a loop-free topology, while at the same time providing redundancy. An 802.1D bridge operation is such that it provides redundant paths between end stations to enable the bridged LANs to

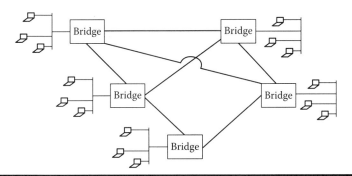

Figure 9.9 Examples of bridge topologies.

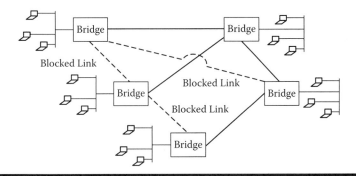

Figure 9.10 Examples of spanning trees.

continue to provide the service in the event of component failure (of bridge or LAN). Features supported by IEEE 802.1D bridges include the following:

1. A bridge is not directly addressed by communicating end stations: frames transmitted between end stations carry the MAC address of the peer-end station in their destination address field, not the MAC address of the bridge (if it has any). The only time a bridge is directly addressed is as an end station for management purposes.
2. All MAC addresses must be unique and addressable within the bridged system.
3. The MAC addresses of end stations are not restricted by the topology and configuration of the bridged system.
4. The quality of the MAC service supported by a bridge is comparable, by design, to that provided by a single LAN.

9.4.1.1.5.1 Relaying

An 802.1D bridge relays individual MAC user data frames between the separate MACs of the LANs connected to its ports. The order of frames of given user priority received on one bridge port and transmitted on another port is preserved. The functions that support the relaying of frames are shown in Table 9.6.

9.4.1.1.5.2 Filtering

A bridge filters frames to prevent unnecessary duplication. For example, frames received at a port are not copied to the same port. Frames transmitted between a pair of end stations are confined to LANs that form a path between those end stations. The functions that support the use and maintenance of filtering information include the following:

1. Automatic learning of dynamic filtering information through observation of bridged system traffic
2. Aging of filtering information that has been automatically learned
3. Calculation and configuration of bridged system topology

9.4.1.1.6 Bridge Protocol Data Units

The restoration algorithms STA and RSTA require topology status messages to be exchanged between Bridge Protocol Entities. If the network topology changes or a bridge or link fails, the

Table 9.6 Relaying Functions of a Bridge

1. Frame reception
2. Discard of the frames received in error
3. Frame discard if the frame type is not user data frame
4. Fame discard following the application of filtering information
5. Frame discard if service data unit size exceeded
6. Forwarding of received frames to other bridge ports
7. Frame discard to ensure that maximum bridge transit delay is not exceeded
8. Selection of outbound access priority
9. Mapping of service data units and recalculation of frame check sequence
10. Frame transmission

	Octct
Protocol Identifier	1
	2
Protocol Version Identifier	3
BPDU Type	4

Figure 9.11   Topology change notification BPDU.

spanning tree algorithm calculates a new spanning tree by sending topology change notification bridge protocol data units (BPDUs) (see Figure 9.11). Unfortunately, the convergence time can range from 45 to 60 s, particularly in a large network.

The configuration algorithm and protocol used in IEEE 802.1D reduce the bridged LAN topology to a single spanning tree. This pares down the complexity of the forwarding process. STP detects and eliminates network loops: when STP detects multiple paths between any two network devices, STP blocks ports until only one path exists between any two network devices. In this fashion, the STA and its associated bridge protocol operate to support, preserve, and maintain the quality of the MAC service. To perform this function, the algorithm performs the following tasks:

1. It configures the active topology of a bridged system of arbitrary topology into a single spanning tree, such that there is at most one data route between any two end stations, thereby eliminating loops.
2. It provides for fault tolerance by automatic reconfiguration of the spanning tree topology in case of bridge failure or a breakdown in a data path, within the confines of the available network components, and for the automatic accommodation of any bridge port added to the bridged system without the formation of transient data loops.
3. It allows for the entire active topology to become stable (with a high probability) within a short, known interval. This minimizes the time for which the service becomes unavailable between any pair of end stations.
4. It allows for the active topology to be predictable and reproducible. This allows the application of configuration management, following traffic analysis, to meet the goals of performance management.
5. It operates transparently to the end stations; the stations are unaware of their attachment to a single LAN or a bridged system.
6. It keeps the communication bandwidth consumed by the bridges in establishing and maintaining the spanning tree to a small percentage of the total available bandwidth. Such bandwidth is independent of the total traffic supported by the bridged system regardless of the total number of bridges or LANs.
7. It keeps the memory requirements associated with each bridge port independent of the number of bridges and LANs in the bridged system.
8. It operates so that bridges do not have to be individually configured before being added to the bridged system, other than having their MAC addresses assigned through normal procedures.

To remove loops, STP defines a tree that spans all the switches in an extended network. STP forces certain redundant data paths into a standby (blocked) state. If one network segment in the STP becomes unreachable, the spanning-tree algorithm reconfigures the spanning-tree topology and reactivates the blocked path to reestablish the link. STP operation is transparent to end stations.

STP configures a simply connected active topology from the arbitrarily connected components of a bridged system. Frames are forwarded through some of the bridge ports in the bridged system and not through others, which are held in a blocking state. At any time, bridges effectively connect just the LANs to which ports in a forwarding state are attached. Frames are forwarded in both directions through bridge ports that are in a forwarding state. Ports that are in a blocking state do not forward frames in either direction but may be included in the active topology, i.e., be put into a forwarding state if components fail, are removed, or are added.

The STA uses the IEEE 802.3 frame format with IEEE 802.2 LLC headers with DSAP set to 0x42 (hexadecimal 42), SSAP set to 0x42, and CTRL set to 0x01 to carry topology information. For the bridges to calculate the spanning tree, they require five values assigned at setup of the bridge:

A fixed multicast address (01:80:C2:00:00:00) for all spanning tree bridges.

1. A unique identifier for each bridge called Bridge ID.
2. A unique identifier for each bridge interface (port) called Port ID.
3. A priority for each port called Port Priority.
4. A cost for each port called Port Cost.

The bridges then send this information to each other via the Configuration BPDUs (see Figure 9.12) and construct a spanning tree by the following steps:

1. Elect a root bridge. The bridge with the lowest Bridge ID value becomes the root of the spanning tree.
2. Determine root path costs. The root path cost is the cost of the path to the root bridge offered by each bridge port.
3. Select a root port and elect a designated bridge for each LAN. Each bridge selects a port with the lowest path cost to the root bridge as the root port. If the lowest path costs are equal, the port with the lowest Port Priority is selected. For each LAN the bridge with the lowest cost path to the root bridge is selected as the designated bridge from all the bridges on that LAN. All bridges disable (set to blocking state) all of the ports except for the single port that is the lowest-cost path to the root and any interface attached to the LANs for which the bridge serves as a designated bridge.
4. Elect a designated port. The designated port for each bridge is the port with the lowest root path cost. If there are two or more ports with equal cost, then first the Bridge ID of the bridges and then the Port ID of the bridges are used as tiebreakers. Thus, a single bridge port is selected as the Designated Port for each LAN. The Designated Port carries all external network traffic to and from the LAN and is in the forwarding state. All network traffic is forwarded toward the root of the spanning tree.

9.4.1.2 Gigabit LANs

As the volume of enterprise network traffic increases, the bandwidth offered by traditional 10 Mbps or 100 Mbps Ethernet LANs becomes inadequate for a growing number of desktop/server computing environments. The introduction of switched Ethernet has alleviated some of these bottlenecks; however, these increased traffic levels still place a burden on the vertical/campus backbone. Advances in end-user applications drive overall requirement for increased bandwidth at campus

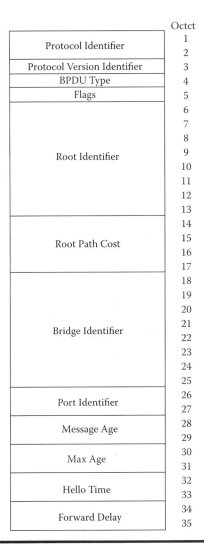

Figure 9.12   Configuration BPDU.

(and at WAN) level. Faster* processors, graphics applications, and general increases in network traffic are forcing the development of new LANs with higher bandwidth. Most Ethernet networks today incorporate devices and cabling capable of 100 Mbps operation. State-of-the-art network servers today can generate network loads of more than a Gbps. In fact, many network backbones already require bandwidth in excess of several Gbps; some applications do as well. At the campus (and building) level, evolving needs will be addressed by GbE (and/or 10 GbE) systems.

In GbE there has been a desire to retain a familiar technology base as faster systems are developed; specifically, there has been a desire to retain key Ethernet principles. GbE allows a graceful transition to higher speeds. Ethernet developers have sought in earnest an extension of Ethernet technology, specifically providing switched segments to the desktops, thereby creating a need for an even higher-speed network technology at *local backbone* and *server* level. Broadband technology

---

* Portions of this material are based directly on various IEEE sources and specifications.

should provide a smooth upgrade path, be cost-effective, support QoS, and not require staff retraining and new tools. GbE provides high-speed connectivity, but does not by itself provide a full set of services such as QoS, automatic redundant failover, or higher-level routing services; these are added via other standards.

The applicable standard is the IEEE 802.3z-1998, which has become Clause 34 thru 42 of the 802.3 specification. This specification was approved by the IEEE in 1998. The work of the IEEE P802.3ab 1000BASE-T Task Force for a UTP version was completed with the approval of IEEE 802.3ab-1999 in 1999. Most of the standardization efforts focused on the physical layer, because the goal of GbE is to retain Ethernet principles and existing upper-layer protocols down to the data-link layer.

Both a full-duplex version of the technology as well as a shared (half-duplex) version has developed that uses CSMA/CD. GbE supports new full-duplex operating modes for switch-to-switch and switch-to-end-station connections, and half-duplex operating modes for shared connections using repeaters and the CSMA/CD access method. GbE is able to utilize Category 5 UTP cabling. Figure 9.13 depicts the PHYs that are available. Market surveys indicate that Category 5 balanced copper cabling is the predominant installed intrabuilding horizontal networking media today. The market acceptance of 100BASE-TX is a clear indication that copper cabling will continue to be the medium of choice for in-building systems wherever it can be applied. This is for simple reasons of economics: UTP is cheaper than a fiber-based horizontal-wiring system. Replacing the near 100 million UTP/LAN runs now deployed in U.S. corporations at an average cost of $150 would cost the

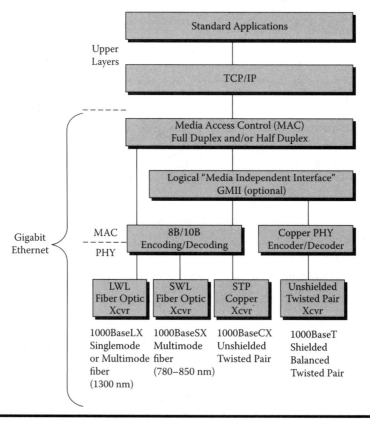

Figure 9.13   GbE PHYs that are available.

industry $15 billion just in the United States. 1000BASE-T is the natural extension of this evolution and can expect broad market acceptance as the demand for network speed increases. 1000BASE-T continues the Ethernet tradition of providing balanced-cost solutions. Gigabit Ethernet offers an upgrade path for current Ethernet installations, leveraging existing end stations, protocol stacks, management tools, and staff training. Vendor support of GbE, in general, and of 1000BASE-T, in particular, has been strong in the past few years, and a plethora of products are now available.

Many applications and environments can benefit from GbE capabilities:

- Building-level backbone, server, and gateway connectivity
- Multimedia, distributed processing, imaging, medical, CAD/CAM and prepress applications
- Aggregation of 100 Mbps switches (e.g., see Figure 9.14)
- Upgrade for large installed base of 10/100 Ethernet
- Vendors are also looking to extend GbE to the metro access/metro core space.

9.4.1.2.1 Compatibility with IEEE Standard 802.3

The development goals for GbE have been to support the following objectives:

- Conformance with CSMA/CD MAC, and physical layer signaling (PLS)
- Conformance with 802.2 architecture
- Conformance with 802 frame

The standard conforms to the CSMA/CD MAC, appropriately adapted for 1000 Mbps use (e.g., packet bursting). In a fashion similar to the 100BASE-T standard, the current physical layers were extended with new PHYs, as appropriate for 1000 Mbps operation over the defined link: a link

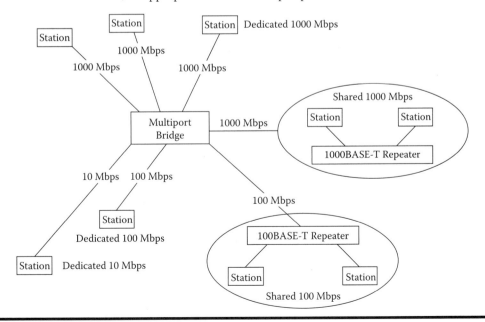

Figure 9.14   Upgradability supported by GbE.

that meets the link requirements of 4 pair Category 5 balanced copper component specifications. 1000BASE-T offers compatibility with the current installed base of tens of millions of CSMA/CD devices, most of which utilize copper cabling systems. Support of 802.3 Auto-Negotiation ensures that 802.3 UTP solutions continue to be autoconfiguring.

Conformance with 802.2 is provided by the overlying 802.3z MAC sublayer. The 1000BASE-T PHY conforms to the Gigabit Media Independent Interface (GMII) specified in 802.3z. Two kilometer network spans, although not supported specifically by 1000BASE-T, will be supported by combination with other members of the 802.3 family of 1000 Mbps standards. The standard is a 1000 Mbps upgrade for 802.3 users based on the 802.3 CSMA/CD MAC. It is the only balanced copper solution for 1000 Mbps capable of providing service over the defined link. As such, it offers an easy upgrade for the millions of users who have installed Category 5 cable plants. It is substantially different from other 802.3 copper solutions in that it supports 1 Gbps operation over the defined link. The standard is a supplement to the existing 802.3 standard.

The cost/performance ratio for 1000BASE-T vis-à-vis 100BASE-TX is about the same as that offered by 100BASE-TX vis-a-vis 10BASE-T at the time of initial introduction (1994). The cost of GbE implementations is 2 to 4 times that of 100BASE-TX. The cost model for horizontal copper cabling is well established. A variety of surveys conducted in the recent past have demonstrated that Category 5 cabling is the dominant cabling in place today. Table 9.7 depicts key features of the two different capabilities of GbE.

Changes that can impact small-packet performance have been offset by incorporating a new feature called *packet bursting* into the CSMA/CD algorithm. Packet bursting will allow servers, switches, and other devices to send bursts of small packets to fully utilize available bandwidth. Devices that operate in full-duplex mode (switches and *buffered distributors*) are not subject to carrier extension, slot time extension, or packet-bursting changes: full-duplex devices will continue to use regular Ethernet 96-bit Inter-Packet Gap (IPG) and 64-byte minimum packet size.

Carrier extension is a way of maintaining IEEE 802.3 minimum/maximum frame size with targeted cabling distances. Nondata symbols are included in a "collision window." The entire extended frame is considered for collision decisions and dropped as appropriate. Carrier extension is a straightforward solution, but it is bandwidth inefficient, because up to 488 padding octets may

Table 9.7 Switched/Shared Configurations

Item	Objective for switched configurations	Objective for shared configurations
Performance	High throughput Long distance	Low cost Short distance
Transmission Modes	Full duplex Half duplex	Half duplex
Media	Multimode fiber Single-mode fiber Copper	Multimode fiber Copper
Applications	Campus backbone Building backbone Wiring closet uplink Servers	Desktop Servers

be sent for small packets. For a large number of small packets, throughput improvement is small when compared to 100 Mbps Ethernet.

Packet bursting is an elaboration of carrier extension. When a station has a number of frames (packets) to send, the first packet is padded to slot time, if needed, using carrier extension. Packets that follow are sent back to back, with a minimum IPG until a timer (called burst timer) of 1500 octets expires. GbE will perform at gigabit wire speeds: as packet size increases, GbE will exceed performance of Fast Ethernet by an order of magnitude; as packet bursting is implemented, GbE will become more efficient at handling small packets.

Repeaters can be used to connect segments of a network medium together into a single collision domain if needed. Different physical signaling systems (e.g., 1000BASE-CX, 1000BASE-SX, 1000BASE-LX, and 1000BASE-T) can be joined into a common collision domain using an appropriate repeater. Bridges can also be used to connect different portions of the network or different signaling systems. When a bridge is so used, each LAN connected to the bridge will comprise a separate collision domain (which is often desirable).

9.4.1.2.2 GbE Standard Details

The 802.3z standard is a large 300-page document, with the following sections:

- IEEE 802.3 Section 34—Introduction to 1000 Mbps baseband network
- IEEE 802.3 Section 35—Reconciliation Sublayer (RS) and Gigabit Media Independent Interface (GMII)
- IEEE 802.3 Section 36—Physical Coding Sublayer (PCS) and Physical Medium Attachment (PMA) sublayer, type 1000BASE-X
- IEEE 802.3 Section 37—Auto-Negotiation function, type 1000BASE-X
- IEEE 802.3 Section 38—Physical Medium Dependent (PMD) sublayer and baseband medium, type 1000BASE-LX (Long Wavelength Laser) and 1000BASE-SX (Short Wavelength Laser)
- IEEE 802.3 Section 39—Physical Medium Dependent (PMD*) sublayer and baseband medium, type 1000BASE-CX (short-haul copper)
- IEEE 802.3 Section 40—Physical Coding Sublayer (PCS), Physical Medium Attachment (PMA) sublayer and baseband medium, type 1000BASE-T
- IEEE 802.3 Section 41—Repeater for 1000 Mbps baseband networks
- IEEE 802.3 Section 42—System Considerations for multisegment 1000 Mbps networks

In terms of ISO/IEC standards, GbE couples an extended version of the ISO/IEC 8802-3 (CSMA/CD MAC) to a family of 1000 Mbps physical layers. The relationships among GbE, the extended ISO/IEC 8802-3 (CSMA/CD MAC), and the ISO/IEC Open System Interconnection (OSI) Reference Model are shown in Figure 9.15. GbE uses the extended ISO/IEC 8802-3 MAC layer interface, connected through a GMII layer to physical layer entities (PHY sublayers) such as 1000BASE-LX, 1000BASE-SX, and 1000BASE-CX, and 1000BASE-T.

In GbE the bit rate is faster, and the bit times are shorter—both in proportion to the change in bandwidth. In full-duplex mode, the minimum packet transmission time has been reduced by a factor of ten. Wiring/floor topologies for 1000 Mbps full-duplex operation are comparable to

---

* Note that this acronym is different from the one used in Section 9.3.1.5.

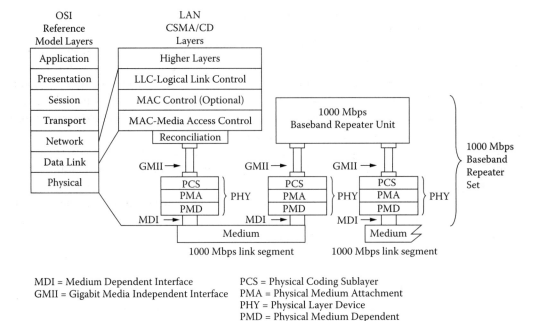

Figure 9.15   GbE protocol model, IEEE 802.3.

those found in 100BASE-T full-duplex mode. In half-duplex mode, the minimum packet transmission time has been reduced, but not by a factor of ten. Cable delay budgets are similar to those in 100BASE-T. The resulting achievable topologies for the half-duplex 1000 Mbps CSMA/CD MAC are similar to those found in half-duplex 100BASE-T.

The GMII provides an interconnection between the MAC sublayer and PHY entities and between PHY layer and Station Management (STA) entities (see Figure 9.16). GMII supports 1000 Mbps operation through its eight-bit wide (octet wide) transmit and receive paths. The Reconciliation Sublayer (RS) provides a mapping between the signals provided at the GMII and the MAC/PLS service definition.

The specification defines the logical and electrical characteristics of the RS and the GMII between CSMA/CD media access controllers and various PHYs. Whereas the Attachment Unit Interface (AUI) was defined to exist between the PLS and PMA sublayers for 10 Mbps DTEs, the GMII maximizes media independence by cleanly separating the data-link and physical layers of the ISO/IEC seven-layer reference model. This allocation also recognizes that implementations can benefit from a close coupling between the PLS or PCS sublayer and the PMA sublayer. This interface has the following characteristics:

1. It is capable of supporting 1000 Mbps operation.
2. Data and delimiters are synchronous to clock references.
3. It provides independent eight-bit-wide transmit and receive data paths.
4. It provides a simple management interface.
5. It uses signal levels compatible with common complementary metal oxide semiconductor (CMOS) digital Application-Specific Integrated Circuit (ASIC) processes and some bipolar processes.
6. It provides for full-duplex operation.

LAN CSMA/CD LAYERS

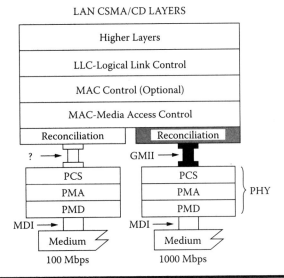

Figure 9.16   Reconciliation Sublayer and the Gigabit Media Independent Interface.

Table 9.8   Physical Layers of GbE

1000BASE-SX Short Wave Length Optical	Duplex multimode fibers
1000BASE-LX Long Wave Length Optical	Duplex single-mode fibers or duplex multimode fibers
1000BASE-CX Shielded Jumper Cable	Two pairs of specialized balanced cabling
1000BASE-T Category 5 UTP	Advanced multilevel signaling over four pairs of Category 5 balanced copper cabling.

Each direction of data transfer is serviced by Data (an eight-bit bundle), Delimiter, Error, and Clock signals. Two media status signals are provided: one indicates the presence of a carrier, and the other indicates the occurrence of a collision. The RS maps the signal set provided at the GMII to the PLS service primitives provided to the MAC.

The GbE standard specifies a family of physical layer implementations. The generic term 1000 Mbps MAC refers to any use of the 1000 Mbps ISO/IEC 8802-3 (CSMA/CD) MAC (the GbE MAC) coupled with any physical layer implementation. The term 1000BASE-X refers to a specific family of physical layer implementations. The 1000BASE-X family of physical layer standards has been adapted from the ANSI X3.230-1994 (Fibre Channel) FC-0 and FC-1 physical layer specifications and the associated 8B/10B data coding method. The 1000BASE-X family of physical layer implementations is composed of 1000BASE-SX, 1000BASE-LX, and 1000BASE-CX. All 1000BASE-X PHY devices share the use of common PCS, PMA, and Auto-Negotiation specifications. The 1000BASE-T PHY uses four pairs of Category 5 balanced copper cabling. The standard also defines its own PCS, which does not use 8B/10B coding (see Table 9.8). From an enterprise network point of view 100BASE-T is very important, as is 1000BASE-LX. For metro access/metro core applications, 1000BASE-LX is important because people have extended the optics reach to cover a (small) metro area (also see Figure 9.17).

Auto-Negotiation provides a 1000BASE-X device with the capability to detect the modes of operation supported by the device at the other end of a link segment, determine common abilities,

	Optical link									Fibre		
	Horizontal			Building backbone			Campus backbone					
	62.5/ 125 µm MMF	50/ 125 µm MMF	10/ 125 µm SMF	62.5/ 125 µm MMF	50/ 125 µm MMF	10/ 125 µm SMF	62.5/ 125 µm MMF	50/ 125 µm MMF	10/ 125 µm SMF	62.5/ 125 µm MMF	50/ 125 µm MMF	10/ 125 µm SMF
8802-3: 1000BASE-SX	N	N		I	N		I	I		I	I	
8802-3: 1000BASE-LX	N	N	N	N	N	N	I	I	N	I	I	I

NOTE— "N" denotes normative support of the media in the standard.
"I" denotes that there is information in the International Standard regarding operations on this media.

Figure 9.17   GbE supported media.

and configure for joint operation. Auto-Negotiation is performed upon link start-up through the use of a special sequence of reserved link code words. Auto-Negotiation is used by 1000BASE-T devices to detect the modes of operation supported by the device at the other end of a link segment, determine common abilities, and configure for joint operation. Auto-Negotiation is performed upon link startup through the use of a special sequence of fast link pulses.

9.4.1.2.3 Physical Sublayers

9.4.1.2.3.1 1000 BASE-X

There is a section of the standard that specifies the PCS and the PMA sublayers that are common to a family of 1000 Mbps physical layer implementations, collectively known as 1000BASE-X. There are currently four PHYs: 1000BASE-CX, 1000BASE-LX, 1000BASE-SX, and 1000BASE-T. The 1000BASE-CX implementation specifies operation over a single copper media: two pairs of 150 Ω balanced copper cabling. 1000BASE-LX specifies operation over a pair of optical fibers using long-wavelength optical transmission. 1000BASE-SX specifies operation over a pair of optical fibers using short-wavelength optical transmission. 1000BASE-T specifies operation over four pairs of Category 5 balanced copper cabling. The term 1000BASE-X is used when referring to issues common to any of three subvariants 1000BASE-CX, 1000BASE-LX, or 1000BASE-SX, but not to refer to 1000BASE-T.

1000BASE-X is based on the PHY standards developed by ANSI X3.230-1994 (Fibre Channel Physical and Signaling Interface). In particular, the standard uses the same 8B/10B coding as Fibre Channel, a PMA sublayer compatible with speed-enhanced versions of the ANSI 10-bit serializer chip, and similar optical and electrical specifications. 1000BASE-X PCS and PMA sublayers map the interface characteristics of the PMD sublayer (including Medium Dependent Interface [MDI]) to the services expected by the Reconciliation Sublayer. 1000BASE-X can be extended to support any other full-duplex medium, requiring only that the medium be compliant at the PMD level. The following are the objectives of 1000BASE-X:

1. Support the CSMA/CD MAC
2. Support the 1000 Mbps repeater
3. Provide for Auto-Negotiation among similar 1000 Mbps PMDs
4. Provide 1000 Mbps data rate at the GMII

5. Support cable plants using 150 Ω balanced copper cabling, or optical fiber compliant with ISO/IEC 11801:1995
6. Allow for a nominal network extent of up to 3 km, including
   a. 150 Ω balanced links of 25 m span
   b. One-repeater networks of 50 m span (using all 150 Ω balanced copper cabling)
   c. One-repeater networks of 200 m span (using fiber)
   d. DTE/DTE links of 3000 m (using fiber)
7. Preserve full-duplex behavior of underlying PMD channels
8. Support a BER objective of 10^{-12}

9.4.1.2.3.2 Physical Coding Sublayer (PCS)

The PCS interface is the GMII that provides a uniform interface to the Reconciliation Sublayer for all 1000 Mbps PHY implementations (e.g., not only 1000BASE-X but also other possible types of gigabit PHY entities). 1000BASE-X provides services to the GMII in a manner analogous to how 100BASE-X provides services to the 100 Mbps MII. The 1000BASE-X PCS provides all services required by the GMII, including the following:

1. Encoding (decoding) of GMII data octets to (from) ten-bit code groups (8B/10B) for communication with the underlying PMA
2. Generating Carrier Sense and Collision Detect indications for use by PHY's half-duplex clients
3. Managing the Auto-Negotiation process, and informing the management entity via the GMII when the PHY is ready for use

The PCS Service Interface allows the 1000BASE-X PCS to transfer information to and from a PCS client. PCS clients include the MAC (via the Reconciliation Sublayer) and repeater.

The PCS comprises the PCS Transmit, Carrier Sense, Synchronization, PCS Receive, and Auto-Negotiation processes for 1000BASE-X. The PCS shields the Reconciliation Sublayer (and MAC) from the specific nature of the underlying channel. When communicating with the GMII, the PCS uses an octetwide synchronous data path, with packet delimiting being provided by separate transmit control and receive control signals. When communicating with the PMA, the PCS uses a ten-bit-wide synchronous data path, which conveys ten-bit code groups. At the PMA Service Interface, code group alignment and MAC packet delimiting are made possible by embedding special nondata code groups in the transmitted code group stream. The PCS provides the functions necessary to map packets between the GMII format and the PMA Service Interface format.

The PCS maps GMII signals into ten-bit code groups, and vice versa, using an 8B/10B lock coding scheme. Implicit in the definition of a code group is the establishment of code group boundaries by a PMA code group alignment function.

The PCS uses a 8B/10B transmission code to improve the transmission characteristics of information to be transferred across the link. The encodings defined by the transmission code ensure that sufficient transitions are present in the PHY bit stream to make clock recovery possible at the receiver. Such encoding also increases the likelihood of detecting any single or multiple bit errors that may occur during transmission and reception of information. In addition, some of the special code groups of the transmission code contain a distinct and easily recognizable bit pattern that assists a receiver in achieving code group alignment on the incoming PHY bit stream.

9.4.1.2.3.3 Physical Medium Attachment (PMA) Sublayer

The PMA provides a medium-independent means for the PCS to support the use of a range of serial-bit-oriented physical media. The 1000BASE-X PMA performs the following functions:

1. Mapping of transmit and receive code groups between the PCS and PMA via the PMA Service Interface
2. Serialization (deserialization) of code groups for transmission (reception) on the underlying serial PMD
3. Recovery of clock from the 8B/10B-coded data supplied by the PMD
4. Mapping of transmit and receive bits between the PMA and PMD via the PMD Service Interface
5. Data loopback at the PMD Service Interface

9.4.1.2.3.4 Physical Medium Dependent (PMD) Sublayer

1000BASE-X physical layer signaling for fiber and copper media is adapted from ANSI X3.230-1994 (FC-PH), which defines 1062.5 Mbps, full-duplex signaling systems that accommodate single-mode optical fiber, multimode optical fiber, and 150 Ω balanced copper cabling. 1000BASE-X adapts these basic physical layer specifications for use with the PMD sublayer and mediums. The MDI, logically subsumed within each PMD, is the actual medium attachment, including connectors, for the various supported media.

9.4.1.2.3.5 Intersublayer Interfaces

There are a number of interfaces employed by 1000BASE-X. Some (such as the PMA Service Interface) use an abstract service model to define the operation of the interface. An optional physical instantiation of the PCS Interface has been defined: the GMII. Another optional physical instantiation of the PMA Service Interface has also been defined, being adapted from ANSI Technical Report TR/X3.18-1997 (Fibre Channel 10-bit Interface).

9.4.1.2.3.6 1000BASE-LX (Long Wavelength Laser) and 1000BASE-SX (Short Wavelength Laser)

There is a section of the standard that specifies the 1000BASE-SX PMD and the 1000BASE-LX PMD (including MDI) and baseband medium for multimode and single-mode fiber. GbE metro rings now being deployed use 1000BASE-LX principles. The operating range for 1000BASE-SX is defined in Table 9.9. A 1000BASE-SX–compliant transceiver supports both multimode fiber media types listed in Table 9.8 (i.e., both 50 and 62.5 μm multimode fiber). A transceiver that exceeds the operational range requirement while meeting all other optical specifications is considered compliant (e.g., a 50 μm solution operating at 600 m meets the minimum range requirement of 2 to 550 m).

The operating range for 1000BASE-LX is defined in Table 9.10. A transceiver that exceeds the operational range requirement while meeting all other optical specifications is considered compliant (e.g., a single-mode solution operating at 5500 m meets the minimum range requirement of 2 to 5000 m). Conditioned launch produces sufficient mode volume so that individual MMF modes do not dominate fiber performance. This reduces the effect of peak-to-peak differential mode delay (DMD) between the launched mode groups and diminishes the resulting pulse-splitting-induced nulls in the frequency response. A conditioned launch is produced by using a single-mode fiber offset-launch mode-conditioning patch cord, inserted at both ends of a full-duplex link, between

Table 9.9 1000BASE-SX

Fiber Type	Modal Bandwidth @ 850 nm (min. overfilled launch) (MHz · km)	Minimum Range (m)
62.5 μm MMF	160	2 to 220
62.5 μm MMF	200	2 to 275
50 μm MMF	400	2 to 500
50 μm MMF	500	2 to 550
10 μm SMF	N/A	Not supported

Table 9.10   1000BASE-LX Operating Range

Fiber Type	Modal Bandwidth @ 1300 nm (min. overfilled launch) (MHz · km)	Minimum Range (m)
62.5 μm MMF	500	2 to 550
50 μm MMF	400	2 to 550
50 μm MMF	500	2 to 550
10 μm SMF	N/A	2 to 5000

Table 9.11   1000BASE-LX Receive Characteristics

Description	Value	Unit
Signaling speed (range)	1.25 ± 100 ppm	GBd
Wavelength (range)	1270 to 1355	nm
Average receive power (max)	~3	dBm
Receive sensitivity	~19	dBm
Return loss (min)	12	dB
Stressed receive sensitivity	~14.4	dBm
Vertical eye-closure penalty	2.60	dB
Receive electrical 3 dB uppercutoff frequency (max)	1500	MHz

the optical PMD MDI and the remainder of the link segment. The single-mode fiber offset-launch mode-conditioning patch cord contains a fiber of the same type as the cable (i.e., 62.5 or 50 μm fiber) connected to the optical PMD receiver input MDI and a specialized fiber/connector assembly connected to the optical PMD transmitter output. The 1000BASE-LX receiver needs to meet the specifications defined in Table 9.11.

Both the 1000BASE-SX and 1000BASE-LX fiber-optic cabling need to meet the specifications defined in Table 9.12. The fiber-optic cabling consists of one or more sections of fiber-optic cable and any connections along the way required to connect sections together. It also includes a connector plug at each end to connect to the MDI. The fiber-optic cable requirements are satisfied by the fibers specified in IEC 60793-2:1992. Types A1a (50/125 μm multimode), A1 (62.5/125 μm multimode), and B1 (10/125 μm single-mode) are supported with the exceptions noted in Table 9.12.

Table 9.12 Optical Cable and Fiber Characteristics

Description	62.5 μm MMF		50 μm MMF		10 μm SMF	Unit
Nominal Fiber Specification Wavelength	850	1300	850	1300	1310	nm
Fiber cable attenuation (max)	3.75	1.5	3.5	1.5	0.5	dB/km
Modal Bandwidth (min; overfilled launch)	160	500	400	400	N/A	MHz · km
	200	500	500	500	N/A	MHz · km
Zero-dispersion wavelength (λ_0)	$1320 \leq \lambda_0 \leq 1365$		$1295 \leq \lambda_0 \leq 1320$		$1300 \leq \lambda_0 \leq 1324$	nm
Dispersion slope (max) (S_0)	0.11 for $1320 \leq \lambda_0 \leq 1348$ and 0.001 $(1458 - \lambda_0)$ for $1348 \leq \lambda_0 \leq 1365$		0.11 for $1300 \leq \lambda_0 \leq 1320$ and $0.001(\lambda_0 - 1190)$ for $1295 \leq \lambda_0 \leq 1300$		0.093	ps/nm² · km

Table 9.13 Transmitter Characteristics at TP2

Description	Value	Unit
Type	(P)ECL	
Data rate	1000	Mh's
Clock tolerance	±100	ppm
Nominal signaling speed	1250	MBd
Differential amplitude (p-p)		
Max (worst case p-p)	2000	mV
Min (opening)	1100	mV
Max (OFF)	170	mV
Raise/Fall time (20–80%)		
Maximum	327	ps
Minimum	85	ps
Differential skew (max)	25	ps

9.4.1.2.3.7 1000BASE-CX (Short-Haul Copper)

GbE specifies the 1000BASE-CX PMD (including MDI) and baseband medium for short-haul copper. 1000BASE-CX has a minimum operating range of 0.1 to 25 m. Jumper cables are used to interconnect 1000BASE-CX PMDs. These cables, however, cannot be concatenated to achieve longer distances. A 1000BASE-CX jumper cable assembly consists of a continuous shielded balanced copper cable terminated at each end with a polarized shielded plug. The transmitter needs to meet the specifications in Table 9.13.

9.4.1.2.3.8 1000BASE-T

The 1000BASE-T PHY is one of the GbE family of high-speed CSMA/CD network specifications. The 1000BASE-T PCS, PMA, and baseband medium specifications are intended for users who want

1000 Mbps performance over Category 5 balanced twisted-pair cabling systems. 1000BASE-T signaling requires four pairs of Category 5 balanced cabling, as specified in ISO/IEC 11801:1995 and ANSI/EIA/TIA-568-A (1995).

This IEEE 802.3ab clause defines the type 1000BASE-T PCS, type 1000BASE-T PMA sublayer, and type 1000BASE-T MDI. Together, the PCS and the PMA sublayer comprise a 1000BASE-T PHY. Section 40 of the IEEE 802.3 document describes the functional, electrical, and mechanical specifications for the type 1000BASE-T PCS, PMA, and MDI. This clause also specifies the baseband medium used with 1000BASE-T. The following are the objectives of 1000BASE-T:

1. Support the CSMA/CD MAC
2. Comply with the specifications for the GMII
3. Support the 1000 Mbps repeater
4. Provide line transmission that supports full- and half-duplex operation
5. Meet or exceed FCC Class A/CISPR or better operation
6. Support operation over 100 m of Category 5 balanced cabling
7. BER of less than or equal to 10^{-10}
8. Support Auto-Negotiation

The 1000BASE-T PHY employs full-duplex base and transmission over four pairs of Category 5 balanced cabling. The aggregate data rate of 1000 Mbps is achieved by transmission at a data rate of 250 Mbps over each wire pair. The use of hybrids and cancellers enables full-duplex transmission by allowing symbols to be transmitted and received on the same wire pairs at the same time. Base and signaling with a modulation rate of 125 Mbaud is used on each of the wire pairs. The transmitted symbols are selected from a four-dimensional five-level symbol constellation. Each four-dimensional symbol can be viewed as a 4-tuple (A_n, B_n, C_n, D_n) of one-dimensional quinary symbols taken from the set {2, 1, 0, –1, –2}. 1000BASE-T uses a continuous signaling system; in the absence of data, Idle symbols are transmitted. Idle mode is a subset of code groups in that each symbol is restricted to the set {2, 0, –2} to improve synchronization. Five-level Pulse Amplitude Modulation (PAM5) is employed for transmission over each wire pair. The modulation rate of 125 MBaud matches the GMII clock rate of 125 MHz and results in a symbol period of 8 ns.

The 1000BASE-T PCS couples a GMII to a PMA sublayer. The functions performed by the PCS comprise the generation of continuous code groups to be transmitted over four channels and the processing of code groups received from the remote PHY. The process of converting data to its code groups is called 4D-PAM5, which refers to the four-dimensional five-level pulse amplitude modulation coding technique used. Through this coding scheme, eight bits are converted to one transmission of four quinary symbols.

1000BASE-T signaling is performed by the PCS, generating continuous code group sequences that the PMA transmits over each wire pair. The signaling scheme achieves a number of objectives, including the following:

1. FEC-coded symbol mapping for data
2. Algorithmic mapping and inverse mapping from octet data to a quartet of quinary symbols and back
3. Uncorrelated symbols in the transmitted symbol stream
4. No correlation between symbol streams traveling both directions on any pair combination
5. Idle mode uses a subset of code groups in that each symbol is restricted to the set {2, 0, –2} to ease synchronization, start-up, and retraining

6. Ability to rapidly or immediately determine if a symbol stream represents data or idle or carrier extension
7. Robust delimiters for Start-of-Stream delimiter (SSD), End-of-Stream delimiter (ESD), and other control signals
8. Ability to signal the status of the local receiver to the remote PHY to indicate that the local receiver is not operating reliably and requires retraining
9. Ability to automatically detect and correct for pair swapping and unexpected crossover connections
10. Ability to automatically detect and correct for incorrect polarity in the connections
11. Ability to automatically correct for differential delay variations across the wire pairs

Table 9.14 depicts the maximum segment lengths for various media.

9.4.1.3 10 Gbps LANs

This section looks at 10 GbE. Efforts took place earlier this decade to extend the existing IEEE802.3 standards to support 10 Gbps data rates and to enhance Ethernet to include more direct support for WAN links. Standards for 10GbE were produced as an extension to the existing IEEE standards, with the basic changes being at the PHY (consisting of the PCS, PMA, and PMD sublayers). Specifically, the goal of the P802.3ae standard is to define 802.3 MAC parameters and minimal augmentation of its operation, physical layer characteristics, and management parameters for transfer of LLC and Ethernet format frames at 10 Gbps using full-duplex operation. The technology is applicable to data centers and metro area environments. 10GbE has two implications for the metro access/metro core:

1. As end users deploy 10GbE LAN systems, the optimized WAN connectivity is in the 1 Gbps range. It follows that 10GbE-based end systems would preferably require a Transparent LAN Service (TLS) WAN service based on this very same technology (or, an alternative, TLS could also be based on SONET/New-Generation SONET). Viewed from this angle, 10GbE is a driver for broadband metro core/metro access systems.
2. 10GbE enables the use of a MAC framing mechanism in the WAN, obviating the need to do either translational bridging at Layer 2 (e.g., remapping a local MAC frame to an AAL5 (ATM Adaptation Layer 5) frame), or remapping at Layer 3 (e.g., remapping a MAC/IP frame to a PPP/SONET frame). Typical traditional Layer 2 protocols used in the WAN

Table 9.14   Maximum Segment Length for Various Media

Media Type	Maximum Segment Length (m)	Maximum Medium Round-Trip Delay per Segment (BT)BT (B"?" Times)
Category 5 UTP Link Segment (1000BASE-T)	100	1112
Shielded Jumper Cable Link Segment (1000BASE-CX)	25	253
Optical Fiber Link Segment (1000BASE-SX. 1000BASE-LX)	316[a]	3192

[a] May be limited by the maximum transmission distance of the link.

include Link Access Procedure D (LAPD, for frame relay), PPP (Point-to-Point Protocol), and the newer Generalized Framing Procedure (GFP) and AAL5.

The second application could have significant relevance to new-generation networks and architectures. The WAN PHY is compatible with SONET/SDH, but cannot directly interconnect with a SONET interface unless a gateway interworking function is used either at the CPE level or at the network edge level, as we discuss later.

9.4.1.3.1 Overview

A desire exists on the part of developers to bring to the market a "higher-speed" (specifically, 10 Gbps) LAN technology that has features that can also be used over the WAN. Prior experience in scaling 802.3 across the range of 1 to 1000 Mbps indicates that the cost balance between adapters, switches, and the infrastructure remains roughly constant. 10GbE is expected to continue this trend at least for building/campus applications. In addition to the traditional LAN space, the standard adds parameters and mechanisms that enable deployment of Ethernet over the WAN operating at a data rate compatible with OC-192c and SDH VC-4-64c payload rate. The new features expand the Ethernet application space to include WAN links to provide a significant increase in bandwidth while maintaining maximum compatibility with the installed base of 802.3 interfaces, previous investment in research and development, and principles of network operation and management. The approach has been to define two families of PHYs: (1) a LAN PHY, operating at a data rate of 10 Gbps; and (2) a WAN PHY, operating at a data rate compatible with the payload rate of OC-192c/SDH VC-4-64c. Note, however, that the WAN PHY does not render the PHY **compliant** with either SONET or SDH at any rate or format and the WAN interface is not intended to **interoperate** directly with interfaces that comply with SONET or SDH standards. 10GbE is defined for full-duplex mode of operation only. Figure 9.18 depicts a simplified protocol model. 10GbE will improve the performance of the following:

■ LAN backbone and server and gateway connectivity
■ Switch aggregation
■ Metropolitan area networks (MANs), WANs, Regional area networks (RANs), and SANs

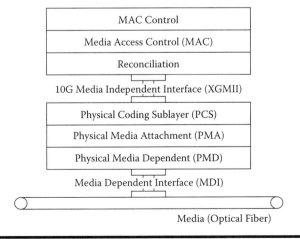

Figure 9.18   Simplified protocol model.

9.4.1.3.1.1 Goals

The principle of scaling the 802.3 MAC to higher speeds has been well established by previous work within 802.3 committees. The 10 Gbps work built on this experience. The design objectives of the Higher Speed Study Group (HSSG) were as follows [THA200101]:

- Preserve the 802.3/Ethernet frame format at the MAC Client service interface
- Meet 802 functional requirements (FRs), with the possible exception of Hamming Distance
- Preserve minimum and maximum FrameSize of the current 802.3 standard
- Support full-duplex operation (only)
- Support star-wired LANs using point-to-point links and structured cabling topologies
- Specify an optional Media Independent Interface (MII)
- Support proposed standard P802.3ad (Link Aggregation)
- Support a speed of 10 Gbps at the MAC/PLS service interface
- Define two families of PHYs (also see Figure 9.18):
  - A LAN PHY, operating at a data rate of 10 Gbps
  - A WAN PHY, operating at a data rate compatible with the payload rate of OC-192c/SDH VC-4-64c (These streams clocked at 9.953 Gbps; payload is approximately 9.29 Gbps) (Physical Coding Sublayers known as 10GBASE-X, 10GBASE-R and 10GBASE-W*)
- Define a mechanism to adapt the MAC/PLS data rate to the data rate of the WAN PHY
- For the LAN PHYs, develop physical layer specifications that support link distances of:
  - At least 65 m over MMF (the solution is cost-optimized for this distance)
  - At least 300 m over installed MMF ("installed" implies all MMF specified in 802.3z [62.5 micron 160/500 MHz × km FDDI-grade is the worst case]).
  - At least 2 km over SMF
  - At least 10 km over SMF
  - At least 40 km over SMF
- Support fiber media selected from the second edition of ISO/IEC 11801.
- The physical layers specified include 10GBASE-S, an 850 nm wavelength serial transceiver that uses two multimode fibers; 10GBASE-L4, a 1310 nm Wide Wavelength Division Multiplexing (WWDM) transceiver that uses two MMFs or SMFs; 10GBASE-L, a 1310 nm wavelength serial transceiver that uses two SMFs; and 10GBASE-E, a 1550 nm wavelength serial transceiver that uses two SMFs.

There is broad market potential for this technology and there is a broad set of applications; multiple vendors and multiple users benefit from the technology. Rapid growth of network and Internet traffic has placed high demand on the existing infrastructure, motivating the development of higher-performance links. The 10 Gbps 802.3 solution extends Ethernet capabilities, providing higher bandwidth for multimedia, distributed processing, imaging, medical, CAD/CAM (computer-aided design/computer-aided manufacturing), data center networking, higher speed wireless LANs, and other existing applications. New opportunities are added when one defines a mechanism to adapt the MAC/PLS data rate to the data rate and framing of the WAN PHY such as SONET/SDH.

As usual, one wants conformance with the 802.3 MAC, the PLS, the 802.2 LLC, and the 802 FR (Functional Requirements). By adapting the existing 802.3 MAC protocol for use at 10 Gbps,

---

* R = 64B/66B encoded without WIS; W = 64B/66B encoded without WIS.

Stack	10 GE LAN PHY		10 GE WAN PHY
	Serial	CWDM	Serial
MAC	10.0 Gbps	10.0 Gbps	10.0 Gbps
PCS	64B/66B	8B/10B	64B/66B SONET framing $x^7 + x^6 + 1$
PMA Interface	XSBI	XAUI	XSBI
PMD	1550 nm DFB 1310 nm FP 850 nm vcsel	1310 CWDM	1550 nm DFB 1310 nm FP 850 nm vcsel
Line Rate	10.3 Gbps	4 × 3.125 Gbps	9.953 Gbps

Figure 9.19   Bit rates for various PHYs.

this standard maintains maximum compatibility with the installed base of over 600 million Ethernet nodes. The standard conforms to the full-duplex operating mode of the 802.3 MAC, appropriately adapted for 10 Gbps operation. Half-duplex operation and CSMA/CD itself will not be supported at 10 Gbps. As was the case in previous 802.3 standards, new physical layers have been defined for 10 Gbps operation. The standard also defines a set of systems management objects that are compatible with Simple Network Management Protocol (SNMP) system management standards. The MIB for 10 Gbps 802.3 will be extended in a manner consistent with the 802.3 MIB for 10/100/1000 Mbps operation. Therefore, network managers, installers, and administrators will see a consistent management model across all operating speeds.

10GbE products are technically feasible and are being developed in a cost-effective manner. For example, bridging equipment that performs rate adaptation between 802.3 networks operating at different speeds has been demonstrated over the years by the broad set of product offerings that bridge 10, 100, and 1000 Mbps. Vendors of optical components and systems are developing, at this time, reliable products that operate at 10 Gbps, and meet worldwide regulatory and operational requirements. Component vendors are confident of the feasibility of physical layer signaling at a rate of 10 Gbps on fiber-optic media using a wide variety of innovative low-cost technologies. A target threefold cost increase of 1000BASE-X with a tenfold increase in available bandwidth in the full-duplex operating mode (for the LAN PHY) results in an improvement in the cost-performance ratio by a factor of 3.

In 10GbE, the bit rate is faster and the bit times are shorter—both in proportion to the change in bandwidth. The minimum packet transmission time has been reduced by a factor of ten. A rate control mode is added to the MAC to adapt the average MAC data rate to the SONET/SDH data rate for WAN-compatible applications of the standard. Achievable topologies for 10 Gbps operation are comparable to those found in 1000BASE-X full-duplex mode and equivalent to those found in WAN applications. There is significant additional supporting material in the standard for a 10 Gigabit Media Independent Interface (XGMII), a 10 Gigabit Attachment Unit Interface (XAUI), a 10 Gigabit Sixteen-Bit Interface (XSBI), and management.

9.4.1.3.1.2 Media
9.4.1.3.1.2.1   LAN/MAN Media
A number of alternative media types have been developed for LAN/MAN environments. Because 10GbE is not expected to connect directly to users' desktops (at least, not yet), the standards are initially based on optical fiber. Optical PHYs include MMF and SMF using serial and parallel links.

9.4.1.3.1.2.2 WAN Media

Support for Ethernet-based communications over long distances is unique to 10GbE and would not be feasible using the original CSMA/CD protocol, because the throughput goes to zero as the variable "a" increases. The full-duplex operation allows 10GbE to operate over long link spans, repeaters, and other transport layers.

The 10GbE WAN physical layer is also defined to be SONET-like. It can be said that 10GbE will be "SONET friendly," even though it is not fully compliant with all the SONET standards. Some SONET features will be avoided: TDM support, performance requirements, and management requirements (the most costly aspects of SONET).

9.4.1.3.1.2.3 Comparison

Table 9.15 provides a brief comparison between the 1 Gbps and 10 Gbps versions of Ethernet. Note once again that the traditional CSMA/CD protocol will not be used, and the fiber will be used as the physical media.

9.4.1.3.2 Snapshot of Technical Details

9.4.1.3.2.1 10GbE Physical Layer

The 10GbE PHY consists of the following sublayers (see Figure 9.20):

1. RS.
2. PCS.
3. PMA.
4. PMD.
5. An optional WAN Interface Sublayer (WIS) is also defined.

As noted earlier, P802.3ae/D3.2 defines the sublayers that implement two families of PHYs: a "LAN PHY" operating at a data rate of 10 Gbps and a "WAN PHY" operating at a data rate and format compatible with SONET STS-192c and SDH VC-4-64c. Seven variants are specified, as seen in Figure 9.21.

The extensive standard specifies a family of physical layer implementations. Table 9.16 specifies the correlation between technologies and required sublayers. The term 10GBASE-X refers to a specific family of physical layer implementations based on the 8B/10B data coding method; the 10GBASE-X

Table 9.15 Comparison between the 1 Gbps and 10 Gbps

	1 Gbps Ethernet	*10 Gbps Ethernet*
Distance	LANs up to 5 km; no intrinsic WAN support	LANs up to 40 km. Direct attachment to SONET/SDH equipment for WANs
MAC	Protocol half-duplex (CSMA/CD) as well as full-duplex	Full-duplex only
PCS	Reuses 8B/10B coding	Established new coding schemes (64B/66B) for 10GBASE-W and 10GBASE-R; uses 8B/10B for 10GBASE-X
Physical media	Optical and copper cabling	Optical cabling only
PMD	Leverages Fibre Channel PMDs	Developed new optical PMDs

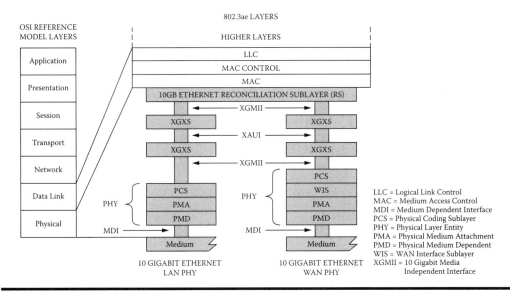

Figure 9.20   10GbE layer diagram.

family of physical layer implementations is composed of 10GBASE-LX4. The term 10GBASE-R refers to a specific family of physical layer implementations based on the 64B/66B data coding method; the 10GBASE-R family of physical layer implementations is composed of 10GBASE-SR, 10GBASE-LR, and 10GBASE-ER. The term 10GBASE-W refers to a specific family of physical layer implementations based on STS-192c/SDH VC-4-64c *encapsulation* of 64B/66B encoded data; the 10GBASE-W family of physical layer standards has been adapted from the ANSI T1.416-1999 (SONET STS-192c/SDH VC-4-64c) physical layer specifications. The 10GBASE-W family of physical layer implementations is composed of 10GBASE-SW, 10GBASE-LW, and 10GBASE-EW. All 10GBASE-R and 10GBASE-W PHY devices share a common PCS specification. The 10GBASE-W PHY devices also require the use of the WIS. A 10GBASE-PHY needs to "talk" to a 10GBASE-PHY protocol peer; it cannot "talk" directly to a SONET protocol peer.

The following are the objectives of 10GBASE-R:

1. Support the full duplex Ethernet MAC
2. Provide 10 Gbps data rate at the XGMII
3. Support LAN PMDs operating at 10 Gbps and WAN PMDs operating at SONET STS-192c/SDH VC-4-64c rate
4. Support cable plants using optical fiber compliant with ISO/IEC 11801: 1995
5. Allow for a nominal network extent of up to 40 km
6. Support a BER objective of 10^{-12}

The generic term *10 Gigabit Ethernet* refers to any use of the 10 Gbps IEEE 802.3 MAC (the 10 Gigabit Ethernet MAC) coupled with any IEEE 802.3 10GBASE physical layer implementation.

Interfaces of interest are as follows:

■ XGMII—The 10 Gigabit Media Independent Interface provides an interconnection between the MAC sublayer (specifically RS) and PHY. This XGMII supports 10 Gbps operation through its 32-bit-wide transmit and receive paths. The Reconciliation Sublayer provides a mapping between the signals provided at the XGMII and the MAC/PLS service definition.

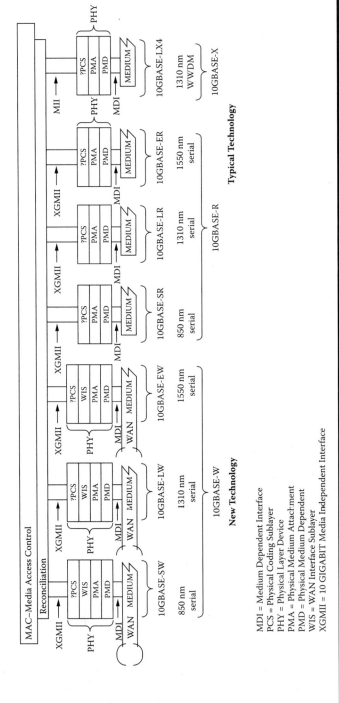

MDI = Medium Dependent Interface
PCS = Physical Coding Sublayer
PHY = Physical Layer Device
PMA = Physical Medium Attachment
PMD = Physical Medium Dependent
WIS = WAN Interface Sublayer
XGMII = 10 GIGABIT Media Independent Interface

Figure 9.21   Seven PHYs, with a view of supportive sublayers.

Table 9.16 Correlation between Technologies and Required Sublayers

Nomenclature	8B/10B PCS & PMA	64B/66B PCS	WIS	Serial PMA	850 nm Serial PMD	1310 nm Serial PMD	1550 nm Serial PMD	1310 nm WWDM PMD	10GBASE-X	10GBASE-R	10GBASE-W
10GBASE-SR		Req.		Req.	Req.					■	
10GBASE-SW		Req.	Req.	Req.	Req.						■
10GBASE-LX4	Req.							Req.	■		
10GBASE-LR		Req.		Req.		Req.				■	
10GBASE-LW		Req.	Req.	Req.		Req.					■
10GBASE-ER		Req.		Req.			Req.			■	
10GBASE-EW		Req.	Req.	Req.			Req.				■

Although the XGMII is an optional interface, it is used extensively in the standard as a basis for the functional specification and provides a common service interface.

■ XGMII Extender Sublayer (XGXS) and XAUI (pronounced "Zowie")—The 10 Gigabit Attachment Unit Interface provides an interconnection between two XGMII Extender sublayers to increase the reach of XGMII. This XAUI supports 10 Gbps operation through its four-lane,* differential-pair transmit and receive paths.† The XGXS provides a mapping between the signals provided at the XGMII and the XAUI. (This interface is also optional.) [10G200301].

Ethernet (including 10GbE) defines a logical MAC-PLS interface between the RS (PHY) and the MAC. The interface operates at a constant 10 Gbps data rate. The interface is defined as a set of service primitives.

9.4.1.3.2.2 Reconciliation Sublayer
P802.3ae/D3.2 defines a Reconciliation Sublayer and optional 10 XGMII‡ (see Figure 9.22). The purpose is to convert the logical MAC-PLS service primitives to electrical signals; it provides a simple, inexpensive, and easy-to-implement interconnection between the MAC sublayer and the PHY.

---

* A lane is a bundle of signals that constitutes a logical subset of a point-to-point interconnect. A lane contains enough signals to communicate a quantum of data or control information between the two endpoints.
† The "AUI" portion is borrowed from the Ethernet Attachment Unit Interface. The "X" represents the Roman numeral for ten and implies ten gigabits per second. The XAUI is designed as an interface extender, and the interface, which it extends, is the XGMII, the 10 Gigabit Media Independent Interface. The XGMII is a 64-signal-wide interface (32-bit data paths for each of transmit and receive) that may be used to attach the Ethernet MAC to its PHY. The XAUI may be used in place of, or to extend, the XGMII in chip-to-chip applications typical of most Ethernet MAC-to-PHY interconnects. The XAUI is a low-pin-count, self-clocked serial bus that is directly evolved from the Gigabit Ethernet 1000BASE-X PHY. The XAUI interface speed is 2.5 times that of 1000BASE-X. By arranging four serial lanes, the 4-bit XAUI interface supports the ten-times data throughput required by 10GbE.
‡ XGMII is optional, but used as the basis for specifications.

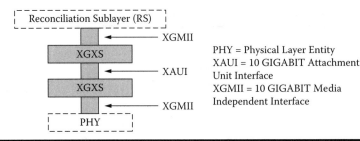

Figure 9.22 Reconciliation Sublayer and 10 Gigabit Media Independent Interface.

9.4.1.3.2.3 Physical Coding Sublayer (PCS)

The PCS sublayer provides for packet delineation and scrambling for the LAN PHY. The transmission code used by the PCS, referred to as 8B/10B, is identical to that specified in Clause 36 of the 802.3 standard as well as ANSI X3.230-1994 (FC-PH), Clause 11. The PCS maps XGMII characters into ten-bit code groups, and vice versa, using the 8B/10B block-coding scheme. Implicit in the definition of a code group is an establishment of code group boundaries by a PCS Synchronization process. The 8B/10B transmission code, as well as the rules by which the PCS ENCODE and DECODE functions generate, manipulate, and interpret code groups are specified in the standard. As seen in Figure 9.21 10GBASE-LX4 is the only PHY utilizing this encoding. The standard also specifies the PCS that is common to a family of 10 Gbps physical layer implementations, known as 10GBASE-R. This PCS can connect directly to one of the 10GBASE-R physical layers: 10GBASE-SR, 10GBASE-LR, and 10GBASE-ER. Alternatively, this PCS can connect to a WIS that will produce the 10GBASE-W encoding (10GBASE-R encoded data stream encapsulated into frames compatible with SONET and SDH networks) for transport by the 10GBASE-W physical layers, namely, 10GBASE-SW, 10GBASE-LW, and 10GBASE-EW. The term 10GBASE-R is used when referring generally to physical layers using the PCS defined here. The 10GBASE-R is based on a 64B/66B code. The 64B/66B code supports data and control characters while maintaining robust error detection. 10GBASE-R PCS maps the interface characteristics of the WIS when present, and the PMA sublayer to the services expected by the Reconciliation and XGXS sublayers. 10GBASE-R can be extended to support any full-duplex medium requiring only that the medium be compliant at the PMA level. 10GBASE-R PCS may be attached through the PMA sublayer to a LAN PMD sublayer supporting a data rate of 10 Gbps or it may be attached to a WAN PMD through the WIS and PMA sublayers. When attached to a WAN sublayer, this PCS adapts the data stream to the WAN data rate.

9.4.1.3.2.4 Physical Media Attachment (PMA) Sublayer

The PMA provides for the serialization and deserialization of the data being transmitted. It is responsible for supporting multiple encoding schemes, because each PMD will use an encoding that is suited to the specific media it supports.

9.4.1.3.2.5 Physical Media Dependent (PMD) Sublayer

A summary of the seven PHY variants is shown in Table 9.17. The data rates of the PMA sublayer, type Serial, are as follows:

Term	Definition
10GBASE-R nominal baud rate	10.3125 Gbps
10GBASE-W nominal baud rate	9.95328 Gbps

Table 9.17   Seven PHY Variants

		10GbE Designation	
Description	*Reach/Fiber*	*LAN PHY*	*WAN PHY*
850 nm serial	~85 m/MMF	10GBASE-SR	10GBASE-SW
1310 nm serial	10 km/SMF	10GBASE-LR	10GBASE-LW
1550 nm serial	40 km/SMF	10GBASE-ER	10GBASE-EW
1310 nm WDM	10 km/SMF ~300 m/MMF	10GBASE-LX4	—

9.4.1.3.3 WAN Interface Sublayer (WIS), Type 10GBASE-W, Metro Ethernet

The WIS defined in Clause 50 of the standard is an optional PHY sublayer that may be used to create a 10GBASE-W PHY that is data-rate and format compatible with the SONET STS-192c transmission format defined by ANSI, as well as SDH's VC-4-64c container specified by the International Telecommunication Union (ITU). The purpose of the WIS is to allow 10GBASE-W equipment to generate Ethernet data streams that may be mapped directly to STS-192c or VC-4-64c streams at the PHY level, without requiring MAC or higher-layer processing. These streams are then carried over a SONET/SDH infrastructure via the use of an interworking unit. This technology is currently contemplated for "metro Ethernet" applications

The WIS, therefore, specifies a *subset* of the logical frame formats in the SONET and SDH standards. In addition, the WIS constrains the effective data throughput at its service interface to the payload capacity of STS-192c/VC-4-64c, i.e., 9.58464 Gbps. Multiplexed SONET/SDH formats are not supported.

The WIS does not render a 10GBASE-W PHY **compliant** with either SONET or SDH at any rate or format. A 10GBASE-W interface is not intended to **interoperate** directly with interfaces that comply with SONET or SDH standards, or other synchronous networks. Operation over electrically multiplexed payloads of a transmission network is outside the scope of this standard. Such interoperation would require full conformance to the optical, electrical, and logical requirements specified by SONET or SDH, and is outside the scope and intent of this standard.

The achievable topologies with the use of a WIS as part of a 10GBASE-W PHY are identical to those implementable without it. From the perspective of the 10 Gbps MAC layer, a 10GBASE-W PHY with a WIS does not appear different (in either the functions or service interface) from a PHY without a WIS, with the exception of sustained data rate. However, a 10GBASE-W interface implementing a WIS may interoperate only with another 10GBASE-W interface that also implements a WIS.

9.4.1.3.3.1 Scope

The WIS clause in the 10GbE standard specifies the functions, features, services, and protocol of the WIS. The WIS may be used with any of the PCS, PMA, and PMD sublayers that are defined for 10GBASE-W; it is placed between the PCS and PMA sublayers within the 10GBASE-W PHY. The WIS is common to all members of the family of 10GBASE-W WAN-compatible PHY implementations, specifically, 10GBASE-SW, 10GBASE-LW, and 10GBASE-EW.

The definition of the WIS is based on the subset of signaling rates and data formats standardized by ANSI T1.416-1999 (Network to Customer Installation Interfaces—Synchronous Optical Network Physical Layer Specification: Common Criteria), which is in turn based on ANSI

T1.105-1995 (Telecommunications—Synchronous Optical Network—Basic Description including Multiplex Structure, Rates, and Formats).

The WIS maps the encoded Ethernet data received (transmitted) from (to) the PCS into a frame structure that has the same format as that defined by T1.416-1999, implementing a minimal number of the standard SONET overhead fields and functions. WIS does not adhere to the electrical and optical aspects of SONET specified by T1.416-1999, as it is intended to be used with PHYs that conform to the corresponding parameters defined by the 10GBASE-W standard; otherwise, a gateway mechanism is needed to use an existing SONET/SDH infrastructure, either at the CPE level or at the network edge device. The WIS meets all requirements of ANSI T1.416-1999 except the following:

1. Section 5 (Jitter)
2. Section 6 (Synchronization)
3. Section 7.2.2 (VT1.5 rate—Electrical Interface)
4. Section 7.4.2 (VT1.5 rate)
5. Section 7.6 (Performance and failure alarm monitoring)
6. Section 7.7 (Performance monitoring functions)
7. Annex A (SONET VT1.5 Line Interface Common Criteria)
8. Annex B (SONET maintenance signals for the NI)
9. Annex C (Receiver jitter tolerance and transfer)

9.4.1.3.3.2 Summary of WIS Functions

The following provides a summary of the principal functions implemented by the WIS. In the transmit direction (i.e., when transferring data from the PCS to the PMA), the WIS performs the following functions:

1. *Mapping* of data units received from the PCS via the WIS Service Interface to the *payload capacity of the SPE* defined for STS-192c
2. Addition of Path Overhead and fixed stuff octets to generate the actual SPE
3. Creation of frames consisting of Line Overhead and Section Overhead octets plus the SPE, and the generation and insertion of Section, Line, and Path Bit Interleaved Parity (BIP)
4. Scrambling of the generated WIS frames
5. Transmission of these frames to the PMA sublayer via the PMA Service Interface

In the receive direction, the functions performed by the WIS include the following:

1. Reception of data from the PMA sublayer via the PMA Service Interface
2. Delineation of octet boundaries as well as STS-192c frame boundaries within the unaligned data stream from the PMA
3. Descrambling of the payload and overhead fields within the incoming frames
4. Processing of the pointer field within the Line Overhead, and delineation of the boundaries of the SPE within the received WIS frames
5. Generation and checking of Bit Interleaved Parity (BIP) within the Section, Line and Path Overheads
6. Removal of Line, Section, and Path Overhead columns, as well as fixed stuff columns, to extract the actual payload field

7. Handling of errors and exception conditions detected within the incoming WIS frame stream, and reporting these errors to Layer Management
8. Mapping of octets extracted from the payload capacity of the incoming SPE to data units that are passed to the PCS via the WIS Service Interface

9.4.2 Rapid Spanning Tree Algorithm

This section looks at mechanisms to achieve faster restoration of LAN/MAN topologies (also known as restoration) when dealing with service-affecting events. We discussed the STA earlier in the chapter. In the case of bridged Ethernet networks faster convergence can be obtained using the RSTA instead of the STA. Faster restoration is particularly important if network planners choose to use the GbE or 10GbE technology in metro environments. Currently, SONET-based architectures offer a 50 ms restoration service, whereas STA-based networks offer a 45–60 s restoration time (based on the size of the network).

9.4.2.1 Motivations

Restoration in WAN and metropolitan networks is complex. In this section we look at the much simpler situation of an enterprise bridge-based network where an STA is used to keep a general topology pruned to a spanning tree by blocking links in normal mode and unblocking them in failure mode. Traditionally, the STP has been used to maintain topology, as discussed earlier. One of the problems with STP is its slow convergence time, as just noted. To reduce the convergence time, a new protocol, the IEEE 802.1w Rapid Spanning Tree Protocol (RSTP), was standardized in the early 2000s. A brief overview is offered in this section, followed by a more extensive discussion.

A debate has already arisen of late whether this protocol will improve the resilience of Ethernet-based backbones enough to enable metropolitan area services to compete with traditional carrier-based services utilizing SONET/SDH services. Although Ethernet-based metropolitan services have gained some penetration, observers say the networks delivering these services need to be as reliable as circuit-switched SONET networks before large numbers of customers will move traffic to them. The question is whether the recently ratified IEEE 802.1w RSTP is the answer to Ethernet's shortcomings. All parties seem to agree that RSTP offers a vast improvement on the 45–60 s it takes the traditional Spanning Tree to help a failed Ethernet link recover. However, they differ on the extent of that improvement—estimates run from 10 ms to a full second or more—and whether it is sufficient for guaranteeing service level agreements (SLAs). The consensus seems to be that RSTP is one component of several needed to make Ethernet as resilient as SONET, which recovers from link outages in 50 ms or less, in the metropolitan area. Recovery times may, however, depend on how one implements the standard. If one combines the technology with other Ethernet technologies—specifically, the Link Aggregation Protocol—it is possible for services providers to guarantee SLAs where they were not traditionally able to get resiliency and recovery time in tens of milliseconds.

Some metropolitan Ethernet equipment vendors disagree with the assertion that RSTP can provide recovery in tens of milliseconds. RSTP's recovery time is closer to 1 s; this is still not in the subsecond category, which does not allow the network in question to carry certain types of traffic or guarantee SLAs. Even in the LAN, users are not seeing recovery times in the 1 s range. Fast

Spanning Tree helps some, but it is still not perfect for some applications. One does not measure failover times of 1 s as of yet; more typically, one sees 10 s from boot up to traffic transport. RSTP lacks the fault-management capabilities that service providers get with SONET and is not designed for ring topologies, which continue to be widely deployed in metro networks [GIM200101].

Some practitioners feel that [Rapid] Spanning Tree is not the right algorithm to show that the problems associated with Ethernet have been solved; the technology still is not viable in a ring environment and often it is hard to deploy a mesh network, especially in the metro. That is why the IEEE is defining the resiliency of Ethernet networks via the RPR. Just as its name implies, RPR is designed for ring topologies carrying packets, but with the same resiliency attributes of a typical SONET ring. A number of Ethernet services providers have asserted that RSTP is better than RPR; however, some researchers believe that RSTP may be unable to scale to be able to support large networks.

Security is another issue of Ethernet VLAN services that RSTP cannot solve. VLAN is a weak technology, overall. If one crosses service provider boundaries with virtual LANs, there is no guarantee that a user's VLAN ID has not already been assigned to some other VLAN. Rapid Spanning Tree can support multiple VLANs, fast reroutes and prevent loops, but security remains the key issue. Service providers have to be careful about how they implement these VLANs, especially across service providers' boundaries. Companies cannot be assured that just because their Ethernet service provider supports RSTP, traffic will be safe. They must consider the totality of the service provisioning environment before deciding whether to subscribe to VLAN Ethernet services. No one technology is going to make Ethernet viable in the metropolitan area network; it is a collection of factors that must come together for us to build the kind of network with rapid failover times like those of SONET. It is also going to take a good implementation of these standards and smart network design [GIM200101].

9.4.2.2 IEEE 802.1w Rapid Spanning Tree Protocol

The sections that follow cover RSTP at the technical level.

9.4.2.2.1 Overview

The standard of interest is "Part 3: Media Access Control (MAC) Bridges—Amendment 2: Rapid Reconfiguration." This amendment to IEEE Std 802.1D, 1998 Edition (ISO/IEC 15802-3:1998) and IEEE Std 802.1t-2001 defines the changes necessary to the operation of a MAC bridge to provide rapid reconfiguration capability. These changes are defined as a series of additions to, and modifications of, the combined text that is generated by applying the editing instructions contained in IEEE Std 802.1t-2001 to the text of IEEE Std 802.1D, 1998 Edition.

As noted earlier, bridged LANs can provide for the following:

1. The interconnection of stations attached to LANs of different MAC types
2. An effective increase in the physical extent, the number of permissible attachments, or the total performance of a LAN
3. Partitioning of the physical LAN for administrative or maintenance reasons
4. Validation of access to the LAN
5. Increased availability of the MAC Service in case of reconfiguration or failure of components of the bridged LAN (new feature with IEEE Std 802.1w)

RSTP offers a reduction in the time taken to reconfigure the active topology of the bridged LAN when changes to the physical topology or its configuration parameters take place. The IEEE 802.1w standard specifies the operation of MAC bridges that attach directly to IEEE 802 LANs. Specifically, the configuration protocol and associated algorithm required for the distributed computation of a Spanning Tree active topology appears in two forms in this standard: one section (Clause 8) specifies a version of the Spanning Tree algorithm and protocol that is consistent with the specification contained in IEEE Std 802.1D, 1998 Edition, discussed earlier; another section (Clause 17) specifies the Rapid Spanning Tree Algorithm and Protocol. The two versions of the algorithm and protocol are capable of interoperating within the same bridged LAN.* In view of the improved performance offered, the IEEE now recommends that the Rapid Spanning Tree algorithm and Protocol be supported in preference to the original version in new MAC bridge implementations.

Specification changes are in the following areas:

1. Definition of a new Protocol Version number (version 2) for use with RSTP.
2. Definition of a new BPDU type (BPDU type 2) to distinguish RST BPDUs from Configuration and Topology Change BPDUs.
3. Inclusion of the port Roles (*Root Port*, *Designated Port*, and *Backup Port*) in the computation of port State (*Discarding*, *Learning*, and *Forwarding*). In particular, a new *Root Port* is able to transition rapidly to *Forwarding*.
4. Signaling to neighboring bridges of a bridge port's desire to be Designated and *Forwarding*, and explicit acknowledgement by the neighboring bridge on a point-to-point link. This allows the port State to transition to the *Forwarding* state without waiting for a timer expiry.
5. Acceptance of messages from a prior Designated bridge even if they conveyed "inferior" information. Additionally, a minimum increment to the Message Age is specified so that messages propagating in this way cannot "go round in circles" for an extensive period of time.
6. Improvements in the propagation of topology change information in such a fashion that the information does not have to be propagated all the way to the Root bridge and back before unwanted learned source address information is flushed from the Filtering Databases.
7. Origination of BPDUs on a port by port basis, instead of transmission on *Designated Port*s following reception of information from the Root.

Also, there are revised specifications of timer values† to accommodate changed behavior in the cases where neighboring bridges do not support RSTP, and the forward delay timers do actually run to completion.

9.4.2.2.1.1 Interworking Issues

Text in the IEEE 802.1w standard points out that the original BPDU formats used in IEEE Std 802.1D, 1998 Edition and prior versions of the standard had been designed with the intent that they would permit straightforward extensions to the protocol. The basis for the intended backward compatibility is that, for an implementation of version X of the protocol, an implementation

---

* It follows that it is not necessary for equipment to support both versions of the Spanning Tree algorithm and protocol.
† The default timer values are chosen in the IEEE 802.1w specification to work effectively; however, some care may be needed in environments where timers have been tuned to their minimum values.

should interpret versions *greater than version X* BPDUs as if they were version X, ignoring any parameters or flags added by the more recent version, and interpret versions *less or equal to version X* BPDUs exactly as specified for the version concerned. For this to work, new versions of the protocol are allowed to add new parameters or flags, but not to redefine the semantics or encoding of any of the parameters and flags that existed in previous versions.

Adoption of this approach would enable a device that correctly implemented version 0 to ignore the protocol version field altogether, and also to ignore any parameters or flags that were not part of the version 0 protocol specification. Unfortunately, although the 1998 and prior revisions of IEEE Std 802.1D are correctly specified in this regard, the interpretation of the words in the standard has not been consistent; consequently, there are implementations of IEEE Std 802.1D in the field that will discard BPDUs that do not carry protocol version 0, or that carry additional flags over and above those specified for version 0. Consequently, the wording in Clause 9 has been made much more explicit with regard to the requirements for protocol version handling, to ensure that this problem is not repeated in future implementations.

To ensure correct interworking between version 2 (RSTP) bridges and version 0 bridges, it has been necessary therefore not simply to define a new protocol version number and additional parameters to go with it, but also to allow version 2 bridges to detect the presence of version 0 bridges on its ports and to use version 0 BPDUs if such a bridge is detected. If a version 0 device is detected, the information necessary to allow requests for, and confirmations of, *Designated Port* transitions to *Forwarding* cannot be exchanged; however, the key element of rapidly transitioning new *Root Ports* to a *Forwarding* state is retained.

The protocol version chosen for RST BPDUs is version 2; version 1 BPDUs (defined for use in Remote Bridging—IEEE 802.1G) are accommodated in the version 2 format by means of a placeholder of zero length for the version 1 protocol information. (Note: Network planners should avoid *intermixing* equipment in the field because of the subtleties involved.)

The reconfiguration time of the STP is significantly improved in RSTP by using port roles (*"Root Port," "Designated Port," "Alternate,"* or *"Backup"*) to select forwarding state transitions. In STP, these transitions are determined by the current and desired forwarding states (*Blocking* or *Forwarding*). A newly selected *"Root Port"* can be moved directly from the *Blocking* to the *Forwarding* state provided that the previously selected *Root Port* is made *Blocking*. Loop-free topology is maintained.

The RSTP transitions accommodate arbitrary reconfiguration during periods of network device and link changes. However, an important application is autoconfiguration of redundant connections as backup "resilient links." Assuming that the "next best" *Root Port* (an *Alternate Port*) has been precomputed, and the *Designated Port* to which that Alternate port is connected is in *Forwarding*, physical connectivity can be restored within the time taken for the physical media to signal link failure (through "link beat" or "loss of light" indication). This could be as little as 10 ms, and does not require the exchange of any BPDUs between the bridges concerned.

Where a link is lost but one of the bridges involved has no precomputed backup port, connectivity can be restored after link failure detection within the time necessary to exchange two BPDUs (one in each direction) on one of the remaining active ports. This is needed to perform the "handshake" between two bridges, where one requests to put its *Designated Port* into *Forwarding*, and the other (a Root or Alternate port) responds by indicating whether its port states are consistent with the requested state change. A *Root Port* will give a positive response (i.e., giving the *Designated Port* permission to transition to *Forwarding*), if the other ports of its bridge are in a state that is consistent with the state change (i.e., they are all "agreed"); otherwise, and also if the port is an Alternate port, the response is negative.

The "handshake" between Designated and Root or Alternate ports mentioned earlier has the effect of moving a cut in the network one bridge nearer the edge of the bridged LAN (i.e., one bridge further away from the Root), as a *Root Port* can signal "agreed" once all of its bridge's *Designated Ports* have been made *Discarding*. These *Designated Ports*, in their turn, request the downstream *Root Ports* for permission to change state to *Forwarding*, and so on, until the edge of the bridged LAN is reached. A worst-case reconfiguration (based on a maximum diameter of 7 for the bridged LAN) would involve the time taken for six such handshakes to take place in sequence before the reconfiguration had been propagated from the point of the original cut to the edge of the LAN (i.e., for the entire network to reconfigure).

Topology anomalies are "inferred" by the absence of expected "bridge hello" messages. The standard recommends a hello time of 2 s, although a range of 1 to 10 s is allowed. If too many hello packets are sent by a large number of bridges, they will take up bandwidth and computation resources around the network. Hence, in some cases a 10 s value may be used by the network engineer that sets up the network. However, even assuming a suggested 2-s figure, ignoring the propagation delay across the network, and ignoring the time needed for the "handshake," the "blind spot" for a failure can be 2 s, or 1 s "on the average," assuming a uniform event probability distribution on a 2 s range, with a failure somewhere in the 2 s interval. An interval of 2 s represents 40 times more time than on a SONET system, and 1 s represents 20 times more time than on SONET.

The specification makes the point that such rapid recovery (in the seconds range) is in significant contrast to the slow (about 50 s) STP reconfiguration times. It provides a basis for improved-availability continuous network operation based on redundant low-cost network devices, with recovery times commensurate with fault-tolerant telecommunications equipment. Using the campus data network for voice applications with the proposed improvement, failure and recovery might result in the loss of only a few speech samples—a "click" on the line rather than loss of a call.

Although RSTP changes the dynamic effects of STP (bridge ports becoming forwarding or blocking at certain times), there is no change in the BPDUs sent between an RSTP bridge and an STP bridge; nor is it a requirement that all bridges in the network should change their behavior, but those that do upgrade benefit from the much reduced reconfiguration delay, and can be introduced arbitrarily into an existing network.

9.4.2.2.2 Support of the MAC Service

9.4.2.2.2.1 Quality of Service Maintenance

Service availability is measured as that fraction of some total reference time during which the MAC Service is provided. The operation of a bridge can increase or lower service availability. Service availability can be increased by automatic reconfiguration of the bridged LAN to avoid the use of a failed component (e.g., link) in the data path. Service availability can be lowered by failure of a bridge itself, through denial-of-service by the bridge, or through frame filtering by the bridge. RSTP aims at maximizing service availability. It is expected that to optimize the service availability, no loss of service or delay in service provision should be caused by bridges, except as a consequence of extraordinary events such as a failure, removal, or insertion of a bridged LAN component, or as a consequence of the movement of an end station, or as a consequence of an attempt to perform unauthorized access.

Frame loss: The MAC Service does not guarantee the delivery of Service Data Units. Frames transmitted by a source station arrive, uncorrupted, at the destination station with high probability. The operation of a bridge introduces minimal additional frame loss.

Frame misordering: The MAC Service permits a small rate of reordering of frames with a given user priority for a given combination of destination address and source address.

Frame duplication: The MAC Service permits a small rate of duplication of frames. The potential for frame duplication in a bridged LAN arises through the possibility of duplication of received frames on subsequent transmission within a bridge, or through the possibility of multiple paths between source and destination end stations.

In IEEE Std 802.1D, 1998 (and earlier-dated specifications), the delays imposed by STP before a port is made *Forwarding* ensure that any frames of a session that were "in transit" prior to a reconfiguration event will have been delivered or discarded before any frames are transmitted on a port that is made *Forwarding* as a result of the reconfiguration event. In a network configured according the original 802.1D standard, the only source of duplicated or misordered frames is an "exceptionally healed" connection between two bridges, for example, as a result of accidental interconnections between shared media hubs. This exceptional situation hypothetically impacts both STP and RSTP; however, RSTP introduces a new means whereby duplication and misordering can occur. RSTP by its design and intent can reduce the delay before a port is made *Forwarding* to very small values; in the case of *Root Port* transitions, the delay can be as short as the hardware can manage it, or in the case of *Designated Port* transitions, as short as two frame transmission times on a single segment. Hence, it is conceivable that a reconfiguration event can take place, and a port be made *Forwarding* as a result, while prior frames of a conversation are still in flight.

RSTP introduces an additional risk of *duplication* of unlearned unicast frames, and of multicast frames, on reconfiguration events. The risk depends on the configuration of the LAN, and the opportunity that the configuration offers for frames to be "in transit" in buffers on alternate paths to the destinations when a reconfiguration event takes place. The probability of frame duplication occurring as a result of a reconfiguration event depends on the frequency of reconfiguration events in the network, the selected network topology, and the implementation details of the equipment used.

It is possible to conceive of a situation where, prior to a reconfiguration event, an end-to-end session was required to transit the maximum diameter of the bridged LAN, and following reconfiguration, the same session only transits a single bridge. This could happen, for example, with a bridge that has a *Root Port* connected to one end of a LAN "diameter" and an Alternate port connected to the other end of the "diameter." Because there could be frames in transit before the reconfiguration, frames transmitted immediately following the reconfiguration could arrive at their destination before the ones in transit, resulting in frame *misordering* as perceived by the recipient. Some LAN protocols are sensitive to misordering; in these cases even a low incidence of misordering could result in perceived problems in networks that support these protocols. As in the case of frame duplication, there is an additional risk of misordering of unicast and multicast frames on reconfiguration events with RSTP.

9.4.2.2.1.2 New Internal Sublayer Service Mechanisms Provided within the MAC Bridge

Some of the rapid state transitions that are possible within RSTP are dependent upon whether the port concerned can only be connected to exactly one other bridge (i.e., it is served by a point-to-point

LAN segment), or can be connected to two or more bridges (i.e., it is served by a shared-medium LAN segment). To this end, in addition to the unit-data service primitives available under the 802.1D specification, the Internal Sublayer Service provided by a MAC entity to the MAC Relay Entity within a bridge makes available a pair of parameters that permit inspection of, and control over, the administrative and operational state of the point-to-point status of the MAC entity by the MAC Relay Entity. These parameters are *operPointToPointMAC* and *adminPointToPointMAC*. From the point of view of determining the value of *operPointToPointMAC*, the MAC is considered to be connected to a point-to-point LAN segment if any of the following conditions are true:

1. The MAC entity concerned contains a Link Aggregation sublayer, and the set of physical MACs associated with the Aggregator are all aggregatable.
2. The MAC entity concerned supports autonegotiation, and the autonegotiation function has determined that the LAN segment is to be operated in full-duplex mode.
3. The MAC entity has been configured by management means for full-duplex operation.

Otherwise, the MAC is considered to be connected to a LAN segment that is not point to point.

9.4.2.2.1.3 STP/STA Timer Values

The recommended values and operational ranges for the essential STA performance parameters are shown in Table 9.18. Because the operation of RSTP is largely insensitive to the choice of timer values, these values are used by RSTP as a "backstop" to the normal operation of the protocol; i.e., to ensure correct protocol operation when encountering exception conditions caused by lost messages or failure to detect hardware state changes, and to allow seamless integration of STP and RSTP bridges in the same bridged LAN.

9.4.3 VLANs

The term *virtual LAN (VLAN)* refers to a collection of devices across a local network that communicate as if they were on the same physical LAN. The IEEE standard defines it as "a subset of the active topology of a bridged Local Area Network." A VLAN is a logical association of ports on a LAN (or LANs). The standards effort has taken the view of the "…establishment of Groups in a

Table 9.18 Spanning Tree Algorithm Timer Values

Parameter	Recommended or Default Value	Fixed Value	Range
Bridge Hello Time	2.0	NA	1.0–10.0
Bridge Max Age	20.0	NA	6.0–40.0
Bridge Forward Delay	15.0	NA	4.0–30.0
Hold Time	NA	Not more than TxHoldCount (17.16.6) BPDUs transmitted in any HelloTime interval	NA

Note: All times are in seconds; NA = Not applicable; Subclause 8.10.2 constrains the relationship between Bridge Max Age and Bridge Forward Delay; Implementations that are conformant to the definition of Hold Time in IEEE Std 802.ID. 1998 Edition are also conformant to the revised definition of Hold Time stated in this table.

Table 9.19   Enterprise VLAN Benefits Advanced by Proponents

VLANs help control traffic	With traditional networks, congestion can be caused by broadcast traffic that is directed to all network devices, regardless of whether they require such broadcast information. VLANs increase the efficiency of the network (at complexity's expense) because each VLAN can be set up to logically group only those devices that must communicate with one another.
VLANs provide "label-based security"	Devices within each VLAN only communicate with member devices in the same VLAN. If a device in VLAN Marketing must communicate with devices in VLAN Sales, the traffic must cross a routing device.
VLANs simplify the change and movement of devices	With traditional networks, administrators spend time dealing with moves and changes. If users move to a different subnetwork, the addresses of each station must be updated manually. In the VLAN environment this can be done administratively or by self discovery.

LAN environment, and the filtering of frames by bridges such that frames addressed to a particular Group are forwarded only on those LAN segments that are required to reach members of that Group…" (ISO/IEC 15802-3). As Ethernet networks become large, the many stations and devices transmitting data within a single broadcast domain can increase "broadcast storms." One can use VLANs to partition the broadcast domain into several domains and thereby decrease the likelihood of broadcast storms. Hence, a VLAN carves out its own single, unique broadcast domain from the larger Ethernet network. Proponents see VLANs as LANs that do not have traditional physical and topological constraints, and position them as software-defined LANs (see Table 9.19).

VLAN technology was developed in the early 1990s for enterprise applications; the protocols are single-organization-centric. Nonetheless, they have been exported to the metro environment, but with a baggage of limitations and lack of robustness. They do not appear to be "the wave of the future" in terms of being the major new carrier-class next-generation network architecture. GbE/VLAN are subject to the problem of congestion. Traffic sources operating under TCP linearly increase their bandwidth usage until resources are exhausted. On packet drop they back off exponentially. Uncontrolled congestion seriously degrades performance: buffers fill up and packets are dropped, resulting in retransmissions (with the vicious cycle of more packet loss and increased latency). The problem builds until throughput collapses. Furthermore, 802.1Q has a limit of only 4096 VLANs, which limits the number of customers that can be supported in an Ethernet network; stacked VLANs and VLAN tag translation capabilities implemented by several vendors alleviate this problem to some extent [RAM200101]. VLAN-based "security" is generally very weak: a simple label on an entity is no security at all, any more than a label on a door in place of a lock would offer any assurance against intrusion. Security can only be achieved with strong methods, specifically, payload encryption. However, traffic segregation based on VLAN port membership does offer some isolation.

From a single VLAN enterprise switch* point of view, any subset of ports (including all ports on the switch) can comprise a VLAN. The switch needs to support VLAN features to be able to group such a set of ports into a logical LAN or VLAN. Not surprisingly, VLANs can be defined across multiple enterprise switches. LAN segments are not restricted by the hardware that physically connects them; rather, the segments are defined by the user groups that the planner can create on the VLAN switches.

---

* Really a multi-port bridge or Layer 2 switch.

Over the past decade, VLANs have seen three technology generations and limited adoption up to now. Generation 1 was based on vendor-proprietary systems; Generation 2 was based on ATM LAN Emulation/Multi-Protocol over ATM (LANE/MPOA); and Generation 3 is IEEE 802.1Q-based (IEEE 802.1Q-1998, IEEE Standard for Local and Metropolitan Area Networks: Virtual Bridged Local Area Networks). Enterprise VLANs enable the planner to construct the broadcast domain without being restricted by physical connections.

Initially VLANs were vendor-specific. An organization implementing VLANs had to acquire all the hardware (NICs, hubs, switches, etc.) from the same vendor. Because of the vendor-specific nature of these early systems, one could not define virtual workgroups across equipment of two vendors. First-generation VLANs had these limitations:

1. Lack of interoperability
2. Scope limitations, by geography
3. Complex implementation and deployment

Second-generation VLANs looked into the use of connection-oriented ATM methods; the complexity of this solution limited deployment considerably. The commercial success of IEEE 802.1Q is still an open question.

VLANs group collections of users into closed user group (CUG) communities. Associated with each VLAN is a VLAN Identifier (VID) (also known as Q-Tag). VLANs promised users connectivity that is technology- and topology-independent; for example, some corporate users could be on a token-ring system whereas others could be on an Ethernet, and yet others on ATM's LANE; yet, with the "miracle" of VLAN all would appear to the user to be on the same segment (it should be noted, however, that practically the same service can be achieved using translational bridging, or just bridging if one used only one MAC type). Hence, VLANs disaggregate the total corporate community of users into subcommunities; software on the switch then rejoins specified switch ports into distinct IP networks (VLANs link to multiple LAN segments at the VLAN switch). Each device attached to a port is on the port's VLAN. In the case where a hub is attached to a VLAN port, every device attached to the hub is on the same VLAN. VLAN trunking is the spanning of multiple VLANs across multiple switches. Where two or more VLAN-capable switches are connected, VLAN trunking allows any port on any switch to be part of any VLAN. This technology may conceivably work as specified in a private enterprise environment, but the forced import into a metro access/metro core environment is problematic because of security considerations. (One way around the security issue is for each user to employ IPsec at the network layer; however, administration of IPsec connections is not trivial.)

In a nutshell, IEEE 802.1Q, the VLAN standard, places a Q-tag in the Ethernet frame header. 802.1Q-aware devices use Q-tags to differentiate VLANs. This allows the same physical port to host multiple 802.1Q VLANs, each representing a different logical network. Without 802.1Q, physical ports alone define the VLAN. Many older Ethernet devices do not recognize 802.1Q. Because 802.1Q lengthens the Ethernet header, older (non-802.1Q) devices can incorrectly identify the 802.1Q tagged packets as "giants"—an Ethernet frame larger than 1518 bytes—and drop them.

According to observers, the campuswide VLAN model is highly dependent upon the 80/20 rule. If 80 percent of the traffic is within a workgroup, then 80 percent of the packets are switched at Layer 2 from client to server. However, if 90 percent of the traffic goes to the enterprise servers in the server farm, then 90 percent of the packets are switched by the one-armed router, defeating the purpose of the VLAN. The scalability and performance of the VLAN model are limited by the characteristics of STP [HAV200201]. Each VLAN is equivalent to a flat bridged network.

In summary, VLAN technology works as designed in an enterprise network environment. Its import into the metro access/metro core space, however, leaves a lot to be desired from an overall performance (availability, restoration, and security) point of view. VLANs can be created based on the following methodologies, which we describe in the subsections that follow:

- Physical port
- 802.1Q tag
- MAC address
- Ethernet, LLC SAP, or LLC/SNAP Ethernet protocol type
- A combination of the foregoing

9.4.3.1 Port-Based VLANs

In a port-based VLAN, a VLAN name is given to a group of one or more ports on the switch. A port can be a member of only one port-based VLAN. As noted earlier, for stations that are members of the different VLANs to communicate, the traffic must be routed; routing may be incorporated in the VLAN switch as an add-on function, or may be done by an external router. This implies that each VLAN must be configured as a router interface with a unique IP address. Routing must occur even if the stations are physically part of the same access module on the switch.

To create a port-based enterprise VLAN that spans two switches, one must: (1) assign the port on each switch to the VLAN and (2) cable the two switches together using one port on each switch per VLAN. At the practical level, in typical hardware, to create multiple VLANs that span two switches in a port-based VLAN, a port on System 1 must be cabled to a port on System 2 *for each VLAN one wants to span the switches.* At least one port on each switch must be a member of the corresponding VLANs as well. Using this daisy-chained approach, one can create multiple enterprise VLANs that span multiple enterprise switches. Each switch must have a dedicated port for each VLAN. Each dedicated port must be connected to a port that is a member of its VLAN on the next switch.

9.4.3.2 Tagged VLANs

Tagged VLANs are basically port-based VLANs that are implemented across two bridges using a single trunk. For untagged traffic (which, at this juncture in the discussion, we assume represents the entire company traffic*), VLAN membership for a port-based VLAN is determined by the Port VLAN Identifier (PVID) assigned to the receiving port.† For this arrangement to function, there needs to be an additional way to convey the VLAN information between the two bridges other than the physical connection discussed in the previous paragraph. This is accomplished by having the VLAN switches add a VLAN tag to every frame that is sent between the two bridges; such frames are known as VLAN-tagged frames and the connection between the two bridges is known as a *Trunk Link*. Tagging is an approach that inserts a marker (called a *tag*) into the Ethernet frame.

---

* Prior to the IEEE standard, one way to have tagged traffic was to purchase both the bridge and the NIC from the same vendor that would have implemented a vendor-proprietary tagging on the NIC-to-bridge link; clearly, this was undesirable.

† Other criteria for VLAN membership, such as protocol type or MAC address, can also be used.

In this environment, each VLAN is assigned an 802.1Q VLAN tag. The tag contains the identification code of a specific VLAN, namely, the VID.

A Trunk Link is a LAN segment used for multiplexing and transporting VLANs between VLAN bridges. All the devices that connect to a Trunk Link must be *VLAN-aware*. VLAN-aware devices are devices that are able to understand VLAN membership and VLAN frame formats. (*VLAN-unaware* devices do not have an understanding of VLAN membership and of VLAN frame formats.) The Trunk Link is a point-to-point LAN segment; there are, therefore, exactly two VLAN-aware bridges attached to this trunk. A Trunk Link could also be a shared-medium LAN segment that has several VLAN-aware bridges attached to it. All frames, including end station frames, on a Trunk Link are VLAN-tagged; that is, they carry a tag header that contains a non-null VID (by implication, there are no VLAN-unaware end stations on a Trunk Link.) An *Access Link* is a LAN segment used to multiplex one or more VLAN-unaware stations into a port of a VLAN bridge. In other words, the Access Link is an 802 LAN segment with stations attached, that is, connected to a VLAN-aware bridge or a number of LAN segments interconnected by bridges. None of the frames on an Access Link carry VLAN identification; i.e., there are no VLAN-tagged frames on an Access Link. Typically, the Access Link is viewed as being on the edge of the VLAN network.

Tagging is the most contemporary way to create VLANs that span multiple Layer 2 switches. To be able to work end to end, the stations in this environment must have an NIC that supports 802.1Q tagging. Using the tagging mechanism, multiple VLANs can span multiple switches using one or more trunks. As noted, in a port-based VLAN, each VLAN requires its own pair of trunk ports. On the other hand, using the tag mechanism, multiple VLANs can span two switches with a single trunk. Another benefit of tagged enterprise VLANs is the ability of a port to be a member of multiple VLANs (e.g., for a server that must belong to multiple VLANs—in a port-based VLAN a port can be a member of only one VLAN.) However, the use of 802.1Q tagged packets gives rise to packets bigger than the current IEEE 802.3/Ethernet maximum of 1518 bytes; specifically, 4 bytes, sometimes more, may be added. This may lead to connectivity problems of non-802.1Q bridges or routes that are placed in the path.

As ports are added to a VLAN with an 802.1Q tag defined, the network administrator will decide whether those ports will use tagging for specific (active) VLANs. The default mode of a VLAN switch is to have all ports assigned to the VLAN named *default* with an 802.1Q VID set to 1; frames arriving on a port with an 802.1Q tag containing a VID of zero are treated as untagged. Not all ports in the VLAN need to be tagged. As traffic from a port is forwarded by the VLAN switch, the switch determines in real-time if each destination port should use tagged or untagged packet formats for the VLAN. The switch adds and removes tags, as required, by the port configuration for the VLAN. Note that frames arriving tagged with a VID that is not configured on a port will be discarded.

As frames transit out of the switch, the switch determines if the destination port requires the frames to be tagged or untagged. All traffic going to and coming from the server is tagged. Traffic going to and coming from the trunk ports is tagged. The traffic that comes from and goes to the other stations on this network is not tagged.

One can configure the enterprise VLAN switch using a combination of port-based and tagged VLANs. A given port can be a member of multiple VLANs, with the understanding that only one of its VLANs uses untagged traffic; that is, a port can simultaneously be a member of one port-based VLAN and multiple tag-based VLANs.

When VLAN-unaware end stations are added to a Trunk Link, the link is then known as a *Hybrid Link*. A Hybrid Link is a LAN segment that has both VLAN-aware and VLAN-unaware devices attached to it. Consequently, a Hybrid Link can carry both VLAN-tagged frames and other (untagged or priority-tagged) frames. It must be kept in mind that, for a given VLAN, all frames transmitted by a specific bridge on a specific hybrid link must be tagged the same way on that link. They must be either all untagged or all tagged, carrying the same VLAN ID. Note that a bridge can transmit a mix of VLAN-tagged frames and untagged frames, but they must be for different VLANs.

9.4.3.3 MAC-Based VLANs

MAC-based VLANs allow physical ports to be mapped to a VLAN based on the source MAC address learned in the Filtering Database (FDB). This feature allows one to designate a set of physical VLAN switch ports that have their VLAN membership dynamically determined by the MAC address of the end station that plugs into the physical port. For example, one could use this application for a roaming user who wishes to connect to a network from one or more conference rooms. In each room, the user plugs into one of the designated ports on the switch and is mapped to the appropriate VLAN. MAC-based VLANs have certain (practical) limitations. For example, ports participating in MAC VLANs must first be removed from any static VLANs; the MAC-to-VLAN mapping can only be associated with VLANs that already exist on the switch; and a port can only accept connections from an end station/host and should not be connected to a Layer 2 repeater device (connecting to a Layer 2 repeater device can cause certain addresses to not be mapped to their respective VLAN if they are incorrectly configured in the MAC-VLAN configuration database).

9.4.3.4 Protocol-Based VLANs

Protocol-based VLANs enable the planner to define a frame/packet filter that the switch uses as the matching criteria to determine if a particular PDU belongs to a particular VLAN. Protocol-based VLANs are most often used when network segments contain hosts running multiple protocols.

9.4.3.5 Filtering Database

A VLAN switch maintains a database of all MAC addresses received on all of its ports. The switch uses the information in this database to decide whether a frame should be forwarded or filtered. Each FDB entry consists of the MAC address of the device, an identifier for the port on which it was received, and an identifier for the VLAN to which the device belongs (frames destined for devices that are not in the FDB are flooded to all members of the VLAN; see Table 9.20).

9.5 SAN-Related Technology

SANs can be viewed as a subset of high-speed networks that support the networking (extension) of the *channel* of a processor. A channel is generally a higher-speed port than a communication port, although this distinction is becoming less of an issue of late. A channel is generally a parallel communication link that needs to be serialized before it can be transported at any distance greater than a few feet. Within the native channel environment, data is known as *block-level data*. One can think of the channel as an extension of the processor's internal bus (although there is a subtle

Table 9.20 FDB Entry Types

Dynamic entries	Entries in the database are removed (aged out) if, after a period of time (aging time), the device has not transmitted. This prevents the database from becoming filled with obsolete entries. Initially, all entries in the database are dynamic. These entries are deleted if the switch is reset.
Non-aging entries	Entries in the database are defined as static, nonaging entries by setting the aging time to zero. These entries do not age, but they are still deleted if the switch is reset.
Permanent entries	These are entries (e.g., up to 256) that are retained in the database if the switch is reset or a power off/on cycle occurs. A permanent entry can either be a unicast or multicast MAC address. Once created, permanent entries stay the same as when they were created: for example, the permanent entry store is not updated when any of the following take place: a VLAN is deleted, a VID is changed, a port mode is changed (tagged/untagged), etc.
Blackhole entries	A blackhole entry enables the switch to discard packets with a specified MAC destination address. Blackhole entries are useful as a security measure or in special circumstances. They are treated like permanent entries in the event of a switch reset and they are never aged out of the FDB.

difference, for the purists). Channel-level communication is applicable to a number of instances (e.g., real-time mirroring), but the recent focus has been on connecting storage devices. Hence, for all intents and purposes, SANs and channel-based communication are thought, of late, as one and the same. (This author wrote what is regarded as the first textbook treatment of WAN-based channel extension technologies, with extensive materials on this topic in the 1991 book *Telecommunications Technology Handbook*, Artech House.) In recent years a variety of switches and routers have been brought to the market by Fibre Channel (FC) vendors that let users consolidate, connect, and more easily manage FC and IP-based storage-area networks.

Channel-based communication has always been problematic, not only because it is intrinsically a parallel-originated high-speed stream, but more importantly, because the developers failed over the years to make use of available telecom standards such as SONET in the wide area, and Ethernet in the local area. Channel-oriented streams can be carried generally in four modes:

■ Native over a channel-specific communication fiber (typically dark fiber), as is the case for FICON and even FC, an ANSI standard
■ Mapped over a physical layer service such as SONET, SDH, or the evolving OTN/ASON
■ Mapped over a data-link layer service such as ATM
■ Most recently, tunneled over a network layer (that is, IP) service

(A service or protocol is "mapped" when it is carried by a service/protocol that operates at the same protocol layer; it is "tunneled" when it is carried within the payload of a protocol that operates at layers higher than the protocol in question.)

Although native or mapped service is typically best from a bandwidth and latency perspective, it may be expensive to support and inflexible (by requiring fiber or high-speed availability at various locations). Tunneled service makes the assumption that IP networking is ubiquitously available as an intranet- or Internet-delivered service, and hence, channel communication based on it

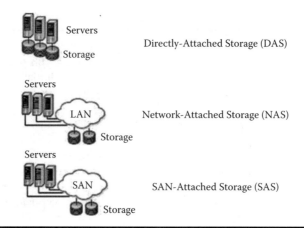

Figure 9.23 Directly attached devices, network-attached storage, SANs.

is more flexible. Tunneled service, however, is faced with bandwidth and latency issues. Midrange applications (e.g., tape backup) can use tunneled services; higher-range applications (e.g., real-time disk mirroring and scientific data-intensive applications) may need native or mapped services.

When storage is all within a data center, SANs can run the native FC medium; when storage is remote, a native, mapped, or tunneled service is required. (Another approach is not to use channel-based communications to begin with, but to use the communication port, specifically GbE or 10GbE, instead. As mentioned, in the past, the channel "port" of a processor, server, or storage system was faster than the "communication" port; these days, both ports can operate at the same speed, and hence, the designer has a choice). Figure 9.23 depicts a typical environment.

9.5.1 Fibre Channel Technology—Native Mode

9.5.1.1 FC

This section looks at some basic concepts of FC. "Fibre" is a generic term used to cover all physical media supported by the FC protocols, including optical fiber, twisted pair, and coaxial cable. Logically, FC is a bidirectional point-to-point serial data channel, designed for high-performance information transport. Physically, FC is an interconnection of one or more point-to-point links. Each link end terminates in a port, and is specified in the Physical Interface (FC-PI) specification and in the Framing and Signaling (FC-FS) specification. FC is defined by a set of ANSI standards, including the following:

- Fibre Channel Framing and Signaling (FC-FS); ANSI NCITS/Project 1331-D; Draft Standard Rev. 1.9, April 9, 2003
- Fibre Channel Physical and Signaling Interface (FC-PH); ANSI INCITS 230-1994 (R1999), formerly ANSI X3.230-1994 (R1999), November 14, 1994
- ANSI X3.297:1997, Information Technology—Fibre Channel—Physical and Signaling Interface-2 (FC-PH-2)
- ANSI X3.303:1998, Fibre Channel—Physical and Signaling Interface-3 (FC-PH-3)
- ANSI X3.272:1996, Information Technology—Fibre Channel—Arbitrated Loop (FC-AL)

- ANSI NCITS 332-1999, Fibre Channel—Arbitrated Loop (FC-AL-2)
- Fibre Channel Switch Fabric—2 (FC-SW-2); ANSI INCITS 355-2001, 2001
- Fibre Channel Switch Fabric—3 (FC-SW-3); ANSI NCITS/Project 1508-D; Draft Standard Rev. 6.3, February 19, 2003
- Fibre Channel Methodologies for Interconnects (FC-MI-2); ANSI NCITS/Project 1599-DT; Draft Standard Rev 2.03, June 4, 2003

FC is structured as a set of hierarchical and related functions, FC-0 through FC-3 (see Figure 9.24). Each of these functions is described as a level. FC does not restrict implementations to specific interfaces between these levels. The physical interface (FC-0) consists of transmission media, transmitters, receivers, and their interfaces. The physical interface specifies a variety of media, and associated drivers and receivers capable of operating at various speeds. The Transmission protocol (FC-1), Signaling protocol (FC-2), and Common Services (FC-3) are fully specified in FC-FS and FC-AL-2. FC levels FC-1 through FC-3 specify the rules and provide mechanisms needed to transfer blocks of information end to end, traversing one or more links. An Upper Level Protocol mapping to FC-FS constitutes an FC-4 that is the highest level in the FC structure. FC-2 defines a suite of functions and facilities available for use by an FC-4. A Fibre Channel Node may support one or more N_Ports (the endpoints for Fibre Channel traffic) and one or more FC-4s. Each N_Port contains FC-0, FC-1, and FC-2 functions. FC-3 optionally provides the common services to multiple N_Ports and FC-4s.

An encapsulated description of the FC functionality follows.* Table 9.21 defines some key terms needed to describe the concepts.

FC is a frame-based, serial technology designed for peer-to-peer communication between devices at gigabit speeds and with low overhead and latency. Figure 9.25 depicts the basic FC environment.

---

* The rest of this section is based on [MON200201].

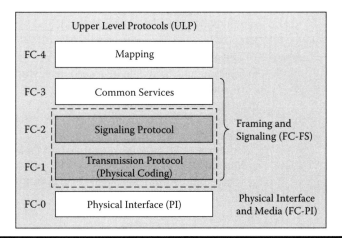

Figure 9.24   FC layers.

Table 9.21   Key FC and iFCP Terms

Address-translation mode	A mode of gateway operation in which the scope of N_PORT fabric addresses for locally attached devices is local to the iFCP gateway region in which the devices reside.
Address-transparent mode	A mode of gateway operation in which the scope of N_PORT fabric addresses for all FC devices is unique to the bounded iFCP fabric to which the gateway belongs.
Bounded iFCP Fabric	The union of two or more gateway regions configured to interoperate together in address-transparent mode.
DOMAIN_ID	The value contained in the high-order byte of a 24-bit N_PORT FC address.
F_PORT	The interface used by an N_PORT to access FC switched fabric functionality.
Fabric	The entity that interconnects N_PORTs attached to it and is capable of routing frames by using only the address information in the Fibre Channel frame.
Fabric Port	The interface through which an N_PORT accesses a Fibre Channel fabric. The type of fabric port depends on the FC fabric topology. In this specification, all fabric port interfaces are considered to be functionally equivalent.
FC-2	The FC transport services layer described in [FCF200201].
FC-4	The FC mapping of an upper-layer protocol, such as [FCP200201], the FC to SCSI mapping.
Fibre Channel Device	An entity implementing the functionality accessed through an FC-4 application protocol.
Fibre Channel Network	A native FC fabric and all attached FC nodes.
Fibre Channel Node	A collection of one or more N_PORTs controlled by a level above the FC-2 layer. A node is attached to a Fibre Channel fabric by means of the N_PORT interface described in [FCF200201] .
Gateway Region	The portion of an iFCP fabric accessed through an iFCP gateway by a remotely attached N_PORT. Fibre Channel devices in the region consist of all those locally attached to the gateway.
Internet Fibre Channel Protocol (iFCP)	Gateway-to-gateway protocol that supports FC Layer 4 FCP over TCP/IP.
iFCP Frame	An FC frame encapsulated in accordance with the FC Frame Encapsulation Specification and iFCP.
iFCP Portal	An entity representing the point at which a logical or physical iFCP device is attached to the IP network. The network address of the iFCP portal consists of the IP address and TCP port number to which a request is sent when creating the TCP connection for an iFCP session.
iFCP Session	An association comprising a pair of N_PORTs and a TCP connection that carries traffic between them. An iFCP session may be created as the result of a PLOGI FC login operation.
Locally Attached Device	With respect to a gateway, a Fibre Channel device accessed through the Fibre Channel fabric to which the gateway is attached.
Logical iFCP Device	The abstraction representing a single Fibre Channel device as it appears on an iFCP network.

N_PORT	An iFCP or FC entity representing the interface to FC device functionality. This interface implements the FC N_PORT semantics specified in [FCF200201]. FC defines several variants of this interface that depend on the FC fabric topology.
N_PORT Alias	The N_PORT address assigned by a gateway to represent a remote N_PORT accessed via the iFCP protocol.
N_PORT fabric address	The address of an N_PORT within the FC fabric.
N_PORT ID	The address of a locally attached N_PORT within a gateway region. N_PORT IDs are assigned in accordance with the Fibre Channel rules for address assignment specified in [FCF200201].
N_PORT Network Address	The address of an N_PORT in the iFCP fabric. This address consists of the IP address and TCP port number of the iFCP Portal and the N_PORT ID of the locally attached Fibre Channel device.
Port Login (PLOGI)	The Fibre Channel Extended Link Service (ELS) that establishes an iFCP session through the exchange of identification and operation parameters between an originating N_PORT and a responding N_PORT.
Remotely Attached Device	With respect to a gateway, a FC device accessed from the gateway by means of the iFCP protocol.
Unbounded iFCP Fabric	The union of two or more gateway regions configured to interoperate together in address-translation mode.

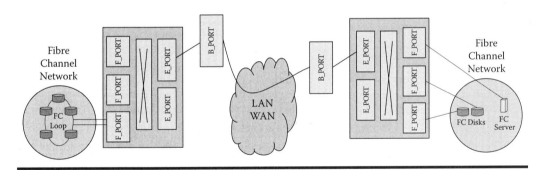

Figure 9.25   Fibre Channel environment.

9.5.1.1.1 The FC Network

The fundamental entity in FC is the FC network. Unlike a layered network architecture, an FC network is largely specified by functional elements and the interfaces between them. As shown in Figure 9.26, these consist, in part, of the following:

1. N_PORTs—The endpoints for FC traffic. In the FC standards, N_PORT interfaces have several variants, depending on the topology of the fabric to which they are attached. As used in this specification, the term applies to any one of the variants.
2. FC devices—The FC devices to which the N_PORTs provide access.
3. Fabric ports—The interfaces within an FC network that provide attachment for an N_PORT. The types of fabric port depend on the fabric topology and are discussed later.

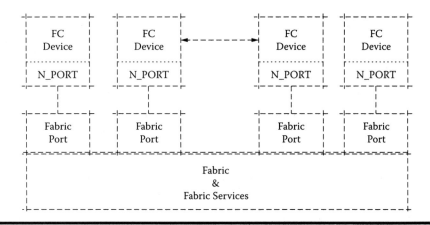

Figure 9.26 A Fibre Channel network.

4. The network infrastructure for carrying frame traffic between N_PORTs.
5. Within a switched or mixed fabric (see following text), a set of auxiliary servers, including a name server for device discovery and network address resolution. The types of service depend on the network topology.

The following sections describe FC network topologies and give an overview of the FC communications model.

9.5.1.1.2 FC Network Topologies

The principal FC network topologies are the following:

1. Arbitrated Loop—A series of N_PORTs connected together in daisychain fashion. In [FCF200201], loop-connected N_PORTs are referred to as NL_PORTs. Data transmission between NL_PORTs requires arbitration for control of the loop in a manner similar to a Token Ring network.
2. Switched Fabric—A network consisting of switching elements, as described in the following text.
3. Mixed Fabric—A network consisting of switches and "fabric-attached" loops. A description can be found in [FCF199701]. A loop-attached N_PORT (NL_PORT) is connected to the loop through an L_PORT and accesses the fabric by way of an FL_PORT.

Depending on the topology, the N_PORT and its means of network attachment may be one of the following:

FC Network Topology	Network Interface	N_PORT Variant
Loop	L_PORT	NL_PORT
Switched	F_PORT	N_PORT
Mixed	FL_PORT via L_PORT	NL_PORT
	F_PORT	N_PORT

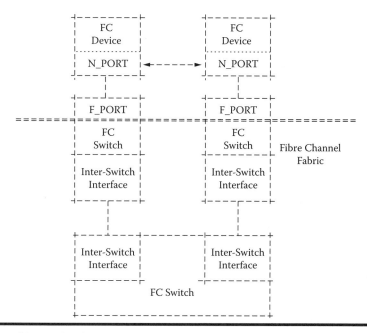

Figure 9.27   Multi-switch Fibre Channel fabric.

The differences in each N_PORT variant and its corresponding fabric port are confined to the interactions between them. To an external N_PORT, all fabric ports are transparent and all remote N_PORTs are functionally identical.

9.5.1.1.3 Switched FC Fabrics

An example of a multi-switch fibre channel fabric is shown in Figure 9.27. The interface between switch elements is either proprietary or the standards-compliant E_PORT interface described by the FC-SW2 specification [FCS200101].

9.5.1.1.4 Mixed FC Fabric

A mixed fabric contains one or more arbitrated loops connected to a switched fabric as shown in Figure 9.28. As noted previously, the protocol for communications between peer N_PORTs is independent of the fabric topology, N_PORT variant, and type of fabric port to which an N_PORT is attached.

9.5.1.1.5 FC Layers and Link Services

As noted earlier, FC consists of the following layers:

■ FC-0—The interface to the physical media
■ FC-1—The encoding and decoding of data and out-of-band physical link control information for transmission over the physical media
■ FC-2—The transfer of frames, sequences, and exchanges comprising protocol information units
■ FC-3—Common services
■ FC-4—Application protocols such as the Fibre Channel Protocol for SCSI (FCP)

(FCP is the ANSI SCSI serialization standard to transmit SCSI commands, data, and status information between a SCSI initiator and SCSI target on a serial link, such as a FC network [FC-2].)

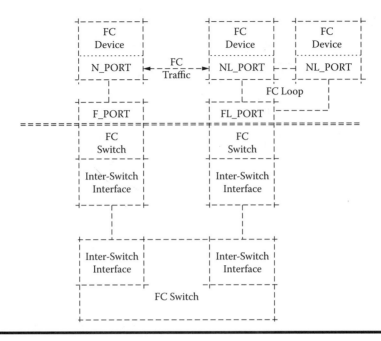

Figure 9.28 Mixed Fibre Channel fabric.

In addition to the layers defined earlier, FC defines a set of auxiliary operations, some of which are implemented within the transport layer fabric, called *link services*. These are required to manage the FC environment, establish communications with other devices, retrieve error information, perform error recovery, and other similar services. Some link services are executed by the N_PORT, whereas others are implemented internally within the fabric. These internal services are described in the next section.

9.5.1.1.6 Fabric-Supplied Link Services

Servers internal to a switched fabric handle certain classes of Link Service requests and service-specific commands. The servers appear as N_PORTs located at the "well-known" N_PORT fabric addresses specified in [FCF200201]. Service requests use the standard FC mechanisms for N_PORT-to-N_PORT communications.

All switched fabrics must provide the following services:

■ Fabric F_PORT server—Services N_PORT requests to access the fabric for communications.
■ Fabric Controller—Provides state-change information to inform other FC devices when an N_PORT exits or enters the fabric (see following text).
■ Directory/Name Server—Allows N_PORTs to register information in a database, retrieve information about other N_PORTs, and discover other devices as described later.

A switched fabric may also implement the following optional services:

■ Broadcast Address/Server—Transmits single-frame, class 3 sequences to all N_PORTs.

- Time Server—Intended for the management of fabricwide expiration timers or elapsed time values and not intended for precise time synchronization.
- Management Server—Collects and reports management information, such as link usage, error statistics, link quality, and similar items.
- Quality-of-Service Facilitator—Performs fabricwide bandwidth and latency management.

9.5.1.1.7 FC Nodes

An FC node has one or more fabric-attached N_PORTs. The node and its N_PORTs have the following associated identifiers:

1. A worldwide unique identifier for the node.
2. A worldwide unique identifier for each N_PORT associated with the node.
3. For each N_PORT attached to a fabric, a 24-bit fabric-unique address having the properties defined later. The fabric address is the address to which frames are sent.

Each worldwide unique identifier is a 64-bit binary quantity having the format defined in [FCF200201].

9.5.1.1.8 FC Device Discovery

In a switched or mixed fabric, FC devices and changes in the device configuration may be discovered by means of services provided by the FC Name Server and Fabric Controller. The Name Server provides registration and query services that allow an FC device to register its presence on the fabric and discover the existence of other devices. For example, one type of query obtains the fabric address of an N_PORT from its 64-bit worldwide unique name. The full set of supported FC name server queries is specified in [FCG200001]. The Fabric Controller complements the static discovery capabilities provided by the Name Server through a service that dynamically alerts an FC device whenever an N_PORT is added or removed from the configuration. An FC device receives these notifications by subscribing to the service as specified in [FCF200201].

9.5.1.1.9 FC Information Elements

The fundamental element of information in FC is the frame. A frame consists of a fixed header and up to 2112 bytes of payload having the structure described later. The maximum frame size that may be transmitted between a pair of FC devices is negotiable up to the payload limit, based on the size of the frame buffers in each FC device and the path maximum transmission unit (MTU) supported by the fabric.

Operations involving the transfer of information between N_PORT pairs are performed through "Exchanges." In an Exchange, information is transferred in one or more ordered series of frames referred to as Sequences.

Within this framework, an upper-layer protocol is defined in terms of transactions carried by Exchanges. Each transaction, in turn, consists of protocol information units, each of which is carried by an individual Sequence within an Exchange.

9.5.1.1.10 FC Frame Format

An FC frame (see Figure 9.29) consists of a header, payload, and 32-bit CRC bracketed by SOF and EOF delimiters. The header contains the control information necessary to route frames between N_PORTs and manage Exchanges and Sequences. The following diagram gives a schematic view of the frame. The source and destination N_PORT fabric addresses embedded in the S_ID and D_ID fields represent the physical addresses of originating and receiving N_PORTs, respectively.

9.5.1.1.11 N_PORT Address Model

N_PORT fabric addresses (see Figure 9.30) are 24-bit values having the format of Figure 9.30 defined by the FC specification [FCF200201]. An FC device acquires an address when it logs into the fabric. Such addresses are volatile and subject to change based on modifications in the fabric configuration.

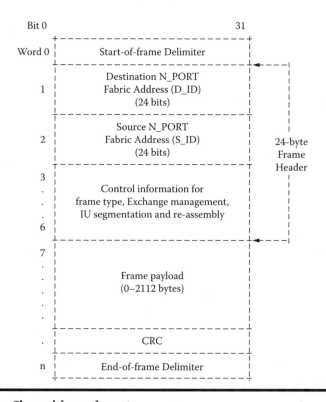

Figure 9.29 Fibre Channel frame format.

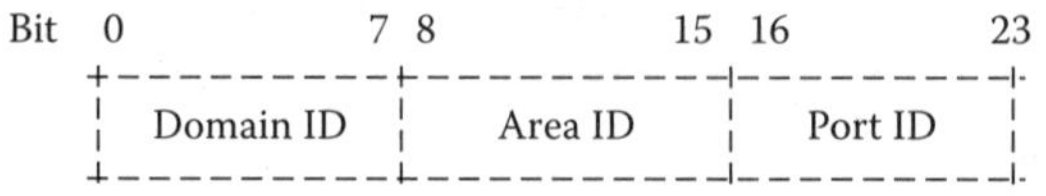

Figure 9.30 Fibre Channel address format.

In an FC fabric, each switch element has a unique Domain ID assigned by the principal switch. The value of the Domain ID ranges from 1 to 239 (0xEF). Each switch element, in turn, administers a block of addresses divided into area and port IDs. An N_PORT connected to a F_PORT receives a unique fabric address consisting of the switch's Domain ID concatenated with switch-assigned area and port IDs.

A loop-attached NL_PORT obtains the Port ID component of its address during the loop initialization process described in [FCA199901]. The area and domain IDs are supplied by the fabric when the fabric login (FLOGI) is executed.

9.5.1.1.12 FC Transport Services

N_PORTs communicate by means of the following classes of service specified in the FC standard ([FCF200201]):

- Class 1—A dedicated physical circuit connecting two N_PORTs.
- Class 2—A frame-multiplexed connection with end-to-end flow control and delivery confirmation.
- Class 3—A frame-multiplexed connection with no provisions for end-to-end flow control or delivery confirmation.
- Class 4—A connection-oriented service, based on a virtual circuit model, providing confirmed delivery with bandwidth and latency guarantees.
- Class 6—A reliable multicast service derived from class 1.*

Classes 2 and 3 are the predominant services supported by deployed FC storage and clustering systems. Class 3 service is similar to User Datagram Protocol (UDP) or IP datagram service. FC storage devices using this class of service rely on the ULP implementation to detect and recover from transient device and transport errors. For classes 2 and 3 service, the FC fabric is not required to provide in-order delivery of frames unless explicitly requested by the frame originator (and supported by the fabric). If ordered delivery is not in effect, it is the responsibility of the frame recipient to reconstruct the order in which frames were sent based on information in the frame header.

9.5.1.1.13 Login Processes

The Login processes are FC-2 operations that allow an N_PORT to establish the operating environment necessary to communicate with the fabric, other N_PORTs, and ULP implementations accessed via the N_PORT. Three login operations are supported:

1. Fabric Login (FLOGI)—An operation whereby the N_PORT registers its presence on the fabric, obtains fabric parameters such as classes of service supported, and receives its N_PORT address.
2. Port Login (PLOGI)—An operation by which an N_PORT establishes communication with another N_PORT.
3. Process Login (PRLOGI)—An operation that establishes the process-to-process communications associated with a specific FC-4 ULP—such as FCP-2, the FC SCSI mapping.

---

* Class 5 was originally envisioned for isochronous traffic, but it has not been further defined in FC-PH.

Because N_PORT addresses are volatile, an N_PORT originating a login (PLOGI) operation executes a Name Server query to discover the FC address of the remote device. A common query type involves use of the worldwide unique name of an N_PORT to obtain the 24-bit N_PORT FC address to which the PLOGI request is sent.

9.5.1.2 10 Gigabit Fibre Channel

The 10 Gigabit Fibre Channel (10GFC) standard* describes in detail extensions to FC signaling and physical layer services introduced in FC-PH to support data transport at a rate in excess of 10 gigabits per second. This standard was developed by Task Group T11 of Accredited Standards Committee NCITS during 2000–2001. 10GFC describes the signaling and physical interface services that may be utilized by an extended version of the FC-2 level to transport data at a rate in excess of 10 gigabits per second over a family of FC-0 physical variants. 10GFC additionally introduces port management functions at the FC-3 level.

9.5.1.2.1 FC-3: General Description

The FC-3 level of 10GFC extends the FC-3 levels of FC-FS and FC-AL-2 by adding a port management interface and register set and low-level signaling protocol. The port management interface and register set provide an interconnection between manageable devices within a port and port management entities.

The Link Signaling Sublayer (LSS) is used to signal low-level link and cable plant management information during the Idle stream. The WIS is an optional sublayer that may be used to create a physical layer that is data-rate and format compatible with the SONET STS-192c transmission format defined by ANSI, as well as the SDH VC-4-64c container specified by ITU. The purpose of the WIS is to support 10GFC data streams that may be mapped directly to STS-192c or VC-4-64c streams at the PHY level, without requiring higher-layer processing. The WIS specifies a subset of the logical frame formats in the SONET and SDH standards. In addition, the WIS constrains the effective data throughput at its service interface to the payload capacity of STS-192c/VC-4-64c, i.e., 9.58464 Gbps. Multiplexed SONET/SDH formats are not supported.

9.5.1.2.2 FC-2: General Description

The FC-2 level of 10GFC extends the FC-2 levels of FC-FS and FC-AL-2 to transport data at a rate of 10.2 Gbps over a family of FC-0 physical variants. 10GFC provides the specification of optional physical interfaces applicable to the implementation of 10GFC ports. These interfaces include the XGMII and the XAUI discussed earlier. One or both of these interfaces may typically be present within a 10GFC port.

> XGMII—The 10 Gigabit Media Independent Interface provides a physical instantiation of 10.2 Gbps parallel data and control transport within FC-2. Its implementation is typically an internal chip interconnect or chip-to-chip interconnect. XGMII supports 10.2 Gbps data transport through its 32-bit-wide data and 4-bit-wide control transmit and receive paths.

---

* This section is based on 10GbE Alliance Tutorial Materials.

XAUI—The 10 Gigabit Attachment Unit Interface provides a physical instantiation of a 10.2 Gbps four-lane serial data and control transport within FC-2 or between FC-2 and lower levels, including FC-1 and FC-0. The XAUI is defined as an XGMII extender. Its implementation is typically a chip-to-chip interconnect, including chips within transceiver modules. The XAUI supports 10.2 Gbps data transport through its four 8B/10B-based serial transmit and receive paths.

9.5.1.2.3 FC-1: General Description

The FC-1 level of 10GFC provides the ability to transport data at a rate of 10.2 Gbps over a family of FC-0 physical variants. 10GFC provides the following FC-1 functions and interfaces:

■ Direct mapping of FC-1 signals to 10GFC Ordered Sets.
■ 8B/10B transmission code that divides FC-2 data and Ordered Sets among four serial lanes.
■ 64B/66B transmission code that supports FC-2 data and Ordered Sets over a single serial lane.
■ An optional physical interface for use by single-lane serial FC-0 variants. This interface is the XSBI.

FC-1 signals convey FC-2 data as well as frame delimiters and control information to be encoded by FC-1 transmission code. The same transfer is possible in the reverse direction.

8B/10B transmission code is the same as that specified in FC-FS. It is intended for 10.2 Gbps data transport across printed circuit boards, through connectors, and over four separate transmitters and receivers. These four transmitters and receivers may be either optically multiplexed to and from a single fiber-optic cable or directly conveyed over four individual fibers.

64B/66B transmission code is intended for 10.2 Gbps data transport across a single fiber-optic cable. The primary reason for the development of this code is to provide minimal overhead above the 10.2 Gbps serial data rate to allow the use of optoelectronic components developed for other high-volume 10 Gbps communications applications such as SONET OC-192.

The 10 Gigabit Sixteen Bit Interface provides a physical instantiation of a 16-bit-wide data path that conveys 64B/66B encoded data to and from FC-0. The XSBI is intended to support serial FC-0 variants.

9.5.1.2.4 FC-0: General Description

The FC-0 level of 10GFC describes the FC link. The FC-0 level covers a variety of media and associated transmitters and receivers capable of transporting FC-1 data. The FC-0 level is designed for maximum flexibility and allows the use of a large number of technologies to meet the broadest range of FC system cost and performance requirements.

The link distance capabilities specified in 10GFC are based on ensuring interoperability across multiple vendors supplying the technologies (both transceivers and cable plants) under the tolerance limits specified in 10GFC. Greater link distances may be obtained by specifically engineering a link based on knowledge of the technology characteristics and the conditions under which the link is installed and operated. However, such link distance extensions are outside the scope of 10GFC.

FC-PI describes the physical link, the lowest level, in the FC system. It is designed for flexibility and allows the use of several physical interconnect technologies to meet a wide variety of system application requirements.

Optical variants. Multiple optical serial physical full-duplex variants are specified to support the transport of encoded FC-1 data transport over fiber-optic medium.

Copper physical variant. A four-lane electrical serial full-duplex physical variant is specified to support the transport of encoded FC-1 data transport over copper medium.

Ports, links, and paths. Each fiber set is attached to a transmitter of a port at one link end and a receiver of another port at the other link end. When a Fabric is present in the configuration, multiple links may be utilized to attach more than one N_Port to more than one F_Port. Patch panels or portions of the active Fabric may function as repeaters, concentrators, or fiber converters. A path between two N_Ports may be made up of links of different technologies. For example, the path may have single-fiber multimode fiber links or parallel copper or fiber multimode links attached to end ports, but may have a single-fiber single-mode fiber link in between.

FC-PI defines the optical signal characteristics at the interface connector receptacle. Each conforming optical FC attachment shall be compatible with this optical interface to allow interoperability within an FC environment. FC links shall not exceed the BER objective (10^{-12}) under any conditions. The parameters specified in this clause support meeting that requirement under all conditions, including the minimum input power level.

The following physical variants are included:

- 850 nm Parallel (four-lane) optics; specified in this standard
- 850 nm Serial; fully specified in IEEE P802.3ae Clause 52
- 850 nm WDM (four-wavelength); specified in this standard
- 1310 nm Serial; fully specified in IEEE P802.3ae Clause 52
- 1310 nm WDM (four-wavelength); fully specified in IEEE P802.3ae Clause 53

850 nm parallel (four-lane). This supports MM Short Wavelength (SW) data links. The laser links operate at the 3.1875 GBd (gigabaud) rate. The specifications are intended to allow compliance with class 1 laser safety. Reflection effects on the transmitter are assumed to be small, but need to be bounded. A specification of maximum Relative Intensity Noise (RIN) under worst-case reflection conditions is included to ensure that reflections do not impact system performance. The receiver shall operate within a BER of 10^{-12} over the link's lifetime and temperature range.

850 nm WDM (four-wavelength). Spectral specifications for the four wavelengths are as follows:

1. 771.5–784.5 nm
2. 793.5–806.5 nm
3. 818.5–831.5 nm
4. 843.5–856.5 nm

9.5.2 FC Technology—Tunneled Modes

This section describes tunneling methods for handling channel communication. The jargon *IP storage* is being used to describe this set of approaches. A number of transport protocol standards, specifically, Internet Small Computer Systems Interface (iSCSI), Fibre Channel over TCP/IP (FCIP), and the Internet Fibre Channel Protocol (iFCP) have emerged of late. This gives organizations additional choices for accessing data over IP networks. IP storage products are also appearing.

The benefits of the tunneled approach to channel communications (*IP storage networking* is the new jargon) relate to leveraging the large installed base of Ethernet and IP intranets, extranets, and Internet. This enables storage to be accessed over LAN, MAN, or WAN environments, without needing to deal with native channel interfaces across the network itself. This is of interest in grid computing. Tunneling enables the rapid deployment of IP-based SANs linking to FC devices. It allows organization to implement enterprise-level solutions based on existing applications that already communicate with the FCP layer alluded to in the previous section. These protocols enable scalable implementations using existing FC storage products via TCP/IP networks of any distance, using standard GbE layer 2 switches and layer 3 routers. They can also be used to facilitate grid computing deployment.

Facilitating the IP-based movement of block-level data that is stored as either direct-attached storage (DAS) or on a FC SAN requires new tunneling (transport) protocols. The tunneling protocols enable organizations to create and manage heterogeneous data storage environments (e.g., for backup, disaster recovery, and grid computing) where DAS and FC SANs can be integrated over a common IP network backbone.

Even without the full power of grid computing, these developments in IP storage networking are being viewed by proponents as a storage virtualization that enables managers to create virtual storage pools among geographically dispersed DAS, network attached storage (NAS), and SAN data resources [SHU200401]. This is kind of an entry-level approach to a full-fledged data grid.

The tunneling protocols that have emerged of late are as follows:

- The Internet Small Computer Systems Interface (iSCSI):
  - iSCSI defines the mechanisms to transmit and receive block storage data over TCP/IP networks by encapsulating SCSI-3 commands into TCP and transporting them over the LAN/intranet/Extranet/Internet via IP (that is, iSCSI SANs can be deployed within LAN, MAN, or WAN environments). TCP provides the required end-to-end reliability. The iSCSI protocol runs on the host initiator and the receiving target device. ISCSI is being developed by the IETF.
- Fibre Channel over TCP/IP (FCIP):
  - FCIP provides a mechanism to "tunnel" FC over IP-based networks. This enables the interconnection of SANs, with TCP/IP used as the underlying reliable wide-area transport. FCIP is a protocol for connecting FC SANs over IP networks. It provides the functionality and speed of FC with the ability to manage the networks using the same tools used today [SNI200501]. FCIP is being developed by the IETF.
- The Internet Fibre Channel Protocol (iFCP):
  - iFCP is a gateway-to-gateway protocol that supports FC Layer 4 FCP over TCP/IP. TCP/IP routing and switching components complement, enhance, or replace the FC fabric; that is to say, the iFCP specification defines a protocol for the implementation of an FC fabric in which TCP/IP switching and routing elements replace FC components: the lower-layer FC transport is replaced with IP-based networks (along with TCP), and standard LANs, such as GbE. The protocol enables the attachment of existing FC storage products to an IP network by supporting the fabric services required by such devices. iFCP supports FCP. It replaces the transport layer (FC-2)

with an IP network (i.e., Ethernet), but retains the upper-layer (FC-4) information, such as FCP. This is accomplished by mapping the existing FC transport services to IP [SNI200401].

These tunneling/IP storage networking protocols are different, but they all deal with transporting block-level data over an IP network. These protocols enable end users to accomplish the following [SNI200402]:

- Leverage existing storage devices (SCSI and FC) and networking infrastructures, such as GbE-based LANs and IP-based intranets.
- Optimize storage resources to be available to a larger pool of applications.
- Reduce the geographic limitations of DAS and SAN access.
- Extend the reach of existing storage applications (backup, disaster recovery, and mirroring), without upper-layer modification.
- Manage storage networks with traditional IP tools.
- Provide enablements: ease of deployment, management, support associated, scalability, and flexibility that come with IP networking; this, in turn, is expected to provide impetus to grid-based solutions (as well as more traditional data center solutions).

iSCSI has been developed to enable access of the embedded base of DAS over IP networks. The protocol enables block-level storage to be accessed from FC SANs using IP-based networks. iSCSI defines the mechanisms to handle block storage applications over TCP/IP networks. At the physical layer, iSCSI supports a GbE interface; this means that systems supporting iSCSI interfaces can be directly connected to standard switches or IP routers. The iSCSI protocol is positioned above the physical and data-link layers and interfaces to the operating system's standard SCSI Access Method command set. iSCSI can be supported over any physical media that supports TCP/IP, but the most typical implementations are on GbE. iSCSI can run in software over a standard GbE NIC, or can be optimized in hardware for better performance on an iSCSI host bus adapter (HBA). iSCSI also enables the access of block-level storage that resides on FC SANs over an IP network via iSCSI-to-Fibre Channel gateways such as storage routers and switches. Initial iSCSI deployments are targeted at small- to medium-sized businesses and departments or branch offices of larger enterprises that have not deployed FC SANs [SHU200401]. (See Figure 9.31 top.) By allowing greater access to DAS devices, possibly in a grid computing setting, these storage resources can be optimally utilized. Applications such as remote backup, disaster recovery, and storage virtualization and grid computing can be supported. The recent standardization efforts in this arena, the iSCSI-compliant products that are becoming available, and the SNIA IP Storage Forum's multi-vendor interoperability validations enable users to rapidly deploy "plug-and-play" IP SAN environments.

FCIP encapsulates FC packets and transports them via IP; it is a tunneling protocol that uses TCP/IP as the transport, while keeping FC services transparent to the end-user devices. FCIP relies on IP-based network services (e.g., alternate routing, QoS, etc.), and on TCP for congestion control and end-to-end integrity (that is, data-error and data-loss recovery.) FCIP is intended to support the installed base of FC SANs, as shown in Figure 9.31 (middle), and the need to interconnect these SANs over a geographic area to support mission-critical environments. This approach enables applications that have been developed to run over SANs to be supported over WANs. This same arrangement can be used to support data grids. SAN extensions (SAN interconnections to meet the needs for remote storage access) provide the high performance and reliability (diversified routing) required for business continuity and disaster recovery, including remote backup/archiving, remote mirroring. FCIP also provides centralized management. By combining IP networking, FCIP allows an organization to extend the interconnectivity of SANs across regional and national distances: FCIP provides the transport for traffic between SANs over LANs, MANs, and WANs.

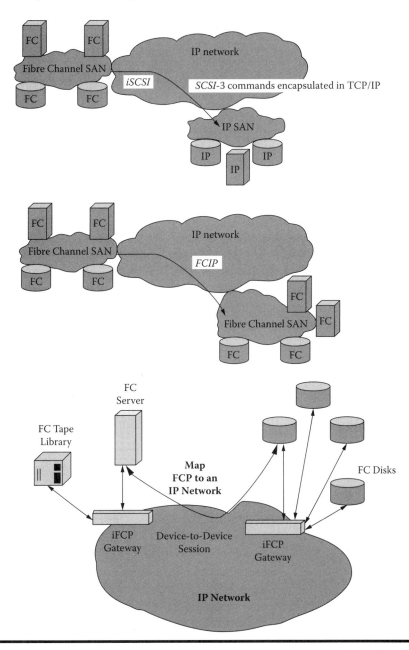

Figure 9.31   Tunneling arrangements. Top: iSCSI permits SCSI-3 commands to be tunneled and delivered reliably over IP networks. Middle: FCIP permits multiple local FC SANs to be interconnected over an IP network backbone. Bottom: iFCP permits FC SANs to be interconnected via IP networks of any distance, using traditional IP network elements (e.g., routers).

It also enables organizations to leverage their current IP infrastructure and management resources to interconnect and extend SANs.

iFCP is a TCP/IP-based protocol for interconnecting FC storage devices or FC SANs using an IP infrastructure in conjunction with, or, better yet, in place of, FC switching and routing elements. iFCP also has the capability to create fully autonomous regions by interconnecting islands of existing FC hub- and switch-based SANs, if present. iFCP represents an ideal customer solution for transitioning from FC to native IP storage networks [SNI200501]. Like FCIP, the primary drivers for iFCP are the large installed base of FC devices, combined with the broad availability of IP networking. Through the use of TCP, iFCP can accommodate deployment in environments where the underlying IP network may not by itself be reliable. iFCP's primary advantage as a SAN gateway protocol is the mapping of FC transport services over TCP, allowing networked, rather than point-to-point, connections between and among SANs without requiring the use of FC fabric elements. Existing FCP-based drivers and storage controllers can safely assume that iFCP, also being FC-based, provides the reliable transport of storage data between SAN domains via TCP/IP, without requiring any modification of those products. iFCP is designed to operate in environments that may experience a wide range of latencies [SNI200401]. iFCP maps FC transport services to an IP fabric, as outlined in Figure 9.31 bottom. Gateways are used to connect existing FC devices to an IP network, and as such, will include physical interfaces for both FC and IP. FC devices (e.g., disk arrays, switches, and HBAs) connect to an iFCP gateway or switch. Each FC session is terminated at the local gateway and converted to a TCP/IP session. The remote gateway or switch receives the iFCP session and initiates an FC session at the remote location. iFCP is a TCP/IP protocol that transports encapsulated FC-4 frame images between gateways. iFCP session endpoints are FC N_Ports [SNI200401]. Table 9.22 compares iFCP and FC. Data Center functionality such as centralized backup, remote mirroring, storage management, and storage virtualization are supported within an iFCP environment because of the ability to create a scalable, peer-to-peer FC/IP storage network [SHU200401].

Table 9.22　Comparison of iFCP and FC

	iFCP	FC
General Services	• IP based • Name services, security key distribution, zoning 　– iSNS, TLS, etc. • Time services 　– /TBS/	• Name services, security key distribution, time services, zone management, fabric configuration services, management services • Based on FC-GS2
Fabric Services	• Class 2, class 3	• Class 1, class 2, class 3 per FC-FS
Routing	• OSPF or any other IP routing protocol	• FSPF

Appendix 9.1: Basic Glossary

10GbE	10 Gigabit Ethernet
AAL5	ATM Adaptation Layer 5
APD	Avalanche Photodetector Diode
ASK	Amplitude Shift Keying
ATM	Asynchronous Transfer Mode
AUI	Attachment Unit Interface
BER	Bit Error Rate
BPDUs	Bridge Protocol Data Units
CAD/CAM	Computer-Aided Design/Computer-Aided Manufacturing
CSMA/CD	Carrier Sense Multiple Access with Collision Detect
DBR	Distributed Bragg Reflector
DCF	Dispersion Compensation Fiber
DSAP	Destination Source Service Access Point
DSF	Dispersion Shifted Fiber
DSL	Digital Subscriber Line
DWDM/CWDM	Dense or Coarse Wavelength Division Multiplexing
ECDL	External Cavity Diode Laser
ESD	End-of-Stream Delimiter
EWB	Extended Wavelength Band
FC	Fibre Channel
FCIP	Fibre Channel over TCP/IP
FCS	Frame Check Sequence
FDB	Filtering Database
FDM	Frequency Division Multiplexing
FEC	Forward Error Correction
FR	Frame Relay
GbE	Gigabit Ethernet
GFP	Generalized Framing Procedure
GMII	Gigabit Media Independent Interface
GMPLS	Generalized MPLS
IPG	Inter-Packet Gap
iSCSI	Internet Small Computer Systems Interface
L2S	Layer 2 Switches
LAN	Local Area Network
LAPD	Link Access Procedure D
LD	Laser Diode
LED	Light Emitting Diode
LLC	Logical Link Control
MAC	Media Access Control
MANs	Metropolitan Area Networks

MDI	Medium Dependent Interface
MMF	Multimode Fiber
MPLS	Multi-Protocol Label Switching
NDSF	Non Dispersion Shifted Fiber
NIC	Network Interface Card
NNI	Network Node Interface
NRZ	Non-Return-to-Zero
NZDSF	Non Zero Dispersion Shifted Fiber
OAM&P	Operations Administration Maintenance and Provisioning
OC	Optical Carrier
OSI	Open System Interconnection
OSS	Operations Support System
PCS	Physical Coding Sublayer
PDU	Protocol Data Unit
PHY	Physical Layer
PLS	Physical Layer Signaling
PMA	Physical Medium Attachment
PMD	Polarization Mode Dispersion
PMD	Physical Medium Dependent
POH	STS Path Overhead
PONs	Passive Optical Networks
PPP	Point-to-Point Protocol
PTE	Path Terminating Equipment
QoS	Quality of Service
RPR	Resilient Packet Ring
RS	Reconciliation Sublayer
RSTA	Rapid Spanning Tree Algorithm
RSTP	Rapid Spanning Tree Protocol
RTP	Real Time Protocol
SAN	Storage Area Network
SLAs	Service Level Agreements
SMF	Single-Mode Fiber
SNAP	SubNetwork Access Protocol
SONET/SDH	Synchronous Optical Network/Synchronous Digital Hierarchy
SPE	Synchronous Payload Overhead
SSAP	Source Service Access Point
SSD	Start-of-Stream delimiter
STA	Spanning Tree Algorithm
STA	Station Management
STP	Spanning Tree Protocol
STS-1	Synchronous Transport Signal Level 1
TCP	Transmission Control Protocol
TLS	Transparent LAN Service
UNI	User-Network Interface
UTP	Unshielded Twisted Pair
VCSEL	Vertical Cavity Surface Emitting Laser

VID	VLAN Identifier
VLAN	Virtual LAN
VOD	Video On Demand
VoIP	Voice-over-IP
VPNs	Virtual Private Networks
VT	Virtual Tributaries
WAN	Wide Area Network
WIS	WAN Interface Sublayer
XAUI	10 Gigabit Attachment Unit Interface
XGMII	10 Gigabit Media Independent Interface
XGXS	XGMII Extender Sublayer
XSBI	10 Gigabit Sixteen-Bit Interface
ZDP	Zero-Dispersion Point

Chapter 10

Evolving MAN/WAN Technologies

This chapter continues the survey of telecom and networking technologies that are applicable to enterprise environments, by focusing on metropolitan area networks (MANs) and briefly on wide area networks (WANs). We briefly discussed MANs in the previous chapter, but did so from a metro Ethernet perspective; the discussion here is more general. Networking is part of the technology architecture that defines the infrastructure resources of an enterprise. Some of the technologies described here are applicable to service providers. However, savvy enterprise architects can also put these networking technologies to work for them—understanding what services are being deployed by carriers will enable enterprise planners to select new state-of-the-art capabilities that benefit the organization's target vision. We focus here more on connectivity-level technologies or physical layer services rather than higher-layer logical services, e.g., IPv4 and IPv6, because the actual corporate communication disbursements depend almost directly on the type of physical layer services selected rather than on the upper-layer capabilities selected (e.g., Enhanced Interior Gateway Routing Protocol versus Open Shortest Path First.) We start out with a bottom-line section where readers interested in general trends for technology architecture planning for enterprise networks, specifically for MANs and WANs, can find some quick pointers. Then we proceed with an assessment of relevant technologies.

10.1 The Technology Architecture Bottom Line for MANs and WANs

Chapter highlights are as follows:

- High-speed metro services (e.g., access) are generally more difficult to obtain than wide area services. MANs often are the de facto bottleneck in a communications system.
- A plethora of existing and evolving services are available in the MAN and WAN, each with their advantages and disadvantages, applicability, and market availability.

■ Currently there are several types of broadband carrier network infrastructures (and related services) in place for consideration by enterprise users, as follows:
  – Transport:
    ■ Async DS1/DS3 systems
    ■ Synchronous Optical Network/Synchronous Digital Hierarchy (SONET/SDH)-based systems
    ■ (Vendor-based) Dense Wavelength Division Multiplexing (DWDM) systems
  – Layer 2 packet:
    ■ Frame networks overlaid on Asynchronous Transfer Mode (ATM) (in decline)
    ■ ATM overlaid on async or sync optical transport (in decline)
    ■ Metro Ethernet
  – Layer 3 packet (data):
    ■ Private lines overlaid on async or sync optical transport
    ■ IP overlaid on ATM
    ■ IP overlaid on async or sync optical transport, for example Packet Over SONET (POS)
    ■ Multi-Protocol Label Switching (MPLS)
■ For high-speed communications, SONET/SDH is the de facto infrastructure technology for communication services at the present time because effectively all communication in the world is taking place over SONET or SDH systems ranging from DS3 (45 Mbps) to OC-768 (39813.12 Mbps).
■ During the past few years, manufacturers and vendors of IP-based equipment claimed that the inefficiencies of time division multiplexing (TDM)-based technology could not accommodate the growth of Internet and data traffic. This, however, is not the case. Even with the emergence of "competitive technologies," SONET penetration is expected to continue to grow.
■ Networks consist of various network elements (NEs), such as add/drop multiplexers (ADMs), switches, and routers, that use signaling protocols to dynamically provision resources and to provide network survivability using protection and restoration techniques.
■ Network management needed by carriers to guarantee high availability by supporting Automatic Protection Switching (APS) requires existence of open industry standards for the User Plane, Control Plane, and Management Plane, for all NEs, for various pieces of networking equipment to properly function together.
  – The *user plane* refers to data forwarding in the transmission path; industry standards deal with transmission parameters (electrical, optical, and mechanical parameters and frame/packet formats).
  – The *control plane* refers to a session setup and teardown mechanism; industry standards allow switches from two different vendors to talk to one another.
  – The *management plane* deals with procedures and mechanisms to deal with fault, configuration, accounting, and performance management.
■ Protection switching exists at Layer 1 (physical layer protection switching), Layer 2 (LAN, Frame Relay, or ATM switching), and Layer 3 (Internal Gateway Protocols, Exterior Gateway Protocols, or MPLS). Typically, Layer 1 protection switching operates at the 50 ms level, Layer 2 in the second-to-multisecond level, and Layer 3 operates on the tens-of-seconds level, as it requires topological information from significant portions of the network.
■ APS is the mechanism used in SONET/SDH to restore service in the case of an optical fiber failure or a NE failure. SONET standards specify restoration of service within 50 ms.

- Fiber cuts are the most common failures in SONET rings; NEs typically have mean time between failure (MTBF) of about 20 years.
- The most common SONET topology for carrier networks is the ring. Rings are preferred as they provide an alternate path to support communication between any two nodes.
- A two-fiber ring can operate as a unidirectional ring or as a bidirectional ring. In a unidirectional ring, traffic is limited to one fiber and it always flows the same direction around the ring; the second fiber is the protection path. With bidirectional designs, information is sent on both fibers; when data is sent between two nodes, it flows over the two fibers connecting them. To provide backup, each fiber in a bidirectional ring can only be utilized to half its capacity.
- Four-fiber rings always operate as bidirectional rings. Full transmission capability is achieved on the working fibers, and the protection fibers are not utilized for traffic under normal conditions.
- At this time DWDM supports large amounts of bandwidth over fiber facilities; the technology is ideal for long-haul WAN applications and can also be used in MAN backbone applications; however, the technology is not ideally suited for direct building access applications (being an overkill and being expensive in this context); here Coarse Wavelength Division Multiplexing (CWDM) may be better suited.
- Passive optical network (PON) technologies are not yet broadly deployed; these technologies are generally targeted to Fiber To The Home (FTTH) applications, rather than for enterprise applications.
- Optical Transport Network (OTN*) addresses requirements of next-generation networks that have a goal of efficiently transporting data-oriented traffic. OTN is based on industrial standards to ensure interoperability among various NE manufacturers. A distinguishing characteristic of the OTN is its ability to transport any digital signal, independent of client-specific aspects, making it a protocol-agnostic technology. OTN services are not generally available at this time.
- The optical transport functions in OTN include multiplexing; cross-connecting, including grooming and configuration; management functions; and physical media functions). OTN makes use of a Data Plane (transport layer) and a Control Plane (signaling and measurement layer).
- Automatically Switched Optical Networks (ASONs) aim at providing the OTN with an intelligent optical control plane for dynamic network provisioning. The ASON model is based on mesh network architectures.
- ASON is an optical/transport network that has dynamic connection capability leading to the following network benefits: traffic engineering of optical channels (bandwidth issues based on actual demand), mesh network topologies and restoration, managed bandwidth to core IP network connectivity, and ability to introduce new optical services. ASON is an emerging service (infrastructure) and is not yet generally available at this juncture.
- The dynamic aspects of ASON (e.g., provisioning and restoration) require complex interactions between the optical control channels (OCCs) and the transport plane. ASON uses an out-of-band control mechanism in which signaling and data paths could make use of different paths through the network.
- Generalized Multi-Protocol Label Switching (GMPLS) extends MPLS to encompass time division (used in SONET/SDH), wavelength (lambdas), and spatial switching. The focus of GMPLS is on the control plane of various OSIRM layers because each of them can use physically diverse data or forwarding planes.

---

* Some have the used the term Intelligent Optical Network (ION) to describe pre-standardization versions of the OTN.

- GMPLS can be understood as a peer-to-peer signaling protocol as it extends MPLS with necessary mechanisms to control routers, DWDM systems, ADMs, and photonic cross-connects.
- MPLS-based services may see major deployment in the near future. ATM services are in decline, at least in the United States.
- Many applications (especially extranet applications, Grid Computing, and virtualization) benefit from the use of Layer 3 virtual private network (VPN) services.

To aid readability, an acronym glossary is provided at the end of the chapter.

10.2 Advances in MAN Technology, Applications, and Opportunities

Major interest has arisen of late regarding MANs because these networks are often the de facto bottleneck in a communications system. To support evolving customer needs, commercial office buildings (in the range of 800,000 or so in the United States alone, or several thousand per city) and other kinds of buildings need to be connected in an effective and high-speed manner to the carrier's network. In metropolitan and long-haul environments, there are major deployments of telco-managed fiber-optic rings that are utilized for narrowband services. These rings, however, currently tend to make use of telephony-centric architectures that may not scale to the demands of packet networks in general, and broadband connectivity in particular. New technologies or architectural designs are, therefore, needed. Requirements in this arena include reducing equipment and operational cost; improving the speed of deployment; supporting bandwidth allocation and throughput; providing resiliency to faults; and giving the user gigabit per second data rates. Emerging metropolitan optical products must be optimized for the *metro edge* portion of the network. Two approaches are now available to address the stated requirements: (1) Ethernet-based extensions of the LAN to a MAN technology (e.g., Gigabit Ethernet [GbE], 10 Gigabit Ethernet [10GbE], Virtual LAN/Rapid Spanning Tree Algorithm [VLAN/RSTA], and Resilient Packet Ring [RPR], already discussed in Chapter 9); and (2) traditional but fast-evolving Synchronous Optical SONET/SDH-based techniques.* In the short term, traditional SONET technology is likely to dominate. Both sets of technologies are addressed in this chapter.

10.2.1 Overview

10.2.1.1 Topological Positioning

A general data network infrastructure usually has three different levels: access networks, metro core networks, and national backbone networks:

- *Access Networks* (also known as metro access) include the local access facilities between a service-providing node (SN), central office (CO), or points of presence (POP) and the customer premises network. The customer premises network comprises building, riser, and campus elements. Ethernet is the dominant technology for the LAN at both the floor and backbone levels. The access link is the "last/first mile" between the metro core/national backbone network and the customer premises. Today, the access network is usually provider-owned;

---

* New technologies/services such as OTN/ASON are emerging but are not yet commercially available on a large scale—see Section 10.2.2.

the access link is mostly based on narrowband copper transmission technologies. The speed of the access link, is, therefore, much lower than Ethernet, Fast Ethernet, GbE, and 10GbE speeds. Fiber deployments in major metro areas aim at removing the access network bottleneck; unfortunately, today only a small fraction (a few percentage points) of buildings is actually on broadband-ready fiber links to the metro core network, and alternative access technologies are not proven and are not widely deployed.

■ *Metro core networks* interface to both the local metro access network and the WAN network. Historically, SONET-based transmission systems have provided MAN connectivity. These systems were originally designed and built to carry voice traffic; as such, they operate in a TDM mode at the physical layer and rely on some added data-link layer (DLL) protocol such as Point-to-Point Protocol (PPP), ATM, or Frame Relay (FR). Most of the traffic growth in these networks is now due to data applications. The critical question is whether the embedded SONET transport infrastructure (which represents billions of dollars of partially depreciated assets in the United States*) is adequate, or optimized, for data traffic.

■ *National backbone networks* have been implemented using a variety of architectures and technologies, but most recently by deploying DWDM systems and securing Optical Carrier-x (OC-x) links (e.g., OC-3, OC-12s, OC-48s) to overlay data networks onto the bearer transport network. A preliminary discussion of these was provided in Chapter 9.

Different technologies and architectures are required for these different portions of the network. The emerging optical networking systems and services have the potential to enable metro carriers to scale up their infrastructure to meet the demand at the metro-access-to-metro-core confluence point. This is desirable because, as noted earlier, there is typically a severe bottleneck in the metropolitan access networks that serve as the bridges between the long-distance core networks and the end-user building and campus networks. Any hope of truly delivering broadband services to customers resides on addressing this issue, and not just on pure technology considerations or on an abstract view of networks without a proper end-to-end view.

10.2.1.2 Business Drivers

End-user organizations (enterprises) have increasing bandwidth needs for intranets, connectivity to backup and storage sites, virtualized IT resources (e.g., Grid Computing), and access to the Internet. As organizations deploy LANs that comprise dedicated (switched) segments based on 100, 1000, or 10,000 Mbps technology, as discussed in Chapter 9, there is a corresponding need for broadband† WAN services, MAN services, and Access Network services. As a heuristic rule of thumb, the WAN/Access requirement is equal to the aggregate LAN speed divided by 100 (or

---

* At an average of 4 ADM per SONET ring and $80,000 per ADM, this would equate to an original install cost of $32B in the United States alone.

† At least two parochial uses of the term *broadband* have occurred in the recent past. Some applied broadband to mean xDSL Internet access, at what turned out to be 384-, 768-, or at most 1,544-kbps; this is far from being broadband in any sense of the word. Others have applied broadband to mean cable-TV based residential services on digital cable. The proper use of the word broadband (according to the International Telecommunications Union) is for a service at speeds *greater than a T1* (1.544 Mbps); hence, to qualify as broadband one needs at least 3.088 Mbps (T1C), 6.312 (T2), 10 Mbps, or more. In fact, many people today consider 100 Mbps, 1 Gbps, or 10 Gbps to be the reference speed for broadband. Current technology even supports speeds of 40–320 Gbps; these, however, are more backbone network speeds rather than user-level speeds.

1000 for less data-intensive users environments/market segments).* Hence, a corporate site with an aggregate LAN traffic of 1 Gbps (e.g., 100 users on 10 Mbps LAN segments), will need 10 Mbps of sustained WAN throughput (or 1 Mbps for less data-intensive user environments); if 100 users were on 100 Mbps segments, the corresponding WAN requirement from such a site will be 100 Mbps (or 10 Mbps for less data-intensive users environments). Today, leading-edge enterprises provide 1000 Mbps access at the desktop; a 100-site location might need a Gbps-level access (or 100 Mbps for less data-intensive users environments). Of course, the actual bandwidth requirement will depend on the type of business that the firm is in.

By volume, up to 70% of corporate WAN traffic is LAN-originated data; less than 10% of WAN traffic is voice. Therefore, the challenge for carriers is how to migrate from their current TDM/ATM-based networks to a world dominated by packet traffic driven by the growth of the Internet and Web Services. In spite of recent advances in optical technologies, there remains an intrinsic need to "disruptively" increase the available metro/WAN throughput. There is the beginning of a trend in a move toward full-speed end-to-end 1 and 10 Gigabit Ethernet in the WAN to support *native-Ethernet* and *IP-over-optics* communication networks. At the beginning of the decade, new service providers emerged that planned to deploy both the evolving and the new technologies and position themselves to deliver new broadband services in the 100, 1000, and 10,000 Mbps range in the metro access and metro core portions of the network, as well as end to end over the long haul. The majority of these plans by these new service providers have not come to fruition (because many of them have gone out of business) and the incumbent providers have continued to retain a strong hold on the network infrastructure. However, some of these incumbent providers are now adopting some newer technologies.

There is reportedly a large market potential for broadband services. It is a well-known fact that less than 5% of commercial buildings in the United States with more than 5000 sq ft of space have fiber connectivity (only between 25,000 and 40,000, depending on the estimate, out of the 800,000 or so commercial office buildings in the United States, not to mention the entire set of 4.6 million commercial buildings [MIN200201]). Therefore, there is a significant opportunity in the next five to ten years to develop products that will support the eventual "mandatory" connectivity that all of these building will need to support their existence in an information/Internet-based economy. The "Fiber Glut" of the early 2000s only existed, if at all, in the long-haul environment, not in metropolitan network environments.

MANs play a vital role in connecting users to WAN services. Traditionally, MANs have been circuit-switched networks that are optimized for voice traffic using the SONET/SDH circuit-switched layer. Many of the current traditionally architected networks deliver data services known as *Private Line*. Private Line services are billable, physically (TDM) segregated, point-to-point circuits that are directly provisioned into segregated bandwidths in the intermachine trunks on the transmission infrastructure; DS-1/DS-3. *Virtual Private Line* services are billable, virtually segregated, point-to-point circuits that are carried over ("encapsulated," "tunneled") common shared bandwidths provisioned in the intermachine trunks on the transmission infrastructure; examples include FR, ATM, and VLAN-based GbE. LANs, on the other hand, are packet-switched networks that are optimized for data traffic using Ethernet technology. This is quickly becoming the dominant traffic source driving bandwidth demands in MANs and WANs.

---

* This is derived by assuming that 10% of the traffic is destined for the outside and that an inside-to-outside concentration of 10-to-1 or, alternatively 100-to-1, is suitable.

Network survivability, high availability, security, and fast restoration are also key desiderata of end users, regardless of their bandwidth needs. The various metro access/metro core architectures need to support most or possibly all of these requirements.

10.2.1.3 Range of Solutions

The consequence of carrying packet traffic on circuit-switched networks is inefficiency at the bandwidth level. New packet-switched MAN and WAN architectures and technologies are needed that are optimized for data traffic with carrier-class operational performance attributes [COL200101]. Will this new architecture be Ethernet-at-the-core metro, or next-generation SONET with Ethernet handoffs? Does the need or desire to deliver an Ethernet handoff to the customer require an Ethernet-at-the-core metro infrastructure, or can such handoffs be supported more cost-effectively and reliably using a next-generation SONET platform that has Ethernet just at the edge? Planners need to understand the trade-off between efficiency, complexity, transparency, flexibility, manageability, and cost-effectiveness. More specifically, metrics might include security, reliability, speed, throughput, access/backbone cost, equipment cost, sustainability, and margins (which also factors in operational management costs).

Recent industry efforts have focused on bringing innovative technology to the metro-edge of the public service network, where, as stated, nearly all the bandwidth scarcity and connectivity bottlenecks currently are. Major recent advances in optical technologies are poised to enable wide-scale deployment of broadband services at least for commercial customers, when the proper end-to-end focus and architectures are taken into account as part of the design process. Several technologies have emerged for providers that want to sell new metro access services to businesses. New metro access services can use Ethernet, DWDM, CWDM, data-aware SONET/SDH (next-generation SONET/SDH), and PON technologies to connect businesses to optical transport for WAN and Internet access.* Optical networking and evolving Ethernet WAN technologies may bring about changes in network design, services, and economics. However, the foremost considerations in actually delivering reliable, ubiquitous, sustainable broadband services are the following:

1. The problem has to be conceived as an end-to-end challenge: just solving a portion of the problem is pointless. Broadband connectivity must include the building riser fiber, the building access fiber, the metro access subnetwork, and the metro core backbone. Therefore, just having broadband DWDM-based networks in the long haul, or in the metro core, or in the POP-to-POP segment without bringing fiber connectivity to major commercial neighborhoods, office buildings, hospitals, industrial campuses, or college buildings will not achieve the intended goal.
2. The equipment cost is typically 15% of the total cost to deliver a service. Hence, a 20% decrease in equipment cost only results in a 3% decrease in total service cost. A new technology or a new piece of equipment needs to show deeper savings to really impact the bottom line. For example, it should reduce equipment costs by, say, 100% or reduce operations cost by 100% (which is typically 20% of the cost to deliver service); in this case the bottom-line

---

* Residential customers will ultimately have access to fiber and intelligent optical networking gear, but in the near term will have to use DSL, cable, and fixed wireless access technologies to meet their demand for increased bandwidth.

savings would be 17.5%, which might be enough for a customer to consider a switch in service/service-provider.*

3. Reliability, security, and carrier-class grade features are a must. Campus-derived service offerings are arguably not sufficiently robust or secure. As users pack larger and larger portions of their corporate traffic onto fewer and fewer broadband facilities, high levels of reliability and security become imperative.

4. Metro broadband communication is neither free nor cheap. End users requiring broadband at the local level need to comprehend the cost issues. The price of long-haul services has gone down significantly in recent years. Unfortunately, these reductions in prices in long-haul services foster an unattainable expectation in end users for very low prices in metro access/metro core. Low prices have so far not been achieved in the metro access/metro core space partially for intellectual reasons: the focus of architects, designers, technologists, and venture capitalists has not been where it needs to be. The focus has been on developing an array of new layer 2 protocols of all kinds, rather than on lowering the per-building fiber access cost, which comprises the spur cost and the in-building equipment cost. However, there are also endogenous issues: local services (e.g., cab ride at $1.50 per mile) are intrinsically more expensive than long-haul services (e.g., air transportation, generally at $0.25 per mile) because of the much smaller base upon which facilities costs can be dispersed (e.g., an access fiber can be shared among a handful of users—say 1 to 4 users—whereas a long-haul fiber can be shared among several thousand users), and because of the economy of scale of the equipment that has to be used. Finally, there are regulatory and open-competition reasons.

These new optical systems aim at delivering an optimized blend of user-preferred Ethernet *access protocols*, broadband speeds, cost-effective fiber-optic "pair-gain," and multimedia support (e.g., high definition video for videoconferencing/telepresence application) via a family of price-per-performance-specific field-upgradeable platforms. This enables new-generation carriers, incumbents, and ISPs to efficiently deploy end-to-end Ethernet services as well as traditional private line services faster, farther, and with greater flexibility than possible until the present time. MANs may include one or more of the following architectures and technologies:

- SONET/SDH
- Next-generation SONET/SDH
- IP over ATM over SONET
- IP over PPP over SONET
- IP over Generic Framing Procedure (GFP) over SONET/SDH
- DWDM (metro core)
- Wide WDM (WWDM), also known as CWDM, for metro access
- Ethernet (Electrical and Electronics Engineers (IEEE) 802.3z Gigabit Ethernet PHY in WAN) with VLAN and STP or RSTP
- Ethernet (IEEE 802.3ae 10 Gigabit Ethernet PHY in WAN or 10 GbE WAN PHY)
- IEEE 802.17 RPR
- OIF (Optical Internetworking Forum) Optical User-to-Network Interface (O-UNI)†
- All-optical networking: OTN and ASON
- IEEE P802.3ah Ethernet in the First Mile and other PON technologies

---

* We assume that the price to the customer has the form $P = (1 + p) * C$, where p is a profit factor ($0.1 \leq p \leq 0.6$) and C is cost.

† This signaling protocol enables the dynamic establishment of optical connections in an intelligent optical network.

Table 10.1 maps some typical customer services to possible underlying technologies. It turns out that a multifaceted carrier is going to need more than a single technology or a single architecture.

A number of factors are relevant to a discourse on new-generation networks that planners may consider deploying in the near future: (1) The recent passing away of many competitive local exchange carriers (CLECs) and smaller Internet service providers (ISPs); (2) the need for cost-effective but financially sound broadband service delivery; (3) the major recent advances in optical technologies; (4) the apparent glut of fiber facilities in the long-haul portion of the network, but the absolute dearth of such facilities for broadband-services-use in the local metro access/metro core segment of the network, and (5) the emergence of new access and backbone architectures, in particular Ethernet-based WAN approaches. Another factor has also become pertinent of late: the need to build distributed, disaster-proof broadband communication networks that allow users to have backup sites in low-rise suburban environments, and the related requirement of bringing the underlying fiber infrastructures to these suburban buildings.

Users and providers both consider Ethernet to be a well-known, well-understood technology with a high comfort level among technical experts and network operators. Industry groups, such as the IEEE, have developed metropolitan fiber architectures with the stated goal of being able to handle data more efficiently than traditional SONET and to bring down the cost for service providers and companies. According to observers, these standards will let companies and service providers deploy metropolitan area optical bandwidth so that it can be distributed efficiently for IP, with a focus on Ethernet. Efforts by the IEEE in developing 802.3ah (Ethernet in the First Mile) and RPR, and by the Internet Engineering Task Force (IETF) in developing Virtual Private LAN services (VPLS), among others, also address these developments. Ethernet in the First Mile is a PON technology that makes use of passive optics. RPR is a packet-based technology that takes advantage of the fact that data flows are less time-dependent than voice. VPLS is a recently evolving standard that delivers a multipoint-to-multipoint Transparent LAN Service (TLS) direct Ethernet connectivity that can span one or more metro areas and that provides connectivity between multiple sites as if these sites were attached to the same Ethernet LAN. In contrast to the current Ethernet multipoint-to-multipoint service offering that is delivered upon a service provider infrastructure composed of Ethernet switches, VPLS uses the IP/MPLS service provider infrastructure. From the service provider's point of view, use of IP/MPLS routing protocols and procedures instead of the Spanning Tree Protocol and MPLS labels instead of VLAN IDs within the service provider infrastructure results in significant improvements in the scalability of the VPLS as a service [CAP200301]. However, before deciding whether to use Ethernet-backbone-based networks or next-generation SONET-based networks to deliver new broadband services, service providers and users should first understand the issues and opportunities surrounding end-to-end Ethernet networks or TLS, and then should begin to incorporate

Table 10.1 "Best-Fit" Mapping between Services and Technologies

	CWDM/DWDM	TDM/SONET	VLAN/GbE	RPR
TLS	x	x	x	x
Private Line	x	x		
Optical Lambda	x			
Channel Extension	x	x		
Multimedia		x	x	x

Ethernet-based paradigms into their service development and deployment plans. Only then can they ascertain the extent of the impact on the proposed network architecture.

Although new Ethernet-based technologies that are being applied to the MAN environment have arisen of late, traditional architectures and technologies, specifically SONET/SDH, have been making major strides of late in improving their price-performance points, sustaining the "assault" from the new alternatives, and cementing themselves as formidable embedded solutions [MER200101]. In recent years major advances in SONET have occurred; these evolving systems are being called next-generation SONET. Because of its field penetration, SONET/SDH will continue to play a key role for years to come, particularly if some of the newer technologies do not get deployed for any number of reasons. At the same time, vendors are adding features to the existing SONET platforms and, in so doing, they are bringing out next-generation SONET/SDH systems, which may play an important role in metro access/metro core deployments up to the present time.

For example, vendors are now beginning to support the International Telecommunications Union (ITU) X.86 and American National Standards Institute (ANSI) T1X1.5 GFP standard for direct Ethernet over SONET (EoS) services. This technology enables new products for LAN-to-LAN connections with fewer network elements: EoS maps Ethernet frames into SONET/SDH payload and as such effectively transforms a portion of the SONET network into an "invisible" tunnel between LANs to provide TLS. There is also interest in GMPLS, because it extends the MPLS control plane to encompass time division (e.g., SONET ADMs), wavelength (optical lambdas), and spatial switching (e.g., incoming port or fiber to outgoing port or fiber).

The SONET/SDH transmission protocol is used by carriers seeking to provide carrier-class services because it provides the needed Operations, Administration, Maintenance, and Provisioning (OAM&P) capabilities. Such capabilities reduce the operations cost (which nearly always exceeds the amortized equipment cost), particularly for large-deployment environments—some of the simplistic management tools available on campus-derived architectures (e.g., VLAN architectures) become significantly problematic from a productivity point of view when the base of NEs reaches the hundreds range. Both the topological and the OAM&P capabilities of SONET are needed by service providers to support large-scale networks.

As noted earlier, in recent years there has been quite a bit of hype on the new GbE/10GbE-based technologies for metro applications. These technologies have been offered as a panacea by proponents. However, the economics presented by vendors are usually very superficial and miss the true test of what it takes to run a carrier function. There is a push to selling of technology rather than services. Not enough objective consideration is being given to robustness, scalability, and provisionability. The idea of a carrier-supported LAN extension to a city level, that is, TLS service, is not such an esoteric concept as it is made out to be today. Bellcore's Switched Multimegabit Data Service (SMDS) and the IEEE 802.6 MAN standard were mid-to-late-1980s carrier-grade broadband services; the former supported up to 34 Mbps and the latter supported 10 Mbps. TLS can be delivered via nonpacket architectures (such as SONET, next-generation SONET, etc.), as well as via packet architectures (such as GbE/VLAN, RPR, etc.) It is interesting to note that both SMDS and IEEE 802.6 services were packet based. Therefore, whatever intrinsic advantages packet technology brings to the table, these advantages are already a "known quantity" and "already tried." If packet represents a breakthrough, the said breakthrough was already commercially available since these 1980s services. A discourse about the commercial success of packet-based TLS/MAN services such as VLAN/RPR, etc., should at least make reference to the (commercial) experience accrued at that time with SMDS and IEEE 802.6. Additionally, one should note that "efficient bandwidth packet technologies" attempt to makes the most parsimonious use of a supposedly plentiful commodity: bandwidth.* Why be so parsimonious in the one resource (at the expense of added equipment costs/expenditures) whose price keeps dropping so rapidly? Furthermore, one notes that going back at least a decade providers of packet-based networks (e.g., frame relay, ATM, etc.) have, almost invariably, overengineered (read: "placed more bandwidth in play than necessary") their networks to hide quality of service (QoS) issues from the user, and keep customers as content as they would have been with a private line service.†

10.2.1.4 Transition Considerations

As discussed in the previous section, new architectural models are emerging and need to be considered by carriers and network architects in end-user organizations; there may be advantages in these new models and technologies. These architectures include GbE- and 10GbE-based backbones using VLAN techniques; SONET and next-generation SONET (where SONET here supports native Ethernet interfaces to the user and provides services in a more cost-effective manner than in the past); metro-optimized WDM (perhaps CWDM), possibly under GMPLS control; and evolving RPR (see Figure 10.1). Customers prefer an Ethernet handoff for carrier services (that is, they are interested in TLS, especially for Internet services); customers want carrier-class, highly reliable, and secure services, especially if they have to funnel most of their corporate traffic (and also voice) over a small set of multimegabit and even possibly multigigabit circuits.

---

* In this context we mean "metro core bandwidth," although one could also include here "long-haul bandwidth."
† Although a packet service is bandwidth-efficient, and therefore, theoretically, cheaper, the statistical nature of the service may/should occasionally show some "warts," this being part of the "bargain." However, to hide these aspects of the service from the user, carriers have tended to overengineer the networks, thereby, adding in more bandwidth than necessary, undoing the supposed advantages of bandwidth parsimony.

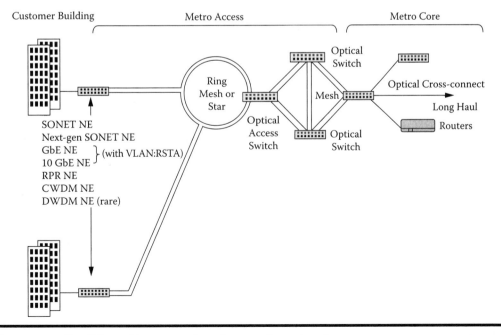

Figure 10.1   Possible architectures of modern carrier networks.

As a consequence of the panoply of architectural choices, carriers (and corporate users) will have to decide between next-generation SONET, metro DWDM, CWDM, optical Ethernet/ GbE VLAN, optical Ethernet/10GbE WAN, and optical Ethernet/RPR. Each technology has advantages and disadvantages, yet all will play a role in the metro market's growth. Some of the questions being posed include the following: "Will metro DWDM solve the metro bandwidth bottleneck? Will next-generation SONET be able to handle the data-centric Internet world? Will easy-to-use, low-cost Ethernet work its way out of the access and into the metro core market?" The transition of the lower layers, particularly the physical layer of the network, is a complex task that must be undertaken diligently, because all higher layers supporting telecom and data communications are dependent on it.

New players (or incumbents applying new strategies) that are going to be successful are those that have a panoply of carrier-class services that are highly reliable and secure. These carriers have to be multi-architecture, multi-technology, multi-service, and multi-QoS oriented. They do not sell technology but services. These carriers give due consideration to GbE/10GbE/ VLAN/RPR/SONET/next-generation SONET/WDM and use all of them by undertaking a sophisticated technical and financial analysis and forgo the superficial conclusions suggested/ implied by the trade press.

Focusing on the IP layer, during the past few years, manufacturers and vendors of IP-based equipment claimed that the inefficiencies of TDM-based technology could not accommodate the growth of Internet and data traffic. If this were the case, the SONET metro market would flatten, and in a few short years, be gone completely. This, however, is not the case. Even with the emergence of "competitive technologies," SONET penetration is expected to continue to grow. At a macro level, the migrations that are occurring from a protocol architecture point of view include (see Figure 10.2) the following:

■ IP-over-ATM to IP-over-SONET—ATM traditionally provided connection-oriented Virtual Channels. A mechanism exists in ATM for supporting QoS. SONET/SDH provides for TDM circuit transport and grooming. Protection and restoration (within 50 ms) are also provided by SONET. The OTN supports the transmission of one or more (SONET) optical channels over a fiber pair; when more than a channel is supported, a WDM technique is needed. For some time now, ATM has been in the process of being replaced/eliminated from very-high-speed connections (at 622 Mbps or higher); in this scenario IP runs directly over SONET, which in turns runs on the OTN. MPLS has been added to the architecture to provide for connection-oriented services.

■ IP-over-SONET to IP-over-Ethernet—Proponents of new metro architecture advocate this approach to broadband networking. Currently, these approaches lack robust OAM&P capabilities, and the cost savings are relatively small, when looking at the entire cost of providing service, not just at equipment cost.

■ IP-over-SONET to IP-over-OTN/ASON (an OTN with a dynamic control plane is called ASON)—In the next stage of the evolution, SONET could (theoretically) also be removed (although the SONET framing is generally thought as of being retained), and IP could run directly over the OTN. In this scenario the IP control plane could interact directly with the control plane of the OTN for dynamic establishment of optical connections. The eventual

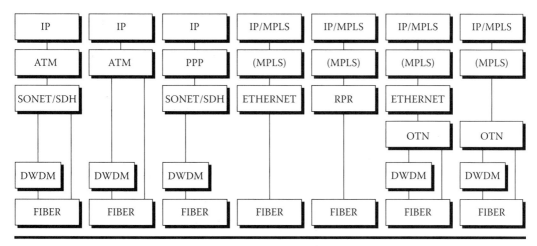

Figure 10.2   Subset of possible approaches/migrations from a protocol point of view.

commercial outcome of this stage remains to be established, particularly with regard to networks provided by carriers (the planner could always develop his or her own private network with full IP-to-OTN interaction, but such a private network will likely be very expensive). The factors affecting the commercial outcome are as follows: (1) full OAM&P capabilities are required by carriers; these capabilities are offered by SONET/SDH, but it is not clear that they are offered by the OTN; (2) the carriers may not want to relinquish provisioning control to users, and Switched Virtual Connections in either Frame Relay or ATM have not taken off; (3) the national network is not a simple cloud of a few nodes under the administrative domain of a single carrier, as often implied or portrayed by vendor presentations; and (4) (as noted) only a small fraction (between 25,000 and 40,000, depending on the estimate) of the 4,600,000 commercial buildings in the United States currently have fiber, making the promise of instantaneous provisionability an impossibility.

10.2.2 Synopsis of Baseline MAN Technologies

This section reviews the following technologies: SONET, next-generation SONET, DWDM, CWDM, all-optical networking, and Ethernet/RPR. The first three technologies (SONET, next-generation SONET, and DWDM) have a local (MAN) as well as a long-haul (WAN) application. The last set of technologies has more of a metro core/metro access focus.

10.2.2.1 Optical Networking Overview

SONET is a North American specification for optical transport originally formulated by the industry in the mid-1980s and codified in the late 1980s/early 1990s into a standard by the American National Standards Institute (ANSI), which sets industry standards in the United States for telecommunications and other industries. SONET principles have also been incorporated into the

SDH recommendations of the ITU, which sets standards for international telecommunications*; SDH is used outside North America.

Deployment of fiber-optic facilities started in the early 1980s. Up to that point the telecommunications infrastructure was built on a hierarchy that was derived from, and suited to, copper or coaxial transmission systems. Throughout the 1980s, these fiber-optic systems were vendor-proprietary, notably based on AT&T technology in the North American market. Other manufacturers introduced systems in Europe and in Japan; however, none of the systems interoperated with each other. Starting in the mid-1980s, and more so in the late-1980s, there was a recognition that standardization across vendors was desirable. In addition to being based on copper/coaxial systems, the traditional digital hierarchy suffered two additional drawbacks:

1. The speeds (e.g., up to DS-3C or 90 Mbps) were not adequate for fiber
2. The hierarchy was asynchronous (that is, it did not rely on a master clock).

SONET (North America) and SDH (Rest of World) were developed in the mid-to-late 1980s to address these issues. As we saw briefly in Chapter 9, SONET/SDH standards define equipment interoperability and addresses the translation of electrical signals to optical signals for transmission over an optical waveguide. The standards require SONET/SDH equipment to include fundamental multiplexing features, transmission features, and operational OAM&P features such as restoration, signaling, performance monitoring, and fault management. Indeed, the widespread use of fiber has been made possible, in part, by the industry's acceptance of SONET/SDH as the standard for transmission functions ("user plane") and OAM&P functions ("management plane"). Work on SONET/SDH standards started in the mid-1980s, but it was only in the late 1980s and early 1990s that market acceptance was achieved. Throughout the 1990s, with the commercialization of the Internet, there was major demand for additional bandwidth. Using SONET/SDH technology, telecommunications companies have gradually expanded their capacity by increasing data transmission rates, to the point that many carriers now routinely transport 2.4 Gbps on fiber (STM–16/OC-48), and deployment of 10 Gbps (STM-64/OC-192) is under way. Work on 40 Gbps STM-256/OC-768 systems is also under way.

During the late 1990s, bandwidth demand was approaching the maximum capacity available in typical networks and carriers. Because of the limitations of *embedded fiber*, today there is a practical ceiling of 2.4 Gbps on many fiber networks, although there are instances where STM–64/OC–192 is also being realized (new construction, of course, can easily accommodate the higher rates). The TDM equipment installed today (specifically, SONET) utilizes but a fraction of the intrinsic capacity of the fiber. Therefore, DWDM techniques were developed to address these issues; DWDM started to gain commercial success in the mid-1990s, with major deployment in the late 1990s.

---

* Outside of North America carriers utilize Synchronous Digital Hierarchy (SDH) standards (SONET can be considered a subset of SDH). TDM systems in North America combines 24 DS-0s into one 1.54-Mbps DS-1 signal. European TDM multiplexes 32 E-0s into one 2.048 Mbps E-1 signal. (The European standard has become common in many parts of the world.) The original goal of the standardization efforts was to efficiently accommodate both the 1.5-Mbps and the 2-Mbps non-synchronous hierarchies in a single synchronization standard. The agreement reached specified a basic transmission rate of 51 Mbps for SONET and a basic rate of 155 Mbps for SDH. SONET and SDH converge at SDH's 155-Mbps base level, defined as STM-1 or "Synchronous Transport Module-1." The base level for SONET is STS-1 (or OC-1) and is equivalent to 51.84 Mbps. Thus, SDH's STM-1 is equivalent to SONET's STS-3 (3 x 51.84 Mbps = 155.5 Mbps). Higher SDH rates of STM-4 (622 Mbps), STM-16 (2.4 Gbps), and STM-64 (9.9 Gbps) have also been defined.

Up to now the industry has focused to a large degree on the long-haul aspect of the business. However, metro edge and metro core needs have also arisen of late, and are ill-served by long-haul-retrofitted solutions that are too expensive for metro edge/metro access applications. Applications of interest include broadband connectivity of the office buildings for IT/intranet connectivity and fiber to the home (FTTH) applications for video and "triple play" services. Metro optical networks and providers need to focus in another direction, namely, access; they need to capitalize on solutions that are more cost-effective in that space, where typical distances are 1–4 mi (e.g., CWDM). As noted earlier, approximately 95% of the office buildings in the United States, not to mention the other commercial buildings, are not on fiber-based systems today; part of the issue relates to the cost of the in-building equipment. However, nobody is going to make any money by deploying $80,000-to-$150,000 DWDM equipment in a building. Per-building equipment costs need to be in the $8,000 to $25,000 range for carriers to be able to deploy sustainable services.

10.2.2.2 First-Generation Optical Networks

A first-generation optical network was based on a ring architecture: SONET/SDH NEs interface with the fiber medium and allow a single lightwave beam ("lambda" or "wavelength") to be carried over the fiber. Data rates up to 2.4 Gbps (OC-48)* were supported. First-generation equipment spanned the 1990–1995 timeframe. To transmit a single wavelength, SONET ADMs use a fixed (nontunable) laser. The handoff to the customer is a DS-3, OC-3c, OC-12c, or OC-48c, or some Layer 2 (e.g., ATM) or Layer 3 (e.g., POS) interface. Typically, a Digital Cross Connect (DXC) at the central office or service node performs a "grooming" function. This user traffic is encapsulated into SONET Layer 1 frames by the CPE device (e.g., a SONET plug-in in a customer's router). The original protocol data unit (PDU), including Layer 2 header and Layer 2 payload (e.g., ATM header/payload), which in turn includes Layer 3 header and Layer 3 payload (e.g., IP header/payload), is transmitted from SONET node to SONET node embedded in the SONET envelope. Multiple SONET links may be involved in one data-link layer link; in turn, multiple data-link layer links are involved in an end-to-end path (e.g., an IP route).

Because a SONET/SDH ring is limited to transmitting only at one wavelength (e.g., 1310 nm), there are capacity limitations in terms of what one can achieve at the fiber level; therefore, each time the capacity of a ring is filled, the service provider has to lay more fiber and add a set of SONET/SDH devices. This is costly in long-haul applications; for metro access/metro core applications, the jury is still out on the advantages of highly packed wavelengths (e.g., 120); however, lower-density systems (e.g., 8, 16, or 32) may be appropriate in the metro core space, and 2-to-4 wavelengths may be fine for metro access applications, if the cost of the devices is within specific ranges. In the metro network case, there is a traditional transmission cost versus multiplexing-cost trade-off for the architecture: in long haul the transmission cost is high; therefore, multiplexing costs are easily justified; in metro applications the transmission cost could be bounded, so the cost of electronics supporting multiplexing, particularly if this is high, may or may not always be justified.

---

* As noted earlier, today 10 Gbps OC-192 systems are also being deployed; 40 Gbps OC-768 is being considered for some special high-end environments.

10.2.2.3 Second-Generation Optical Networks

The second generation of optical networking saw the introduction of DWDM technologies to the existing SONET environment. In this architecture, DWDM terminals are inserted into point-to-point segments of fiber rings (or even at every point on a ring) where more than just the single-wavelength capacity is required. By multiplexing up to 80 channels (in the second generation, and more in the third generation), the capacity of the ring is expanded several dozen times. It needs to be noted immediately, however, that the cost of DWDM gear is not trivial (e.g., $120,000 or more per node, with the cost being a function of the number of wavelengths supported), and so, although easily justifiable at the long-haul level, it remains a design cost issue for metro access networks (and to some extent also for metro core networks). Typically, for each DWDM channel added, a SONET device needs to be "stacked" in front of the DWDM terminal to provide the wavelength source. This also drives a proliferation of cross-connect systems because more electronic traffic needs to be routed and groomed. Because of cost, the ideal application for this technology is long haul [KOF200001].

10.2.2.4 Third-Generation Optical Networks

The third generation of optical networking has evolved to deal with the cost/performance issues associated with SONET and DCSs deployments just discussed. Third-generation equipment spans the 2000+ timeframe. At a high level, this equipment accomplishes the following:

1. Incorporates the SONET, DWDM, and cross-connect functions into a fewer number of discrete, cost-reduced devices.
2. Adds more intelligence to optical networking, specifically by enabling routing/switching at the wavelength level. (This is also often referred to as enabling "mesh" capability in the optical network.)

These optical networks comprise DWDM systems connected to intelligent Optical Cross Connects (OXC). OXCs support the basic functions of SONET/SDH equipment, including restoration, signaling, performance monitoring, fault management, and multiplexing. With this design, SONET/SDH equipment is vectored even further to the edge of the network to manage the lower-speed interfaces and mixtures of protocols. This allows the core optical network to handle the high-speed traffic, which makes the core easy to build and manage. It is worth noting that the traditional SONET/SDH protocol is still used in the network, albeit in a different way. The traditional SONET/SDH OAM&P features are required by carriers and are performed in an efficient manner by SONET NEs. The goal of the OXC is to remove the expensive SONET/SDH equipment layer, but not the protocol itself. Again, because of cost, the ideal application for this technology is still long haul.

Although equipment cost is important, however, it tends to be only 10–15% of the total cost incurred by a carrier, and reflected in the service charges. Hence, equipment cost reduction is important, but its overall true effect has to be understood. For example, reducing a piece of equipment from $10 to $8.70 (a 13% decrease) only reduces the total cost of a service from $100 to $98.7, or a mere 1.3% net reduction. As implied by our earlier discussion, the edge equipment cost reduction has to be in the 100% to 1000% range. In our example, the cost would have to go from $10 to $5, or better yet, from $10 to $1. In the latter case, the total service cost would go from $100 to $91, or about a 10% reduction. Even this is not all that significant, but if the OAM&P costs are reduced from say $25 (as typical, in proportion) to $15, then the service cost reduces by

20%, which is where customers start to show interest in examining an alternative to an embedded service they would have. The criticality of the 100% to 1000% cost reduction is made clear when some carriers stated publicly that they needed 67 broadband customers in a building to deliver sustainable breakeven services. A mere 10–30% equipment cost reduction is meaningless. This implies that "disruptive" technology is needed.

10.2.2.5 Expanding the Infrastructure to Support Higher Capacity

As implied in the foregoing paragraphs, during the recent past carriers have had three possible solutions to the problem of increased bandwidth demand, particularly at the long-haul level:

- Install new fiber.
- Invest in new TDM technology to achieve higher bit rates.
- Deploy Dense Wavelength Division Multiplexing.

Installing New Fiber to Meet Capacity Needs: Traditionally, carriers have expanded their networks by deploying new fiber and new ancillary transmission equipment. Unfortunately, such deployment tends to be costly: the budgetary cost to deploy the additional fiber cable, excluding costs of associated support systems and electronics, is in the neighborhood of $50,000–$70,000 per mile (costs are higher in downtown urban centers). Although this figure varies from place to place, installing new fiber can be a major project. In many instances, a third party (e.g., a railroad, a cable TV company), or even a competitor, owns the right of way of the cable route or right of entry for the premises needed to house transmission equipment. For these reasons, the brute-force deployment of additional fiber is often somewhat of an impractical or last-resort solution for many carriers, for both the long-haul and the metro access/metro core space.

Higher-Speed TDM—Deploying STM-64/OC-192 (10 Gbps): As indicated earlier, STM–64/OC–192 is becoming an option for carriers seeking higher capacity. However, there are technical issues affecting this solution, restricting its applicability. The majority of the existing fiber plant is single-mode fiber that has high dispersion in the 1550 nm window, making STM–64/OC–192 transmission difficult to achieve in a reliable fashion. In fact, dispersion has a 16 times greater effect with STM–64/OC–192 equipment than with STM–16/OC–48. As a result, effective STM–64/OC–192 transmission requires either some form of dispersion compensating fiber or entire new fiber builds using nonzero dispersion shifted fiber (NZDSF). Newer fiber can also be 50% more expensive than traditional single-mode fiber, impacting the $70,000 per mile just cited. Polarization Mode Dispersion (PMD), which impacts the distance a light pulse can travel without signal degradation, is of particular concern for STM-64/OC–192. As transmission speeds increase, dispersion problems grow significantly, thereby reducing the distance a signal can travel; this is a major concern in long-haul applications. Specifically, PMD appears to limit the reliable reach of STM–64/OC–192 to about 50 mi on most embedded fiber. Although there is a debate within the industry over the extent of PMD problems, some key issues are known:

  - PMD is an issue in the conventional SMF plant that comprises the vast majority of the existing fiber plant.

– PMD varies significantly from cable to cable and is also affected by environmental conditions, making it difficult to determine ways to offset its effect on high-bit-rate systems.

– Carriers are forced to test their constituent spans of fiber to determine their compatibility with STM–64/OC–192; in many cases, PMD will rule out its deployment altogether.

DWDM as an Upgrade Path: DWDM (discussed in some greater detail later) is a technology that allows multiple information streams to be multiplexed and transmitted simultaneously over a single fiber. DWDM technology utilizes a composite optical signal carrying multiple information streams, each transmitted on a distinct optical wavelength. The DWDM approach multiplies the baseline 2.4 Gbps system capacity by up to 80, 120, or 160 times, providing a major increase in throughput while utilizing the embedded fiber. DWDM technology has been available for over a decade, but the early applications were restricted to providing two or four widely separated "wideband" wavelengths. Only in the past few years has the technology evolved to the point that multiple wavelengths can be densely packed and integrated into a transmission system. By conforming to the ITU channel plan (the "ITU Grid"), such a system ensures interoperability with other equipment. Sixteen channel systems supporting 40 Gbps in each direction over a fiber pair are commercially available; systems that have entered the market in the recent past that can support 32 channels operating at 10 Gbps each, for a total of 320 Gbps. To transmit 40 Gbps over 700 km using a traditional system would require 16 separate fiber pairs with regenerators placed every 35 km for a total of 320 regenerators. A 16-channel DWDM system, on the other hand, uses a single fiber pair and four amplifiers positioned every 120 km for a total of 20 regenerators to transmit over 700 km. The most common form of DWDM uses a fiber pair: one for transmission and one for reception. Systems do exist in which a single fiber is used for bidirectional traffic, but these configurations must sacrifice performance and reliability. The benefits of DWDM for increasing capacity are clear; however, this increase does not come for free, as the cost can be as high as $10,000 per lambda, and in some cases even more. Up to the present time, DWDM has only been cost-effective for long-haul applications.

10.2.2.6 SONET Technology

SONET/SDH is a standard intended to support interworking of optical equipment at various speeds. Interworking is achieved by defining a set of optical parameters, data-framing formats, clocking speeds, and OAM&P mechanisms. It also provides excellent restoration capabilities (less than 50 ms). In addition, DWDM has enabled carriers to derive near-terabits-per-second speeds on fiber. SONET is broadly deployed in North America. SONET has proved useful in multiplexing legacy services, as well as in providing point-to-point high-quality high-speed links. SONET provides several capabilities that are of interest to carriers and users:

1. An electrical and optical transmission standard
2. A multiplexing hierarchy
3. An extensive OAM&P capability
4. A restoration apparatus

Speeds of 2.4 and 9.95 Gbps (typically shown as 10 Gbps) are readily available. Systems operating at 40 Gbps are now under development. Lower speeds are also supportable. The issue is, however, that although costs (per bit) have decreased significantly, traditional carriers have tended to keep the price of point-to-point SONET links relatively high. Therefore, many users seeking speeds higher than those offered by Frame Relay services have been forced to use, for a period of time, ATM-based approaches of sharing the bandwidth with other users. Some high-end users have, nonetheless, availed themselves of a quantum leap to more native services, such as POS.

Basic goals of SONET include the following:

- Compatibility of equipment between vendors who manufacture to the standard (often referred to as "midspan meet")
- Synchronous networking
- Enhanced OAM&P
- More efficient add/drop multiplexing
- Standards-based survivable rings/meshes
- A Layer 1 infrastructure for transport of services such as IP, ATM, and 10GbE WAN PHY.

SONET defines Optical Carrier (OC) levels and electrically equivalent Synchronous Transport Signals (STSs) for the fiber-optic based transmission hierarchy. Multiplexing is accomplished by combining (or interleaving) multiple lower-order signals (1.5 Mbps, 45 Mbps, etc.) into higher-speed circuits (51 Mbps, 155 Mbps, etc.).

When using SONET, voice interfaces (e.g., DS-1s and DS-3s), high-speed data (e.g., private lines, IP, 10GbE), and video can be accepted by various types of service edge adapters. A service adapter maps the signal into the payload envelope of the STS-1 or onto a virtual tributary (VT); a VT is a construct (principally) to support DS-1s.* New streams can be transported by a SONET system by adding new service adapters at the edge of the SONET network. All inputs are converted to a STS-1 signal. Several synchronous STS-1s are multiplexed together in either a single- or two-stage process to form an electrical STS-n signal (n ≥ 1); STS multiplexing is performed at the Byte Interleave Synchronous Multiplexer. As noted earlier, the architectural evolution that has taken place since the mid-1990s in regard to "private-line-like" services is as follows: the first generation consisted of ATM-over-SONET architectures; the second generation consisted of IP (directly) over SONET (e.g., with POS); and the third generation is 10GbE WAN PHY over SONET.

SONET uses a basic transmission rate of STS-1—equivalent to 51.84 Mbps. Higher-level signals are multiples of the base rate. For example, STS-3 is three times the rate of STS-1 (3 × 51.84 = 155.52 Mbps). An STS-12 rate is 12 × 51.84 = 622.08 Mbps. SDH is built on 155.52 Mbps modules and multiples thereof. The frame comprises two main elements: (1) transport overhead and (2) the synchronous payload envelope (SPE). The synchronous payload envelope can also be partitioned into two parts: (2.a) the STS path overhead and (2.b) the payload. The signal is transmitted byte by byte beginning with byte one, reading left to right from row one to row nine. The entire frame is transmitted in 125 μs. Once the payload is multiplexed into the synchronous payload envelope, it can be transported and switched through SONET without having to be examined and possibly demultiplexed at intermediate nodes.

SONET carries substantial management information, allowing expanded OAM&P capabilities compared with previous systems such as DS-1 and DS-3. The management information has several layers. Path-level overhead is carried end to end; it is added to DS-1 signals when they are mapped into virtual tributaries and for STS-1 payloads that travel end to end. Line overhead is for the STS-n signal between STS-n multiplexers. Section overhead is used for communications

---

* Streams such as DS-1s are first bit- or byte-multiplexed into virtual tributaries.

between adjacent network elements, such as regenerators. Transport overhead comprises section overhead and line overhead. The STS-1 path overhead is part of the synchronous payload envelope [NOR200201].

SONET provides a plethora of restoration schemes. Some consider SONET's allocated backup capacity a drawback, but with the continued introduction of DWDM technology, bandwidth issues should become less of an overwhelming driving design criterion. PC manufacturers have "overcome" their memory-preciousness mind-set and are liberally using memory in favor of ever-increasing power and ever-increasing-user-friendliness aspects of the PC. It is high time for network designers and carriers to do the same: "overcome" the link-capacity-preciousness mind-set and liberally use bandwidth in favor of ever-increasing service portfolios and ever-increasing network simplification; network simplification leads to major operational OAM&P cost savings for them, which, as they realize, are the highest costs to a carrier.

Tracking the technology evolution, OC-192 SONET systems have emerged in the recent past that can transport an OC-192 (10 Gbps) on one fiber pair. These can be deployed discretely (as a simple SONET/SDH system), or in conjunction with a WDM system. The majority of embedded fiber in long-haul networks, however, is standard, single-mode (ITU G.562-defined) fiber with dispersion in the 1550 nm window, which limits the distance for OC-192 transmission. The majority of the legacy fiber plant cannot support high-bit-rate TDM. Earlier-vintage fiber has some attributes that lead to significant dispersion and would, therefore, be incompatible with high-bit-rate TDM.

State-of-the-art OC-192 SONET technology is a viable alternative for new fiber builds because the fiber parameters can be controlled through placement of the appropriate fiber type and because new fiber-handling procedures can be accommodated. However, for existing fiber applications, the ability to install 10 Gbps TDM systems depends on fiber properties such as chromatic and polarization mode dispersion, which may differ from fiber span to fiber span. In addition, high-rate TDM systems require specialized fiber-handling and termination procedures when compared to lower rate OC-48 systems. In contrast, current DWDM systems can transport up to 32 wavelengths at OC-48 each, giving an aggregate capacity of 80 Gbps on one fiber pair. This means WDM technology surpasses TDM in terms of the aggregate capacity offered on a single fiber pair, while maintaining the same fiber-handling procedures developed for OC-48 TDM systems [ALL199701]. SONET and WDM systems typically have built-in forward error correction (FEC) features that provide a 10^{-15} BER.

OC-768 systems were beginning to be considered for possible plant deployment at press time.

10.2.2.7 Next-Generation SONET and Related Optical Architectures

"Next-generation SONET" is a collection of vendor-advanced approaches to improve the cost-effectiveness of traditional SONET in a broadband data context. The term was coined ealier in the decade. Although traditional SONET approaches to packet data transport can provide support for LAN/MAN/WAN connectivity needs in midspeed (e.g., 10–100 Mbps) situations, these approaches generally do not adequately address the full requirements of emerging data-centric high-capacity networks (e.g., 1–10 Gbps). Such requirements can be better served by new TLS-friendly technologies; equipment vendors have also realized that no single technology can do it all, and have begun to combine technologies into network elements that enable service providers to easily add new services [LEE200101]. Next-generation SONET/SDH systems go in this direction, and it is possible that next-generation SONET may enjoy easier market penetration than the Ethernet-based MAN technologies.

As a technology, next-generation SONET systems are not "revolutionary," but rather are "evolutionary." At the network topology level these systems are generally similar or identical to traditional SONET/SDH systems. Basically, next-generation systems are "data-aware" SONET NEs that have direct 100 Mbps, 1 Gbps, or 10 Gbps Ethernet handoff, in addition to traditional handoffs.* Typical industry headlines included the following: "There is a hot new product category emerging in the industry, but no one seems to know exactly what it is. Some call it next-generation SONET, others call it the Multi-Service Provisioning Platform (MSPP). And since neither term has been clearly defined, vendors are making up their own definitions and then claiming to be market leaders" [GIM200101,GIM200102]. There is no standard definition (i.e., published by a standards body) of what "next generation" means; as just noted, various vendors have developed various vendor-initiated packaging of functions deemed to be of value to data-intensive metro access/metro core applications. Typically, the user handoff is Ethernet or SONET, whereas the network side is either SONET/TDM, RPR-like (pre-RPR), or a combination.

The reasons for the growth in next-generation SONET are quoted as being as follows:

■ Ability to interoperate with existing SONET networks
■ New system architectures that allow simple capacity and service upgrades
■ New enabling technologies that increase network revenue-generating capacity by as much as an order of magnitude
■ Native data and video interfaces that reduce network elements
■ Functionality that combines DCS, edge routing, and ADM functionality into a single NE for reduced overlay and purpose-built networks.

Figure 10.3 depicts a protocol-model view of both traditional and next-generation SONET. In next-generation SONET equipment one looks for cheaper transport and cheaper network elements, but with a full complement of OAM&P capabilities. Because of its emphasis on customer-ready interfaces (such as Ethernet), next-generation SONET is generally more applicable to the metro access portion of the network (rather than the metro core). Next-generation systems provide an improved IP delivery solution. In the past, carriers typically built overlay networks to accommodate different characteristics of the various media (voice, data, video, and Internet), because there was no single technology or product that could meet the requirements for each service. Next-generation SONET systems aim at addressing these requirements. In addition, these systems can also be used in conjunction with embedded systems [GIM200101].

Incumbent providers that also support traditional lower-speed data services beyond just TLS have additional design considerations. Traditional SONET approaches generally do not adequately address the broad mix of traditional circuit-based services plus the TLS service: to incumbents considering POS channels, traditional ATM, or Frame Relay, serious drawbacks in the critical areas of cost-effectiveness, scalability, manageability, survivability, and service flexibility quickly become apparent with these traditional approaches when compared to next-generation SONET solutions, as shown in Table 10.2. According to Nortel Networks statistics, these systems can provide savings to the operator of up to 70% over traditional solutions [NOR200102]. Multi-service next-generation SONET platforms support a mix of traditional and newer (TLS) services, enabling the end-to-end delivery of 10 Gbps data streams, including 10GbE, POS, Fibre Channel, ESCON, FICON, and GbE. These platforms enable the delivery of traditional and new service

---

* Next-generation SONET NEs are cheaper than traditional NEs because of advances in technology and because they do not support voice-originated capabilities such as a complex VT mechanism.

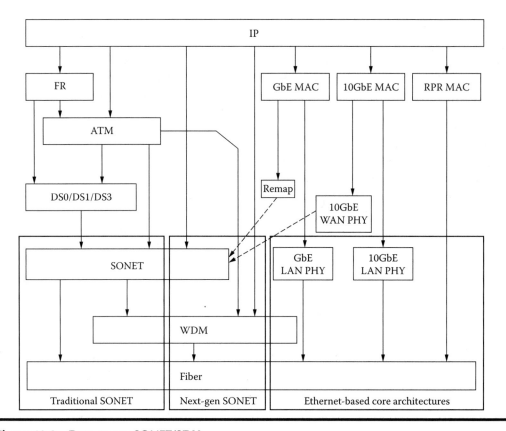

Figure 10.3   Data-aware SONET/SDH.

offerings such as data center interconnect, storage area networking, VLANs, and VPNs. The new platforms also provide low-cost native LAN interfaces, eliminating the need for more expensive TDM transport interfaces in customer equipment or additional customer premises systems (such as T1/T3 multiplexers) to access the backbone. Typical equipment available at press time had the following features:

- Carrier-grade reliability
- Protocol and bit-rate independence
- Ethernet switching integrated directly into the optical layer
- Up to 32 protected wavelengths, 64 unprotected
- Per-wavelength protection switching
- Built-in DWDM capabilities with bandwidth scalable to 2.5 Gbps per wavelength (10 Gbps future)

As seen in Figure 10.4, there are a number of variants of next-generation SONET products. Traditional SONET provides a robust physical-layer protection, but it employs a rigid multiplexing hierarchy that is not well-suited to data-centric line rates (although it has definitions for VTs for DS-1s and DS2s). For example, a 10BASE-T Ethernet interface (10 Mbps) delivered in a SONET network is traditionally mapped to an STS-1 (51 Mbps), effectively wasting 40 Mbps

Table 10.2 Comparing Architectural Alternatives

Packet Transport Alternatives	Issues
Traditional ATM	• More expensive • No built-in redundancy • Many hard-to-manage permanent virtual circuits (PVCs) required
Frame Relay	• Limited bandwidth • Many hard-to-manage PVCs required
Packet Over SONET Channels	• Not scalable • Inefficient bandwidth usage • Many hard-to-manage point-to-point corrections required
Fiber Optic Inter-Repeater Link (FOIRL)	• Limited bandwidth • Primarily short-haul solution • Inefficient use of fiber resources • No built-in redundancy • No end-to-end management
Router Based Packet Transport Rings	• Limited support for mixed services • Limited support for long-haul, high-capacity applications • Not based on carrier-grade network elements • Proprietary technology
Next-generation SONET	• Scalable • Cost-effective, bandwidth-efficient • Connectionless • Full support for mixed packet data and TDM services • Short-haul or long-haul, high capacity up to 1.6 Tops • Survivable with inherent resilience • Easily manageable • Carrier-grade equipment • Open industry standards

worth of link capacity or 80%. 100 Mbps Ethernet is mapped to an STS-3c (155 Mbps). Next-generation SONET technologies leverage virtual concatenation to right-size the bandwidth of the data-centric connection. The Virtual Tributary mechanism maps DS-1 and DS2 signals onto the SONET payload in an efficient manner. Some argue, therefore, that there is a further need to define VTs that are data-oriented, e.g., 10 Mbps and 100 Mbps (and combinations thereof). For example, a 10BASE-T interface could be mapped to 7 SONET VT1.5s, resulting in an increase of approximately 95% in transport efficiency. Vendors leveraging virtual concatenation typically provide a software-based approach to creation, deletion, and modification of these right-sized SONET connections. Such technology enables new services such as user-based subscription and bandwidth-on-demand [LEE200101].

Savvy planners understand that as bandwidth becomes a commodity, the engineering urge to optimize just one variable in the system (namely, bandwidth efficiency) is counterproductive in the total scheme of things, much the same way PC suppliers have come to understand that it is better to be (somewhat) memory-usage inefficient (with PCs having 64 MB for RAM or more), in

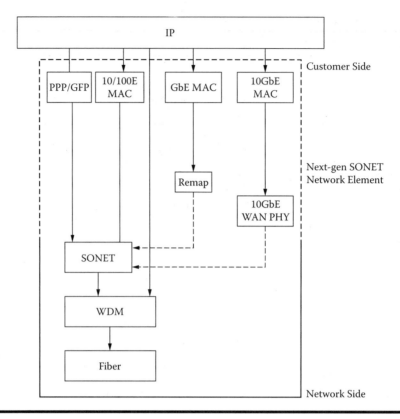

Figure 10.4 Variants of next-generation SONET.

favor of user simplicity (via the use of a GUI-based OS such as Windows), as noted earlier.* One approach to addressing the trunk-side bandwidth efficiency is to employ Statistical TDM (STDM) rather than TDM means. This could save, say, 50% of the metro core bandwidth. However, a typical metro-level backbone ring costs $5000 MRC and can easily support 16 buildings; this equates to $313 per building per month. Improving efficiency by 100% would reduce the backbone cost

---

* Fortunately, we are not the only ones recognizing this, although, prima facie, there are very few people who have made this mental shift. The following quote (Nortel's White Paper, "A Layered Architecture for Metro Optical Networks," 56018.25/08-00, August 2000) supports the thesis: "While the economic values of Ethernet seem compelling, the issue is how Quality of Service (QoS) and Service Level Agreements (SLAs) can be enforced by the carrier. This has been one of the key propositions behind ATM versus Ethernet. The need to enforce QoS within SLAs was based on an assumption of a scarcity of bandwidth. While this assumption has been true in the past, today's bandwidth has been doubling every nine months, twice the rate of Moore's law for chip capacity. With prices of 2.5 G and 10G products dropping rapidly coupled with metro DWDM products, the cost per megabit is dropping rapidly for metro optical services. Hence, the significant operational costs and complexity of enforcing QoS to customers can be resolved simply by recognizing that bandwidth is no longer a scarce resource. Rather than expending significant resources to micro-manage bandwidth, it is suggested to advocate throwing bandwidth at the problem. Rather than QoS, it is recommended to enforce class of service (CoS) for most applications. The engineering of the network with significant bandwidth capacity will reduce the complexity of enforcing stringent QoS guidelines. Furthermore, any cost of provisioning additional bandwidth will be more than offset by a savings in operational costs. In today's tight market for network management resources, the savings in operational costs become the overriding critical path item versus incremental capital spending for bandwidth."

to $156 per month. Although not implying that one should ignore savings here and savings there, this implies that the real value of next-generation SONET systems must be principally in providing new services, followed by reducing operations costs followed by reducing NE costs, followed by reducing backbone transmission costs (through better bandwidth efficiency). Pure bandwidth efficiency by itself is of limited value.

Edge solutions need to support flexible 10 Mbps, 100 Mbps, and 1 Gbps interfaces to meet a wide range of end-user requirements. Occasionally there may be a need for user information rates to be assigned in increments of 10 Mbps for flexible service level agreements and additional scalability. Some vendors push hard on this feature.* However, as bandwidth becomes a commodity, the precise amount of bandwidth on a link becomes less of a differentiating factor for various providers. Value-added solutions will be of increased interest to the end user compared to just pure bandwidth solutions. Frankly, there is relatively little incentive for a provider that has just incurred a nontrivial expense bringing a building online to fine-tune the billing, to distinguish, for example, between a customer's needs requiring 58 Mbps today, 59 Mbps tomorrow, and 57 Mbps the day after tomorrow. It appears at the practitioner's level that customers are more likely to be interested in 10 Mbps on a 10 Mbps interface; 50 Mbps or 100 Mbps on a 100 Mbps interface; and 50 Mbps, 100 Mbps, 200 Mbps, 500 Mbps, or 1000 Mbps on a 1000 Mbps interface. The fine-grained 1 Mbps granularity that some equipment vendors are bringing out appears to have rather limited commercial value; after all, if bandwidth is (expected to be) so abundant in the future, why be so precise about the amount of the commodity delivered?

So, although bandwidth efficiency is important, transport bandwidth efficiency is not the linchpin that will make or break the deployment of broadband at the enterprise level. Principally, enterprise locations need affordable, timely, reliable, broadband *connectivity*; efficiency of the payload is just an element of the overall desiderata. ATM was the multiplexing (read, efficient payload) par excellence: once the "cell tax" was "paid," near perfect packing of any bursty stream can be achieved, typically with overall overbooking ratios of 5 or 10 (which more than compensate for the 20% or so of tax overhead). Yet, ATM has not seen major deployment just on the basis of bandwidth efficiency (and QoS). The main reason was the operational cost for both the user and the carrier; both the user and the carrier had to deploy completely new equipment and establish new procedures (at both ends) for fault management, capacity management, accounting management, performance management, and security management. The overall operational cost proved to be too high, in spite of the major bandwidth efficiency achieved with overbooking ratios of 5 to 10 times.

MSPPs combine transport, switching, and routing platforms into an integrated system with which service providers can offer bundled services flexibly, ostensibly at lower cost. By incorporating many service interfaces in one device, MSPPs may eliminate the need for extra devices to deliver intelligent optical services. Proponents also claim MSPPs improve SONET's efficiency in transporting multi-service traffic. Next-generation SONET platforms, however, do much the same thing. MSPPs grew out of the next-generation SONET market. The MSPP category is really an umbrella category that includes next-generation SONET, and the lines are blurry between the two. Original next-generation SONET boxes were single-platform SONET ADM, perhaps with

* A chef in Roman times was to be commended if he could cook and use the minimal possible amount of salt without wasting a gram (salt being scarce and people being paid in "salt," from which word the word *salary* comes from). Today nobody would be impressed by a chef who claims he or she could save the restaurant 1 g of salt per day in serving 100 people. So why would anyone be impressed when a vendor can save 1 Mbps on a 1 Gbps stream compared to another vendor (who does not save the 1 Mbps)?

an integrated cross-connect capability, and Ethernet capabilities made possible through a service interface. Then MSPP start-ups started emerging and taking this model and adding other functions to it, such as Layer 2 switching and Layer 3 routing.

10.2.2.8 DWDM Systems

WDM and high-capacity DWDM have seen major deployment in the United States since the late 1990s, particularly for long-haul or metro core applications. By using frequency division multiplexing (FDM) techniques on a fiber transmission system, one can achieve "fiber optic pair gain," where multiple signals (called *lambdas*) operating at different frequencies can individually carry OC-48 or OC-192 channels between endpoints.* A WDM greatly increases the traffic-carrying capacity of existing fiber spans by combining two or more optical signals of different wavelengths on a single fiber pair.† These days, therefore, WDM is viewed as operating at the optical layer; SONET is viewed as an overlay onto this newly established layer. The ITU has defined a set of standard wavelengths for manufacturers to use in DWDM to facilitate interworking between equipment. So far this technology has been optimized for, and has seen major deployment in, long-haul networks, based on very *traditional cost-of-transmission-versus-cost-of-multiplexing economic tradeoff considerations.*‡

DWDM coupler devices perform the actual multiplexing/demultiplexing of the different optical wavelengths. Systems carrying from 2 to 1000 channels have been demonstrated, with typical commercial systems in the field carrying 16, 32, or 64 channels operating at the OC-48 (2.5 Gbps) or OC-192 (10 Gbps) data rates. High-end commercially available DWDMs can deliver up to 320 Gbps of capacity; these are 32-channel systems with each channel operating at 10 Gbps (OC-192 SONET/SDH). Optical technology nearing commercial deployment can now provide 10 Gbps on a single lambda and support up to 160 lambdas over a single fiber pair for long distance networking services (more lambdas are achievable in laboratory systems). In 2007, Core Optics, Inc. announced that they were able to transmit 10 lambdas at 111 Gbps each over a fiber 2,400 km long (1.1 Tbps). In 2008, Alcatel-Lucent stated that they were able to transmit 160 lambdas each at 100 Gbps, for a combined bandwidth of 16.4 Tbps over a single fiber. However, both of these were lab tests and not commercial products. 16-channel DWDMs have been deployed throughout the carrier infrastructure, and 32-channel systems (and higher) are also entering the field.§ A 16-channel system in essence provides a virtual 16-fiber cable, with each frequency channel serving as a unique STM–16/OC–48 carrier. Advances in aggregate bandwidth have been seen in recent years in commercially deployed systems, from 400 Gbps on high-end systems evolving to 800 Gbps; near-term projections are in the terabit per second range. One also observes DWDM channel growth: whereas the current range is OC-192 (10 Gbps), the projected range is OC-768 (40 Gbps). The availability of mature supporting technologies, like quality demultiplexers and

---

* One can also carry a non-SONET framed signal; however, the majority of systems now deployed are used as adjuncts to SONET, namely, they carry a SONET signal.

† It is also possible to pack both a send and a receive signal onto a single strand, but most telecom systems utilize a fiber *pair*.

‡ The methodologies embodied in these trade-off considerations are really no different from the trade-off considerations of the 1950s when considering deploying 12-channel analog loop carrier as contrasted with deploying 12 distinct analog loops; or, from considerations in the 1970s in considering deploying 24-channel digital loop carrier as contrasted with deploying 24 distinct (analog) loops.

§ For example, some systems could support 64 channels unprotected or 32 channels protected.

Erbium Doped Fiber Amplifiers (EDFA), has enabled DWDM high-channel counts to be commercially delivered. Systems with DWDM systems have been used extensively in the long-haul space and typically cost from $100K to $1 million or more.

Going back at least half a century, network designers have looked for simple, straightforward methods for migration of networks to higher performance levels. Throughout the 1950s and 1960s, analog, and later on, digital, carrier systems of ever-increasing capacity were being developed. A carrier system is a multiplexed transmission system supporting multiple channels. Fiber-optic (light-wave) systems have been deployed at least since 1979 (then operating at DS-3 rates). 90 Mbps systems (FT3C) were deployed as early as 1983. In the mid-to-late 1980s, systems supporting 400–565 Mbps emerged, followed by systems operating at 800–1100 Mbps. In the early 1990s, systems operating at 1600–2200 Mbps (1.6–2.2 Gbps) emerged. Finally, SONET/SDH systems emerged supporting up to 2.4 Gbps (OC-48); 10 Gbps (OC-192) systems have been introduced in the past couple of years, and 40 Gbps systems are under development. These advances are based on TDM technologies, where the clock driving the on/off Intensity Modulation (IM) light process is driven at a higher pulse rate. As one approaches the limit as to how short the light pulse can be made, there are at least two other methods to increase the carrying capacity on the fiber waveguide: (1) coherent transmission, a variant of full FDM; and (2) WDM, which is in effect a space division multiplexing method. Although coherent methods offer perhaps the best long-term opportunity for maximum throughput, they currently suffer from technical, engineering, and cost drawbacks. Therefore, WDM methods have enjoyed significant market penetration in the long-haul segment in the United States and abroad.

The proliferation of bandwidth-intensive applications has driven demand for broadband connectivity and transport in the recent past. DWDM increases the capacity of the embedded optical fiber base by adding "pair-gain" methods to the transmission channel. A DWDM optical backbone allows carriers to expand capacity in any portion of their network, thus addressing specific problem areas that may be congested. However, any network planner knows that as one moves closer and closer to the core, the need for bandwidth becomes more intensive and concentrated, whereas at the edges of the network the needs are less intensive and concentrated; therefore, the long-haul core is the more natural "habitat" for DWDM technology rather than the metro access and metro core space. In long-haul networks, the primary value provided by DWDM in combination with optical line amplifiers is the cost-effective transmission of high aggregate bit rates over large distances on a single fiber pair. The large distances in long-haul networks make deploying new fiber challenging. Long-haul carriers have traditionally been the first to embrace advances in transmission technologies to gain additional capacity while leveraging their existing equipment [ALL199701].

The agnostic nature of DWDM technology allows multiple networks (ATM, IP, SONET, etc.) to share the same optical core, but possibly with some bandwidth inefficiencies (e.g., one can map a GbE link directly over a lambda, but one will be dedicating a channel to support 1 Gbps where one could otherwise derive 10 Gbps/OC-192). DWDM provides a means for carriers to integrate diverse technologies of their existing networks onto one physical infrastructure. DWDM systems are bit-rate and format independent and can accept any combination of interface rates and formats, although SONET tributaries are the most common. DWDM provides a "grow as you go" infrastructure; the "grow as you go" approach is implemented by adding the lambda plug-ins over time.* However, many observers now believe that there was an overestimation of the demand in

---

* For the purpose of sizing the market in the foregoing discussion, however, we assumed that the entire system was deployed on Day 1.

the late 1990s and early 2000s, at least in the long-haul and Internet segments of the market, and that terabit per second system will not be needed in the near term.

10.2.2.9 DWDM Opportunities and Application Scope

Because of its costs, at this time DWDM is more suited to longer-reach applications. This situation could change in the future if developers were to begin to grasp what the real requirements are in the metro access/metro core space. For long-haul applications, DWDM offers a cost-effective complement to OC-48/OC-192 TDM technology that is embodied in SONET/SDH systems: assuming a decent-quality fiber plant, WDM methods enable the planner to maximize network capacity and address service scalability needs. And because it defers—or eliminates—the capital outlays and long lead times associated with deploying new fiber cable, DWDM is a useful solution for high-growth routes that have an immediate need for additional bandwidth. According to vendors, carriers that are building or expanding their long-haul networks could find DWDM to be an economical way to incrementally increase capacity, rapidly provision needed expansion, and "future-proof" their infrastructure against unforeseen bandwidth demand. Network wholesalers can take advantage of DWDM to lease capacity, rather than entire fibers, either to existing operators or to new market entrants. However, in aggregate, DWDM technology is not cheap. Systems can cost from $50K to $100,000 per lambda, particularly when redundant and long-reach applications are considered; furthermore, these figures do not include the cost of the repeaters. Power consumption and floor space requirements are usually high, and unless tunable laser systems are available, complex design/engineering and sparing disciplines are involved, with plug-ins specific to given lambdas being required. Furthermore, "future-proofing" may in fact imply that after a route upgrade, there is no need for additional equipment for several years; this is, therefore, bad news for equipment suppliers.

DWDM is well suited for long-distance telecommunications operators that use either point-to-point or ring topologies. The availability of 16, 32, or 64 new transmission channels, where there used to be one, improves an operator's ability to expand capacity and simultaneously set aside backup bandwidth without installing new fiber. Proponents make the case that this large amount of capacity is critical to the development of self-healing rings. By deploying DWDM terminals, an operator can construct a protected 40 Gbps ring with 16 separate communication signals using only two fibers. However, unless there is a major underlying engine continuously driving the demand through the roof, this kind of technology is a "one-time (in a long time) upgrade," with obvious market-sizing implications.

There has been a lot of hype in the recent past about metro DWDM. Proponents of DWDM make the claim that the acceptance of the technology will drive the expansion of the optical layer throughout the telecommunications network and allow service operators to exploit the bandwidth capacity that is inherent in optical fiber, but that has gone largely untapped until now. The widespread introduction of this technology, however, could at the same time lead to a long-haul bandwidth glut and price disruptions,* and set expectations for price points at the metro access/metro core that may or may not be achievable. Finally, one finds with some satisfaction the following quotes: "With so much unused fiber, when will metro nets really need WDM? What are the requirements for 40 Gbps systems? What are the new economic trade-offs between transparency and grooming? And which

---

* For example, note this quote from J. McQuillan, "Broadband Networking at the Crossroad," NGN 2001 Promotional materials, October 11, 2001: "10 years of price competition in voice have been compressed into three years for Internet prices. And price erosion is accelerating: a contract for an OC-3 from New York to Los Angeles for the year 2002 dropped in price by 92% in just four months."

of the new service providers will succeed?" [MCQ200101]. At the metro level, repackaged products can cost from $100,000 per building all the way to $250,000 per building. This is totally untenable, because carriers generally need to keep their in-building costs to be no more than $20,000 to have any chance of being profitable. Furthermore, the high building cost is multiplicative: every building in the ring would require the expensive optics. Although high-cost DWDM might be acceptable for point-to-point applications (not rings with 8, 16, or 32 buildings on them), and for long-haul, it is most often unacceptable in the metro access space (it could occasionally have an application in the metro core space).

The pertinent question for the current discussion is whether DWDM has practical application to the metro access/metro core space. The reality is that in its general form DWDM has some (limited) applicability to metropolitan environments, probably for a handful of POP-to-POP rings. If DWDM systems now in the market were redesigned to be optimized according to the requirements for metropolitan environments, there could be increased applicability. If the systems were redesigned to meet specific price points, then their applicability would be enhanced. When the long-haul industry saw major retrenchments at the turn of the decade, a number of optical vendors took the easy course of relabeling the equipment that had been developed by them for long-haul applications and pasted a "metro DWDM" label onto the equipment while at the same time generating new marketing collaterals, rather than redeveloping, as would have been more appropriate, equipment that is optimized and right-sized for metro access/metro core applications from both density and cost points of view. It appears that, at least for the next few years, the opportunity for metro DWDM is somewhat limited. As noted earlier, this technology may see some penetration in a metro core application of POP-to-POP rings, but extremely limited application in the metro access segment. A price of $10,000 per dropped "lambda" ($20,000 for a redundant system with two "lambdas") is desirable for metro access, particularly when the component cost of metro optics to build 8 or 16 channels CWDM, WWDM, or even DWDM, is actually about $2000 per lambda or less. In particular, if systems are designed in such a manner that each building needs to incur the full cost even though only one or two lambdas are dropped off at that building, then the equipment will see very limited penetration at the metro access level.

Systems with DWDM technology have been used extensively in the long-haul space and typically cost from $100,000 to $1 million or more. There are economic advantages in using DWDM when the transmission costs are high, such as in long-haul applications. Such use is justified by standard transmission-versus-multiplexing cost calculations. For example, to transmit 40 Gbps over 600 km using a traditional system would require 16 separate fiber pairs with regenerators placed every 35 km for a total of 272 regenerators. A 16-channel DWDM system, on the other hand, uses a single fiber pair and four amplifiers positioned every 120 km for a total of 600 km. At the same time, new Extended Wavelength Band (EWB) fiber is being introduced that allows a wider range of operation for the transmission system; some Coarse Wavelength Division Multiplexing equipment (which is more ideal for metropolitan environments) will make use of the E-band.

Even in long-haul applications, design considerations aimed at optimizing the cost profile are not always straightforward. In particular, TDM-only solutions supporting increasing speed have kept pace with a number of advances in the WDM technology during the mid-to-late 1990s, at least for medium-size trunking applications (up to 10 Gbps). For example, a TDM-based solution has only one 10 Gbps SONET terminal. A WDM system that transports an aggregate capacity of 10 Gbps requires four 2.5 Gbps terminals in addition to a WDM terminal per end. Because TDM technology has typically quadrupled its capacity for a cost multiplier of 2.5, the 10 Gbps solution appears to be more cost-effective. However, if the TDM system also requires four 2.5 Gbps terminals to provide the first stage of multiplexing, the 10 Gbps solution might actually be more costly (note that if the 2.5 Gbps terminals are already in the network, they represent a sunk cost and might not be included in the cost analysis.)

Before optical line amplifiers were developed and deployed, higher-speed TDM-based systems were more cost-effective than WDM because the TDM systems allowed multiple lower-speed electronic regenerators at a point in the network to be replaced with a single higher-speed regenerator at that point in the network; originally, this was not the case with the WDM design. The introduction of optical line amplifiers with the ability to amplify the entire ITU grid frequencies simultaneously allows multiple lower-speed electronic regenerators at a site to be replaced with one optical amplifier, making WDM more cost-effective in this context.

10.2.2.10 DWDM Technological Advances

Modulation on a fiber in a traditional system is unipolar amplitude shift keying (ASK), which is another name for amplitude modulation (AM); in the optics world the term IM is used to describe ASK/AM. Traditional systems ASK-modulate a light beam at, for example, 1310 nm. In a simple modulation environment like IM, clock speed determines the digital throughput of the system; for example, if the clock is 2.4 GHz, then the bit rate is 2.4 Gbps. Because the optical domain is large (the infrared spectrum where telecommunications optics operates in has a bandwidth of 10^{14} Hz), one should theoretically be able to derive between 10^{14} bps and 10^{15} bps; this is between 0.5×10^5 (50,000) and 0.5×10^6 (500,000) times more than achievable on a system with a single ASK-modulated signal operating at some fixed frequency.* Hence, if one were to employ IM-based systems operating at practically spaced spectral points, one should be able to obtain additional throughput. In effect, what one wants to do is to use FDM techniques in conjunction with the digital ASK-based modulation employed at each of the frequencies. This methodology is called WDM (or DWDM when 16 or more frequencies are used).

WDM amplifier technology has improved significantly in the past few years. It is now mature and it is used in many networks. As already noted, WDM technology started with systems that carried 2, then 4, then 16, then 32, etc., light beams. Systems with 160+ channels are now available. For example, some systems could support 64 unprotected channels or 32 protected channels. A 16-channel system in essence provides a virtual 16-fiber cable, with each frequency channel serving as a unique STM–16/OC–48 carrier. Advances in aggregate bandwidth have been seen in recent years, from 400 Gbps on high-end systems evolving to 800 Gbps; near-term projections are in the terabit per second range. One also observes DWDM channel growth: whereas the current range is OC-192 (10 Gbps), the projected range is OC-768 (40 Gbps). The availability of mature supporting technologies, such as precise demultiplexers and EDFAs, has enabled DWDM with 8, 16, and even higher channel counts to be commercially delivered. These

---

* In practical terms, not the entire 10^{14} Hz spectrum can be used because of the attenuation characteristics of the fiber. Perhaps 200 nm (e.g., 1300–1400 nm and 1500–1600 nm) can be used. Noting that f = c/λ, 1300 nm equates to a frequency of 2.30×10^{14} Hz and 1400 nm equates to a frequency of 2.14×10^{14} Hz; the bandwidth is then 1.64×10^{13}, and with 1 to 10 bits per Hz, one here obtains a digital throughput of 16 to 160 Tbps. 1500 nm equates to a frequency of 2.00×10^{14} Hz and 1600 nm equates to a frequency of 1.87×10^{14} Hz; the bandwidth is then 1.25×10^{13}, and with 1 to 10 bits per Hz, one here obtains a digital throughput of 12 to 125 Tbps. Hence, the total theoretical digital throughput is around 300 Tbps, or 100,000 more than a 2.4-Gbps-based system. Another limiting issue is amplifier performance. Although no one has achieved these kinds of theoretical results, it is clear that the fiber can carry much more information than is achievable on a standard pre-DWDM system.

amplifiers support transmission of multiple OC-48 (2.4 Gbps), OC-192 (10 Gbps), and evolving OC-768* signals over conventional and (newer) NZDSF fiber. There are three primary technologies used to perform the multiplexing and demultiplexing functions: (1) thin-film filters, (2) fiber Bragg gratings, and (3) arrayed wave guides.

Transmitter modules (TxM) are responsible for sending input signals, whereas receiver modules (RxM) are responsible for receiving output signals. Each wavelength enters and leaves the DWDM system separately through Tx and Rx. TxM and RxM consist of passive and active components. The passive components (isolators, couplers, attenuators, detectors, and DWDM mux and demux components) are used to route and guide the wavelengths through the network. The active components (modulators, transmission lasers, and wavelength lockers) are used to create, modulate, or amplify the wavelengths. TxMs and RxMs can also be packaged together as a transceiver; a transceiver transports input and output light signals through the system, whereas TxM and RxM can only transport light in one direction. The most common form of DWDM uses a fiber pair—one for transmission and one for reception. Systems exist in which a single fiber is used for bidirectional traffic, but these configurations must sacrifice some fiber capacity by setting aside a guard band to prevent channel mixing; they also degrade amplifier performance, as well as reliability.

Although WDM has been a known technology for several years, its early application was restricted to providing two or four widely separated "wideband" wavelengths. During the mid-to-late 1990s, the technology evolved to the point that parallel wavelengths could be densely packed and integrated into a transmission system, with multiple signals in the 192 to 200 THz range. DWDM multiplexing and demultiplexing requires separating and combing wavelengths.

In WDM, multiple wavelengths of light carry the data channels to an optical multiplexer, where they are combined for transport over a single fiber pair. As noted earlier, essential to WDM technology is the optical amplifier, particularly for long-haul applications (typically, these amplifiers do not have uses in metro applications). Optical amplifiers maintain continuity by amplifying the multiple signals simultaneously as they travel down the fiber. The initial amplifier technology was EDFA; now new extended-band amplifiers are being studied and developed. These amplifiers carry the signal to optical demultiplexers, where they are split into the original channel. Semiconductor optical amplifies have been proposed for use in optical cross-connects for wavelength conversion in the optical domain and for amplification of a large number of ports. Support technologies include (1) optical components (mux/demux devices and dispersion compensation) and (2) design enhancements to overcome fiber nonlinearities (causes signals to be distorted in transmission). The DWDM wavelengths fall within two bands: a "blue" band between 1527.5 and 1542.5 nm and a "red" band between 1547.5 and 1561 nm. Each band is dedicated to a particular direction of transmission.

EDFA allows the following:

- Amplification in the optical domain (no optical-to-electrical-to-optical conversion required)
- Amplification of multiple signals simultaneously
- Format independence (analog, digital, pulse, etc.)

---

* 40 Gbps transmission systems are now the "next frontier" in optical communication. At the transmitter end, appropriate source modulation is critical to deal with effects such as fiber dispersion and nonlinearity. Modulation requirements for efficient transmission at 40 Gbps impact chirp, drive voltages, insertion loss, extinct ratio, power-handling capability, and wavelength dependence. Components such as LiNbO3, GaAs Polymer, and integrated electro-absorption modulators may play a role in this context.

- 20–30 dB gain and output power
- Bit-rate independence when designed for the highest bit rate
- Current bandwidth: 30 nm in the 1530–1560 nm range (80 nm in the future is possible)
- High bandwidth that can be extended with improved designs

Typical repeaters (amplifiers) enable 32 channels to be inserted and spaced 0.8 nm apart in field-deployable systems. One needs flat gain performance in the bandwidth of the amplifier, as well as high power; high power is critical in long-haul applications where one needs to transmit over long distances. Long-haul applications require periodic regeneration to ensure sufficient signal strength and quality at the receiving end. This results in substantial repeater bays adding to the total transmission system cost. Although the cost of one regenerator may appear to be small, these costs can dominate when multiplied over the total length of a route, especially for heavy routes where there might be several systems contained within the same fiber sheath.

The wavelengths of the light output by laser diodes have been chosen to minimize transmission loss across the fiber cable span and to utilize the highest sensitivity ranges of receivers. The most commonly used wavelengths employed by laser diodes are centered around 850, 1310, and 1550 nm. The ITU has recently standardized a grid of wavelengths for use in DWDM systems. This grid defines a minimum channel spacing of 100 GHz in the frequency domain corresponding to approximately 0.8 nm in the wavelength domain [ALL199701].

ITU has defined in standard G.692 a channel optical frequency grid based on 100 GHz spacing from a reference frequency of 193.1 THz = 1552.52 nm. A channel plan describes a number of factors that need to be taken into account in an optical communications network, including number of channels, channel spacings and width, and channel center wavelengths. Although this grid defines the standard, users are free to use wavelengths in arbitrary ways and to choose from any part of the spectrum. Users can also deviate from the grid by extending the upper or lower bounds or by spacing the wavelengths more closely, typically at 50 GHz, to double the number over channels.

DWDM systems with open interfaces give carriers the flexibility to support SONET/SDH, asynchronous (e.g., DS-3), ATM, Frame Relay, and other protocols over the same fiber pair. Proprietary systems, in which SONET/SDH equipment is integrated into the optical multiplexer/demultiplexer unit, are usable for simple point-to-point configurations; however, they require costly additional transmission equipment when deployed in meshed networks. DWDM systems that comply with the ITU channel plan reassure carriers that they can employ equipment from a variety of suppliers, although, generally, carriers do not mix equipment from two suppliers on the same ring, typically because of network management (and more generally, OAM&P) considerations.

As the need for expansion arises, WDM and TDM technology could be considered to reduce the number of fibers that would otherwise be required. WDM technology has traditionally been considered more expensive than TDM. One reason is that a WDM solution requires a separate SONET terminal for each channel in addition to the WDM terminal. One way to address this issue would be to retire and replace these electronic systems, assuming that they have fully depreciated. However, carriers that are bottom-line positive in financial metrics are not fond of retiring working equipment. Early deployments of WDM (in the early 1990s) were based on *wideband* technology: one terminal operates in the 1310 nm range and the other in the 1550 nm range. Although this is a cost-effective solution for applications with restricted reach (distance), wideband WDM systems, which tend to consist of little more than an optical coupler and splitter, suffer from the absence of maintenance capabilities and scalability for long-haul applications

[ALL199701]. However, if they are priced right, these WWDM (or CWDM) solutions, perhaps with some added features, may be applicable to metro applications.

More recently, *narrowband or dense WDM* systems have been deployed. With DWDM, the outputs of 2, 4, 8, 16, or more SONET terminals are optically multiplexed into one fiber pair. As noted earlier, the wavelengths used are all within the 1550 nm range to allow for optical amplification using EDFA technology to maximize reach (stated differently, the EDFA operates in this optical region). The wavelength of the optical output from a SONET network element is roughly centered at 1310 or 1550 nm with an approximate tolerance of ±20 nm. Such wavelengths would have to be so widely spaced that after optical multiplexing only a few would be within the EDFA passband. Therefore, DWDM systems must translate the output wavelength from the SONET NE to a specific, stable, and narrow-width wavelength in the 1550 nm range that can be multiplexed with other similarly constrained wavelengths. The device that does the translation function is sometimes called a *transponder*.

High-end DWDM systems are designed with extended-reach optics support for the major fiber types in use today, including non-dispersion-shifted fiber (NDSF), dispersion-shifted fiber (DSF), and NZDSF fibers (e.g., Alcatel-Lucent TrueWave™ Classic/Plus and Corning SMF-LS™/ LEAF™). Long-haul systems typically need large cabinets; this makes the systems expensive from an equipment, power, environment, space, maintenance, sparing, design, and troubleshooting point of view, limiting their applications in the metro access/metro core segment.

The original DWDM systems were optimized for long-haul interexchange applications; therefore, these WDM systems support mainly point to point or linear configurations. Although these systems provide fiber capacity relief, the management of add, drop, and pass-through traffic must be done manually. Current-generation DWDM products can perform linear ADM functions in long-haul or interexchange applications. These products also support ring topologies; ring topologies increase the reliability and the survivability of the user-level connection. Products that support ring or mesh configurations are more suited to metro applications.

Photonic networking is the next-generation application of WDM technology. Future systems providing end-to-end photonic networking will have the ability to manage individual nonfixed wavelengths utilizing tunable lasers. OADM capability offers the ability to add or drop wavelengths from a single fiber without the use of a SONET terminal. Additional flexibility will come from cross-connect capability at the optical layer (OXC), combined with DWDM and OADM functionality. Photonic networking achieves multiplexing and cross-connecting strictly in the optical domain, significantly reducing the number of back-to-back electro-optic conversions and the cost of the network. However, full photonic networking is not here today at the commercial/ deployment level: not all of the types of NEs just discussed were available or broadly deployed at press time.

Current-generation systems still lack full flexibility and affordability that is required in metro applications. Because the wavelengths that are added and dropped are fixed, there is no mechanism to increase the add/drop capacity without physically reconfiguring the system. Networking in a TDM network is provided by multiplexers, such as traditional linear and ring ADMs, and cross-connects. These NEs must convert the optical signal to an electrical signal before performing their specific function, then convert the result back to an optical signal for transmission on the next span; this back-to-back electro-optic conversion is a major cost component of these network elements.

DWDM has a number of advantages even over the latest TDM STM–64/OC–192 option. However, one needs to recognize that there are instances in which TDM may offer a better solution than DWDM. Recently introduced fiber NZDSF, for example, is flexible enough for the latest TDM equipment, but it is expensive and may limit the ability of carriers to migrate to the greater bandwidth available through DWDM at STM–16/OC–48 rates.

10.2.2.11 DWDM Advocacy for Metro Access/Metro Core

We have already hinted at the limitations of DWDM for metro applications. The following observations from a key vendor are refreshing: "Although capacity per fiber is important in the local networks, the value equation is different because the topologies and traffic patterns are more meshed, resulting in shorter spans with less capacity per span. The capacity demand is still within the realm of TDM technology and the cost advantages of optical amplification cannot be fully exploited because of the shorter distances. As such, WDM technology must bring a richer set of values to meet the diverse challenges of the local network." [ALL199701].

In long-haul networks, the major portion of the network transport cost is due to the numerous regenerators along a link (typically every 35–70 mi). Normally, not only does one need to do the amplification, but one also needs an optical-to-electrical conversion, further followed by an electrical-to-optical conversion. Utilizing optical line amplifiers reduces this cost by eliminating the back-to-back electro-optic conversion. As the cost of optical amplifier technology drops, WDM becomes increasingly more economical in long-haul networks. However, in local networks, where distances are shorter, the bulk of the core network transport cost is due to the multiplexers and cross-connects; in the *access* network it is the cost of the fiber spur. Hence, reductions in the cost of these components will prove advantageous to the bottom line. The one major factor driving the potential success of DWDM in metro access/metro core is the cost per unit (specifically per lambda) per building. The cost per lambda should be in the $2,000–10,000 range; the cost per building should be in the $10,000–20,000 range; and the system should carry 4, 8, or 16 protected lambdas (8, 16, or 32 distinct lambdas).

One key consideration must be how many broadband customers actually reside in one building. The practical answer is between two and four. Hence, the deployment of high-channel capacity WDM systems in the metro access is ineffective from a financial point of view and is an overkill. Even if one assumes that there are eight buildings on a ring and each building has three broadband customers per building that a carrier is able to bring online, it needs to be noted that the typical WAN speed today is 10–100 Mbps; this equates to a maximum 2.4 Gbps per ring, which fits very well the profile of a next-generation SONET solution. If the bandwidth need grows fourfold, an OC-192 next-generation SONET solutions would still be adequate. However, again, it is important to understand that the issue is more financial than technical: if a DWDM solution were to enjoy cost parity with a next-generation solution, then the planner would have no problem selecting the former over the latter.

The issues in metro optical networks are significantly different from those in the long haul. Whereas long-haul networks are focused on lowering the cost per bit for point-to-point transport, metro networks are more concerned with cost-effective connectivity to a multitude of endpoints (that is, connectivity to a large set of buildings), service transparency, end-user protocol support, and speed of provisioning as well as end-to-end connectivity. During the 1990s, the metro network was primarily concerned with the transport of voice-based TDM circuits (DS-1, DS-3) for private line services. In the recent past, the issues related to metro network are now how to support the emergence of data services based on IP/Ethernet and lambdas, as well as how to support the continued growth of legacy TDM. Another related issue is to how to architect the metro network to support the shift from legacy TDM to a data-centric network based on IP.

Nearly all enterprise data traffic now originates in Ethernet format (10/100/GbE), whereas the backbone is built on optical rates of 2.5 and 10 Gbps with STS-1 granularity. This is why it is important for metro WDM devices to support the data-oriented interfaces; this would not be a requirement for long-haul DWDM. On the other hand, a traditional (telco) metro optical network continues to focus primarily on legacy DS-1 and DS-3 granularity within the MAN and through to the backbone. A full-featured metro WDM must support both the traditional interfaces as well as the new data interfaces. Enterprise routers currently do support direct OC-3c, OC-12c, and OC-48c/192c WAN links. These private line interfaces on end-user equipment (that is, on intranet routers) are widely deployed because of their ubiquitous deployment throughout metro optical networks (e.g., extensive deployment of SONET transport and cross-connects). However, this comes at a cost: high-end SONET plug-ins can cost upward of $50,000. Therefore, it is desirable to include these interfaces in the NE, because of the economies of scale that can be secured by network providers, which can then be passed on to the enterprise user.

Equipment vendors working on WDM are realizing that data-oriented services are now consuming more network capacity than voice, because of increasing numbers of users and escalating capacity demands from each user. The protocols, bit rates, and interfaces used by the enterprise networks that support these applications are different from those used in the carrier networks. The former are increasingly Ethernet-based; the latter are typically OC-x based. Conversion between the two domains is needed. This conversion can be done by the user and would have to be done at multiple places where the enterprise network touches the carrier's network; or, better yet, it could be done by the carrier on behalf of the user. One example may suffice: carriers have come to realize that it is better to carry voice over distances in digital format. However, the network does not impose that requirement on the user: all residential users generate analog voice over their telephone handsets and the network adapts the user's signal into a digital signal that is better suited for network handling. Similarly, because all enterprise networks are now based on Ethernet/IP/TCP technology, it would be preferable for the carrier's network to accept this handoff and then convert it, if necessary, to a SONET/WDM format. Because Ethernet interfaces are very cost-effective for the end user compared to traditional WAN interfaces, TLS-based services (supported by Ethernet-ready edge NEs) would be an attractive offering to corporations. They also save costs for the network provider by eliminating adaptation functions to ATM; although ATM can support speeds of tens of Mbps, it does not support interfaces operating at 1 or 10 Gbps equally well. Native data interfaces for other protocols on edge NEs, such as ESCON or FICON, would provide similar values depending on user-specific requirements.

At the end of the day, however, native data interfaces are not necessarily intrinsic to WDM only. As noted earlier, next-generation SONET aims at supporting these same interfaces. Hence, the choice between WDM and next-generation SONET is really (beyond initial cost) a traffic engineering consideration: how much growth can be anticipated in a metro access subnetwork.

By deploying a WDM-based photonic network, the service provider gains an access or inter-office transport infrastructure that is flexible and scalable. However, planners need to ascertain that what could turn out to be a high NE cost does not become multiplicative and all 8, 16, or 32 buildings on the ring are each forced to incur a high nodal cost. Although a long-haul network may be a 2-point link, or at most be a ring/mesh with a half-a-dozen or so high-capacity points (say, in several states), metro access rings typically have a larger number of nodes on them, unless a nonredundant building access is utilized. A 16-building access ring using next-generation SONET with a $30,000 device would cost the provider $480,000 in nodal equipment; a ring using DWDM with a $60,000 device would cost the provider $960,000.

There are certain key OAM&P implications for metro core WDM networks as well. At this time long-haul applications do not require dynamic management of individual wavelengths. Therefore, one optical surveillance channel carried on a dedicated wavelength is sufficient to control and monitor all remote WDM network elements such as optical line amplifiers. Photonic networks in metropolitan access and interoffice applications manage individual wavelengths. Because individual wavelengths have different endpoints and take different paths across the network, one optical surveillance channel carried on a separate wavelength is not sufficient. Fault information is required for, and must accompany, each wavelength. Per-wavelength fault information is needed for fault detection and isolation, which are necessary to support survivability mechanisms and trigger fast maintenance and repair.actions. In photonic networks, service providers can also verify the connectivity and monitor the performance of each connection [ALL199701].

Proponents make the case that with metro DWDM, user requests for increased bandwidth or different protocols can be filled quickly, so the network provider can realize increased revenue. This may be true in the metro core network, but is unlikely that it can be achieved in general in the metro access. New services such as optical-channel leased lines that provide end-to-end protocol and bit-rate independent connections can be offered, affording new revenue for the network provider. In WDM-based photonic networks, transport interfaces that are specific to protocol and bit rates are no longer required, minimizing the network provider's inventory and operating costs.

On the other hand, it is important to keep in mind that the market for traditional handoff from intranet routers will continue to exist for many years. The camp that supports native data interfaces asks the following rhetorical question: "Given that WAN traffic from the enterprise into the metro network is primarily Ethernet data today and likely to continue to dominate in the future, should the conventional view that legacy private lines services are the most efficient means for metro optical networking be challenged?" In the long term (three to five years out) metro optical networking based on Ethernet native LAN interfaces is likely to become common. This is because there is additional cost for Ethernet router vendors to adapt native data interfaces into private line interfaces (DS-1, DS-3, and OC-N) using what is referred to as "telecom adapters." The additional cost translates into private line interfaces costing as much as 3 to 4 times higher than native LAN interfaces (100BaseT and GbE). In addition, the cost of GbE interfaces is expected to drop rapidly as their deployment rises in enterprise networks. Bandwidth growth has been limited to private-line-like bandwidth increments such as DS-1, DS-3, or OC-x. Because these private line interfaces are provisioned as physical connections from the customer premises onto the metro network, incremental bandwidth needs require new physical connections to be established. However, as noted earlier, the reality is that the legacy interfaces will be around for a number of years. Clearly, most carriers have invested billions of dollars in SONET optical products, ATM switches, and DCS cross-connects; hence, they are highly motivated to price and design these services right, to achieve a return on their investment, particularly in the new telecom economics market. Eventually, carriers will migrate to new technologies; the challenge is how to make a graceful migration from the embedded network to a network based on data-oriented interfaces.

10.2.2.12 Coarse Wavelength Division Multiplexing

CWDM appears to be a reasonably good technology for metro access applications if certain extensions are developed by the vendors. In principle, CDWM can be used by metropolitan area carriers that wish to keep the cost-per-building low, so that they can turn a positive net bottom line [DRI200101]. Prima facie, CDWM technology may be used effectively until either (1) the cost of

DWDM remains higher than that of CWDM, or (2) the bandwidth requirement per enterprise building exceeds 10, 40, or 320 Gbps. Unless the cost of DWDM comes down significantly, CWDM has a window of opportunity for the foreseeable future in the metro access/metro core space. It is going to be a challenge to deploy a bottom-line positive metro access metro core operation; among other things, the cost per building has to be kept low. Optical equipment vendors that have developed long-haul DWDM equipment will find that they cannot simply relabel the product by taking a "long-haul DWDM" system and repainting the word "metro" over "long-haul" to secure a cost-effective "metro DWDM" product. However, some advancements are going to be needed before CWDM technology becomes poised for wide-scale deployment. In particular, it is crucial that CWDM systems be enhanced with strong network management/OSS tools, so that networks based on these NEs can be cost-effectively supported in terms of provisioning, alarming, and fault restoration.

CWDM is an implementation of WDM technology that is applicable to metro access applications, as well as short- to medium-haul networks. Because CWDM uses low-cost, uncooled lasers and wide-band multiplexers and demultiplexers instead of the more expensive cooled lasers found in standard DWDM systems, it provides a much more affordable solution.

Typically, there is no (immediate) need for 32 channels in the access network. From a power budget point of view, designers may want to limit themselves to 8 (or 16) buildings per ring. Utilizing 32 lambdas would equate to 4 lambdas per building. Providing 40 Gbps (4 × 10 Gbps) or 10 Gbps (4 × 2.5 Gbps) is currently an overkill; this simply builds an expensive and non-revenue-producing "inventory" of capacity that will not be able to be utilized (in a profitable manner) for the foreseeable future. Therefore, it makes sense to provide an inexpensive way for carriers to use WDM. Low-cost transceiver optics, along with inexpensive passive components for CWDM using 8 channels, 12 channels, or 16 channels, make this approach a viable solution. As noted earlier, however, one of the critical issues yet to be fully addressed is OAM&P support: unfortunately, CWDM technology has not yet developed to the point where (1) a well-recognized architecture for "standard" deployment exists, and (2) a set of operational disciplines in the OAM&P context (supported by feature-rich OSSs) exists. Hence, the de facto alternative to CWDM-based metropolitan systems, at this time, is next-generation SONET.

CWDM and DWDM differ noticeably in the spacing between adjacent wavelengths. DWDM packs many channels into a small usable spectrum, spacing them 1 to 2 nm apart; DWDM systems support a high channel count, but also require expensive cooling equipment and independent lasers and modulators to ensure that adjacent channels do not interfere. CWDM systems, on the other hand, use 10 to 25 nm spacings, with 1300 or 850 nm lasers that drift less than 0.1 nm/C. This low drift eliminates the need for cooling equipment, which, in turn, reduces the total system cost. As a result, CWDM systems support less total bandwidth than DWDM systems, but with 8 to 16 channels, each operating between 155 Mbps and 3.125 Gbps (and soon 10 Gbps), these systems can deliver bandwidths ranging from 1 Gbps to over 100 Gbps [CIS200201]. Typical systems support eight wavelengths, data rates up to 2.5 Gbps per wavelength, and distances up to 50 km.

CWDM uses lasers with a wide channel wavelength spacing. In contrast, DWDM, which is widely used in long-haul networks and some metro core networks (particularly those with large diameters), uses lasers with much narrower wavelength spacing, typically 0.8 or 0.4 nm. The wide channel spacing of CWDM means a lower system cost can be achieved. This lower equipment cost is the result of a lower transmitter cost (because no temperature and wavelength control is needed), as well as a lower optical mux/demux cost (due to wider tolerance on the wavelength stability and bandwidth).

Table 10.3 Key Parameters for a Typical CWDM System

CWDM Series		Unit
Center Wavelength λ_c	1471.0, 1491.0, 1511.0, 1531.0, 1551.0, 1571.0, 1591.0, 1611.0	nm
Passband Bandwidth	$\lambda_c \pm 6.5$	nm
Insertion Loss	<4.5	dB
In-Band Ripple	<0.5	dB
Polarization Dependent Loss (PDL)	<0.1	dB
Adjacent Band Isolation	>25	dB
Return Loss without Connectors	>45	dB
Directivity	>55	dB
Operating Power	300	mW
Operating Temperature	0–70	°C
Storage Temperature	40–85	°C
Fiber Type	Coming SMF-28	
Fiber Package	900 µm loose tube	

Table 10.3 depicts key parameters for a typical CWDM system. The pragmatic bottom line is that the opportunity to add two to eight wavelengths per fiber in metro/short-haul applications allows network designers to increase capacity without installing costly DWDM systems.

CWDM represents significant costs savings—from 25% to 50% at the component level over DWDM, both for equipment OEMs and service providers. CWDM products cost about $3500 per wavelength. That is half the price of its regular product, which typically sells for $7500 per wavelength. Traditional CWDM only scales to about eight wavelengths, but for metro access applications, this may be adequate. Also, vendors have found ways to combine CWDM with its regular DWDM blades that allow the system to scale up to 20 wavelengths. CWDM system architecture can benefit the metro access market because it takes advantage of the inherent natural properties of the optical devices and eliminates the need to artificially control the component characteristics.

The typical CWDM optical elements are as follows:

CWDM Uncooled Coaxial Lasers: Distributed-feedback multiquantum well (DFB/MQW) lasers are often used in CWDM systems. These lasers typically come in eight wavelengths and feature a 13 nm bandwidth. Wavelength drift is typically only 5 nm under normal office conditions (say, with a 50°C total temperature delta), making temperature compensation unnecessary. For additional cost savings, the lasers do not require external gratings or other filters to achieve CDWM operation. They are available with or without an integral isolator.

CWDM Transmitters/Receivers: OC-48 CWDM transmitters typically use an uncooled DFB laser diode and are pigtailed devices in a standard 24-pin DIP package. Six to eight channels are supported (six channels: 1510 to 1610 nm; two additional channels are located at 1470 and at 1490 nm.) The OC-48 receiver typically uses an APD photodetector, has a built-in DC-DC converter, and employs a PLL for clock recovery. Transmission distances of up to 50 km are achievable with these modules.

CWDM Wavelength-Division Multiplexers/Demultiplexers: These come in four- or eight-channel modules, typically use thin-film filters optimized for CWDM applications, with filtering bands matched to the CWDM wavelengths. Filters need to feature low insertion loss and high isolation between adjacent channels.

CWDM Optical Add/Drop Modules (OADMs): These are available in various configurations with one, two, or four add and drop channels using the same thin-film filters as the CWDM mux and demux modules.

DWDM* systems typically use wavelength separations of 200 GHz (1.6 nm), 100 GHz (0.8 nm), or 50 GHz (0.4 nm), with future systems projected to have even narrower spacing at 25 GHz or less. The operating wavelengths of DWDM systems are defined according to a standardized frequency/wavelength grid developed by the ITU, which was discussed in the previous chapter.

DFB lasers are used as sources in DWDM systems. The laser wavelength drifts about 0.08 nm/degree centigrade with temperature. DFB lasers are cooled to stabilize the wavelength from drifting outside the passband of the multiplexer and demultiplexer filters as the temperature fluctuates in DWDM systems. CWDM systems use DFB lasers that are not cooled. They are specified to operate from 0 to 70°C, with the laser wavelength drifting only about 5–6 nm over this range (e.g., 0.1 nm/C). This wavelength drift coupled with the variation in laser wavelength of up to ±3 nm due to laser die manufacturing processes yields a total wavelength variation of about 12 nm. The optical filter passband and laser channel spacing must be wide enough to accommodate the wavelength variation of the uncooled lasers in CWDM systems. Channel spacing in these systems is typically 20 nm with a channel bandwidth of 13 nm. CWDM systems offer some key advantages over DWDM systems for applications that require channel counts on the order of 16 or less. These benefits include costs, power requirements, and size.

The cost difference between CWDM and DWDM systems can be attributed to hardware and operating costs. Although DWDM lasers are more expensive than CWDM lasers, the cooled DFB lasers provide cost-effective solutions for long-haul transport and large metro rings requiring high capacity. In both of these applications, the cost of the DWDM systems is amortized over the large number of customers served by these systems. Metro access networks, on the other hand, require lower-cost and lower-capacity systems to meet market requirements, which are based largely on what the customer is willing to pay for broadband services.

The price of DWDM transceivers is typically four to five times more expensive than that of their CWDM counterparts. The higher DWDM transceiver costs are attributed to a number of factors related to the lasers. The manufacturing wavelength tolerance of a DWDM laser die compared to a CWDM die is a key factor. Typical wavelength tolerances for DWDM lasers are on the order of ± 0.1 nm; whereas manufacturing wavelength tolerances for CWDM laser die are ± 2 to 3 nm. Lower die yields thus drive up the costs of DWDM lasers relative to CWDM lasers. In addition, packaging DWDM laser die for temperature stabilization is more expensive than the uncooled CWDM coaxial laser packaging.

The cost difference between DWDM and the CWDM multiplexers and demultiplexers, based on thin-film filter technology contributes to lower overall system costs in favor of CWDM as well. CWDM filters are inherently less expensive to manufacture than the DWDM filters because of the fewer number of layers in the filter design. Typically, there are approximately 150 layers for a 100 GHz filter design used in DWDM systems, whereas there are approximately 50 layers in a 20 nm CWDM filter. The result is higher manufacturing yields for CWDM filters: specifically, production of three times as many CWDM devices when the alignment tolerances are relaxed relative to those for DWDM devices. The CWDM filter costs about 50% less than the DWDM filter,

---

* Most of the rest of this section is based on [NEB200201].

and, the cost is projected to drop by a factor of three in the next two to three years as automated manufacturing takes hold. The adoption of new filter and multiplexing/demultiplexing technologies is expected to decrease costs even further.

The operating costs of optical transport systems depend on maintenance and power. Although maintenance costs are assumed to be comparable for both CWDM and DWDM systems, the power requirements for DWDM are significantly higher. For example, DWDM lasers are temperature-stabilized with Peltier coolers integrated into their module package. The cooler along with the associated monitor and control circuitry consumes around 4 W per wavelength. Meanwhile, an uncooled CWDM laser transmitter uses about 0.5 W of power. The transmitters in an eight-channel CWDM system consume approximately 4 W of power, whereas the same functionality in a DWDM system can consume up to 30 W. As the number of wavelengths in DWDM systems increase along with transmission speeds, power and the thermal management associated with them become a critical issue for board designers. The lower power requirement resulting from the use of uncooled lasers in CWDM systems has positive financial implications for system operators. For example, the cost of battery backup is a major consideration in the operation of transport equipment. Minimizing operating power and the costs associated with its backup, whether in a central office or a wiring closet, reduces operating costs.

CWDM lasers are significantly smaller than DWDM lasers. Uncooled lasers are typically constructed with a laser die and monitor photodiode mounted in a hermetically sealed container with a glass window. These containers are aligned with a fiber pigtail or an alignment sleeve that accepts a connector. The container plus sleeve forms a cylindrical package called a Transmitter Optical Subassembly (TOSA). A typical TOSA is approximately 2 cm long and 0.5 cm in diameter. Cooled lasers are offered in either a butterfly or dual inline laser package and contain the laser die, monitor photodiode, thermistor, and Peltier cooler. These lasers are about 4 cm long, 2 cm high, and 2 cm wide. These devices are almost always pigtailed, requiring fiber management, a heat sink, and corresponding monitor and control circuitry. The size of a DWDM laser transmitter typically occupies about five times the volume of a CWDM transmitter.

CWDM systems supporting two to eight wavelengths have been commercially available for some time. Newer systems now scale to 16 wavelengths in the 1290–1610 nm spectrum. Today, most CWDM systems are based on 20 nm channel spacing from 1470 to 1610 nm with some development occurring in the 1300 nm window for 10 GbE. With conventional fiber, wavelengths in the 1400 nm region suffer higher optical loss owing to the attenuation peak caused by residual water present in most of the installed fiber today. Although this additional loss can limit system performance for longer links, it is not an obstacle to CWDM deployment in most metro access spans. New fiber that eliminates the "water attenuation peak" is offered by at least two of the primary fiber vendors for use in metro links with loss budgets that mandate lower fiber attenuation. EWB fibers will easily support 16 channels, whereas conventional SMF easily supports 12 channels.

CWDM systems development and standards efforts come at a critical time for metro access service providers. Work is under way for the transport plane, but additional work is needed in the management plane, as noted earlier. One organization working to define standards for CWDM systems in the 1400 nm region is the Commercial Interest Group (CIG). CIG participants include component suppliers, system vendors, and service providers. The groups' focus to date has been primarily on defining the CWDM wavelength grid and investigating the cost/performance comparisons of DWDM versus CWDM architectures. The CWDM wavelength grid under consideration for proposal is divided into three bands. The "O-Band" consists of 1290, 1310, 1330, and 1350 nm. The "E-Band" consists of 1380, 1400, 1420, and 1440 nm. The "S+C+L-Band" consists of eight wavelengths from 1470 to 1610 nm in 20 nm increments. These wavelengths take advantage of the full optical-fiber spectrum, including the legacy optical sources at 1310, 1510, and 1550 nm, while maximizing the number of channels. The 20 nm channel spacing supports lower component costs with the use of uncooled lasers and wideband filter. It also avoids the high-loss 1270 wavelength and maintains a 30 nm gap for adjacent band isolation [GEO200101].

10.2.2.13 All-Optical Networks

At the beginning of this decade there was a lot of fanfare about the Optical Transport Network (OTN) and the companion Automatic Switched Optical Network (ASON). The OTN is intended to be an evolution of the carrier's network plant. OTN addresses the requirements of next-generation networks that have a goal of efficiently transporting data-oriented traffic. OTN is designed for the transmission of multiple wavelengths per fiber, which is characteristic DWDM systems; SONET was developed to handle one optical signal per physical channel. At the same time, a need has emerged of late for networks capable of transporting a variety of heterogeneous types of signals directly over wavelengths carried on the same optical backbone. This need is in fact addressed by the OTN.

In the early 2000s, the ITU reached agreement on several new standards for next-generation optical networks capable of transporting transparent wavelength services, SONET/SDH services, and data streams (Ethernet, Fibre Channel, ATM, Frame Relay, and IP). The new standards provide the ability to combine multiple client signals within a wavelength, to facilitate optimal utilization of transport capacity, and to realize improved cost-effectiveness of transport capacity, while allowing switching at service rates of 2.5, 10, and 40 Gbps. The new standards also specify optical equipment functions such as performance monitoring, fault isolation, and alarming. ITU Recommendations G.709 and G.872 define an OTN consisting of optical channels within an optical multiplex section layer, within an optical transmission section layer network; the optical channels are the individual light paths (beams). OTN makes use of a data plane (transport layer) and a control plane (signaling and management layer).

Existing TDM SONET/SDH networks were originally designed for voice and medium-speed leased line (point-to-point dedicated) services. In some instances (e.g., outermost edges of the network), the growing trend of data traffic could pose some technical challenges to TDM SONET/SDH networks, especially in relation to the bursty and asymmetrical nature of such traffic (however, one needs to keep in mind that in the core of a large data/IP network like the Internet or a corporate intranet backbone, contrary to trade press assertions, data traffic is neither bursty nor asymmetric.) At the same time, DWDM technology, which was initially introduced to increase transport capacity, is currently available for implementing advanced optical networking functionality. The existing carrier transport networks are expected to evolve to next-generation optical networks; the expectation is that these networks will fulfill new emerging requirements such as fast and automatic end-to-end provisioning, optical rerouting and restoration, support of multiple clients and client types, and interworking of IP-based and optical networks. A mechanism that supports an IP over OTN protocol stack (and the underlying communications infrastructure) is a candidate for providing high bandwidth on demand and flexible, scalable support for QoS for transmission of multimedia services with low jitter, latency, and loss [NAT200301].

OTN makes use of an optical channel layer: each wavelength λ is wrapped in an envelope that consists of a header (for overhead bytes) and a trailer (for FEC functions.) The payload section allows for existing network protocols to be mapped (wrapped), thus making OTN protocol independent. OTN NEs can receive, generate, and transmit management and control information throughout the network, making performance monitoring and other network management possible on a per-λ basis. The FEC supports error detection and correction (unlike SONET's simple error monitoring, FEC has intrinsic mechanisms to correct errors and achieve BER levels of 10^{-12}–10^{-15}).

OTN is composed of a set of optical NEs, specifically OXCs, interconnected by optical fiber links, that are able to provide functionality of transport, multiplexing, routing, management, supervision, and survivability of optical channels carrying client signals. OXCs switch wavelength channels between their input and output fibers, and are used to establish optical paths. The OTN provides the ability to route wavelengths, and therefore, when deployed in a ring topology, it has the same survivability capabilities as SONET/SDH rings. Furthermore, the OTN has the ability to improve survivability by reducing the number of electro-optical network elements; these elements are, in principle, prone to failures.

The OTN is designed to provide a cost-effective, high-capacity, survivable, and flexible transport infrastructure. The elimination of multiple service network overlays and the elimination of fine-granularity sublayers implies a reduction in the number and types of NEs and a concomitant reduction in capital and operating costs for the network provider.

The optical transport functions include the following:

- Multiplexing functions
- Cross-connect function, including grooming and configuration
- Management functions, and
- Physical media functions

A distinguishing characteristic of the OTN is its ability to transport any digital signal, independent of client-specific aspects (making it protocol agnostic). The flexibility of OTN is built on the protocol and bit-rate independence of the information-carrying optical beams in the fiber waveguide. This transparency enables the OTN to carry many different types of traffic over an optical channel regardless of the protocol (GbE, 10 GbE, ATM, SONET, etc.) or bit-rate (155 Mbps, 1.25 Gbps, 2.5 Gbps, and so on). GFP provides a means for packing nonvoice traffic into a SONET or OTN frame. A virtual concatenation mechanism called the Link Capacity Adjustment Scheme (LCAS) provides additional flexibility. With conformant implementation, interworking between equipment from different vendors is achievable.

In OTN there are two networks layers: an optical network layer and the user's network layer. Routers, switches, and other equipment that comprise the user's network establish connections over the underlying network through User Network Interfaces (UNIs) (also known as Client Network Interface (CNI)). In the ITU-T model the network consist of clients; clients may be multiplexers, DWDM systems, an Ethernet switches, or other devices. Clients connect into the network through one of three types of network interfaces: UNIs, external-network-to-network interfaces (E-NNIs), and internal-network-to-network interfaces (I-NNIs):

- The UNI specifies how users can access the providers' networks; only the basic information is transferred over this interface, namely, the name and address of the endpoint, authentication and admission control of the client, and connection service messages.
- Service providers are required to share more information within their domains and between the different providers. E-NNIs support the exchange of reachability information, authentication and admission control information, and connection service information.

■ The I-NNIs enable devices to get the topology or routing information for the carrier's network along with connection service information necessary to optionally control network resources. Devices within the optical network rely on I-NNIs to access network information.

As is the case in SONET, OTN defines a network hierarchy, here known as the Optical Transport Hierarchy (OTH). OTH's basic unit, the Optical Transport Module (OTM), supports higher transport data rates by bundling together wavelengths; OTMs can span multiple wavelengths of different carrying capacities (by contrast, to support higher speeds SONET's STS-1s are concatenated at the electrical level).

Clients can request three types of circuits via the interfaces defined earlier, as follows:

■ *Provisioned circuits* (also called hard-permanent circuits): These are basically a "leased line" service. Through the use of a network management station or a manual process, each NE along a required path is configured with the required information to establish a connection between two endpoints.
■ *Signaled circuits*: These are established dynamically by the endpoint that requests connectivity and bandwidth. To establish a connection with an endpoint, these types of connections require network-addressing information.
■ *Hybrid connections*: These circuits have provisioned connections into the Automatic Switched Transport Network (ASTN), but then rely on switched connections within the ASTN to connect with other end nodes (these connections are also known as Soft Provisioned Connections [SPCs]). To the end node an SPC and a regular permanent circuit appear identical.

One of the major advantages of OTN is its backward-compatible formulation, specifically, support for existing SONET/SDH protocols without changing the format, bit rate, or timing. The OTN allows transmission of different data packet types using the new GFP mapping; this mapping reduces the protocol layers between the fiber and the IP layer and thus much efficient use of bandwidth. The mapping capability advantages position the OTN as a protocol-agnostic carrier allowing service transparency for SDH/SONET, Ethernet, ATM, IP, MPLS, and other protocols/clients.

To achieve the design goals of seamless restorability, uniform grade of service, and bandwidth optimization, standards are needed. ITU-T Recommendations G.872, G.709, and G.959.1, the initial set of standards in the OTN series approved at the turn of the decade, address the OTN architecture, interface frame format, and physical layer interfaces, respectively. This work is carried out by Study Group 15 of the ITU. The ITU-T G.709, *Network Node Interface for the Optical Transport Network*, provides the basic standard specification for OTN. OTN elements' transport of a client signal over an optical channel is based on the digital signal wrapping technique defined in the ITU-T G.709 recommendation; the wrapper provides transmission protection using FEC. The OTN architecture is further defined under ITU-T G.872, *Architecture of Optical Transport Networks*. By complying with ITU-T G.709, network nodes from various vendors can interoperate, although in actual practice carriers rarely if ever mix transport equipment from two vendors. OTN provides carrier-class robustness.

In addition to basic transport, there is also interest in real-time provisioning of λs. ITU-T has grouped these new signaling architectures into two protocol-independent framework models: the general ASTN and the more specific ASON. Bandwidth-on-demand (also called *instant provisioning* by some) requires a signaling protocol to set up the paths or connections. Work on signaling is being defined in the ASTN and ASON specifications. The Optical Internetworking Forum

(OIF) has taken the ITU-T ASTN and ASON models and extended the signaling capabilities of the IETF's GMPLS.

In what follows, a more detailed survey of key recommendations is provided. OTN-related recommendations developed by the study group include the following:

- G.709, "Network node interface for the Optical Transport Network (OTN)" (February 2000, Amendment 1: Nov 2001.) (This recommendation is also referred to as Y.1331, and is being renumbered G.7090) This recommendation provides the requirements for the OTH signals at the Network Node Interface, in terms of the following:
- Definition of an Optical Transport Module of order *n* (OTM-n)
- Structures for an OTM-n
- Formats for mapping and multiplexing client signals
- Functionality of the overheads

An amendment to Recommendation G.709 entitled "Interfaces for Optical Transport Networks" describes the mappings for TDM-multiplexed signals in the OTN, as well as extensions to allow even higher-bit-rate signals to be carried using virtual concatenation.

- ITU-T Recommendation G.7041/Y.1303, "Generic Framing Procedure (GFP)," specifies interface mapping and equipment functions for carrying packet-oriented payloads including IP/PPP, Ethernet, Fibre Channel, and ESCON (Enterprise Systems Connection)/FICON (Fiber Connection) over optical and other transport networks. This recommendation, together with ITU-T Recommendation G.709 on Interfaces for Optical Transport Networks, provides the full set of mappings necessary to carry IP traffic over DWDM systems.
- ITU-T Recommendation G.7710/Y.1701, "Common Equipment Management Function Requirements," is a generic equipment management recommendation, and was derived from knowledge gained through the development of SONET and SDH equipment management recommendations. This recommendation provides the basis for management of equipment for new transport network technologies, including the optical transport network.
- G.871, "Framework of Optical Transport Network Recommendations," October 2000, provides a framework for coordination among the various activities in ITU-T on OTN, to ensure that recommendations covering the various aspects of OTN be developed in a consistent manner. As such, this recommendation provides references for definitions of high-level characteristics of OTN, along with a description of the relevant ITU-T Recommendations that were expected to be developed, together with the timeframe for their development. This is also numbered Y.1301.
- G.872, "Architecture of Optical Transport Network" (February 1999, Revision November 2001), describes the functional architecture of OTNs using the modeling methodology described in ITU-T G.805. The OTN functionality is described from a network-level viewpoint, taking into account an optical network-layered structure, client characteristic information, client/server layer associations, networking topology, and layer network functionality providing optical signal transmission, multiplexing, routing, supervision, performance assessment, and network survivability. This recommendation is limited to the functional description of OTNs that support digital signals. The support of analog or mixed digital/analog signals is not included. A revision includes (among other features), the ability to support TDM signals over the OTN.

- ITU-T Recommendation G.798, "Characteristics of Optical Transport Network Hierarchy Equipment Functional Blocks," specifies the characteristics of OTN equipment, including supervision, information flow, processes, and functions to be performed by this equipment.
- ITU-T Recommendation G.8251, "The Control of Jitter and Wander within the Optical Transport Network," includes the network limits for jitter and wander, as well as jitter and wander tolerances required of equipment for OTNs. These parameters relate to the variability of the bit rate of signals carried over the optical transport network.
- ITU-T Recommendation G.874, "Management Aspects of the Optical Transport Network Element," specifies applications, functions, and requirements for managing optical networking equipment utilizing operations support systems (OSSs). It covers the areas of configuration management, fault management, and performance management for client optical network elements.
- ITU-T Recommendation G.874.1, "Optical Transport Network Protocol-Neutral Management Information Model for the Network Element View," provides a means to ensure consistency among the models for OTN equipment for specific management protocols, including CMISE (Common Management Information Service Element), CORBA (Common Object Request Broker Architecture), and SNMP (Simple Network Management Protocol).

At face value it is desirable to migrate to a single infrastructure, to reduce OAM&P costs. This is the goal of OTN. The move to this next target, however, will not happen overnight. Field trials of OTN supporting over 1 Tbps (40 Gbps × 25 light beams) were already underway at the time of publication. It is not clear when OTN-based technology will be deployed in the United States on a broad scale, but a 2013-or-beyond expectation would not be totally unreasonable.

While waiting for deployment of the OTN, enterprise users will continue to have access to SONET-based services. Although carrying data traffic across an access ring SONET link is not bandwidth-efficient on that initial edge ring, it is all relative: this is not different from when a user gets a T1 tail (1.544 Mbps) to support a 384 kbps fractional T1 line or a frame relay circuit with a 64 kbps Committed Information Rate (CIR). This is why there is grooming, where outer-edge traffic is repacked into multiplexed links of higher payload concentration. Carriers build networks using hierarchical sets of rings, not one giant ring that spans a metropolitan area. Ignoring the fact that bandwidth may, in fact, be a commodity at this juncture, virtual concatenation mechanisms have been developed of late to enable channels in SONET to be combined to support improved efficiencies. At a grooming point in the network, Ethernet streams, for example, could be multiplexed and carried across VT1.5-6v (10.368 Mbps) links instead of an STS-1 link; similarly, 100 Mbps Ethernet links could be multiplexed and carried across an STS-2c (103.68 Mbps) link instead of an STS-3c (155.520 Mbps) link.

10.2.2.14 Automatically Switched Optical Networks

Developers have argued that it would, in principle, be useful to have the ability for the end user to set up optical connections from and to various points in the network, in real-time and as needed. The ASTN/ASON mechanisms discussed here aim at providing the OTN with an intelligent optical control plane for dynamic network provisioning; subtending capabilities include network survivability, protection, and restoration. ASTN specifications have been under development in the ITU in the recent past, and were being positioned as the global framework for intelligent optical networking. The architectural choices for the interaction between IP and optical network layers, particularly the routing and signaling aspects, are key to the successful deployment of next-generation networks [ABO200201].

As we have seen, with today's DWDM technology the capacity of a single fiber can be increased 160-fold compared with a typical approach. DWDM, however, does not hold the ultimate solution to address bandwidth demand. Carrier-grade standards-supported work for next-target (next-generation) intelligent optical networks has been undertaken under the ASTN and ASON specifications of the ITU-T. The ASTN/ASON construct aims at providing the OTN with an intelligent optical control plane incorporating dynamic network provisioning, along with mechanisms for network survivability, protection, and restoration. In effect, a hierarchy has been built with fibers at the bottom, followed by groups of λs, individual λs, SONET/SDH tributaries, and packet-switch-capable connections at the top. As connections are established at each level of the hierarchy, they need to be propagated to other NEs in the system to establish higher-level connections. Dynamic routing necessitates information exchange between neighboring nodes to support the discovery of topology information; to achieve this, the out-of-band control plane is augmented with a link layer node-to-node protocol. The ASTN/ASON model is based on mesh network architectures; mesh topologies are now, in fact, being deployed by service providers. The ASTN/ASON specifications are framework models and they are protocol independent, but they do require a choice of protocols to operate, such as GMPLS.

The ASON family of standards from ITU-T Study Group 15 builds on OTN standards completed earlier in the decade. The deployment of an ASTN/ASON-enabled infrastructure enables carriers to support circuit provisioning in relatively short times, e.g., minutes; to have dynamic restoration and resiliency; to achieve flexible service selection and dynamic resource allocation; and to provide interdomain, intercarrier QoS. In certain ways, the ASTN/ASON model is relatively traditional (evolutionary) and incorporates aspects of other network technologies, such as the PSTN and ATM, (although GMPLS is based on IP specifications).

Proponents claim that these new standards can create business opportunities for network operators and service providers, giving them the means to deliver end-to-end, managed bandwidth services efficiently, expediently, and at reduced operational cost. ASON standards can also be implemented to add dynamic capabilities to new optical networks or established SONET/SDH networks. Service provider benefits could include the following:

- Increased revenue-generating capabilities through fast turn-up and rapid provisioning, as well as wavelength-on-demand services to increase capacity and flexibility
- Increased return on capital from cost-effective and survivable architectures that help protect current and future network investments from forecast uncertainties
- Reduced operations cost through more accurate inventory and topology information, resource optimization, and automated processes that eliminate manual steps

ASON control mechanisms provide support for both switched wavelength and subwavelength connection services in OTNs to provide bandwidth on demand. Wavelength connection services make use of an entire optical wavelength (e.g., at 1550 nm), whereas subwavelength services use a channel within a wavelength.

The ASON control mechanisms also enable fast optical *restoration*. Traditionally, transport networks have used protection rather than restoration to provide reliability for connections; with protection, connections are moved to dedicated or shared routes in the event of a failure of a fiber or network equipment. With restoration, the endpoints can reestablish the connection through an alternative route as soon as a loss of the original connection is detected. Restoration provides a functional advantage for carriers because it makes better use of the network capacity, and, with a control plane signaling standard, it can be performed faster than with restoration systems available today.

An ASON infrastructure is fairly complex, with major NE-to-NE real-time interactions required. Therefore, it is critical that standards be available. ASON architecture defines a set of reference points (interfaces) that allows ASON clients to request network services across those reference points. The protocols that run over ASON interfaces are not specified in the basic ASON specifications [MAY200101,MAY200102]. IP-based protocols such as GMPLS can be considered so that the ASON/ASTN work can benefit from the protocol design work done by the IETF [ABO200201]. The ASON model distinguishes reference points (representing points of protocol information exchange) defined (1) between an administrative domain and a user also known as UNI, (2) between (and when needed within) administrative domains also known as external network-network interface (E-NNI), and (3) between areas of the same administrative domain and when needed between control components (or simply controllers) within areas also known as internal network–network interface (I-NNI) [ALA200301]. Clients (e.g., end-user routers) can request three different types of circuits over the UNI using a signaling protocol: provisioned, signaled, and hybrid.

To realize the ASTN/ASON, signaling standards are needed. GMPLS and OIF Optical User-to-Network Interface (O-UNI) were considered by the ITU-T in the early part of the decade; the ITU-T, however, has also considered alternative proposals to these, including a modified form of the signaling and routing mechanisms used by ATM's private network-to-network interface (PNNI). The GMPLS suite of protocol provides support for controlling different switching technologies or applications. These include support for requesting TDM connections, including SONET/SDH (see ANSI T1.105 and ITU-T G.707, respectively), as well as OTN (see ITU-T G.709); furthermore, it can be used to support the ASON control plane (as defined in G.8080) and ASON routing requirements (as identified in G.7715) [ALA200301]. GMPLS is a suite of protocol extensions to MPLS to make it applicable to the control of non-packet-based switching, and particularly, optical switching. One proposal is to use GMPLS protocols to upgrade the control plane of optical transport networks. The following ASTN/ASON standardization bodies, forums, and consortia are currently involved in the standardization process:

- ITU-T SG 15 on optical and other transport network infrastructures
- ITU-T SG 4 on the Telecommunications Management Network (TMN)
- ITU-T SG 13 on next-generation network operation and maintenance
- ITU-T SG 16 for the transport of multimedia
- ITU-T SG 17 on data networks
- ITU-R WP 9B for radio relay system
- OMG on CORBA technology
- IETF Working Groups in Operations and Management, Transport, and Routing
- OIF (Signaling, Architecture, Carrier, and OAM&P WGs)
- ATIS Committee T1X1 on transport management aspects
- ATIS Committee T1M1 on generic management aspects
- TeleManagement Forum (MTNM and IPNM Teams)
- W3C on XML
- IEEE 802 on Ethernet management
- Metro Ethernet Forum (MEF) on Ethernet management

ITU-T Recommendation G.807, the first standard in the ASTN series approved, addressed the network-level architecture and requirements for the control plane of ASTN independent of specific transport technologies. Agreement was reached in the recent past on other standards in the ASON, including the following:

- ITU-T Recommendation G.8080/Y.1304, "Architecture for the Automatically Switched Optical Network (ASON)," specifies the architecture and requirements for the automatic switched transport network as applicable to SDH transport networks, defined in recommendation G.803, and Optical Transport Networks, defined in Recommendation G.872. This new Recommendation is based on requirements specified in Recommendation G.807. The reference architecture is described in terms of the key functional components and the interactions among them. This recommendation describes the set of control plane components that are used to manipulate transport network resources to provide the functionality of setting up, maintaining, and releasing connections. The use of components allows for the separation of call control from connection control and the separation of routing and signaling. G.8080 takes path-level and call-level views of an optical connection and applies a distributed call model to the operation of these connections. In the area of optical signaling, the ITU-T has been involved in the creation of a standardized architecture for optically signaled networks. A number of different approaches have been suggested for signaling, including GMPLS and possibly other protocols.*
- ITU-T Recommendation G.7712/Y.1703, "Architecture and Specification of Data Communication Network (DCN)," specifies the architecture and requirements for a data network to support the exchange of ASON messages in addition to the traditional TMN communication. These communications take place among the transport plane, control plane, and management plane for ASON signaling and network management.
- ITU-T Recommendation G.7713/Y.1704, "Distributed Call and Connection Management," gives the requirements for distributed connection management (DCM) for both the UNI and the NNI. The requirements in this recommendation specify the signaling communications between functional components to perform automated connection operations, such as setup and release of connections. It describes DCM messages, attributes, and state transitions in a protocol-neutral fashion.
- ITU-T Recommendation G.7714/Y.1705, "Generalized Automatic Discovery Techniques," describes automatic discovery processes that support distribution connection management. Applications of automatic discovery addressed include neighbor discovery and adjacency discovery. The requirements, attributes, and discovery methods are described in a protocol-neutral fashion.

The dynamic aspects of the ASTN/ASON (e.g., provisioning and restoration) require complex interactions between the OCCs and the transport plane. In turn, this implies an interaction between the signaling and routing protocols. The result is an out-of-band control mechanism in which the signaling and data paths could make use of different paths through the network.

GMPLS has been getting a lot of attention in this context. GMPLS extends MPLS to encompass time-division (e.g., SONET/SDH, PDH, G.709), wavelength (lambdas), and spatial switching

---

* However, the past 35 years have shown that neither X.25 SVCs, nor Frame Relay SVCs, nor ATM SVCs have seen commercial success; we venture to guess that in the short term switched light paths are not going to see major commercial success either for end-user enterprise applications.

(e.g., incoming port or fiber to outgoing port or fiber). The focus of GMPLS is on the control plane of these various layers because each of them can use physically diverse data or forwarding planes [MAN200401]. GMPLS largely consists of the following [ATO200101,PAP200501]:

- Extensions to the dynamic routing protocols' Intermediate System—Intermediate System (IS-IS) and Open Shortest Path First (OSPF) to provide management applications with the topology of the optical network, optical NE capabilities, resource availability, etc.
- Extensions to the signaling protocols Constraint-based Routing Label Distribution Protocol (CR-LDP) and Reservation Protocol with Traffic Engineering (RSVP-TE) to establish, maintain, and tear down optical paths
- A new Link Management Protocol (LMP), for control channel management and link information exchange between neighboring optical NEs

10.2.2.15 Architectural Principles for ASON

The* existing transport networks provide SONET/SDH and WDM services whose connections are provisioned via network management. This process is both slow (weeks to months) relative to the switching speed and costly to the network providers. An ASON is an optical/transport network that has dynamic connection capability. It encompasses SONET/SDH, wavelength, and potentially, fiber connection services in both Optical-Electrical-Optical (OEO) and all-optical networks. There are a number of added values related to such a capability [ABO200201]:

Traffic engineering of optical channels: Where bandwidth assignment is based on actual demand patterns.

Mesh network topologies and restoration: Mesh network topologies can in general be engineered for better utilization for a given demand matrix. Ring topologies might not be as efficient because of the asymmetry of traffic patterns.

Managed bandwidth to core IP network connectivity: A switched optical network can provide bandwidth and connectivity to an IP network in a dynamic manner compared to the relatively static service available today.

Introduction of new optical services: The availability of switched optical networks will facilitate the introduction of new services at the optical layer. Those services include bandwidth on demand and optical virtual private networks (OVPNs).

ASON defines a control plan architecture that allows the setup and teardown of calls (and the connections that support a call) as a result of a user request. To achieve global coverage and the support of multiple client types, the architecture is described in terms of components and a set of reference points and rules must be applied at the interface points between clients and the network, and between networks [MAY200102].

---

* This section is based on its entirety on the IETF draft: O. Aboul-Magd, B. Jamoussi, S. Shew, Gert Grammel, Sergio Belotti, Dimitri Papadimitriou, IPO WG, Internet Draft, draft-ietf-ipo-ason-02.txt, Automatic Switched Optical Network (ASON) Architecture and Its Related Protocols, March 2002. Copyright (C) The Internet Society. All Rights Reserved. This document and translations of it may be copied and furnished to others, and derivative works that comment on or otherwise explain it or assist in its implementation may be prepared, copied, published, and distributed, in whole or in part, without restriction of any kind, provided that the above copyright notice and this paragraph are included on all such copies and derivative works.

In ASON architecture there is the recognition that the optical network control plane will be subdivided into domains that match the administrative domains of the network, as we alluded to earlier. The transport plane is also partitioned to match the administrative domains. Within an administrative domain the control plane may be further subdivided, e.g., by actions from the management plane. This allows the separation of resources into, for example, domains for geographic regions, that can be further divided into domains that contain different types of equipment. Within each domain, the control plane may be further subdivided into routing areas for scalability, which may also be further subdivided into sets of control components. The transport plane resources used by ASON will be partitioned to match the subdivisions created within the control plane.

The interconnection between domains, routing areas and, where required, sets of control components is described in terms of reference points. The exchange of information across these reference points is described by the multiple abstract interfaces between control components. The physical interconnection is provided by one or more of these interfaces. A physical interface is provided by mapping an abstract interface to a protocol. The reference point between an administrative domain and an end user is the UNI. The reference point between domains is the E-NNI. The reference point within a domain between routing areas and, where required, between sets of control components within routing areas is the I-NNI.

The difference between the I-NNI and the E-NNI is significant. I-NNI is applied in a single routing area where all equipment support the same routing protocol and detailed routing information could be exchanged between the different nodes. On the other hand, E-NNI is mainly concerned with reachability between domains that employ different routing and protection methodologies.

ASON is an emerging service (infrastructure) and is not yet generally available at this juncture.

10.2.2.16 Ethernet-Based Solutions

VLAN-based architectures extending GbE into the metro access/metro core space received considerable attention at the beginning of the decade. Metro access/metro core implementations of GbE backbones utilize VLAN technology. VLANs have been developed for enterprise applications and focus on enterprise issues; its protocols are single-organization-centric. Nonetheless, they have been exported to the metro environment, but with a baggage of limitations and lack of robustness. They do not appear to be "the wave of the future" in terms of being the major new carrier-class next-generation-network architecture.

Prima facie, Ethernet accommodates data requirement more easily than legacy networks that depend so heavily on channelization and ATM switching. According to proponents, GbE over metro fiber will become the standard for local distribution-loop deployment in five to ten years. Proponents posit that after proving its viability at the metro core, GbE is poised to enter carriers' local distribution loops. This potential migration to fiber-optic Ethernet is the result of three forces: the heterogeneous traffic as the access network moves to a converged network environment, the economic benefits offered by greater scalability and flexibility in supporting increasing numbers of users demanding higher bandwidth, and technology extensions putting GbE on par with ATM [SHA200101].

Corporate planners have considered these technologies either to interconnect dispersed geographic locations or for access to the Internet. Although this technology is relatively inexpensive, allowing the in-building equipment cost to range from $5,000 to $10,000, it also has a number of major technical limitations. These limitations include no traffic management and virtually nonexistent robustness to failure (the time needed to reconfigure around a failure is greater by a factor of 1000 compared to time required with a SONET/WDM environment). Compared with SONET and with the IEEE 802.17 Resilient Packet Ring, raw GbE backbones for metropolitan applications leave a lot to be desired. Many dismiss a raw GbE-based metro backbone as inferior technology. Ethernet-based systems must overcome at least four implementation obstacles:

- Support for QoS and security
- Support for differentiated service pricing and billing
- Rugged, carrier-grade equipment
- Support for legacy media (e.g., PSTN, twisted-pair, and wireless)

Ethernet-based backbone architectures use (back-to-back) bridges, although they typically are full-duplex transmission arrangements. A bridge is a frame filtering and forwarding device. Network reconfiguration time is slow, as indicated earlier, and the IEEE recommends a maximum diameter of seven bridges* in the network, although some carriers have built rings consisting of a higher number of drops. In a traditional bridging environment, frames destined for a user on the same side (segment) as the sender are kept confined to that segment, and therefore do not take up bandwidth on the segments of other users. In other words, the bridge segments the LAN into several collision domains, and therefore, increases the achievable local network throughput per device. Bridges do flood broadcast messages, multicast messages, and unknown unicast messages to all segments; therefore, all the bridged segments in the campus or building together form a single broadcast domain.

An edge GbE LAN bridge is a device that injects frames destined for a remote segment onto the "carrying" backbone. In some implementations of TLS, this backbone is dedicated to that specific user, therefore the security,† throughput, and performance can be controlled by design. The designer can either dedicate a physical link or a virtual link (e.g., ATM). In GbE-based backbones, however, all traffic from all users connected to that backbone share the common higher-speed backbone. A similar approach was tried by some carriers in the early 1990 using Fiber Distributed Data Interface (FDDI). In the earlier days of FDDI backbones, the arriving traffic was 10 Mbps per segment, and the FDDI ring could easily support the aggregate traffic as long as the number of subnetworks was in the range of 10 to 20 (depending on the traffic leaving the constituent subnetworks). The same holds true for a (campus) GbE backbone that interconnects a number of 100 Mbps subordinate LANs. However, today's GbE-based metro-backbone networks accept traffic arriving on the customer side at full 1Gbps, and then load this traffic, with that of several other customers also arriving at 1Gbps, on a single shared 1Gbps backbone. This quickly becomes problematic from a throughput and delay point of view.

An 80/20 rule is generally accepted in the design of enterprise network: 80% of the traffic stays inside and 20% exits to the WAN. On a GbE interface, if the traffic from a customer is, on the average, 200 Mbps, then fewer than five customers can be supported on that metro ring. Nominal overbooking of 3 Gbps has been tried on metro-GbE systems by some carriers, but the underlying

---

* For example, refer to Annex F and other sections in the IEEE 802.1w-2001 standard.
† One way to deal with the security issue is to either force the customer to use IPsec, which has administrative complexity, or for the carrier to deploy and manage routers with IPsec, which can be expensive from both a hardware as well as an operational point of view.

assumption must be that the actual traffic from the customer on the GbE interface must be only in the 1 to 200 Mbps range. Some edge equipment vendors have attempted to incorporate traffic shaping, but results have been disappointing. Burstiness only helps to a modest extent: burstiness has been greatly overrated over the years: as networks become more highly utilized, as people depend more and more on communications, as network gateway points (e.g., routers) aggregate and concentrate data from large portions of an organization (even from the entire organization), the traffic acquires almost a deterministic profile, exiting the concentration point at a sustained rate equating the channel speed, particularly during the busy hours.

The IEEE standard defines a VLAN as "a subset of the active topology of a bridged Local Area Network." A VLAN is a logical (association of ports on a) LAN (or LANs). The standards effort have taken the view of the "…establishment of Groups in a LAN environment, and the filtering of frames by bridges such that frames addressed to a particular Group are forwarded only on those LAN segments that are required to reach members of that Group…" (ISO/IEC 15802-3). From a single VLAN enterprise switch (really a multi-port bridge or Layer 2 Switch) point of view, any subset of ports (including all ports on the switch) can comprise a VLAN. The switch needs to support VLAN features to be able to group such a set of ports into a logical LAN or VLAN. Not surprisingly, VLANs can be defined across multiple enterprise switches. LAN segments are not restricted by the hardware that physically connects them; rather, the segments are defined by the user groups that the planner can create on the VLAN switches.

VLAN technology in general was initially developed in the early 1990s for campus applications, where security was not a concern. VLAN technology works as designed in an enterprise network environment. Its import into the metro access/metro core space, however, leaves a lot to be desired. It is one thing not to deliver Citibank's data into JPMorgan's building, and not to deliver Citibank's data and JPMorgan's data into Wachovia's building, and not to deliver Citibank's data and JPMorgan's data and Wachovia's data into Wells Fargo's building. It is all-together another matter to in fact deliver Citibank's data and JPMorgan's data and Wachovia's data into a Wells Fargo's building and hope that no one in the competitor's building takes the trouble to "promiscuously" read the data of the competitors by simply accessing the edge device and taking off all such information with an inexpensive Ethernet protocol analyzer, and be discouraged just by a nonrestrictive label in front of the data.* This is IP-routing-in-the-Internet-deja-vu, where, in principle, anyone with access to the backbone can read any data in the clear regardless of what the label (IP address) in front of the packet says. This is particularly problematic when the equipment is deployed in a customer's own closet or data center rather than in a common space, such as a basement, although even the latter case is cause for concern in an Ethernet-based environment.

Reconfiguration time is also a most critical element of a network [GIM200102]. Because optical access networks carry high volumes of critical traffic, the level of reliability and robustness traditionally reserved for core networks must also be implemented in access networks. Reliability

---

* Although a SONET ring also carries data from multiple users, the different data streams are kept in different channels, which is not the case in a VLAN situation where all the data is aggregated into the same channel. By way of analogy, it is true that all the valuables at a bank are kept in the same vault (read, backbone link), but these valuable are not all thrown into a large box which is accessible to every user (read, VLAN channel) every time they go into the vault looking for something they own, but are kept in individual safety boxes (read, SONET channels) which can only be opened by the proper owner, in a confidential manner.

(and related measures) is evaluated both in terms of the ability to replace a failed link and reestablish communications, as well as the time needed to affect such change. All the GbE metro VLAN networks that were deployed in the early 2000s utilized the traditional Spanning Tree Algorithm/ Spanning Tree Protocol (STA/STP), which has a convergence time of between 50 s and 1 min. The problem is that the service restoration time under the STA is about 1000 times slower than with SONET-based technology. To address this issue and partly ameliorate the restoration issue, the IEEE recently published a new standard, the IEEE 802.1w Rapid Spanning Tree Protocol (RSTP).

RSTP offers an improvement on the 50 s it takes traditional Spanning Tree to enable a failed Ethernet path to be swapped with an alternate path and to recover. Stakeholders differ on the extent of that improvement (estimates run from 10 msec in an optimal [but likely unachievable] case to a full second or more in more typical environments), and whether it is sufficient for guaranteeing service level agreements (SLAs) that commercial customers need. This is why nearly every article that has appeared in the open press about carriers with GbE metro technology describes how these carriers provided services to this school, university, or college. Their services would never be adequate for the financial, insurance, and real estate (FIRE) industry, for government agencies, medical institutions, or mission-critical operations. Reconfiguration times in the centi-second range are required.

The bottom line is that although RSTP is an improvement, it is still not clear that it can support carrier-class services. Note that the specification of RSTP as it appears in Clause 17 of IEEE 802.1w is explicitly designed to be compatible with the STP as specified in Clause 8 of IEEE Std 802.1D, 1998 Edition and prior revisions of the standard, and computation of the Spanning Tree is identical between STP and RSTP.

GbE/VLANs are subject to the problem of congestion. Traffic sources operating under TCP linearly increase their bandwidth usage until resources are exhausted. On packet drop they back off exponentially. Uncontrolled congestion seriously degrades performance: buffers fill up and packets are dropped, resulting in retransmissions (with the vicious cycle of more packet loss and increased latency). The problem builds until throughput collapses: users of these kinds of networks have reported utilization on MAN and WAN links in the range of 35–45%. This is why the RPR effort spent so much time on the issue of QoS and fairness. Delivering real-time delay-sensitive frames over the network requires minimum delay, and minimum delay variation. A network that transfers both loss-sensitive and delay-sensitive traffic will have to intelligently hide the load and the resources that the loss-sensitive traffic consumes from the delay-sensitive traffic, otherwise, service providers will be reluctant to use such delay-sensitive frames, and their applications will be limited [MOR200201]. As is known, an excessive amount of jitter and wander can adversely affect both digital and analog signals used to transport voice and video services. Network output wander specifications' compliance at synchronous network nodes are necessary to ensure satisfactory network performance (e.g., slips, error bursts). Availability issues and outages are also problems. Studies show that metro fiber cables break very often. A fiber link's MTBF is typically 1 failure every 10–20 km per year and the fiber link's MTTR is 12–24 hr [BUS200101]. 802.1Q has a limit of only 4096 VLANs. This limits the number of customers that can be supported in an Ethernet network. Stacked VLANs and VLAN tag translation capabilities implemented by several vendors alleviate this problem to some extent [RAM200101].

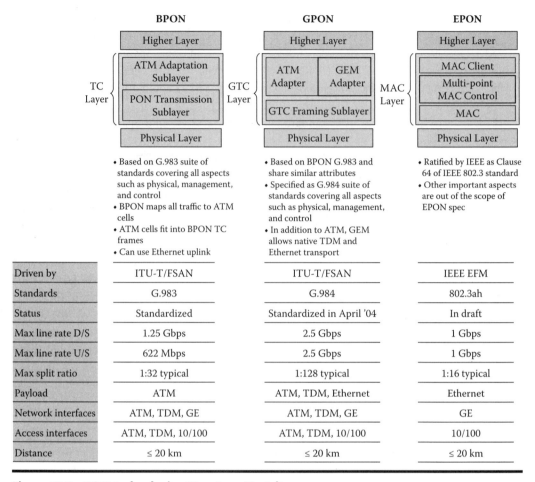

Figure 10.5   PON technologies (Courtesy: Nortel).

10.2.2.17 Passive Optical Network (PON)

PON technologies are being considered for FTTH deployments "triple play" services. Three major passive optical network (PON) technologies under consideration by service providers: Broadband PON (BPON), Gigabit PON (GPON), and Ethernet PON (EPON). These PON technologies are at different stages of maturity and offer slightly different sets of capabilities. The work of the IEEE P802.3ah Ethernet in the First Mile Task Force is now complete with the approval of IEEE Std 802.3ah-2004 at the June 2004 IEEE Standards Board meeting. We limit our discussion here on this topic just by calling attention to Figure 10.5, which provides an overview of the three major classes of services being contemplated. These services do not have immediate applications to typical enterprise users.

10.3 Advances in WAN Technology, Applications, and Opportunities

The need for increased WAN bandwidth becomes clear as the planner upgrades the office LANs to higher speeds, e.g., to GbE or 10GbE. Some key WAN technologies that have played an important role in the recent past and are expected to continue to play a role in the near future are POS, MPLS, VPNs, Frame Relay, ATM, and metro optical solutions. This section limits the discussion to MPLS.

10.3.1 The Concept of Overlay

For all intents and purposes, WAN connectivity these days translates into IP support over the wide area. Many efforts over the past 15 years regarding IP support can be boiled down to two issues:

1. Carriage of IP PDUs
2. Functionality of IP or network layer

There are three basic ways to carry IP:

- A pure IP network with high-power routers and high-speed point-to-point links interconnecting these routers with some kind of (appropriate) topology
- An overlay mechanism where IP is carried by an underlying network such as ATM or Frame Relay
- A hybrid network with a mixed layer 2/layer 3 mechanism, such as MPLS

There are two ways to envision the network layer:

- Keep the network layer nimble
- Augment the network layer functionality to include other features (e.g., QoS)

Combinatorially, therefore, there are six approaches to handle layer 3 networking, as shown in Table 10.4.

Some argue that there are emerging requirements such as traffic engineering (selecting certain special routes through the network), support for VPNs, QoS-enabled communications, security, and so on, that cannot be supported by existing connectionless networks and that extensions are therefore needed. Purists, on the other hand, argue against the idea of overlays and extensions. Purist argue in favor of a "nimble" network layer without extensions or overlays: many different applications are carried over the network layer that operates over many different link/physical technologies. Anything that "thickens the Internet waist is seen as heresy" [GUE200101]. These purists prefer to leave the network layer as is and build on top of it, if needed, and not build into it.

Table 10.4 Possible Approach to IP in Modern Networks

	Classical/Pure (including POS)	Over ATM	Over MPLS
No L3 extensions	Typical of today	Typical of yesterday	Maybe in future
With L3 Extensions	Not successful (e.g., RSVP)	Redundant functionality	Redundant functionality

These IP purists make the case that the following questions need to be answered before an extension is advanced:

1. How many users need a given functionality?
2. What are users willing to pay for the functionality?
3. How much do different solutions cost?

Past attempts at extending the network layer have failed in the view of purists because each approach tended to be a "big solution for a small problem," and such solutions had a higher cost than the corresponding saving. There may be solutions that are "good enough," without requiring a systemwide upgrade of the Internet. Three examples can be considered to make the case: (1) multicast, (2) QoS, and (3) traffic engineering.

The Integrated Services *(intserv)* approach to QoS can be viewed as an extension. In terms of who needs it, the answer can be that either all users need it (if it can be easily administered), or no one needs it, if a few users rob the rest of the population of reliable throughput. Willingness to pay remains an open issue. In terms of cost, there is significant control path (management) cost. Today there is no meaningful deployment of *intserv*/RSVP: people either use overprovisioning or IP-centric *diffserv* [GUE200101].

Some see MPLS in the same light [GUE200101]. The motivations, according to these observers, were that (1) there is a need to control network performance to support the SLAs that users require; and (2) this should be done in a way to reduce capital expense and make better use of existing solutions (having to obsolete $60–100 billion of internetworking equipment every three years is a self-serving predicament that only helps the vendors of such equipment, and few others). Further motivations were that (3) IP networks are too unpredictable owing to routing instability. The answer offered to address these issues is the extensive MPLS apparatus. However, such apparatus has major OAM&P overhead in keeping the network tuned. Some see it as a "technology is search of a problem": from fast PDU forwarding, to traffic engineering, to optical control plane. Purists argue that incremental changes to IP could provide a large majority of the benefits that MPLS offers.

In conclusion, IP purist make the case to keep the network layer "nimble"; run IP directly over SONET, WDM, or WAN Ethernet (WIS). The argument is that if a function is really important, that it will be added by the pressure of the market (e.g., FEC or retransmission on wireless links.)

The rest of the chapter takes a neutral view and looks at some of the common overlay/extension approaches that have been highlighted in this section. Some hold these extensions dear whereas others see them in a skeptical light.

10.3.2 MPLS and VPNs

MPLS protocols allows high-performance label switching of IP packets: network traffic is forwarded using a simple label, as described in RFC 3031 [RFC3031]. MPLS is a decade-old set of standards that provides a link-layer-independent transport framework for IP. MPLS runs over ATM, Frame Relay, Ethernet, and point-to-point packet-mode links. MPLS-based networks use existing IP mechanisms for addressing of elements and for routing of traffic. MPLS adds connection-oriented capabilities to the connectionless IP architecture. It is the industry-accepted manifestation of the "Network Layer/Layer 3/Tag/IP" Switching" technology that developed from various sources in the mid-to-late 1990s.

In an MPLS domain, when a stream of data traverses a common path, a Label Switched Path (LSP) can be established using MPLS signaling protocols. At the ingress Label Switch Router

(LSR), each packet is assigned a label and is transmitted downstream. At each LSR along the LSP, the label is used to forward the packet to the next hop. By combining the attributes of Layer 2 switching and Layer 3 routing into a single entity, MPLS provides [PUL200101]: (1) enhanced scalability by way of switching technology; (2) support of CoS- and QoS-based services (Differentiated Services/*diffserv*, as well as Integrated Services/*intserv*); (3) elimination of the need for an IP-over-ATM overlay model and its associated management overhead; and (4) enhanced traffic shaping and engineering capabilities. Table 10.5 depicts some of the features of MPLS that make it

Table 10.5   Application-Oriented Features of MPLS

Aggregation of PDU streams	In MPLS the Label-stacking mechanism can be used to perform the aggregation within Layer 2 itself. Typically, when multiple streams have to be aggregated for forwarding into a switched path, processing is required at both Layer 2 and Layer 3. The top label of the MPLS label stack is used to switch PDUs along the label-switched path, whereas the rest of the label stack is "application specific."
Explicit/improved routes	MPLS supports explicit routes (a route has not been set up by normal IP hop-by-hop routing, but rather an ingress/egress node has specified all or some of the downstream nodes of that route).
Improved performance	MPLS enables higher data transmission performance owing to simplified packet forwarding and switching mechanisms.
Link-layer independence	MPLS works with any type of link layer medium such as ATM, Frame Relay, Packet-over-SONET, Ethernet, etc.
QoS support	Explicit routes provide a mechanism for QoS/constraint routing, etc. As an example, some of the initial deployment of the MPLS was over ATM infrastructures; in other cases it could be over a metro-optical network. In the ATM scenario the core LSRs and edge LSRs can allocate QoS to different user requirements and map them to different ATM Virtual Channels (VCs) supporting different ATM QoS. As the edge LSRs are the ingress to the ATM overlay network, it is responsible for efficiently classifying the IP flows and mapping to the ATM QoS.
Scalability of network-layer routing	A key MPLS goal was to achieve a better and efficient transfer of PDUs in the current IP networks. Combining the routing knowledge at Layer 3 with the ATM switching capability in ATM devices results in a better solution. In the MPLS scenario, it is sufficient to have adjacencies with the immediate peers. The edge LSRs interact with the adjacent LSR, and this is sufficient for the creation of LSPs for the transfer of data.
Traffic engineering (TE)	MPLS supports traffic engineering (a process of selecting the paths chosen by data traffic to balance the traffic load on the various links, routers, and switches in the network). Key performance objectives of TE are (1) Traffic-oriented: includes those aspects that enhance the QoS of traffic streams; and (2) resource-oriented: includes those aspects that pertain to the optimization of resource utilization.
Virtual private network support	VPN is an application that uses the label stacking mechanisms. At the VPN ingress node, the VPN Label is mapped onto the MPLS Label stack and packets are label-switched along the LSP within the VPN until they emerge at the egress. At the egress node, the label stack is used to determine further forwarding of the PDUs.

a useful networking technology. QoS is where MPLS can find its technical sweet spot in supporting voice applications. The improved traffic management, the QoS capabilities, and the expedited packet forwarding via the label mechanism can be a significant technical advantage to voice.

MPLS can be logically and functionally divided into two elements to provide the label switching functionality:

1. MPLS Forwarding/Label Switching Mechanism
2. MPLS Label Distribution Mechanism

10.3.2.1 MPLS Forwarding/Label Switching Mechanism

The key mechanism of MPLS is the Forwarding/Label Switching function. This is an advanced form of packet forwarding that replaces the conventional longest-address-match-forwarding with a more efficient label-swapping forwarding algorithm. The IP header analysis is performed once at the Ingress of the LSP for the classification of PDUs. PDUs that are forwarded via the same next hop are grouped into a "Forwarding Equivalence Class" (FEC)* based on one or more of the following parameters:

Address prefix
Host Address
Host Address and QoS

The FEC to which the PDU belongs is encoded at the edge LSRs as a short fixed-length value known as a "label" (see Figure 10.6). When the PDU is forwarded to its next hop, the label is sent along with it. At downstream hops, there is no further analysis of the PDU's network layer header. Instead, the label is used as an index into a table; the entry in the table specifies the next hop, and a new label. The incoming label is replaced with this outgoing label, and the PDU is forwarded to its next hop. Labels usually have a local significance and are used to identify FECs on the basis of the type of the underlying network. For example, in ATM networks, the virtual Path Identifier (VPI) and Virtual Channel Identifier (VCI) are used in generating the MPLS label; in Frame Relay networks, the Data Link Control Identifier (DLCI) is used. In ATM environments the labels assigned to the FECs (PDUs) are the VPI/VCI of the virtual connections established as a part of the LSP. In Frame Relay environments, the labels assigned to the FECs (PDUs) are the DCLIs.

---

* Do not confuse this with Forward Error Correction.

Label: Label Value, 20 bits
Exp: Experimental Use, 3 bits
S: Bottom of Stack, 1 bit
TTL: Time to Live, 8 bits

Figure 10.6   MPLS label.

Label Switching has been designed to leverage the Layer 2 switching function done in the current data link layers such as ATM and FR. It follows that the MPLS Forwarding mechanism should be able to update the switching fabrics in ATM and FR hardware in the LSR for the relevant sets of LSPs, which can be switched at the hardware level [FUT200101]. In the Ethernet-based networks, the labels are short headers placed between the data-link headers and the data-link layer PDUs.

10.3.2.2 MPLS Label Distribution Mechanism

The MPLS architecture does not assume a single label distribution protocol. The distribution of labels in MPLS is accomplished in two ways:

Utilizing the Resource ReSerVation Protocol (RSVP) signaling mechanism to distribute labels mapped to the RSVP flows
Utilizing the Label Distribution Protocol (LDP)

Label Distribution using RSVP. RSVP [RFC2205] defines a *session* to be a data flow with a particular destination and transport-layer protocol. From the early 1990s to the late 1990s, RSVP was being considered just for QoS purposes in IP networks. When RSVP and MPLS are combined, a flow or session can be defined with greater generality. The ingress node of an LSP can use a variety of means to determine which PDUs are assigned a particular label. Once a label is assigned to a set of PDUs, the label effectively defined the *flow* through the LSP. Such an LSP is referred to as an *LSP tunnel* because the traffic flowing through it is opaque to intermediate nodes along the label-switched path. The label request information for the labels associated with RSVP flows will be carried as part of the RSVP *Path* messages and the label-mapping information for the labels associated with RSVP flows will be carried as part of the RSVP *Resv* messages [FUT200101]. The initial implementers of MPLS chose to extend RSVP into a signaling protocol to support the creation of LSPs that could be automatically routed away from network failures and congestion.

The use of RSVP as a signaling protocol for traffic engineering is quite different from that envisioned by its original developers in the mid-1990s [SEM200001]:

■ A number of extensions were added to the base RSVP specification [RFC2205 and RFC2209] to support the establishment and maintenance of explicitly routed LSPs.
■ RSVP signaling takes place between pairs of routers (rather than pairs of hosts) that act as the ingress and egress points of a traffic trunk. Extended RSVP installs a state that applies to a collection of flows that share a common path and a common pool of shared network resources, rather than a single host-to-host flow. By being able to aggregate numerous host-to-host flows into each LSP tunnel, extended RSVP significantly reduces the amount of RSVP state that needs to be maintained in the core of a service provider's network.
■ RSVP signaling installs distributed state related to packet forwarding, including the distribution of MPLS labels.
■ The scalability, latency, and traffic overhead concerns regarding RSVP's soft state model are addressed by a set of extensions that reduce the number of refresh messages and the associated message-processing requirements.
■ The path established by RSVP signaling is not constrained by conventional destination-based routing, so it is a good tool to establish traffic-engineering trunks.

The initial implementers of MPLS had a number of reasons to choose to extend RSVP rather than design an entirely new signaling protocol to support traffic-engineering requirements [SEM200001]:

- With the proposed extensions, RSVP provides a unified signaling system that delivers everything that network operators needed to dynamically establish LSPs.
- Extended RSVP creates an LSP along an explicit route to support the traffic-engineering requirements of large service providers.
- Extended RSVP establishes LSP state by distributing label-binding information to the LSRs in the LSP.
- Extended RSVP can reserve network resources in the LSRs along the LSP (the traditional role of RSVP). Extended RSVP also permits an LSP to carry best-effort traffic without making a specific resource reservation.

RSVP can serve a dual role in MPLS: for label distribution and for QoS support.

Label Distribution using the Label Distribution Protocol. LDP is a set of procedures and messages by which LSRs establish LSPs through a network by mapping network-layer routing information directly to data-link-layer switched paths. These LSPs may have an endpoint at a directly attached neighbor (this being comparable to IP hop-by-hop forwarding), or may have an endpoint at a network egress node, enabling switching via all intermediary nodes. LDP associates an FEC with each LSP it creates. The FEC associated with an LSP specifies which PDUs are "mapped" to that LSP. LSPs are extended through a network as each LSR "splices" incoming labels for an FEC to the outgoing label assigned to the next hop for the given FEC.

The messages exchanged between the LSRs are classified into the four categories:

- Discovery messages: Used to announce and maintain the presence of an LSR in a network
- Session messages: Used to establish, maintain, and terminate sessions between LSP peers
- Advertisement messages: Used to create, change, and delete label mappings for FECs
- Notification messages: Used to provide advisory information and to signal error information

The LDP uses the Transmission Control Protocol (TCP) for session, advertisement, and notification messages. TCP is utilized to provide reliable and sequenced messages. Discovery messages are transmitted using the User Datagram Protocol (UDP). These messages are sent to the LSP port at the *all routers on this subnet* group multicast address.

Discovery messages provide a mechanism for the LSRs to indicate their presence in a network. LSRs send the *Hello* message periodically. When an LSR chooses to establish a session with another LSR discovered via the *Hello* message, it uses the LDP initialization procedure (this is done using TCP). Upon successful completion of the initialization procedure, the two LSRs are LSP peers, and may exchange *advertisement* messages. The LSR requests a label mapping from a neighboring LSR when it needs one, and advertises a label mapping to a neighboring LSR when it wishes the neighbor to use a label.

The reader interested in this topic may consult a number of references, including [MIN200301].

10.3.2.3 VPNs

A VPN emulates a private network infrastructure over a shared public network, typically the Internet. The term *virtual* refers to the fact that there is no privately managed underlying physical network. The term *private* refers to the fact that access is restricted only to a defined set of entities. In particular, IP VPNs emulate a private network over a shared MPLS or IP network. Layer 2 VPNs emulate Frame Relay, ATM, or Ethernet services over an MPLS or IP infrastructure. RFC 2764, *A Framework for IP-Based Virtual Private Networks*, is a useful baseline document. IPsec-based networks have been around for a number of years, as also have Layer 2 VPNs.

Two metrics to evaluate VPNs are (1) administrative complexity and (2) scalability, security, and overhead. From a price/performance view, IPsec has the highest capital expenditure, the lowest MRC (Monthly Recurring Charge), and the worst performance, because of overhead and software encryption. The technology specified in RFC 2547 is exactly the opposite. Layer 2 VPNs are somewhere in the middle. Regarding extranet connectivity support, all three can be used, but IPsec and Layer 2 VPNs are the easiest to implement and control.

As noted earlier, MPLS improves traffic engineering and bandwidth management on IP networks and enables new network services, including RFC 2547 Layer 3 VPNs and Layer 2 VPNs. Proponents see MPLS* as having many advantages over other VPN tunneling technologies: they support label stacks for hierarchy and scaling. Also, they support explicit paths for traffic engineering, with bandwidth allocation and QoS. They provide a short header for low overhead. IPsec is best for mobile users, remote access, and for enterprises that can afford capital expenditures or require encryption. RFC 2547 is best suited for enterprises that prefer fully managed services, can afford the least amount of capital investments, and only utilize IP in the WAN. Layer 2 VPNs are best for enterprises that are comfortable with managing their own routers and addressing architecture, or use other protocols besides IP.

---

* IPSec VPNs are MPLS-agnostic.

Appendix 10.1: MAN/WAN Acronym List

10GbE	10 Gigabit Ethernet
ADM	Add/Drop Multiplexer
AM	Amplitude Modulation
APS	Automatic Protection Switching
ASK	Amplitude Shift Keying
ASON	Automatically Switched Optical Networks
ATM	Asynchronous Transfer Mode
BPON	Broadband PON
CIR	Committed Information Rate
CLECs	Competitive Local Exchange Carriers
CMISE	Common Management Information Service Element
CNI	Client Network Interface
CO	Central Office
CORBA	Common Object Request Broker Architecture
CR-LDP	Constraint-based Routing Label Distribution Protocol
CWDM	Coarse Wavelength Division Multiplexing
DCN	Data Communication Network
DCS	Digital Cross Connect
DLCI	Data-Link Control Identifier
DLL	Data-Link Layer
DSF	Dispersion-Shifted Fiber
DWDM	Dense Wavelength Division Multiplexing
DXC	Digital Cross Connect
EDFA	Erbium Doped Fiber Amplifiers
E-NNIs	External-Network-to-Network Interfaces
EoS	Ethernet over SONET
EPON	Ethernet PON
ESCON	Enterprise Systems Connection
EWB	Extended Wavelength Band
FDDI	Fiber Distributed Data Interface
FDM	Frequency Division Multiplexing
FEC	Forward Error Correction, or
FEC	Forwarding Equivalence Class
FICON	Fiber Connection
FR	Frame Relay
FTTH	Fiber To The Home
GbE	Gigabit Ethernet
GFP	Generic Framing Procedure
GMPLS	Generalized Multi-Protocol Label Switching
GPON	Gigabit PON
IM	Intensity Modulation
I-NNIs	Internal-Network-to-Network Interfaces
IS-IS	Intermediate System - Intermediate System
ISPs	Internet Service Providers

LCAS	Link Capacity Adjustment Scheme
LDP	Label Distribution Protocol
LMP	Link Management Protocol
LSP	Label Switched Path
LSR	Label Switch Router
MAN	Metropolitan Area Networks
MEF	Metro Ethernet Forum
MPLS	Multi-Protocol Label Switching
MSPP	Multi-Service Provisioning Platform
MTBF	Mean Time Between Failure
NDSF	Non-Dispersion-Shifted Fiber
NEs	Network Elements
NZDSF	Non-Zero Dispersion-Shifted Fiber
OADMs	Optical Add/Drop Modules
OAM&P	Operations, Administration, Maintenance, and Provisioning
OCCs	Optical Control Channels
OC-x	Optical Carrier-x
OEO	Optical-Electrical-Optical
OSPF	Open Shortest Path First
OSS	Operations Support Systems
OTH	Optical Transport Hierarchy
OTM	Optical Transport Module
OTN	Optical Transport Network
O-UNI	Optical User-to-Network Interface
OVPN	Optical Virtual Private Networks
OXC	Optical Cross Connects
PDU	Protocol Data Unit
PMD	Polarization Mode Dispersion
PNNI	Private Network-to-Network Interface
PON	Passive Optical Network
POP	Points Of Presence
POS	Packet Over SONET
PPP	Point-to-Point Protocol
QoS	Quality of Service
RPR	Resilient Packet Ring
RSTA	Rapid Spanning Tree Algorithm
RSTP	Rapid Spanning Tree Protocol
RSVP-TE	Reservation Protocol with Traffic Engineering
SLAs	Services Level Agreements
SN	Service-providing Node
SONET/SDH	Optical Network/Synchronous Digital Hierarchy
SPCs	Soft Provisioned Connections
SPE	Synchronous Payload Envelope
STA/STP	Spanning Tree Algorithm/Spanning Tree Protocol
STDM	Statistical TDM
STSs	Synchronous Transport Signals

TCP	Transmission Control Protocol
TDM	Time Division Multiplexing
TLS	Transparent LAN Service
TMN	Telecommunications Management Network
UDP	User Datagram Protocol
UNIs	User Network Interfaces
VCI	Virtual Channel Identifier
VLAN	Virtual LAN
VPI	Virtual Path Identifier
VPLS	Virtual Private LAN services
VPN	Virtual Private Network
VT	Virtual Tributary
WANs	Wide Area Networks
WWDM	Wide WDM

Chapter 11

Networking in SOA
Environments*

11.1 Introduction and Overview

Chapters 9 and 10 provided a survey of some (but certainly not all) broadband networking services and technologies that can be used by architecture planners at institutions and enterprises. There we focused on connectivity-level technologies or physical-layer services because the actual corporate communication disbursements track almost directly the type of physical-layer services selected rather than the upper-layer capabilities. However, users also require a gamut of higher-level capabilities that go beyond basic connectivity. This chapter examines how these advanced network services can be architected by institutional users and service providers using service-oriented networking techniques. These techniques have the potential of increasing flexibility, time to market, and cost-effectiveness.

Organizations have become highly dependent on their network infrastructures. Already, in the mid-1990s, it was recognized that

> "...we have reached a state where *the corporation is the network*. Hence, the entire business viability of a corporation may well depend on the network it has in place..." [MIN199601].

This point is underscored by the importance of the network to a bank, a brokerage firm, an online business such as reservations or E-commerce, the aviation industry, or the military, to just name a few. It follows that organizations seek to have networks with high availability and self-healing capabilities. Requirements for availability in the 99.999% range are common for many institutional networks. Carriers and service providers need to deploy network infrastructures that meet these needs. A properly designed network will achieve high availability.

---

* This chapter was contributed by Gary Smith, The SOA Network (www.soanetworkarchitect.com).

To be successful, organizations must respond on a routine basis to quickly evolving market opportunities, customer demands, competitive threats, and regulatory mandates. As discussed or implied in previous chapters, *automation agility* is a basic requirement for business operations: corporate stakeholders seek enhanced yet customized solutions, and they expect these solutions to have immediate, cost-effective, and global geographic deployment. Unfortunately, in a typical enterprise, the IT infrastructure is often composed of a multitude of applications, platforms, operating systems, and networks. This predicament quickly leads to an environment of discrete silos of computing resources. In turn, the proliferation of silos and associated operational complexity diminish the organization's ability to adapt in a timely manner.

The network has now become the intrinsic platform for business solutions that enable enterprisewide communications and collaboration. Therefore, one can begin to address a subset of the overall silo issue by deploying a Service-Oriented Network (SON). A SON is a service-based architecture for the development, deployment, and management of network services, typically focusing on connection-oriented and overlay networks [SOU200601]. One approach to achieving this is with Service-Oriented Architecture (SOA) constructs. A slightly different but related concept is embodied in Service-Oriented Architecture Networking (SOAN). SOAN is a framework for building SOA *Networks*, specifically, a mechanism for distributing SOA components across a network, and have these components available on demand. Both these issues are the topics of this chapter.

To aid readability, an acronym glossary is provided at the end of the chapter.

Although it may not be practical to take a statically standardized approach to all business applications, architects can benefit their organizations by taking a uniform approach to the network so that it becomes the common connectivity fabric for all applications, computing resources, and video and voice communication. The network is pervasive, affecting all fixed and mobile devices, end users, and even entities outside the enterprise, such as supply-chain partners. It enables resources across the enterprise—even those in discrete silos—to deliver business agility by integrating IT assets with critical business processes, creating a platform for application optimization, and achieving process improvements. The network also has the ability to consolidate security and identity services so that the integrity of business applications, as they migrate, can be maintained. Also, the network can support the virtualization of resources such as storage, firewalls, or policy enforcement. An intelligent network creates the kind of dynamic, application- and service-aware infrastructure that a nonintegrated infrastructure is unable to provide [MIL200701].

The emergence of Web Services (WSs) technologies has triggered a major paradigm shift in distributed computing. Distributed computing can be supported by any number of models and approaches; however, it is useful when some kind of (de facto) industry standard is used. One such standard is Distributed Object Architecture (DOA). DOA makes use of technologies such as Common Object Request Broker (CORBA), Distributed Component Object Model (DCOM), Distributed Communications Environment (DCE), and Remote Method Invocation (RMI).

However, at this time one is seeing a general transition from DOA to SOAs. The emergence of approaches based on WSs has triggered a major paradigm shift in distributed computing. As covered in earlier chapters, in a SOA environment, a set of network-accessible operations and associated resources are abstracted as a "service." The SOA vision allows for a service to be described in a standardized fashion, published to a service registry, discovered, and invoked by a service consumer. SOAs make use of technologies such Web Services Description Language (WSDL); Simple Object Access Protocol (SOAP); and Universal Discovery, Description and Integration (UDDI). Like all its predecessors, SOA promises to provide ubiquitous application integration. It also promises to provide platform-independent standards that enable application integration and dynamic any-to-any real-time connectivity locally or even across distributed networks. Although the nature of SOA is different from previous architecture approaches, traditional architecture modeling approaches can be built upon and used to describe SOA.

Original applications of SOA were related to software application development, as we covered in Chapter 8. However, at this juncture, SOA is finding direct applications in networking; furthermore, applications are making use of networks to reach SOA business-logic functional modules. A number of SOA concepts were discussed in Chapter 8; some of them are revisited here, but with the aforementioned focus. Specifically, the goals of this chapter are the following:

1. To expand upon the impact of SOA, specifically on network infrastructure and how this network infrastructure and vendors' products are evolving as SOA itself continues to change in response to WS standards and as vendors better understand the business value that SOA and SOA networking can bring to the business. For example, network providers need to devise a novel way of developing services and SOA-based methods are being presented as a reasonable solution for this problem. The service composition mechanisms play an important role: a new service can be created by composing a primitive group of services. This recursive definition is important because it enables the construction of more complex services above a set of extant ones. For example, a virtual private network (VPN) service may be constructed through the composition of services for connection management, authentication, fault management, and resource management. These services can be distributed in the service provider's network, some executing in the central office computers, and others close or inside the switching equipments [SOU200601]. This is the concept of SON with SOA constructs, i.e., the application of SOA principles to a variety of network services.
2. To discuss SOA as a way of connecting applications across a network via a common communications protocol. From this perspective, SOA is an architectural style for building integrated software applications that use services available in a network, such as the corporate intranet or public Internet. In theory, this allows developers to treat applications as services that can be orchestrated into complex business processes more quickly by using other methods irrespective of where these services are located or on what platform they reside. This is the concept of SOA networking: SOAN is a set of mechanisms to support the deployment of network-centric SOA infrastructure solutions to enable reliable, consistent, and predictable communications between WSs.

It should be noted, however, that there is currently a gap between what the SOA potential is and what the currently available off-the-shelf products are. This gap comes to light when vendors flush out specific requirements needed to meet the needs of their customers and implement this functionality into product offerings. In a competitive marketplace, this productization is often an iterative approach in which vendors must strike a balance: there are business imperatives of continuing to deliver additional functionalities to provide added business value; and at the same time, generate revenue streams from these products. Often, from the end user's perspective, it may seem that vendors do not know where they are heading, but in reality it is a "chicken and egg" process in which concepts must be validated by customer use. Therefore, one sees that many of the SOA products are continuing to evolve, as of press time, as vendors better understand customer use, standards mature, and competition increases. SOA networking is in a state of flux, and the industry is coming to terms with the value the SOA network infrastructure will bring to the table and how much "intelligence" or business logic should reside within the network itself. This is similar to the process in the networking world, as vendors try to identify needs and deliver value. One of the challenges in the networking world has always been the question of how much intelligence (i.e., business logic) should be in the network. In fact, now, SOA may help answer that question.

Two major trends are affecting SOA networking as vendors iteratively build and deploy SOA solutions. They are as follows:

1. Many SOA platforms have been built on a core message-oriented middleware (MOM) or Enterprise Service Bus (ESB), and these SOA platforms are constantly evolving as features and functionalities are added. At the high end, SOA platforms will likely evolve into Integration Centric-Business Process Management Suites (IC-BPMS); at the low end, SOA platform functionalities (mainly ESB functionality) are being commoditized from application servers into embedded network appliances.

2. The focus of SOA adoption is moving from enterprise SOA to business-to-business (B2B) SOA (also known as extended enterprise SOA), requiring the management of services beyond the immediate enterprise where these services are being deployed, over a more distributed network infrastructure between more partners.

These two trends present challenges not only in the productizing SOA platforms and associated SOA infrastructure in general, but also, specifically, in the SOA network infrastructure. The objective of SOA networking is to support the deployment of network-centric SOA infrastructure solutions to enable reliable, consistent, and predictable communications between WSs deployed across a distributed enterprise or between enterprises.

To support the most sophisticated enterprise application integration and business processes, SOA networks must solve a number of problems:

- **Ubiquitous, secure, and reliable messaging:** As SOA evolves and the IT environment is transforming from a few, large applications to a network of many shared services, there are a number of factors such as reliable messaging, security, policy management, and ubiquity, which become more important. SOA platforms for internal enterprise integration are challenging in their own right, but managing distributed services beyond the enterprise is even more of a challenge when a network is introduced.

- **Enterprise SOA interoperability and mediation:** An enterprise IT environment is characterized by many incompatibilities in areas such as software platforms, standards adoption, service sophistication, invocation patterns, developer capabilities, and so on. These factors must be mitigated to enable seamless service sharing within and between enterprises. Sharing services through loose coupling lies at the foundation of the benefits of SOA, enabling business agility, lowering IT cost, and reducing time to market for new applications. These incompatibilities between heterogeneous SOA environments create obstacles to service sharing and therefore must be removed as we move from Enterprise SOA to B2B SOA if we want to achieve the goals of SOA.

Middleware is a traditional way of making disparate applications "communicate" with one another without actually being integrated. However, middleware itself is an application that introduces its own layer of maintenance and management; it also has limitations in terms of extensibility and adaptability. However, as SOA and Web 2.0 evolve, the network has the capability to complement and enhance this evolution, as desktop environments embrace WSs directly. By embedding XML translation, message routing, and event notification within the network, service-oriented environments are optimized with efficiency gains in file transfers, database synchronizations, e-mail, and Web acceleration, among other processes [MIL200701].

Table 11.1 provides a basic glossary for architectural terms employed in this chapter.

Table 11.1 Basic Service-Oriented Architecture Glossary

Application-Oriented Networking (AON)	A vendor-specific concept defined before SOA was commonly adopted in the industry and is primarily focused on routing, performance, managing quality of service (QoS), and security.
Business Process Management (BPM)	A discipline combining software capabilities and business expertise through people, systems, and information to accelerate time between process improvements, facilitating business innovation [IBM200701].
Business-to-Business (B2B) SOA (also known as Extended Enterprise SOA)	SOA-based mechanisms for automating business interactions between suppliers, customers, and trading partners, allowing companies to better share information and optimize processes across the value chain from better demand forecasting to streamlined manufacturing to more responsive customer service. B2B SOA allows firms to [TIB200701] achieve the following: • Reuse internal services by extending them to trading partners. • Build composite applications that extend from their back-end systems to their partner's back-end systems for end-to-end process automation. • Insulate trading partners from the underlying technology framework through a flexible solution that decouples process, protocols, transports, and payloads. • Engineer partner processes and services once, and reuse across all trading partners.
Common Object Request Broker Architecture (CORBA)	Object Management Group's open, vendor-independent architecture and infrastructure that computer applications use to work together over networks. A CORBA-based program from any vendor, on almost any computer, operating system, programming language, and network can interoperate with a CORBA-based program from the same or another vendor, on almost any other computer, operating system, programming language, and network. Because of the easy way that CORBA integrates machines from so many vendors, with sizes ranging from mainframes through minis and desktops to hand-helds and embedded systems, it is the middleware for large (and even not-so-large) enterprises. One of its most important, as well most frequent, uses is in servers that must handle large number of clients at high hit rates with high reliability. CORBA works behind the scenes in the computer rooms of many of the world's largest Web sites; ones that you probably use daily. Specializations for scalability and fault-tolerance support these systems [OMG200701].

(continued)

Table 11.1 Basic Service-Oriented Architecture Glossary (continued)

Enterprise Service Bus (ESB)	A connectivity infrastructure for integrating applications and services by performing the following actions between services and requestors: *routing* messages between services, *converting* transport protocols between requestor and service, *transforming* message formats between requestor and service, and *handling* business events from disparate sources [IBM200701].
eXtensible Mark-up Language (XML)	A structured language that was published as a W3C Recommendation in 1998. It is a metalanguage because it is used to describe other languages, the elements they contain, and how those elements can be used. These standardized specifications for specific types of information make them, along with the information that they describe, portable across platforms.
Integration Centric - Business Process Management Suites (IC-BPMS)	Integration capabilities products that support process improvement and that have evolved out of the enterprise application integration (EAI). Originally, this space was dominated by proprietary, closed-framework solutions; at this time these products are based on SOA and on standards-based integration technology. Vendors have added embedded enterprise service bus (ESB) and Business Process Management (BPM) capabilities.
Message-oriented middleware (MOM)	A client/server infrastructure that increases the interoperability, portability, and flexibility of an application by allowing the application to be distributed over multiple heterogeneous platforms. It reduces the complexity of developing applications that span multiple operating systems and network protocols by insulating the application developer from the details of the various operating system and network interfaces. Application programming interfaces (APIs) that extend across diverse platforms and networks are typically provided by the MOM. Applications exchange messages that can contain formatted data, requests for action, or both.
Service orientation	A way of thinking about business processes as linked, loosely coupled tasks supported by services. A new *service* can be created by composing a primitive group of *services*. This recursive definition is important because it enables the construction of more complex services above a set of existent ones [SOU200601].
Service-Oriented Architecture (SOA)	An IT architecture based on the concept of delivering reusable, business services that are underpinned by IT components in such a way that the providers and the consumers of the business services are loosely coupled, with no knowledge of the technology, platform, location or environment choices of each other [STA200502]. It embodies business-driven IT architectural approach that supports integrating business as linked, repeatable business tasks, or services. SOA helps businesses innovate by ensuring that IT systems can adapt quickly, easily and economically to support rapidly changing business needs [IBM200701]. In an SOA, resources are made available to other participants in the network as independent services that are accessed in a standardized way.

Service-Oriented Architecture Networking (SOAN)	Infrastructure for building SOA networks. Mechanism for distributing SOA components across a network, and have these components available on demand.
Service-Oriented Network (SON)	A service oriented architecture for the development, deployment, and management of network services, focusing on connection oriented and overlay networks [SOU200601].
Service-Oriented Network Architecture (SONA)	Cisco Systems' architectural framework that aims at delivering business solutions to unify network-based services such as security, mobility, and location with the virtualization of IT resources.
Service-Oriented Networking (SON)	The application paradigm that utilizes services distributed across a network as fundamental functional elements.
Service-Oriented Computing (SOC)	The computing paradigm that utilizes services as fundamental elements for developing applications [PAP200301].
Simple Object Access Protocol (SOAP)	A standard of the W3C that provides a framework for exchanging XML-based information.
SOA infrastructure	A simplified, virtualized, and distributed application framework that supports SOA.
Universal Discovery, Description and Integration (UDDI)	A standardized method for publishing and discovering information about Web Services. UDDI is an industry initiative that attempts to create a platform-independent, open framework for describing services, discovering businesses, and integrating business services. UDDI deals with the process of discovery in the SOA (WSDL is often used for service description, and SOAP for service invocation). Being a Web service itself, UDDI is invoked using SOAP. In addition, UDDI also defines how to operate servers and how to manage replication among several servers.
Web 2.0	System/approach that encompasses a range of technologies, tools, techniques, and standards that focus on enabling people to increase the social factor—how people connect with one another to improve how software works. Key principles involve use of lightweight programming models and standards, and techniques such as mash-ups, wikis, tagging, and blogs for richer user interfaces and improved use of data [IBM200701].
Web Services (WSs)	A software system designed to support interoperable machine-to-machine interaction over a network. It has an interface described in a machine-processable format (specifically WSDL). Other systems interact with the Web service in a manner prescribed by its description using SOAP messages, typically conveyed using HTTP with an XML serialization in conjunction with other Web-related standards [IBM200701].
	Web Services provide standard infrastructure for data exchange between two different distributed applications (grids provide an infrastructure for aggregation of high-end resources for solving large-scale problems). Web Services are expected to play a key constituent role in the standardized definition of grid computing, because they have emerged as a standards-based approach for accessing network applications.

(continued)

Table 11.1   Basic Service-Oriented Architecture Glossary (continued)

Web Services Description Language (WSDL)	An XML-based language used to describe Web Services and how to locate them; it provides information on what the service is about, where it resides and how it can be invoked.
Web Services Networking	Assembly of a more complex service from service modules that reside on different nodes connected to a network.
XML Networking	An approach that provides integration services by inspecting the full context of the application transaction and adding XML standards-based intelligence on top of the TCP/IP stack. An XML-enabled network provides greater control, flexibility, and efficiency for integrating applications than integration brokers [CIS200701].

11.2 XML, Web Services, and SOA Networking

The SOA networking evolution timeline follows but lags the SOA evolution itself. The evolution of SOA can be described as a continuum—from eXtensible Markup Language (XML) to WS to SOA. This evolution will likely continue to evolve to business process management (BPM). Likewise, the evolution of SOA networking has followed this continuum: from XML networking to WS networking to SOA networking; it will likely continue to evolve over time. This trend is driven by the desire of businesses to integrate with partners and have more intelligent exchanges with them, which inherently means exchanging more data and metadata.

Although the evolution continues, it does not mean that SOA networking is the solution for all applications and environments. For example, XML networking may be adequate for environments where a simple exchange of documents is needed. WS networking may be adequate for the simple exchange of structured data between databases. SOA networking is used to describe the management of services within and between homogenous and heterogeneous SOA environments.

11.2.1 XML Networking

In a Web environment, Hypertext Markup Language (HTML) is used to display information and XML is used to structure data in a representation that can be easily understood and agreed upon between a number of parties. Agreeing on the same data representation allows for easier exchange of documents and data. XML is a foundation for SOAP messaging, which in turn is the foundation of WS and SOA networking. XML networking is usually used for the simple exchange of XML documents over a network and is focused on the lower level of the stack.

11.2.2 WS Networking

As noted, WSs build upon XML and SOAP, and allow for the exchange of structured data, using a commonly agreed upon standards-based communications framework. This framework allows for organizations to communicate the numerous incompatibilities that exist between them as well as build more intelligent exchanges. Exposing WSs to the network requires a common interface called WSDL, which is built upon the SOAP messaging standard. UDDI is also part of this first generation of WS standards and allows for discovery of services beyond the immediate enterprise. UDDI, however, has not yet become popular for discovering services even though many vendors have adopted the support of service registries (UDDI v3.0). WS networking is based on standards and has been adopted primarily as B2B solutions for the exchange of structured data. These exchanges presently tend to be very limited in scope and are not usually implemented as part of an overall SOA architecture; therefore, they are not to be used for orchestrating, choreographing, or communicating services between SOA environments. It must be noted that building a bunch of WSs is not equivalent to architecting a SOA environment and, therefore, networking a bunch of WSs is not the same as SOA networking.

11.2.3 SOA Networking

The evolution of XML and WSs continues to move beyond simple exchange of documents and database records to support of distributed SOA environments. XML and WSs have become building blocks for an architectural platform—SOA. Although standards bodies such as OASIS (Organization for the Advancement of Structured Information Standards) are working on providing a common framework (SOA–RM) for understanding SOA and the related concepts, these concepts are still at a very high level of abstraction and do not specifically address the network as part of an overall SOA solution. Because standards bodies have not defined the terminology around networking in SOA environments, the following definitions have been put together to describe networking terminology used in the industry, although they may not be commonly accepted. The following definitions will help clarify what SOA networking is and is not.

11.2.3.1 Services Networking

The term *Services Networking* has been used to describe a network of WSs, but it is too general a term to know whether it denotes an architected SOA environment or not. As previously outlined, this could be just the exchange of WSs as in WS networking.

11.2.3.2 Service-Oriented Networking

The term *Service-Oriented Networking* (SON) is being used by the IT industry to describe networking of "distributed (Web) services" in networked environments. The term is also being used by the telecom industry to describe delivery and the composition of "network services," i.e., voice, video, and IPTV network-based applications. These network services and the service delivery (SDP) platform used to deliver these solutions in telecom environments may or may not be based on SOA principles. Finally, the term is also being used in the context of *service virtualization,* where *service* is a generic term describing various network services, such as security, identity, presence, etc. To add to the confusion, there may be instances where a network service is equivalent to a WS, and vice versa, but this may not always be the case.

There is some ambiguity surrounding the term SON, because it is not clear what is meant by a service and whether these services are "Web Services" or "network services"; it is also unclear whether these services are being used in SOA environments.

11.2.3.3 SOA Networking

The term *SOA Networking* (SOAN) relates to the networking of services in service-oriented environments (which can be homogeneous or heterogeneous) and is based on SOA principles. WSs are used in these environments to support the deployment of SOA architectures. Presently, most deployments are focused on primarily homogenous environments. However, as we move to the networking between heterogeneous environments, it becomes necessary to mediate between these environments. SOAN is presently being used interchangeably with SON; but is not as ambiguous as SON, because it clearly includes the term *SOA* in its definition. SOAN is based on XML, SOAP, and WSs, but it does not encompass XML and WSs networking, because it is possible to have the exchange of XML documents or WSs without being used in a SOA. SOAN is used to describe the use of WSs and associated messaging used to support a SOA. In SOAN more of the business logic starts to become distributed in the network itself, and the differentiation between what is an application and what is a network is replaced with the notion of *services* and *business processes*. Ideally, these business processes can be composed of services irrespective of distance, location, and platforms.

Figure 11.1 depicts an example of a SOA-based network [SOU200601]. To be consistent with the terminology associated with SOA, such as SOA platforms, SOA infrastructure, etc., the term *SOA Networking* has been adopted and used here.

The markets for XML, WS, and SOA are currently experiencing consolidation.

11.2.3.4 Service-Oriented Network Architecture

Service-Oriented Network Architecture (SONA) is a vendor-specific architectural framework that aims at delivering business solutions to unify network-based services such as security, mobility, and location with the virtualization of IT resources. SONA is composed of layers; so, as applications migrate to Web-based services, this architectural approach enables each layer to complement

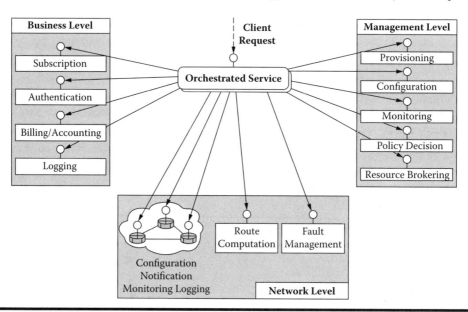

Figure 11.1 A service-oriented architecture for developing network services (after deSouza and Cardoza).

the functionality of the other layers, thereby presenting a loosely coupled framework. SONA's layers are the following [MIL200701]:

- Applications layer—This includes all software used for business purposes (e.g., enterprise resource planning) or collaboration (e.g., conferencing). As Web-based applications rely on XML schema and become tightly interwoven with routed messages, they become capable of supporting greater collaboration and more effective communications across an integrated networked environment.
- Integrated network services layer—This is a layer that optimizes communications between applications and services by taking advantage of distributed network functions such as continuous data protection, multi-protocol message routing, embedded quality of service (QoS), I/O virtualization, server load balancing, SSL VPN, identity, location, and IPv6-based services. These intelligent network-centric services can be used by the application layer through either transparent or exposed interfaces presented by the network.
- Network systems layer—This is a layer that provides the corporate campus, the data center, and remote branches a broad suite of collaborative connectivity functions, including peer-to-peer, client-to-server, and storage-to-storage connectivity.

11.2.3.5 Application-Oriented Networking

Application-Oriented Networking (AON) is a vendor-specific concept defined before SOA was commonly adopted in the industry and is primarily focused on routing, performance, and managing QoS associated with different types of applications. Because services are actually smaller composable units than an application, AON typically does not address applications that are built upon services in a SOA environment. AON is focused on the networking of applications and associated acceleration, performance, QoS, and managing of applications over networks. It preceded SOA; therefore, it is not built upon WSs and SOA principles, which call for the reuse and composability of services. Applications built upon these types of services by their very nature are much more dynamic than traditional applications because services having different characteristics or principles are associated with their use. The two major differences are composability and reuse. Supposedly, AON is part of SONA.

11.3 Network Architecture Framework

Many network architectural frameworks have been articulated over the years. The most commonly used and accepted networking framework is the International Organization for Standardization's (ISO) Open Systems Interconnection (OSI) Reference Model (OSIRM). For purposes of this analysis, the OSI reference model will be used and built upon. This model is also consistent with the model used to describe network infrastructure and data communications in The Open Group Architecture Framework (TOGAF). A SOAN framework will build on the OSIRM, which describes the components that help articulate in more detail the need of networking in SOA environments.

Figure 11.2 shows the SOA Networking Architecture Framework (SNAF) (also known as SOAN Architecture Framework) and the mapping from the ISO OSIRM to the SOAN model. This is an arbitrary grouping of functionalities based on the current view of functionality being implemented by SOAN software and devices. The major difference between the OSI and SNAF

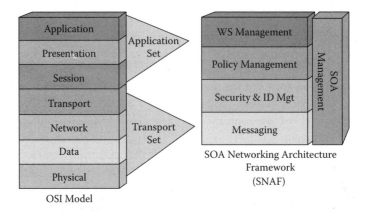

Figure 11.2   SOA networking architecture framework (SNAF).

models is that the latter is focused on the upper layers of the model—layers 4–7, i.e., the application layer; in SNAF there is less of a clear demarcation point between layers 1–4 and 5–7 than there has been in the past. Note that the grouping and management of layers 5–7 are becoming more important from WS and SOA aspects. SOAP messaging is essentially an overlay on other networks, primarily IP; it operates above the transport layer, Layer 4.

Using SNAF, we will first talk about the lower levels of the stack—messaging, which includes routing, transformation, etc., and then security, which includes identity and access management. From there, we will address the upper layers of the model—outlining policy management, WS management, and SOA management, where true value is being delivered to enterprises.

11.4 XML and SOAP Messaging

This overview of XML and SOA messaging in the context of the SNAF is limited in nature because our focus area is the upper layers of the stack.

11.4.1 XML Messaging

XML is an extensible language because it enables the definition of many classes of documents. XML is designed to make it easy to define document types, author and manage documents, and transmit and share them in a distributed environment. SOAP is built upon XML.

11.4.2 Basic SOAP Messaging

SOAP messaging has become the leading standard for use with WS and is being adopted by MOM vendors in addition to other protocols.

SOAP is a lightweight protocol for exchange of XML-based information in distributed environments and is designed to allow transparent intermediaries to perform processing on behalf of the service components within a SOA (see Figure 11.3).

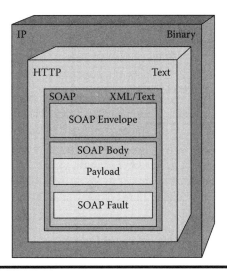

Figure 11.3 SOAP message structure.

11.4.2.1 Representational State Transfer (REST)

REST is gaining in popularity as many believe that WS standards are taking too long to be developed and feel that there is too much overhead associated with this SOAP messaging. REST has been growing in popularity as a solution to meet requirements of many applications.

REST Web Services architecture conforms to the W3C's Web Architecture, and leverages the architectural principles of the Web, building its strength on the proven infrastructure of the Web. It utilizes the semantics of HTTP whenever possible and most of the principles, constraints, and best practices published by the W3C's Technical Architecture Group (TAG) also apply [HHE200401]. The term REST was first introduced by Roy Fielding to describe the Web architecture. A REST Web Service is an SOA based on the concept of "resource." A resource is anything that has a Universal Resource Identifier (URI). A resource may have zero or more representations. Usually, people say that a resource does not exist if no representation is available for that resource. A REST Web Service requires the following additional constraints [HHE200301]:

1. Interfaces are limited to HTTP. The following semantics are defined:
   - HTTP GET is used for obtaining a representation of a resource. A consumer uses it to retrieve a representation from a URI. Services provided through this interface must not incur any obligation from consumers.
   - HTTP DELETE is used for removing representations of a resource.
   - HTTP POST is used for updating or creating the representations of a resource.
   - HTTP PUT is used for creating representations of a resource.
2. Most messages are in XML, confined by a schema written in a schema language such as XML Schema from W3C or RELAX NG.
3. Simple messages can be encoded with URL encoding.
4. Service and service providers must be resources while a consumer can be a resource.

REST Web Services require little infrastructure support apart from standard HTTP and XML processing technologies, which are now well supported by most programming languages and platforms. REST Web Services are simple and effective because HTTP is the most widely available interface, and it is good enough for most applications. In many cases, the simplicity of HTTP simply outweighs the complexity of introducing and additional transport layer.

11.4.3 Advanced SOAP Messaging

Basic SOAP messaging capabilities have been implemented in the first released standards. However, additional advanced messaging capabilities of WS.* extensions are being put forth: WS-ReliableMessaging (WSRM), WS-BusinessActivity, WS-Policy, WS-Context, etc.

Until the advanced messaging capabilities of the proposed WS.* extensions become commonplace, many messaging applications will have to be augmented with custom SOAP headers to implement interim solutions and manage more complex message exchanges.

11.5 SOA Security, Identity Management, and Access Control

The SOA security layer within the SOAN Architecture Framework is driven by general SOA principles, security challenges under SOA, and the architectural requirements designed to ensure that the SOA platform can be invoked securely. Although SOA security is fundamentally different from what we are used to, this is a mandatory baseline needed for deploying and managing services. The real value is delivered in the upper layers of the model.

11.5.1 Basic SOA Security

Our present security models are for the most part modeled on client/server relationships, which are simply outdated in the service-oriented world of security. We must model our security architecture based on services and the fact that these services can be reused between provider and consumers. Also, it must be based on the fact that processes will replace the notion of applications and that these processes are made up of services.

Service-oriented collaboration and composition is fundamentally different and requires a different approach. Most of today's security architecture is based on the assumption that both clients and servers are collocated either physically on the same LAN or logically on a connected network through a virtual private network (VPN). Therefore, perimeter-based security relies on traditional solutions, such as DMZ's, firewalls, and intrusion detection, to address security threats. The resulting security policies associated with this type of perimeter-based architecture will also primarily be perimeter focused.

In SOA environment, perimeter-based security models are generally inadequate. The primary goal of building a SOA is to facilitate net-centric information sharing and collaboration:

- Business functionality, previously inaccessible unless, for instance, physically sitting in front of a terminal, will become service-enabled and exposed to external consumers via standard WS protocols.
- Consumers, which may be services themselves, can dynamically discover services and make use of their data in real-time.
- Services are inherently location independent and not necessarily even bound to a physical location. The network addresses or endpoints of services are published in a service registry such as UDDI, but can change over time as services are relocated during normal system evolution or for failover reasons during system maintenance.

■ Service consumers and providers may belong to different physical networks or even different organizations. These networks or organizations may be governed by entirely different security policies.

Therefore, in a net-centric environment, the focus on perimeter-based security models must be augmented with an application or a service level view of security. With both models in mind, the emphasis is not placed on physical ownership and control but on network identities, trust, and authorized access to resources by both users and other principals.

Security within a net-centric environment has its own challenges:

■ **Firewall limitations**—Allowing inbound Hypertext Transfer Protocol (HTTP) access to WSs opens up servers to potential attack that may not be detectable by conventional firewall products. For example, a malicious SOAP message may be constructed to cause internal application buffer overflow, although looking completely benign to the firewall and the HTTP server. Recently, many new XML firewall products have emerged that attempt to protect WSs at the SOAP level, but their effectiveness has not been closely studied, and the positioning of those products within the entire enterprise security architecture is not yet clear.

■ **Service level security semantics**—Most of the standardization efforts have focused on defining the wire formats needed for security information exchange. The standards largely ignore the similar challenge of defining the mechanism by which different parties interface with one another to achieve security goals such as authentication and authorization. For example, Security Association Markup Language (SAML) defines the XML structures and protocols for sending authentication assertions, but it does not prescribe who should pass what information to whom, when information should be passed, or how such information may be used.

■ **Interoperability of security solutions**—Because of the lack of standard profiling at the service interface level, WS security products in the market today are not fully interoperable even though they all claim to be compliant with WS security standards. Further, many are point solutions that do not meet all requirements of U.S. Department of Defense (DoD) enterprise security architecture, and are not capable of extending beyond enterprise boundaries.

■ **Secure composition and orchestration**—As WS enterprises proliferate, there is an increasing need for multiple services to interact among one another within a joint business process or workflow. This situation presents many security challenges. For example, SOAP is not a full-blown messaging protocol and does not have inherent provisions for a service consumer to specify destinations or the "itinerary" of an invocation sequence. As a result, the SOAP message might be replayed to unintended third parties bearing the same operation signature.

■ **Multiple security domains and classification levels**—Current guard technologies are not yet connection oriented and must evolve to support XML and SOAP message security.

■ **Security versus performance**—A Public Key (PK)-enabled security architecture involves many computation-intensive tasks such as message signing, encryption, and certificate validation. Sending a properly signed message may be many times slower than a less secure version, and there is usually a direct inverse relationship between performance and security. Cautious planning and effective optimization techniques are necessary to ensure that a secured SOA environment will meet operational requirements.

- **Impacts on existing policies and processes**—Current certification and accreditation (C&A) policies generally require identification of system boundaries, whereas in a SOA-based network, trust relationships are established more dynamically. One possible solution is to define the C&A boundaries in the WS interfaces.

The primary goal of security architecture is to ensure services within the SOA Foundation that can be invoked securely. As with every critical distributed system, there is a set of key security requirements that must be met:

- **Authentication**—Service providers will in most cases require that consumers be authenticated before accepting a service request. Service consumers will also need to authenticate service providers when a response is received. Different authentication mechanisms should be supported, and these mechanisms should be configurable and interchangeable according to service-specific requirements.
- **Authorization**—In addition to authentication of a service consumer, access to a service will also require the consumer to possess certain privileges. These privileges feed an authorization check that is usually based on access control policies—who can access a service and under what conditions, for example. Different models may be used for authorization, such as mandatory or role-based access control. The authorization implementation should also be extensible to allow for domain- or Community of Interest (COI)-specific customizations.
- **Confidentiality**—The messages or documents that are carried over the underlying communication transport have to be reported so that they cannot be made available to unauthorized parties. Sometimes only a fragment of the message or document (e.g., wrapped within a certain XML tag) may need to be kept confidential.
- **Data integrity**—Protection has to be provided against unauthorized alteration of messages during transit.
- **Non-repudiation**—Protection has to be provided against false denial of involvement in a communication. Non-repudiation ensures that a sender cannot deny a message already sent and a receiver cannot deny a message already received. A more common form of non-repudiation for messaging systems is sender non-repudiation, which only ensures that a sender cannot deny a message already sent. Non-repudiation is especially important in monetary transactions and security auditing.
- **Manageability**—The security architecture should also provide management capabilities for security functions. These may include, but are not limited to, credential management, user management, and access control policy management.
- **Accountability**—This includes secure logging and auditing, which is also required to support non-repudiation claims. In addition, the following additional requirements are specific to or are also important in a SOA environment.
- **Interoperability**—Interoperability is the cornerstone of SOAs, and the security architecture must preserve it to the maximum extent possible. Major security integration points in the architecture—such as those between service consumers and service providers, and between service providers and the security infrastructure—must have stable, consistent interfaces based on widely adopted industry and government standards. These interfaces enable each domain or organization to implement its own market-driven solution while maintaining effective interoperability.
- **Modeling tailored constraints in security policies**—In a traditional security domain, resources and services are often protected by a uniform set of security rules that are not

granular enough to meet specific application needs. Under a SOA, service provider requirements may vary in terms of how they need to be protected. For example, one service may require X.509-certificate-based authentication, whereas another may only need username/password authentication. Further, because clients that access a resource may or may not be from the local domain, different "strengths" of authentication and access control may be required. Consequently, security policies must be expressive and flexible enough to be tailored according to a variety of parameters (e.g., principal attributes).

■ **Allowing integration with existing Information Assurance (IA) solutions, products, and policies**—The SOA-based security architecture is not intended to replace an existing investment in security infrastructure. On the contrary, a flexible IA solution should be designed to leverage existing IT investments without initiating any redundant development efforts. Seamless integration with existing security tools and applications also increases the overall stability of the enterprise.

■ **Securing other infrastructure services within the SOA**, such as discovery, messaging, mediation, and service management.

■ **Unobtrusiveness**—The architecture should be unobtrusive to other service implementations. More specifically, to deploy into the new security architecture, a service provider shall not have to
  - Be constrained to use any one particular programming language
  - Port an existing service implementation to a specific hardware platform
  - Modify an existing implementation against any vendor-specific API interface
  - Recompile or rebuild existing code sets

11.5.2 Identity Management and Access Control

Effective control of identity management services for a SOA will require the use of policies that define the identity-specific requirements of each interaction, such as how a consumer of a business function service must be authenticated or what their rights to access particular information are. Because these identity services depend on identity data, it will be necessary to maintain a reconciled and unified view of identity information.

Regulatory compliance will also exert its influence. Concerns about identity theft will require role-based approaches to security that grade authentication and authorization to more accurately reflect the risks of all parties in a transaction.

Another factor to take into account is that services will increasingly depend on collaboration between service providers. This means that there will be a need for federation among service providers; once a user has been authenticated by one service, no further authentication would be required.

All of this means that identity management must be delivered as a set of horizontal, resource-agnostic capabilities, as opposed to vertical, resource-specific, fragmented silos.

Any architectural blueprint for identity management must be based on a clear separation of identity management concerns, with identity management capabilities delivered as a set of distributed infrastructure services, underpinned by a federated identity data repository.

Resources access these services through policy-based mediation, which also serves to control the monitoring and audit functions required to mitigate risk, and enforce and demonstrate compliance. Identity data must be managed throughout its life cycle, from core data maintenance through to provisioning and deprovisioning, by a set of processes implemented using automated workflow and process management technologies, to increase efficiency, enforce consistency, and facilitate integration of identity management and business processes. Open standard protocols and data formats bridge the gaps between the layers to facilitate interoperability between the architectural components and the broader IT infrastructure.

11.6 Security Policy

Security policy focuses on the actual configuration and description policies for nonfunctional features of specific SOA elements that describe and configure low-level security and reliability settings of specific services such as WS-Security and WS-SecurePolicy.

11.7 Policy Management

In the narrow sense of the term, policy is focused on the description and configuration of certain nonfunctional features of specific SOA elements that typically are associated with the rules around security and identity management. However, policy management in SOA environments is meant to take on a broader meaning. Policy management can take on additional functionality in the form of constraint and compliance policies, while at the same time being applied to services delivered to a wider audience than just internal users—for example, clients and partners. **Constraint policies** represent constraints (typically nonfunctional) or contractual agreements that need to be fulfilled like a service level agreement (SLA). **Compliance policies** are simple thresholds that identify either existing or desired compliance to specification and standards, for example, to WS.* policy or WSDL specifications.

Policy management is an underlying capability of SOA and provides flexibility and configurability, and the business service interface layer is a convenient and architecturally sound place to apply the policies for technical operation. The real value added to SOA lies in its ability to move beyond the basic management and security of services and cross into the business domain, where higher levels of business management and associated policies can be deployed and managed. Security is important and is the baseline that is required for all SOA Infrastructure deployments. However, the real value delivered to the business lies in the higher levels of the stack, where the policy management and capabilities of SOA can be exploited. Most of the emphasis is presently focused on SOA Governance, but this is expected to evolve beyond the enterprise.

11.7.1 Policy Life Cycle Management Process

Policy management can be considered in terms of a process (see Figure 11.4). Generally, a process is made up of the following steps, which are common to all processes: **Plan -> Do -> Check-> Correct**. In terms of a Policy Life Cycle Management Process, the process is made up of Policy Administration, Policy Deployment, Policy Monitoring, and Policy Enforcement. Because it is a closed-loop process, the resulting enforcement needs to be fed back to the policy creation, where the effectiveness of the policies can be measured and modified if necessary.

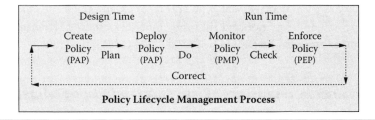

Figure 11.4   Policy Life-Cycle Management Process.

11.7.2 Policy Administration Point

The Policy Administration Point (PAP) is any functional component that supports the centralized definition and authoring of policies, and remote distribution of these policies to one or more Policy Enforcement Points (PEPs). Vendor-provided authoring tools for creating and administering various classes of policies are business-based, content-based, message-based, and session-handling policies. The PAP distributes policies to the PEPs for execution and enforcement. PAPs are evolving and include reporting tools to identity exceptions and the ability to modify policies. Policies also need to be captured to a repository and recorded so that they may later be auditable.

11.7.3 Policy Monitoring Point

A Policy Monitoring Point (PMP) usually captures real-time collection and statistics analysis for display. This management console provides visibility into the management of a distributed network of PEPs and the status of these enforcements. In addition, these consoles log, aggregate measurements, and highlight significant events. The data is correlated and analyzed, and visualization of data is fed in by the various PEPs. The PMP and PAP can be integrated into a visually oriented management tool, such as a Business Automation Monitoring (BAM) Tool, to monitor business processes as well as policies.

11.7.4 Policy Enforcement Points

A PEP can be implemented in software or as a stand-alone network device. It is any hardware-based, high-performance functional component that intercepts, inspects, filters, and performs content-aware policy-driven processing on application messages and their payloads. The PEP may execute diverse policies and lower-level message functionalities outlined previously, such as addressing transformation, routing, caching, compression, and other content-handling functions. The specific packaging functionality varies among vendor implementations and can be packaged in software or hardware (firmware). PEP functionality can also be implemented in conjunction with other network device functionalities, such as coprocessors, proxies, gateways, blade servers, routers, grids, and other configurations.

In the narrow sense of the term, policy management is associated with the management of security, identity management, access control, and application performance management. However, in the world of SOA, policy management has been broadened to encompass the management of other processes (on a service-by-service basis) and based on the Plan, Do, Check, and Correct process. In the regulated, post-Enron world, and with the need for vendors to provide return on investment, policy life cycle management now encompasses governance, compliance, and risk. However, many policy administration and authoring tools allow for the authoring of user-defined policies, and in some instances these could be user-defined policies.

11.7.5 Governance, Compliance, Risk, SLA, and User-Defined Policies

Software development compliance is a small subset of an organization's overall "business compliance" efforts, and policy life-cycle management is seen as a way to help organizations support it (see Figure 11.5).

11.7.5.1 SOA Governance, Risk, and Compliance (GRC)

The policy in SOA is a broad process that can be applied to a variety of different processes, and more recently the focus has been on **SOA governance** of the software development process. Governance is usually expressed in terms of the management of one's own environment. This may be in response to internal or external forces. **Compliance** requires governance, but governance alone is not sufficient to demonstrate compliance unless specific goals and measurements related to the regulations have been put in place and fulfilled. This means that a business-driven process must not only have measurement, policy, and control mechanisms in place, but it must also be auditable. To be auditable, many implementations include repositories to store and manage services. **Risk** is a measurement between the actual state and the desired state, and in terms of Policy Life-Cycle Management Process, it could be measured by the delta between the policy definitions and results of policy enforcement.

With compliant development environments, executives can manage risk associated with development. Project teams can have more control and predictability across their project. This implies an ongoing program to respond quickly to changing regulatory environments, thus hopefully reducing risk. Governance, and compliance are instances of policy life-cycle management, but there are other applications too.

11.7.5.2 Service Level Agreements and Contracts

SLAs and contracts could also be theoretically managed through the same Policy Life-Cycle Management Process. SLAs address situations when access thresholds or latencies need to be managed on a service-by-service basis. SLA management is being used with increasing frequency in general outsourcing, E-business, and B2B applications. Metrics such as processing time, messages per hour, rejected transaction counts, etc., are then compared by policy enforcement to the desired level. The result then drives some sort of corrective action, which may be simply reporting, the auditing of results and violations, or changing SLAs or contract agreements.

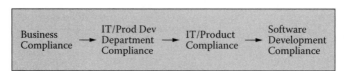

Figure 11.5 Organization compliance hierarchy.

11.7.5.3 User-Defined and Managed Policy

To generalize even further, policies are essentially processes. In the broadest sense, policies can also be user defined. The whole Web 2.0 movement is about putting service coordination (mashups) in the hands of the end users. Although it is uncertain how far this will go, it is gaining momentum and some companies are looking at the ability of users to define and manage policies (within limits). For example, some cellular companies allow users to manage a rate plan dollar amount to be managed between various media offerings.

11.8 WS Management and Monitoring

WS management is focused on monitoring the overall health of the system, managing performance and uptime of the systems, and allowing for the administration and management of the integration system. The typical functionalities include system installation, provisioning, configuration, user creation service monitoring, service level management, alert management, etc.

These tools can be integrated into an overall network management solution.

11.9 Business-Level SOA Management and Analysis

As SOA implementation matures within enterprises, there is a need to manage the overall health of the business. The focus of business-level SOA management is to monitor and report on the business processes, applications, services, and infrastructure, including hardware, software (O/S, middleware), network devices, and storage.

11.9.1 Business-Level SOA Management

The management of SOA occurs on various levels, the most important being the business services layer—the inventory of SOA-based services that deliver core business capabilities in a modular, incrementally composable way to facilitate the composition of any business process between suppliers, partners, or customers. Also important are lower-level interfaces built around the needs of particular applications. For both of these types of interfaces, SOA management solutions can monitor and manage SOA activity by providing visibility into SOAP messaging and viewing the request-response messages flow into and out of services. This can be done without having to manage the service implementation.

Not only does management allow visibility into SOAP messaging, SOA appliances can also intercept and interpret content that resides in those messages. Therefore, SOA management solutions can implement additional functions, such as enforcing policies for security and governance, collecting business data from service flows, or providing a basic level of application integration through mediation.

SOA management covers the following categories:

1. Policy-based management
2. Business process management—end-to-end management services used
3. Interoperability—mediation between homogenous and heterogeneous environments

Beyond simple WS applications, business service management relates to the management of SOA. Comprehensive SOA management also can include other features, such as alerting and exception management, deployment management, logging and auditing support and business analysis, and correlated event, message, and policy logs.

11.9.2 Business Activity Monitoring (BAM)

These tools sit at the highest level of the stack and provide the highest levels of business integration services. These are the tools that monitor the health of the business. They provide the monitoring capability for business processes and transactions.

11.9.3 Networked Business Intelligence

Business intelligence (BI) is a continuum that starts with the collection of data, analysis of that data, and its transformation into actionable knowledge that can be used to manage the day-to-day operations of the business and predict future opportunities and risks to the business (see Figure 11.6). Most BI is focused on gathering data from within the enterprise. The use of Networked BI implies that the boundaries of this continuum can move beyond the enterprise. In this scenario, more information and metadata can be gathered and analyzed from beyond the immediate enterprise—the extended enterprise and partners.

11.10 SOA Interoperability

In completely homogenous SOA environments, managing services between service requestors and service providers is relatively straightforward, and ESB provides this functionality today in what we call **Enterprise SOA**. However, as we move beyond the enterprise into more distributed heterogeneous environments, mediation is usually required to broker between various environments (**B2B SOA**); although this functionality may be implemented by ESBs, more of it, and associated logic, is moved to the network to implement limited ESB capabilities.

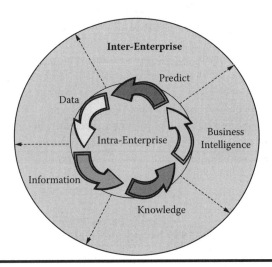

Figure 11.6 Knowledge discovery continuum.

The reality is that business services will likely be used in heterogeneous SOA environments by a variety of internal and external users, and these users will have a wide variety of interoperable technologies and applications. Therefore, mediation capabilities become more important to mediate between different standards and versions of those standards (**standards mediation**), between different protocols (**protocol mediation**), and between asynchronous and synchronous communications (**message exchange pattern (MEP) mediation**).

To accommodate these differences, service implementations must do either of the following: have an interface for each variation, force others to adapt to their services, or mediate between the two environments. Because SOA is about flexibility and abstraction away from particular platforms or specific implementations, management usually provides for some limited mediation capabilities.

WS-Policy (specification, not a standard at the time of writing) defines a policy framework about how organizations are going to exchange information between incompatible environments.

The WSDL tells you where to send the SOAP request and what the operations are; there are more if a requestor and a service provider are going to actually work together. There are a lot of other considerations that are not API related—security mechanisms, credentials, encryption, reliable messaging, etc.—which simply cannot be expressed in a WSDL.

WS-Policy will become the fundamental mechanism to mediate between all types of systems.

11.11 WS Standards

11.11.1 Basic Standards

When WSs first emerged as a distributed computing alternative, there were two core standards associated with it: WSDL (common interface standard), and SOAP (common messaging format). However, as the first WS began emerging in early adopter enterprises, many concerns were voiced: "If everything is openly exposed using a common interface standard communicating over HTTP, how will I control access to my services?"; "Given the simplicity of the SOAP envelope, how will a message expose its desired destination?"; and "Given the inherent unreliability of Internet-standard protocols, how can I guarantee that messages are delivered in support of business-critical applications?"

Key standards and specifications for WSs are as follows (also see Figure 11.7):

> *XML: Extensible Mark-Up Language*—An extensible language because it enables the definition of many classes of documents. XML is designed to make it easy to define document types, author and manage documents, and transmit and share them in a distributed environment.
> *SOAP: Simple Object Access Protocol*—A lightweight protocol for exchange of XML-based information in a distributed environment.
> *WS-Policy: Web Services Policy*—A fledgling specification; it aims to handle policies around SOAP-based WSs, including but not limited to security policies.
> *WSDL: Web Services Description Language*—An XML-based syntax for describing WSs.
> *BPEL: Business Process Execution Language*—XML-based language for the specification of business processes. Basically, it underpins business processes in an SOA.
> *UDDI: Universal Description, Discovery, and Integration*—UDDI defines a registry architecture. It is a place to store, share and discover WSs.
> *WS-Security: Web Services Security*—A specification—not yet a standard—for handling security in a SOA.

In addition to these basic standards, additional standard extensions have been added.

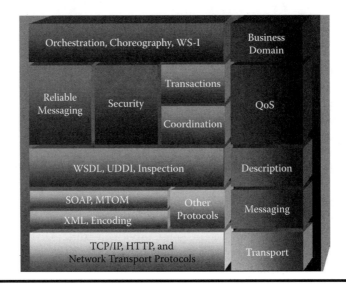

Figure 11.7   Web Services standards stack.

11.11.2 WS-* Standards Extensions

Increasingly, additional standards have emerged to tackle most of these issues, such as WS-Security and WS-Addressing (arguably the two most widely adopted WS-* standards).

More recently, WS-ReliableMessaging has emerged to provide a standard means of enabling a variety of advanced reliable messaging techniques. In a nutshell, WS-ReliableMessaging defines a transport-independent protocol that enables a variety of reliable messaging techniques between distributed services, including "at least once" delivery, "exactly once" delivery, and "in order" delivery. WS-ReliableMessaging has been coauthored by IBM, Microsoft, Tibco, and BEA. Support for the standard has begun emerging in products from established market makers, in addition to certain start-up vendors.

11.11.3 WS-I Basic Profiles

The **WS-I Basic Profile**, a specification from the Web Services Interoperability (WS-I) industry consortium, provides interoperability guidance for core WS specifications such as SOAP, WSDL, and UDDI. The profile uses WSDL to enable the description of services as sets of endpoints operating on messages. When complete, the package of deliverables produced in conjunction with the WS-I Basic Profile will be as follows [IBM200201]:

- **Use cases and usage scenarios:** Use cases and usage scenarios capture business and technical requirements, respectively, for the use of WSs. These requirements reflect the classes of real-world requirements supporting WS solutions, and provide a framework to demonstrate the guidelines described in WS-I Profiles.
- **Profiles:** Profiles are comprised of a set of named and versioned WS specifications together with a set of implementation and interoperability guidelines recommending how the specifications may be used to develop interoperable WS.

- **Sample applications:** Sample applications demonstrate the implementation of applications that are built from WS usage scenarios and use cases, and that conform to a given set of profiles. Implementations of the same sample application on multiple platforms, languages, and development tools demonstrate interoperability in action, and provide readily usable resources for the WS practitioner.
- **Testing tools:** Testing tools are used to monitor and analyze interactions with a WS to determine whether or not the messages exchanged conform to WS-I Profile guidelines.

The WS-I process begins with the definition of use cases that describe how WSs can be applied to meet real-world business needs. These use cases are then decomposed into usage scenarios supporting various aspects of the use cases and design patterns. The usage scenarios describe the ways in which WSs are employed in the context of the collected use cases. This work aids in the demonstration of how WS specifications are used individually, in concert with one another, or both. Use case analysis forms the foundation for the definition of profile requirements.

11.11.3.1 WS- Basic Profile 1.0

WS- Basic Profile 1.0 is a set of nonproprietary WS specifications. It deals with the following (among other things): Conformance of Artifacts; Conformance of Services, Consumers and Registries; Messaging; XML Representation of SOAP Messages; SOAP Processing Model; Use of SOAP in HTTP; Service Descriptions; WSDL Schema Definitions; Types and Port Types; Bindings; Use of XML Schema; and Service Publication and Discovery. It incorporates the following specifications by reference, and defines extensibility points within them:

- Simple Object Access Protocol (SOAP) 1.1
- Extensible Markup Language (XML) 1.0 (Second Edition)
- RFC2616: Hypertext Transfer Protocol—HTTP/1.1
- RFC2965: HTTP State Management Mechanism

The profile was developed according to a set of principles that together form the philosophy of the profile, as it relates to bringing about interoperability. The guidelines were as follows:

No guarantee of interoperability: It is impossible to completely guarantee the interoperability of a particular service. However, the profile does address the most common problems that implementation experience has revealed to date.
Application semantics: Although communication of application semantics can be facilitated by the technologies that comprise the profile, ensuring the common understanding of those semantics is not addressed by it.
Testability: When possible, the profile makes statements that are testable. However, such testability is not required. Preferably, testing is achieved in a nonintrusive manner (e.g., examining artifacts "on the wire").
Strength of requirements: The profile lays down strong requirements (e.g., MUST, MUST NOT) wherever feasible; if there are legitimate cases where such a requirement cannot be met, conditional requirements (e.g., SHOULD, SHOULD NOT) are used. Optional and conditional requirements introduce ambiguity and mismatches between implementations.
Restriction versus relaxation: When amplifying the requirements of referenced specifications, the profile may restrict them, but does not relax them (e.g., change a MUST to a MAY).

Multiple mechanisms: If a referenced specification allows multiple mechanisms to be used interchangeably, the profile selects those that are well understood, widely implemented, and useful. Extraneous or underspecified mechanisms and extensions introduce complexity and therefore reduce interoperability.

Future compatibility: When possible, the profile aligns its requirements with in-progress revisions to the specifications it references (e.g., SOAP 1.2, WSDL 1.2). This aids implementers by enabling a graceful transition, and ensures that WS-I does not "fork" from these efforts. When the profile cannot address an issue in a specification it references, this information is communicated to the appropriate body to ensure its consideration.

Compatibility with deployed services: Backward compatibility with deployed WSs is not a goal for the profile, but due consideration is given to it; the profile does not introduce a change to the requirements of a referenced specification unless doing so addresses specific interoperability issues.

Focus on interoperability: Although there are potentially a number of inconsistencies and design flaws in the referenced specifications, the profile only addresses those that affect interoperability.

Conformance targets: Where possible, the profile imposes requirements on artifacts (e.g., WSDL descriptions, SOAP messages) rather than the producing or consuming software's behaviors or roles. Artifacts are concrete, making them easier to verify and therefore making conformance easier to understand and less error prone.

Lower-layer interoperability: The profile speaks to interoperability at the application layer; it assumes that interoperability of lower-layer protocols (e.g., TCP, IP, Ethernet) is adequate and well understood. Similarly, statements about application-layer substrate protocols (e.g., SSL/TLS, HTTP) are only made when there is an issue affecting WSs specifically; WS-I does not attempt to ensure the interoperability of these protocols as a whole. This ensures that WS-I's expertise in and focus on WS standards is used effectively.

11.11.3.2 WS- Basic Profile 1.1

This profile is derived from the Basic Profile 1.0 by incorporating any errata to date and separating out those requirements related to the serialization of envelopes and their representation in messages. Such requirements are now part of the Simple SOAP Binding Profile 1.0, identified with a separate conformance claim. This separation is made to facilitate composability of Basic Profile 1.1 with any profile that specifies envelope serialization, including the Simple SOAP Binding Profile 1.0 and the Attachments Profile 1.0. A combined claim of conformance to both the Basic Profile 1.1 and the Simple SOAP Binding Profile 1.0 is roughly equivalent to a claim of conformance to the Basic Profile 1.0 plus published errata. This profile, composed with the Simple SOAP Binding Profile 1.0, supersedes the Basic Profile 1.0. The Attachments Profile 1.0 adds support for SOAP with attachments, and is intended to be used in combination with this profile.

11.12 SOA Platform Functionality, Components, and SOA Infrastructure

Up to this point it was important to prepare the ground and to outline a common framework for SOA; next, it was also important to discuss the various layers within that architecture and associated functionalities needed to implement within a SOA. From this point on, we will now be able to discuss, at a high level, how the functionalities previously discussed are grouped and actually implemented as SOA platforms, components, SOA infrastructure, and SOA network infrastructure.

The management of WS in a collocated SOA environment has proved to be more complex than originally envisioned, and subsequently the management of WSs in a distributed SOA environment has turned out to be even more complex than originally envisioned.

What is important to remember is that this analysis is only a snapshot in time and that the baseline for what is considered a *SOA platform* is based on functionality that continues to evolve. In addition to the fact that the SOA platform functionality continues to be enriched by additional features/functionality, the SOA platform is also evolving as SOA adoption continues to grow.

The evolution can actually be characterized as taking place in two dimensions:

1. First and most obvious is that as the bottom layers of the stack become more standardized and commoditized, there is a tendency to move to higher levels of the stack, where the real business value addition can take place.
2. The second dimension is to leverage from what has been learned within the enterprise to move beyond the enterprise and start to expose services to lines of business within the enterprise, to trusted partners, and unknown partners. In this dimension the services are now beginning to be exposed beyond the firewall and impact networks. Historical trends have shown us that functionality such as routing, fire-walling, and load balancing have been offloaded from application servers and commoditized and migrated into network devices.

Actual functionality supported and implementations as outlined earlier are implemented by vendors in a variety of ways and may or may not include features/functionality outlined here.

11.12.1 SOA Platform Functionality

The current view of SOA platforms largely supports application delivery, integration, management, security, identity management, and overall SOA management within an enterprise (see Figure 11.8). However, as services become more distributed, these SOA platforms must consider these functionalities only on a wider plane. As the evolution of SOA management moves to encompass partners, suppliers and customers and the distributed nature of SOA management will encompass and impact the networks.

Presently, most efforts are focused on enterprise integration, and at a very high level the functionality can be characterized by a set of about a half-dozen groupings. At this point there is no concern regarding how these capabilities actually get implemented. The next section will outline how this functionality gets packaged into a product.

Although somewhat of a moving target, a *Full Suite SOA Platform* generally consists of the following grouping of basic functionality:

1. **Business Model** defines how the business goals and desires influence process and service definitions.
2. **Enterprise Business Process** defines tools, processes, and technology for orchestrating services.
3. **Service Definition** specifies definition and requirements of a service.
4. **Service Bus Functionality** (Enterprise Service Bus or Services Network) defines the communications technologies for applications integration.

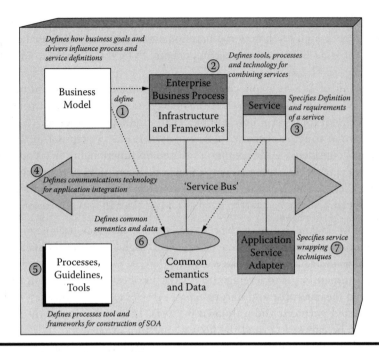

Defines how business goals and drivers influence process and service definitions

② *Defines tools, processes and technology for combining services*

Business Model

define ①

Enterprise Business Process

Infrastructure and Frameworks

Service

③ *Specifies Definition and requirements of a serivce*

④ *Defines communications technology for application integration*

'Service Bus'

Defines common semantics and data ⑥

⑤ Processes, Guidelines, Tools

Common Semantics and Data

Application Service Adapter

Specifies service wrapping ⑦ *techniques*

Defines processes tool and frameworks for construction of SOA

Figure 11.8 SOA platform functionality.

5. **Development Environment** defines processes, tools, and frameworks for developing a SOA.
6. **Common Semantics and Data Repository** defines common semantics and metadata.
7. **Application Service Adapters** specifies service-wrapping techniques.

11.12.2 SOA Platform Components

The functionality outlined earlier can generally be grouped into the following physical components of a SOA platform. The actual implementation by vendors will vary substantially from vendor to vendor. Also, some vendors may only implement certain aspects of this functionality, whereas there are others who offer full suites.

11.12.2.1 Enterprise Service Bus (ESB) Component

The core of most SOA implementations is typically built upon middleware in the form of an ESB. One definition describes ESB functionality as follows: "Delivers all of the interconnectivity capabilities required to leverage the services implemented across the entire architecture, including transport services, event services, and mediation services." This is only one definition of an ESB, and there are a variety of definitions for ESBs; however, the best way of describing an ESB is by outlining the functionality or capabilities of an ESB. The ESB usually has more or less the following functionality incorporated into it:

Routing—The ability to channel a request to a particular service provider on deterministic or variable routing criteria. Types of routing can be static or deterministic routing, content-based routing, policy-based routing, or complex rules-based routing.

Message Transformation—The ability to convert the structure and the format of the incoming business service requests to the structure and format expected by the service provider.

Message Enhancement—The ability to add or modify the information contained in the message as required by the service provider. Examples of message enhancements are as follows.

Protocol Transformation—The ability to accept one type of protocol from the consumer as input (i.e., SOAP/JMS) and then communicate to the service provider through a different protocol (i.e., IIOP).

Service Mapping—The ability to translate a business service into a corresponding service implementation and provide binding and location information.

Message Processing—The ability to manage state and perform request management by accepting an input request and ensuring delivery back to the client via message synchronization.

Process Choreography—The ability to manage complex business processes that require the coordination of multiple *business services* to fulfill a single business service request.

Service Orchestration—The ability to manage the coordination of multiple *implementation services*.

Transaction Management—The ability to provide a single unit of work for a business service request by providing a framework for the coordination of multiple resources across multiple disparate services.

Security—The ability to protect enterprise services from unauthorized access.

11.12.2.2 ESB Adapters

In addition to an ESB itself, ESB adapters are often needed to provide bridging capabilities between legacy applications, prepackaged applications, enterprise data stores, and the ESB to incorporate services that are delivered through existing applications into a SOA environment.

11.12.2.3 Registry

A registry acts as a central catalog of business services. A registry typically fulfills the following functionality (actual implementation varies between vendors):

Store service descriptions—Information about their endpoints (the network resource where the service functionality is implemented), and the other technical details that a consumer requires to invoke the service, such as protocol bindings and message formats

Catalog services—Services categorized and organized

Publish new services—Publish new services into the registry and to browse and search for existing services

Service history—Maintains service history, allowing users to see when a service was published or changed

11.12.2.4 Repository

A repository is used to store policies and other metadata related to the management and governance of services. A governance repository should support the following basic capabilities:

An information model or taxonomy—This represents and stores organizational and regulatory policies that can be translated into rules enforced by the SOA governance system. It should be possible for policies and rules to be interpreted by people or machines (and sometimes both) as appropriate.

Auditable—Audit capabilities for tracking the trail of changes and authorizations applied to assets in the repository context.

IMA—Identity management capabilities and role-based access controls to ensure that only appropriate parties have access to policies.

Notification—A notification system and content validation capabilities to provide additional assurances those policies are well formed, consistent, and properly applied.

11.12.3 SOA Infrastructure

IT infrastructure historically was implemented as a series of complementary but independent technology layers, and traditionally, there has been a clear abstraction between the computing platforms and the network infrastructure. However, with WSs, implementations demand a systemic view that starts at the network and works its way up the OSIRM stack and beyond. Because business logic can be distributed, enforced, and monitored throughout a distributed network, there is no clear abstraction as there has been in the past. However, for purposes of analysis, this discussion will follow the traditional tiers of Business, Application, and Infrastructure (which includes network infrastructure) and an optional orchestration layer added for composition and orchestration of services. (See Figure 11.9.)

As SOA platforms themselves evolve and as capabilities are commoditized into applications servers and network devices, we see the network infrastructure taking on more capabilities.

11.13 SOA Network Infrastructure

The infrastructure, particularly network infrastructure, plays an important part in most information technology architectures, and as we are beginning to see, this is also true for architectural approaches such as SOA (this is the reason for the coverage in Chapters 9 and 10). Although the original view of a "Services Network" was one in which WSs would allow the network to work

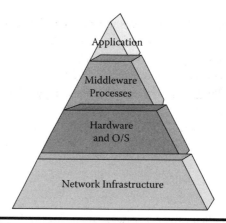

Figure 11.9 Architecture components.

as a "Network Service Bus" (as opposed to an ESB) where services could be composed, orchestrated, and discover reusable, substitutable, and commoditized services regardless of the location or platform; in reality, the road to delivering this vision has been more rough than first thought. Although the Internet is pretty much ubiquitous, there are a number of fallacies that presently are limiting this vision from coming to fruition.

An article written by L. Peter Deutsch, a noted computer scientist, has publicized what has become known in software engineering circles as the "Eight Fallacies of Distributed Computing." He first presented them in a talk he gave to the researchers and engineers at Sun Microsystems Labs in 1991. At the time Deutsch first presented the fallacies, there were only seven. He added the eighth sometime later.

The eight fallacies are as follows:

1. The network is reliable.
2. Latency is zero.
3. Bandwidth is infinite.
4. The network is secure.
5. Topology does not change.
6. There is one administrator.
7. Transport cost is zero.
8. The network is homogenous.

WSs are, in their essence, distributed applications. These fallacies, in addition to a number of other reasons, have prompted network managers to deploy SOA network devices: to overcome the fallacies outlined, offload applications servers in the data centers, speed content-specific messages through the network backbone, enforce SOA security policies at the intranet perimeter, and enforce governance policies.

In the case of SOA, the SOA network infrastructure is essentially an overlay on top of an IP infrastructure in the form of SOAP messaging, which uses the HTTP protocol (see Figure 11.10). Other transport mechanisms are available.

Although SOA networking is still in a state of flux and some question its viability, the industry is coming to terms with the value SOA network infrastructure is bringing to the table. The following

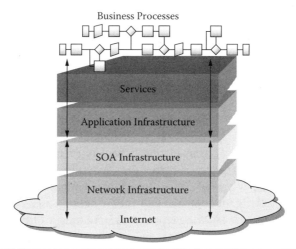

Figure 11.10   SOA network infrastructure.

trends will make it more likely that SOA network infrastructure will play a more dominant role in future SOA deployments than it has in the past.

11.13.1 Trends Affecting SOA Network Infrastructure

Two current major trends influencing SOA network infrastructure can be discerned as vendors iteratively build and deploy SOA solutions. These trends also migrate to, and ultimately impact and raise the awareness of, SOA networking infrastructure as well:

1. **Core SOA platforms, which are traditionally built upon ESB functionality, continue to evolve.**
   a. **SOA platforms are still evolving and increasing in functionality**—The majority of SOA platforms have grown out of middleware solutions—now more often ESBs. The core of most SOA platforms is built upon these ESBs and over time additional complementary functionality and components are being built around these platforms, i.e., registry, repository, etc., to support the composing services and orchestrate business processes. SOA platforms, with ESB as their core, are expected to continue to grow in features/functionality and will evolve into Integration-Centric Business Process Management Suites (IC-BPMSs). Platforms that can deploy and manage services are evolving into platforms that can also deploy and orchestrate services into business processes. (See Figure 11.11.)
   b. **Economies of embedding functionality into network devices (SOA appliances)**— The second trend is taking place is at the lower end of the spectrum. Here, basic ESB capabilities such as routing, messaging, transformation, security, etc, are migrating from application servers to specialized semiconductor technology, which is then embedded into network devices. Past history shows that as functionality in application servers become stable, this functionality becomes commoditized and embedded into firmware within network appliances. Rudimentary functionality and patterns inherited from ESBs are migrating to the network and provide for the majority of the capabilities of low-end ESBs (often called SOA Appliances), although in some limited functions: routing, message processing, message transformation, protocol transformation, service mapping, and security.
   Although the move to add increased functionality to ESBs and SOA platforms does not directly affect the SOA infrastructure, one can see how this functionality migrates to the low end when economies of scale allow for productization into embedded network devices.
2. **SOA adoption is evolving from enterprise SOA to B2B SOA**—A second major trend that is impacting SOA network infrastructure is that SOA adoption is evolving from Enterprise SOA to B2B SOA, requiring services to be deployed and managed over distributed network infrastructure.
   – Current productization of SOA platforms has occurred without taking into consideration the underlying network infrastructure. Typically, these SOA platforms were built upon ESBs that use WS standards but were focused primarily on interenterprise application integration. Early adoption and efforts have been focused on enterprise integration, where applications silos are being replaced with more agile SOA environments and concerns of interoperability, security, etc., have not been at the forefront of product development efforts. Focus has been on application integration to get "one view of the customer" or to combine information to be viewed at a corporate portal. (See Figure 11.12.)

– As SOA adoption within the enterprise matures, future product development efforts will turn to integration functionality outside of the immediate enterprise and turn to integration efforts with trusted partners for B2B applications such as extended ERP, supply-chain management, etc.; eventually, the focus will be on unknown partners in a "Global" SOA Network. The first phase of SOA adoption has been primarily intra-enterprise. The challenge of the second phase of adoption is to enable interoperability between various homogenous, particularly heterogeneous SOA environments, where a number of different SOA platforms may be deployed. Interoperability between SOA environments require more emphasis on security, identity, and WS management as messaging moves over intranets and the public Internet.

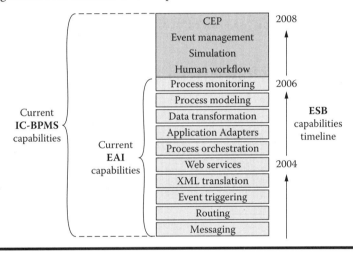

Figure 11.11   Evolving ESB functionality.

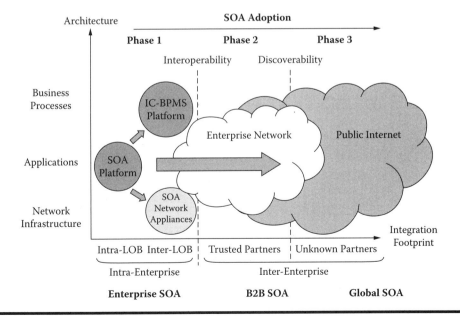

Figure 11.12   SOA adoption phases.

– Finally, the third phase of SOA adoption is where discoverability allows for the identification of commoditized and substitutable services from unknown partners—a **global SOA network**. The vision of SOA is the ability to eventually evolve to a point where business processes could use substitute services from the best and most economical provider no matter where these services are physically located.

In summary, the second major trend impacting SOA network infrastructure is the emphasis of moving to more heterogonous environments where the network will be impacted more by phases 2 and 3 of SOA adoption.

It is important to know the current trends at both macro and micro levels, so that we can understand what was the past and what will be the future prioritization for productization of SOA functionality into SOA platforms, SOA infrastructure, and SOA network infrastructure.

11.13.2 SOA Network Software versus Hardware Network Infrastructure

ESB functionality inherited from the core SOA platform is being commoditized from application services into SOA network appliances. This core functionality of the SOA network appliances comes from ESBs. This, along with additional functionality needed to deploy these devices in distributed heterogeneous networked environments, acts as distributed Policy Enforcement Points for policy management and the ability to network these devices together and manage from a central location; all are driving the future functionality requirements for these devices.

11.13.3 SOA Network Device Functionality

Most traditional network devices, such as routers and load balancers, are not content-aware; instead, they typically intercept packets and make forwarding decisions based on information in the outer protocol packet headers, including HTTP, SSL, and TCP/IP. What makes SOA network appliances different is their ability to intercept, inspect, interpret, enforce, and act upon metadata associated with the content—*content-based routing*. In addition, some of these devices are able to perform *policy-based routing* and act as Policy Enforcement Points in support of Policy Life-Cycle Management Processes. The core functionality of these devices is inherited from Enterprise Service Buses as ESB functionality is commoditized from application servers to embedded network appliances. In fact, many of these devices today are capable of pretty much all of the ESB functionality (but to a much more limited extent) previously outlined except for Transaction Management, Service Orchestration, and Process Choreography. Although SOA network devices may be deployed to assist in Service Orchestration and Process Choreography, they do not actually have this capability built in, but rather facilitate these capabilities.

SOA network appliance functionality can be generally characterized by the following high-level functionalities:

Message handling—The core functionality of many appliances are inherited from core capabilities outlined earlier when ESB capabilities were described.

Message routing—As the complexity and size of networks increased, specialized networking devices called routers were used to offload routing processes from applications servers. Message routing of XML traffic is the most basic functionality required to route traffic. The core functionality of these devices, as their name *routers* implies that they used for routing of SOAP messages through a network. Routing can be classified into the following types of routing.

Static or deterministic routing—The routing of traffic between given pairs of endpoints is preprogrammed.

Content-based routing—SOAP messages can be intercepted, inspected, and routed based on the type of content it contains.

Policy-based routing—Most appliances provide some narrowly defined sets of policies associated with security. Increasingly, as competition and natural evolution move to support new business requirements, these devices may support a broad set of policies that include governance, risk, compliance, and even user-defined policies, depending upon how the device has been designed and deployed. In the Policy Life-Cycle Management Process outlined earlier, the networking device allows for policy-based processing, where this device acts as a policy enforcement point and connects to a policy administration and policy management solution.

Complex rules-based routing—As these devices take on the management of more policies, their decisions could be automated with rules.

Message processing—Acceleration of XML processing enables the offloading of extremely processor-intensive operations such as encryption/decryption, signature validation, XML parsing, XML schema validation, from application servers, database servers, and ESB.

Message transformation—In addition to processing messages on input, message transformation allows for messages to be transformed to a different message structure and format. This is typically based on XSL transformations.

Message enhancement—Message enhancement allows for the adding of additional information that may be required for some application and/or functionality.

Protocol transformation—Protocol transformation focuses on transforming the message structure and not the message payload. XML and SOAP messages can be transported over protocols other than HTTP. These protocols could be other TCP/IP protocols for transmission over the Internet, such as SMTP and FTP, or they could be proprietary reliable messaging protocols used within companies, such as IBM's MQ Series or TIBCO's Rendezvous. Mediating XML messages between these transports and middleware protocols is a common function preformed by many XML/SOA network appliances.

Service mapping (service virtualization)—Service mapping allows for the simple creation of service applets that may be used for some applications and/or functionality.

Security—Security is also a core requirement of many XML/SOA appliances.

SLA and policy management—Mechanisms for SLA enforcement are needed. This functionality can be performed by XML/SOA Appliances. As solutions continue to grow, the competition increases, resulting in a host of additional features. Policy management is also critical.

11.13.4 SOA Network Device Components

The following is a generic classification of SOA networking devices that are often called XML/SOA Network Appliances or just XML/SOA Appliances. The tendency in the industry is to package more and more functionality in firmware/hardware over time as functionality becomes commoditized and WS standards become more widely formalized and adopted. In the past, application server functionality such as routing, firewalls, load balancing, and other functionalities over time tend to migrate to the network infrastructure. Today, XML processing overhead of WSs and SOA and other functionalities can be offloaded from application platforms and software middleware to the network to enable the advantages of a Service-Oriented Architecture.

SOA network appliances all provide routing, and generally provide basic acceleration and security functionality. In addition to basic capabilities such as routing, acceleration, and security, these devices also need to be able to be networked into an overall SOA solution. These devices, therefore, need to be able to interface with a SOA management solution, and support the latest standards and certification requirements. This list is a broad classification of XML/SOA network appliances.

11.13.4.1 Acceleration Appliances

Early in the introduction of these devices they were typically focused on simple message processing: XML processing and acceleration. At that time there was a concern that with the increase of XML traffic, applications using XML messaging would choke network traffic because XML processing consumes a large percentage of applications resources. When parsing, query, validation, and transformation of messages are left to application servers, the overall costs increase. By offloading this functionality to 64-bit architecture, fast XML classification, stream processing technology, and specialized semiconductor technology, SOA network appliances can be used to offload and act as coprocessor devices, providing overall increased performance and application server requirements for back-end applications.

11.13.4.2 Integration Appliances

These devices are designed to route XML traffic and to make the integration of applications easy to do, and in most applications act as a low-end cost-effective ESB solution where a larger ESB solution would not be economical. XML integration typically implements the simplest form of routing.

11.13.4.3 Security Appliances

The following are two types of common XML/SOA network devices:

XML/SOA Security Gateways (Firewalls)—Also referred to as XML/SOA firewalls, the primary function of these devices is to manage security. These devices are separate from internal computer systems; they are specialized firewalls used to provide security for XML messaging and frequently reside in organizations DMZ. Typically, they include support for all leading directory, identity, access control, single sign on (SSO), and federation services. These devices provide flexibility for SOA and security architects in defining and enforcing identity-driven SOA security policies leveraging SSO session cookies, Kerberos tickets, SAML assertions, and PKI.

XML/SOA VPN—The XML virtual private network or XML VPN works like a traditional SSL VPN by "tunneling" a secure encryption connection across public networks so two machines can interoperate securely; the XML VPN allows for secure connections between WS providers and consumers. An XML VPN can be used in EAI or SOA B2B configurations and mitigates the security risk for certain security policy enforcement issues that may arise otherwise.

11.13.4.4 SOA Appliances

SOA platform vendors for the most part have not embraced the need or the concept of SOA appliances in their overall SOA deployments. There could be a number of reasons for this: SOA adoption and productization has moved beyond enterprise SOA; SOA appliances are not seen as being mature enough; the market is waiting for the leaders to deliver products that set benchmarks in functionality; standards are not mature enough, etc.

11.13.4.5 Interoperability Appliances

XML/SOA Networking Gateways—The majority of SOA deployments are focused on integration within an enterprise or lines of business (lob) within enterprises that typically are homogeneous environments. However, as SOA adoption increases, there will be increased demand to interconnect heterogeneous SOA environments. The role that appliances play in this environment is to bridge or mediate between different environments.

11.13.5 SOA Network Management Software

Centralized management and enforcement of message-level security and policies, along with the ability to manage WS, has become the baseline for most SOA network management software. Like the rest of the components of an overall SOA solution, the requirements and expectations are continually moving up the value-added stack. More and more vendors' WS management solutions are incorporating policy life-cycle management, business process management, business activity monitoring, as well networked business intelligence into their solutions.

11.13.6 SOA Network Configurations

XML/Appliances can be deployed in a number of configurations and often can be deployed to support simple XML network configurations and more complex SOA network configurations. The focus here will be on SOA network configurations.

11.14 Vendor-Specific Implementations

Table 11.2 is a list of capabilities available SOA network appliances that were on the market at press time. The actual vendor packaging of this functionality in vendor's product offerings varies widely and can be implemented either in software or firmware/hardware, or a combination of both. Some vendors provide general-purpose appliance platforms that can be software-enabled through software keying to address a wide variety of deployment applications, from simple acceleration to more complex SOA interoperability. Other vendors have application-specific integration appliances focused specifically on integration only, whereas other vendors focus specifically on security applications, and yet others such as IBM have taken a lead by integrating SOA appliances into their overall SOA solutions.

Table 11.2   List of XML/SOA Appliances Features

Functional Grouping	Features
SOA Management	Business Intelligence Support
	Business Activity Monitoring (BAM)
	Vendor Abstraction
	SOA Platform Integration
	Service Virtualization
	Autodiscovery of Services
	UDDI/WSIL
Web Services Management	Network Management Integration
	SNMP Support
	Application Performance Management
	Performance Management
	Configuration
	Provisioning
Policy Management	User-Defined Policies
	Governance
	Risk
	Compliance
	Policy Administration
	Policy Monitoring
	Policy Enforcement
	SLA-Based Routing
	Policy-Based Routing
	Content-Based Routing
Security, Identity Management, and Access Control	AV (Anti Virus)
	Service/Operation Authorization Control
	Security Audit
	Security Policy Enforcement
	Federation and SAML Support
	Single Sign On (SSO) Integration
	Client Authentication
	XACML (eXtensible Access Control Markup Language)
	Message/Element Privacy and Integrity
	Public Key Infrastructure (PKI) Management
	WSDL Security
	XML VPN for B2B, EAI
	XML Threat/Intrusion Protection
	CDL (Choreography Description Language)
	Secure Sockets Layer (SSL) Channel Security
XML/SOAP Messaging	Optimization
	Caching Schemes and Learning
	Protocol Translation
	Load Balancing
	Transport and MOM Mediation

Functional Grouping	Features
	Compression
	Acceleration
	Message Transformation and Enhancement
	Schema Validation
	Message Integrity
	Parsing
	Filtering
	Route Forwarding
	Routing

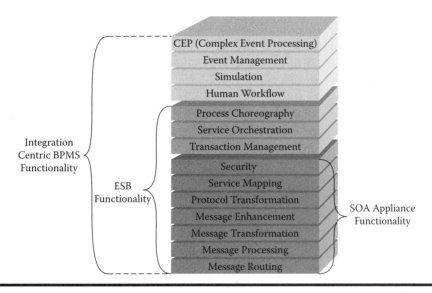

Figure 11.13 ESB and SOA appliance functionality.

11.15 Future of Networking in SOA Environments

Often, the road we take to get to a vision is tempered by reality, where vendors take iterative steps prioritizing requirements into the product development process as standards maturity and product revenue streams allow. Enterprises need to be sold on the business value for them to adopt these new technologies into their enterprise infrastructure. The productization of the SOA vision into reality and consumer adoption continues to evolve, over time. What is considered to be a "SOA platform" continues to evolve and economies allow for the commercialization of some of that functionality to migrate from application servers to embedded SOA networking devices. SOA networking has arisen because the functionality—whether it is implemented in an ESB or services network—is migrating to the network in the form of network appliances. There are numerous advantages of having this functionality offloaded from applications servers to network devices:

■ *Lower overall hardware costs*—Economies allow for functionality to be moved from application servers to the network in the form of application-specific devices.
■ *Lower software development costs*—Network devices abstract away a lot of complexity of service development that developers and architect should not have to be concerned with.

For intelligent communications to take place, we need to move beyond the simple exchange of data. However, until such time this happens, we need to exchange the context of communication exchanges in the form of metadata. XML, WS, and SOA allow for standards and architecture to do this.

Appendix 11.1: Basic Glossary

AON	Application-Oriented Networking
APIs	Application Programming Interfaces
B2B	Business-to-Business
B2B SOA	Business-to-Business SOA
BAM	Business Acctivity Monitoring
BI	Business Intelligence
BPEL	Business process execution language
BPM	Business Process Management
CORBA	Common Object Request Broker
DCE	Distributed Communications Environment
DCOM	Distributed Component Object Model
DOA	Distributed Object Architecture
EAI	enterprise application integration
ESB	Enterprise Service Buses
GRC	Governance, Risk, and Compliance
HTML	Hypertext Markup Language
IC-BPMS	Integration Centric—Business Process Management Suites
MEP	Message Exchange Pattern
MOM	Message-Oriented Middleware
PAP	Policy Administration Point
PEP	Policy Enforcement Points
PMP	Policy Monitoring Point
QoS	Quality of Service
REST	Respresentational State Transfer
RMI	Remote Method Invocation
SDP	Service Delivery Platform
SLA	Service Level Agreement
SOA	Service Oriented Architecture
SOAN	Oriented Architecture Networking
SOAN	Service Oriented Architecture Networking
SOAP	Simple Object Access Protocol
SOC	Service-Oriented Computing
SON	Service-Oriented Network
SONA	Service-Oriented Network Architecture
TOGAF	The Open Group Architecture Framework

UDDI	Universal Discovery, Description and Integration
VPN	Virtual Private Network
WSDL	Web Services Description Language
WSs	Web Services
XML	eXtensible Mark-up Language

Chapter 12

Server/Storage Virtualization and Grid Computing for Commercial Enterprise Environments

12.1 Introduction

Grid computing* (or more precisely, a *grid computing system*) is a virtualized distributed computing environment. Such an environment aims at enabling the dynamic runtime selection, sharing, and aggregation of geographically distributed autonomous resources on the basis of the availability, capability, performance, and cost of these computing resources, and simultaneously, also on the basis of an organization's specific baseline or burst-processing requirements [MIN200701]. When people think of a grid, the idea of an interconnected system for the distribution of electricity, especially a network of high-tension cables and power stations, comes to mind. In the mid-1990s the grid metaphor was reapplied to computing, by extending and advancing the 1960s concept of "computer time sharing." The grid metaphor strongly illustrates the relation with, and the dependency on, a highly interconnected networking infrastructure. Off-the-shelf products supporting virtualization and server consolidation are now available and are deployed in many Fortune 500 companies.

This chapter is a survey of the grid computing field as it applies to corporate environments and focuses on what the potential advantages of the technology in these environments are. The goal

---

* The material in this chapter is summarized from the article "Grid Computing For Commercial Enterprise Environments," contained in the textbook *Handbook on Information Technology in Finance* (International Handbooks on Information Systems), edited by F. Schlottmann, D. Seese, and C. Weinhardt, Springer Verlag, New York, April 2008.

is to serve as a familiarization vehicle for the interested information technology (IT) professional. It should be noted at the outset, however, that no claim is made herewith that there is a single or unique solution to a given computing problem; grid computing is one of a number of available solutions in support of optimized distributed computing. Corporate IT professionals, for whom this text is intended, will have to perform appropriate functional, economic, business-case, and strategic analyses to determine which computing approach ultimately is best for their respective organizations. Furthermore, it should be noted that grid computing is an evolving field, and so there is not always one canonical, normative, universally accepted, or axiomatically derivable view of "everything grid-related"; it follows that occasionally we present multiple views, multiple interpretations, or multiple perspectives on a topic, as it might be perceived by different stakeholders of communities of interest.

This chapter begins the discussion by providing a sample of what a number of stakeholders define grid computing to be, along with a survey of the industry. The precise definition of what exactly this technology encompasses is still evolving, and there is not a globally accepted normative definition that is perfectly nonoverlapping with other related technologies. Grid computing emphasizes (but does not mandate) geographically distributed, multiorganization, utility-based, outsourcer-provided, networking-reliant computing methods. For a more complete treatment of the topic, the reader is referred to the textbook by this author entitled *A Networking Approach to Grid Computing*, Wiley, 2005.

Virtualization is a well-known concept in networking from Virtual Channels in Asynchronous Transfer Mode to virtual private networks, virtual LANs, and virtual IP addresses. However, an even more fundamental type of virtualization is achievable with today's ubiquitous networks: machine cycle and storage virtualization through the auspices of grid computing and IP storage. Grid computing is also known as *utility computing*, what IBM calls *on-demand computing*.

Grid computing is a virtualization technology that was talked about in the 1980s and 1990s and entered the scientific computing field in the past ten years. The technology is now beginning to make its presence felt in the commercial computing environment. In the past couple of years there has been a lot of press and market activity, and a number of proponents see major penetration in the immediate future. VMware (EMC), IBM, and Oracle, among others are major players in this space.

Grid computing cannot really exist without networks (the grid), because the user is requesting computing or storage resources that are located miles or continents away. The user need not be concerned about the specific technology employed in delivering the computing or storage power: all the user wants and gets is the requisite service. One can think of grid computing as a middleware that shields the user from the raw technology itself. The network delivers the job requests anywhere in the world and returns the results, based on an established service level agreement.

The advantages of grid computing are that there can be a mix and match of different hardware in the network; the cost is lower because there is a better, statistically averaged, utilization of the underlying resources; also, there is higher availability because if a processor were to fail, another processor is automatically switched in service. Think of an environment of a Redundant Array of Inexpensive Computers (RAIC), similar to the concept of RAID.

Grid computing is intrinsically network based: resources are distributed all over an intranet, an extranet, or the Internet. Users can also get locally based virtualization by using middleware such as VMware that allows a multitude of servers right in the corporate data center to be utilized more efficiently. Typically, corporate servers are utilized for less than 30–40% of their available computing power. Using a virtualization mechanism, the firm can improve utilization, increase availability, reduce costs, and make use of a plethora of mix-and-match processors; at a minimum, this drives to server consolidation.

Security is a key consideration in grid computing. The user wants to get services in a trustworthy and confidential manner. Then, there is the desire for guaranteed levels of service and predictable, reduced costs. Finally, there is the need for standardization, so that a user with an appropriate middleware client software can transparently access any registered resource in the network. Grid computing supports the concept of the Service-Oriented Architecture, where clients obtain services from loosely coupled service-provider resources in the network. As covered in previous chapters, Web Services (WSs) based on the Simple Object Access Protocol (SOAP) and Universal Description, Discovery, and Integration (UDDI) protocols are now the key building blocks of a grid environment [MIN200601].

Server consolidation and infrastructure optimization help organizations consolidate servers and increase utilization rates, greatly reduce power and cooling costs, and manage and automate IT processes for maximum availability, performance, and scalability. A virtual infrastructure is a dynamic mapping of physical resources to business needs. Although a virtual machine represents the physical resources of a single computer, a virtual infrastructure represents the physical resources of the entire IT environment, aggregating x86 computers and their attached network and storage into a unified pool of IT resources. For example, a typical approach to virtualization (e.g., used by VMware) inserts a thin layer of software directly on the computer hardware or on a host operating system. This software layer creates virtual machines and contains a virtual machine monitor or "hypervisor" that allocates hardware resources dynamically and transparently so that multiple operating systems can run concurrently on a single physical computer without the user even "knowing" it [VNW200701].

12.2 What Is Grid Computing and What Are the Key Issues?

In its basic form, the concept of grid computing is straightforward: with grid computing, an organization can transparently integrate, streamline, and share dispersed, heterogeneous pools of hosts, servers, storage systems, data, and networks into one synergistic system to deliver agreed-upon service at specified levels of application efficiency and processing performance. Additionally, or alternatively, with grid computing an organization can simply secure commoditized "machine cycles" or storage capacity from a remote provider, on demand, without having to own the "heavy iron" to do the "number crunching." Either way, to an end user or application this arrangement (ensemble) looks like one large, cohesive, virtual, transparent computing system [DEV200301,MCC200301]. Broadband networks play a fundamental enabling role in making grid computing possible, and this is the motivation for looking at this technology from the perspective of communication.

According to IBM's definition [ZHA200201,HAW200301], "a grid is a collection of distributed computing resources available over a local or wide area network that appear to an end user or application as one large virtual computing system. The vision is to create virtual dynamic organizations through secure, coordinated resource-sharing among individuals, institutions, and resources. Grid computing is an approach to distributed computing that spans not only locations but also organizations, machine architectures, and software boundaries to provide unlimited power, collaboration, and information access to everyone connected to a grid." "…The Internet is about getting computers to talk together; grid computing is about getting computers to work together. The grid will help elevate the Internet to a true computing platform, combining the qualities of service of enterprise computing with the ability to share heterogeneous distributed resources—everything from applications, data, storage and servers."

Another definition, this one from The Globus Alliance (a research and development initiative focused on enabling the application of grid concepts to scientific and engineering computing), is as follows [GLO200301]: "The grid refers to an infrastructure that enables the integrated, collaborative use of high-end computers, networks, databases, and scientific instruments owned and managed by multiple organizations. Grid applications often involve large amounts of data or computing and often require secure resource sharing across organizational boundaries, and are thus not easily handled by today's Internet and Web infrastructures."

Yet another industry-formulated definition of grid computing is as follows [FOS199901, FOS200201]: "A computational grid is a hardware and software infrastructure that provides dependable, consistent, pervasive, and inexpensive access to high-end computational capabilities. A grid is concerned with coordinated resource sharing and problem solving in dynamic, multi-institutional virtual organizations. The key concept is the ability to negotiate resource-sharing arrangements among a set of participating parties (providers and consumers) and then to use the resulting resource pool for some purpose. The sharing that we are concerned with is not primarily file exchange but rather direct access to computers, software, data, and other resources, as is required by a range of collaborative problem-solving and resource-brokering strategies emerging in industry, science, and engineering. This sharing is, necessarily, highly controlled, with resource providers and consumers defining clearly and carefully just what is shared, who is allowed to share, and the conditions under which sharing occurs. A set of individuals or institutions defined by such sharing rules form what we call a virtual organization (VO)."

Whereas the Internet is a network of communication, grid computing is seen as a network of computation: the field provides tools and protocols for resource sharing of a variety of IT resources. Grid computing approaches are based on coordinated resource sharing and problem solving in dynamic, multi-institutional VOs. A short list of examples of possible VOs include: application service providers, storage service providers, machine-cycle providers, and members of industry-specific consortia. These examples, among others, represent an approach to computing and problem solving based on collaboration in data-rich and computation-rich environments [KES200101,MYE200301]. The enabling factors in the creation of grid computing systems in recent years have been the proliferation of broadband (optical-based) communications, the Internet, and the World Wide Web (WWW) infrastructure, along with the availability of low-cost, high-performance computers using standardized (open) operating systems [CHE200201,FOS199901,FOS200101]. The role of communications as a fundamental enabler will be emphasized throughout this chapter.

Prior to the deployment of grid computing, a typical business application had a dedicated server platform of servers and an anchored storage device assigned to each individual server. Applications developed for such platforms were not able to share resources, and from an individual server's perspective, it was not possible, in general, to predict, even statistically, what the processing load would be at different times. Consequently, each instance of an application needed to have its own excess capacity to handle peak usage loads. This predicament typically resulted in higher overall costs than would otherwise need to be the case [HAN200301]. To address these lacunae, grid computing aims at exploiting the opportunities afforded by the synergies, the economies of scale, and the load smoothing that result from the ability to share and aggregate distributed computational capabilities, and deliver these hardware-based capabilities as a transparent service to the end user.* To reinforce the point, the term *synergistic* implies "working together so that the total effect is greater than the sum of the individual constituent elements." From a service provider perspective, grid computing is somewhat akin to an application service provider (ASP) environment, but with a much-higher level of performance and assurance [BUY200301]. Specialized ASPs known as grid service providers (GSPs) are expected to emerge to provide grid-based services, including, possibly, "open-source outsourcing services."

Grid computing started out as the simultaneous application of the resources of many networked computers to a single scientific problem [FOS199901]. Grid computing has been characterized as the massive integration of computer systems [WAL200201]. Computational grids have been used for a number of years to solve large-scale problems in science and engineering. The noteworthy fact is that, at this juncture, the approach can already be applied to a mix of mainstream business problems. Specifically, grid computing is now beginning to make inroads into the commercial world, including financial services operations, making the leap forward from such scientific venues as research laboratories and academic settings [HAN200301].

The possibility exists, according to the industry, that with grid computing companies can save as much as 30% of certain key line items of the operations budget (in an ideal situation), which is typically a large fraction of the total IT budget [SUN200301]. Companies yearly spend, on the average, 6%† of their top line revenues on IT services; for example, a $10 billion/year Fortune 500 company might spend $600 million/year on IT. Grid middleware vendors make the assertion that *cluster computing* (aggregating processors in parallel-based configurations) yields reductions in IT costs and costs of operations that are expected to reach 15% by 2005 and 30% by 2007–2008 in most early adopter sectors, according to the industry. Use of *enterprise grids* (middleware-based environments to harvest unused "machine cycles," thereby displacing otherwise-needed growth costs) is expected to result in 15% savings in IT costs by the year 2007–2008, growing to a 30% savings by 2010 to 2012 [COH200301]. This *potential* saving is what this chapter is all about.

In 1994 this author published the book *Analyzing Outsourcing, Reengineering Information, and Communication Systems* (McGraw-Hill), calling attention to the possibility that companies could save 15–20% or more in their IT costs by considering outsourcing—the trends of the mid-2000s have, indeed, validated this (then) timely assertion [MIN199501]. At this juncture, we call early attention to the fact that the possibility exists for companies to save as much as 15–30% of certain key line items of the IT operations (run-the-engine) budget by using grid computing or related computing or storage virtualization technologies. In effect, grid computing, particularly the utility computing aspect, can be seen as another form of outsourcing. Perhaps, utility computing will be the next phase of outsourcing and be a major trend in the upcoming decade. Evolving grid computing standards can be used by companies to deploy a next-generation kind of "open source outsourcing" that has the advantage of offering portability, enabling companies to easily move their business among a variety of pseudocommodity providers.

This chapter explores practical advantages of grid computing and what is needed by an organization to migrate to this new computing paradigm, if it so chooses. This chapter is intended for practitioners and decision makers in organizations (not necessarily for software programmers) that want to explore the overall business opportunities afforded by this new technology. At the same

---

* As implied in the opening paragraphs, a number of solutions in addition to grid computing (e.g., virtualization) can be employed to address this and other computational issues—grid computing is just one approach.
† The range is typically 2–12%.

time, the importance of the underlying networking mechanism is emphasized. For any kind of new technology, corporate and business decision makers typically seek answers to questions such as these: (1) "What is this stuff?"; (2) "How widespread is its present/potential penetration?"; (3) "Is it ready for prime time?"; (4) "Are there firm standards?"; (5) "Is it secure?"; (6) "How do we bill it, as it's new?"; and (7) "Tell me how to deploy it (at a macro level)." Table 12.1 summarizes these and other questions that decision makers, CIOs, CTOs, and planners may have about grid computing. Table 12.2 lists some of the concepts embodied in grid computing and other related technologies.

Grid computing is also known by a number of other names (although some of these terms have slightly different connotations) such as *grid* (the term *the grid* was coined in the mid-1990s to denote a proposed distributed computing infrastructure for advanced science and engineering), *computational grid, computing on demand, on-demand computing, just-in-time computing, platform computing, network computing, computing utility* (the term used by this author in the late 1980s [MIN198701]), *utility computing, cluster computing,* and *high-performance distributed computing.* With regard to nomenclature, in this text, besides the term *grid computing,* we will also interchangeably use the term *grid* and *computational grid.* In this chapter, we use the term *grid technology* to describe the entire collection of grid computing elements, middleware, networks, and protocols.

To deploy a grid, a commercial organization needs to assign computing resources to the shared environment and deploy appropriate grid middleware on these resources, enabling them to play various roles that need to be supported in the grid (e.g., scheduler, broker, etc.) Some minor application retuning or parallelization may, in some instances, be required; data accessibility will also have to be taken into consideration. A security framework will also be required. If the organization subscribes to the service provider model, then grid deployment would mean establishing adequate access bandwidth to the provider, some possible application retuning, and the establishment of security policies (the assumption being that the provider will itself have a reliable security framework).

The concept of providing computing power as a utility-based function is generally attractive to end users requiring fast transactional processing and scenario-modeling capabilities. The concept may also be attractive to IT planners looking to control costs and reduce data center complexity. The ability to have a cluster, an entire data center, or other resources spread across a geography connected by the Internet (or alternatively, connected by an intranet or extranet), operating as a single transparent virtualized system that can be managed as a service, rather than as individual constituent components, likely will over time increase business agility, reduce complexity, streamline management processes, and lower operational costs [HAN200301]. Grid technology allows organizations to utilize numerous computers to solve problems by sharing computing resources. The problems to be solved might involve data processing, network bandwidth, or data storage, or a combination thereof.

In a grid environment, the ensemble of resources is able to work together cohesively because of defined protocols that control connectivity, coordination, resource allocation, resource management, security, and chargeback. Generally, the protocols are implemented in the middleware. The systems glued together by a computational grid may be in the same room or may be distributed across the globe; they may be running on homogenous or heterogeneous hardware platforms; they may be running on similar or dissimilar operating systems; and they may be owned by one or more organizations. The goal of grid computing is to provide users with a single view or mechanism that can be utilized to support any number of computing tasks: the grid leverages its extensive informatics capabilities to support the number crunching needed to complete the task and all the user perceives is, essentially, a large virtual computer undertaking his or her work [DEV200301].

Table 12.1 Issues of Interest and Questions That CIOs/CTOs/Planners Have About Grid Computing

What is grid computing and what are the key issues?
  Grid benefits and status of technology
  Motivations for considering computational grids
  Brief history of grid computing
  Is grid computing ready for prime time?
  Early suppliers and vendors
  Challenges
  Future directions
What are the components of grid computing systems/architectures?
  Portal/user interfaces
  User security
  Broker function
  Scheduler function
  Data management function
  Job management and resource management
Are there stable standards supporting grid computing?
  What is OGSA/OGSI?
  Implementations of OGSI
  OGSA services
  Virtual organization creation and management
  Service groups and discovery services
  Choreography, orchestration, and workflow
  Transactions
  Metering service
  Accounting service
  Billing and payment service
  Grid system deployment issues and approaches
  Generic implementations: Globus Toolkit
Security considerations—can grid computing be trusted?
What are the grid deployment/management issues?
  Challenges and approaches
  Availability of products by categories
  Business grid types
  Deploying a basic computing grid
  Deploying more complex computing grid
  Grid operation
What are the economics of grid systems?
  The chargeable grid service
  The grid payment system
How does one pull it all together? Communication and networking infrastructure
  Communication systems for local grids
  Communication systems for national grids
  Communication systems for global grids

Table 12.2   Definitions of Some Key Terms

Grid computing	• Virtualized distributed computing environment that enables the dynamic "runtime" selection, sharing, and aggregation of geographically distributed autonomous (autonomic) resources based on the availability, capability, performance, and cost of these computing resources, and simultaneously, also based on an organization's specific baseline or burst-processing requirements.
	• Enables organizations to transparently integrate, streamline, and share dispersed, heterogeneous pools of hosts, servers, storage systems, data, and networks into one synergistic system to deliver agreed-upon service at specified levels of application efficiency and processing performance.
	• An approach to distributed computing that spans multiple locations or multiple organizations, machine architectures, and software boundaries to provide power, collaboration, and information access.
	• Infrastructure that enables the integrated, collaborative use of computers, supercomputers, networks, databases, and scientific instruments owned and managed by multiple organizations.
	• A network of computation: namely, tools and protocols for coordinated resource sharing and problem solving among pooled assets ... allows coordinated resource sharing and problem solving in dynamic, multi-institutional virtual organizations.
	• Simultaneous application of the resources of many networked computers to a single problem ... concerned with coordinated resource sharing and problem solving in dynamic, multi-institutional virtual organizations.
	• Decentralized architecture for resource management and a layered hierarchical architecture for implementation of various constituent services.
	• Combines elements such as distributed computing, high-performance computing, and disposable computing, depending on the application.
	• Local, metropolitan, regional, national, or international footprint. Systems may be in the same room or may be distributed across the globe; they may running on homogenous or heterogeneous hardware platforms; they may be running on similar or dissimilar operating systems; and they may owned by one or more organizations.
	• Types: (1) Computational grids: machines with set-aside resources stand by to number-crunch data or provide coverage for other intensive workloads; (2) Scavenging grids: commonly used to locate and exploit machine cycles on idle servers and desktop machines for use in resource-intensive tasks; and (3) Data grids: a unified interface for all data repositories in an organization, and through which data can be queried, managed, and secured.
	• Computational grids can be local, enterprise grids (also called intragrids), and Internet-based grids (also called intergrids). Enterprise grids are middleware-based environments to harvest unused "machine cycles," thereby displacing otherwise-needed growth costs.
	• Other terms (some with slightly different connotations): computational grid, computing on demand, on-demand computing, just-in-time computing, platform computing, network computing, computing utility, utility computing, cluster computing, and high-performance distributed computing.

Virtualization	• An approach that allows several operating systems to run simultaneously on one large computer (e.g., IBM's z/VM operating system lets multiple instances of Linux coexist on the same mainframe computer).
	• More generally, it is the practice of making resources from diverse devices accessible to a user as if they were a single, larger, homogenous, locally available resource.
	• Dynamically shifting resources across platforms to match computing demands with available resources: the computing environment can become dynamic, enabling autonomic shifting applications between servers to match demand.
	• The abstraction of server, storage, and network resources to make them available dynamically for sharing by IT services, both internal to and external to an organization. In combination with other server, storage, and networking capabilities, virtualization offers customers the opportunity to build more efficient IT infrastructures. It is seen by some as a step on the road to utility computing.
	• A proven software technology that is rapidly transforming the IT landscape and fundamentally changing the way that people compute [VMW200701].
Clusters	• Aggregating of processors in parallel-based configurations, typically in the local environment (within a data center); all nodes work cooperatively as a single unified resource.
	• Resource allocation is performed by a centralized resource manager and scheduling system.
	• Comprising multiple interconnected independent nodes that cooperatively work together as a single unified resource; unlike grids, cluster resources are typically owned by a single organization.
	• All users of clusters have to go through a centralized system that manages allocation of resources to application jobs. Cluster management systems have centralized control, complete knowledge of system state and user requests, and complete control over individual components.
(Basic) Web Services (WSs)	• Web Services (WSs) provide standard infrastructure for data exchange between two different distributed applications (grids provide an infrastructure for aggregation of high-end resources for solving large-scale problems).
	• Web Services are expected to play a key constituent role in the standardized definition of grid computing, because they have emerged as a standards-based approach for accessing network applications.
Peer-to-peer (P2P)	• P2P is concerned with same general problem as grid computing, namely, the organization of resource sharing within virtual communities.
	• The grid community focuses on aggregating distributed high-end machines such as clusters, whereas the P2P community concentrates on sharing low-end systems such as PCs connected to the Internet.
	• Similar to P2P, grid computing allows users to share files (many-to-many sharing). With grid, the sharing is not only in reference to files, but also other IT resources.

In recent years one has seen an increasing roster of published articles, conferences, tutorials, resources, and tools related to this topic [DEV200301]. Distributed virtualized grid computing technology, as we define it today, is still fairly new, it being only a decade in the making. However, as already implied, a number of the basic concepts of grid computing go back as far as the mid-1960s and early 1970s. Recent advances, such as ubiquitous high-speed networking in both private and public venues (e.g., high-speed intranets or high-speed Internet), make the technology more deployable at the practical level, particularly when looking at corporate environments.

As far back as 1987, this author was advocating the concept of grid computing in internal Bell Communications Research White Papers (e.g., in Special Reports SR-NPL-000790—an extensive plan written by the author listing progressive data services that could be offered by local telcos and RBOCs, entitled "A Collection of Potential Network-Based Data Services" [MIN198701]). In a section called *"Network for a Computing Utility,"* it was stated:

> The proposed service provides the entire apparatus to make the concept of the Computing Utility possible. This includes as follows: (1) the physical network over which the information can travel, and the interface through which a guest PC/workstation can participate in the provision of machine cycles and through which the service requesters submit jobs; (2) a load sharing mechanism to invoke the necessary servers to complete a job; (3) a reliable security mechanism; (4) an effective accounting mechanism to invoke the billing system; and, (5) a detailed directory of servers ... Security is one of the major issues for this service, particularly if the PC is not fully dedicated to this function, but also used for other local activities. Virus threats, infiltration and corruption of data, and other damage must be appropriately addressed and managed by the service; multi-task and robust operating systems are also needed for the servers to assist in this security process... The Computing Utility service is beginning to be approached by the Client/Server paradigm now available within a Local Area Network (LAN) environment... This service involves capabilities that span multiple 7-layer stacks. For example, one stack may handle administrative tasks, another may invoke the service (e.g., Remote Operations), still another may return the results (possibly a file), and so on... Currently no such service exists in the public domain. Three existing analogues exist, as follows: (1) timesharing service with a centralized computer; (2) highly-parallel computer systems with hundreds or thousands of nodes (what people now call cluster computing), and (3) gateways or other processors connected as servers on a LAN. The distinction between these and the proposed service is the security and accounting arenas, which are much more complex in the distributed, public (grid) environment... This service is basically feasible once a transport and switching network with strong security and accounting (chargeback) capabilities is deployed, as shown in Figure ... A high degree of intelligence in the network is required ... a physical network is required ... security and accounting software is needed ... protocols and standards will be needed to connect servers and users, as well as for accounting and billing. These protocols will have to be developed before the service can be established ...

12.3 Potential Applications and Financial Benefits of Grid Computing

Grid proponents take the position that grid computing represents a "next step" in the world of computing, and that grid computing promises to move the Internet evolution to the next logical level. According to some ([YAN200401,YAN200301,CHU200201], among others), "utility computing is a positive, fundamental shift in computing architecture," and many businesses will be completely transformed over the next decade by using grid-enabled services, as these businesses integrate not only applications across the Internet but also raw computer power and storage. Furthermore, proponents prognosticate that the resulting infrastructure will be able to connect multiple regional and national computational grids, creating a universal source of pervasive and dependable computing power that will support new classes of applications [BER200301].

Most researchers, however, see grid computing as an evolution, not revolution. In fact, grid computing can be seen as the latest and most complete evolution of more familiar developments, such as distributed computing, the Web, peer-to-peer (P2P) computing, and virtualization technologies [IBM200301]. Some applications of grid computing, particularly in the scientific and engineering arena include, but are not limited to the following [BUR200302]:

- Distributed supercomputing/computational science
- High-capacity/throughput computing: large-scale simulation/chip design and parameter studies
- Content sharing, e.g., sharing digital contents among peers
- Remote software access/renting services: ASPs and WSs
- Data-intensive computing: drug design, particle physics, and stock prediction
- On-demand, real-time computing: medical instrumentation and mission-critical initiatives
- Collaborative computing (E-science, E-engineering, ...): collaborative design, data exploration, education, and E-learning
- Utility computing/service-oriented computing: new computing paradigm, new applications, new industries, and new business.

The benefits gained from grid computing can translate into competitive advantages in the marketplace. For example, the potential exists for grids to achieve the following [IBM200301,CHE200201]:

- Enable resource sharing
- Provide transparent access to remote resources
- Make effective use of computing resources, including platforms and datasets
- Reduce significantly the number of servers needed (25–75%)
- Allow on-demand aggregation of resources at multiple sites
- Reduce execution time for large-scale data processing applications
- Provide access to remote databases and software
- Provide load smoothing across a set of platforms
- Provide fault tolerance
- Take advantage of time zone and random diversity (in peak hours, users can access resources in off-peak zones)

■ Provide the flexibility to meet unforeseen emergency demands by renting external resources for a required period instead of owning them
■ Enable the realization of a virtual data center

As an example, VMware customers who have adopted the virtual infrastructure solutions have reported "dramatic" results, including [VMW200701]:

■ 60–80% utilization rates for x86 servers (up from 5–15% in nonvirtualized PCs)
■ Cost savings of more than $3000 annually for every workload virtualized
■ Ability to provision new applications in minutes instead of days or weeks
■ 85% improvement in recovery time from unplanned downtime

Naturally, there also are challenges associated with a grid deployment, this field being new and evolving. As implied earlier, there is a discernable IT trend toward virtualization and on-demand services. Virtualization* (and the supporting technology) is an approach that allows several operating systems to run simultaneously on one large computer. For example, IBM's z/VM operating system lets multiple instances of Linux coexist on the same mainframe computer. More generally, virtualization is the practice of making resources from diverse devices accessible to a user as if they were a single, larger, homogenous, locally available resource. Virtualization supports the concept of dynamically shifting resources across platforms to match computing demands with available resources: the computing environment can become dynamic, enabling autonomic shifting applications between servers to match demand [OTE200401]. There are well-known advantages in sharing resources, as a routine assessment of the behavior of the M/M/1 queue (memoryless/memoryless/1 server queue) versus the M/M/m queue (memoryless/memoryless/m servers queue) demonstrates: a single more powerful queue is more efficient than a group of discrete queues of comparable aggregate power. Grid computing represents a development in virtualization—as we have stated, it enables the abstraction of distributed computing and data resources such as processing, network bandwidth, and data storage to create a single system image; this grants users and applications seamless access (when properly implemented) to a large pool of IT capabilities. Just as an Internet user views a unified instance of content via the Web, a grid computing user essentially sees a single, large virtual computer [IBM200301]. "Virtualization"—the driving force behind grid computing—has been a key factor since the earliest days of electronic business computing.

Studies have shown that when problems can be parallelized, as in the case of data mining, records analysis, and billing (in a bank, securities company, financial services company, insurance company, etc.), then significant savings are achievable. Specifically, when a classical model may require, say, $100,000 to process 100,000 records, a grid-enabled environment may take as little as $20,000 to process the same number of records. Hence, the bottom line is that Fortune 500 companies have the potential to save 30% or more in the run-the-engine costs on the appropriate line item of their IT budget.

Grid computing can also be seen as part of a larger rehosting initiative and underlying IT trend at many companies (where alternatives such as Linux or possibly Windows operating systems could, in the future, be the preferred choice over the highly reliable but fairly costly UNIX solutions). Although each organization is different and the results vary, the directional cost trend is

---

* Virtualization can be achieved without grid computing; but many view virtualization as a step toward the goal of deploying grid computing infrastructures.

believable. Vendors engaged in this space include, but are not limited to, IBM, Hewlett-Packard, Sun, and Oracle. IBM uses "*on demand*" to describe its initiative; HP has its *Utility Data Center* (UDC) products; Sun has its *N1 Data-Center Architecture;* and Oracle has the *10 g family* of "grid-aware" products. Several software vendors also have a stake in grid computing, including, but not limited to, Microsoft, VMware, Computer Associates, Veritas Software, and Platform Computing [BED200301]. VMware was one of the leading suppliers of virtualization software at press time.*

Commercial interest in grid computing is on the rise, according to market research published by Gartner. The research firm estimated that 15% of corporations adopted a utility (grid) computing arrangement in 2003, and the market for utility services in North America was expected to increase from $8.6 billion in 2003 to more than $25 billion in 2006. By 2006, 30% of companies were expected to have some sort of utility computing arrangement, according to Gartner [BED200301]. One can infer from published statements that IBM expects the sector to move into hypergrowth, with "technologies … moving 'from rocket science to business service'," and the company had a target of doubling its grid revenue during that year [FEL20301]. According to economists, proliferation of high-performance cluster and grid computing and WSs applications will yield substantial productivity gains in the United States and worldwide over the next decade [COH200301].

A recent report from research firm IDC concluded that 23% of IT services were expected to be delivered from offshore centers by 2007 [MCD200301]. Grid computing may be a mechanism to enable companies to reduce costs, yet keep the jobs, intellectual capital, and data from migrating abroad. Although distributed computing does enable "remoting" functions, with grid computing this remoting can be done to some in-country regional—rather than Third World—location (just as electric and water grids have regional or near-countries scope, rather than having far-flung Third World remote scope). IT jobs that migrate abroad (particularly if terabytes of data about U.S. citizens and the U.S. government become the resident ownership of politically unstable Third World countries), have, in the opinion of this researcher, national security/homeland security risk implications, in the long term.

Although grids have advantages (e.g., potential reduction in the number of servers from 25 to 50% and related run-the-engine costs), some companies have reservations about immediately implementing the technology. Some of this hesitation relates to the fact that the technology is new, and in fact may be overhyped by the potential provider of services. Other issues may be related to "protection of turf": eliminating vast arrays of servers implies reduction in data center space, reduction in management span of control, reduction in operational staff, reduction in budget, etc. This is the same issue that was faced in the 1990s regarding outsourcing (e.g., see [MIN199501]). Other reservation may relate to the fact that infrastructural changes are needed, and this may have a short-term financial disbursement implication. Finally, not all situations, environments, and applications are amenable to a grid paradigm.

---

* VMware Infrastructure 3 is being positioned by the vendor as a tool for creating a self-optimizing IT infrastructure today with the most widely deployed software suite for optimizing and managing industry-standard IT environments through virtualization. VMware Infrastructure 3 is the next generation of industry-leading infrastructure virtualization software that virtualizes servers, storage, and networking, allowing multiple unmodified operating systems and their applications to run independently in virtual machines while sharing physical resources. The suite delivers virtualization, management, resource optimization, application availability, and operational automation capabilities [VMW200701].

12.4 Grid Types, Topologies, Components, Layers—A Basic View

Grid computing embodies a combination of a decentralized architecture for resource management, and a layered hierarchical architecture for the implementation of various constituent services [GRI200301]. A grid computing system can have local, metropolitan, regional, national, or international footprints. In turn, the autonomous resources in the constituent ensemble can span a single organization, multiple organizations, or a service provider space. Grids can be focused on the pooled assets of one organization or span virtual organizations that use a common suite of protocols to enable grid users and applications to run services in a secure, controlled manner [MYE200301]. Furthermore, resources can be logically aggregated for a long period of time (say, months or years) or for a temporary period of time (say, minutes, days, or weeks).

Grid computing often combines elements such as distributed computing, high-performance computing, and disposable computing, depending on the application of the technology and the scale of the operation. Grids can, in practical terms, create a virtual supercomputer out of existing servers, workstations, and even PCs, to deliver processing power not only to a company's own stakeholders and employees, but also to its partners and customers. This metacomputing environment is achieved by treating such IT resources as processing power, memory, storage, and network bandwidth as pure commodities. Similar to an electricity or water network, computational power can be delivered to any department or any application where it is needed most at any given time, based on specified business goals and priorities. Furthermore, grid computing allows chargeback on a per-usage basis rather than for a fixed infrastructure cost [HAN200301].

Present-day grids encompass the following types [DEV200301]:

- Computational grids, where machines with set-aside resources stand by to number-crunch data or provide coverage for other intensive workloads
- Scavenging grids, commonly used to find and harvest machine cycles from idle servers and desktop machines for use in resource-intensive tasks (scavenging is usually implemented in a way that is unobtrusive to the owner or user of the processor)
- Data grids which provide a unified interface for all data repositories in an organization, and through which data can be queried, managed, and secured.

As already noted, no claim is made herewith that there is a single solution to a given problem; grid computing is one of the available solutions. For example, although some of the machine-cycle inefficiencies can be addressed by virtual servers/rehosting (e.g., VMware, MS VirtualPC and VirtualServer, LPARs from IBM, partitions from Sun and HP, which do not require a grid infrastructure), one of the possible approaches to this inefficiency issue is, indeed, grid computing. Grid computing does have an emphasis on geographically distributed, multiorganization, utility-based (outsourced), networking-reliant methods, whereas clustering and rehosting have more (but not exclusively) of a data-center-focused, single-organization-oriented approach. Organizations will need to perform appropriate functional, economic, and strategic assessments to determine which approach is, in the final analysis, best for their specific environment. (This chapter is on grid computing; hence, our emphasis is on this approach, rather than other possible approaches such as pure virtualization).

Figures 12.1, 12.2, and 12.3 provide a pictorial view of some grid computing environments. Figure 12.1 depicts the traditional computing environment where a multitude of often-underutilized servers support a disjoint set of applications and datasets. As implied by this figure, the typical IT environment prior to grid computing operated as follows: A business-critical application

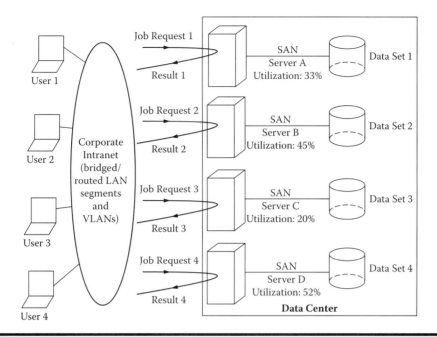

Figure 12.1   Standard computing environment.

runs on a designated server. Because the average utilization may be relatively low, during peak cycles the server in question can get overtaxed. As a consequence of this instantaneous overtaxation, the application can slow down, experience a halt, or even stall. In this traditional instance, the large dataset that this application is analyzing, exists only in a single data store (note that although multiple copies of the data could exist, it would not be easy with the traditional model to synchronize the databases if two programs independently operated aggressively on the data at the same time). Server capacity and access to the data store place limitations on how quickly desired results can be returned. Machine cycles on other servers are unable to be constructively utilized, and available disk capacity remains unused [IBM200301].

Figure 12.2 depicts an organization-owned computational grid; here, a middleware application running on a Grid Computing Broker manages a smaller set of processors and an integrated data store. A computational grid is a hardware and software infrastructure that provides dependable, consistent, pervasive, and inexpensive access to high-end computational capabilities. In a grid environment, workload can be broken up and sent in manageable pieces to idle server cycles. Not all applications are necessarily instantly migratable to a grid environment, without at least some redesign. Because legacy business applications may, a priori, fit such class of applications, a number of Fortune 500 companies are indeed looking into how such legacy applications can be modified or retooled such that they can be made to run on grid-based infrastructures.

A scheduler sets rules and priorities for routing jobs on a grid-based infrastructure. When servers and storage are enabled for grid computing, copies of the data can be stored in formerly unused space and easily made available [IBM200301]. A grid also provides mechanisms for managing the distributed data in a seamless way [PAD200301,FOS199901]. A grid middleware provides facilities to allow the use of the grid for applications and users. Middleware such as Globus [FOS199701], Legion [GRI199701], and UNICORE (UNiform Interface to Computer Resources)

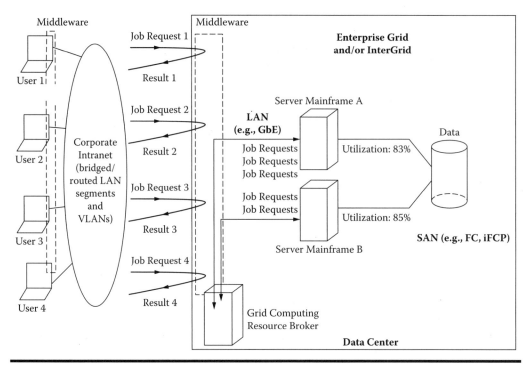

Figure 12.2   Grid computing environment (local implementation).

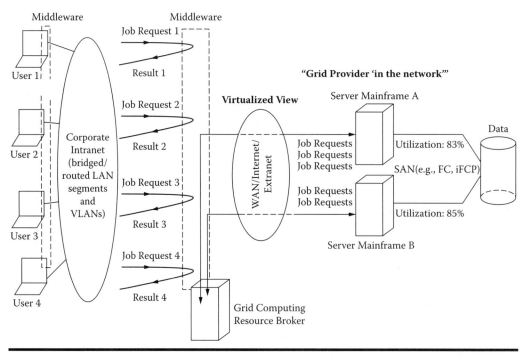

Figure 12.3   Grid computing environment (remote implementation).

[HUB200101] provide software infrastructure to handle various challenges of computational and data grids [PAD200301].

Figure 12.3 depicts the utility-oriented implementation of a computational grid. This concept is analogous to electric power network (grid), where power generators are distributed but the users are able to access electric power without concerning themselves about the source of energy and its pedestrian operational management [GRI200301]. As suggested by these figures, grid computing aims to provide seamless and scalable access to distributed resources. Computational grids enable the sharing, selection, and aggregation of a wide variety of geographically distributed computational resources (such as supercomputers, computing clusters, storage systems, data sources, instruments, and developers), and presents them as a single, unified resource for solving large-scale computing and data-intensive applications (e.g., molecular modeling for drug design, brain activity analysis, and high-energy physics). An initial grid deployment at a company can be scaled over time to bring in additional applications and new data. This allows gains in speed and accuracy without significant cost increases. Several years ago, this author coined the phrase "the corporation is the network" [MIN199701]. Grid computing supports this concept very well: with grid computing, all a corporation needs to run its IT apparatus is a reliable high-speed network to connect it to the distributed set of virtualized computational resources not necessarily owned by the corporation itself.

Grid computing started out as a mechanism to share the computational resources distributed all over the world for basic science applications, as illustrated pictorially by Figure 12.4 [PAD200301,FOS199901]. However, other types of resources, such as licenses or specialized equipment, can now also be virtualized in a grid computing environment. For example, if an

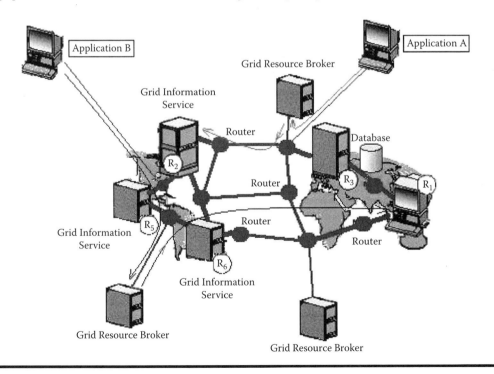

Figure 12.4   Pictorial view of World Wide InterGrid.

organization's software license agreement limits the number of users that can be using the license simultaneously, license management tools operating in grid mode could be employed to keep track of how many concurrent copies of the software are active. This will prevent the number from exceeding the allowed number, as well as scheduling jobs according to priorities defined by the automated business policies. Specialized equipment that is remotely deployed on the network could also be managed in a similar way, thereby making it unnecessary for the organization to purchase multiple devices, in much the same way today that people in the same office share Internet access or printing resources across a LAN [HAN200301].

Some grids focus on data federation and availability; others focus on computing power and speed. Many grids involve a combination of the two. For end users, all infrastructural complexity stays hidden [IBM200301]. Data (database) federation makes disparate corporate databases look as though the constituent data is all in the same database. Significant gains can be obtained if one can work on all the different databases, including selects, inserts, updates, and deletes as if all the tables existed in a single database.* Almost every organization has significant unused computing capacity, widely distributed among a feudal arrangement of PCs, midrange platforms, mainframes, and supercomputers. For example, if a company has 10,000 PCs, at an average computing power of 333 MIPS, this equates to an aggregate 3 tera (10^{12}) floating-point operations per second (TFLOPS) of potential computing power. As another example, in the United States there are an estimated 300 million computers; at an average computing power of 333 MIPS, this equates to a raw computing power of 100,000 TFLOPS. Mainframes are generally idle 40% of the time; Unix servers are actually "serving" something less than 10% of the time; most PCs do nothing for 95% of a typical day [IBM200301]. This is an inefficient situation for customers. TFLOPS-speeds that are possible with grid computing enable scientists to address some of the most computationally intensive scientific tasks, from problems in protein analysis that will form the basis for new drug designs, to climate modeling, to deducing the content and behavior of the cosmos from astronomical data [WAL200201].

Many scientific applications are also data intensive, in addition to being computationally intensive. By 2006, several physics projects were producing multiple petabytes (10^{15} byte) of data per year. This has been called *peta-scale* data. PCs now ship with up to 100 GB of storage (as much as an entire 1990 supercomputer center) [FOS200202]: 1 petabyte would equate to 10,000 of these PCs, or to the PC base of a smaller Fortune 500 company. Data grids also have some immediate commercial applications. Grid-oriented solutions are the way to manage this kind of storage requirement, particularly from a data access perspective (more than just from a physical storage perspective.) As grids evolved, the management of peta-scale data became burdensome. The confluence and combination of large dataset size, geographic distribution of users and resources, and computationally intensive scientific analyses prompted the development of data grids, as noted earlier [PAD200301,CHE199901]. Here, a data middleware (usually part of general-purpose grid middleware) provides facilities for data management. Various research communities have developed successful data middleware such as Storage Resource Broker (SRB) [BAR199801], Grid Data Farm [TAT200201], and European Data Grid Middleware.

---

* The "federator" system operates on the tables in the remote systems, the "federatees." The remote tables appear as virtual tables in the federator database. Client application programs can perform operations on the virtual tables in the federator database, but the real persistent storage is in the remote database. Each federatee views the federator as just another database client connection. The federatee is simply servicing client requests for database operations. The federator needs client software to access each remote database. Client software for IBM Informix®, Sybase, Oracle, etc., would need to be installed to access each type of federatee [IBM200301].

These middleware tools have been effective in providing framework for managing high volumes of data, but they are often incompatible.

The key components of grid computing include the following [DEV200301]:

■ Resource management: The grid must be aware of what resources are available for different tasks.
■ Security management: The grid needs to ensure that only authorized users can access and use the available resources.
■ Data management: Data must be transported, cleansed, parceled, and processed.
■ Services management: Users and applications must be able to query the grid in an effective and efficient manner.

More specifically, grid computing can be viewed as comprising a number of logical hierarchical layers. Figure 12.5 depicts a first view of the layered architecture of a grid environment. At the base of the grid stack, one finds the *grid fabric*, namely, the distributed resources that are managed by a local resource manager with a local policy; these resources are interconnected via local-, metropolitan-, or wide-area networks. The grid fabric includes and incorporates networks; computers such as PCs and processors using operating systems such as Unix, Linux, or Windows; clusters using various operating systems; resource management systems; storage devices; and databases. The *security infrastructure* layer provides secure and authorized access to grid resources. Above this layer, the *core grid middleware* provides uniform access to the resources in the fabric; the middleware is designed to hide complexities of partitioning, distributing, and load balancing. The next layer, the *user-level middleware* layer consists of resource brokers or schedulers responsible for aggregating resources. The *grid programming environments and tools* layer includes the compilers, libraries, development tools, and so on, that are required to run the applications (resource brokers manage the execution of applications on distributed resources using appropriate scheduling strategies, whereas grid development tools grid-enable applications.) The top layer consists of *grid applications* themselves [CHE200201].

Building on this intuitive idea of layering, it would be advantageous if industry consensus were reached on the series of layers. Architectural standards are now under development by the Global Grid Forum (GGF). The GGF is an industry advocacy group; it supports community-driven processes for developing and documenting new standards for grid computing. The GGF is a forum for exchanging information and defining standards relating to distributed computing and grid technologies. GGF is fashioned after the Grid Forum, the eGrid European Grid Forum,

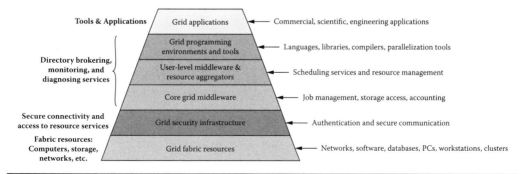

Figure 12.5   One view of grid computing layers.

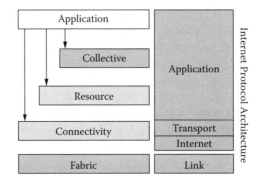

Figure 12.6 Layered grid architecture, global grid forum. (This presentation is licensed for use under the terms of the Globus Toolkit Public License. See http://www.globus.org/toolkit/download/license.html for the full text of this license.)

and the Grid Community in the Asia-Pacific. GGF is focusing on open grid architecture standards [ZHA200201]. Technical specifications are being developed for architectural elements: e.g., security, data, resource management, and information. Grid architectures are being built based on Internet protocols and services (for example, communication, routing, name resolution, etc.). The layering approach is used to the extent possible because it is advantageous for higher-level functions to use common lower-level functions. The GGF's approach has been to propose a set of core services as basic infrastructure, as shown in Figure 12.6. These core services are used to construct high-level, domain-specific solutions. The design principles are the following: keep participation cost low, enable local control, support for adaptation, and use the "IP hourglass" model of many applications using a few core services to support many fabric elements (e.g., operating systems). In the meantime, Globus Toolkit™ has emerged as the de facto standard for several important connectivity, resource, and collective protocols. The toolkit, a "middleware plus" capability, addresses issues of security, information discovery, resource management, data management, communication, fault detection, and portability [GLO200301].

12.5 Comparison with Other Approaches

It is important to note that certain IT computing constructs are not grids, as we discuss next. In some instances, these technologies are the optimal solution for an organization's problem; in other cases, grid computing is the best solution, particularly if in the long-term one is especially interested in supplier-provided utility computing.

The distinction between clusters and grids relates to the way resources are managed. In the case of clusters (aggregating of processors in parallel-based configurations), the resource allocation is performed by a centralized resource manager and scheduling system; also, nodes cooperatively work together as a single unified resource. In the case of grids, each node has its own resource manager and such a node does not aim at providing a single system view [BUY200301]. A cluster comprises multiple interconnected independent nodes that cooperatively work together as a single unified resource. This means all users of clusters have to go through a centralized system that manages the allocation of resources to application jobs. Unlike grids, cluster resources are almost always owned by a single organization. Actually, many grids are constructed by using clusters or traditional parallel systems as their nodes, although this is not a requirement. An example of grid that contains clusters as its nodes is the NSF TeraGrid [GRI200301]; another example, the World Wide Grid, has many nodes that are clusters located in organizations such as NRC Canada, AIST-Japan, N*Grid Korea, and University of Melbourne. Although cluster management systems such as Platform's Load Sharing Facility, Veridian's Portable Batch System, or Sun's Sun Grid Engine can deliver enhanced distributed computing services, they are not grids themselves. These cluster management systems have centralized control, complete knowledge of system state and user requests, and complete control over individual components (such features tend not to be characteristic of a grid proper) [FOS200201].

Grid computing also differs from basic WSs, although it now makes use of these services. WSs have become an important component of distributed computing applications over the Internet [GRI200401]. The WWW is not (yet, in itself) a grid: its open, general-purpose protocols support access to distributed resources but not the coordinated use of those resources to deliver negotiated qualities of service [FOS200201]. So, because the Web is mainly focused on communication, grid computing enables resource sharing and collaborative resource interplay toward common business goals. WSs provide standard infrastructure for data exchange between two different distributed applications, whereas grids provide an infrastructure for aggregation of high-end resources for solving large-scale problems in science, engineering, and commerce. However, there are similarities as well as differences: (1) similar to the case of the WWW, grid computing keeps complexity hidden: multiple users experience a single, unified experience; and (2) WSs are utilized to support grid computing mechanisms: these WSs will play a key constituent role in the standardized definition of grid computing, because they have emerged in the past few years as a standards-based approach for accessing network applications. The recent trend is to implement grid solutions using WSs technologies; for example, the Globus Toolkit 3.0 middleware is being implemented using WSs technologies. In this context, low-level grid services are instances of WSs (a grid service is a WS that conforms to a set of conventions that provide for controlled, fault-resilient, and secure management of stateful services) [GRI200301,FOX200201].

Both *peer-to-peer* (P2P) and grid computing are concerned with the same general problem, namely, the organization of resource sharing within VOs. As is the case with P2P environments, grid computing allows users to share files, but unlike P2P, grid computing allows many-to-many sharing; furthermore, with grid computing, the sharing is not only in reference to files but other resources as well. The grid community generally focuses on aggregating distributed high-end machines such as clusters, whereas the P2P community concentrates on sharing low-end systems such as PCs connected to the Internet [CHE200201]. Both disciplines take the same general approach to solving this problem, namely, the creation of overlay structures that coexist with, but need not correspond in structure to, underlying organizational structures. Each discipline has made technical advances in recent years, but each also has—in current instantiations—a number of limitations: there are complementary aspects regarding the strengths and weaknesses of the two approaches that suggest the interests of the two communities are likely to grow closer over time [IAM200301]. P2P networks can amass computing power, as does the SETI@home project, or share contents, as Napster and Gnutella have done in the recent past. Given the number of grid and P2P projects and forums that began worldwide at the turn of the decade, it is clear that interest in the research, development, and commercial deployment of these technologies is burgeoning [CHE200201].

Grid computing also differs from *virtualization*. Resource virtualization is the *abstraction* of server, storage, and network resources to make them available dynamically for sharing by IT services—both inside and outside an organization. Virtualization is a step along the way on the road to utility computing (grid computing) and, in combination with other server, storage, and networking capabilities, offers customers the opportunity to build, according to advocates, an IT infrastructure without hard boundaries or fixed constraints [HEP200201]. Virtualization has somewhat more of an emphasis on local resources, whereas grid computing has more of an emphasis on geographically distributed interorganizational resources. The universal problem that virtualization is solving in a data center is that of dedicated resources. Although this approach does address performance, it lacks fine granularity. Typically, IT managers take an educated guess as to how many dedicated servers they will need to handle peak loads, by purchasing extra servers, and then later finding out that a significant portion of these servers are grossly underutilized. A typical data center has a large amount of idle infrastructure, bought and set up online to handle peak traffic for different applications. Virtualization offers a way of moving resources from one application to another dynamically. However, specifics of the desired virtualizing effect depend on the specific application deployed [SME200301]. Three representative products at the time of this writing are EMC's VMware, HP's Utility Data Center, and Platform Computing's Platform LFS. With virtualization, the logical functions of the server, storage, and network elements are separated from their physical functions (e.g., processor, memory, I/O controllers, disks, switches). In other words, all servers, storage, and network devices can be aggregated into independent pools of resources. Some elements may even be further subdivided (server partitions, storage LUNs) to provide an even more granular level of control. Elements from these pools can then be allocated, provisioned, and managed—manually or automatically—to meet the changing needs and priorities of one's business. Virtualization can span the following domains [HEP200201]:

1. Server virtualization for horizontally and vertically scaled server environments—Server virtualization enables optimized utilization, improved service levels, and reduced management overhead.
2. Network virtualization enabled by intelligent routers, switches, and other networking elements supporting virtual LANs—Virtualized networks are more secure and more able to support unforeseen spikes in customer and user demand.
3. Storage virtualization (server, network, and array-based)—Storage virtualization technologies improve the utilization of current storage subsystems, reduce administrative costs, and protect vital data in a secure and automated fashion.
4. Application virtualization—This enables programs and services to be executed on multiple systems simultaneously. This computing approach is related to horizontal scaling, clusters, and grid computing, where a single application is able to cooperatively execute on a number of servers concurrently.
5. Data center virtualization, whereby groups of servers, storage, and network resources can be provisioned or reallocated on the fly to meet the needs of a new IT service or to handle dynamically changing workloads [HEP200201].

Grid computing deployment, although potentially related to a rehosting initiative, is not just rehosting. As Figure 12.7 depicts, rehosting typically implies the reduction of a large number of servers (possibly using some older or proprietary OS) to a smaller set of more powerful and more modern servers (possibly running on open source OSs). This is certainly advantageous from an operations, physical maintenance, and power and space perspective. There are savings associated with rehosting. However, applications are still assigned specific servers. Grid computing, on the other hand, permits the true virtualization of the computing function, as seen in Figure 12.7. Here applications are not preassigned a server, but the "runtime" assignment is made based on real-time considerations. (Note: In the bottom diagram, the hosts could be collocated or spread all over the world. When local hosts are aggregated in tightly coupled configurations, they tend

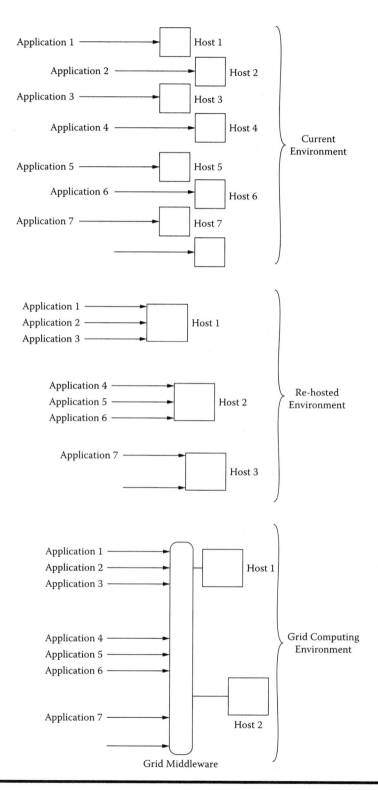

Figure 12.7   A comparison with rehosting.

to generally be of the cluster parallel-based computing type; such processors, however, can also be non-parallel-computing-based grids, e.g., by running the Globus Toolkit. When geographically dispersed hosts are aggregated in distributed computing configurations, they tend to generally be of the grid computing type and not running in a clustered arrangement—Figure 12.7 does not show geography, and the reader should conclude that the hosts are arranged in a grid computing arrangement.)

In summary, like clusters and distributed computing, grids bring computing resources together. Unlike clusters and distributed computing, which need physical proximity and operating homogeneity, grids can be geographically distributed and can be heterogeneous. Similar to virtualization technologies, grid computing enables the virtualization of IT resources. Unlike virtualization technologies, which virtualize a single system, grid computing enables the virtualization of broad-scale and disparate IT resources [IBM200301]. Scientific community deployments such as the distributed data processing system being deployed internationally by "Data Grid" projects (e.g., *GriPhyN, PPDG, EU DataGrid*), NASA's *Information Power Grid*, the *Distributed ASCI Supercomputer* system that links clusters at several Dutch universities, the *DOE Science Grid* and *DISCOM Grid* that link systems at DOE laboratories, and the *TeraGrid* mentioned previously being constructed to link major U.S. academic sites, are all bona fide examples of grid computing. A multi-site scheduler such as Platform's MultiCluster can reasonably be called a first generation grid. Other examples of grid computing include the distributed computing systems provided by Condor, Entropia, and United Devices, which make use of idle desktops; P2P systems such as Gnutella, which support file sharing among participating peers; and a federated deployment of the Storage Resource Broker, which supports distributed access to data resources [FOS200201].

12.6 A Quick View of Grid Computing Standards

One of the challenges with any computing technology is getting the various components to communicate with one another. Nowhere is this more critical than when trying to get different platforms and environments to interoperate. It should, therefore, be immediately evident that the grid computing paradigm requires standard, open, general-purpose protocols and interfaces. Standards for grid computing are now being defined and are beginning to be implemented by the vendors [DEV200301, CAT200301]. To make the most effective use of the computing resources available, these environments need to utilize common protocols [BRO200301]. Standards are the "holy grail" for grid computing.

Regarding this issue, proponents make the case that we are now indeed entering a new phase of grid computing where standards will define grids in a consistent way—by enabling grid systems to become easily built "off-the-shelf" systems. Standard-based grid systems have been called "Third-Generation Grids," or 3G Grids by some. First-generation grids or "1G Grids" involved local "metacomputers" with basic services such as distributed file systems and sitewide single sign-on, upon which early-adopter developers created distributed applications with custom communications protocols. Gigabit test beds extended 1G grids across distance, and attempts to create "Metacenters" explored issues of interorganizational integration. 1G grids were totally custom-made proofs of concept [CAT200301]. 2G grid systems began with projects such as Condor, I-WAY (the origin of Globus), and Legion (origin of Avaki), where underlying software services and communications protocols could be used as a basis for developing distributed applications and services. 2G grids offered basic building blocks, but deployment involved significant customization and filling in many gaps. Independent deployments of 2G grid technology today involve enough customized extensions that interoperability is problematic, and interoperability among 2G grid systems is very difficult. This is why the industry needs 3G grids [CAT200301].

By introducing standard technical specifications, 3G grid technology will have the potential to allow both competition and interoperability not only among applications and toolkits but also among implementations of key services. The goal is to mix and match components; but this potential will only be realized if the grid community continues to work at defining standards [CAT200301]. The Global Grid Forum community is applying lessons learned from 1G and 2G grids and from WS technologies and concepts to create 3G architectures [CAT200301].

GGF has driven initiatives such as the Open Grid Services Architecture (OGSA). OGSA is a set of specifications and standards that integrate and leverage the worlds of WSs and grid computing (WSs are viewed by some as the "biggest technology trend" in the last five years [LEH200301]). With this architecture, a set of common interface specifications support the interoperability of discrete, independently developed services. OGSA brings together Web standards such as XML (eXtensible Markup Language), WSDL (Web Service Definition Language), UDDI (Universal Description, Discovery, and Integration), and SOAP (Simple Object Access Protocol), with the standards for grid computing developed by the Globus Project [MCC200301]. The Globus Project is a joint effort on the part of researchers and developers from around the world that focuses on grid research, software tools, test beds, and applications. As TCP/IP (Transmission Control Protocol/Internet Protocol) forms the backbone for the Internet, the OGSA is the backbone for grid computing. The recently released Open Grid Services Infrastructure (OGSI) service specification is the keystone in this architecture [CAT200301].

In addition to making progress on the standards front, grid computing as a service needs to address various issues and challenges. Besides standardization, some of these issues and challenges include security, true scalability, autonomy, heterogeneity of resource access interfaces, policies, capabilities, pricing, data locality, dynamic variation in availability of resources, and complexity in creation of applications [GRI200301].

It should be noted, however, that at the current time the more successful virtualization suites are vendor specific.

12.7 A Pragmatic Course of Investigation on Grid Computing

To identify possible benefits to their organizations, planners should understand grid computing concepts and the underlying networking mechanisms. Practitioners interested in grid computing are asking basic questions [DEV200301]: What do we do with all of this stuff? Where do we start? How do the pieces fit together? What comes next? As implied by the introductory but rather encompassing foregoing discussion, grid computing is applicable to enterprise users at two levels:

1. Obtaining computing services over a network from a remote computing service provider
2. Aggregating an organization's dispersed set on uncoordinated systems into one holistic computing apparatus

As noted earlier, with grid computing, organizations can optimize computing and data resources, pool such resources to support large-capacity workloads, share the resources across networks, and enable collaboration [IBM200301]. Grid technology allows the IT organization to consolidate and numerically reduce the number of platforms that need to be kept operating.

Practitioners should look at networking as not only the best way to understand what grid computing is, but more importantly, the best way to understand why and how grid computing is important to IT practitioners (rather than "just another hot technology" that gets researchers excited but never has much effect on what network professionals see in the real world).

One can build and deploy a grid of a variety of sizes and types: for large or small firms, a single department or the entire enterprise, and enterprise business applications or scientific endeavors. Similar to many other recent technologies, however, grid computing runs the risk of being over-hyped. CIOs need to be careful not to be to oversold on grid computing: a sound, reliable, conservative economic analysis is, therefore, required that encompasses the true total cost of ownership (TCO) and assesses the true risks associated with this approach.

Like the Internet, grid computing has its roots in the scientific and research communities. After about a decade of research, open systems are poised to enter the market. Coupled with a rapid drop in the cost for communication bandwidth, commercial-grade opportunities are emerging for Fortune 500 IT shops searching for new ways to save money. All of this has to be properly weighted against the commoditization of machine cycles (just buy more processors and retain the status quo) and against reduced support cost by way of subcontinent outsourcing of said IT support and related application development (just move operations abroad, but otherwise retain the status quo). During the past ten years or so, a tour-de-force commoditization has been experienced in computing hardware platforms that support IT applications at businesses of all sizes. Some have encapsulated this rapidly occurring phenomenon with the phrase "IT does not matter." The price-disrupting predicament brought about by commoditization affords new opportunities for organizations, although it also has conspicuous process- and people-dislocating consequences. Grid computing is yet another way to capitalize on this Moore-Law-driven commoditization.

Already we have noted that at its core grid computing is, and must be, based on an open set of standards and protocols that enable communication across heterogeneous, geographically dispersed environments. Therefore, planners should track the work that the standards groups are doing. It is important to understand the significance of standards in grid computing, how they affect capabilities and facilities, what standards exist, and how they can be applied to the problems of distributed computation [BRO200301].

There is effort involved with resource management and scheduling in a grid environment. When enterprises need to aggregate resources distributed within their organization and prioritize allocation of resources to different users, projects, and applications based on their quality-of-service (QoS) requirements (call these service level agreements), these enterprises need to be concerned about resource management and scheduling. The user QoS-based allocation strategies enhance the value delivered by the utility. The need for QoS-based resource management becomes significant whenever more than one competing application or user need to utilize shared resources [GRI200301].

Regional economies will benefit significantly from grid computing technologies, as suggested earlier in the chapter, assuming that two activities occur [COH200301]: First, the broadband infrastructure needed to support grid computing and WSs must be developed in a timely fashion (this being the underlying theme of this text); and second, that states and regions attract (or grow from within) a sufficient pool of skilled computer and communications professionals to fully deploy and utilize the new technologies and applications.

A number of commercial-grade products are now available, for example, VMware ESX Server. By decoupling the entire software environment from its underlying hardware infrastructure, virtualization enables the aggregation of multiple servers, storage infrastructure, and networks into shared pools of resources that can be delivered dynamically, securely, and reliably to applications as needed. This approach enables organizations to build a computing infrastructure with high levels of utilization, availability, automation, and flexibility using building blocks of inexpensive industry-standard servers [VMW200701]. Virtualization is a proven software technology that is rapidly transforming the IT landscape and fundamentally changing the way that people compute. Today's powerful x86 computer hardware was originally designed to run only a single operating system and a single application, but virtualization makes it possible to run multiple operating systems and multiple applications on the same computer at the same time, increasing the utilization and flexibility of hardware. In essence, virtualization lets a planner transform hardware into software. Use software such as VMware ESX Server to transform or virtualize the hardware resources of an x86-based computer—including the CPU, RAM, hard disk, and network controller—to create a fully functional virtual machine that can run its own operating system and applications just like a real computer. Multiple virtual machines share hardware resources without interfering with one another so that the IT planner can safely run several operating systems and applications at the same time on a single computer. The VMware approach to virtualization inserts a thin layer of software directly on the computer hardware or on a host operating system. However, virtualizing a single physical computer is just the beginning. Virtualization software offers a robust virtualization platform that can scale across hundreds of interconnected physical computers and storage devices to form an entire virtual infrastructure.

Appendix: A Basic Architecture Glossary

This appendix provides a basic glossary of architectural and technology terms, synthesized from a number of industry sources. This glossary is not intended to be exhaustive.

10 Gigabit Ethernet (10GbE): Ethernet local area network (LAN) systems operating at 10000 Mbps (10 Gbps) (IEEE Std. 802.3ae-2002.) The 10 Gbps IEEE P802.3ae solution extends Ethernet capabilities, providing higher bandwidth for multimedia, distributed processing, imaging, and other super-high-speed applications by improving the performance of (1) LAN, backbone, server and gateway connectivity; (2) switch aggregation functions; and (3) the metropolitan area network (MAN), wide area network (WAN), regional area network (RAN), and storage area network (SAN) environments.

Application Modeling: Specifying the functionality and design of an application in a separate step using a modeling language, such as UML, before coding starts. May include a requirements-gathering step, and follow a formal methodology [OMG200501].

Application-Oriented Networking (AON): Application-Oriented Networking (AON) is a vendor-specific concept defined before SOA was commonly adopted in the industry and is primarily focused on routing, performance, managing quality of service (QoS), and security.

Architect: A high-level role responsible for the overall work effort of creating the architecture and design of the system. More specialized roles, such as enterprise architect, application architect, Service-Oriented Architecture architect, lead designer (for microdesign-level tasks such as class modeling, sequence diagrams, and so forth), and infrastructure architect are actually responsible for various architectural work efforts that constitute the design phase of the project [MIT200601].

Architecture Description: A formal description of an information system, organized in a way that supports reasoning about the structural properties of the system. It defines the components or building blocks that make up the overall information system, and provides a plan from which products can be procured, and systems developed, that will work together to implement the overall system. It thus enables one to manage one's own overall IT investment in a way that meets the needs of the business [TOG200501].

Architecture Description Languages (ADLs): Mechanisms to describe software architectures via special-purpose languages. ADLs have the disadvantage of not providing adequate support for separating several kinds of concerns across different viewpoints [FER200401].

Architecture Description, IEEE 1471-2000: A collection of artifacts that document the architecture.

Architecture Development Method: TOGAF Architecture Development Method [SYS200501].

Architecture Framework: A tool that can be used for developing a broad range of different architectures. Typically, a collection of guidelines for developing and documenting architectures. The framework provides rules and guidance for developing and presenting architectural descriptions. The products defined by the framework are the work products of architecture development, the descriptive artifacts that communicate the architecture [SYS200501].

The framework should describe a method for designing an information system in terms of a set of building blocks, and for showing how the building blocks fit together. The framework should contain a set of tools and provide a common vocabulary. It should also include a list of recommended standards and compliant products that can be used to implement the building blocks.

Architecture, ANSI: Per ANSI/IEEE Std 1471-2000 architecture is "the fundamental organization of a system, embodied in its components, their relationships to each other and the environment, and the principles governing its design and evolution."

Architecture, IEEE 1471-2000: A system's fundamental organization, embodied in its components, their relationships to one another and to the environment, and the principles guiding its design and evolution. This definition/formulation is more focused on the architecture of a single system rather than an entire enterprise.

Architecture, The Object Management Group: A specification of the parts and connectors of the system and the rules for the interactions of the parts using the connectors [OMG200501].

Architecture, The Open Group Architecture Framework (TOGAF): TOGAF embraces but does not strictly adhere to ANSI/IEEE Std 1471-2000 terminology. In TOGAF, architecture has two meanings depending upon its contextual usage: (1) A formal description of a system, or a detailed plan of the system at component level to guide its implementation; (2) the structure of components, their interrelationships, and the principles and guidelines governing their design and evolution over time [TOG200501].

Blade Servers: High-density compact server consisting of packing these "slim-format" computers in high-count cabinets (chassis) with shared assets (e.g., power, cooling, networking, etc.). This arrangement requires less power and physical space than a traditional rack of servers. Blades are typically arranged vertically (like books in a bookshelf.) A blade generally includes a limited number of components (processor, memory, and optional hard drive); the chassis supports in-rack power distribution, local server access/console (keyboard/mouse), and networking access.

Business-analyst: A high-level role responsible for the business analysis and business process management (BPM) work activities. The business analyst performs use case identification and creates functional specifications for each use case. This high-level role implies that the analyst might also take on more specialized tasks during the project [MIT200601].

Business Architecture: An architectural formulation of the business function.

Business Function: A description of all business elements and structures that are covered by the enterprise.

Business Process Management (BPM): A discipline combining software capabilities and business expertise through people, systems, and information to accelerate time between process improvements, facilitating business innovation [IBM200701].

Business-to-Business (B2B) SOA (also known as Extended Enterprise SOA): SOA-based mechanisms for automating business interactions between suppliers, customers, and trading partners, allowing companies to better share information and optimize processes across the value chain from better demand forecasting to streamlined manufacturing to more responsive customer service. B2B SOA allows firms to [TIB200701] achieve the following:

- Reuse internal services by extending them to trading partners.
- Build composite applications that extend from their back-end systems to their partner's back-end systems for end-to-end process automation.
- Insulate trading partners from the underlying technology framework through a flexible solution that decouples process, protocols, transports, and payloads.
- Engineer partner processes and services once and reuse across all trading partners.

Clinger–Cohen Act of 1996: Also known as the Information Technology Management Reform Act (ITMRA). Act authorized a chief information officer (CIO) for all federal agencies; it makes the CIO responsible for developing, maintaining, and facilitating the implementation of a sound and integrated information technology architecture (ITA) (i.e., enterprise architecture).

Clusters:

- Aggregating of processors in parallel-based configurations, typically in local environment (within a data center); all nodes work cooperatively as a single unified resource.
- Resource allocation is performed by a centralized resource manager and scheduling system.
- Comprises multiple interconnected independent nodes that cooperatively work together as a single unified resource; unlike grids, cluster resources are typically owned by a single organization.
- All users of clusters have to go through a centralized system that manages allocation of resources to application jobs. Cluster management systems have centralized control, complete knowledge of system state and user requests, and complete control over individual components.

Commercial Off-The-Shelf (COTS): Products that can be purchased and used by the enterprise with minimal or no customization as an application supporting a given business functions.

Common Object Request Broker Architecture (CORBA): Object Management Group's open, vendor-independent architecture and infrastructure that computer applications use to work together over networks. A CORBA-based program from any vendor, on almost any computer, operating system, programming language, and network can interoperate with a CORBA-based program from the same or another vendor, on almost any other computer, operating system, programming language, and network. Because of the easy way that CORBA integrates machines from so many vendors, with sizes ranging from mainframes through minis and desktops to hand-helds and embedded systems, it is the middleware for large (and even not-so-large) enterprises. One of its most important, as well as most frequent, uses is in servers that must handle a large number of clients at high hit rates with high reliability. CORBA works behind the scenes in the computer rooms of many of the world's largest Web sites; ones that you probably use daily. Specializations for scalability and fault-tolerance support these systems [OMG200701].

Concerns, IEEE 1471-2000: Key interests that are critically important to the stakeholders in the system and determine the acceptability of the system. Concerns may pertain to any aspect of the system's functioning, development, or operation, including considerations such as performance, reliability, security, distribution, and migration/scalability.

Core Architecture Data Model (CADM): A formal model defining the data organization for a repository of C4ISR/DoDAF-compliant architectural products (artifacts). The CADM provides a common schema for repositories of architectural information. Tool builders or vendors providing support for DoDAF-style architecture descriptions typically implement the CADM with a database [SYS200501].

Data Grid: A kind of grid computing grid used for housing and providing access to data across multiple organizations; users are not focused on where this data is located as long as they have access to it [MIN200501].

Deployment Manager: Individual responsible for deploying the application code on the infrastructure in various environments (for example, testing, staging, and production) and all the work efforts required for seamless deployment applicable to all environments (such as developing installation scripts, configuration management, and so on) [MIT200601].

Developer: A high-level role responsible for the implementation of the solution. Again, more specialized actors within this role might actually carry out the work, such as a database programmer, a Java developer, a Web developer, and a business process choreographer, to name a few. Developers work on specific layers of the application stack, and each requires specialized skills for that layer [MIT200601].

DoD Architecture Repository System: A DoD repository for approved architecture information compliant with the DoDAF [SYS200501].

Enterprise: Any collection of corporate or institutional task-supporting functional entities that has a common set of goals or a single mandate. In this context, an enterprise is, but is not limited to, an entire corporation, a division or department of a corporation, a group of geographically dispersed organizations linked together by common administrative ownership, a government agency (or set of agencies) at any level of jurisdiction, and so on. This also encompasses the concept on an extended enterprise, which is a logical aggregation that includes internal business units of a firm along with partners and suppliers [TOG200501].

Enterprise Architecture Program Management Office: Program Management Office established in 2002, in accordance with directions issued by the Associate Director for Information Technology and E-Government, Office of Management and Budget (OMB).

Enterprise Architecture, Minoli: Define a Function Block m at version n, FB(m,n), as comprising the following:

$$FB(m,n) = \{F(m,n), I(m,n,j), D(m,n,j), PI(m,n,j)\} \text{ for some } 1 < m < w$$

where

F(m,n) is a set of (enterprise IT) functions that Function Block m can undertake at version n;

I(m,n,j) is equal to "1" if Function Block FB(m,n) has an interface with Function Block FB(j,n) for j = 1, 2, ..., x where x is the number of Function Blocks under consideration in this architecture, and 0 otherwise;

D(m,n,j) is the set of data that is exchanged over interface I(m,n,j) for all j where I(m,n,j) = 1; and

PI(m,n,j)} is the protocol used to exchange data over interface I(m,n,j) for all j where I(m,n,j) = 1.

Finally, assume that a (nonoverlapping) partition exists such that

$$\{FB(m,n)\} = P(1,n) \ U \ P(2,n) \ U \ P(3,n)\ldots U \ P(y,n) \ \text{for} \ m = 1, 2, \ldots, x.$$

Then enterprise architecture A(n) is defined as

$$A(n) = \{P(k,n)\}, \ k = 1, 2, \ldots, y$$

Note: We also call the set {P(k,n)}, k = 1, 2, ..., y the architecture description.

Enterprise Architecture, this text: The following components:
- The enterprise architecture description (of the current or target state)
- The enterprise standards set
- The enterprise approved equipment list
- The roadmap along with (migration) strategies

Enterprise Service Bus (ESB): A connectivity infrastructure for integrating applications and services by performing the following actions between services and requestors: routing messages between services, converting transport protocols between requestor and service, transforming message formats between requestor and service, and handling business events from disparate sources [IBM200701].

eXtensible Mark-up Language (XML): A structured language that was published as a W3C Recommendation in 1998. It is a metalanguage because it is used to describe other languages, the elements they contain, and how those elements can be used. These standardized specifications for specific types of information make them, along with the information that they describe, portable across platforms.

Fibre Channel over IP (FCIP): A protocol for transmitting Fibre Channel (FC) data over an IP network. It allows the encapsulation/tunneling of FC packets and transport via Transmission Control Protocol/Internet Protocol (TCP/IP) networks. Gateways are used to interconnect FC Storage Area Networks (SANs) to the IP network and to set up connections between SANs. The protocol enables applications developed to run over FC SANs to be supported under IP, enabling organizations to leverage their current IP infrastructure and management resources to interconnect and extend FC SANs.

Grid Computing: (aka Utility Computing) An environment that can be built at the local (data center), regional, or global level, where individual users can access computers, databases, and scientific tools in a transparent manner, without having to directly take into account where the underlying facilities are located.

Virtualized distributed computing environment that enables the dynamic "runtime" selection, sharing, and aggregation of geographically distributed autonomous (autonomic) resources based on the availability, capability, performance, and cost of these computing resources, and simultaneously, also based on an organization's specific baseline or burst-processing requirements. Grid computing enables organizations to transparently integrate, streamline, and share dispersed, heterogeneous pools of hosts, servers, storage systems, data, and networks into one synergistic system, to deliver agreed-upon service at specified levels of application efficiency and processing performance. Grid computing is an approach to distributed computing that spans multiple locations or multiple organizations, machine architectures, and software boundaries to provide power, collaboration, and information access. Grid computing is infrastructure that enables the integrated, collaborative use of computers, supercomputers, networks, databases, and scientific instruments owned and managed by multiple organizations. Grid computing is a network of computation: namely, tools and protocols for coordinated resource sharing and problem solving among pooled asset ... allows coordinated resource sharing and problem solving in dynamic, multi-institutional virtual organizations [MIN200501].

Grid Computing Synonyms: (some with slightly different connotations): Computational grid, computing-on-demand, on-demand computing, just-in-time computing, platform computing, network computing, computing utility, utility computing, cluster computing, and high performance distributed computing [MIN200501].

Grid Computing Topologies: Local, metropolitan, regional, national, or international footprint. Systems may be in the same room, or may be distributed across the globe; they may be running on homogenous or heterogeneous hardware platforms; they may be running on similar or dissimilar operating systems; and they may owned by one or more organizations [MIN200501].

Grid Computing Types: (1) Computational grids: machines with set-aside resources stand by to "number-crunch" data or provide coverage for other intensive workloads; (2) Scavenging grids: commonly used to locate and exploit CPU cycles on idle servers and desktop machines for use in resource-intensive tasks; and (3) Data grids: a unified interface for all data repositories in an organization through which data can be queried, managed, and secured. Computational grids can be local, Enterprise grids (also called Intragrids), and Internet-based grids (also called Intergrids.) Enterprise grids are middleware-based environments that harvest unused "machine cycles," thereby obviating otherwise-needed growth costs [MIN200501].

Grid Service: A Web service that conforms to a set of conventions (interfaces and behaviors) that define how a client interacts with a grid capability [MIN200501].

Information Architecture: An architectural formulation of the Information Function via a data model.

Information Function: A comprehensive identification of the data, the data flows, and the data interrelations required to support the business function. The identification, systematization, categorization, and inventory/storage of information are always necessary to run a business, but these are essential if the data-handling functions are to be automated.

Integration Centric-Business Process Management Suites (IC-BPMS): Integration capabilities products that support process improvement and that have evolved out of the enterprise application integration (EAI). Originally, this space was dominated by proprietary, closed-framework solutions; at this time these products are based on SOA and on standards-based integration technology. Vendors have added embedded enterprise service bus (ESB) and business process management (BPM) capabilities.

Internet FCP (iFCP): A protocol that converts Fibre Channel (FC) frames into Transmission Control Protocol (TCP) enabling native Fibre Channel devices to be connected via an IP network. It comprises encapsulation protocols for IP storage solutions where the lower-layer FC transport is replaced with TCP/IP and GbE. The protocol enables existing FC storage devices or Storage Area Network (SAN) to attach to an IP network. The operation is as follows: FC devices, such as disk arrays, connect to an iFCP gateway or switch. Each FC session is terminated at the local gateway and converted to a TCP/IP session via iFCP. A second gateway or switch receives the iFCP session and initiates an FC session. In iFCP, Transmission Control Protocol/Internet Protocol (TCP/IP) switching and routing elements complement and enhance, or replace, FC SAN fabric components.

Internet Small Computer System Interface (iSCSI): A protocol that serializes Small Computer System Interface (SCSI) commands and converts them to Transmission Control Protocol/Internet Protocol (TCP/IP). Encapsulation protocols for IP storage solutions for the support of Direct Attached Storage (DAS) (specifically SCSI-3 commands) over IP network infrastructures (at the physical layer, iSCSI supports a GbE interface so that systems supporting iSCSI interfaces can be directly connected to standard GbE switches or IP routers; the iSCSI protocol sits above the physical and data-link layers).

IP Storage (Internet Protocol Storage): Using IP and GbE to build Storage Area Networks (SANs). Traditional SANs were developed using Fibre Channel (FC) transport, because it provided gigabit speeds compared to 10 and 100 Mbps Ethernet used to build messaging networks at that time. FC equipment was costly, and interoperability between different vendors' switches was not completely standardized. As Gigabit Ethernet and IP have become commonplace, IP storage enables familiar network protocols to be used, and IP allows SANs to be extended throughout the world. Network management software and experienced professionals in IP networks are also widely available.

Internet FCP (iFCP) is a gateway-to-gateway protocol that allows the replacement of FC fabric components, allowing attachment of existing FC-enabled storage products to an IP network.

Metro Fibre Channel Protocol (mFCP) is another proposal for handling IP storage. It is identical to iFCP, except that Transmission Control Protocol (TCP) is replaced by User Datagram Protocol (UDP).

Internet Small Computer System Interface (iSCSI) is a transport protocol for SCSI that operates on top of TCP. It provides a new mechanism for encapsulating SCSI commands on an IP network. iSCSI is a protocol for a new generation of storage end-nodes that natively use Transmission Control Protocol/Internet Protocol (TCP/IP) and replaces FCP with a pure TCP/IP implementation. iSCSI has broad industry support.

Fiber Channel Over Internet Protocol (FCIP) is FC over TCP/IP. Here, FC uses IP-based network services to provide the connectivity between the SAN islands over local area networks (LANs), metropolitan area networks (MANs), or wide area networks (WANs). FCIP relies on TCP for congestion control and management and upon both TCP and FC for data error and data loss recovery. FCIP treats all classes of FC frames in the same way as datagrams.

IT Operations Manager : Individual responsible for supporting the activities essential for ongoing support of the application when it is up and running, especially in the production environment. This role might also be responsible for collecting the run-time data from the application and analyzing the results against service level agreements (SLA) requirements [MIT200601].

Message-Oriented Middleware (MOM): A client/server infrastructure that increases the interoperability, portability, and flexibility of an application by allowing the application to be distributed over multiple heterogeneous platforms. It reduces the complexity of developing applications that span multiple operating systems and network protocols by insulating the application developer from the details of the various operating system and network interfaces. Application programming interfaces (APIs) that extend across diverse platforms and networks are typically provided by the MOM. Applications exchange messages that can contain formatted data, requests for action, or both.

Metro Ethernet : Ethernet-based carrier-provided services in metropolitan area network (MAN) and wide area network (WAN) environments. One of the goals is to formalize the idea of carrier-class Ethernet; this is defined as a service in a WAN/MAN Ethernet environment that matches the reliability and quality of service (QoS) that carriers have enjoyed with Synchronous Optical NETwork (SONET), Synchronous Digital Hierarchy (SDH), and Asynchronous Transfer Mode (ATM).

Multi-Protocol Label Switching (MPLS): A newly introduced telecommunications (carrier-provided) service that is IP-based. MPLS is a hybrid Layer 2–Layer 3 service that attempts to bring together the best of both worlds: Layer 2 and Layer 3, ATM and IP. During the past 25 years corporates have sought improved packet technologies to support intranets, extranets, and public switched data networks such as the Internet. The progression went from X.25 packet-switched technology to Frame Relay technology, and also, on a parallel track, cell relay/Asynchronous Transfer Mode (ATM) technology. In the meantime, throughout the 1980s and 1990s, IP-based connectionless packet services (a Layer 3 service) continued to make major inroads. IP, however, has limited quality-of-service (QoS) capabilities by itself. Therefore, the late 1990s and early 2000s saw the development of MPLS as a way to provide a better QoS framework, based on improved packet handling [MIN200201,MIN200301].

MPLS is a late-1990s set of specifications that provides a link-layer-independent transport mechanism for IP. The specification-development work is carried out by the Internet Engineering Task Force (IETF). MPLS protocols allow high-performance label switching of IP packets: network traffic is forwarded using a simple label apparatus as described in RFC 3031. By combining the attributes of Layer 2 switching and Layer 3 routing into a single entity, MPLS provides (1) enhanced scalability by way of switching technology, (2) support of class of service (CoS) and QoS-based services (Differentiated Services/diffserv, as well as Integrated Services/intserv); (3) elimination of the need for an IP-over-ATM overlay model and its associated management overhead; and, (4) enhanced traffic shaping and engineering capabilities. In addition, MPLS provides a gamut of features that support virtual private networks (VPNs).

The basic idea of MPLS involves assigning short fixed-length labels to packets at the ingress to an MPLS cloud (based on the concept of forwarding equivalence classes). Throughout the interior of the MPLS domain, the labels attached to packets are used to make forwarding decisions (usually without recourse to the original packet headers). A set of powerful constructs to address many critical issues in the (eventually) emerging diffserv Internet can be devised from this relatively simple paradigm. One of the most significant initial applications of MPLS is in traffic engineering (TE). (It should be noted that even though the focus is on Internet backbones, the capabilities described in MPLS TE are equally applicable to traffic engineering in enterprise networks.)

Peer-To-Peer (P2P):
- P2P is concerned with the same general problem as Grid Computing, namely, the organization of resource sharing within virtual communities.
- Grid community focuses on aggregating distributed high-end machines such as clusters, whereas the P2P community concentrates on sharing low-end systems such as PCs connected to the Internet.
- Like P2P, Grid Computing allows users to share files (many-to-many sharing). With the latter, the sharing is not only in reference to files, but also other IT resources.

Service Orientation: A way of thinking about business processes as linked, loosely coupled tasks supported by services. A new service can be created by composing a primitive group of services. This recursive definition is important because it enables the construction of more complex services above a set of existent ones [SOU200601].

Service-Oriented Architecture (SOA): SOA describes an IT architecture based on the concept of delivering reusable, business services that are underpinned by IT components in such a way that the providers and the consumers of the business services are loosely coupled, with no knowledge of the technology, platform, location or environment choices of each other [STA200502]. It embodies business-driven IT architectural approach that supports integrating business as linked, repeatable business tasks, or services. SOA helps businesses innovate by ensuring that IT systems can adapt quickly, easily and economically to support rapidly changing business needs [IBM200701]. In an SOA, resources are made available to other participants in the network as independent services that are accessed in a standardized way.

Service-Oriented Architecture Networking (SOAN): Infrastructure for building SOA networks. Mechanism for distributing SOA components across a network, and have these components available on demand.

Service-Oriented Computing (SOC): The computing paradigm that utilizes services as fundamental elements for developing applications [PAP20301].

Service-Oriented Network (SON) : A service oriented architecture for the development, deployment, and management of network services, focusing on connection oriented and overlay networks [SOU200601].

Service-Oriented Network Architecture (SONA): Cisco Systems' architectural framework that aims at delivering business solutions to unify network-based services such as security, mobility, and location with the virtualization of IT resources.

Service-Oriented Networking (SON): The application paradigm that utilizes services distributed across a network as fundamental functional elements.

Simple Object Access Protocol (SOAP): A standard of the W3C that provides a framework for exchanging XML-based information. A lightweight protocol for exchange of XML-based information in a distributed environment.

SOA infrastructure: A simplified, virtualized, and distributed application framework that supports SOA.

Software Architecture: The organizational structure of an IT system. Structures of the IT system, which comprise software components, the externally visible properties of those components, and the relationships among them [BAS199701]. An architecture can be recursively decomposed into parts that interact through interfaces, relationships that connect parts, and constraints for assembling parts. Parts that interact through interfaces include classes, components, and subsystems (from UML 1.3).

Stakeholders, IEEE 1471-2000: Individuals that have key roles in, or concerns about the system: for example, as users, developers, or managers. Different stakeholders with different roles in the system will have different concerns. Stakeholders can be individuals, teams, or organizations.

Storage: Infrastructure (typically in the form of appliances) that is used for the permanent or semi-permanent online retention of structured (e.g., databases) and unstructured (e.g., business/e-mail files) corporate information. Typically includes (1) a controller that manages incoming and outgoing communications as well as the data steering onto the physical storage medium (e.g., RAIDs [redundant arrays of independent disks], semiconductor memory, etc.); and (2) the physical storage medium itself. The communications mechanism could be a network interface (such as Gigabit Ethernet), a channel interface (such as Small Computer System Interface [SCSI]), or a SAN Interface (i.e., Fibre Channel [FC]).

Storage Appliance: A storage platform designed to perform a specific task, such as NAS, routers, virtualization, etc.

Storage Virtualization: Software subsystems (typically middleware) that abstract the physical and logical storage assets from the host systems.

System: A collection of components organized to accomplish a specific function or set of functions (IEEE Std. 610.12-1990). A system can be described by one or more models, possibly from different viewpoints.

Systems (Applications) Solution Architecture: An architectural definition of the systems/application solution function.

Systems (Applications) Solution Function: The function that aims at delivering/supplying computerized IT systems required to support the plethora of specific functions needed by the business function.

Technology Infrastructure Architecture: An architectural formulation (description) of the technology infrastructure function.

Technology Infrastructure Function: The complete technology environment required to support the information function and the (systems/application) solution function.

Tester: A role responsible for performing activities required to test the application before it is deployed in a production environment. The tester creates test scripts directly from the functional requirements that illustrate the use case. These test scripts are then executed with various input conditions to validate the desired output conditions. The more thorough the test cases and their execution, the more robust is the application, minimizing the chances of surprises during runtime [MIT200601].

The Open Group: A vendor-neutral and technology-neutral consortium seeking to enable access to integrated information, within and among enterprises, based on open standards and global interoperability (HYPERLINK "http://www.opengroup.org/architecture/togaf/") [TOG200501].

The Open Group Architecture Framework (TOGAF): TOGAF is a framework—a detailed method and a set of supporting tools—for developing an enterprise architecture. It is described in a set of documentation published by The Open Group on its public Web server, and may be used freely by any organization wishing to develop an enterprise architecture. TOGAF was developed by The Open Group's members, working within the Architecture Forum. Now in Version 8.1 (with Version 9 expected by 2007). The original development of TOGAF Version 1 in 1995 was based on the Technical Architecture Framework for Information Management (TAFIM), developed by the U.S. Department of Defense (DoD). The DoD gave The Open Group explicit permission and encouragement to create TOGAF by building on the TAFIM, which itself was the result of many years of development effort and many millions of dollars of U.S. government investment. Starting from this sound foundation, the members of The Open Group's Architecture Forum have developed successive versions of TOGAF each year and published each one on The Open Group's public Web site [TOG200501].

Tiered Storage: A process for the assignment of different categories of data to different types of storage media. The purpose is to reduce total storage cost and optimize accessibility. Organizations are reportedly finding cost savings and improved data management with a tiered-storage approach. In practice, the assignment of data to particular media tends to be an evolutionary and complex activity. Storage categories may be based on a variety of design/architectural factors, including levels of protection required for the application or organization, performance requirements, and frequency of use. Software exists for automatically managing the process based on a company-defined policy. Tiered storage generally introduces more vendors into the environment, and interoperability is important.

An example of tiered storage is as follows: Tier 1 data (e.g., mission-critical files) could be effectively stored on high-quality Directly Attached Storage (DAS) (but relatively expensive) media such as double-parity RAIDs (redundant arrays of independent disks). Tier 2 data (e.g., quarterly financial records) could be stored on media affiliated with a storage area network (SAN); this media tends to be less expensive than DAS drives, but there may be network latencies associated with the access. Tier 3 data (e.g., e-mail backup files) could be stored on recordable compact discs (CD-Rs) or tapes. (Clearly, there could be more than three tiers, but the management of the multiple tiers then becomes fairly complex.)

Another example (in the medical field) is as follows: Real-time medical imaging information may be temporarily stored on DAS disks as a Tier 1, say for a couple of weeks. Recent medical images and patient data may be kept on Fibre Channel (FC) drives (tier-2) for about a year. After that, less frequently accessed images and patient records are stored on AT Attachment (ATA) drives (tier-3) for 18 months or more. Tier 4 consists of a tape library for archiving.

Universal Discovery, Description and Integration (UDDI): A standardized method for publishing and discovering information about Web Services. UDDI is an industry initiative that attempts to create a platform-independent, open framework for describing services, discovering businesses, and integrating business services. UDDI deals with the process of discovery in the SOA (WSDL is often used for service description, and SOAP for service invocation). Being a Web Service itself, UDDI is invoked using SOAP. In addition, UDDI also defines how to operate servers and how to manage replication among several servers.

Use cases: Use cases are a means for specifying required usages of a system. Typically, they are used to capture the requirements of a system, that is, what a system is supposed to do. The key concepts associated with use cases are actors, use cases, and the subject. The subject is the system under consideration to which the use cases apply. The users and any other systems that may interact with the subject are represented as actors. Actors always model entities that are outside the system. The required behavior of the subject is specified by one or more use cases, which are defined according to the needs of actors. Strictly speaking, the term use case refers to a use case type. An instance of a use case refers to an occurrence of the emergent behavior that conforms to the corresponding use case type. Such instances are often described by interaction specifications. Use cases, actors, and systems are described using use case diagrams [UML200501].

View, IEEE 1471-2000: A representation of an entire system from the perspective of a related set of concerns.

Virtual infrastructure: A virtual infrastructure is a dynamic mapping of physical resources to business needs [VMW200701].

Virtualization:
- An approach that allows several operating systems to run simultaneously on one (large) computer (e.g., IBM's z/VM operating system lets multiple instances of Linux coexist on the same mainframe computer).
- More generally, it is the practice of making resources from diverse devices accessible to a user as if they were a single, larger, homogenous, locally available resource.

- Dynamically shifting resources across platforms to match computing demands with available resources: the computing environment can become dynamic, enabling autonomic shifting applications between servers to match demand.
- The abstraction of server, storage, and network resources to make them available dynamically for sharing by IT services, both internal to and external to an organization. In combination with other server, storage, and networking capabilities, virtualization offers customers the opportunity to build more efficient IT infrastructures. Virtualization is seen by some as a step on the road to utility computing.
- Virtualization is a proven software technology that is rapidly transforming the IT landscape and fundamentally changing the way that people compute [VMW200701].

Web 2.0: System/approach that encompasses a range of technologies, tools, techniques, and standards that focus on enabling people to increase the social factor—how people connect with one another to improve how software works. Key principles involve use of lightweight programming models and standards, and techniques such as mash-ups, wikis, tagging, and blogs for richer user interfaces and improved use of data [IBM200701].

Web Services (WSs): A software system designed to support interoperable machine-to-machine interaction over a network. It has an interface described in a machine-processable format (specifically WSDL). Other systems interact with the Web Service in a manner prescribed by its description using SOAP messages, typically conveyed using HTTP with an XML serialization in conjunction with other Web-related standards [IBM200701].

Web Services provide standard infrastructure for data exchange between two different distributed applications (grids provide an infrastructure for aggregation of high-end resources for solving large-scale problems). Web Services are expected to play a key constituent role in the standardized definition of grid computing, because Web Services have emerged as a standards-based approach for accessing network applications.

Web Services Description Language (WSDL): An XML-based language used to describe Web Services and how to locate them; it provides information on what the service is about, where it resides and how it can be invoked.

Web Services Networking: Assembly of a more complex service from service modules that reside on different nodes connected to a network.

XML Networking: XML networking provides integration services by inspecting the full context of the application transaction and adding XML standards-based intelligence on top of the TCP/IP stack. An XML-enabled network provides greater control, flexibility, and efficiency for integrating applications than integration brokers [CIS200701].

Zachman Framework: A framework developed by John Zachman providing a view of the subjects and models needed to develop a complete enterprise architecture. The framework is described pictorially by a two-dimensional tableau. A picture of this framework is available at the Zachman Institute for Framework Advancement (ZIFA) Web site (HYPER-LINK "http://www.zifa.com"). The Zachman Framework is a widely used approach for developing or documenting an enterprisewide information systems architecture. Zachman based his framework on practices in traditional architecture and engineering. This resulted in an approach that on the vertical axis provides multiple perspectives of the overall architecture, and on the horizontal axis a classification of the various artifacts of the architecture.

References

[10G200301] 10GbE Alliance Tutorial Materials. 2003.

[ABO200201] O. Aboul-Magd, B. Jamoussi, S. Shew, G. Grammel, S. Belotti, and D. Papadimitriou, "Automatic Switched Optical Network Architecture and Its Related Protocols," IPO WG, Internet Draft, draft-ietf-ipo-ason-02.txt, March 2002. Copyright © The Internet Society. All Rights Reserved. This document and translations of it may be copied and furnished to others, and derivative works that comment on or otherwise explain it or assist in its implementation may be prepared, copied, published and distributed, in whole or in part, without restriction of any kind, provided that the above copyright notice and this paragraph are included on all such copies and derivative works.

[ALA200301] W. Alanqar et al., "Requirements for Generalized MPLS (GMPLS) Routing for Automatically Switched Optical Network (ASON)," draft-ietf-ccamp-gmpls-ason-routing-reqts-00.txt, December 2003.

[ALL199701] B. Allen and S. Wong, Nortel White Paper: Is WDM Ready For Local Networks? Document 56005.25-05-99, 1997.

[AMB200301] J. Ambrosio, "MDA: What is in the standard?," 7/1/2003, http://www.enterprise-architecture.info/Images/MDA/MDA what is in the standard.PDF

[ATO200101] Promotional material from Atos Origin—Systems Integration Telecom Technologies Business Unit, Paris, France, http://www.marben-products.com

[BAR199801] C. Baru, R. Moore, A. Rajasekar, and M. Wan. "The sdsc storage resource broker," Proceedings of IBM Centers for Advanced Studies Conference. IBM, 1998.

[BAS199701] L. Bass, P. Clements, and R. Kazman, *Software Architecture in Practice*, Addison-Wesley, Reading, MA, 1997.

[BED200301] A. Bednarz and D. Dubie, "How to: How to get to utility computing," *Network World*, 12/01/03.

[BEL199001] Bellcore, *Telecommunications Transmission Engineering*, 1990, Piscataway, NJ, ISBN 1-878108-04-2.

[BER200301] F. Berman, G. Fox, and A. J. Hey, Eds., *Grid Computing: Making the Global Infrastructure a Reality*, May 2003, Wiley, New York.

[BIR200601] R. Bird, "Fiber Optics 101: A Primer," 101COMMUNICATIONS, White Paper, 2006, 9121 Oakdale Ave., Suite 101, Chatsworth, CA 91311, http://certcities.com/editorial/features/story.asp?EditorialsID=25

[BPM200201] Business Process Modeling Language Version 1.0, November 13, 2002, Copyright © 2002, BPMI.org. All Rights Reserved. This document and translations of it may be copied and furnished to others, and derivative works that comment on or otherwise explain it or assist in its implementation may be prepared, copied, published and distributed, in whole or in part, without restriction of any kind, provided that the above copyright notice and this paragraph are included on all such copies and derivative works.

[BPM200301] Business Process Modeling Notation, Working Draft (1.0) August 25, 2003, Copyright 2003, BPMI.org. All Rights Reserved, This document is the first working draft of the BPMN specification submitted for comments from the public by members of the BPMI initiative on August 25, 2003. It supersedes any previous version. It has been produced based on the work of the members of the BPMI Notation Working Group. This document and translations of it may be copied and furnished to others, and derivative works that comment on or otherwise explain it or assist in its implementation may be prepared, copied, published and distributed, in whole or in part, without restriction of any kind, provided that the above copyright notice and this paragraph are included on all such copies and derivative works.

[BPM200501] Business Process Management Initiative (BPMI.ORG), http://www.bpmi.org

[BRO200301] M. C. Brown, "Grid Computing—Moving to a Standardized Platform," August 2003, IBM's Developerworks Grid Library, IBM Corporation, 1133 Westchester Avenue, White Plains, New York 10604, United States, www.ibm.com

[BUR200302] R. Buyya, "Delivering Grid Services as ICT Commodities: Challenges and Opportunities, Grid and Distributed Systems (GRIDS) Laboratory," Department of Computer Science and Software Engineering, The University of Melbourne, Melbourne, Australia, IST (Information Society Technologies) 2003, Milan, Italy.

[BUS200101] I. Busi and V. Mascolo, "Network Requirements for RPR," IEEE 802.17, March 2001.

[BUY200301] R. Buyya, Frequently Asked Questions, Grid Computing Info Centre, *GridComputing Magazine*.

[CAP200301] M. Capuano, "VPLS: Scalable Transparent LAN Services," Whitepaper, Juniper Networks, Inc., 1194 North Mathilda Avenue, Sunnyvale, CA 94089 USA.

[CAT200301] C. Catlett, "The Rise of Third-Generation Grids," Global Grid Forum Chairman, Grid Connections, Fall 2003, Volume 1, Issue 3, The Global Grid Forum, 9700 South Cass Avenue, Bldg 221/A142, Lemont, IL, 60439, USA.

[CHE199901] A. Chervenak, I. Foster, C. Kesselman, C. Salisbury, and S. Tuecke, "The Data Grid: Towards an Architecture for the Distributed Management and Analysis of Large Scientific Datasets," 1999.

[CHE200201] M. Chetty, and R. Buyya, Weaving Computational grids: How Analogous Are They With Electrical Grids?, *Computing in Science and Engineering*, July/August 2002, IEEE.

[CHE200401] D. Chen and F. Vernadat, "Standards on enterprise integration and engineering—state of the art," *International Journal of CIM*, Vol. 17, (2004), No. 3, pp. 235–253.

[CHU200201] L.-J. Zhang, J.-Y. Chung, and Q. Zhou, "Developing Grid Computing Applications, Part 1: Introduction of a Grid Architecture and Toolkit for Building Grid solutions," October 1, 2002, Updated November 20, 2002, IBM Corporation, 1133 Westchester Avenue, White Plains, New York 10604, United States.

[CIM200501] CIMOSA: Engineering and Integration, Germany. The CIMOSA Association (COA) is a non-profit organization involved in promotion of Enterprise Engineering and Integration based on CIMOSA and its active support in national, European and international standardization. http://www.cimosa.de

[CIS200201] Cisco, WDM-Based Metropolitan-Area Deployment of SRP and PoS with the Cisco ONS 15190, Cisco White Paper.

[CIS200701] S. Da Ros, "Boosting the SOA with XML networking," *The Internet Protocol Journal*, Vol. 9, Number 4. Cisco Systems.

[CLE200501] P. Clements, "1471 (IEEE Recommended Practice for Architectural Description of Software-Intensive Systems)," CMU/SEI-2005-TN-017, Software Architecture Technology Initiative, July 2005, Carnegie-Mellon Software Engineering Institute, http://www.sei.cmu.edu/publications/documents/05.reports/05tn017/05tn017.html#chap03

[COH200301] R. B. Cohen and E. Feser, Grid Computing, Projected Impact in North Carolina's Economy and Broadband Use Through 2010, Rural Internet Access Authority, September 2003.

[COL200101] N. Cole, J. Hawkins, M. Green, R. Sharma, and K. Vasani, "Resilient Packet Rings for Metro Networks," a report by Resiliant Packet Ring (RPR) Alliance, 2001.

[DEV200301] developerWorks staff, "Start Here to learn about Grid Computing," August 2003, IBM Corporation, 1133 Westchester Avenue, White Plains, New York 10604, United States.

[DOD200301] DoD Architecture Framework, version 1.0, (http://www.aitcnet.org/dodfw/).

[DRI200101] J. C. Dries, "InGaAs Avalanche Photodiodes Enable Low-Cost CWDM-Based Metropolitan Area Networks," Cahners ECN *Cahners Business Information* (www.cahners.com).

[FAR199601] K. Farooqui, L. Logrippo, and J. de Meer, "Introduction into the ODP Reference Model," 2/14/96, Department of Computer Science, University of Ottawa, Ottawa K1N 6N5, Canada; Research Institute for Open Communication Systems Berlin (GMD-FOKUS), D10623 Berlin, Hardenbergplatz 2, Germany.

[FCA199901] dpANS X3.XXX-199X, "Fibre Channel Arbitrated Loop (FC-AL-2)," revision 7.0, NCITS Project 1133D, April 1999.

[FCF199701] TR-20-199X, "Fibre Channel Fabric Loop Attachment (FC-FLA)," revision 2.7, NCITS Project 1235-D, August 1997.

[FCF200201] dpANS INCITS.XXX-200X, "Fibre Channel Framing and Signaling (FC-FS), Rev 1.70, INCITS Project 1331D, February 2002.

[FCG200001] dpANS X3.XXX-200X, "Fibre Channel Generic Services -3 (FC-GS3)," revision 7.01, INCITS Project 1356-D, November 2000.

[FCP200201] dpANS T10, "Fibre Channel Protocol for SCSI, Second Version," revision 8, INCITS Project 1144D, September 2002.

[FCS200101] dpANS X3.XXX-2000X, "Fibre Channel Switch Fabric -2 (FC-SW2)," revision 5.2, INCITS Project 1305-D, May 2001.

[FEA200101] Federal Enterprise Architecture, http://www.feapmo.gov/

[FEA200102] The Federal Enterprise Architecture Framework, Version 1.1, http://www.cio.gov/index.cfm?function=documents and section=Architecture%20and%20Infrastructure%20Committee

[FEA200503] Segment Data Architecture Best Practices Analysis, HUD EA Practice Support, CLIN 004.2; SOW 1.4.1.1, Contract C-DEN-01916, February 22, 2005.

[FEL200301] W. Fellows, "IBM'S Grid Computing Push Continues," *Gridtoday*, Daily News and Information for the Global Grid Community, October 6, 2003: Vol. 2 No. 40, published by Tabor Communications Inc, 8445 Camino Santa Fe, San Diego, California 92121, (858) 625-0070.

[FER200401] L. F. Fernández-Martínez and C. Lemus-Olalde, "Improving the IEEE std 1471-2000 for Communication among Stakeholders and Early Design Decisions," Proceeding (418) Software Engineering—2004.

[FOS199701] I. Foster and C. Kesselman, "Globus: A Metacomputing Infrastructure Toolkit," *The International Journal of Supercomputer Applications and High Performance Computing*, 11(2): 115–128, 1997.

[FOS199901] I. Foster and C. Kesselman, (Eds.). *The Grid: Blueprint for a Future Computing Infrastructure*, Morgan Kaufmann Publishers, San Francisco, CA 1999.

[FOS200101] I. Foster, C. Kesselman, and S. Tuecke, *International Journal of High Performance Computing Applications*, 15(3), 200, (2001).

[FOS200201] I. Foster, "What is the Grid? A Three Point Checklist," Argonne National Laboratory and University of Chicago, July 20, 2002, Argonne National Laboratory, 9700 Cass Ave, Argonne, IL, 60439, Tel: 630 252-4619, Fax: 630 252-5986, foster@mcs.anl.gov

[FOS200202] Foster, I., "The Grid: A New Infrastructure for 21st Century Science," *Physics Today*, 55(2), 42–47. 2002.

[FOX200201] G. Fox, M. Pierce, D. Gannon, and M. Thomas, Overview of Grid Computing Environments, GFD-I.9, February 2003, Copyright © Global Grid Forum (2002). The Global Grid Forum, 9700 South Cass Avenue, Bldg 221/A142, Lemont, IL, 60439, USA. This document and translations of it may be copied and furnished to others, and derivative works that comment on or otherwise explain it or assist in its implementation may be prepared, copied, published and distributed, in whole or in part, without restriction of any kind, provided that the above copyright notice and this paragraph are included on all such copies and derivative works.

[FUT200101] Future Software Limited, MultiProtocol Label Switching White Paper, Chennai, India, 2001, www.futsoft.com

[GEO200101] J. George, "Optical Architectures and Fibers," IEEE EFM Meeting—Hilton Head NC, 3/12-15 2001.

[GIM200101] T. Gimpelson, "Metro Vendors Question Spanning Tree Standard," *Network World*, August 6, 2001.

[GIM200101] T. Gimpelson, "MSPPs, next-gen SONET Mixing Optical Signals," The Edge, 10/09/01.

[GIM200102] T. Gimpelson, "Metro Vendors Question Spanning Tree Standard," *Network World*, August 6, 2001.

[GIM200102] T. Gimpelson, "Nortel's Alternative for Metro Ethernet Recovery," *Network World*, 10/01/01.

[GLO200301] Globus Alliance, Press Releases, C/o Carl Kesselman, USC/Information Sciences Institute, 4676 Admiralty Way, Suite 1001, Marina del Rey, CA 90292-6695, Tel: 310 822-1511 x338, Fax: 310 823-6714, carl@isi.edu, http://www.globus.org, info@globus.org

[GLO200301] The Global Grid Forum, 9700 South Cass Avenue, Bldg 221/A142, Lemont, IL, 60439, USA, http://www.ggf.org

[GRE200101] D. Greenfield, "Optical Standards: A Blueprint for the Future," *Network Magazine*, 10/05/01.

[GRI199701] A. S. Grimshaw, W. A. Wulf, and the Legion Team, "The legion vision of a worldwide virtual computer," *Communications of the ACM*, 40(1): 39–45, January 1997.

[GRI200301] Grid Computing Info Centre (GRID Infoware), Enterprise Architect Magazine: Grid Computing, Answers to the Enterprise Architect Magazine Query, http://www.cs.mu.oz.au/~raj/GridInfoware/gridfaq.html

[GRI200301] http://www.gridcomputing.com/

[GRI200401] Grid Computing using .NET and WSRF.NET Tutorial, GGF11, Honolulu, June 6, 2004.

[GUE200101] R. Guerin, "To Overlay or Not to Overlay," NGN 2001 Proceedings, Boston, MA.

[HAN200301] M. Haney, "Grid Computing: Making Inroads into Financial Services," 24 April 2003, Issue No: Volume 4, Number 5, IBM's Developerworks Grid Library, IBM Corporation, 1133 Westchester Avenue, White Plains, New York 10604, United States, www.ibm.com

[HAV200201] G. Haviland, "Designing High-Performance Campus Intranets with Multilayer Switching," Cisco White Paper, 2002, Cisco Networks, San Jose, CA.

[HAW200301] T. Hawk, IBM Grid Computing General Manager, Grid Computing Planet Conference and Expo, San Jose, 17 June 2002. Also as quoted by Globus Alliance, Press Release, July 1, 2003.

[HEP200201] Hewlett-Packard Company, HP Virtualization: Computing without boundaries or constraints, Enabling an Adaptive Enterprise, HP Whitepaper, 2002, Hewlett-Packard Company, 3000 Hanover Street, Palo Alto, CA 94304-1185 USA, Phone: (650) 857-1501, Fax: (650) 857-5518, www.hp.com

[HHE200301] H. He, "What Is Service-Oriented Architecture," Online resource: webservices.xml.com, September 30, 2003.

[HHE200401] H. He, "Implementing REST Web Services: Best Practices and Guidelines, "Online resource: webservices.xml.com, August 11, 2004.

[HUB200101] V. Huber. UNICORE: A Grid Computing environment for distributed and parallel computing. Lecture Notes in Computer Science, 2127: 258–266, 2001.

[IAM200301] I. Foster and A. Iamnitchi, On Death, Taxes, and the Convergence of Peer-to-Peer and Grid Computing, 2nd International Workshop on Peer-to-Peer Systems (IPTPS'03), February 2003, Berkeley, CA.

[IBM200201] Chris Ferris, "First look at the WS-I Basic Profile 1.0, Features of the Profile," IBM, http://www.ibm.com/developerworks/webservices/library/ws-basicprof.html

[IBM200301] IBM Press Releases. IBM Corporation, 1133 Westchester Avenue, White Plains, New York 10604, United States, www.ibm.com

[IBM200701] IBM, "Service Oriented Architecture—SOA," Service Oriented Architecture Glossary, IBM Corporation, 1 New Orchard Road, Armonk, New York 10504-1722, United States.

[IEA200501] J. Schekkerman, Institute For Enterprise Architecture Developments (IFEAD), "Trends in Enterprise Architecture 2005," Reports of the Third Measurement, December 2005, Edition 1.0, Suikerpeergaarde 4, 3824BC Amersfoort, The Netherlands.

[IEA200502] Institute for Enterprise Architecture, Enterprise Architecture Tools, February 2005, http://www.enterprise-architecture.info/EA_Tools.htm

[IEE200001] IEEE Std 1471-2000 IEEE Recommended Practice for Architectural Description of Software-Intensive Systems-Description.

[IES200501] Institute for Enterprise Architecture, Standards, http://www.enterprise-architecture.info/EA_Tools.htm

[ISO199301] ISO/IEC 10038 Information technology—Telecommunications and information exchange between systems—Local Area Networks—Media Access Control (MAC) Bridges, (also ANSI/IEEE Std 802.1D-1993), 1993.

[ISO199801] ISO/IEC 15802-3 Information technology—Telecommunications and information exchange between systems—Local and Metropolitan Area Networks—Common specifications—Part 3: Media Access Control (MAC) bridges (also ANSI/IEEE Std 802.1D-1998), 1998.

[ITU200101] ITU Public Relations, "Recommendations adopted by Study Group 15 in October 2001," http://www.itu.int/newsroom/Recs/SG15Recs.html

[KEL200501] D. A. Kelly, "Enterprise Service Bus," Ebizq, The Insider's Guide to Business Integration, 12/18/2005, 271 North Avenue, Suite 1210, New Rochelle, NY 10801, (914) 712-1500, http://www.ebizq.net/hot_topics/esb/features/6579.html

[KES200101] I. Foster, C. Kesselman, and S. Tuecke, "The anatomy of the grid: Enabling scalable virtual organizations," *International Journal of High Performance Computing Applications*, 15(3). 200–222. 2001.

[KOC200501] C. Koch, "Koch's IT Strategy, Chicken and Egg," *CIO Magazine*, March 11, 2005, http://www.cio.com/blog_view.html?CID=3266

[KOC200502] C. Koch, "Enterprise Architecture: A New Blueprint For The Enterprise," *CIO Magazine*, March 1, 2005.

[KOF200001] S. Koffler and L. Franklyn, "Optical Networking: A Focus on the Metro Opportunities," Wachovia (formerly Wachovia Securities), New York, 2000.

[KOS200301] K. Kosanke, "Business Process Modeling and Standardisation," 2003, CIMOSA Association e.V. c/o K. Kosanke, Stockholmer Str., Böblingen, Denmark.

[KOS200501] K. Kosanke, "ISO Standards for Interoperability: a comparison" CIMOSA Association e.V., Stockholmer Str. 7, D-71034 Böblingen, Germany.

[KOU199901] B. Koufos, M. Hamdan, E. Olson, M. Parikh., and R. Whyte, "Synchronous optical network (SONET)," December 20, 1999, Polytechnic University Publications, Brooklyn New York.

[LAZ200101] Lazar, M. et al., "Alternate Addressing Proposal," OIF Contribution, OIF2001.21, January 2001.

[LEE200101] G. Lee, "SONET: A Viable Solution to the Metro Access Network Bottleneck?," Opticalbiznet.com, June 2001.

[LEH200301] M. Lehmann, "Who Needs Web Services Transactions?," *Oracle Magazine*, http://otn.oracle.com/oraclemagazine, November/December 2003.

[LUO200501] M. Luo, B. Goldshlager, and L. J. Zhang, "Designing and Implementing Enterprise Service Bus (ESB) and SOA Solutions," IBM White Paper (SOA and Web Services Center of Excellence, IBM Global Services, IBM Global Services, IBM T. J. Watson Research Center), 2005.

[MAC200501] D. MacVittie, S. Doherty, C. Franklin Jr., T. Wilson, and B. Boardman, "This Old Data Center State of the Art Designs and Technology Trends," *Network Computing*, May 26, 2005.

[MAH200501] Q. H. Mahmoud, "Service-Oriented Architecture (SOA) and Web Services: The Road to Enterprise Application Integration (EAI)," Sun Developer Network, April 2005, Sun Microsystems, Inc., 4150 Network Circle, Santa Clara, CA 95054, Phone: US 1-800-555-9SUN; International 1-650-960-1300, http://java.sun.com/developer/technicalArticles/WebServices/soa/

[MAN200401] E. Mannie, (Ed.), "Generalized Multi-Protocol Label Switching (GMPLS) Architecture," IETF, Request for Comments: 3945, October 2004.

[MAY200101] Mayer, M (Ed.), "Requirements for Automatic Switched Transport Networks (ASTN)," ITU G.8070/Y.1301, V1.0, May 2001.

[MAY200102] M. Mayer (Ed.), "Architecture for Automatic Switched Optical Networks (ASON)," ITU G.8080/Y1304, V1.0, October 2001.

[MCC200301] M. McCommon, "Letter from the Grid Computing Editor: Welcome to the New DeveloperWorks Grid Computing Resource," Editor, Grid Computing resource, IBM, April 7, 2003.

[MCD200301] P. McDougall, Offshore 'Hiccups In An Irreversible Trend' December 1, 2003, *InformationWeek*, CMP Media Publishers, Manhasset, NY.

[McQ200101] J. McQuillan, "Broadband Networking at the Crossroad," NGN 2001 Promotional materials, October 11, 2001.

[MDA200301] J. Miller and J. Mukerji, OMG MDA Guide Version 1.1.1, Document Number omg/2003-06-01, June 12, 2003.

[MER200101] M. Merard and S. Lumetta, "Architectural Issues for Robust Optical Access," *IEEE Communications Magazine*, July 2001, pages 116 ff.

[MEY200501] F. Meyer, "How Integration Appliances Simplify and Accelerate SOA Implementation," White Paper, Cast Iron Systems, Inc., 2593 Coast Avenue, Suite 200, Mountain View California 94043, United States May 2005.

[MIL200701] M. Milinkovich, "Agility Principle: Service-Oriented Network Architecture," 07/12/2007, Service-Oriented Network Architecture, http://www.ebizq.net, Cisco Systems.

[MIN198701] D. Minoli, A Collection of Potential Network-Based Data Services, Bellcore/Telcordia Special Report, SR-NPL-000790, 1987, Piscataway, NJ.

[MIN199301] D. Minoli, *Enterprise Networking—From Fractional T1 to SONET*, Frame Relay to BISDN, Artech House, Norwood, MA, 1993.

[MIN199501] D. Minoli, *Analyzing Outsourcing, Reengineering Information and Communication Systems*, McGraw-Hill, 1994/5.

[MIN199601] D. Minoli and A. Alles, *LAN, ATM, and LAN Emulation Technologies*, Artech House, Norwood, MA, 1996.

[MIN199701] D. Minoli and A. Schmidt, *Client/Server over ATM: Making Use of Broadband to Support Client/Server Applications,* Prentice Hall, Englewood Cliffs, NJ, 1997.

[MIN200201] D. Minoli, P. Johnson, and E. Minoli, *Planning and Designing Next-Generation Optical Metro Access/Metro Core Networks—Ethernet-based Approaches*, McGraw-Hill, New York, 2002.

[MIN200201] D. Minoli, *Voice Over MPLS*, McGraw-Hill, New York, 2002.

[MIN200301] D. Minoli, *Telecommunication Technologies Handbook*, 2nd edition, Artech House, Norwood, MA, 2003.

[MIN200501] D. Minoli, *A Networking Approach to Grid Computing*, 2005, Wiley, New York.

[MIN200601] D. Minoli, "Metro Ethernet: Where's the beef?" *Network World*, December 11, 2006.

[MIN200601] D. Minoli, "The Virtue of Virtualization," *Network World*, February 27, 2006.

[MIN200701] D. Minoli, "Service Oriented Architecture Modeling: An Integrated Approach to Enterprise Architecture Definition that spans the Business Architecture, the Information Architecture, the Solution Architecture, and the Technology Architecture," *Handbook of IT in Finance,* Springer, 2008.

[MIN200701] D. Minoli, Grid computing for commercial enterprise environments, contained in the textbook *Handbook on Information Technology in Finance (International Handbooks on Information Systems),* F. Schlottmann, D. Seese, and C. Weinhardt, (Eds.), Springer-Verlag, October 2007.

[MIT200601] T. Mitra, "Business-driven Development," January 13, 2006, *IBM developerWorks*, On-line Magazine, http://www-128.ibm.com/developerworks/webservices/library/ws-bdd/

[MON200201] C. Monia, R. Mullendore, F. Travostino, W. Jeong, and M. Edwards, iFCP—A Protocol for Internet Fibre Channel Networking, IP Storage Working Group December 2002, Internet Draft, draft-ietf-ips-ifcp-14.txt. "Copyright © The Internet Society, December 2002. All Rights Reserved. This document and translations of it may be copied and furnished to others, and derivative works that comment on or otherwise explain it or assist in its implementation may be prepared, copied, published and distributed, in whole or in part, without restriction of any kind, provided that the above copyright notice and this paragraph are included on all such copies and derivative works.

[MOO200401] J. Moore, "This year's model: Business process," April 19, 2004, FCW.COM, FCW Media Group, http://www.fcw.com/article82653-04-19-04-Print, FCW Media Group, 3141 Fairview Park Drive, Suite 777, Falls Church, Va. 22042, tel. 703-876-5100.

[MOR200201] G. Mor, "Jitter and Wander of High-priority Traffic in RPR Environment," IEEE 802.17 materials.

[MYE200301] T. Myer, "Grid Computing: Conceptual flyover for developers," May 2003, IBM Corporation, 1133 Westchester Avenue, White Plains, New York 10604, United States.

[NAT200301] National Communications System, Internet Protocol Over Optical Transport Networks, Technical Information Bulletin 03-3 Ncs Tib 03-3, December 2003, Office Of The Manager, National Communications System, 701 South Court House Road, Arlington, Virginia, 22204-2198.

[NEB200201] The white paper by Marcus Nebeling, CWDM: Lower Cost for More Capacity in the Short Haul," Fiber Network Engineering, Inc., Livermore CA, 94550, info@fn-eng.com

[NOR200102] White Paper: An Optical Ethernet Business Case for Incumbent Local Exchange Carriers—A Nortel Networks Business Case, September 2001, Publication 56049.

[NOR200201] Nortel Corporation, SONET 101 White Paper (Doc. 56118.11), Ottawa, Canada.

[NOR200401] Ultra Broadband Access, Unleashing the Power of PON, Nortel White Paper, Nortel Networks, 8200 Dixie Road, Suite 100, Brampton, Ontario L6T 5P6, 2004.

[OAS200601] OASIS, Post Office Box 455, Billerica, MA 01821, USA, http://www.uddi.org/faqs.html

[OMG200501] Object Management Group, Inc., 250 First Ave. Suite 100, Needham, MA 02494, USA, Ph: +1-781-444 0404, Email: info@omg.org, http://www.omg.org

[OMG200701] OMG, Oject Management Group, 140 Kendrick Street, Building A Suite 300, Needham, MA 02494, U.S.A.

[OTE200401] M. Otey, "Grading Grid Computing," *SQL Server Magazine*, January 2004, published by Windows and .Net Magazine Network, a Division of Penton Media Inc., 221 E. 29th St., Loveland, CO 80538.

[PAD200301] P. Padala, "A Survey of Grid File Systems," Editor, GFS-WG (Grid File Systems Working Group), Global Grid Forum, September 19, 2003. The Global Grid Forum, 9700 South Cass Avenue, Bldg 221/A142, Lemont, IL, 60439, USA.

[PAP200301] M. P. Papazoglou and D. Georgakopoulos, "Service-oriented computing: Introduction," *Communications of the ACM*, Vol. 46, No. 10, pp. 24–28, October 2003.

[PAP200501] D. Papadimitriou and J. Drake et al, "Requirements for Generalized MPLS (GMPLS) Signaling Usage and Extensions for Automatically Switched Optical Network (ASON)," Request for Comments: 4139, July 2005.

[PAT200501] A. Patrizio, "What You Need to Begin an SOA Deployment with IBM Rational SDP," DevX Skillbuilding from IBM DeveloperWorks Whitepaper, December 22, 2005, Jupitermedia, 23 Old Kings Highway South Darien, Connecticut 06820, http://www.devx.com/ibm/Article/30191

[PUL200101] R. Pulley and P. Christensen, "A Comparison of MPLS Traffic Engineering Initiatives," A White Paper by NetPlane Systems, Inc., www.netplane.com

[RAJ200101] Rajagopalan, B. (Ed.), "User Network Interface (UNI) 1.0 Signaling Specifications," OIF Contribution, OIF2000.125.7, October 2001.

[RAM200101] V. Ramamurti and G. Young "Ethernet Transport over RPR," IEEE 802.17 September 2001 Submission, IEEE, Piscataway, NJ, USA.

[RFC2205] Braden et al., "Resource ReSerVation Protocol (RSVP)—Version 1 Functional Specification," RFC-2205, September 1997.

[RFC3031] E. Rosen, A. Viswanathan, and R. Callon, "Multiprotocol Label Switching Architecture," January 2001.

[SCH200501] J. Schekkerman, How to Survive in the Jungle of Enterprise Architecture Frameworks: Creating or Choosing an Enterprise Architecture Framework , 222 pages; 2nd edition; Trafford Publishing; catalogue #03-1984; ISBN 1-4120-1607-X.

[SEI200201] J. Siegel, "Making the Case: OMG's Model-driven Architecture," http://www.sdtimes.com/news/064/special1.htm

[SEM200001] C. Semeria, "RSVP Signaling Extensions for MPLS Traffic Engineering," White Paper, Juniper Networks, Inc., 2000.

[SHA200101] R. Sharer, "Fiber-Optic Ethernet in the Local Loop," *Lightwave*, July 2001.

[SHA200201] D. Shahane, "Building Optical Control Planes: Challenges and Solutions," *Communication Systems Design*, January 7, 2002.

[SHI200001] R. Shirey, Internet Security Glossary, RFC 2828, May 2000, Copyright © The Internet Society (2000). All Rights Reserved. This document and translations of it may be copied and furnished to others, and derivative works that comment on or otherwise explain it or assist in its implementation may be prepared, copied, published and distributed, in whole or in part, without restriction of any kind, provided that the above copyright notice and this paragraph are included on all such copies and derivative works.

[SHU200401] J. Shurtleff, IP storage: A review of iSCSI, FCIP, and iFCP, iSCSI Storage/IP network Storage Trend and News, iSCSI Storage Publications, 2004, P.O. Box 7317, Golden, CO, 80304-0100, info@iscsistorage.com, http://www.iscsistorage.com

[SME200301] M. Smetanikov, HP Virtualization a Step toward Planetary Network, Web Host Industry Review (theWHIR.com) April 15, 2003. Web Host Industry Review, Inc. 552 Church Street, Suite 89, Toronto, Ontario, Canada M4Y 2E3, (p) 416-925-7264, (f) 416-925-9421.

[SNI200401] SNIA IP Storage Forum White Paper Internet Fibre Channel Protocol (iFCP)—A Technical Overview, SNIA Archives and Promotional Materials. 2004. 500 Sansome Street, Suite #504, San Francisco, CA, 94111. SNIA hereby grants permission to use this document solely as set forth below, provided that the user complies with and agrees to the terms and conditions set forth below. (1) The user may reproduce, distribute, or display publicly this document (in its entirety). In any reproduction, distribution, or display, the user must not remove any copyright or other proprietary notices or these terms and conditions from this document. (2) The user may also incorporate this document, or portions of this document, into other documents or works of authorship, including without limitation articles and books. For any such use, the user must include a reasonably prominent copyright notice acknowledging the SNIA's copyright in any content in this document and a reasonably prominent acknowledgment crediting the SNIA for granting permission for the use of this document. The user must not assert any claims of ownership or proprietary rights, including without limitation seeking copyright registration, of or in any content in this document; and the user must not otherwise seek to limit or restrict others' ability to use this document subject to these terms and conditions. (3) In any use of this document whatsoever, the user may not alter, change, or otherwise modify any of the content in this document. However, in using a diagram from this document, the user may make certain limited changes to the diagram: (a) solely as reasonably necessary to show the placement or interaction of a product (including a planned or hypothetical product) with or relative to the components shown in the diagram; (b) that are text annotations superimposed upon a diagram, solely as reasonably necessary to comment on or explain the diagram, the Shared Storage Model, or other related proposals, research, or analysis; or (c) that are simple graphical annotations (such as arrows, circles, or other geometric figures) to show interaction, relations, groupings, or subsets, solely as reasonably necessary to comment on or explain the diagram, the Shared Storage Model, or other related proposals, research, or analysis. (4) When making any such changes to a diagram permitted under Section 3, above, the user must include a reasonably proximate and prominent notice both of the changes and that any such changes are the sole responsibility of the user (in addition to any notices required by Section 2, above). (5) Notwithstanding anything to the contrary, the user must not make any change to any diagram that: (a) changes the SNIA Shared Storage Model itself (as described in this document); (b) extends the SNIA Shared Storage Model to cover products or applications for which it was not intended (as described in this document); or (c) misrepresents the SNIA Shared Storage Model (as described in this document) in any way, for example, by omitting significant portions of a diagram. (6) Furthermore, the user may make no use of this document that might in any way suggest the SNIA endorses, sponsors, or is affiliated with the user or any products, services, or content provided by the user. The user may not use the names "Storage Networking Industry Association" or "SNIA" to endorse or promote any product, service, or content provided by the user incorporating, based on, or otherwise derived from this document, without prior, express, written permission. However, nothing in these terms and conditions precludes a member of the SNIA from noting it is a member of the SNIA.

[SNI200402] The Storage Networking Industry Association's (SNIA) IP Storage Forum, "Clearing the Confusion: A Primer on Internet Protocol Storage," SNIA Archives and Promotional Materials. 2004. SNIA was incorporated in December 1997 and is a registered 501-C6 non-profit trade association. 500 Sansome Street, Suite #504, San Francisco, CA 94111.

[SNI200501] The Storage Networking Industry Association's (SNIA), Press Releases, Promotional Material, and Archives. 2005. SNIA was incorporated in December 1997 and is a registered 501-C6 non-profit trade association. 500 Sansome Street, Suite #504, San Francisco, CA 94111.

[SOU200601] V. A. S. M. de Souza and E. Cardozo, "SOANet—A service oriented architecture for building compositional network services," *Journal of Software*, Vol. 1, No. 2, August 2006.

[SPE199201] S. H. Spewak, *Enterprise Architecture Planning*, Wiley, New York, 1992.

[STA200502] Staff, "Enterprise-Class SOA Management with webMethods Servicenet, Leveraging a Web Services Infrastructure Platform to deliver on the promise of SOA," January 2006, White Paper, December 2005, webMethods, Inc., 3877 Fairfax Ridge Road, South Tower, Fairfax, VA 22030, USA.

[STA200503] Staff, "Service-Oriented Architecture: Revolutionizing IT Systems Development," White Paper, December 2005, webMethods, Inc., 3877 Fairfax Ridge Road, South Tower, Fairfax, VA 22030, USA.

[STA200504] Staff, "Making the Transformation to Service-Oriented Architecture: Capitalizing on the Next Revolution in IT," January 2005, White Paper, December 2005, webMethods, Inc., 3877 Fairfax Ridge Road, South Tower, Fairfax, VA 22030, USA.

[STA200505] Staff, "Overcoming the Roadblocks to SOA Success: Realizing the Value of Service-Oriented Architectures," Above All Software, Inc., June 2005, One Lagoon Drive, Suite #110, Redwood City, CA 94065, Office: 650.232.2900, http://www.aboveallsoftware.com/

[STA200601] Staff, "Service Oriented Architecture—An Introduction," India Web Developers, Stylus Systems Pvt. Ltd., # 924, 5 A Cross, I Block, HRBR Layout, Kalyan Nagar, Bangalore—560043, India, http://www.indiawebdevelopers.com/articles/SOA.asp

[STA200601] Staff, "SOA (service-oriented architecture)—Research Center: Applications," *Network World*, 118 Turnpike Road Southborough, MA 01772-9108, Tel. 800-622-1108, http://www.networkworld.com/details/6187.html

[STA200602] Staff, "New to SOA and Web Services," DeveloperWorks, IBM Whitepaper, IBM Corporation, 1133 Westchester Avenue, White Plains, New York 10604, United States, http://www-128.ibm.com/developerworks/webservices/newto/

[SUN200301] Sun Networks Press Release, "Network Computing Made More Secure, Less Complex With New Reference Architectures, Sun Infrastructure Solution, September 17, 2003. Sun Microsystems, Inc., 4150 Network Circle, Santa Clara, CA 95054, Phone: 1-800-555-9SUN or 1-650-960-1300.

[SUN200601] Sun Developer Network, "Java Message Service API Overview" Web page, http://java.sun.com/products/jms/overview.html

[SYS200501] Systems and Software Consortium, Glossary, http://www.software.org/pub/architecture/pzdefinitions.asp

[SYS200502] Systems and Software Consortium, Architecture, http://www.software.org/pub/architecture/default.asp

[TAT200201] O. Tatebe, Y. Morita, S. Matsuoka, N. Soda, and S. Sekiguchi. "Grid datafarm architecture for petascale data intensive computing," In Henri E. Bal, Klaus-Peter Lohr, and Alexander Reinefeld (Eds.), Proceedings of the Second IEEE/ACM International Symposium on Cluster Computing and the Grid (CCGrid2002), pages 102–110, Berlin, Germany, 2002. IEEE, IEEE Computer Society.

[TEA200001] The Treasury Enterprise Architecture Framework, Version 1.0, http://www.treas.gov/offices/management/cio/teaf/arch_framework.doc

[THA200101] J. Thatcher, July 2001 IEEE Presentations on 10 GbE, IEEE, Piscataway, NJ, USA.

[TIB200701] TIMCO Promotional Materials, 3303 Hillview Avenue, Palo Alto, CA 94304.

[TOG200501] TOGAF, Preliminary Phase: Framework and Principles, http://www.opengroup.org/architecture/togaf8-doc/arch/p2/p2_prelim.htm

[TOG200502] TOGAF documentation, The Open Group.

[UMI200401] Unified Modeling Language (UML) Specification: Infrastructure Version 2.0 ptc/04-10-14 Accompanied by ptc/2004-10-16 (Normative XMI and XML Schema Files), November 2004. Subject to all of the terms and conditions below, the owners of the copyright in this specification hereby grant you a fully-paid up, non-exclusive, nontransferable, perpetual, worldwide license (without the right to sublicense), to use this specification to create and distribute software and special purpose specifications that are based upon this specification, and to use, copy, and distribute this specification as provided under the Copyright Act; provided that: (1) both the copyright notice identified above and this permission notice appear on any copies of this specification; (2) the use of the specifications is for informational purposes and will not be copied or posted on any network computer or broadcast in any media and will not be otherwise resold or transferred for commercial purposes; and (3) no modifications are made to this specification.

[UML200501] Unified Modeling Language: Superstructure Version 2.0, formal/05-07-04, August 2005. Subject to all of the terms and conditions below, the owners of the copyright in this specification hereby grant you a fully-paid up, non-exclusive, nontransferable, perpetual, worldwide license (without the right to sublicense), to use this specification to create and distribute software and special purpose specifications that are based upon this specification, and to use, copy, and distribute this specification as provided under the Copyright Act; provided that: (1) both the copyright notice identified above and this permission notice appear on any copies of this specification; (2) the use of the specifications is for informational purposes and will not be copied or posted on any network computer or broadcast in any media and will not be otherwise resold or transferred for commercial purposes; and (3) no modifications are made to this specification.

[VMW200701] VMware Promotional Materials, VMware, Inc. World Headquarters, 3401 Hillview Ave, Palo Alto, CA 94304. http://www.vmware.com

[WAL200201] M. Waldrop, "Hook enough computers together and what do you get? A new kind of utility that offers supercomputer processing on tap," MIT Enterprise Technology Review, May 2002, Technology Review, One Main Street, 7th Floor, Cambridge, MA, 02142, Tel: 617-475-8000, Fax: 617-475-8042.

[YAN200301] Enterprise Computing and Networking Report on Utility Computing in Next-Gen IT Architectures, Yankee Group, August 2003 Yankee Group, 31 St. James Avenue (aka the Park Square Building), Boston MA 02116, (617) 956–5000.

[YAN200401] Enterprise Computing and Networking Report on Performance Management Road Map for Utility Computing, Yankee Group, February 2004. Yankee Group, 31 St. James Avenue (aka the Park Square Building), Boston MA 02116, (617) 956–5000.

[ZHA200201] L.-J Zhang, J.-Y Chung, and Q. Zhou, Developing Grid Computing applications, Part 1: Introduction of a Grid architecture and toolkit for building Grid solutions, October 1, 2002, Updated November 20, 2002, IBM's Developerworks Grid Library, IBM Corporation, 1133 Westchester Avenue, White Plains, New York 10604, United States, www.ibm.com

[ZIF200501] Zachman Institute for Framework Advancement (ZIFA), http://www.zifa.com/

INDEX

Index

T